Cape Town & the Garden Route

"All you've got to do is decide to go and the hardest part is over.

So go!"

TONY WHEELER, COFOUNDER – LONELY PLANET

THIS EDITION WRITTEN AND RESEARCHED BY

Simon Richmond

Lucy Corne

Contents

MLRAMOS/GETTY IMAGES ©

ALLAN BAXTER/GETTY IMAGES ©

(left) **Bo-Kaap p58** Colourful houses and cobbled streets

(above) **Cape Town Stadium p110** Contemporary architecture

(right) **Kirstenbosch Botanical Gardens p126** Local flora

LARANIK/SHUTTERSTOCK ©

Green Point & Waterfront p104

East City, District Six, Woodstock & Observatory p80

City Bowl, Foreshore, Bo-Kaap & De Waterkant p52

Cape Flats & Northern Suburbs p151

Gardens & Surrounds p92

Sea Point to Hout Bay p116

Southern Suburbs p124

Simon's Town & Southern Peninsula p137

Welcome to Cape Town & the Garden Route

The Mother City, home to soaring Table Mountain, golden beaches and bountiful vineyards, is an old pro at capturing people's hearts.

Natural Wonders

Table Mountain National Park defines the city. The flat-topped mountain is the headline act, but there are many other equally gorgeous natural landscapes within the park's extensive boundaries. Cultivated areas, such as the historic Company's Gardens, Kirstenbosch Botanical Gardens and Green Point Park, also make exploring the city a pleasure. Follow the lead of locals by taking advantage of the abundant outdoor space: learn to surf; go hiking or mountain biking; tandem-paraglide off Lion's Head; abseil off the top of Table Mountain – just a few of the many activities on offer.

Design Delights

Human creativity is also self-evident here – it's one of the things that made the city a World Design Capital in 2014. From the brightly painted facades of the Bo-Kaap and the bathing chalets of Muizenberg to the Afro-chic decor of its restaurants and bars and the striking street art and innovation incubators of the East City and Woodstock, this is one great-looking metropolis. The informal settlements of the Cape Flats are a sobering counterpoint, but these townships also have enterprising projects that put food from organic market gardens on tables, or stock gift shops with attractive souvenirs.

Proudly Multicultural

Christian, Muslim, Jewish, Hindu and traditional African beliefs coexist peacefully in this proudly multicultural city. Given South Africa's troubled history, such harmony has been hard-won and remains fragile: nearly everyone has a fascinating, sometimes heartbreaking story to tell. It's a city of determined pioneers – from the Afrikaner descendants of the original Dutch colonists and the majority coloured community to the descendants of European Jewish immigrants and more recent Xhosa (isiXhosa) migrants from the Eastern Cape. They all bring unique flavours to Cape Town's rich creole melting pot.

Beyond the City

Wrenching yourself away from the magnetic mountain and all the delights of the Cape Peninsula is a challenge, but within an hour you can exchange urban landscapes for the charming towns, villages and bucolic estates of Winelands destinations, such as Stellenbosch and Franschhoek. Hermanus is a prime whale-watching location, and also a base from which to organise shark-cave diving. Further afield, the delights of the Garden Route unfold, with more inspiring scenery to be viewed on thrilling drives down the coast and over mountain passes.

HOUGAARD MALAN PHOTOGRAPHY/GETTY IMAGES ©

Why I Love Cape Town

By Simon Richmond, Author

Mother Nature surpassed herself when crafting the Mother City. Whether jogging along Sea Point Promenade, climbing up Lion's Head in the dawn light, clambering over giant boulders at Sandy Bay or driving the amazing coastal roads down to Cape Point, I never fail to feel my spirits soar as I take in the breathtakingly beautiful vistas. You don't need to break a sweat: sipping wine on a historic farm in Constantia or enjoying a picnic at an outdoor concert in Kirstenbosch Botanical Gardens are equally memorable ways to commune with Cape Town's great outdoors.

For more about our authors, see p296.

Top: Cape Point (p139)

Cape Town's Top 10

1

Table Mountain (p94)

1 Whether you take the easy way up and down on the revolving cableway or put in the legwork and climb, attaining the summit of Table Mountain is a Capetonian rite of passage. Weather permitting, your rewards are a panoramic view across the peninsula and a chance to experience some of the park's incredible biodiversity. Schedule time for a hike: the park's 245 sq km include routes to suit all levels of fitness and ambition, from gentle ambles to spot *fynbos* (literally 'fine bush', primarily proteas, heaths and ericas) to the five-day, four-night Hoerikwaggo Trail.

Garden & Surrounds

Robben Island (p109)

2 A World Heritage Site, the former prison on Robben Island is a key location in South Africa's long walk to freedom. Nelson Mandela and other Freedom struggle heroes were incarcerated here, following in the tragic footsteps of earlier fighters against the various colonial governments that ruled over the Cape. Taking the boat journey here and the tour with former inmates provides an insight into the country's troubled history – and a glimpse of how far it has progressed on the path to reconciliation and forgiveness. BELOW: NELSON MANDELA'S CELL

Green Point & Waterfront

GUNTER LENZ/GETTY IMAGES ©

2

MARK HARRIS/GETTY IMAGES ©

Kirstenbosch Botanical Gardens *(p126)*

3 There's been European horticulture on the picturesque eastern slopes of Table Mountain since Jan van Riebeeck's time in the 17th century, but it was British imperialist Cecil Rhodes, owner of Kirstenbosch Farm and surrounding properties, who really put the gardens on the map when he bequeathed the land to all Capetonians. Today it's a spectacular showcase for the Cape floral kingdom, also declared a World Heritage Site. Take in the view from the new treetop walkway known as the Boomslang.

Southern Suburbs

District Six Museum *(p82)*

4 Some 40 years on from when most of the homes in the inner-city suburb of District Six were demolished, and their multiethnic owners and tenants shifted to separate, blighted communities in the Cape Flats, the area remains largely barren. A visit to the illuminating, moving museum here is a must to understand the history of what was destroyed here, and the impact it had on the lives of former residents and on all of Cape Town. You can also arrange a walking tour of the area, led by a former resident.

East City, District Six, Woodstock & Observatory

3

V&A Waterfront

(p106)

5 Cape Town's top sight in terms of visitor numbers, the V&A Waterfront is big, busy and in a spectacular location, with Table Mountain as a backdrop. There's a pirate's booty of consumer opportunities, from chic boutiques to major department stores, plus plenty of cultural and educational experiences, including walking tours of its well-preserved heritage buildings and public sculptures, the excellent Two Oceans Aquarium (a firm family favourite) and the new Zeitz MOCAA museum of contemporary art, set to open in 2017. Be sure to board a harbour cruise, too – preferably at sunset.

Green Point & Waterfront

Cape of Good Hope *(p139)*

6 The spectacular journey out to Cape Point, the tip of the peninsula protected within Table Mountain National Park, is a trip you're going to want to make: rugged cliffs shoot down into the frothing waters of the Atlantic Ocean; giant waves crash over the enormous boulders at Africa's most southwesterly point; and the Flying Dutchman Funicular runs up to the old lighthouse for fantastic views. Afterwards you can relax on lovely beaches such as the one at Buffels Bay, which is lapped by the slightly warmer waters of False Bay.

Simon's Town & Southern Peninsula

Franschhoek *(p165)*

7 Franschhoek is the smallest – but for many the prettiest – Cape Winelands town. Nestled in a spectacular valley, Franschhoek bills itself as the country's gastronomic capital, and you won't find too many people arguing that point. You may have a tough time deciding where to eat – the main road is lined with top-notch restaurants, some of them among the best in the country. The surrounding wineries likewise offer excellent food and no shortage of superb wine. Add a clutch of art galleries and some stylish guesthouses and it really is one of the loveliest towns in the Cape.

Day Trips & Wineries

6

Bo-Kaap *(p58)*

8 Painted in vivid colours straight out of a packet of liquorice allsorts, the jumble of crumbling and restored heritage houses and mosques along the cobblestoned streets of the Bo-Kaap are both visually captivating and a storybook of inner-city gentrification. A stop at the Bo-Kaap Museum is recommended to gain an understanding of the history of this former slave quarter. Also, try Cape Malay dishes at one of the area's several restaurants, or stay in one of the homes turned into guesthouses and hotels, including the lovely, antique-filled Dutch Manor.

City Bowl, Foreshore, Bo-Kaap & De Waterkant

Surfing along the Garden Route *(p183)*

9 The Garden Route is known for its outdoor pursuits on both land and sea. The coast between Mossel Bay and Plettenberg Bay boasts some of the Western Cape's best surf, great whether you're a pro or just starting out. Herold's Bay and Victoria Bay, near George, are particularly pretty spots to catch a wave, and offer excellent beaches for nonsurfing travel companions. In Victoria Bay you can try a beginner lesson or rent a board and join the experts on a more challenging day trip.

The Garden Route

10

Kalk Bay *(p141)*

10 This delightful False Bay fishing village – named after the kilns that produced lime from seashells, used for painting buildings in the 17th century – offers an abundance of antique, arts and craft shops, and great cafes and restaurants, as well as a daily fish market at its harbour. A drink or meal at institutions such as the Brass Bell pub or Live Bait restaurant – nearly as close to the splashing waters of False Bay as you can get without swimming – are fine ways to pass the time.

Simon's Town & Southern Peninsula

What's New

Urban Farms & Farmers Markets

The Mother City is proverbially going back to its historical roots with an emerging urban-farm movement. Leading the way is the Oranjezicht City Farm, with its associated Saturday farmers market, and the food-security activists Tyisa Nabanye, who have crafted a biodynamic market garden in Tamboerskloof, where they hold the Erf 81 Food Market on Sundays. Also check out the VOC Vegetable Garden, newly planted in the Company's Gardens. (p100, p102 & p57)

Tree Canopy Walkway

Nicknamed the Boomslang ('tree snake'), this sculptural walkway through the treetops of Kirstenbosch was built to celebrate the botanical gardens' centenary. (p126)

Public Art

A red house on Long St and a regularly changing set of art installations on Sea Point Promenade – just some of the new sculptures in Cape Town. (p59 & p118)

Zeitz MOCAA

Until the Thomas Heatherwick–designed museum opens in the Waterfront's former grain silos in 2017, there's a pavilion where you can view part of this outstanding collection of Southern African art. (p107)

Woodstock Rising

The edgy inner-city suburb continues its uneven gentrification with the success of the Woodstock Exchange, the Woodstock Co-op and arty new backpackers Wish U Were Here. (p90 & p202)

Langa Quarter

Aiming to bring vibrant arts and cultural life to a section of South Africa's oldest planned township. Also check out the new theatre at the Guga S'Thebe Arts & Cultural Centre. (p153 & p153)

First Thursdays

Zigzag between the clusters of art galleries and event spaces on Church and Bree Sts in the City Bowl to experience this vibrant monthly event. (p74)

Snorkelling with Seals

Swim alongside wide-eyed and playful Cape fur seals off their home on rocky, smelly Duiker Island, a short, bouncy boat ride out of Hout Bay Harbour. (p123)

Watershed

A shed like no other, this imaginatively designed bright-yellow hangar at the Waterfront is a treasure trove of the best of Capetonian crafts, design and fashion. (p113)

Flagship

Journeys down towards Cape Point just got a whole lot more delicious with the opening of this fine-dining set-course lunch venue and boutique hotel. (p147)

For more recommendations and reviews, see **lonelyplanet.com/cape-town**

Need to Know

For more information, see Survival Guide (p243)

Currency
South African rand (R)

Language
English, Afrikaans, Xhosa

Visas
Australian, UK, US and most Western European citizens can get a 90-day entry permit on arrival.

Money
ATMs are widely available. Credit cards are accepted at most businesses, but some smaller food places, including weekly markets, are cash-only.

Mobile Phones
South Africa uses the GSM digital standard; check compatibility with your phone provider. Local SIM cards are easy to buy.

Time
South Africa Standard Time (GMT/UTC plus two hours)

Tourist Information
The head office of **Cape Town Tourism** (Map p268; ☎021-487 6800; www.capetown.travel; Pinnacle Bldg, cnr Burg & Castle Sts, City Bowl) is centrally located and there are plenty of satellite offices around the city, including one at the airport.

Daily Costs

Budget: Less than R500
- Dorm bed: R160
- Gourmet burger: R60
- Local beer: R20
- Hiking in Table Mountain National Park: free
- MyCiTi bus from City Bowl to Camps Bay: R9.80

Midrange: R500–2500
- Hotel room: R1000–1500
- Township/cultural tour: R450
- Kirstenbosch Summer Sunset Concert ticket: R135
- Meal with wine at Waterfront restaurant: R350–450

Top End: More than R2500
- Hotel room: R3000–5000
- Meal at Aubergine: R700–1000
- Full-day gourmet wine tour: R2000
- Thirty-minute helicopter flight: R2700
- Three-hour cruise on luxury yacht: R34,600

Advance Planning

Three months before Book Robben Island tour; reserve table at the Test Kitchen; train for hiking in Table Mountain National Park.

Three weeks before Book a township/cultural tour; check listings for theatre shows and for Kirstenbosch Summer Sunset Concerts.

One week before See what gigs and club events are coming up; buy online tickets for Table Mountain Cableway.

Useful Websites

Cape Town Magazine (www.capetownmagazine.com) Online magazine with its finger on Cape Town's pulse.

Cape Town Tourism (www.capetown.travel) The city's official tourism site is stacked with info.

Lonely Planet (www.lonelyplanet.com/cape-town) Destination information, hotel bookings, traveller forums and more.

WHEN TO GO

Summer (Dec–Feb) brings warm, dry weather and lively festivals. Winter (Jun–Aug) is wet, cool and windy. Neither has extremes of temperature.

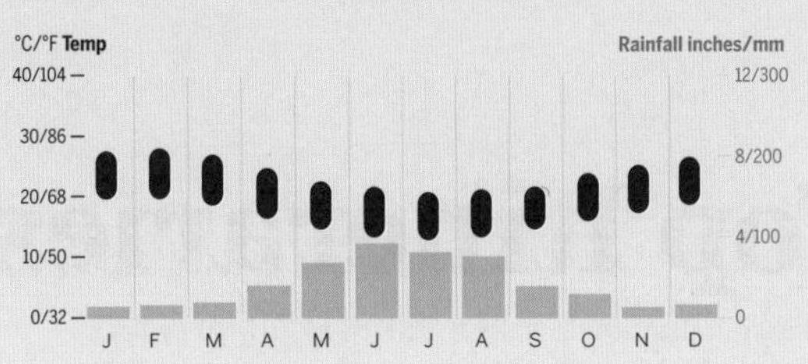

Arriving in Cape Town

Cape Town International Airport MyCiTi bus to Cape Town Train Station is R75; the Backpacker Bus shared minivan taxi is R180 to city-centre hotels and hostels; a private taxi is around R250.

Cape Town Train Station Long-distance trains and buses arrive at this centrally located terminal; a taxi ride to most central locations will be under R50.

V&A Waterfront Jetty 2 or Duncan Dock Where international cruise ships dock.

For much more on **arrival,** see p249

Getting Around

Contact the **Transport Information Centre** (☎0800 656 463) for timetables.

➡ **Car hire** Budget around R300 per day and R400 for a tank of petrol.

➡ **City Sightseeing Cape Town** Hop-on, hop-off routes good for orientation of the city.

➡ **MyCiTi buses** For city-centre and Atlantic Coast routes.

➡ **Cape Metro Rail** For trips to Southern Suburbs, False Bay and Stellenbosch.

➡ **Shared minibus taxis** Useful from City Bowl along Atlantic Coast to Sea Point or townships.

➡ **Private taxis** Many with rates from R10 per kilometre. Book to ensure a pick-up.

For much more on **getting around,** see p250

Sleeping

There are plenty of budget backpackers, charming guesthouses and five-star pamper palaces, but reserve well in advance, especially if visiting during school holidays (from mid-December to the end of January). All places will slash their rates from May to October in the quiet winter season. Rates usually include a value-added tax (VAT) of 14% and, often, the 1% tourism promotion levy. Also check whether secure parking is included in your hotel rate, otherwise you could be charged anything up to R100 extra per day to park your car.

Useful Websites

➡ **SA-Venues.com** (www.sa-venues.com)

➡ **Cape Town Tourism** (www.capetown.travel)

➡ **Portfolio Collection** (www.portfoliocollection.com)

➡ **Lonely Planet** (lonelyplanet.com/south-africa/cape-town/hotels)

For much more on **sleeping,** see p198

CAPE TOWN'S MICROCLIMATES

Pack a raincoat and umbrella for Cape Town's 'four seasons in one day'. The peninsula's geography creates microclimates, so you can be basking in the sun on one side of the mountain and sheltering from chilly rain and winds on the other. It's no accident that Newlands is so lush in comparison to Cape Point – it receives four times as much rain annually.

Top Itineraries

Day One

Gardens & Surrounds (p92)

Skip the line at the kiosk by printing a web-ticket for the **Table Mountain Cableway**. The revolving car provides 360-degree views as you ascend this mesmerising 60-million-year-old mountain. From the upper cableway station it's about an hour's round-trip hike to the 1088m summit at Maclear's Beacon.

Lunch Locals love Jason Bakery (p66) and Tamboers Winkel (p98).

City Bowl, Foreshore, Bo-Kaap & De Waterkant (p52)

After a postprandial stroll through the **Company's Gardens**, browse the craft stalls in **Greenmarket Square**, then head uphill into the old Cape Malay quarter, the **Bo-Kaap**, where cobblestoned streets are lined with brightly painted houses. There's more good shopping here, in stores such as **Monkeybiz** and **Streetwires**. Continue over into the gay-friendly **De Waterkant** for more prettily restored cottages and the buzzing malls of the Cape Quarter.

Dinner Enjoy tapas and wine at Chef's Warehouse & Canteen (p67).

Sea Point to Hout Bay (p116)

Catching the sunset with a cocktail in hand is a must – whether it be from along **Sea Point Promenade** or the strip of touristy restaurants and cafe-bars lining picturesque **Camps Bay**.

Day Two

District Six & City Bowl (p80 & p52)

Learn about the city's troubled past at the **District Six Museum**. Join the 11am tour of the 350-year-old **Castle of Good Hope**, then watch the noon key ceremony. Across the road is the handsome old Cape Town City Hall.

Lunch Kitchen (p85) offers delicious food fit for First Ladies.

Woodstock & Salt River (p80)

Check out Woodstock's contemporary galleries such as **Stevenson**, as well as the abundant street art. In nearby Salt River there's more art at **What If The World** (in a converted synagogue), and the fabulous retail collection at the **Old Biscuit Mill**; if it's Saturday don't miss the **Neighbourgoods Market** that happens here, offering the cream of the region's artisan food purveyors and product designers.

Dinner La Perla (p119) serves excellent Italian, along with water views.

Green Point & Waterfront (p104)

More than just a mega shopping mall, the **V&A Waterfront** is worth exploring for its carnival-like atmosphere, well-preserved Victorian architecture and the chance to join a harbour cruise. It's also where you board the boat out to World Heritage–listed **Robben Island** (for which you should book ahead).

Day Three

Southern Suburbs (p124)

Explore the beautiful **Kirstenbosch Botanical Gardens**, covering some 5 hectares of the eastern slopes of Table Mountain, to learn more about the richly endowed Cape floral kingdom. A wander around lovely **Wynberg Village**, packed with old thatched-roof cottages, is also a pleasure. Alternatively, admire the paintings in the **Irma Stern Museum**.

Lunch Gourmet delights await at La Colombe (p133).

Southern Suburbs (p124)

Spend a blissful afternoon exploring the wineries on the **Constantia Valley Wine Route**. Target the historic ones, such as **Groot Constantia**, with its beautifully restored homestead and wine cellar, and **Klein Constantia**, producer of Napoleon's favourite tipple. **Steenberg Vineyards** has an excellent contemporary tasting room and restaurant – not to mention delicious wines.

Dinner Tuck into top-quality pizza at Massimo's (p120).

Sea Point to Hout Bay (p116)

Motor over Constantia Neck; if it's not too late in the day, drop by the hidden ceramics gallery **Art in the Forest**. Enjoy the view of Hout Bay, beer in hand, from the deck of the **Chapman's Peak Hotel** or beachside pub **Dunes**. If it's Friday night, the **Bay Harbour Market** will have live music and tasty eats.

Day Four

Simon's Town & Southern Peninsula (p137)

Time to explore the peninsula's deep south. Take the Atlantic Coast route, including spectacular **Chapman's Peak Drive**, past Noordhoek's broad sweep of sand and the surfing hot spots of Kommetjie and Scarborough. Hit the very southwestern tip of Africa, found within the **Cape Point** section of Table Mountain National Park.

Lunch Try the Lighthouse Cafe (p146) in Simon's Town for seafood.

Simon's Town & Southern Peninsula (p137)

Also part of the park is **Boulders**, home to a thriving colony of super-cute African penguins, who waddle around and over the giant boulders that give this secluded False Bay beach area its name. The historic naval yard of **Simon's Town** is just up the road; take a cruise around the harbour or potter around its antique and gift stores.

Dinner Glam it up at Tiger's Milk (p147) in Muizenberg.

Simon's Town & Southern Peninsula (p137)

Continue around False Bay to charming **Kalk Bay**, an old fishing village packed with more great places to find arty buys and tasty nibbles. Freshen up with a dip in one of the sea pools here or in nearby **St James**. Muizenberg's convivial **Slow Life** offers live music, as does the **Blue Bird Garage Food & Goods Market** on Friday nights.

If You Like...

Beaches

Muizenberg Beach Colourful Victorian chalets, warm(ish) water and fun surfing. (p141)

Clifton 3rd Beach Where the gay community leads, Capetonians follow. (p118)

Buffels Bay Tranquil, with sweeping views across False Bay and a sea pool for safe swimming. (p139)

Sandy Bay The nudist beach also has amazing giant rock formations to explore. (p118)

Noordhoek Beach Magnificently broad, overlooked by Chapman's Peak and with a shipwreck in the sand. (p143)

Viewpoints

Table Mountain Sweeping vistas across the city and peninsula. (p94)

Bloubergstrand Picture-perfect view of Table Mountain north of the city. (p153)

Cape of Good Hope Walk to just above the Cape's original lighthouse. (p139)

Chapman's Peak Drive Take in the elegant sweep of horseshoe-shaped Hout Bay. (p123)

Signal Hill Hear the cannon fire and look out over the Waterfront. (p97)

Free Attractions

V&A Waterfront Buskers, outdoor events, seals, historic buildings, public artworks and the comings and goings of the harbour. (p106)

Table Mountain National Park No charge for hiking the myriad

Beach huts, Muizenberg (p141)

trails on the main mountain, up Lion's Head or along Signal Hill. (p64)

Street Art District Six and Woodstock are dotted with impressive large-scale works. (p84)

Nelson Mandela Gateway Learn about the Freedom struggle and life in the prison before heading to Robben Island. (p109)

Parks & Gardens

Company's Gardens Stroll through these historic gardens, marvelling at ancient trees and pretty flower beds. (p56)

Green Point Urban Park Enjoy the lovely eco-legacy of World Cup 2010 at this new park showcasing biodiversity. (p110)

Oranjezicht City Farm A beautifully laid-out urban farm on the slopes of Table Mountain. (p100)

Prestwich Memorial Garden Attractive city-centre space dotted with a collection of quirky sculptures and installations by Capetonian artists. (p66)

Arderne Gardens The oldest collection of trees in the southern hemisphere is a lovely place to escape the crowds. (p131)

Babylonstoren Explore the blissful garden of edible and medicinal plants at this elegantly reimagined wine and fruit estate. (p171)

Art Collections

South African National Gallery Prime examples of the nation's art are exhibited in this elegant building. (p97)

Michaelis Collection Old masters and new works in the Old Town House on Greenmarket Sq. (p59)

Stevenson Major commercial gallery for contemporary artists, with interesting thematic exhibitions. (p89)

Irma Stern Museum Former home of the pioneering expressionist artist, with a lovely garden. (p129)

Casa Labia Cultural Centre Beautifully restored interiors at this Muizenberg villa, converted to an arts and cultural space. (p141)

New Church Museum Focuses on contemporary Southern African art. (p98)

Historical Insights

District Six Museum Shines a light on the destroyed multicultural inner-city area. (p82)

Robben Island Book ahead for visits to the former prison of Mandela and other freedom fighters. (p109)

Bo-Kaap Museum Learn about the people of the Cape Malay community in this colourful district. (p58)

Iziko Slave Lodge Exhibits on the history of slaves and their descendants. (p60)

South African Museum Lots of natural history, fine examples of San rock art and an African Cultures Gallery. (p97)

South African Jewish Museum Traces the routes of Jewish migration and settlement in the country; has a section on the Holocaust. (p96)

Hidden Gems

Rust en Vreugd Elegant 18th-century mansion and garden in the midst of the city. (p97)

For more top Cape Town spots, see the following:

- Eating (p32)
- Drinking & Nightlife (p35)
- Entertainment (p37)
- Shopping (p39)
- Sports & Activities (p41)
- GLBT Travellers (p43)
- Wineries (p45)

Art in the Forest Ceramics gallery and art complex overlooking the Constantia valley. (p135)

Tintswalo Atlantic Not staying at this luxe lodge? Call to see if you can visit for lunch or dinner. (p207)

Enmasse Thai massage the modern way, in a historic building tucked away in Gardens. (p103)

The Luxe Life

Status Luxury Vehicles Cruise Cape Town's roads in a top-marque convertible, or have a chauffeur drive it for you. (p251)

Prins & Prins Go shopping for diamonds and other precious jewels at this emporium based in a historic City Bowl house. (p77)

Klûk & CGDT Haute couture from a former apprentice to John Galliano. (p78)

Belmond Mount Nelson Hotel Not a guest? Come for afternoon tea or visit the Planet bar and restaurant. (p205)

Sports Helicopters Hire a chopper and take some photos of the peninsula that will really impress your friends. (p115)

Month by Month

TOP EVENTS

Cape Town Minstrel Carnival, January

Infecting the City, March

Design Indaba, February

Cape Town Fringe, September

Adderley St Christmas Lights, December

January

Expect packed hotels and restaurants, crowds at the beaches and traffic on main coastal roads. Some restaurants, cafes and shops close for the first week or so of the month.

Cape Town Minstrel Carnival

Tweede Nuwe Jaar (2 January) sees satin- and sequin-clad minstrel troupes march through the city for the traditional Kaapse Klopse (Cape Town Minstrel Carnival), with smaller marches on Christmas Eve and New Year's Eve. From January into early February there are competitions between troupes at Athlone Stadium. (www.capetown-minstrels.co.za)

J&B Met

South Africa's richest horse race – with a R2.5 million jackpot – is an occasion for big bets and even bigger hats. Usually held on the last Saturday in January at Kenilworth Racecourse (p135). (www.jbscotch.co.za)

February

Check for classical concerts at the Cape Town International Summer Music Festival. The city goes into lockdown for the opening of Parliament in the first week of February so avoid anything but essential travel.

Design Indaba

This creative convention brings together the worlds of fashion, architecture, visual arts, crafts and media from late February to early March, usually at the Cape Town International Convention Centre. A two-week film festival at the Labia kicks off proceedings. (www.designindaba.com)

March

The cultural calendar cranks up with a series of arts and music festivals. Cyclists take over the streets (and many of the city's hotels) for the Cape Town Cycle Tour, so forget driving around town on the day of the event.

Cape Town Carnival

Held in the middle of the month on the Walk of Remembrance (the former Fan Walk) in Green Point, this city-sponsored parade and street party celebrates the many facets of South African identity. (www.capetowncarnival.com)

Infecting the City

Cape Town's squares, fountains, theatres and museums are the venues for this innovative performing arts festival, featuring artists from across the continent. (www.infectingthecity.com)

Cape Town Cycle Tour

Held on a Saturday in the middle of March, the world's largest timed cycling event attracts more than 30,000 contestants. The route circles Table Mountain, heads down the Atlantic Coast and along Chapman's Peak Dr. (www.cycletour.co.za)

Cape Town International Jazz Festival

Cape Town's biggest jazz event, attracting big names from both South Africa and overseas, is usually held at the Cape Town International Convention Centre at the end of March. It includes a free concert in Greenmarket Sq. (www.capetownjazzfest.com)

April

The weather starts to chill from now through early October, so bring warmer clothes and be prepared for rainy, blustery days.

Just Nuisance Great Dane Parade

Not an April Fools' joke – every 1 April a dog parade is held at Jubilee Sq in Simon's Town to commemorate Able Seaman Just Nuisance, a Great Dane who was a Royal Navy mascot during WWII. (www.simonstown.com/tourism/nuisance/nuisance.htm)

Old Mutual Two Oceans Marathon

Held in early April, this 56km marathon kicks off in Newlands and follows a similar route to the Cape Town Cycle Tour around Table Mountain, with about 9000 competitors. (www.twooceansmarathon.org.za)

Freedom Swim

Only thick-skinned and strong swimmers should apply for the solo and team relay events of this swim from Murray's Bay, on Robben Island, to Bloubergstrand. It's held around Freedom Day (27 April). (www.freedomswimseries.co.za)

May

Head to Kirstenbosch, Constantia and the Winelands to enjoy the blaze of autumnal colours laid on by Mother Nature.

Franschhoek Literary Festival

As if you needed another reason to visit this delightful Winelands town, this literary festival attracts the cream of locally based and expatriate South African writers. (www.flf.co.za)

Good Food & Wine Show

Cape Town goes gourmet with this four-day event held at the Cape Town International Convention Centre. (www.goodfoodandwineshow.co.za)

July

Winter in Cape Town can be very blustery and wet, but it's also one of the best times to spot whales off the peninsula's coast.

Cape Town World Music Festival

Held over Mandela Day weekend (around 18 July), this celebration of global beats and rhythms takes over City Hall and parts of the Grand Parade. (www.capetownworldmusicfestival.com)

Cape Town Fashion Week

Fashionistas line the catwalks to spot the hottest work from local designers and pick up the latest trends. (www.mbfashionweeksa.co.za)

September

South Africa's creative community comes out to play in the Mother City: Creative Week (www.creativeweekct.co.za) happens around the same time as the Loerie Awards, which recognise regional creative excellence.

Cape Town Fringe

A jamboree of the performing arts, organised in conjuction with the respected Grahamstown Festival, peppers the Mother City with interesting happenings for 11 days in late September and early October. (www.capetownfringe.co.za)

October

Outsurance Gun Run

Starting from Mouille Point, this popular half-marathon (21km) is the only time that the Noon Gun on Signal Hill gets fired on a Sunday – competitors try to finish the race before the gun goes off. (www.outsurance.co.za/gunrun)

November

Cape Town can be lovely in the spring, although the wind may drive you a little crazy. The Galileo outdoor cinema (www.thegalileo.co.za) starts screenings in Kirstenbosch, the Waterfront and the Winelands.

Kirstenbosch Summer Sunset Concerts

These Sunday afternoon concerts run through until

April; expect everything from arias performed by local divas to a funky jazz combo. There's always a special concert for New Year's Eve. (www.sanbi.org/events/kirstenbosch)

Cape Town International Kite Festival

Held in mid-November, in support of the Cape Mental Health Society, is this colourful gathering of kite enthusiasts at Zandvlei, near Muizenberg. (www.capementalhealth.co.za)

December

This is the top holiday season, so book well ahead for tickets for popular attractions and to get reservations at top restaurants. New Year's Eve is busy, with fireworks at the Waterfront – one of many special events across the city.

Adderley St Christmas Lights

Thousands turn out for a concert in front of Cape Town Train Station, followed by a parade along illuminated Adderley St. A night market is also held in the Company's Gardens starting around 20 December.

Mother City Queer Project

There's always a wacky fancy-dress theme for this massive, gay-friendly dance party, which everyone seems to turn out for. (www.mcqp.co.za)

(Top) Setting for Kirstenbosch Summer Sunset Concerts (p21)
(Bottom) Performer, Cape Town Minstrel Carnival (p20)

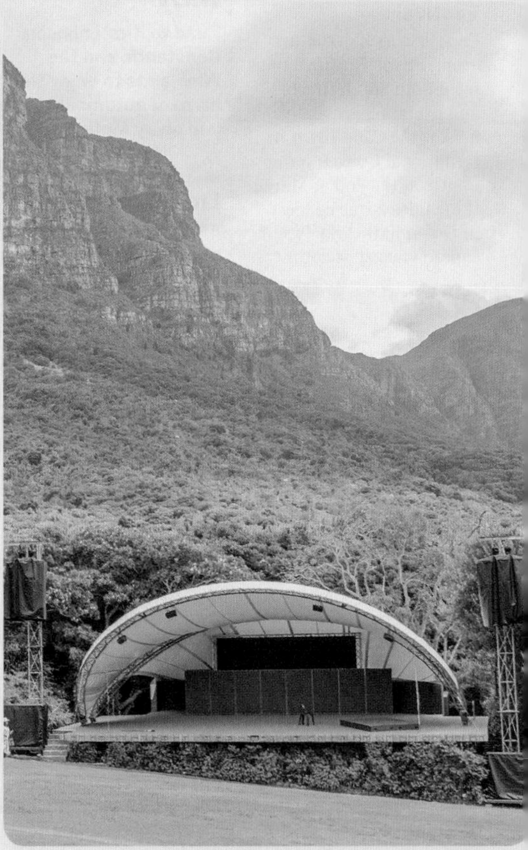

GROBLER DU PREEZ/SHUTTERSTOCK ©

GALLO IMAGES/CONTRIBUTOR/GETTY IMAGES ©

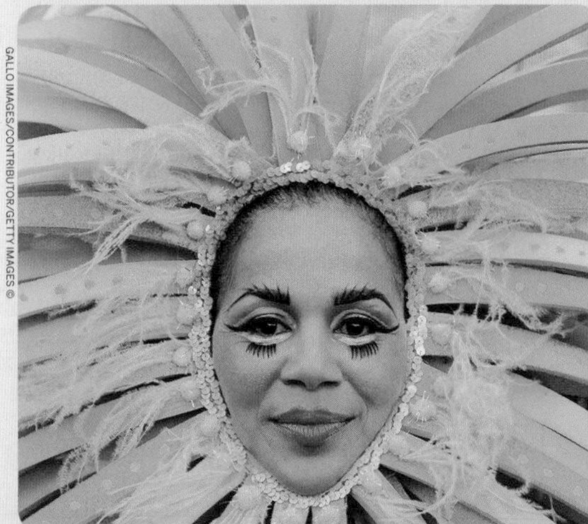

With Kids

Soft sand beaches, the mountain and its myriad activities, wildlife spotting, the carnival atmosphere of the Waterfront and much more: Cape Town takes the prize as a lekker *(Afrikaans for 'brilliant') location for family vacations.*

Beaches & Boats

There's no shortage of beaches, with those on the False Bay side of the peninsula lapped by warmer waters than those on the Atlantic Coast. Good choices include Muizenberg (p141), St James (p142), or lovely Buffels Bay (p139) at Cape Point.

Boat tours (p108) are abundant: *Tommy the Tugboat* and the *Jolly Roger Pirate Boat* are at the Waterfront, while cruises leave from the harbours at Simon's Town and Hout Bay.

Playgrounds & Parks

There are two inventively designed playgrounds at Green Point Park; Mouille Point (p110) has a big play area, toy train, maze and golf-putting course. Sea Point Promenade (p118) also has playgrounds, and swimming at the pavilion. In Vredehoek, there's a good playground beside Deer Park Café (p99). The amusement park Ratanga Junction (p158) offers thrill rides for teens, as well as plenty for smaller kids.

Animals, Birds & Sea Life

Check out local marine life at the excellent Two Oceans Aquarium (p115); birds and monkeys at Hout Bay's World of Birds (p119) or the wetland reserve of Intaka Island (p153); a happy-footed African penguin colony at Boulders (p144); wild ostriches, baboons and dassies at Cape Point (p139); and shy hippos at Rondevlei Nature Reserve (p143). Farm animals live at Oude Molen Eco Village (p158) and at Imhoff Farm (p144), where you can arrange camel rides!

Interesting Museums

Science and technology is made fun at the Cape Town Science Centre (p84), where there's usually some special activity scheduled. The South African Museum (p97) offers giant whale skeletons and star shows at the attached planetarium. The Castle of Good Hope (p54), with its battlements, museums and horse and carriage rides, offers an entertaining visual history lesson.

Shopping & Eating

Toy and kids' clothing stores are found at all the major shopping malls. For a fine selection of secondhand items, a play area and kids' yoga, visit **Merry Pop Ins** (Map p268; ☎021-422 4911; www.merrypopins.co.za; 201 Bree St, City Bowl; ⏲9.30am-5pm Mon-Thu, 9am-4pm Fri, 10am-2pm Sat; 🚌Upper Loop/Upper Long). The Book Lounge (p90) has a great kids' book section and story readings.

Weekly markets, including Neighbourgoods (p89), Bay Harbour Market (p122) and Blue Bird Garage (p148), have play areas and kid-friendly food. For fish and chips try the Waterfront, Hout Bay and Simon's Town.

NEED TO KNOW

- Try **Cape Town Kids** (www.capetownkids.co.za) for local places and events that will appeal to kids, or **Child Mag** (www.childmag.co.za) for a South African parenting guide.
- Hire a local babysitter from **Super Sitters** (☎073 976 5107, 021-551 7082; www.supersitters.net).

Like a Local

Extremes of wealth in Cape Town mean a chasm separates the life of a typical resident in Crossroads from one in Clifton. However, there are opportunities for visitors to experience the city with insight and sensitivity to local communities of all circumstances.

Weekly Shopping

Joining the long-established Trafalgar Pl flower market (p65) and the bric-a-brac vendors at Milnerton Flea Market (p157) is a trendy breed of artisan food and designer goods and crafts markets. Neighbourgoods (p89) – the original – remains one of the best, although it's so busy each Saturday you may prefer the outdoor Oranjezicht City Farm (p100) or Tokai Forest (p135) markets. Muizenberg locals gather on Friday nights for the bash at the Blue Bird Garage (p148, with great live jazz), while the inhabitants of Hout Bay do the same at the Bay Harbour Market (p122), also very popular during the day on Saturday and Sunday. The Cape Point Vineyards market (p148) on Thursday evening also draws crowds.

Outdoor Activities

Capetonians take full advantage of the magnificent national park in the midst of their city, gathering for weekly hikes (set your alarm to join the 6am Wednesday hike up Lion's Head, p97, for example), sunbathing on beaches or picnics in parks. Don't miss the chance to attend one of the vibey Sunday concerts (p21) held throughout the summer at Kirstenbosch Botanical Gardens.

Surfing has a huge following. If you don't know how, there are several operations ready to teach you in Muizenberg or Table Bay; the more ambitious can try kiteboarding or stand-up paddleboarding. Yachties will always be welcome to join in the Wednesday twilight races at the Royal Cape Yacht Club (p79).

Cyclists should check out the monthly **Moonlight Mass** (www.moonlightmass.co.za) social bike ride, and Promenade Mondays (p123) at Sea Point.

Township Experiences

Cultural tours will give you some insight into life in Cape Town's many poor townships; we particularly like the ones that get you out on the streets, such as the Run Cape Town (p25) 10km jog through Gugulethu, or Juma Mkwela's (p26) street-art tours in Khayelitsha. For a more immersive experience book a night in a township guesthouse or homestay (p210; they're all run by wonderful women), eat at a restaurant such as the buzzy braai (barbecue) joints Mzoli's (p154) in Gugulethu or Nomzamo (p154) in Langa, or volunteer to assist with a charitable project (p248).

Parties & Performances

All Capetonians love a *jol* (party) – preferably one that involves dressing up! The Mother City Queer Project (p22) in December and the Cape Town Minstrel Carnival (p20) and subsequent competitions in January and February are the biggest. Other regularly hosted themed parties and events include raucous **Renegade Bingo** (www.facebook.com/rbingo).

Attending a book launch at the Book Lounge (p90) or a concert at intimate spaces such as Studio 7 (p122), Straight No Chaser (p101), Youngblood Africa (p64) or Alma Café (p134) are other entertaining ways to get down with locals. The First Thursdays and Thursday Late art gallery events (p74) turn parts of the City Bowl and Woodstock into roving street parties.

Tours

If you're short on time, have a specific interest, or want some expert help in seeing Cape Town, there's a small army of tour guides and companies to assist you. The best will provide invaluable insight into local food and wine, flora and fauna, and history and culture.

SEB OLIVER/GETTY IMAGES ©

Lonely Planet's Top Choices

City Sightseeing Cape Town (☎021-511 6000; www.citysightseeing.co.za; adult/child 1 day R170/80, 2 days R270/170) These hop-on, hop-off buses, running two routes, are perfect for a quick orientation, with commentary available in 16 languages. The open-top double-deckers also provide an elevated platform for photos. Buses run at roughly half-hourly intervals between 9am and 4.30pm, with extra services in peak season.

Coffeebeans Routes (Map p278; ☎021-461 3572; www.coffeebeansroutes.com; 22 Hope St, Gardens; tours from R800; 🚌Roodehek) The concept – hooking up visitors with interesting local personalities, including musicians, artists, brewers and designers – is fantastic. Among innovative routes are ones focusing on South Africa's recent revolutionary history, creative enterprises and organic and natural wines.

Awol Tours (Map p280; ☎021-418 3803; www.awoltours.co.za; Information Centre, Dock Rd, V&A Waterfront; 🚌Nobel Square) Discover Cape Town's cycle lanes on this superb city bike tour (three hours; R500), leaving daily from Awol's Waterfront base. Other pedalling itineraries include the Winelands, Cape Point and the township of Masiphumelele – a great alternative to traditional township tours. Also offers guided hikes on Table Mountain (from R1000).

Uthando Township Tour (☎021-683 8523; www.uthandosa.org; 9 Princes Rd, Harfield Village; tours R650) These township tours cost more because half of the money goes towards the social upliftment projects that the tours visit and are specifically designed to support. Usually three or so projects are visited: they could be anything from an organic farm to an old folks' centre.

Run Cape Town (☎072 920 7028; www.runcapetown.co.za; tours R450) Go sightseeing while you get a workout on this innovative company's variety of running routes across the city, both within Table Mountain National Park and further afield in Gugulethu and Darling.

City Walking & Cycling Tours

VoiceMap (www.voicemap.me) This locally developed website and app provides high-quality self-guided walking tours that you can download to your smartphone or listen to on your computer. Narrated by local experts, they provide insight into corners of the city sometimes overlooked by regular guided tours.

Good Hope Adventures (☎021-510 7517; www.goodhopeadventures.com; 3-5hr tours R250-500) Go underground on these fascinating walking tours as you explore the historic tunnels and canals that run beneath the city. You'll need to wear old shoes and clothes and have a torch. Not for the claustrophobic!

Cape Town on Foot (Map p268; ☎021-462 2252; www.wanderlust.co.za; tours R200; ⏱11am Mon-Fri, 10am Sat) These 2½-hour walking tours, leaving from Cape Town Tourism's office on Burg St, cover the central city sights and are led by a knowledgeable guide speaking either English or German.

Day Trippers (☎021-511 4766; www.daytrippers.co.za) Many of this long-established outfit's tours include the chance to go cycling. Their city cycle tour is R360.

Township & Cultural Tours

The best township tours provide a clear understanding of the Mother City's split nature and the challenges faced by the vast majority of Capetonians in their daily lives. They also reveal that these lives are not uniformly miserable and deprived, and that there are many inspiring things to see and do and people to meet.

Typically lasting half a day, township tours usually involve travel in a car or small bus, but there are also walking, cycling and even running tours, if you'd prefer.

NEED TO KNOW

Advance booking Necessary for most tours. Sometimes tours will run only if there's a minimum number of people (eg four in the group).

Where to meet? Check whether the tour company will pick you up from your accommodation and if that's included in the tour cost.

Who benefits? Ask township tour operators how much of the fee goes to help people in the townships – not all tours are run by or benefit residents.

Juma Mkwela (☎073 400 4064; juma.mkwela@gmail.com; Woodstock/Khayelitsha tours R200/500) Zimbabwean Juma is a talented street artist who lives and works in Khayelitsha, where he leads excellent walking tours of the street art brightening up the area around Khayelitsha station. He also used to be based in Woodstock, so is the go-to guide for insight into the rich stock of street art there.

Laura's Township Tours (☎082 979 5831; www.laurastownshiptours.co.za; tours from R400) Gugulethu-based Laura Ndukwana gets rave reviews for her tours of her 'hood. She also runs a breakfast club, where she feeds 40 kids daily before they go to school. Itineraries include a Sunday-morning visit to a charismatic evangelist church, and cooking tours (R700).

Andulela Creative (☎021-790 2592; www.andulela.com; cooking tours from R795) Offers a variety of cultural and culinary-themed tours, including an African cooking tour in Gugulethu and a Cape Malay one in Bo-Kaap.

Vamos (☎072 499 7866; www.vamos.co.za; walking/cycling tours R270/350) Personable guide Siviwe Mbinda is one of the cofounders of this company, offering two- to three-hour walking and cycling tours around Langa. Itineraries often include a performance by the Happy Feet gumboot dance troupe that Siviwe established. They can also arrange homestays in Langa.

Dinner@Mandela's (☎021-790 5817, 083 471 2523; www.dinneratmandelas.co.za; tours R295) A highly recommended alternative or addition to daytime township tours is this evening tour and dinner combination at Imizamo Yethu, which runs Monday and Thursday from 7pm (with pick-ups in the city centre). The meal, which includes African traditional dishes and is veggie-friendly, is held at Tamfanfa's Tavern and is preceded by lively African dancing and a choir singing.

Township Tours SA (☎083 719 4870; tours R85) Afrika Moni can guide you on a two-hour walking tour of Imizamo Yethu (it's on the blue line of the City Sightseeing Cape Town bus), including a visit to a *sangoma* (traditional medicine practi-

JOHN SNELLING/GETTY IMAGES ©

Greenmarket Square (p59)

tioner, usually a woman), a drink of home brew at a shebeen (unlicensed drinking establishment), a look at some art projects and the township museum. Bookings essential.

Transcending History Tours (☎084 883 2514; http://sites.google.com/site/capeslave routetours; 2½hr tours from R200) Lucy Campbell is the go-to academic for these tours, which offer a deeper insight into the rich and fascinating indigenous and slave history of the Cape.

Nature Tours

Hiking and walking tours can be arranged in Table Mountain National Park (p28) and around the Rondevlei Nature Reserve (p143).

Boat trips to spot sharks, whales and pelagic birds can be arranged in Simon's Town (p150).

Birdwatch Cape (☎072 635 1501; www.bird watch.co.za; half-/full-day tours R2000/3200) offers informative tours pointing out the many unique species of the Cape bird kingdom.

Winery Tours

African Story (☎073 755 0444; www. africanstorytours.com; tours R650) Full-day tours include wine, cheese and chocolate tastings at four estates in the Stellenbosch, Franschhoek and Paarl regions.

Bikes 'n Wines (☎074 186 0418; www.bikesn wines.com; half-/full-day tours from R500/1150) These carbon-negative pedalling tours through the Cape's wineland areas cover full- or half-day itineraries (over 30km to 50km) in Stellenbosch, Franschhoek, Elgin and Grabouw, Wellington, Hermanus and the Cape Peninsula.

Easy Rider Wine Tours (☎021-886 4651; www. winetour.co.za; tours R500) Reliable Stellenbosch-based operation. The day kicks off with a cellar tour and includes visits (usually) to Boschendal and Fairview, as well as a few other estates.

Gourmet Wine Tours (☎021-705 4317, 083 229 3581; www.gourmetwinetours.co.za; half-/ full-day tours from R1400/2000) Stephen Flesch, a former chairman of the Wine Tasters Guild of South Africa, has over 35 years of wine-tasting experience and runs tours to the wineries of your choice.

Vine Hopper (☎021-882 8112; www.vinehop per.co.za; 1-/2-day pass R250/440, day trip R500) A hop-on, hop-off bus with two routes, each covering six estates, the Hopper departs hourly from Stellenbosch Tourism (where you can buy tickets). They also offer a full-day tour that includes brandy and sparkling wine cellars.

Wine Flies (☎021-462 8011; www.wineflies. co.za; tours R650) Fun trips taking in four to five estates, including cellar and vineyard walking tours, cheese, olives and chocolate tastings.

Table Mountain National Park

Stretching from Signal Hill to Cape Point, this 220-sq-km park is a natural wonder. With granite and sandstone mountains, boulder-strewn beaches and shady forests, it's a great venue for a host of adventure activities, including hiking, cycling, climbing, water sports and wildlife-watching.

SPROETNIEK/GETTY IMAGES ©

Climber, Table Mountain's west face

Park Highlights

- Spend a night sleeping at one of the tented camps (p208) and hiking some, if not all, of the Hoerikwaggo Trail.
- Ride the cableway (p94) and enjoy the view from the top of the mountain without the slog.
- Paddle with a colony of African penguins at Boulders (p144).
- Journey to Africa's most southwestern tip at Cape Point (p139).
- Climb Lion's Head (p97) for an awesome view over Table Bay and down the Twelve Apostles.
- Go mountain biking in Tokai Forest (p131) or Silvermine (p141).

Table Mountain National Park by Area

Covering about 73% of the Cape Peninsula, the park is made up of many different areas. The following are the key sections to visit:

Table Mountain The park's main attraction is here; climb it, or ride the cableway to within easy walking distance of the summit. (p94)

Lion's Head An easier climb than the main mountain; provides 360-degree views of the mountain, coastline and city. (p97)

Signal Hill Home of the Noon Gun; access by car from Kloof Nek Rd or on foot from Bo-Kaap or Sea Point. (p64)

Oudekraal A picnic area and popular dive site on the Atlantic Coast. (p119)

Back Table Follow the old bridle path up the back of Table Mountain from Constantia Nek to the series of reservoirs. (p129)

Kirstenbosch Botanical Gardens The gardens themselves are managed separately but adjoin sections of the park: hike up the mountain along Skeleton Gorge or Nursery Ravine, or join the contour path that connects across to Constantia Nek through the Cecilia Plantation. (p126)

Tokai Forest A popular, shaded picnic site with an arboretum, as well as hiking, mountain-biking and horse-riding trails. (p131)

Silvermine Nature Reserve Set in the middle of the Southern Peninsula, this section of the park offers boardwalks alongside a river and the reservoir, as well as hikes to caves and magnificent viewpoints. (p141)

Boulders Sheltered sandy coves on False Bay and a reserve protecting a colony of 2100 African penguins. (p144)

Cape of Good Hope The peninsula's tip is protected by this 77.5-sq-km reserve, including the most southwestern point of Africa. (p139)

Hiking & Climbing

There are scores of routes on Table Mountain alone, covering everything from easy strolls to extreme rock climbing. Entrance fees have to be paid for the Boulders, Cape of Good Hope, Oudekraal, Silvermine and Tokai sections of the park, but otherwise the routes are freely open. Signage is improving, but it's far from comprehensive and even with a map it's easy to get lost. Be sure to read about safety before setting off, and consider hiring a guide.

Popular Routes

Platteklip Gorge (p94) is the most straightforward route up the mountain, but if you want less of a slog the Pipe Track (p95) is preferable (though it takes roughly double the time). Climbing Lion's Head (p97), and the walk from the upper cable-way station to Maclear's Beacon (p95), the highest point of the mountain, are both easily achievable.

Possibilities for overnight hikes include the two-day, one-night, 33.8km Cape of Good Hope Trail (p140), and the five-day, four-night, 75km Hoerikwaggo Trail (p140) running the full length of the peninsula from Cape Point to the upper cableway station.

Guided Walks

As well as the companies listed here, Abseil Africa (p95), Awol Tours (p252) and Downhill Adventures (p103) offer guided hikes in the park. Hiking clubs that arrange day and weekend hikes include **Cape**

Table Mountain NP

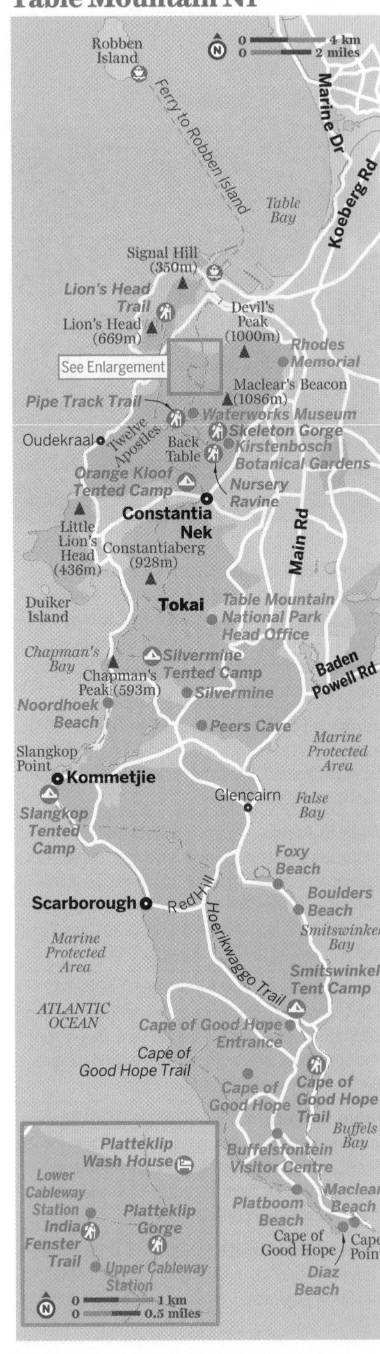

JACQUES MARAIS/GETTY IMAGES ©

View from Table Mountain

Union Mart Hiking Club (www.cumhike.co.za); **Trails Club of South Africa** (www.trailsclub.co.za); and **Mountain Club of South Africa** (Map p278; 021-465 3412; www.mcsacapetown.co.za; 97 Hatfield St, Gardens; Government Avenue).

Venture Forth (086 617 3449, 021-510 3137; www.ventureforth.co.za; from R570 per person) Excellent guided hikes and rock climbs with enthusiastic, savvy guides.

Walk in Africa (021-785 2264; www.walkinafrica.com) Steve Bolnick, an experienced and passionate safari and mountain guide, runs this company. Its five-day, four-night Mountain in the Sea walk runs from Platteklip Gorge to Cape Point, partly following the Hoerikwaggo Trail.

South African Slackpacking (082 882 4388; www.slackpackersa.co.za; per person from R300) Registered nature guide Frank Dwyer runs this operation, which offers one-day and multiday hikes.

Table Mountain Walks (021-715 6136; www.tablemountainwalks.co.za; per person from R450) Offers a range of guided day hikes in different parts of the park, from ascents of Table Mountain to rambles through Silvermine.

Christopher Smith (061 103 7398; www.tablemountain.my-hiking.com) This personable and knowledgeable freelance guide is National Park–trained and has plenty of experience guiding along the Hoerikwaggo Trail and other routes.

Safety First

Just because Table Mountain National Park is on the doorstep of the city doesn't make this wilderness area, extending above 1000m, any less dangerous and unpredictable. Accidents on the mountain are common, often due to a climbing expedition gone wrong; more people have died on Table Mountain than on Mt Everest. Mountain fires have also claimed their victims, and muggings on the slopes of Table Mountain and Lion's Head are unfortunately not rare events.

There are some 50 staff patrolling the park but it covers such a large area they cannot be everywhere, so be well prepared before setting off. Even if taking the cableway to the summit, be aware that the weather up top can change very rapidly. The main emergency numbers are 086 110 6417 to report fires, poaching, accidents and crime, and 021-948 9900 for Wilderness Search and Rescue.

Hiking Tips

Hike with long trousers. Much of the *fynbos* (literally 'fine bush', primarily proteas, heaths and ericas) is tough and scratchy. There's also the seriously nasty blister bush (its leaves look like those of continental parsley); if you brush against this plant cover the spot immediately – exposure to sunlight activates the plant's toxins, which can leave blisters on your skin that may refuse to heal for years.

- Tell someone the route you're planning to climb and take a map (or better still, a guide).
- Stick to well-used paths. Don't be tempted to take shortcuts.
- Take plenty of water, some food, weatherproof clothing and a fully charged mobile phone.
- Wear proper hiking boots or shoes and a sun hat.
- Don't climb alone – park authorities recommend going in groups of four.
- Don't leave litter on the mountain or make a fire on the mountain – they're banned.

Discount Cards

Providing unlimited access to South Africa's national parks for a year are various types of **Wild Cards** (www.wildcard.co.za). International visitors must purchase the All Parks Cluster card (individual/couple/family R1770/2770/3310). South African citizens and Cape Town residents can buy a My Green Card (R110), which allows 12 entries per year to any of Table Mountain National Park's pay points. Either card can be bought at the park's information centres.

VISITOR INFORMATION

Table Mountain National Park Head Office (Map p288; ☎021-712 2337; www.tmnp.co.za; Tokai Manor House, Tokai Rd, Tokai; ⊙8am-5pm Mon-Fri)

Boulders Visitor Centre (Map p292; ☎021-786 2329; 1 Kleintuin Rd, Seaforth, Simon's Town; ⊙8am-4pm)

Buffelsfontein Visitor Centre (Map p293; ☎021-780 9204; Cape of Good Hope; ⊙9am-4pm Mon-Thu, to 3pm Fri)

Slingsby Maps (www.slingsbymaps.com)

Books

To read more about the park and what you can do in it, we recommend the following:

➡ *Mountains in the Sea: Table Mountain to Cape Point* (John Yeld)

➡ *Best Walks in the Cape Peninsula* (Mike Lundy)

➡ *A Walking Guide for Table Mountain* (Shirley Brossy)

➡ *Table Mountain Activity Guide* (Fiona McIntosh)

Eating

It's a wonder that Capetonians look so svelte on the beach because this is one damn delicious city to dine in – probably the best in the whole of Africa. There's a wonderful range of cuisines to sample, including local African and Cape Malay concoctions, superb seafood fresh from the boat and chefs working at the top of their game.

Dining Trends

Cape Town is in the midst of a craze for the low-carb, high-fat diet locally known as 'Banting'. You'll see Banting menu options, such as pizza with a base made from cauliflower, at several places; there are even dedicated Banting restaurants (actually not that great).

Thankfully, there's also been a spike in places offering vegetarian and vegan dishes that are both healthy and delicious. In tune with the Mediterranean climate, more restaurants offer small-plate or tapas-style menus for lighter meals or mix-and-match dining.

The other trend of note is the rise of supper club and 'underground' restaurants, such as Spasie (p70) and **Secret Eats** (www.thesecreteats.com); sign up to their newsletters to find out about their events. If you'd like to dine in a Capetonian's home, **Pozay** (www.pozay.com) can arrange it.

Seafood Galore

Explore local types of fish, including kingklip, or even snoek – a very meaty, mackerel-on-steroids type of fish that is delicious barbecued (or 'braaied' as they say in these parts). Watch out for the many small bones, though.

If you see 'line fish' advertised, it means the catch of the day. Deliciously fresh crayfish can also be had – for a price. Before ordering, make sure what you're eating isn't on the endangered list: details can be found at the **Southern African Sustainable Seafood Initiative** (SASSI; www.wwfsassi.co.za).

Cape Malay Cuisine

This intriguing mix of Malay and Dutch styles, which originated in the earliest days of European settlement, marries pungent spices with local produce. It can be stodgy, with some dishes on the sweet side, but is still well worth trying.

The Cape Malay dish you'll commonly see is *bobotie,* usually made with lightly curried minced beef or lamb topped with savoury egg custard, and served on a bed of turmeric-flavoured rice with a dab of chutney on the side. Some sophisticated versions of *bobotie* use other meats and even seafood.

There's also a great variety of *bredies* – pot stews of meat or fish and vegetables. *Dhaltjies* (chilli bites) are very moreish deep-fried balls of chickpea-flour batter mixed with potato, coriander and spinach. Mild curries are popular and are often served with *rootis,* similar to Indian roti bread but doughier. Also from Indian cooking are samosas, triangular pockets of crisp fried pastry enclosing a spicy vegetable filling. Meat lovers should try *sosaties,* which is a Cape Malay–style kebab.

Desserts include *malva* pudding, a delicious sponge traditionally made with apricot jam and vinegar, and brandy pudding (true Cape Malay cuisine – strongly associated with the Muslim community – contains no alcohol). Also try *koeksusters,* a doughnut dipped in syrup.

African & Afrikaner Cuisine

The staple for most blacks in the townships is rice or else mealie pap (maize porridge), often served with a fatty stew. It isn't especially appetising, but it's cheap. The same goes for the *smilies* (sheep's heads) that you'll see boiled up and served on the streets. Other dishes include *samp* (a mixture of maize and beans), *imifino* (maize meal and vegetables) and *chakalaka* (a tasty fry-up of onions, tomatoes, peppers, garlic, ginger, sweet chilli sauce and curry powder).

Grilled meats, seasoned and sauced on the braai (barbecue), is a dish that cuts across the colour bar as well as being the keystone of traditional Afrikaner cuisine. The Voortrekker heritage comes out in foods such as biltong (deliciously moreish dried beef and venison) and rusks, perfect for those long journeys into the hinterland. *Boerewors* (spicy sausage) is the traditional sausage, and plenty of recipes make use of game; some include venison, which will be some type of buck.

Eating by Neighbourhood

- **City Bowl, Foreshore, Bo-Kaap & De Waterkant** Most options are clustered in City Bowl and De Waterkant, with a scattering of Cape Malay cafes in the Bo-Kaap. (p66)
- **East City, District Six, Woodstock & Observatory** Check out Lower Main Rd in Observatory and the hipster cafes in East City and Woodstock. (p85)
- **Gardens & Surrounds** Kloof St has many good places to eat, several with great views of Table Mountain. (p98)
- **Green Point & Waterfront** Prime seaside views, but choose carefully at the Waterfront, where some places are tourist traps. (p110)
- **Sea Point to Hout Bay** Sea Point's dining scene goes from strength to strength. Camps Bay offers plenty of pricey beachside dining. (p119)
- **Southern Suburbs** Go for a picnic in Kirstenbosch, or fine dining at the wineries of Constantia. (p132)
- **Simon's Town & Southern Peninsula** Great for harbourside seafood served fresh off the boat. (p145)
- **Cape Flats & Northern Suburbs** Traditional African food at township restaurants and roadside braais. (p154)

NEED TO KNOW

Price Ranges

These price ranges represent the cost of an average main dish:

$	less than R75
$$	R75 to R150
$$$	more than R150

Opening Hours

Many restaurants and cafes are closed Sunday.

Cafes 7.30am-5pm Mon-Fri, 8am-3pm Sat

Restaurants 11.30am-3pm & 6-10pm Mon-Sat

Reservations

Reservations are recommended for all top-end restaurants and many popular midrange places too, particularly over busy holiday periods. Top places, such as the Test Kitchen (p86), need reserving several months in advance; some will also require advance payment.

Guides & Blogs

Rossouw's Restaurants (www.rossouwsrestaurants.com) Sprightly criticism of Cape Town's restaurants online; also publishes an annual print guide.

Eat Out (www.eatout.co.za) Online reviews and annual magazine guide with Cape Town and Western Cape reviews.

Once Bitten (www.oncebitten.co.za) Reviews and features by the *Mail & Guardian* journalist Brent Meersman.

BYO

Most restaurants are licensed, but some allow you to bring your own wine for little or no corkage fee. Call ahead to check.

Smoking

Smoking in restaurants is permitted only if there is a separate room where smokers are seated.

Tipping

Leaving 10% is standard, and more if the service is good.

Lonely Planet's Top Choices

Chef's Warehouse & Canteen Liam Tomlin's globally inspired tapas, matched with excellent wines. (p67)

Hallellujah Small-plates gem with an Asian-meets-African flair. (p99)

Ferdinando's Fabulous 'secret' pizzeria run by a fun couple and their cute dog. (p98)

La Mouette Reasonably priced fine dining in a lovely Sea Point courtyard and house. (p120)

La Colombe A new Constantia location but still the same sublime cooking from Scot Kirton. (p133)

Greenhouse Edible artistry marries interesting flavours and cooking techniques. (p133)

Best by Budget

$

Kleinsky's Delicatessen Jewish-style cafe baking their own bagels in Sea Point. (p119)

Kitchen Fabulous cafe with the First Lady's seal of approval. (p85)

Clifford & Sandra's Township food cooked with love at Khayelitsha market. (p154)

$$

Olympia Café & Deli Dig into huge bowls of mussels at this Kalk Bay institution. (p146)

La Boheme Delicious Spanish-style tapas and other small plates in Sea Point. (p119)

Pot Luck Club The more affordable operation of top chef Luke Dale-Roberts. (p86)

$$$

Chef's Table Book ahead for one of the four tables in the Mount Nelson's kitchen. (p99)

Aubergine Fine dining at its best at this long-standing Gardens restaurant. (p100)

Best by Cuisine

African

Africa Café Dishes from around the continent. (p68)

Addis in Cape Ethiopian feast eaten with your fingers; plenty of vegetarian options. (p68)

Cape Malay

Bo-Kaap Kombuis Great views high up in the Bo-Kaap; also serves vegetarian dishes. (p69)

Jonkershuis Casual brasserie-style restaurant at Groot Constantia. (p133)

Italian

Pesce Azzurro Delicious, rustic Italian pasta and seafood dishes. (p86)

La Perla Classy dining on Sea Point's prom since 1959. (p119)

95 Keerom Award-winning pasta from chef Giorgio Nava. (p69)

Japanese

Kyoto Garden Sushi Unbeatable selection of sushi and sashimi. (p99)

Izakaya Matsuri Relaxed Japanese-pub-style eatery with an expert sushi chef. (p69)

Downtown Ramen Hipster hang-out dishing up spicy noodles. (p86)

Indian

Bombay Brasserie Feasts fit for a maharaja. (p69)

Masala Dosa Crispy lentil pancakes and tasty curries on Long St. (p67)

Chandani Woodstock long-runner, serving curries with panache. (p86)

Vegetarian & Vegan

Plant Organic wines alongside vegan delights, including cakes. (p66)

Raw and Roxy Healthy, vegan cafe, newly minted in Woodstock. (p86)

Nü Fresh salads, wraps and juices in Green Point. (p111)

Best Deli Cafes

Giovanni's Deli World Bursting with flavourful products; great for coffee. (p111)

Melissa's Pay by weight for delicious breakfast and lunch buffets. (p99)

Bread, Milk & Honey Impressive lunch buffet spread and takeaway options. (p67)

Best Gourmet Cafes

Starlings Cafe Charming breakfast and lunch spot in the southern suburbs. (p132)

Four&Twenty Cafe & Pantry Toast of Wynberg for its baked goods and lovely meals. (p133)

Hemelhuijs Stylish, arty interior and adventurous cooking. (p67)

Best Seafood

Ocean Jewels Fantastic fish cafe in the Woodstock Exchange. (p85)

Live Bait At Kalk Bay harbour, so you know the fish is fresh. (p146)

Best for Families

Cafe Paradiso Cooking classes for kids at this convivial Italian joint. (p99)

Deer Park Café Playground right next to this popular hillside cafe. (p99)

Drinking & Nightlife

Cape Town didn't become known as the 'Tavern of the Seas' for nothing. There are scores of bars – with stunning views of either beach or mountain – in which to sip cocktails, fine wines or craft beers. If strutting your stuff on the dance floor is more your thing, then there's bound to be a club to suit.

Join the Jol

The busy nights are Wednesday, Friday or Saturday when you'll see how the locals like to party, or *jol*, as they say here. But it's not all about drinking and dancing. Cape Town's nightlife embraces cabaret and comedy venues, and live-music gigs from jazz to rap, as well as hybrid events such as First Thursdays (p74).

What to Drink

There are abundant opportunities to sample the Cape's wines in bars and restaurants and at the cellar door. Cocktails are also popular, and the best mixologists incorporate local flavours and artisanal spirits into their liquid creations.

European beer-making on the Cape also has a long history here: Pieter Visagle is said to have first brewed ale on the banks of the Liesbeek River in 1658. At Newlands Brewery (p131), major brands such as Castle and Black Label are pumped into barrels and 750mL (quart) and 330mL ('dumpy') bottles. Another popular mass-market brand is Windhoek, brewed in Namibia.

Microbrewing is booming, too, with craft brewers clustering in Woodstock and Salt River, where you'll find the likes of Devil's Peak, Riot Factory and Garigista, among others. Beer lovers should mark their calendar for the **Cape Town Festival of Beer** (www.capetownfestivalofbeer.co.za) at the end of November.

Clubbing

Cape Town's club scene is firmly plugged into the global dance network, so expect star appearances by international DJs. Trance parties, such as **Vortex** (www.intothevortex.co.za) and **Alien Safari** (www.facebook.com/aliensafari), held outdoors an hour or so from the city centre, happen throughout the year; check the respective websites for details or make some enquiries at backpacker hostels.

Drinking & Nightlife by Neighbourhood

NEED TO KNOW

Opening Hours

Bars noon-midnight; but some stay open much later

Clubs 8pm-4am; but most don't get going until well after midnight

Cover Charges

From R20 to R100 for clubs, depending on the event.

Tipping

It's the norm to tip bartenders 10%.

Event Tickets

Computicket (www.computicket.com)

Webtickets (www.webtickets.co.za)

Facts

- The alcohol content of beer is around 5% – stronger than UK or US beer.
- It's OK to drink the tap water.

Information

Tonight (www.iol.co.za/tonight)

Cape Town Magazine (www.capetownmagazine.co.za)

More Than Food (www.morethanfood.co.za)

The Next 48 Hours (www.48hours.co.za)

Thunda (www.thunda.com)

The Night Life (www.thenightlife.co.za)

Craft Beer Blogs

Craft Beer Project (www.thecraftbeerproject.co.za)

The Brewmistress (www.brewmistress.co.za)

Lonely Planet's Top Choices

Publik Excellent wines from some of the Cape's more boutique and lesser-known vineyards. (p70)

Weinhaus + Biergarten Craft beers, good eats and live music in a city-centre courtyard. (p70)

Banana Jam Go-to bar for local craft beer enthusiasts, plus tasty Caribbean food. (p133)

Brass Bell Classic Kalk Bay pub – so close to the water you could jump in. (p147)

Truth Cafe-bar with a steampunk theme where the waitstaff wear jaunty hats. (p87)

Honest Chocolate Cafe Homage to fine dark chocolate in liquid, solid, ice-cream and cake form. (p70)

Best Sea Views

Dunes Bring your sunscreen and towel – you're right next to Hout Bay's beach. (p121)

Tobago's Bar & Terrace Splendid sunset views from this Granger Bay hideaway. (p112)

Blue Peter Admire Table Mountain and Robben Island from this Bloubergstrand pub. (p156)

Best Cocktails & Spirits

Bascule Sign up for a whisky tasting or simply enjoy the view of the marina with your dram. (p112)

Vista Bar Refreshing and inventive drinks menu at the One & Only's lounge bar. (p112)

Orphanage Dark, sophisticated and stylish bar with creative libations. (p70)

Best Beers

Forrester's Arms Classic Southern Suburbs pub with an outdoor garden and kid's play area. (p134)

Taproom Showcase for Devil's Peak beers, with a spectacular view of the mountain. (p87)

Beerhouse Get very merry sampling their 99 brands of ale. (p71)

Best Coffee

Bean There Feel good sipping fair-trade coffee. (p72)

Deluxe Coffeeworks Hang out at their roastery in the Yard. (p72)

Hout Bay Coffee Expertly made drinks and luscious cakes. (p121)

Espressolab Microroasters Global coffee blends treated with the same respect as fine wines. (p87)

Best Clubbing

Assembly Dance the night away in an old furniture factory. (p88)

Waiting Room Peer down on Long St from this grooving attic and rooftop bar. (p71)

Shimmy Beach Club Glam-to-the-max club and restaurant with a small fake beach. (p112)

Best African Beats

aMadoda Braai Township-style BBQ and shebeen in Woodstock. (p87)

Buyel' Embo Village DJ events and live music at this hip Khayelitsha complex. (p155)

Entertainment

Rappers and comedians performing in a mix of Afrikaans and English; a cappella township choirs and buskers at the Waterfront; theatre on the streets and in old churches; intimate performances in suburban living rooms – the Mother City dazzles with a diverse and creative range of entertainment, with live music a particular highlight.

All that Jazz

Many world-renowned jazz artists began their careers in Cape Town, perhaps because the free-flowing nature of the genre is so well suited to such a relaxed, cosmopolitan city. Although there are few permanent jazz venues, it's a rare night that there's not a jazz jam on somewhere in the city; check www.capetownjazz.com for details.

All other forms of live music can be enjoyed here, too. The line-up for the celebrated Sunday afternoon concerts at Kirstenbosch Botanical Gardens (p21) reads like a who's who of the South African music scene, skipping right across the genres.

Dance & Theatre

Capetonians also love dance. Apart from the **City Ballet** (www.capetowncityballet.org.za) there's also **Jazzart Dance Theatre** (www.jazzart.co.za), South Africa's oldest modern dance company, and the **Cape Dance Company** (www.capedancecompany.co.za) and associated Cape Youth Dance Company, made up of talented youths aged 13 to 23. Shows can be seen at Artscape and the Baxter Theatre, which along with the Fugard form a trinity of top performing-arts venues.

More intimate performance venues, such as the Kalk Bay Theatre, Theatre on the Bay, the various studios at the University of Cape Town Hiddingh Campus in Gardens and the studio theatre above Alexander Bar & Cafe, also thrive.

Comedy & Cinema

Capetonian comedians whose shows you should keep an eye out for include TV star Marc Lottering (www.marclottering.com) and Kurt Schoonraad, who hosts the Jou Ma Se Comedy Club.

At shopping malls, the **Ster Kinekor** (www.sterkinekor.com) and **Nu Metro** (www.numetro.co.za) multiplexes show the latest international movies and the occasional art-house title. The Fugard's Bioscope screens digital broadcasts of shows by the Bolshoi, Royal Opera House and Royal Ballet.

Entertainment by Neighbourhood

- **City Bowl, Foreshore, Bo-Kaap & De Waterkant** Artscape, classical concerts at the old town hall and events at bars and clubs along Long St. (p74)
- **East City, District Six, Woodstock & Observatory** The Fugard Theatre and live gigs at the Assembly and Tagore. (p88)
- **Green Point & Waterfront** Cape Town Stadium for occasional concerts by international stars; the Waterfront for free music and other entertainment. (p113)
- **Southern Suburbs** Shows at the Baxter Theatre and outdoor concerts at Kirstenbosch Botanical Gardens. (p134)

NEED TO KNOW

Tickets

Computicket (www.computicket.com)

Webtickets (www.webtickets.co.za)

Quicket (www.quicket.co.za)

Information

Cape Town Magazine (www.capetownmagazine.com)

What's On! (www.whatson.co.za)

The Next 48 Hours (www.48hours.co.za)

Tonight (www.iol.co.za/tonight)

Readings

Find book readings at the **Book Lounge** (p90) and **Kalk Bay Books** (p149), and poetry performances on Monday at **A Touch of Madness** (p86).

Film & Music Festivals

Encounters (www.encounters.co.za) Documentary films, June.

Shnit (www.capetown.shnit.org) Short film fest, October.

Wavescape Surf Film Festival (www.wavescapefestival.com) December movie fest.

Cape Town Electronic Music Festival (www.ctemf.com) Three-day event in February.

Cape Town Music Week (www.capetownmusicweek.com) Local acts, late September/early October.

Rocking the Daisies (www.rockingthedaisies.com) Three-day music fest, October.

Lonely Planet's Top Choices

Baxter Theatre Premier theatre and performing arts complex in a striking 1970s building. (p134)

Fugard Theatre Vibrant addition to city's theatre and cinema scene set in a converted church. (p88)

Studio 7 Great acoustic sets, close-up and personal, at this Sea Point lounge. (p122)

Assembly Live music and DJ performance space, also hosts events. (p88)

Kirstenbosch Summer Sunset Concerts Picnic while top South African musicians play the beautiful outdoors. (p21)

Best Theatre

Artscape Behemoth of the Capetonian arts scene, hosting big and small shows alike. (p74)

Alexander Bar & Cafe Upstairs studio space hosts some of Cape Town's most innovative theatre and cabaret. (p71)

Theatre on the Bay Classy venue for plays and light entertainment in Camps Bay. (p122)

Best Music

Bands & Big Acts

Grandwest Casino Plush venue hosting regular concerts by major international singers and bands. (p157)

Cape Town Stadium One Direction, the Eagles and Michael Bublé have all played here. (p110)

Acoustic Sets

Studio 7 Music club in a living room hosts gigs by top local and international musicians. (p122)

Alma Café Cosy and popular venue for intimate gigs in southern suburbs. (p134)

Slow Life Live music and sometimes comedy gigs on Friday and Saturday nights in Muizenberg. (p147)

Jazz & African

Straight No Chaser Tiny jazz club, run by a hardcore jazz cat. (p101)

Crypt Jazz Restaurant Book ahead for shows in the crypt of St George's Cathedral. (p74)

Classical

Cape Town City Hall Home base for the Cape Philharmonic Orchestra. (p63)

Casa Labia Cultural Centre Recitals are held in the ornately decorated salon of this heritage mansion in Muizenberg. (p141)

Best Movies

Labia Retro-cool cinema in Gardens specialising in art-house titles. (p101)

Pink Flamingo Monday-night movies at the rooftop trailer park of the Grand Daddy Hotel. (p75)

Galileo Open Air Cinema From November to April at the Waterfront, Kirstenbosch and Hillcrest Estate in Durbanville. (p113)

Best Cabaret & Comedy

Jou Ma Se Comedy Club Laugh along with South Africa's leading comics at the Waterfront. (p113)

Stardust The waitstaff can really belt out a tune. (p88)

Evita se Perron Theatre legend Pieter-Dirk Uys' Darling home for his satirical cast of characters. (p180)

Shopping

Bring an empty suitcase because the chances are that you'll be leaving Cape Town laden with booty. There's a practically irresistible range of products on offer, including traditional African crafts, ceramics, fashion, fine wines and contemporary art. You'll also find antiques and curios from all over Africa, but shop carefully as there are many fakes among the originals.

Art & Design

Local design came to the fore during Cape Town's stint as World Design Capital in 2014. The best places to tap into what's likely to be the next big thing are the weekly markets such as Neighbourgoods (p89) and the collective designer spaces such as Woodstock Exchange (p90) and Woodstock Foundry (p91). Running alongside the annual Design Indaba (p20) festival is the Southern Guild show for local design – it also has a permanent gallery (p89) in Woodstock.

Commercial galleries stocking a broad range of visual arts are big in both the City Bowl and Woodstock areas, with the highlight of the month being the First Thursday events that show openings often coincide with. There are also some particularly talented ceramicists here, including Barbara Jackson and Clementina van der Walt (www.clementina.co.za).

Ethical Shopping

Shopping here can also effect positive change, as when proceeds from your purchase of some township-produced goods go towards helping people struggling with poverty, or towards supporting projects to deal with health issues such as HIV/AIDS or education.

A great one-stop shop for many such items is the Watershed (p113). Here you'll find established brands, such as **Wola Nani** (www.wolanani.co.za), specialising in picture frames and papier-mâché bowls, and the beaded works of **Monkeybiz** (www.monkeybiz.co.za), alongside up-and-coming businesses such as the fashion accessories of **Lulu K** (www.lulukdesigns.com) or Cool-tabs (made from recycled can tabs).

Fashion for All

Scout the boutiques on Long and Kloof Sts for upcoming designers and affordable streetwear from the likes of **Unknown Union** (www.unknownunion.co.za) or **Strato** (www.wearstrato.com). More couture clothing is produced by **Stefania Morland** (www.stefaniamorland.com) and **Klûk CGDT** (www.klukcgdt.com).

Shopping by Neighbourhood

- **City Bowl, Foreshore, Bo-Kaap & De Waterkant** Long St offers up an eclectic retail mix; African crafts can be found in Greenmarket Sq. (p75)
- **Gardens & Surrounds** Kloof St has several fashion boutiques, galleries and gift stores. (p101)
- **Green Point & Waterfront** There's Victoria Wharf mall and plenty of other retail action in Cape Town's premier shopping destination. (p113)
- **Simon's Town & Southern Peninsula** Kalk Bay offers a brilliant mix of crafts, antique and fashion boutiques. (p135)

NEED TO KNOW

Opening Hours

Shops 8.30am-5pm Mon-Fri, 8.30am-1pm Sat

Malls 9am-9pm daily

Bargaining

When buying handicrafts from street hawkers and at some market stalls, some bargaining is expected. It's not a sophisticated game, though, so don't press too hard.

Taxes & Refunds

A value-added tax (VAT) of 14% is included in prices. Foreign visitors can reclaim some of their VAT expenses upon departure at the airport.

Events

Design Indaba (p20) Local and international designers across various media swap ideas and show products in late February and early March.

Rondebosch Potters Market (p125) Held on the second-last Saturdays of March and November.

Lonely Planet's Top Choices

Watershed Outstanding selection of local crafts, design and fashion at the Waterfront. (p113)

Old Biscuit Mill Fabulous retail and Saturday's Neighbourgoods Market. (p89)

Kalk Bay Modern Fine art, jewellery and fabrics beside the sea. (p148)

KIN Finely curated selection of contemporary arts and crafts, ideal for superior souvenirs. (p102)

Best Fashion

Unknown Union Statement pieces, as well as more casual clothing, on Kloof St. (p102)

South African Market Showcase for local fashion and jewellery, alongside other design products. (p75)

Grandt Mason Originals Beautiful fabrics are used to create one-off shoes and boots. (p90)

Best Ceramics

Art in the Forest Sells established and developing talents; the profits help a worthy cause. (p135)

Imiso Ceramics Creative clay art at the Biscuit Mill. (p89)

Pottershop Great selection by local ceramicists, including discounted rejects (with barely noticeable faults). (p149)

Best Contemporary Art

Stevenson Often humorous, subversive work in shows at this Woodstock gallery. (p89)

Goodman Gallery Cape Represents luminaries like William Kentridge, as well as up-and-coming artists. (p89)

Luvey 'n Rose Mash-up of collectable antiques and works by key South African and African artists. (p75)

Best Crafts

Red Rock Tribal Eclectic selection, ranging from tin-can planes to old Ethiopian silver. (p149)

Mogalakwena Colourful stitched panels and other Pedi crafts from the Limpopo province. (p76)

African Image Fab range of new and old crafts and artefacts at reasonable prices. (p76)

Best Weekly Markets

Oranjezicht City Farm Fresh locally grown produce, edible treats and crafts. (p100)

Blue Bird Garage Fun Friday-night bash in Muizenberg, with tons of food, some fashion and crafts. (p148)

Bay Harbour Market Seaside market that's great for souvenirs, food and relaxing at the weekend. (p122)

Best Books & Music

Book Lounge Hub of Cape Town's literary scene, with a packed schedule of readings and events. (p90)

Clarke's Bookshop Best range of books on South Africa and the continent. (p77)

African Music Store Take home CDs and DVDs for memories of a highly musical city. (p76)

Best Ethical Products

Montebello Artists studios scattered around a central craft shop, stocking a great range of gifts. (p135)

Streetwires They can build anything out of wire here – including life-sized sculptures of Mandela. (p78)

Monkeybiz Rainbow-coloured beadwork crafts, made by local township women. (p78)

Sports & Activities

Want to get active? You've come to the right place. Cape Town is a nirvana for the adventure-sport enthusiast, with operators lining up to ensure you don't go home without having experienced an adrenaline rush. Capetonians are also avid sports fans – attending a football, rugby or cricket game here is highly recommended.

Getting Active

With wind-whipped waves and Table Mountain on hand, surfing, hiking and rock climbing are hugely popular and can easily be organised. For adventures such as shark-cage diving or paragliding, you'll need to travel out of the city or wait for the ideal weather conditions.

But it's not all about thrill-seeking: the Mother City is also a fabulous location for golf, a bike ride or a canter along the beach on horseback. There are plenty of gyms and swimming pools, too.

Spectator Sports

SOCCER

The biggest game on the Cape is soccer (football, known locally as *diski*). Cape Town has two teams in the national **Premier Soccer League** (www.psl.co.za): **Santos** (www.thepeoplesteam.co.za) and **Ajax Cape Town** (www.ajaxct.com). If either of these teams is playing the nation's top soccer teams, the Kaizer Chiefs and the Orlando Pirates (both based in Johannesburg), you'll have to fight for tickets, which start at R40. The season runs from August to May, with matches played at either Cape Town Stadium or Athlone Stadium.

CRICKET

Capetonians have a soft spot for cricket, and Sahara Park Newlands is where all top national and international games are played. The game was the first of the 'whites-only' sports to wholeheartedly adopt a nonracial attitude, and development programs in the townships have paid dividends: hailing from Langa is Thami Tsolekile, who played three test matches for South Africa as wicket keeper. The local team is the **Cape Cobras** (www.wpca.org.za).

RUGBY

Rugby (union, not league) is the traditional Afrikaner sport. Games are held at the Newlands Rugby Stadium, with the most popular matches being those in the Super 14 tournament – teams from South Africa, Australia and New Zealand compete from late February until the end of May.

Sports & Activities by Neighbourhood

- **Gardens & Surrounds** Hiking, climbing and abseiling in Table Mountain National Park. (p94)
- **Sea Point to Hout Bay** Swimming or kayaking at Sea Point; diving at Oudekraal; snorkelling with seals at Hout Bay. (p123)
- **Southern Suburbs** Watching sport at Newlands; hiking up the mountain from Kirstenbosch; zip-lining in Constantia. (p136)
- **Simon's Town & Southern Peninsula** Surfing, horse riding, kayaking, mountain biking and hiking are all big down towards Cape Point. (p150)
- **Northern Suburbs** Head here to windsurf, kitesurf, sandboard and skydive. (p156)

NEED TO KNOW

Contacts & Information

Pedal Power Association (www.pedalpower.org.za)

Table Mountain Bikers (www.tablemountainbikers.co.za)

TASKS: The African Sea Kayak Society (www.seakayak.co.za/tasks)

Wavescape Surfing South Africa (www.wavescape.co.za)

Western Province Golf Union (www.wpgu.co.za)

South African Rugby Union (www.sarugby.net)

The Soccer Pages (www.thesoccerpages.com)

Cycling Events

Cape Town Cycle Tour (p20) Held on a Saturday in early March; with more than 30,000 entrants each year it's the largest bicycle race in the world.

Absa Cape Epic (www.cape-epic.com) An eight-day mountain-biking event with a Western Cape route that changes each year.

Tickets

Computicket (www.computicket.com)

Webtickets (www.webtickets.co.za)

Lonely Planet's Top Choices

Hiking in Table Mountain National Park Hire a guide so you don't get lost, and learn more about the Cape floral kingdom. (p28)

Abseil Africa Dangle from a rope off the edge of Table Mountain and take in the view. (p95)

Downhill Adventures Offering a range of adrenaline-fuelled activities, from mountain biking to surf safaris. (p103)

Animal Ocean Flip around with Cape fur seals off Duiker Island, either snorkelling or diving. (p123)

Skateboarding Join the boarders at Promenade Mondays and the Mill St Bridge Skate Park. (p123)

Best Sports Venues

Sahara Park Newlands Judge for yourself whether this is the world's best-looking cricket ground. (p135)

Newlands Rugby Stadium Local team the Stormers play at this home of South African rugby. (p135)

Best Swimming

Sea Point Pavilion Classic art deco complex with several pools and diving boards. (p123)

Buffels Bay One of the best ocean rock pools within the Cape of Good Hope nature reserve. (p139)

Best Aerial Adventures

Cape Town Tandem Paragliding Pretend you're James Bond as you paraglide off Lion's Head. (p103)

Cape Town Helicopters Amazing bird's-eye view across the peninsula. (p115)

SA Forest Adventures Zip-line across a ravine overlooking Constantia's vineyards. (p136)

Best Sailing

Waterfront Charters Clink champagne glasses at sunset on a cruise across Table Bay. (p114)

Yacoob Tourism Speed-boat jaunts or a cruise on a catamaran. (p114)

Ocean Sailing Academy Sailing courses, tailored to all skill levels. (p115)

Best for Diving

Two Oceans Aquarium Learn to dive and get into the tank with the aquarium's sharks and other sea creatures. (p115)

Into the Blue Sea Point operation that can also arrange shark-cage diving. (p123)

Pisces Divers Dive sites in False Bay with this Simon's Town–based operation. (p150)

Best Golfing

Metropolitan Golf Club Stunning location between Cape Town Stadium and Green Point Park. (p115)

Milnerton Golf Club Magnificent position overlooking Table Bay, with great views of Table Mountain. (p158)

Best Surfing, Windsurfing & Kakayking

Gary's Surf School Stand on a board within a day, or you don't pay for the lesson. (p150)

Surfstore Africa Learn to kitesurf or stand-up paddle-board (SUP). (p150)

Kaskazi Kayaks Close encounters with dolphins, seals and penguins while paddling on the Atlantic. (p115)

GLBT Travellers

Africa's pinkest city is a glam-to-the-max destination that any GLBT traveller should have on their bucket list. De Waterkant, the queer precinct, is welcoming to everyone, from Cape Town's finest drag queens to leathered-up Muscle Marys. Throughout the year the city hosts several gay festivals and events.

GLBT Rights & Challenges

During apartheid, gay male erotic contact was illegal. (Female same-sex conduct never was, however: as in other formerly British colonies such activities were considered simply unthinkable!) With democracy, South Africa became the first country in the world to enshrine gay and lesbian rights in its constitution. There's an equal age of consent and GLBT people are legally entitled to marry, too.

Sadly, alternative lifestyles are not embraced by all South Africans. In 2014, a 21-year-old coloured gay man was brutally murdered in a gay hate crime in the Western Cape. It is not uncommon for lesbians in black communities to be subjected to 'corrective rape'. Anti-hate-crime legislation exists, but the laws are rarely put into action.

In the News

Happier news recently in Cape Town has been the establishment of the **Pride Shelter Trust** (www.prideshelterturst.com), Africa's first autonomous GBLT crisis centre, which has been in operation since 2011.

Cape Town's lesbian community has been striking out with the women-only parties **M.I.S.S** (Make It Sexy Sisters; www.facebook.com/MISSmakeitsexysisters), and the Unofficial Pink Parties, which are lesbian-run but welcoming to everyone.

Also in 2014, **SA Leather South Africa** (www.sal.qw.co.za) voted to become a pansexual organisation – previously it had been men-only. If you fancy going hiking with gays and gay-friendly folk while in the Mother City, check out the **Cape Town Gay Hiking Club** (www.facebook.com/groups/6068816435).

Gay Language

Moffie, the local term for a homosexual, comes from the Afrikaans word for glove; it's also the title of the flamboyant leaders of the performance troupes in the Cape Town Minstrel Carnival (p20). Among gays, *moffie* has come to be used like 'queer' – in an affirmative way to repudiate its negative connotations.

Older Capetonian gays will also remember an apartheid-era code language, called 'Gayle', in which women's names stand in for certain words; for example, 'Beaulah' for 'beautiful' and 'Hilda' for 'ugly'.

GLBT by Neighbourhood

- **De Waterkant** This compact 'gaybourhood' is at its cruisiest on Friday and Saturday nights. (p73)
- **Gardens & Surrounds** Inner-city 'hoods with a sprinkling of GLBT-run and -friendly businesses. (p92)
- **Sea Point to Hout Bay** Sea Point has long had a gay vibe; Clifton 3rd is the beach for the beautiful, and Sandy Bay for nudists. (p116)

NEED TO KNOW

Information

The Pink Map (www.mapmyway.co.za/printed-maps)

Pink South Africa (www.pinksa.co.za)

GayCapeTown4u.com (www.gaycapetown4u.com)

Gaynet Cape Town (www.gaynetcapetown.co.za)

Mamba (www.mambaonline.com)

Mambagirl (www.mambagirl.com)

Magazines & Newspapers

Pink Tongue Free monthly newspaper covering local GLBT news and events.

Out Africa Magazine (www.outafricamagazine.com) Free quarterly publication.

Support

Triangle Project (www.thetriangleproject.org) One of the leading gay support organisations, offering legal advice and a range of education programs.

Lonely Planet's Top Choices

Glen Boutique Hotel Glam Sea Point digs and Cape Town's best 'straight-friendly' hotel. (p206)

Crew Bar The most happening of De Waterkant's clubs, with muscular bar men. (p73)

Sugarhut Venue for the fab lesbian Unofficial Pink Party events. (p87)

Clifton 3rd Beach See and be seen on the cruisiest of Clifton's quartet of beaches. (p118)

Deon Nagel's Gat Party Learn to dance Afrikaans-style. (p157)

Sandy Bay Shed your clothes and inhibitions at this gorgeous nude beach. (p118)

Best GLBT Stays

Purple House Go B&B or self-catering – it's all good. (p202)

Colette's Women-friendly B&B with pet ducks in Pinelands. (p210)

Village Lodge The rooftop bar and pool are its pulling factor. (p202)

De Waterkant House One of several gay-friendly Village & Life properties. (p202)

Huijs Haerlem Gay-owned (but not exclusively gay) Sea Point guesthouse. (p206)

Best GLBT Bars & Clubs

Alexander Bar & Café Classy venue with theatre that puts on a great range of shows. (p71)

Amsterdam Action Bar & Backstage Watch the comings and goings of the Gay Village from its streetside balcony. (p73)

Bar Code Leather and latex rule; depending on the night, clothing may be optional. (p73)

Beaulah Fun club for the girls – but welcoming to the boys, too. (p73)

Best GLBT Eats

Beefcakes Burger bar with campy bingo, drag shows and topless muscle-boy waiters. (p69)

Lazari Ditch the diet: the cakes and bakes here are divine. (p99)

Cafe Manhattan Pioneer of De Waterkant gay scene, given a recent revamp. (p73)

Masala Dosa Add a bit of spice to your diet at this gay-owned Long St restaurant. (p67)

La Petite Tarte Darling spot when it's time for tea and cake. (p69)

Best GLBT Festivals & Events

Cape Town Pride (www.capetownpride.org) End of Feburary; in De Waterkant.

Out in Africa: SA International Gay & Lesbian Film Festival (www.oia.co.za) November; in Cape Town.

Globeflight Pink Loerie Mardis Gras & Arts Festival (www.pinkloerie.co.za) End of April, early May; in Knysna.

Miss Gay Western Cape (www.missgay.co.za) November; beauty pageant in Cape Town.

MCQP (www.mcqp.co.za) December; fancy-dress dance party in Cape Town.

Wineries

With over 200 wine farms within a day's drive, Cape Town is the natural hub for touring the Western Cape's Winelands. This is where South Africa's wine industry began back in the 17th century; by 2013, the annual harvest of grapes was close to 1.5 million tonnes, of which 79% were used for wine and other alcoholic beverages.

Growing Industry

Scores of new wine producers join the industry each year. While many are content to remain as micro-wineries, honing their wines to perfection, others are seeking to capitalise on the industry's popularity by adding museums, restaurants, accommodation, walking trails and other attractions. We review the more notable of these, along with vineyards that are renowned for their fine wines.

Planning Your Wine Tour

Just starting out? Heed the following and you'll never be caught confusing your *vin rouge* with your vanity.

STARTING OFF

Call ahead to any estates you want to visit to make sure they're open and not too crowded (some get very busy from December to February). Allow around an hour for tasting at each estate. It's worth joining at least one cellar tour – these can be fascinating. Appoint a designated driver; for those without their own wheels, there are plenty of guided tours (p27) of the Winelands.

TASTING

Many (but not all) cellars will charge you for tasting – usually a little, sometimes a lot, and often refundable with a minimum purchase. You might get to take home the logo-branded glass you tasted from – it saves them the washing up, and gives you a souvenir. Usually the server (who might even be the winemaker at a small family winery) will guide you through the range, starting with whites (dry, then less dry), moving through reds, then on to sweet and fortified wines. To get the most out of it all, give the wine a deep sniff and swirl a little around in your mouth – then spit that out in the spittoon provided (save swallowing for the ones you really like). Drain the glass before moving on, but don't bother rinsing – better a stray drop of different wine than risk dilution!

AGEING

Producers will usually sell their wine soon after it's bottled, and most of it is then ready to drink. Even many serious red wines these days are designed to give youthful pleasure – though an estate may recommend waiting a year or longer to get the benefit of mature flavours. Good restaurants will often sell particular reds and whites after some bottle-ageing.

BUYING

Intercontinental delivery is expensive, so check the cost before buying a crate. Wine prices vary hugely, of course: there's a big bulge between R50 and R150 for good reds and whites, and an increasing number of grand wines going for much higher than that.

NEED TO KNOW

Advance Reading

Platter's South African Wine Guide (www.wineonaplatter.com) The definitive annual guide to the nation's wines, providing tasting notes and star ratings for thousands of bottles.

Exploring the Cape Winelands of South Africa (Doris Jansen and Kay Leresche; 2013) Pictorial guide to 101 wineries.

Love Your Wine (Cathy Marston; 2015) Will help you get to grips with wine tasting. Marston also regularly updates her *Unwined* blog (www.cathymarston.co.za).

Wine of the New South Africa (Tim James; 2013) Profiles of 150 of South Africa's leading wineries. Also see James' blog *Grape* (www.grape.co.za).

Courses

Cape Wine Academy (www.capewineacademy.co.za) Runs wine appreciation courses in Stellenbosch, Cape Town and other locations around the Western Cape.

Fynbos Estate (www.fynbosestate.co.za) Hands-on winemaking courses in the Paardeberg mountains, 15km outside Malmesbury (an hour's drive from Cape Town).

International Wine Education Centre (www.thewinecentre.co.za) A variety of courses are taught by Cape Town–based wine expert Cathy Marston and other local experts.

Brandy

The Western Cape Brandy Route links up distilleries at 13 wineries; for more information contact the **South African Brandy Foundation** (☎021-882 8954; www.sabrandy.co.za). The Van Ryn Brandy Cellar (p162) in Stellenbosch makes world-class brandy and runs superb tours.

Wineries by Region

➡ **Constantia** South Africa's oldest wine farm area, with 10 wineries on the route (all within 30 minutes' drive south of the city centre). (p127)

➡ **Durbanville** Around 20 minutes' drive north of the city centre, this coastal region offers 12 vineyards, some with spectacular views. (p156)

➡ **Stellenbosch** The first region to promote a 'wine route', it remains South Africa's largest, with more than 200 wineries and five subroutes to follow. (p160)

➡ **Helderberg** Some 30 wineries are scattered around the False Bay towns of Somerset, Gordon's Bay and Strand. (p161)

➡ **Franschhoek** With 48 wineries, including some of South Africa's most innovative. Ideal for those who like to drink rather than sip and spit, as several wineries are within walking or cycling distance of the town centre. (p165)

➡ **Paarl** Another centuries-old vine-growing region – particularly known for its shiraz and viognier – with 27 wineries to visit. (p169)

➡ **Darling** Five wineries around an hour's drive north of Cape Town. (p180)

➡ **Elgin** This route lies along Sir Lowry's Pass in the Hottentots Holland Mountains and covers 29 wine estates and cider makers. (p178)

➡ **Robertson** There are 48 wineries in the Robertson Wine Valley along scenic Route 62, about 1½ hours' drive east of Cape Town. (p173)

➡ **Hemel-en-Aarde** Covering 15 wineries, this route starts 5km west of Hermanus, about 1½ hours' drive southeast of Cape Town. (p175)

Lonely Planet's Top Choices

Babylonstoren New wines and artisan food on a magnificently reimagined estate with a gorgeous culinary garden. (p171)

Solms-Delta Excellent museum, inventive wines, local music, indigenous garden and a beautiful riverside picnic area. (p167)

Groot Constantia Museum, restaurants and beautiful grounds at this historic estate, where winemaking in South Africa began. (p127)

Vergelegen Handsome heritage building, rose gardens and a revamped restaurant. (p161)

Fairview Great-value wine and cheese tasting – plus tower-climbing goats! (p171)

Spice Route Combines complex reds, chocolate, craft beer and glass-blowing. (p171)

Best Tastings

Klein Constantia Sip Vin de Constance, the sweet wine that's said to have the power to mend a broken heart. (p128)

Meerlust Estate Its tasting room is decorated with the owner's collection of posters and a fine history of the winery. (p162)

Durbanville Hills Enjoy wines paired with chocolates, biltong or tapas-style dishes under the shade of olive trees. (p156)

Boschendal Tastings held beneath the oldest oaks on this historic estate; cellar and vineyard tours, too. (p166)

Best Sparkling Wine

Graham Beck Sample the award-winning bubbles of this Robertson winery. (p174)

Steenberg Vineyards Gorgeous contemporary tasting bar and lounge at southern end of Constantia. (p127)

Villiera Produces several excellent Méthode Cap Classique wines. (p161)

Haute Cabrière Marvel at *sabrage:* the method of slicing open a bottle of bubbly with a sword. (p168)

Best Food

Waterkloof French chef Gregory Czarnecki has won awards for his creative cuisine at the restaurant here. (p161)

Buitenverwachting Blissful picnics in this old Constantia estate, as well as a cafe and fine-dining restaurant. (p128)

La Motte Wine-pairing lunches and dinners are served at the Pierneef à la Motte restaurant. (p166)

Tokara Excellent fine dining available, as well as the deli for less fancy lunches. (p163)

Best for Families

Blaauwklippen On weekends there are horse-and-carriage rides around the estate. (p162)

Spier Birds of prey displays, Segway tours through the vines, two restaurants, and picnics to enjoy in the grounds. (p161)

Villiera View antelope, zebras and various bird species on a wildlife drive around the farm. (p161)

Paul Cluver Wines Mountain-biking trails, concerts and a kids' theatre festival at their forest ampitheatre. (p178)

Best Views

Durbanville Hills Offers a splendid view of Table Bay and Table Mountain from its stone-clad bastion. (p156)

Beau Constantia Swoon at the panorama of the Constantia Valley from the tasting room and wine and sushi bar. (p128)

Mont Rochelle Enjoy lunch with a view of the town and the mountains beyond. (p168)

Cape Point Vineyards (Glorious sunsets over Noordhoek beach from the vineyard. p148)

Best Accommodation

Grande Provence Rent out the gorgeously decorated cottages on this beautiful property. (p167)

Chamonix There's a wide variety of places to stay on this Franschhoek estate. (p168)

Babylonstoren Super-chic guest rooms, crafted from old workers' cottages. (p171)

Best for Art

Glen Carlou Among the 65 international artists in this winery's collection are works by Gilbert and George, Frank Stella and James Turrell. (p172)

Grande Provence Its splendid gallery showcases contemporary South African art. (p167)

Tokara Offers a fine art collection, plus a fantastic deli/sculpture gallery. (p163)

La Motte Host to a prime collection of works by South African artist Jacob Hendrik Pierneef. (p166)

Explore Cape Town & the Garden Route

CAPE TOWN'S **TOP SIGHTS**

Neighbourhoods at a Glance

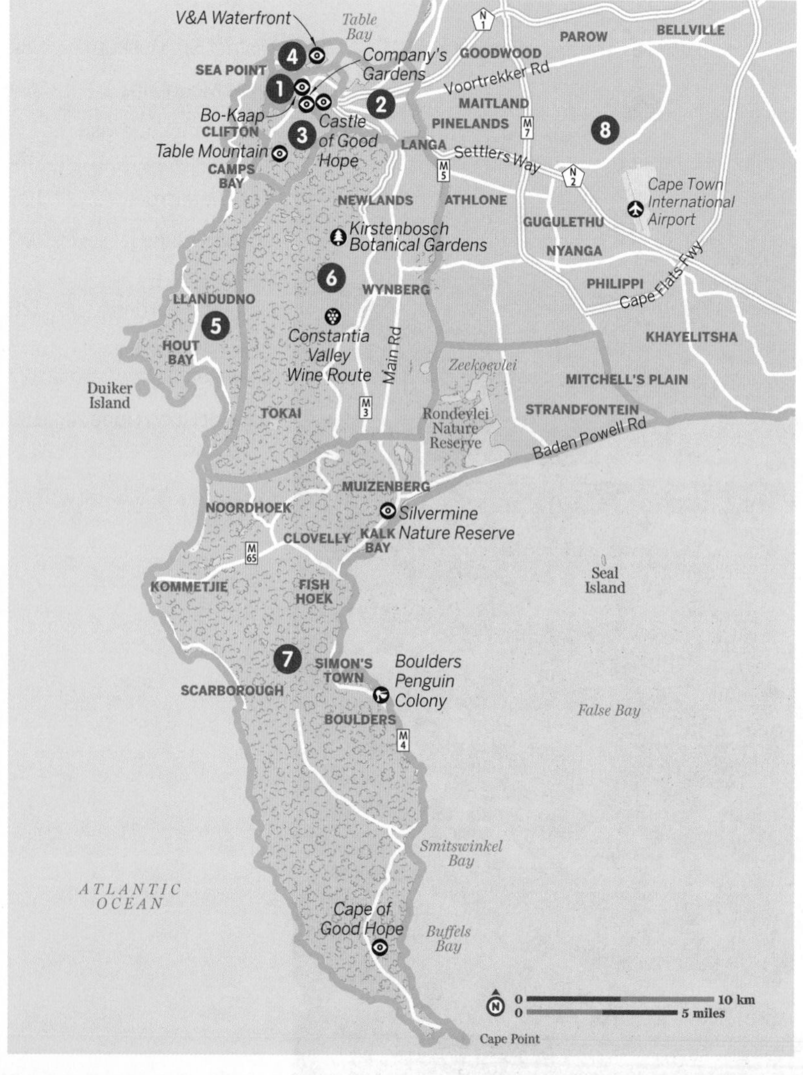

❶ City Bowl, Foreshore, Bo-Kaap & De Waterkant p52

The City Bowl, where the Dutch first set up shop, includes many historic sights and businesses. Landfill created the Foreshore district in the 1940s and 1950s, now dominated by Duncan Dock and the convention centre. Tumbling down Signal Hill are the colourfully painted houses of the Bo-Kaap and, to the northeast, Cape Town's pink precinct De Waterkant, a retail and party hub.

❷ East City, District Six, Woodstock & Observatory p80

Immediately east of the City Bowl is a creative industries enclave that occupies part of what was once the mixed residential area of District Six – now a series of empty plots awaiting development. Woodstock and Salt River continue to attract the attention of developers and the art set, but are yet to fully gentrify. Bohemian rules at Observatory near Cape Town University.

❸ Gardens & Surrounds p92

Ranging from the cluster of museums at the south end of the Company's Gardens, up the slopes of Table Mountain, is the wider area known as Gardens. Neighbourhoods here include Tamboerskloof, Oranjezicht, Higgovale and Vredehoek – all desirable residential suburbs with views of Table Bay and immediate access to Table Mountain. Kloof St and Kloof Nek Rd are the main retail strips.

❹ Green Point & Waterfront p104

Green Point's common includes an imaginatively landscaped park and the Cape Town Stadium, built for the 2010 FIFA World Cup. Fronting Table Bay is the V&A Waterfront shopping, entertainment and residential development (commonly known simply as the Waterfront), as well as the residential Mouille Point.

❺ Sea Point to Hout Bay p116

Sea Point blends into ritzier Bantry Bay and Clifton before culminating in the prime real estate of Camps Bay. Beyond here, urban development is largely curtailed by the national park until you reach delightful Hout Bay, which has good access to both the city and the vineyards of Constantia.

❻ Southern Suburbs p124

The lush eastern slopes of Table Mountain are covered by the areas known collectively as the Southern Suburbs. Here you'll find Kirstenbosch Botanical Gardens, the rugby and cricket grounds of Newlands, the centuries-old vineyards of Constantia and the shady forests of Tokai.

❼ Simon's Town & Southern Peninsula p137

On the False Bay side of the peninsula are the charming communities of Muizenberg, Kalk Bay and Simon's Town, plus the penguins living at Boulders. More wildlife and incredible landscapes are protected within the national park at Cape Point. On the Atlantic Coast side, Kommetjie is beloved by surfers, and the broad beach at Noordhoek by horse riders.

❽ Cape Flats & Northern Suburbs p151

The vast townships and coloured suburbs southeast of Table Mountain are known collectively as the Cape Flats. Cheek by jowl with Langa, but a world apart, is the garden suburb of Pinelands. North along Table Bay lie Milnerton and Bloubergstrand, while inland is the wine-growing district of Durbanville.

City Bowl, Foreshore, Bo-Kaap & De Waterkant

CITY BOWL & FORESHORE | BO-KAAP & DE WATERKANT

Neighbourhood Top Five

1 Learn about the history of Cape Town at the **Castle of Good Hope** (p54), the 17th-century pentagonal stone fortress built by the Dutch to guard Table Bay.

2 Explore the cobbled streets of the rainbow-painted **Bo-Kaap** (p58).

3 Wander the lush, historic **Company's Gardens** (p56).

4 Discover the City Bowl's eclectic selection of art galleries at the **First Thursdays** (p74) monthly event.

5 Browse the craft market on cobbled **Greenmarket Sq** (p59) and admire the surrounding art deco architecture.

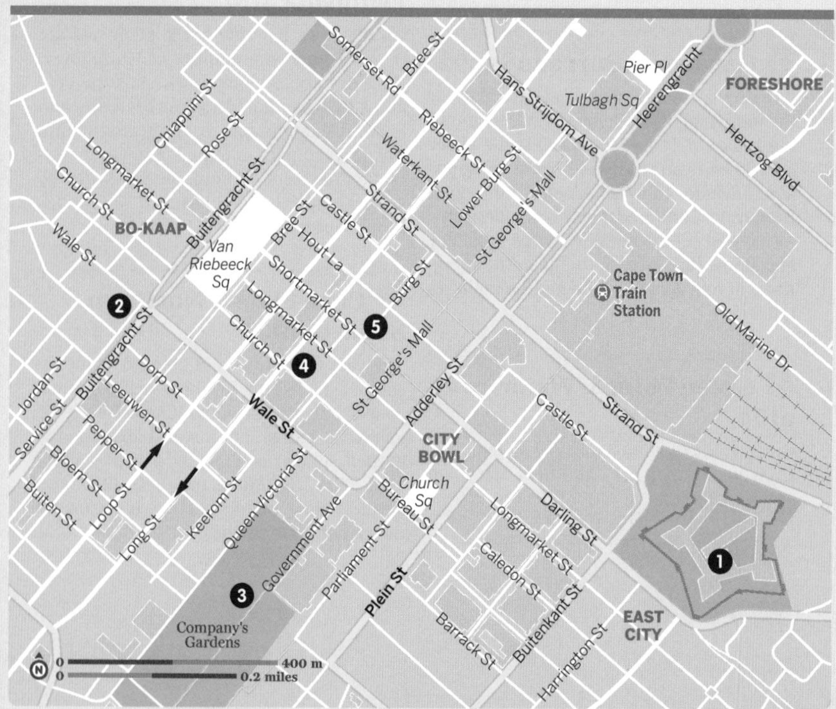

For more detail of this area see Map p268 and p272

Explore City Bowl, Foreshore, Bo-Kaap & De Waterkant

The City Bowl, bordered by Buitenkant St to the southeast, Buitengracht St to the northwest, and Orange St and Annandale Rd to the south, is the Mother City's commercial and historical heart, home to the castle and garden set out by the original Dutch settlers, as well as the nation's parliament and newest skyscrapers. During the day it bustles with colourful street life, from the art and souvenir stalls lining the length of St George's Mall to the flower sellers of Trafalgar Pl off Adderley St. You'll most likely spend at least a couple of days looking around the sights in this part of town, and a night or two on Long and Bree Sts where you'll find many restaurants, cafes and bars.

Other parts of the City Bowl turn deathly quiet come nightfall, though this is changing as more and more old office blocks and commercial buildings are transformed into swanky apartments. New buildings are also going up in the Foreshore, the bleak swathe of reclaimed land between Strand St and Table Bay, including an extension to the Cape Town convention centre.

Further to the west, up the slopes of Signal Hill, is the Bo-Kaap, a predominantly Muslim area of brightly painted houses where time is measured by the regular calls to prayer from the suburb's many mosques. Immediately to its northeast is De Waterkant, a chic party district much favoured by Cape Town's gay community.

Local Life

- **Markets** Buy a bunch of roses or proteas from the flower vendors at Trafalgar Pl flower market (p65).
- **Party** Bar- and restaurant-hop along Bree and Long Sts, look out for events at Youngblood Africa (p64).
- **Parades** Cheer on the marchers in the Cape Town Minstrel Carnival (p20) parades on New Year's Eve and 2 January.

Getting There & Away

- **Walk and cycle** Fine as there's lots of street security. There are dedicated cycle routes, too, but motorists sometimes block them.
- **Bus** Golden Acre Bus Terminal is next to the Grand Parade. MyCiTi bus routes converge at Adderley and Civic Centre.
- **Shared taxi** Plenty of these stop on Strand and Long Sts.
- **Train** Cape Metro Rail trains and long-distance buses terminate at Cape Town Train Station.

Lonely Planet's Top Tip

At the south end of St George's Mall near a slab of the Berlin Wall, the **Earth-Fair Food Market** (www.earthfairmarket.co.za; 11am-3pm Thu) is a good place to buy artisan food products or grab a healthy lunch; if it's raining the market moves inside Mandela Rhodes Pl.

Best Places to Eat

- Chef's Warehouse & Canteen(p67)
- Bombay Brasserie (p69)
- Hemelhuijs (p67)
- Africa Café (p68)
- Plant (p66)

For reviews, see p66.

Best Places to Drink

- Publik (p70)
- Weinhaus + Biergarten (p70)
- Honest Chocolate Cafe (p70)
- Beerhouse (p71)
- Orphanage (p70)

For reviews, see p70.

Best Places to Shop

- Africa Nova (p78)
- Streetwires (p78)
- Monkeybiz (p78)
- South African Market (p75)
- Luvey 'n Rose (p75)

For reviews, see p75.

WALTER BIBIKOW/GETTY IMAGES ©

TOP SIGHT
CASTLE OF GOOD HOPE

Less than a century ago, the sea lapped up to the bluestone walls of the Castle of Good Hope. South Africa's oldest surviving colonial building is the headquarters for the Western Cape military command, as well as the location of a couple of interesting museums and a spectacular backdrop for annual events such as the military tattoo.

History

Designed to protect the logistical and financial interest of the Dutch East India Company (Vereenigde Oost-Indische Compagnie; VOC) the fortress was constructed between 1666 and 1679, and replaced the original 1652 clay and timber structure commissioned by VOC commander Jan van Riebeeck just two days after setting foot on the shores of Table Bay.

VOC governor Simon van der Stel moved into the castle in 1680; it was under his instructions that the main gate was moved from the seaside of the fortress to between Leerdam and Buuren bastions where it remains today. In 1795, when the Dutch lost the Battle of Muizenburg to the British, the castle was taken over without a single shot being fired there. The flag of the Batavian Republic fluttered from the ramparts between 1803 and 1806 when the British once more returned to power.

Never lovers of the Dutch fortress, Cape Town's British rulers tried several times to have the castle demolished but to no avail. In 1922 the old South African flag was raised over the castle, to be replaced in 1994 by the new postdemocracy South African flag. There are military units still stationed here and every year in early November they perform alongside other members of the armed

DON'T MISS

- ➡ Walking the fortifications
- ➡ Castle Military Museum
- ➡ William Fehr Collection
- ➡ Traditional military ceremonies

PRACTICALITIES

- ➡ Map p268
- ➡ www.castleofgood hope.co.za
- ➡ cnr Castle & Darling Sts, City Bowl, entrance on Buitenkant St
- ➡ adult/child Mon-Sat R30/15, Sun R25/10
- ➡ 9am-4pm
- ➡ P
- ➡ Castle

forces at the **Cape Town Military Tattoo** (www.capetattoo.co.za).

Layout

Shaped as a pentagon, the castle has defensive bastions jutting out from its five corners, each of which is named after the official titles of the Prince of Orange (from left to right from the entrance: Buuren, Catzenellenbogen, Nassau, Oranje and Leerdam). Climb up to and around these to take in the fort's layout, and for the panoramic view across the Grand Parade and towards Table Mountain.

Across the fort's centre and around its walls are various buildings, some of which continue to be used by the military. You can peep into the torture chamber, see a replica of the forge, and see the 18th-century bakery (Het Bakhuys) and the Dolphin Pool, so called because of the ornate dolphin fountain at its centre.

Museums

The interesting **Castle Military Museum** occupies the castle's original bayside entrance. Inside you can see examples and vivid paintings of different military uniforms down the centuries as well as a very good exhibition on the Anglo-Boer War, and a shop selling military memorabilia.

A large chunk of the **William Fehr Collection** (www.iziko.org.za) of oil paintings, furniture, ceramics, metal and glassware is displayed in the former Governor's Quarters. Temporary exhibitions on a range of more contemporary themes are also held here. The businessman William Fehr started his collection in the 1920s with South African–related paintings, later adding furniture and other art objects; much of it has been on display at the castle since the 1950s, with works on paper mainly being shown in Rust en Vreugd (p97).

Fronting the former Governor's Quarters is a beautifully restored 18th-century balcony with pediment bas-relief created by the German sculptor Anton Anreith.

Next door is the **Secunde's House**, formerly the Cape's vice governor's home. There's no original furniture here but the rooms are designed to reflect what they would have looked like during the 17th, 18th and 19th centuries. Restoration has revealed some of the house's original wall paintings.

KEY CEREMONY

A traditional key ceremony is performed at 10am and noon from Monday to Friday. At 10am, a key is used to open a wicket gate within the main castle gate after which a bell is rung and sentries take up positions. A small cannon is fired on the outer Bailey and the key is then returned to the Governor's quarters. The noon ceremony repeats the process but in reverse. On public holidays, volunteer guides from the **Canon Association of South Africa** (www.caosa.org.za) hold public demonstrations of how to fire a cannon.

Guided tours are included in the admission fee and run at 11am, noon and 2pm. Hour-long horse and carriage rides (www.ctcco.co.za) are extra, and bookings are advised.

TUNNEL TOURS

For an underground perspective on the castle, sign up for one of the tunnel tours offered by **Good Hope Adventures** (goodhopeadventures.com), which start from the Castle parking area on Darling St.

MICHAELJUNG/SHUTTERSTOCK ©

TOP SIGHT
COMPANY'S GARDENS

What was once the vegetable patch for the Dutch East India Company (Vereenigde Oost-Indische Compagnie; VOC) is now a city-centre oasis, where many locals can be found relaxing on the lawns in the shade of centuries-old trees. The primary focus is the Public Garden but many other interesting buildings and landmarks are found around the garden's main pedestrian thoroughfare, Government Ave.

DON'T MISS

- Public Garden
- De Tuynhuis
- Delville Wood Memorial
- National Library of South Africa
- Centre for the Book

PRACTICALITIES

- Map p268
- City Bowl
- 7am-7pm
- Dorp/Leeuwen

History

The Company's Gardens began to be cultivated in April 1652 as soon as the VOC's first officials arrived at the Cape. *Grachten* (irrigation channels) were dug to lead water from the streams that flowed down Table Mountain and these eventually determined the shape not only of the garden but also of the city's original streets and boundaries. By the end of the 17th century, pathways, fountains and even a menagerie had been established in the area.

It was during the 19th century that the gardens began to take on the shape that they have today. Chunks of the grounds were carved off for buildings including St George's Cathedral, the Houses of Parliament and the South African Museum. In 1848 the lower part of the area became a public Botanical Garden and in the 1920s the construction of the **Delville Wood Memorial** radically changed the upper part of the garden close to the South African Museum.

Public Garden

Planted with a fine collection of botanical specimens, including frangipanis, African flame trees, aloes and roses, the **Public Garden** is the area's highlight. The oldest recorded specimen is a Saffron pear tree, in the region of 300 years old and still bearing fruit.

The squirrels that scamper around were imported from North America by the politician and mining magnate Cecil Rhodes (see p60). A bronze **statue** of Rhodes was erected in

1908 on a plinth carved with the phrase 'Your hinterland is there' as the imperialist points towards the heart of the continent.

Also to be found here is a small aviary; a fake 'slave bell' erected in 1911; a rose garden designed in 1929; and the **VOC Vegetable Garden**, newly installed but inspired by the original market garden – some of the food grown here is used in the garden's restaurant.

Along Government Avenue

The original Company's Gardens was bisected by the oak-lined Government Ave, which has entrances off Wale St between St George's Cathedral and the Houses of Parliament, and Orange St. Along here, peer through ornate gates at **De Tuynhuis** (The Garden House), a handsome building originally constructed in 1700 as a visitor's lodge. From the front gate you'll just about be able to make out the VOC's monogram on the pediment – as close as you'll get since De Tuynhuis is now an official office of South Africa's president, and off-limits to tourists. The design of the parterre garden dates from 1788 and was recreated in the 1960s.

Further south along Government Ave you'll pass the South African National Gallery, the Great Synagogue and the tree-shaded, grassy lawns of the Paddocks, where game animals were once kept. The only animals here now are made of plaster – the lions created by Anton Anreith in 1805 that grace the Lioness Gateway just behind the South African Museum.

Surrounding Buildings & Statues

The **National Library of South Africa** (☎021-424 6320; www.nlsa.ac.za; 5 Queen Victoria St; ⏰9am-5pm Mon-Fri; 📶; 🚌Dorp), facing the north end of the gardens, is a neoclassical building based on the Fitzwilliam Museum in Cambridge, UK. Exhibitions are held here; enter to admire the central rotunda.

The **Centre for the Book** (☎021-423 2662; www.nlsa.ac.za/NLSA/centreforthebook; 62 Queen Victoria St; ⏰8am-4pm Mon-Fri; 📶; 🚌Upper Long/Upper Loop), housed in a grand domed building to the east of the park, first opened in 1913. It has a beautiful central reading room and is sometimes used for concerts.

Two **statues of Jan Smuts** (1870–1950), former general and prime minister, stand at opposite ends of Government Ave. The more attractive and abstract one by Sydney Harpley is in front of the South African National Gallery. When the statue was unveiled in 1964, a storm of protest resulted in the more traditional second statue by Ivan Mitford-Barberton beside the Slave Lodge.

VISITOR INFORMATION

On the Queen Victoria St side of the Public Garden, the Visitor Information Centre has an exhibition on the gardens' development. You can also pick up a good booklet with a self-guided trail of the area's major landmarks.

The Delville Wood Memorial honours the 2000-plus South African soldiers who fell during a five-day WWI battle. The ensemble's elements include Alfred Turner's sculptures of Castor and Pollux, representing the unity of British and Boer soldiers, Anton van Wouw's statue of General Henry Lukin (who gave the order to advance on Delville Wood) and a WWI artillery gun.

EATING

Shaded by giant old eucalyptus trees, the recently revamped Company Garden's Restaurant (p68) is a lovely place for a meal or drink. The wicker hanging basket seats and sculptures there were created by blind craftspeople.

ESPIEGLE/GETTY IMAGES ©

TOP SIGHT
BO-KAAP

Literally meaning 'Upper Cape', the Bo-Kaap, with its vividly painted low-roofed houses strung along narrow cobbled streets, is one of the most-photographed sections of the city. Initially a garrison for soldiers in the mid-18th century, this is where freed slaves started to settle after emancipation in the 1830s.

DON'T MISS

- Chiappini St
- Rose St
- Bo-Kaap Museum
- Auwal Mosque

PRACTICALITIES

- Map p268
- Dorp/Leeuwen

Centre of Muslim Life

There are 10 mosques in the Bo-Kaap including the **Auwal Mosque** (34 Dorp St), the oldest place of Islamic worship in South Africa, established by Iman Abdullah Ibn Qadi Abdus Salaam (also known as Tuan Guru) in 1798. This Indonesian prince served time on Robben Island, where he wrote three copies of the Quran from memory, one of which is on display inside the mosque. The mosque is closed to visitors, but is accessible on a tour with Gamidah Jacobs of **Lekka Kombuis** (079-957 0226; lekkakombuis@mweb.co.za; 81 Wale St; cooking class from R400, cooking class & tour from R600) who also runs cooking classes in her historic turquoise-painted home on Wale St.

Bo-Kaap Museum

Drop by the small but interesting **Bo-Kaap Museum** (www.iziko.org.za; 71 Wale St; adult/child R20/10; 10am-5pm Mon-Sat), which provides some insight into the lifestyle of a 19th-century Cape Muslim family. The most interesting exhibit is the selection of black-and-white photos of local life displayed in the upstairs room. The house itself, which was built between 1763 and 1768, is the oldest in the area.

Picturesque Streets

The Bo-Kaap didn't used to be so well kept; the bright paint jobs are actually a post-democracy development, with the most picturesque streets being Chiappini, Rose and Wale. However, parts of the area remain evidently poor, so it's a good idea to stick to the main streets when walking here after dark.

SIGHTS

City Bowl & Foreshore

CASTLE OF GOOD HOPE MUSEUM
See p54.

COMPANY'S GARDENS GARDENS
See p56.

BO-KAAP AREA
See p58.

LONG STREET ARCHITECTURE
Map p268 (Dorp/Leeuwen) A stroll along Long St is an essential element of a Cape Town visit. This busy commercial and nightlife thoroughfare, partly lined with Victorian-era buildings featuring lovely wrought-iron balconies, once formed the border of the Muslim Bo-Kaap. Along it you'll find the **Palm Tree Mosque** (185 Long St; Dorp), dating from 1780 and closed to the public; the **SA Mission Museum** (021-423 6755; 40 Long St; 9am-6pm Mon-Fri; Mid-Long) FREE, the oldest Mission church in South Africa; and the city's newest public art installation, *Open House*.

By the 1960s, the street had fallen into disrepute and it remained that way until the late 1990s, when savvy developers realised the street's potential. The most attractive section runs from the junction with Buitensingel St north to around Strand St. By day browse the antique shops, second-hand bookshops or street-wear boutiques; by night party at the host of bars and clubs that line the strip.

MICHAELIS COLLECTION AT THE OLD TOWN HOUSE MUSEUM
Map p268 (www.iziko.org.za; Greenmarket Sq, City Bowl; adult/child R20/10; 10am-5pm Mon-Sat; Church/Longmarket) On the south side of Greenmarket Sq is the beautifully restored Old Town House, a Cape rococo building dating from 1755 that was once City Hall. It now houses the impressive art collection of Sir Max Michaelis. Dutch and Flemish paintings and etchings from the 16th and 17th centuries (including works by Rembrandt, Frans Hals and Anthony van Dyck) hang side by side with contemporary works – the contrasts between old and new are fascinating.

GREENMARKET SQUARE ARCHITECTURE, MARKET
Map p268 (City Bowl; Church/Longmarket) This cobbled square is Cape Town's second-oldest public space after the Grand Parade. It hosts a lively and colourful crafts and souvenir market daily. Apart from the Old Town House, the square is also surrounded by some choice examples of art deco architecture, including **Market House**, an elaborately decorated building with balconies and stone-carved eagles and flowers on its facade.

Next to Market House, the dazzling-white **Protea Insurance Building** was built in 1928 and renovated in 1990. Opposite is **Shell House**, once the South African headquarters of Shell, now a hotel and restaurant.

On the corner of Shortmarket St is **Namaqua House**; Baran's cafe here has a wraparound balcony providing a great view over the square. **Kimberley House** (34 Shortmarket St; Groote Kerk) is built of

OPEN HOUSE

As part of Cape Town's 2014 World Design Capital (WDC) program the Western Cape Government launched a R1 million competition for a permanent artwork to sit on a plinth on the corner of Dorp and Long Sts. The brief was that not only should the artwork celebrate 20 years of democracy for South Africa, but that it should also depict the history, diversity and future aspirations of Cape Town, as well as the WDC slogan: 'Live Design, Transform Life'.

From 16 finalists the winning design **Open House** (Map p268; cnr Dorp & Long Sts, City Bowl; Dorp/Leeuwen), by Kimberley-born artist Jacques Coetzer, was chosen in December 2014. Rising up three storeys to 10.5m, the bright-red house facade, with stairs and balconies, is envisioned as a place where people can go to speak, sing, cry or simply wave to passersby. Coetzer drew inspiration from corrugated metal structures, RDP homes (see p230) and Long St itself.

sandstone and decorated with an attractive diamond-theme design.

CHURCH STREET MARKET, MONUMENT

Map p268 (City Bowl; Church/Longmarket) The pedestrianised portion of this street, between Burg and Long Sts, hosts a **flea market** (8am-3pm Mon-Sat) and has several art galleries. At the Burg St end *The Purple Shall Govern* memorial is a piece of graphic art by Conrad Botes commemorating a 1989 anti-apartheid march. Outside the AVA Gallery is the *Arm Wrestling Podium* by Johann van der Schijff.

HOUSES OF PARLIAMENT NOTABLE BUILDING

Map p268 (021-403 2266; www.parliament.gov.za; Parliament St, City Bowl; tours 9am-2pm Mon-Fri; Roeland) FREE A tour around parliament is fascinating, especially if you're interested in the country's modern history. Opened in 1885, the hallowed halls have seen some pretty momentous events; this is where British prime minister Harold Macmillan made his 'Wind of Change' speech in 1960, and where President Hendrik Verwoerd, architect of apartheid, was stabbed to death in 1966. Call ahead and present your passport to gain entry.

IZIKO SLAVE LODGE MUSEUM

Map p268 (021-467 7229; www.iziko.org.za; 49 Adderley St, City Bowl; adult/child R30/15; 10am-5pm Mon-Sat; Groote Kerk) Dating back to 1660, the Slave Lodge is one of the oldest buildings in South Africa. Once home to as many as 1000 slaves, the lodge has a fascinating history; it has also been used as a brothel, a jail, a mental asylum, a post office, a library and the Cape Supreme Court in its time. Today, it's a museum mainly devoted to the history and experience of slaves and their descendants in the Cape.

Until 1811 the building housed slaves in damp, insanitary, crowded conditions; up to 20% died each year. The slaves were bought and sold just around the corner on Spin St.

The walls of the original Slave Lodge flank the interior courtyard, where you can find the tombstones of Cape Town's founder, Jan van Riebeeck, and his wife, Maria de la Queillerie. The tombstones were moved here from Jakarta where Van Riebeeck is buried.

The museum also has artefacts from ancient Egypt, Greece, Rome and the Far East on the 1st floor.

MUTUAL HEIGHTS ARCHITECTURE

Map p268 (cnr Parliament & Darling Sts, City Bowl; Darling) Clad in rose- and gold-veined black marble, Mutual Heights is the most impressive of the City Bowl's collection of art deco structures. It's decorated with one of the longest continuous stone friezes in the world, designed by Ivan Mitford-Barberton and chiselled by master

CECIL RHODES: EMPIRE BUILDER

Empire builder Cecil John Rhodes (1853–1902) was a legend in his own lifetime. When he arrived in South Africa in 1870, he was a sickly, impoverished son of an English vicar. The climate obviously agreed with Rhodes, as he not only recovered his health but went on to found De Beers mining company (which in 1891 owned 90% of the world's diamond mines) and become prime minister of the Cape at the age of 37, in 1890.

As part of his dream of building a railway from the Cape to Cairo (running through British territory all the way), Rhodes pushed north to establish mines and develop trade. He established British control in Bechuanaland (later Botswana) and the area that was to become Rhodesia (later Zimbabwe). His grand ideas of empire went too far, though, when he became involved in a failed uprising in the Boer-run Transvaal Republic in 1895. An embarrassed British government forced Rhodes to resign as prime minister in 1896, but Rhodesia and Bechuanaland remained his personal fiefdoms.

Rhodes never married (there's been much debate over whether he was gay); late in his life he became entangled in the schemes of the glamorous and ruthless Princess Radziwill, who was later jailed for her swindles. His health again in decline, Rhodes returned to Cape Town in 1902, only to die from his ailments, at the age of 49, at his home in Muizenberg. Rhodes' reputation was rehabilitated by his will: he devoted most of his fortune to the Rhodes scholarship, which sends recipients to Oxford University; and his land and many properties in Cape Town were bequeathed to the nation.

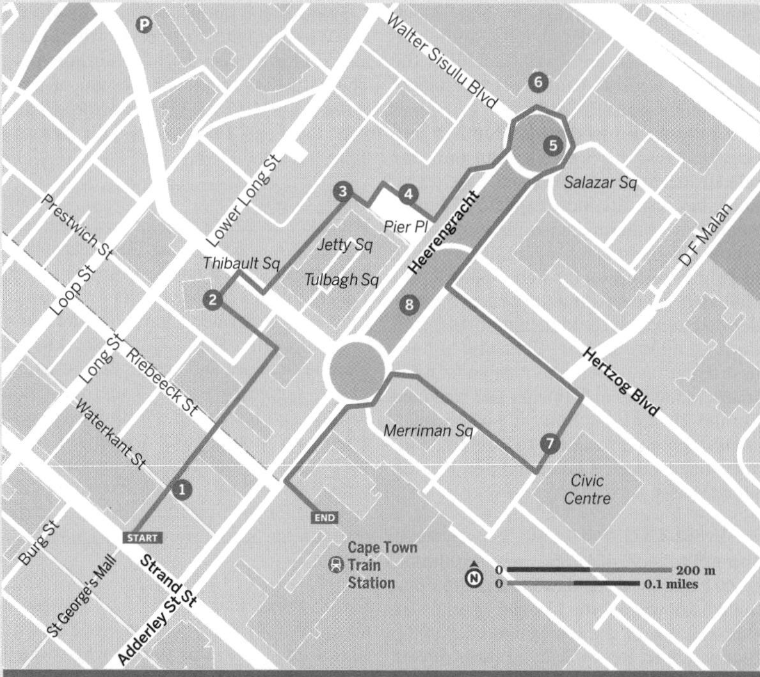

Neighbourhood Walk
Foreshore Public Art Walk

START CORNER ST GEORGE'S MALL & STRAND ST, FORESHORE
END CAPE TOWN TRAIN STATION
LENGTH 1KM; ONE HOUR

The Foreshore isn't big on sightseeing, but on this walk you can explore around the concrete towers and plazas and take in sculptures both old and new.

On pedestrianised St George's Mall, opposite Waterkant St, is Brett Murray's quirky statue 1 **Africa**. This African-curio bronze statue, sprouting bright-yellow Bart Simpson heads, is typical of Murray's satirical style and caused much public debate on its unveiling in 2000.

At the end of St George's Mall turn left into Thibault Sq, surrounded by some of the Foreshore's oldest skyscrapers including the ABSA Centre. In the square you can view 2 **Mythological Landscape**, a steel and bronze piece by John Skotnes that celebrates diversity.

Cross Mechau St and continue towards 3 **Jetty Square** where a school of steel sharks by Ralph Borland respond to passersby by swivelling on their poles.

Around the corner 4 **Pier Place** is scattered with the lifelike statues of people by Egon Tania.

In the middle of the roundabout at the Foreshore end of Heerengracht is a statue of the Portuguese sailor 5 **Bartholomeu Dias**, the first European recorded to have rounded the Cape of Good Hope in 1488. Across the road, beside the Cape Town International Convention Centre, is the 8m-tall, red-painted man 6 **Olduvai** by Gavin Younge, a piece inspired by the Rift Valley and great lakes of East Africa.

Return towards the city down Heerengracht, detouring left on Hertzog Blvd. Near the Civic Centre is Edoardo Villa's 7 **The Knot**, which looks like a giant red paper clip bent out of shape. Back on Heerengracht, opposite Cape Town Train Station, are statues of 8 **Jan van Riebeeck and Maria de la Queillerie**, the first Dutch boss of Cape Town and his wife. This is apparently the spot where they stepped ashore in 1652.

stonemasons the Lorenzi brothers. Much of the building's original detail and decoration have been preserved, including the impressive central banking space (sadly not open for general viewing).

Commissioned by the Old Mutual financial company, this was once not only the tallest structure in Africa bar the Pyramids, but also the most expensive. Unfortunately the building's opening in 1939 was eclipsed by the start of WWII. Additionally, its prime position on the Foreshore was immediately made redundant when the city decided to extend the land 2km further into the bay. Old Mutual started moving its business out of the building to Pinelands in the 1950s. Made into apartments and renamed Mutual Heights in 2002, it kicked off a frenzy among developers to convert similarly long-neglected and empty city-centre office blocks.

ST GEORGE'S CATHEDRAL CATHEDRAL

Map p268 (☎021-424 7360; www.sgcathedral.co.za; 1 Wale St, City Bowl; Groote Kerk) Commonly known as the People's Cathedral, this was one of the few places of worship that was open to people of all races during apartheid. Classical concerts are sometimes held here; see the website for details as well as times of daily services. The interior is a cool retreat, but also search out the **Siyahamba Labyrinth** in the cloisters, a paved circular walking path to aid meditation and spiritual relief.

Designed by Sir Herbert Baker at the turn of the 19th century, the church's official name is the Cathedral Church of St George the Martyr in Cape Town. Archbishop Desmond Tutu presided here and made the cathedral a focus of opposition to the Afrikaner regime.

Look around the exhibition in the Memory & Witness Centre in the crypt, where you'll also find the Crypt Jazz Restaurant (p74). The cathedral remains a beacon of hope through its HIV/AIDS outreach program – note the Cape Town AIDS quilt hanging above the north door.

GROOTE KERK CHURCH

Map p268 (☎021-422 0569; www.grootekerk.org.za; Church Sq, City Bowl; ⏰10am-2pm Mon-Fri, services 10am & 7pm Sun; Groote Kerk) The highlights of the mother church of the Dutch Reformed Church (Nederduitse Gereformeerde Kerk; NG Kerk) are its mammoth organ and ornate Burmese teak pulpit, carved by master sculptors Anton Anreith and Jan Graaff. The building's otherwise an architectural mishmash, with parts dating from the 1704 original and other bits from 1841. While here ponder the fact that for the first 100 years or so of the church's life, slaves were sold immediately outside.

CHURCH SQUARE MONUMENT

Map p268 (City Bowl; Groote Kerk) Groote Kerk fronts on to this square where you'll find a **statue of Jan Hendrik**, one-time editor of the *Zuid Afrikaan* newspaper and a key figure behind the drafting of the 1909 South African constitution. There's also the **Slavery Memorial** – 11 low, black granite blocks engraved with the names of slaves or words relating to slavery, resistance and rebellion. Various events are staged here during First Thursdays (p74). Facing the church from the other side of the square is the handsome old National Mutual Building, parts of which date to 1905; it now houses the Iziko Social History Centre.

CITY WALK

Announced at the end of 2014, the City Walk project will be added to the marketing campaign for the city's big six sights (Table Mountain, Robben Island, Cape Point, V&A Waterfront, Groot Constantia and Kirstenbosch Botanical Gardens) to make it the magnificent seven.

The City Walk aims to promote the street life of the City Bowl. The route starts in the Company's Gardens, runs down St George's Mall, across Strand St to Waterkant St, where it will follow the Walk of Remembrance to terminate at Prestwich Memorial Park. Free wi-fi along the route will provide digital interactive opportunities for historical interpretation to supplement street signage revealing some of the city's hidden stories. Street food, public art, events and entertainment such as busking will also be part of the mix, as well as a revamp for the market stalls strung along St George's Mall.

ROCK GIRL BENCHES

As you wander around the City Bowl, as well as up on Signal Hill, at Lion's Head and along the Waterfront, keep your eyes peeled for the colourful mosaic-decorated benches created by **Rock Girl** (www.rockgirlsa.org). This inspiring project was started by human-rights lawyer Michelle India Baird in 2010 when she was volunteering at the Red River School in the crime-ridden Cape Flats suburb of Manenberg. There was an urgent need to create safe places there for young girls and boys to sit and not be harassed by gangsters.

Several prominent Capetonian artists and designers, including Lovell Friedman, Laurie Wiid van Heerden, Atang Tshikare, Paul du Toit and Lyall Sprong, have since become involved in creating the benches, of which there are currently 37. Most of those in central Cape Town are twinned with a sister bench in the townships, such as Gugulethu, where there's one at the **Amy Biehl Memorial**, and Khayelitsha at the **Grassroot Soccer Football for Hope Centre**.

In the City Bowl along St George's Mall there's a bench at **Krotoa Place** (Map p268; St George's Mall & Castle St; 🚌Strand) commemorating the 17th-century Khoe-San woman Krotoa van Meerhof who acted as an interpreter for Jan van Riebeeck, married a Dutch settler, and ended her life, aged just 32, imprisoned on Robben Island.

In Prestwich Memorial Garden (p66) there are three benches: *Time Out* by artist Paul du Toit, in the shape of a symbolic Rock Girl; an over-sized wooden bench by Mark Thomas (who also designed the Boomslang at Kirstenbosch Botanical Gardens); and a metal and wooden one by Laurie Wiird van Heerden inside Truth Coffee. You'll find others at the southern end of Long St and in the lobby of the Cape Town International Convention Centre. If you go for a surf in Llandudno or Muizenberg, look out for benches there as well.

For the World Design Capital project **Wonder Women** (#WDC519), Rock Girl have partnered with architect Mokena Makeka to create life-size steel statues of up to 10 iconic South African heroines including Albertina Sisulu, Miriam Makeba, Adelaide Tambo and Nadine Gordimer. The plan is to locate them along the Walk of Remembrance (the former Fan Walk) in Green Point.

SLAVE TREE — MONUMENT

Map p268 (Spin St, City Bowl; 🚌Groote Kerk) A small circular plaque in the traffic island on Spin St marks the location of the Slave Tree under which slaves were sold until emancipation in 1834. During World Design Capital year this spot became more prominent as the location of an official art project (www.wdccapetown2014.com/projects/project/377): the temporary sculpture may still be in place when you pass by.

GRAND PARADE & AROUND — SQUARE

Map p268 (Darling St, City Bowl; 🚌Darling) A prime location for Cape Town's history, the Grand Parade is where: the Dutch built their first fort in 1652; slaves were sold and punished; and crowds gathered to watch Nelson Mandela's first address to the nation as a free man after 27 years in jail, made from the balcony of the old town hall. A market is held on part of the square, which is also used for parking.

Facing the parade is the grand Edwardian **Cape Town City Hall**, now used occasionally for music and cultural events. Nearby Drill Hall, dating from 1889 and where Queen Elizabeth II celebrated her 21st birthday, has been sensitively restored and turned into the city's **Central Library** (☎021-467 1500; ⏰9am-8pm Mon, 9am-6pm Tue-Thu, 8.30am-5.30pm Fri, 9am-2pm Sat).

WE ARE STILL HERE — MONUMENT

Map p268 (cnr Longmarket & Parade Sts, City Bowl; 🚌Lower Buitenkant) Mosaic artists Lovell Friedman and Leora Lewis are the creators of this powerfully moving artwork just outside the Central Library. A mosaic of ceramic tiles forms the image of a child and is surrounded by drawings and written contributions from street children. Look closely and you'll see each tile contains the print of an advert placed in the Cape *Government Gazette* between 1841 and 1921 calling for ownership of destitute children.

KOOPMANS-DE WET HOUSE MUSEUM

Map p268 (☎021-481 3935; www.iziko.org.za; 35 Strand St, City Bowl; adult/child R20/10; ⏰10am-5pm Mon-Fri; 🚌Strand) Step back two centuries from 21st-century Cape Town when you enter this classic example of a Cape Dutch town house, furnished with 18th- and early 19th-century antiques. It's an atmospheric place with ancient vines growing in the courtyard and floorboards that squeak just as they probably did during the time of Marie Koopmans-de Wet, the socialite owner after whom the house is named.

EVANGELICAL LUTHERAN CHURCH CHURCH

Map p268 (☎021-421 5854; www.lutheranchurch.org.za; 98 Strand St, City Bowl; ⏰10am-2pm Mon-Fri; 🚌Strand) FREE Converted from a barn in 1780, the first Lutheran church in the Cape has a carved wood pulpit that's a masterwork by the German sculptor Anton Anreith. A pair of muscular Herculeses (symbolising the power of faith) hold up the front two corners of the pulpit, above which four cherubs fly and a rococo canopy hangs. Anreith's work can also be seen in Groote Kerk and at Groot Constantia.

Martin Melck House (Map p268; ☎021-405 1540; adult/child R40/25; ⏰9.30am-4.30pm Mon-Sat; 🚌Strand), the old parsonage next door dating from 1783 and named after the merchant who had it built, is used for various temporary exhibitions. In the courtyard to its rear is the live jazz and restaurant venue Manenberg's @ The Camissa Courtyard (p75).

HERITAGE SQUARE ARCHITECTURE

Map p268 (www.heritage.org.za/heritage_square_project.htm; 90 Bree St, City Bowl; 🅿; 🚌Church/Longmarket) This beautiful collection of Cape Georgian and Victorian buildings was saved from the wrecking ball in 1996. The complex includes the Cape Heritage Hotel (p201), several restaurants, Signal Hill Wines (p77) and a courtyard in which a vine has been growing since the 1770s, making it the oldest such plant in South Africa. It still produces grapes from which wine is made.

YOUNGBLOOD AFRICA GALLERY

Map p268 (☎021-424 0074; www.youngbloodafrica.com; 70-72 Bree St, City Bowl; ⏰9am-5pm Mon-Fri, 10am-5pm 1st & 3rd Sat; 🚌Church/Mid-Long) FREE The artworks of young South Africans are displayed in this impressive multilevel gallery space and creative studio, where you'll also find the **beautiful life** cafe. Check the website for frequent evening events including concerts and performances that could be anything from a swinging electronic gypsy jazz band to classical music in the dark.

MUSEUM OF GEMS & JEWELLERY MUSEUM

Map p268 (☎021-422 1090; www.prinsandprins.com; Huguenot House, cnr Loop St & Hout Lane, City Bowl; ⏰9am-5pm Mon-Fri, to 1pm Sat; 🚌Church/Mid-Long) FREE A chance to see inside the mid-18th-century Huguenot House, mainly occupied by the diamond merchants and jewellers Prins & Prins (p77). There's no pressure to buy on the tour, during which you can see the remains of neoclassical wall paintings depicting the 19th-century owners, the Van Wielligh family. Most of the displays are in the basement where the jewellers also work.

Bo-Kaap & De Waterkant

NOON GUN VIEWPOINT

(Military Rd, Bo-Kaap) FREE At noon, Monday to Saturday, a cannon is fired from the lower slopes of 350m-high Signal Hill, which separates Sea Point from the City Bowl; you can hear it all over town. Traditionally, this allowed the burghers in the town below to check their watches. It's a stiff walk up here through the Bo-Kaap – take Longmarket St and keep going until it ends, just beneath the gun emplacement (which is off limits). The view is phenomenal.

You can also drive or take a taxi up Signal Hill along Military Rd, accessed off Kloof Nek Rd.

PRESTWICH MEMORIAL MEMORIAL

Map p268 (cnr Somerset & Buitengracht Sts, De Waterkant; ⏰8am-6pm Mon-Fri, 2pm Sat & Sun; 🚌Strand) FREE Construction in 2003 along nearby Prestwich St unearthed many skeletons. These were the unmarked graves of slaves and others executed by the Dutch in the 17th and 18th centuries on what was then known as Gallows Hill. The bones were exhumed and this memorial building, with an attractive facade of Robben Island slate, was created. It includes an ossuary

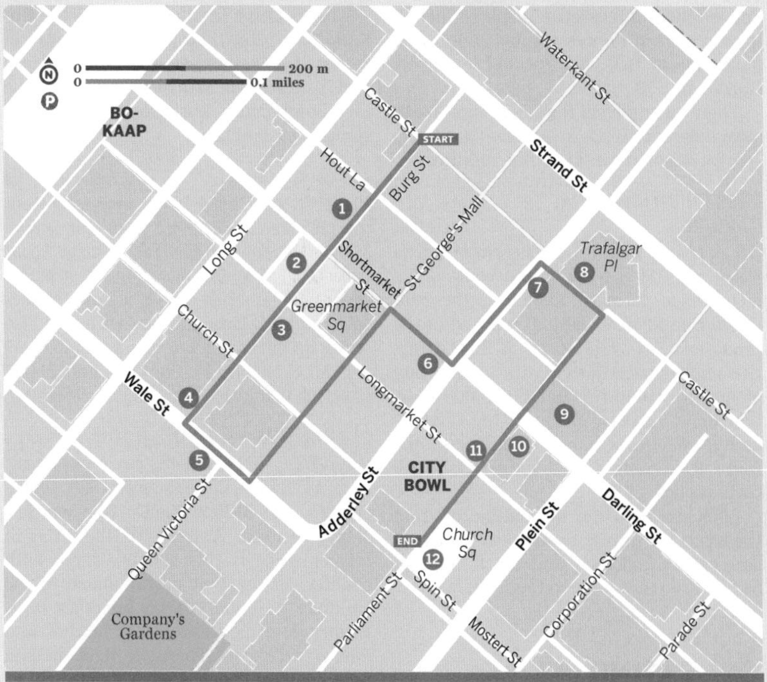

Neighbourhood Walk
Art & Architecture Walk

START CAPE TOWN TOURISM, CORNER CASTLE & BURG STS, CITY BOWL
END CHURCH SQ
LENGTH 1.5KM; ONE HOUR

A building boom in Cape Town during the 1930s resulted in the city centre having a remarkable number of grand art deco buildings. This walk takes you past some of the key buildings. At 24 Burg St is 1 **New Zealand House**, designed by WH Grant in a style known as Cape Mediterranean. Ahead is 2 **Greenmarket Square** (p59), which hosts a daily crafts and souvenir market. Three-quarters of the buildings surrounding the square hail from the 1930s, the main exception being the 3 **Old Town House**, completed in 1761, and now an art gallery.

At the junction of Burg and Wale Sts, the 4 **Waalburg Building** has a facade decorated with bronze and Table Mountain–stone panels depicting scenes of South African life. Opposite is the 5 **Western Cape Legislature**, its grey bulk enlivened by stone-carved animal heads.

Turn into St George's Mall and continue to Shortmarket St, where a right turn will bring you to the junction with Adderley St. Here is the 6 **First National Bank**, completed in 1913, and one of the final projects of Sir Herbert Baker: pop inside to see some of the bank's original fittings. Head up Adderley St, past the 7 **Former Standard Bank**, a grand building topped by a statue of Britannia, and turn right into 8 **Trafalgar Place**, home to Cape Town's flower sellers since 1860.

At the end of Trafalgar Pl is the 9 **General Post Office**. The ground floor is clogged by market stalls, but look above them to view colourful painted panels of Cape Town scenes.

Emerge onto Darling St to face 10 **Mutual Heights** (p60). At the crossing of Parliament and Longmarket Sts is 11 **Mullers Opticians**, a beautifully preserved art deco shopfront. A few steps further along Parliament St is 12 **Church Square** (p62) and Groote Kerk, mother church of the Dutch Reformed Church, facing the old National Building.

and excellent interpretive displays, including a replica of the remarkable 360-degree panorama of Table Bay painted by Robert Gordon in 1778.

There's a branch of the coffee shop **Truth** (www.truthcoffee.com; ⏲8am-6pm Mon-Fri, to 2pm Sat & Sun) in the memorial building.

PRESTWICH MEMORIAL GARDEN — SCULPTURE

Map p272 (cnr Somerset & Buitengracht Sts, De Waterkant; Strand) Along the Walk of Remembrance (formerly known as the 2010 World Cup's Fan Walk) and one end of the proposed City Walk (p62) is this attractive public space dotted with a collection of quirky sculptures and installations by Capetonian artists, including the rainbow arch *It's Beautiful Here* by Heath Nash, the *Full Cycle Tree* by KEAG and several Rock Girl benches (p63).

Look down to see the outline of tram tracks: horse-drawn trams once ran past here, along Somerset and down through Sea Point to terminate in Camps Bay.

EATING

While the City Bowl is packed with restaurants and cafes, many places are closed on Sundays. The Cape Quarter shopping centre is the nexus around which De Waterkant's dining scene revolves. The Bo-Kaap has a few dining options up its sleeves, too; locals swear by the takeaway grilled chicken and other meats served up by the guy near the corner of Rose and Wale Sts.

City Bowl & Foreshore

★PLANT — VEGAN $

Map p268 (www.plantcafe.co.za; 8 Buiten St, City Bowl; mains R40-65; ⏲7am-7pm Mon & Tue, 7am-10pm Wed-Fri, 8.30am-11.30pm Sat, 9am-3pm Sun; ; Upper Loop/Upper Long) As the name suggests, Plant serves only vegan food, and it's so tasty that you may become converted to the cause. Mock cheese and egg substitutes are incorporated in sandwiches and salads, and giant portobello mushrooms or a mix of flaked potato and seaweed do service as alternative burgers. The vegan cupcakes and brownies are delicious.

There's also a smaller branch in the **Bo-Kaap** (Map p268; Urban Hub, 142 Buitengracht Service St, Bo-Kaap; mains R40-65; ⏲9am-5pm Mon-Fri, to 3pm Sat; Dorp/Leeuwen), but the City Bowl branch keeps longer hours and serves wine and beer.

JASON BAKERY — BAKERY, CAFE $

Map p268 (☎021-424 5644; www.jasonbakery.com; 185 Bree St, City Bowl; mains R50; ⏲7am-3.30pm Mon-Fri, 8am-2pm Sat; Upper Loop/Upper Long) Move fast to secure a seat at this super-popular street-corner cafe that makes splendid breakfasts and sandwiches. It also serves decent coffee, Brewers & Union beers and MCC bubbles by the glass and bottle. Good job that it also has a takeaway counter.

CLARKE'S BAR & DINING ROOM — AMERICAN $

Map p268 (☎021-422 7648; www.clarkesdining.co.za; 133 Bree St, City Bowl; mains R55; ⏲7am-5pm Mon, 7am-10.30pm Tue-Sat, 8am-3pm Sun; Dorp/Leeuwen) A focus of the Bree St hipster scene is this convivial spot with counter seating that pays homage to the US diner tradition. All-day breakfast dishes include grilled cheese sandwiches and *huevos rancheros*. There are Reubens and pork-belly sandwiches from lunchtime, as well as burgers and mac and cheese. Hidden behind is the **Pit**, a skate park and DJ/band venue, which is usually open Wednesday (6pm to late) for boarding, and on the occasional Thursday and Friday for events.

LOLA'S — INTERNATIONAL $

Map p268 (www.lolas.co.za; 228 Long St, City Bowl; mains R40-50; ⏲8am-4.30pm Sat-Wed, to 10.30pm Thu & Fri; ; Upper Loop/Upper Long) This old dame of the Long St scene has kept her looks and the vibe remains relaxed. The breakfasts, including sweetcorn fritters and eggs Benedict, are still good. Linger over a drink and watch Long St's passing parade, or drop by on Thursday and Friday evenings when it offers up a short and sweet menu of street-food dishes.

SABABA — MIDDLE EASTERN $

Map p268 (www.sababa.co.za; 231 Bree St, City Bowl; mains R30-50; ⏲8am-4pm Mon-Fri; Upper Loop/Upper Long) The newer Bree St outlet of Sababa, which has been going in Sea Point's Piazza St John for years, is a spotlessly white space serving delicious falafel sandwiches, salads, sweets and drinks. They can rustle up a takeaway box of goodies and sell you a copy of their cookbook. You'll also find them at the Oranjezicht City Farm market (p100) on Saturday.

MASALA DOSA INDIAN $

Map p268 (☎021-424 6772; www.masaladosa.co.za; 167 Long St, City Bowl; mains R40-85; ⌚lunch & dinner Mon-Sat; 🚌Dorp) Bollywood chic rules at this colourful South Indian culinary outpost serving decent *dosas* (lentil pancakes) and *thalis* (set meals with a variety of curries).

LATITUDE 33 INTERNATIONAL $

Map p268 (www.lat33.co.za; 165 Bree St, City Bowl; mains R55-90; ⌚7am-3pm Mon-Fri, 8.30am-1pm Sat; 📶; 🚌Dorp/Leeuwen) There's lots to like at this cafe-boutique-gallery named after Cape Town's geographical location. The surfer-chic cafe serves a good range of drinks, French toast made with farmer's white bread or panettone, crispy chicken-schnitzel sandwiches and burgers. Upstairs there's a boutique stocking beach-friendly fashions from Australia, and a gallery displaying the detailed portrait art of one of the owners.

CRUSH SANDWICHES $

Map p268 (☎021-422 5533; www.crush.co.za; 100 St George's Mall, City Bowl; mains R20-30; ⌚7am-5pm Mon-Fri, 9am-3pm Sat; 🚌Groote Kerk) Offers freshly squeezed juices, smoothies and tasty wraps that prove healthy eating need not be boring.

WOZA! AFRICAN $

Map p268 (☎021-422 0053; www.wozafood.co.za; Church St, City Bowl; mains R20-40; ⌚7am-5pm Mon-Fri; 🚌Groote Kerk) Friendly guys will guide you through this brightly painted, inviting corner cafe to the basement, where you can see the tureens of chicken and beef stew cooking, alongside – for the braver eater – green tripe. The breakfast special is served all day, along with a variety of local baked goods including huge muffins.

BREAD, MILK & HONEY SANDWICHES, SALADS $

Map p268 (☎021-461 8872; www.breadmilkhoney.co.za; 10 Spin St, City Bowl; mains R30-50; ⌚7am-4pm Mon-Fri; 🚌Groote Kerk) The spirited debate of politicos and bureaucrats from nearby parliament rings through this smart family-run cafe. The menu is delicious: the cakes and desserts are especially yummy and they have a pay-by-weight daily lunch, as well as plenty of stuff to go.

SOUTH CHINA DIM SUM BAR CHINESE $

Map p268 (289 Long St, City Bowl; mains R40-50; ⌚12.30-3pm & 6.30-10pm Tue-Fri, 11.30am-3pm & 6.30-10pm Sat; 🚌Upper Loop/Upper Long) No frills, and the service can be very slow, but the food – succulent dumplings, savoury noodles, spring rolls and home-made iced teas – is authentic and worth the wait. The decor of packing-crate stools and tattered Bruce Lee posters has a rustic, Asian cafe charm.

ROYALE EATERY BURGERS $

Map p268 (www.royaleeatery.com; 279 Long St, City Bowl; mains R60-70; ⌚lunch & dinner Mon-Sat; 🚌Upper Loop/Upper Long) Gourmet burgers are grilled to perfection here; downstairs is casual and buzzy while upstairs is a restaurant where you can book a table. For something different try the Big Bird ostrich burger.

CAFÉ MOZART INTERNATIONAL $

Map p268 (www.themozart.co.za; 37 Church St, City Bowl; mains R50-80; ⌚9am-4pm Mon-Fri, 8am-3pm Sat; 📶; 🚌Church/Longmarket) Sample food from the 'table of love', or order a coffee and sandwich at this charming cafe with street-side tables amid the daily flea market. Inside upstairs is a lovely quiet space, like your great-aunt's parlour, in which to net surf and catch up on emails on your laptop.

★CHEF'S WAREHOUSE & CANTEEN TAPAS $$

Map p268 (☎021-422 0128; www.chefswarehouse.co.za; Heritage Sq, 92 Bree St, City Bowl; tapas set for 2 R350; ⌚noon-3pm & 4-8pm Mon-Fri, noon-2.30pm Sat; 🚌Church/Longmarket) Hurry here for a delicious and very generous spread of small plates from chef Liam Tomlin and his talented crew. Flavours zip around the world, from squid with a tangy Vietnamese salad to comforting coq au vin. If you can't get a seat (there are no bookings) there's the takeaway hatch **Street Food** in the space under the stoop. Capetonian chefs come here to shop for ingredients and kitchen items, so browse the shop afterwards for a great selection of cookbooks and other culinary treats.

★HEMELHUIJS INTERNATIONAL $$

Map p272 (☎021-418 2042; www.hemelhuijs.co.za; 71 Waterkant St, Foreshore; mains R60-120; ⌚9am-4pm Mon-Fri, to 3pm Sat; 📶; 🚌Strand)

A quirky yet elegantly decorated space – think deer heads with broken crockery and contemporary art – showcases the art and culinary creations of Jacques Erasmus. The inventive food is delicious and includes lovely fresh juices, daily bakes and signature dishes such as Sandveld potato and saffron gnocchi with blackened quail breast and smoked aubergine.

★AFRICA CAFÉ AFRICAN **$$**

Map p268 (021-422 0221; www.africacafe.co.za; 108 Shortmarket St, City Bowl; set banquets R250; 6-11pm Mon-Sat; Church/Longmarket) Touristy, yes, but still one of the best places to sample African food. Come with a hearty appetite as the set feast comprises some 15 dishes from across the continent, of which you can eat as much as you like. The talented staff go on song-and-dance walkabout around the tables midmeal.

COMPANY GARDEN'S RESTAURANT INTERNATIONAL **$$**

Map p268 (021-423 2919; Company's Gardens, Queen Victoria St, City Bowl; mains R50-85; 7am-6pm; ; Dorp/Leeuwen) Restaurant wizards Madame Zingara have sprinkled their magic on the old Company's Gardens cafe, transforming it into a chic contemporary space with charming outdoor features such as a giant chess set and wickerwork nests to play in. Menu items run from excellent breakfasts (try the French toast) to a lunch buffet table (R85).

ADDIS IN CAPE ETHIOPIAN **$$**

Map p268 (021-424 5722; www.addisincape.co.za; 41 Church St, City Bowl; mains R95-125; noon-10.30pm Mon-Sat; ; Church/Longmarket) Sit at a low basket-weave table and enjoy tasty Ethiopian cuisine served traditionally on plate-sized *injera* (sourdough pancakes), which you rip up and eat with in place of cutlery. There's a good selection of vegetarian and vegan dishes. Also try the homemade *tej* (honey wine) and authentic Ethiopian coffee.

BORAGE BISTRO INTERNATIONAL **$$**

Map p272 (021-418 992; www.borage.co.za; 7B Ground fl, Portside Bldg, cnr Buitengracht St & Hans Strijdom Ave, Foreshore; mains R85-105; noon-3.30pm Mon-Thu, noon-3.30pm & 6.30-8.30pm Fri, 8am-noon Sat; Lower Loop/Lower Long) We were promised that the beef ragu would be 'life changing' at this slick, lofty-ceiling bistro; that's larding it, but the cooking here is certainly very flavoursome, inventive and accomplished. Book ahead for the Friday-night à la carte dinners, and for the supper club every second Thursday night, a bargain at R140 for a set three-course menu.

DEAR ME INTERNATIONAL **$$**

Map p268 (021-422 4920; www.dearme.co.za; 165 Longmarket St, City Bowl; mains R50-130, 5/8-course dinners R460/580; 7-3pm Mon-Fri, 6.30-10pm Thu & Fri; ; Church/Longmarket) High-quality ingredients, creatively combined and served by gracious staff in a pleasant space – what more could you wish for? Well, there's a deli and bakery section, too. Reservations are essential for the excellent gourmet dinners.

BOCCA ITALIAN **$$**

Map p268 (021-422 0188; www.bocca.co.za; cnr Bree & Wale Sts, City Bowl; pizzas R70-120; noon-10pm; Dorp/Leeuwen) The superb Neapolitan-style softer crust pizzas with creative toppings (kimchi, pork sausage and ginger on the Lady Zaza) fly out of the brick oven at this new and already very popular operation. The menu covers other contemporary-style Italian dishes and sharing plates.

6 SPIN ST RESTAURANT INTERNATIONAL **$$**

Map p268 (021-461 0666; www.6spinstreet.co.za; 6 Spin St, City Bowl; mains R75-160; 10am-10pm Mon-Fri, 6-10pm Sat; Groote Kerk) Robert Mulders brings his personable restaurant skills and famous double-baked cheese soufflé to the elegant surrounds of this Sir Herbert Baker–designed building. You might also try Moroccan lamb with couscous or linefish roasted with a garlic crust. The space doubles as an art gallery, which you're welcome to look around whether eating or not.

Every second Saturday a tango night is held here.

BIRDS CAFÉ INTERNATIONAL **$$**

Map p268 (021-426 2534; 127 Bree St, City Bowl; mains R50-120; 8am-4pm Mon-Sat, 6-10pm Wed-Sat; Church/Longmarket) There are new operators at this rustic cafe in a grand old Dutch building. The cooking is patchy, so it's probably best to stick with simpler dishes such as the quiche and laudable cakes. They're also dabbling in the Capetonian trend for tapas to supplement their dinner menu – portions are huge though, so go easy on the ordering!

★**BOMBAY BRASSERIE** INDIAN **$$$**

Map p268 (021-819 2000; www.tajhotels.com; Wale St, City Bowl; mains R70-110, tasting menus from R325; 6-10.30pm Mon-Sat; Groote Kerk) Far from your average curry house, the Taj Hotel's main restaurant, hung with glittering chandeliers and mirrors, is darkly luxurious. Chef Harpreet Longani's cooking is creative and delicious, and the presentation spot on, as is the service. Go on a spice journey with one of the tasting menus.

BISTRO BIZERCA FRENCH, CONTEMPORARY **$$$**

Map p268 (021-423 8888; www.bizerca.com; Heritage Sq, 98 Shortmarket St, City Bowl; mains R110-150; 12.30-2.30pm & 6.30-9.30pm Mon-Fri; Church/Longmarket) French chef Laurent Deslandes' food, including succulent beef cheeks, is expertly prepared and bursting with flavour. Menu items, chalked up on a blackboard, are explained at the table by the knowledgeable waitstaff. The courtyard, an outdoor dining space within Heritage Sq, is also a plus.

SAVOY CABBAGE MODERN SOUTH AFRICAN **$$$**

Map p268 (021-424 2626; www.savoycabbage.co.za; 101 Hout Lane, City Bowl; mains R110-165; noon-2.30pm Mon-Fri, 7-10.30pm Mon-Sat; Church/Longmarket) The long-running Savoy Cabbage remains a great place for inventive cooking and gives diners the chance to try local game meats such as eland and springbok. Also try the legendary tomato tart if it's on the menu.

95 KEEROM ITALIAN **$$$**

Map p268 (021-422 0765; www.95keerom.com; 95 Keerom St, City Bowl; mains R60-400; 12.30-2pm Mon-Fri, 7pm-10.30pm Mon-Sat; Upper Loop/Upper Long) Bookings are essential for this chic Italian restaurant, with an olive tree the centrepiece of the 1st floor. Chef-patron Giorgio Nava lays on the Italian accent with a trowel in his table-side presentations, but you can't fault his splendid pasta.

Meat lovers might want to try Nava's premium steak restaurant **Carne SA** (Map p268; 021-424 3460; www.carne-sa.com; 70 Keerom St, City Bowl; mains R100-400; Upper Loop/Upper Long), which is just across the street; there's also a branch on Kloof St.

Bo-Kaap & De Waterkant

LA PETITE TARTE CAFE **$**

Map p272 (021-425 9077; Shop A11, Cape Quarter, 72 Waterkant St, De Waterkant; mains R50-80; 8.30am-4pm Mon-Fri, to 2.30pm Sat; Alfred) Fancy teas by Mariage Frères and delicious homemade, sweet and savoury French-style tarts are served at this adorable cafe with streetside tables.

LOADING BAY LEBANESE **$**

Map p272 (021-425 6320; www.loadingbay.co.za; 30 Hudson St, De Waterkant; mains R50-75; 8am-5pm Mon-Fri, 9am-4pm Sat, 9am-2pm Sun; Old Fire Station) Hang with De Waterkant's style set at this spiffy cafe serving coffee with 'microtextured milk' (it's heated only to 70°C) and bistro-style dishes such as crispy bacon and avocado on toast. Book for the Thursday-evening burger nights – the patties, both premium beef and vegetarian, are top-grade. There's an attached boutique offering menswear fashion lines from overseas labels and the Aesop skincare range.

BEEFCAKES BURGERS **$**

Map p272 (021-425 9019; www.beefcakes.co.za; 40 Somerset Rd, De Waterkant; burgers R55-85; noon-midnight; Gallow's Hill) Flamingos, feather boas, fairy lights, topless barmen – yup, Beefcakes is as camp as a row of tents and a fave *jol* (party) for groups. There's bitchy bingo on Tuesday and drag shows on other nights, starring characters such as Mary Scary and Princess Pop. The burgers? They're fine, but not what you really come for.

★**IZAKAYA MATSURI** JAPANESE **$$**

Map p272 (021-421 4520; www.izakayamatsuri.com; Shop 6, The Rockwell, Schiebe St, De Waterkant; mains R40-110; Alfred) Genial Arata-san serves some of the best sushi and rolls to be found in Cape Town, along with other Japanese *izakaya* pub-grub including noodles and tempura. When the weather's warm tables shift from the attractive interior hung with giant white and red paper lanterns out to the courtyard area.

BO-KAAP KOMBUIS CAPE MALAY **$$**

Map p268 (021-422 5446; www.bokaapkombuis.co.za; 7 Aug St, Bo-kaap; mains R75-95; noon-4pm & 6-9.30pm Tue-Sat, noon-4pm Sun) You'll receive a hospitable welcome from Yusuf and Nazli and their staff at this spectacularly located restaurant, high up in Bo-Kaap. The panoramic views of Table Mountain and Devil's Peak alone make it worth visiting. There are all the traditional Cape Malay dishes on the menu plus vegetarian options such as sugar bean curry. There's also a few guesthouse and self-catering rooms for rent.

BIESMIELLAH CAPE MALAY **$$**
Map p268 (021-801 1765; www.biesmiellah.co.za; cnr Wale St & Pentz Rd, Bo-Kaap; mains R75-100; noon-10pm Mon-Sat; Dorp/Leeuwen) Not big on atmosphere, Biesmiellah nonetheless offers authentic and spicy Cape Malay and Indian food in a room decorated with tapestries of Mecca. It's all halal and no alcohol is served.

ANATOLI TURKISH **$$**
Map p272 (021-419 2501; www.anatoli.co.za; 24 Napier St, De Waterkant; meze R40-50, mains R110; 6.30-10.30pm Mon-Sat; Alfred) You can always rely on this atmospheric Turkish joint that's a little piece of Istanbul in Cape Town. Make a meal out of the delicious meze, both hot and cold, or try the kebabs.

SPASIE INTERNATIONAL **$$$**
Map p268 (076 947 9231; www.facebook.com/spasieunderground; 97 Church St, Bo-Kaap; dinner R650; 7-11pm Wed-Fri; Dorp/Leeuwen) Each week different, talented chefs get to be creative at this supper club in a Bo-Kaap warehouse. Four dishes are paired with wines and served at a long communal table. It's like going to a fancy but rather relaxed dinner party. Bookings are essential for this and the cash-only Wednesday 'speakeasy' evenings of street food, booze and lewd card games.

GOLD AFRICAN **$$$**
Map p272 (www.goldrestaurant.co.za; 15 Bennett St, De Waterkant; set menu R295; 6.30-10pm; Alfred) Occupying an enormous warehouse space, one part decorated with an organ salvaged from an old church, Gold offers an Africa-wide safari of tastes, from Xhosa corn pot breads and Cape Malay samosas to Tunisian spiced chicken wings and Zanzibar black bean and carrot stew, one of several vegetarian dishes that are part of the set menu. Arrive at 6.30pm to take part in a 30-minute drumming session (extra R95). The staff perform shows throughout the night, too.

DRINKING & NIGHTLIFE

City Bowl & Foreshore

★**PUBLIK** WINE BAR
Map p268 (www.publik.co.za; 81 Church St, City Bowl; 4-10pm Mon & Tue, to midnight Wed-Fri; Church/Longmarket) By night gourmet butchers Frankie Fenner Meat Merchants morphs into this relaxed, unpretentious bar, where the owners do a brilliant job at digging out hidden gems of the Cape's wine scene. Taste drops from sustainably farmed vineyards, interesting and unusual varietals and rare vintages. The tasting flight of five wines is a great deal at R100.

★**HONEST CHOCOLATE CAFE** CAFE, BAR
Map p268 (www.honestchocolate.co.za; 64 Wale St, City Bowl; 8am-4pm Mon-Fri, 9am-2pm Sat; Dorp/Leeuwen) Following a successful crowdfunding campaign, Honest Chocolate, who make their artisan sweet treats at the Woodstock Exchange (p90), have launched this homage to fine dark chocolate in liquid, solid, ice-cream and cake form. It's a chocoholic's dream come true, with even vegan and gluten-free options.

Even better, Wednesday to Saturday evenings they also run an intimate **bar**, specialising in gin, at the back of the building's secluded courtyard.

★**WEINHAUS + BIERGARTEN** BEER
Map p268 (www.facebook.com/bierandwine; 110 Bree St, City Bowl; noon-midnight; ; Church/Longmarket) To the rear of St Stephen's Church, this cool hang-out specialises in imported craft beers by Brewers & Union and, in summer, has ping-pong and fairly frequent live gigs in the courtyard outside; check their Facebook page for details. Ethically sourced meats are used in tasty sandwiches, hot dogs and braais (barbeques).

★**ORPHANAGE** COCKTAIL BAR
Map p268 (021-424 2004; www.theorphanage.co.za; cnr Orphange & Bree Sts, City Bowl; 5pm-2am Mon-Thu & Sat, to 3am Fri; Upper Loop/Upper Long) Named after the nearby lane, the mixologists here prepare tempting artisan libations with curious names including Knicker-Dropper Glory, Dollymop and Daylight Daisy, using ingredients

as varied as peanut butter, kumquat compote and 'goldfish'! It's dark, sophisticated and stylish, with outdoor seating beneath the trees on Bree.

★BEERHOUSE BAR

Map p268 (www.beerhouse.co.za; 223 Long St, City Bowl; Upper Loop/Upper Long) With 99 brands of ale, both local and international, and several more local craft beers on tap, beer lovers will think they've died and gone to heaven at this brightly designed and spacious joint in the heart of Long St. The balcony is a great spot from which to watch the world go by.

HOUSE OF MACHINES CAFE, BAR

Map p268 (www.thehouseofmachines.com; 84 Shortmarket St, City Bowl; 7am-4pm Mon, to midnight Tue-Sat; Church/Mid-Long) Combining a motorbike workshop with barbers, a boutique and a live music/DJ space, this is a homage to Americana, with tasty, inventive bourbon cocktails, US craft beers and Evil Twin Coffee from NYC.

ORCHARD ON LONG JUICE BAR

Map p268 (211 Long St, City Bowl; 9am-5pm Mon-Fri, 9am-3pm Sat; ; Dorp/Leeuwen) Eye-popping displays of fresh fruits and vegetables lure in the Long St passing parade for the super-healthy and tasty juice mixes and smoothies here. Try Dr Ozzy's Lemonade, which has a peppery kick, or Fine Lady, which promises an improved complexion. The wraps, sandwiches and salads are all vegetarian, too.

WAITING ROOM BAR

Map p268 (021-422 4536; 273 Long St, City Bowl; cover Fri & Sat R30; 7pm-2am Mon-Sat; Upper Loop/Upper Long) Climb the narrow stairway beside the Royale Eatery to find this hip bar decorated in retro furniture with DJs spinning funky tunes. Climb even further and you'll eventually reach the roof deck, the perfect spot from which to admire the city's glittering night lights.

ALEXANDER BAR & CAFÉ GAY, COCKTAIL BAR

Map p268 (www.alexanderbar.co.za; 76 Strand St, City Bowl; 11am-1am Mon-Sat; Strand) Playwright Nicholas Spagnoletti and software engineer Edward van Kuik are the driving duo behind this fun, eccentric space in a gorgeous heritage building. Use antique telephones on the tables to chat with fellow patrons, place an order at the bar or send a telegram to someone you might have your eye on.

See the website for details of shows in the **studio theatre** upstairs.

MOTHER'S RUIN COCKTAIL BAR

Map p268 (082 455 2223; www.facebook.com/mothersruincpt; 219 Bree St, City Bowl; 4-11.30pm Mon-Thu, to 1am Fri & Sat; Upper Long/Upper Loop) There are over 70 types of gin served at this relaxed, friendly place including their own concoctions infused with things like mango chutney and ginger beer. Sip your G&T or cocktail in the cosy lounge rooms or back courtyard hung with fairy lights.

LOCAL KNOWLEDGE

LOVING CAPE TOWN'S COFFEE SCENE

Cape Town's booming artisan coffee scene is documented in the blog **I Love Coffee** (www.ilovecoffee.co.za), compiled by Cindy Taylor and two colleagues. She shared with us some of her favourite places to sample the best roasted beans:

'I did my first interview for the blog at Deluxe Coffeeworks (p72); the Kiwi owner Judd now has his roastery in the Yard (p98) where there's always something crazy going on – in a good way. In contrast, having a coffee at Tribe Woodstock (p88) is as comfortable as being at home; they have also have Tribe 112 (p88) in town.

I work in Woodstock so if I want a really good cup I go to Rosetta Roastery (p87), who only do single origin coffee; they roast very specifically to make their coffees distinct. It's a similar approach as that at Espressolab Microroasters (p87) but Rosetta are less the purists – if you want to put sugar in your coffee that's fine by them!

Truth (p87) on Buitenkant has an amazing vibe with loud music and stunning interior design – it's more than just a coffee shop; and I support Bean There (p72) for promoting fair-trade policies, being personally involved with the farmers and providing information on where their coffee comes from.'

TJING TJING BAR

Map p268 (www.tjingtjing.co.za; 165 Longmarket St, City Bowl; ⌚4pm-late Tue-Fri, 6.30pm-late Sat; 📶; 🚇Church/Longmarket) This slick rooftop bar, perched above Dear Me (p68), is a stylish hang-out for cocktails and wine. The barnlike interior has exposed beams, a photo mural of Tokyo and a scarlet lacquered bar. Check the website for details of special events including free wine tastings (5pm to 7pm Wednesdays).

FORK WINE

Map p268 (☎021-424 6334; www.fork-restaurants.co.za; 84 Long S, City Bowl; ⌚noon-11pm Mon-Sat; 🚇Church/Longmarket) Whether you just want to graze on a few tapas-style dishes (each R45 to R60) or cobble together a full meal, this super-relaxed venue is the business, serving inventive if not strictly Spanish nibbles alongside excellent wines, many by the glass.

LA PARADA BAR

Map p268 (☎021-426 0330; 107 Bree St, City Bowl; ⌚noon-10pm Mon-Sat, to 9pm Sun; 🚇Church/Longmarket) *Cerveza*-quaffing and tapas-munching crowds spill out from this spacious and authentically Spanish looking bar all days of the week. The basement DJ space the **Catacombs** is open 7pm to late Wednesday to Saturday.

BEAN THERE COFFEE

Map p268 (www.beanthere.co.za; 58 Wale St, City Bowl; ⌚7.30am-4pm Mon-Fri, 9am-2pm Sat; 🚇Dorp/Leeuwen) Not much other than fair-trade coffees from across Africa and a few sweet snacks are served in this chic cafe, which has space to spread out and a relaxed vibe despite all the caffeine.

HARD PRESSED CAFE CAFE

Map p272 (www.hardpressed.co.za; 4 Bree St, Foreshore; ⌚7.30am-5.30pm Mon-Fri, 9.30am-2.30pm Sat; 🚇Lower Loop/Lower Long) At the base of the Portside, Cape Town's newest and tallest building, this groovy cafe gives others a run for their money with their expertly made coffees and delicious coconut and date cake. They also sell (and play) old LPs.

DELUXE COFFEEWORKS COFFEE

Map p268 (25 Church St, City Bowl; 🚇Longmarket) A pioneer of the artisan coffee scene, Deluxe is a tiny cafe with what looks like a giant kit model for a Vespa hanging on the wall. Ask the baristas if you can have one of the burlap coffee bags as a souvenir.

TWANKEY BAR COCKTAIL BAR

Map p268 (www.tajhotels.com; Taj Hotel, cnr Adderley & Wale Sts, City Bowl; ⌚3-11pm Mon-Thu, to 2.30am Fri & Sat; 🚇Groote Kerk) For those not familiar with the conventions of British theatre, this elegant bar is named after pantomime dame Widow Twankey – which also happens to be the nickname for the shepherdess statue on the building's corner facade. The cocktails are good and there's super-fresh oysters and other tasty bar snacks.

JULEP BAR COCKTAIL BAR

Map p268 (www.julep.co.za; Vredenburg Lane, City Bowl; ⌚5pm-2am Tue-Sat; 🚇Upper Loop/Upper Long) Occupying the ground floor of a former brothel, this favourite with local hipsters, serving cocktails and tapas, will set you apart from the riff-raff on nearby Long St.

NEIGHBOURHOOD BAR

Map p268 (☎021-424 7260; www.goodinthehood.co.za; 163 Long St, City Bowl; ⌚noon-late Mon-Sat; 🚇Dorp/Leeuwen) At this relaxed bar and casual restaurant, styled after British gastropubs, the colour divide of Cape Town melts away. The long balcony is a good place to cool off or keep tabs on Long St, and you can enjoy two-for-one cocktails 4pm to 7pm Monday to Thursday.

COLOURBOX STUDIOS CLUB

(☎072 437 5183; www.colorboxstudios.co.za; 3 Industry St, Paarden Eiland; 🚇Woodstock) Seek out alternative dance events, such as vintage soul and R&B nights curated by **Vinyl Digz** (www.facebook.com/VinylDIGZ), at this free-flowing experimental events space in the industrial area of Paarden Eiland.

LEOPOLD 7 BREWERY

Map p274 (☎071 370 1246; www.leopold7.com; Duncan Rd, Foreshore; ⌚8am-6pm Mon-Sat; 🚇Foreshore) One of Cape Town's newest craft breweries has set up shop next to the Yacht Club. They only make a Belgian-style amber ale which includes seven ingredients – hence the brewery's name which is also a reference to a brewer who worked in the same spot 150 years ago.

KAMILI CAFE

Map p268 (www.kamilicoffee.co.za; cnr Long & Shortmarket Sts, City Bowl; ⌚7am-6pm Mon-Fri, 9am-2pm Sat; 🚇Church/Longmarket) The old

Purple Turtle dive bar has morphed into this stripped-back, on-trend coffee roasters and cafe. It's connected to the **Imperial Bar**, which is also a cool, colourful space for a drink when you need a break from the Long St hustle.

31 CLUB

Map p268 (☎021-421 0581; www.thirtyone.co.za; 31st fl, ABSA Bldg, 2 Riebeeck St, Foreshore; cover R50; Adderley) Taking its name from the lofty storey it occupies, this glitzy club provides stunning views of the city should you need a breather from the dance floor.

COCO CLUB

Map p268 (www.cococpt.co.za; 70 Loop St, City Bowl; cover R30; 9pm-3am Tue-Sun; Church/Mid-Long) The latest glam incarnation for this perpetually name-changing venue. It promises a crowd of beautiful people, so check your looks in the mirror before chancing your luck with the bouncers.

I LOVE MY LAUNDRY CAFE, BAR

Map p268 (www.ilovemylaundry.co.za; 59 Buitengracht St, City Bowl; 7am-7pm; ; Church/Longmarket) Primarily, this is a laundry, which is hidden behind a shopfront festooned with colourful, arty whatnots and wine, as the place triples up as a cafe-bar, gift shop and wine cellar. Come for a glass of wine or a coffee along with a plate of steamed Korean dumplings, the main food offering. There are branches on Bree and Buitenkant Sts, too.

Bo-Kaap & De Waterkant

CREW BAR GAY, CLUB

Map p272 (www.crewbar.co.za; 30 Napier St, De Waterkant; cover from 10pm Fri & Sat R20; 7pm-2am Sun-Thu, to 3.30pm Fri & Sat; Alfred) The best place for gays and the gay friendly to dance the night away – it helps that there are hunky bar dancers dressed in skimpy shorts and glitter. Downstairs it's hands in the air to the latest pop and dance anthems, while upstairs (usually only open weekends) the beats are harder and more eclectic.

BEAULAH LESBIAN

Map p272 (www.beaulahbar.co.za; 1st fl, 24 Somerset Rd, De Waterkant; cover R20; 9pm-4am Fri & Sat; Alfred) This fun gay-friendly bar and dance venue, up a floor from the street, has a devoted crowd of young boys and girls who are always ready to bop to the DJ's poppy tunes.

AMSTERDAM ACTION BAR & BACKSTAGE GAY

Map p272 (www.amsterdambar.co.za; 10-12 Cobern St, De Waterkant; 5pm-late; Alfred) The action is mainly on the upper level where dark rooms and cubicles provide a venue for punters to dabble in whatever or whomever they fancy. At ground level, the streetside balcony is a popular spot to smoke and watch the comings and goings.

There's a pool table in the nonsmoking area, a small boutique for a fashion makeover (or sex toy), and in the connected **Backstage** bar, a live midnight shower show by the twinky barman.

BAR CODE GAY

Map p272 (☎021-421 5305; www.leatherbar.co.za; 18 Cobern St, De Waterkant; 10pm-1am Wed & Thu, 10pm-4am Fri & Sat, 9pm-1am Sun; Alfred) Leather and latex daddies and their acolytes gather at this small bar with a cosy dark room upstairs. Check the website to make sure you're dressed (or undressed) appropriately for whatever theme is on that night, otherwise you might not be let in.

CAFE MANHATTAN GAY

Map p272 (☎021-421 6666; www.manhattan.co.za; 74 Waterkant St, De Waterkant; 9.30am-2am; Alfred) The pioneer and stalwart of De Waterkant's gay scene remains a highly popular bar and restaurant, not least for its wraparound deck which provides a dress circle on the passing scene. It's recently been taken over by the Madame Zingara group and given a zhush of industrial-meets-cowboy chic.

FIREMAN'S ARMS PUB

Map p272 (☎021-419 1513; www.firemansarms.co.za; cnr Buitengracht & Mechau Sts, De Waterkant; Alfred) Here since 1906, the Fireman's is a Capetonian institution. Inside, the Rhodesian and old South African flags remain pinned up alongside a collection of firemen's helmets and old ties. Come to watch rugby on the big-screen TV, grab some seriously tasty pizza or down a lazy pint or two. Thursday is quiz night.

ORIGIN COFFEE, TEA

Map p272 (☎021-421 1000; www.originroasting.co.za; 28 Hudson St, De Waterkant; 7am-5pm

LOCAL KNOWLEDGE

FIRST THURSDAYS & CITY BOWL GALLERIES

The hit event **First Thursdays** (www.first-thursdays.co.za; 5-9pm 1st Thu of month) is centred on the galleries and design shops clustered around Church and Bree Sts – it's a chance to dip into the local art scene, and a roving street party. Church Sq is the open canvas for anything from debates to giant Scrabble games. Food trucks gather around Van Riebeek Sq and in Upper Bree St, where you're also likely to encounter buskers on Orphan Lane.

Sister event, **Thursday Late**, is usually held on the third Thursday of the month and focuses on the East City and Woodstock areas.

Regular participants in First Thursdays (and places worthy of a visit in their own right include): AVA Gallery (p78), Commune.1 (p77), Luvey 'n Rose (p75), Youngblood Africa (p64), Chandler House (p76), the Pit behind Clarke's (p66), the gallery at 6 Spin St (Map p268) and Cape Gallery (p77).

Mon-Fri, 9am-2pm Sat & Sun; ; Alfred) Apart from great coffee, the traditional bagels here are pretty awesome too. Book ahead for the coffee and tea appreciation courses (R500).

LOS MUERTOS CAFE

Map p268 (www.losmuertosmc.com; 42 Dorp St, Bo-Kaap; 8am-5pm Mon-Fri, 9am-1.30pm Sat; Dorp/Leeuwen) Part of the Capetonian trend of combining motorbike/bicycle works with a coffee shop, Los Muertos is a curious, hipster neighbour for the southern hemisphere's oldest mosque across the road. It stock its own biker fashions and surfboards, too.

ENTERTAINMENT

ARTSCAPE THEATRE

Map p272 (021-410 9800; www.artscape.co.za; 1-10 DF Malan St, Foreshore; Civic Centre) Consisting of three different-sized auditoriums, this behemoth is the city's main arts complex. Theatre, classical music, ballet, opera and cabaret shows – Artscape offers it all. If you're into swing and salsa, **Que Pasa** (www.quepasa.co.za; classes per hour from R70) also run regular classes at the Jazzart Studio here.

The desolate area means it's not recommended to walk around here at night; there's plenty of secure parking though.

CRYPT JAZZ RESTAURANT JAZZ

Map p268 (079 683 4658; www.thecryptjazz.com; 1 Wale St, City Bowl; cover R65; 6.30am-midnight Tue-Sat; Groote Kerk) Occupying part of the vaulted stone crypt, this restaurant in St George's Cathedral (p62), which serves a continent-hopping menu of dishes, is best visited for its live jazz. Concerts start at either 7pm or 8pm and last most of the evening. Some very accomplished performers take to the stage here; for some concerts booking ahead is advisable.

PIANO BAR LIVE MUSIC

Map p272 (www.thepianobar.co.za; 47 Napier St, De Waterkant; noon-midnight Mon-Thu, noon-2am Fri, 4.30pm-3am Sat, 4.30-11pm Sun; Alfred) Proving a hit with one and all in the heart of De Waterkant is this slick music revue bar and restaurant with a nightly line-up of different performers. Expect top-class pianists, jazz singers and players.

ONPOINTE DANCE STUDIOS DANCE

Map p268 (www.onpointedancestudio.wordpress.com; 5th fl, 112 Loop St, City Bowl; tickets R70, classes from R150; ; Dorp/Leeuwen) Theo Ndindwa and Tanya Arshamian use dance to change the lives of kids in the townships. On the first Friday of the month this studio, where classes are held, hosts **Art in the City with iKapa Dance**, a wonderful chance to meet up with a host of local dance companies and watch them perform in a very relaxed environment.

CAPE PHILHARMONIC ORCHESTRA CLASSICAL MUSIC

Map p268 (CPO; www.cpo.org.za; Darling St, City Bowl, entrance Corporation St; tickets from R130; Darling) The old Cape Town City Hall (p63) is home base for the Cape Philharmonic Orchestra (CPO). The auditorium to the rear of the building has very good acoustics that are also taken advantage of by local choirs.

The CPO has been working hard to ensure its musicians reflect the ethnic breakdown of the Western Cape more closely. To this end it has formed the Cape Philharmonic Youth Orchestra and the Cape Philharmonic Youth Wind Ensemble, with around 80% of members coming from disadvantaged communities.

CAPE TOWN INTERNATIONAL CONVENTION CENTRE CONCERT VENUE

Map p272 (CTICC; 021-410 5000; www.cticc.co.za; 1 Lower Long St, Foreshore; Convention Centre) Since opening in 2003, the CTICC has barely paused for breath, packing in a busy annual program of musical performances, exhibitions, conferences and other events, such as the Cape Town International Jazz Festival (p21) and Design Indaba (p20). An extension to the complex is rising up on the plot between the current building and Artscape, almost doubling its size.

In the main entrance hall, *Baobabs, Stormclouds, Animals and People* is a giant relief sculpture, a collaboration between Brett Murray and the late San artist Tuoi Steffaans Samcuia of the !Xun and Khwe San Art and Cultural Project.

PINK FLAMINGO CINEMA

Map p268 (021-423 7247; www.granddaddy.co.za/pinkflamingo; 38 Long St, City Bowl; tickets from R100; Church/Mid-Long) On Mondays, from as early as August to as late as April, the Grand Daddy Hotel's rooftop trailer park of Airstream caravans is the venue for this alfresco cinema screening old-school classics. The regular ticket gets you entrance plus a bag of popcorn and a welcome drink; for R250 you also get a gourmet picnic. Booking online is essential.

MARCO'S AFRICAN PLACE LIVE MUSIC

Map p268 (021-423 5412; www.marcosafricanplace.co.za; 15 Rose Lane, Bo-Kaap; noon-midnight Tue-Fri, 3pm-midnight Sat-Mon; Old Fire Station) Marco Radebe's highly popular African restaurant (mains R120 to R140) offers top-class entertainment from a range of singers, dancers and bands each night. Musical styles including the local marimba, Afro-jazz, traditional Xhosa beats and the Congolese kwasa-kwasa. Alongside enjoy game-meat platters, Xhosa dishes including *smilies* (sheep's heads) and home-brewed African beer.

MAMA AFRICA LIVE MUSIC

Map p268 (021-426 1017; www.mamaafricarestaurant.co.za; 178 Long St, City Bowl; diner/non-diner R10/15; 6.30pm-2am Mon-Sat; Dorp/Leeuwen) At this eternally popular tourist venue the three resident bands each play a couple of gigs a week featuring marimba and other swinging African sounds. Diners can choose from a range of game dishes (mains R120). Bookings are essential on weekends, otherwise squeeze into a spot by the Snake Bar.

MANENBERG'S @ THE CAMISSA COURTYARD JAZZ

Map p268 (021-839 5126; www.facebook.com/groups/469188873223545; 96 Strand St, City Bowl; 6-10.30pm; Strand) This renowned jazz joint was originally on Adderley St; after a long break it has reopened in the courtyard of Martin Melk House and is the passion project of local DJ and celebrity Clarence Ford. The music kicks off around 8pm; a menu of local and Indian dishes is served.

SHOPPING

City Bowl & Foreshore

★SOUTH AFRICAN MARKET FASHION, CRAFTS

Map p268 (SAM; www.ilovesam.co.za; Bree St, City Bowl; 9am-5pm Mon-Fri, 10am-2pm Sat; Church/Longmarket) A spacious loft space above La Parada is a showcase for local design talent across fashion, jewellery, homewares, stationery and artworks. There's a great selection of men's, women's and kids wear here including the cute graphic T-shirts of Mingo Lamberti.

★LUVEY 'N ROSE ARTS

Map p268 (083 557 7156; www.luveynrose.co.za; 66 Loop St, City Bowl; 9am-5pm Mon-Fri, to 2pm Sat; Church/Longmarket) This smashing gallery, next to Prins & Prins but something of a hidden gem, mashes up collectable antiques and works by key South African and African artists such as Walter Battiss with more contemporary stuff from emerging talents. It doubles as a cafe and cigar lounge, a smart move to encourage visitors to linger and browse the eclectic art and design.

AFRICAN MUSIC STORE MUSIC

Map p268 (☎021-426 0857; 134 Long St, City Bowl; ⏰9am-6pm Mon-Fri, to 2pm Sat; 🚌Dorp/Leeuwen) The range of local music here, including jazz, kwaito (a form of township music), dance and trance recordings, can't be surpassed; and the staff are knowledgeable about the music scene. You'll also find DVDs and other souvenirs.

CHANDLER HOUSE ARTS, HOMEWARES

Map p268 (www.chandlerhouse.co.za; 53 Church St, City Bowl; ⏰10am-5pm Mon-Fri, to 2pm Sat; 🚌Church/Longmarket) Michael Chandler showcases his quirky ceramic homewares and decorative pieces in this well-edited collection of imaginative local arts and crafts, which includes cushions, prints and playful design pieces.

MERCHANTS ON LONG FASHION, GIFTS

Map p268 (www.merchantsonlong.com; 34 Long St, City Bowl; ⏰10am-6pm Mon-Fri, to 2pm Sat; 🚌Church/Mid-Long) This 'African salon store', in one of Long St's more beautiful buildings and boasting a terracotta art nouveau facade, is a gallery of top contemporary design – from fashion to stationery – sourced from across the continent. There's also a cafe.

AFRICAN IMAGE ARTS & CRAFTS

Map p268 (www.african-image.co.za; cnr Church & Burg Sts, City Bowl; ⏰9am-5pm Mon-Fri, to 2pm Sat; 🚌Church/Longmarket) African Image has a fab range of new and old crafts and artefacts at reasonable prices, including the funky, colourful pillow covers and aprons of Shine Shine. You'll find a lot of township crafts here, as well as wildly patterned shirts.

MOGALAKWENA ARTS & CRAFTS

Map p268 (☎021-424 7488; www.mogalakwena.com; 3 Church St, City Bowl; ⏰9am-4pm Mon-Fri, by appointment Sat; 🚌Groote Kerk) This attractive gallery is on two levels; downstairs you'll find regularly changing exhibitions of local crafts such as pottery, while upstairs has permanent displays of colourful stitched panels depicting rural scenes and other Pedi crafts from the Limpopo province. They make charming gifts.

ALEXANDRA HÖJER ATELIER FASHION

Map p268 (☎021-424 1674; www.alexandrahojer.com; 156 Bree St, City Bowl; ⏰10am-5pm Mon-Fri, to 2pm Sat; 🚌Upper Loop/Upper Long) Swedish immigrant Alexander Höjer has her workshop here, fronted by a boutique stocking her chic men's and women's fashions in tailored linen, denim, cotton and leather. The distressed T-shirts are neatly packaged in boxes decorated with snaps of her rock-and-roll Dad.

Höjer also has a small boutique outlet in the Lifestyle on Kloof mall.

MISSIBABA & KIRSTEN GOSS ACCESSORIES, JEWELLERY

Map p268 (229 Bree St, City Bowl; ⏰10am-6pm Mon-Fri, to 2pm Sat; 🚌Upper Loop/Upper Long) Two fashion businesses share premises here: **Missibaba** (www.missibaba.com), the brand of Woodstock-based designer Chloe Townsend, who hand-makes colourful bags, belts and other accessories, some with craft input from the townships; and jeweller **Kirsten Goss** (www.kirstengoss.com), who takes inspiration from South Africa for her gold-plated sterling silver pieces.

AFRICANDY HOMEWARES

Map p268 (www.africandy.com; 64 Wale St, City Bowl; ⏰9am-5pm Mon-Fri; 🚌Dorp/Leeuwen) From a small shopfront beneath the Commune.1 gallery, Africandy sell their well-edited range of creative products, including hanging mobiles, limited-edition prints, and asymmetric bowls cast in concrete.

MA SE KINNERS CHILDREN, TOYS

Map p268 (1B-C Church St, City Bowl; ⏰8am-7pm Mon-Fri, to 4pm Sat; 🚌Groote Kerk) Meaning 'Mother's Children' but also slang for 'How's it going?', this attractive new place stocks high-quality, locally made kids clothing and soft toys as well as ceramics, art and other things for grown-ups. There are plans to open a cafe here, too.

WILD OLIVE BEAUTY

Map p268 (☎021-422 2777; www.wildolive.eu; 29 Pepper St, City Bowl; ⏰10am-5pm Mon-Fri, to 1pm Sat; 🚌Dorp/Leeuwen) Olive oil and other locally sourced organic ingredients are used for the high-quality bath, body and perfumery products, including scented candles, displayed in this chic artisan apothecary.

PAN AFRICAN MARKET ARTS & CRAFTS

Map p268 (76 Long St, City Bowl; ⏰8.30am-5.30pm Mon-Fri, to 3.30pm Sat; 🚌Church/Longmarket) A microcosm of the continent, with a bewildering range of arts and crafts (which you should certainly bargain over). There's also the cheap cafe **Timbuktu**, with seating on the balcony overlooking Long St, a tailor and music shop, and the publishers of the pan-African newspaper *Chronic Chimurenga* (www.chimurenga.co.za), all packed into three floors.

TRIBAL TRENDS ARTS & CRAFTS

Map p268 (☎021-423 8008; Winchester House, 72-74 Long St, City Bowl; ⏰9am-5pm Mon-Fri, to 2pm Sat; 🚌Church/Longmarket) Colour-coordinated items pack this emporium of all things African, tribal and crafty. It supports local artists, who sell some of their beadwork and jewellery here.

CLARKE'S BOOKSHOP BOOKS

Map p268 (☎021-423 5739; www.clarkesbooks.co.za; 199 Long St, City Bowl; ⏰9am-5pm Mon-Fri, 9.30am-1pm Sat; 🚌Dorp/Leeuwen) Take your time leafing through the best range of books on South Africa and the continent, with a great secondhand section upstairs. If you can't find what you're looking for here, it's unlikely to be in any of the other many bookshops along Long St (although there's no harm in browsing).

IMAGENIUS ARTS & CRAFTS

Map p268 (☎021-423 7870; www.imagenius.co.za; 117 Long St, City Bowl; 🚌Church/Longmarket) Set over three levels, this treasure-trove of modern African design offers an eclectic range, including ceramics, beachwear, jewellery and printed fabrics. There are stylish gift cards, boxes and wrapping, too.

SIGNAL HILL WINES WINE

Map p268 (www.winery.synthasite.com; Heritage Sq, 100 Shortmarket St, City Bowl; ⏰11am-6pm Mon-Fri, also noon-4pm Sat Dec-Mar; 🚌Church/Longmarket) Appropriately, Heritage Sq, which has the oldest vine in South Africa still producing grapes, is the location for the tasting room of Signal Hill Wines, the country's only city-based winery. They offer small, rare batches of their wines which are made from grapes harvested from a small vineyard at the foot of Table Mountain.

CAPE GALLERY ARTS

Map p268 (☎021-423 5309; www.capegallery.co.za; 60 Church St, City Bowl; ⏰9.30am-5pm Mon-Fri, 10am-2pm Sat; 🚌Church/Longmarket) Packed with a wide range of local artworks at a range of price points. Look for the humorous colourful pieces by David Kuijers, puppets and ceramics.

LUCKY FISH CLOTHING, CRAFTS

Map p268 (www.luckyfish.mobi; 43 Long St, City Bowl; ⏰8am-7.30pm Mon-Thu, 8am-6pm Fri, 9am-4pm Sat; 🚌Church/Mid-Long) A very groovy little shop stocking a great range of locally produced souvenirs, from Electric Zulu print T-shirts and cute Bokkie shoes to African music CDs.

COMMUNE.1 ARTS

Map p268 (☎021-423 5600; www.commune1.com; 64 Wale St, City Bowl; ⏰10am-5pm Tue-Fri, to 2pm Sat; 🚌Dorp/Leeuwen) Greg Dale's gallery, in a historic building that was once a mortuary, is primarily focused on sculpture and installations, exhibiting established and emerging South African artists.

MEMEME FASHION

Map p268 (☎021-424 0001; www.mememe.co.za; 121 Long St, City Bowl; ⏰9.30am-6pm Mon-Sat; 🚌Church/Longmarket) A forerunner of the funky boutiques blooming along Long St, started by award-winning sculptor and fashion designer Doreen Southwood in 2001. It's a showcase for young Capetonian designers and labels such as Adam & Eve, Morphe Odonata and the shoe designer Buqisi Ruux from Nairobi.

MUNGO & JEMIMA FASHION

Map p268 (☎074 083 0777; www.mungoandjemima.com; 108 Long St, City Bowl; ⏰9.30am-6pm Mon-Fri, 10am-2pm Sat; 🚌Church/Longmarket) It may sound like a kid's puppet show, but this cute boutique showcases pretty clothes for adults by local labels such as Coppelia and Good, and accessories such as Ballo glass frames (www.ballo.co.za), made from recycled paper and off-cut timber in Woodstock.

OLIVE GREEN CAT JEWELLERY

Map p268 (☎021-424 1101; www.olivegreencat.com; 77 Church St, City Bowl; ⏰9.30am-5pm Mon-Fri; 🚌Church/Longmarket) At the studio of Philippa Green and Ida-Elsje you'll find the work of two talented jewellery designers, both of whom have caught international attention. Green's signature pieces are her chunky Perspex cuffs, hand-stitched with patterns and graphic text, while Elsje specialises in delicate earrings and necklaces. They also collaborate on the striking Situ range of diamond jewellery.

PRINS & PRINS JEWELLERY

Map p268 (☎021-422 0148; www.prinsandprins.com; 66 Loop St, City Bowl; ⏰9am-5pm Mon-Fri, to 1pm Sat; Church/Mid-Long) An old Huguenot House makes a suitably salubrious venue for investing in some of South Africa's mineral wealth, in wearable form.

SKINZ ACCESSORIES
Map p268 (021-424 3978; www.skinzleather.co.za; 86 Long St, City Bowl; 9am-5pm Mon-Fri, 10am-2pm Sat; Church/Longmarket) If you want a little something made from exotic leather or animal skins – think zebra, springbok, crocodile and ostrich – then this is your place. It does regular cowhide leather too, but doesn't that sound boring compared to purple-dyed crocodile?

SKINNY LA MINX CRAFTS
Map p268 (www.skinnylaminx.com; 201 Bree St, City Bowl; 10am-5pm Mon-Fri, to 2pm Sat; Upper Loop/Upper Long) The designs of Heather Moore, printed on cotton and cotton-linen mix, can be found in several other shops, but here you can view the full range made up into cushions, table runners, lampshades and the like, plus you can purchase cloth by the metre.

AVOOVA CRAFTS
Map p268 (www.avoova.com; 97 Bree St, City Bowl; 9am-5pm Mon-Fri, to 1pm Sat; Church/Longmarket) Stocks the beautiful ostrich eggshell–decorated accessories made by Avoova – each one is a unique piece. You'll also find Masai beadwork from Kenya here, and a few other carefully selected crafts.

EYE MUSIC, VINTAGE
Map p268 (44A Bloem St, City Bowl; 7am-7pm Mon-Fri, 10am-4pm Sat; Upper Loop/Upper Long) After years of collecting comics, records, cameras, graphic prints and other pop culture and retro collectables, the team behind this quirky and certainly eye-catching gallery-shop-cafe have turned sellers. They also stock vinyl platters and CDs by local artists such as the Kalahari Surfers.

LONG STREET ANTIQUE ARCADE ANTIQUES
Map p268 (021-423 3585; www.theantiquearcade.co.za; 127 Long St, City Bowl; 9am-5pm Mon-Fri, 10am-2pm Sat; Dorp/Leeuwen) Browse the booths in this compact arcade, offering a range of antiques and bric-a-brac, and you're likely to find something of interest, from old books and pieces of silverware to art and furniture. There are several more antique and curio stores on Long St if you can't find what you're looking for here.

KLÛK & CGDT FASHION
Map p272 (083 377 7780; www.kluk.co.za; 43-45 Bree St, City Bowl; 9am-5pm Mon-Fri, to 2pm Sat; Lower Loop/Lower Long) The showroom and atelier of Malcolm Klûk (once apprentice to John Galliano) and Christiaan Gabriel du Toit are combined here. Expect haute couture, with similarly haute prices, and some more affordable prêt-à-porter pieces.

AVA GALLERY ARTS
Map p268 (021-424 7436; www.ava.co.za; 35 Church St, City Bowl; 10am-5pm Mon-Fri, to 1pm Sat; Church/Longmarket) Exhibition space for the nonprofit Association for Visual Arts (AVA), which shows some very interesting work by local artists. Pick up signed prints of works by the famous local cartoonist Zapiro.

Bo-Kaap & De Waterkant

★AFRICA NOVA ARTS & CRAFTS
Map p272 (www.africanova.co.za; Cape Quarter, 72 Waterkant St, De Waterkant; 9am-5pm Mon-Fri, 10am-5pm Sat, 10am-2pm Sun; Alfred) One of the most stylish and desirable collections of contemporary African textiles, arts and crafts. You'll find potato-print fabrics made by women in Hout Bay, Karin Dando's mosaic trophy heads, Ronel Jordaan's handmade felt rock cushions (which look like giant pebbles) and a wonderful range of ceramics and jewellery. There's a smaller branch at the Watershed (p113) at the Waterfront.

★STREETWIRES ARTS & CRAFTS
Map p268 (www.streetwires.co.za; 77 Shortmarket St, Bo-Kaap; 8.30am-5pm Mon-Fri, 9am-1pm Sat; Church/Longmarket) The motto is 'anything you can dream up in wire we will build'. And if you visit this social project, designed to create sustainable employment, and see the wire sculptors at work, you'll see what that means! It stocks an amazing range, including working radios and chandeliers, life-sized animals and artier products such as the Nguni Cow range.

★MONKEYBIZ ARTS & CRAFTS
Map p268 (www.monkeybiz.co.za; 43 Rose St, Bo-Kaap; 9am-5pm Mon-Thu, 9am-4pm Fri, 10am-1pm Sat; Church/Longmarket) Colourful beadwork crafts, made by local township women, are Monkeybiz' super-successful

stock in trade – you'll find their products around the world but the largest selection is here. Profits are reinvested back into community services such as soup kitchens and a burial fund for artists and their families.

BARAKA GIFTS

Map p272 (021-425 8883; www.barakashop.co.za; Shop 13A, Cape Quarter, Dixon St, De Waterkant; 10am-5.30pm Mon-Fri, 10am-3.30pm Sat, 11am-3.30pm Sun; Alfred) Baraka means 'blessing' in Arabic. Co-owner Gavin Terblanche has an eclectic eye for what works as a gift or quirky piece of home decor. Products include handmade leather journals and photo albums by Terblanche's own company **Worlds of Wonder** (www.worldsofwonder.co.za).

FRAZER PARFUM BEAUTY

Map p268 (www.frazerparfum.com; 3 Rose St, De Waterkant; 10am-5pm Tue-Fri; Old Fire Station) Tammy Violet Frazer, granddaughter of the inventor of Oil of Olay, is the creative perfumer behind this bespoke collection of luxury scents. Beguiling names such as After the Rains incorporate exotic local ingredients and come packaged in beautiful bottles and containers.

CAPE QUARTER SHOPPING CENTRE

Map p272 (021-421 0737; www.capequarter.co.za; 72 Waterkant St, De Waterkant; 9am-6pm Mon-Fri, 9am-4pm Sat, 10am-4pm Sun; Alfred) Cape Quarter is split over two adjacent locations. The newer, larger block is anchored by a snazzy branch of the supermarket **Spar** (Map p272; 7am-9pm Mon-Sat, 8am-9pm Sun), handy if you're self-catering in the area – or indeed staying in one of the complex's luxury penthouse apartments. A food and goods market is held on the upper floors every Friday from 4pm.

ATLAS TRADING COMPANY FOOD

Map p268 (021-423 4361; 94 Wale St, Bo-Kaap; 8am-5pm Mon-Thu, 8am-noon & 2-5pm Fri, 8.30am-12.45pm Sat; Leeuwen) The pungent smell of over 100 different herbs, spices and incenses perfumes the air at this cornerstone of the Bo-Kaap's Cape Muslim community.

BURR & MUIR ANTIQUES

Map p268 (021-418 1296; www.burrmuir.com; The Mirage, cnr Strand & Hudson Sts, De Waterkant; 9am-5pm Mon-Fri, 10am-2pm Sat; Old Fire Station) If you're after something art nouveau, art decor or of 20th-century design, then this expertly curated dealer is the place to head. The displays are like a mini museum.

SPORTS & ACTIVITIES

LONG ST BATHS SWIMMING

Map p268 (www.capetown.gov.za/en/SportRecreation/Pages/LongStreetBaths.aspx; cnr Long & Buitensingel Sts, City Bowl; adult/child R5.50/1.50; 7am-7pm; Upper Loop/Upper Long) Dating from 1906, these nicely restored baths, featuring painted murals of city-centre life on the walls, are heated and very popular with the local community. The Turkish steam baths (R48) are a great way to sweat away some time, especially during the cooler months.

Women are admitted to the steam baths from 9am to 6pm Monday, Thursday and Saturday, and from 9am to 1pm on Tuesday; men from 1pm to 7pm on Tuesday, from 8am to 7pm on Wednesday and Friday, and from 8am to noon on Sunday.

ROYAL CAPE YACHT CLUB SAILING

Map p274 (021-421 1354; www.rcyc.co.za; Duncan Rd, Foreshore; Foreshore) The club is at the far eastern end of Duncan Dock with access through the gate on South Arm Rd within the V&A Waterfront. If you have sailing knowledge, show up on Wednesday afternoons around 4.30pm to take part in the Twilight series of races – you'll be assigned a boat for the race, which starts at 5.30pm.

East City, District Six, Woodstock & Observatory

DISTRICT SIX | WOODSTOCK | SALT RIVER | OBSERVATORY

Neighbourhood Top Five

❶ Learn about Cape Town's troubled past at the **District Six Museum** (p82), which is as much *for* the people of the destroyed inner city as it is about them.

❷ Browse the **Old Biscuit Mill** (p89) for retail therapy and gourmet eats.

❸ Discover South African artists at **galleries** (p89) such as Stevenson and What If The World.

❹ Enjoy top-class theatre and digital movie events at the **Fugard** (p88).

❺ Admire the dazzling **street art** (p84) brightening up East City, District Six and Woodstock.

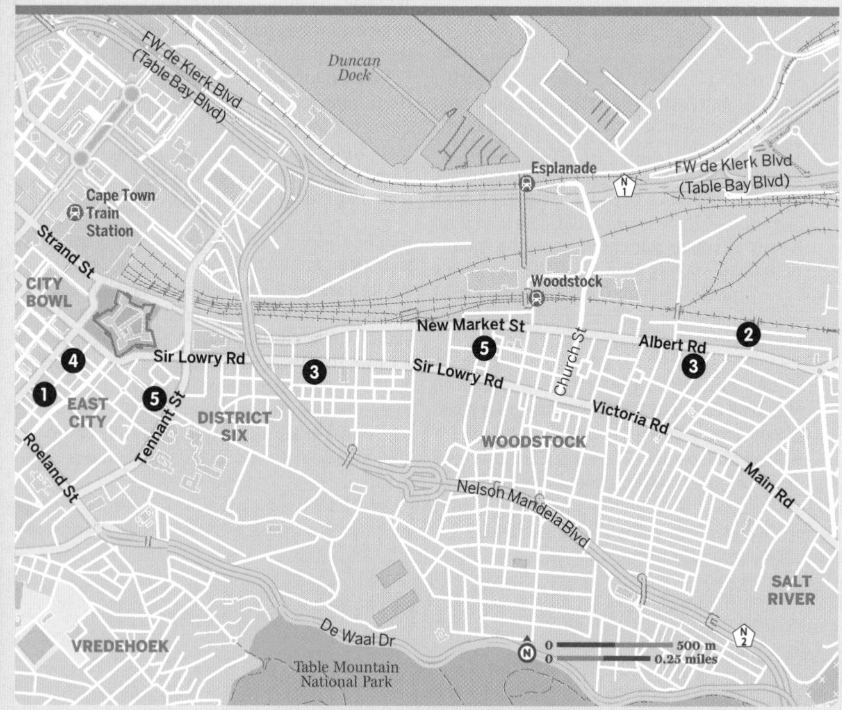

For more detail of this area see Map p274 and p276

Explore East City District Six, Woodstock & Observatory

East of the City Bowl are a string of working-class, industrial suburbs that are regenerating and partly gentrifying. The process is patchy and controversial and has long been so – this is where you'll find the largely empty lots of District Six, a multicultural area destroyed during apartheid.

Creative industries, cafes and bars are clustered at the the East City end of District Six. Moving further eastwards, Woodstock and Salt River continue their upwardly mobile trajectory, with the Woodstock Exchange, the Woodstock Foundry, Woodstock Co-op and Salt Circle Arcade being the prime redevelopments following in the wake of the phenomenal Old Biscuit Mill. The opening of several major and minor Cape Town galleries, joining pioneers such as Greatmore Studios, has put the region on the art-lovers' map. This area is also the canvas for the city's most striking street art, and a hub for the city's blooming craft-beer scene.

Further east is Observatory, named after the first Royal Observatory established nearby in 1820; the site remains the headquarters of the South African Astronomical Observatory. Commonly known as 'Obs', the suburb has long been a bohemian, racially mixed area, even during apartheid. It's popular with students attending the nearby University of Cape Town and the Medical School at Groote Schuur Hospital. Several fine backpacker hostels and lively, inexpensive restaurants make it a great base for budget travellers.

Local Life

- **Markets** Neighbourgoods (p89) every Saturday is the big one, but get there early to avoid jostling crowds.
- **Design** Pick up the *Woodstock Design District Map*, the key to discovering local craftspeople and artists, at Southern Guild (p89).
- **Books** Broaden your intellectual horizons and be entertained by one of many fascinating readings or book launches at the Book Lounge (p90).

Getting There & Away

- **Walk** Fine from the City Bowl to East City, and during daylight around the main roads of Woodstock and Salt River. Proceed with caution at night.
- **Bus and shared taxi** City buses and shared minibus taxis plough the route between the city and Observatory along Sir Lowry and Victoria Rds.
- **Train** Cape Metro trains stop at Woodstock, Salt River and Observatory.

Lonely Planet's Top Tip

Gallery openings, late-night shopping, food trucks and street parties feature across the East City and Woodstock on **Thursday Late** (www.first-thursdays.co.za), the third Thursday of the month.

Best Places to Eat

- Pot Luck Club (p86)
- Kitchen (p85)
- Test Kitchen (p86)
- Pesce Azzurro (p86)
- Ocean Jewels (p85)

For reviews, see p85.

Best Places to Drink

- Taproom (p87)
- Espressolab Microroasters (p87)
- aMadoda Braai (p87)
- Truth (p87)
- Lady Bonin's Tea (p87)

For reviews, see p87.

Best Places to Shop

- Old Biscuit Mill (p89)
- Neighbourgoods Market (p89)
- Book Lounge (p90)
- Southern Guild (p89)
- Woodstock Exchange (p90)

For reviews, see p89.

TOP SIGHT
DISTRICT SIX MUSEUM

It's impossible not to be emotionally touched by this museum which celebrates the once lively multiracial area that was destroyed during apartheid, its 60,000 inhabitants forcibly removed. Inside the former Methodist Mission Church home interiors have been re-created, alongside photographs, recordings and testimonials, all of which build an evocative picture of a shattered but not entirely broken community.

Noor Ebrahim's Story

The best way to understand the events of District Six is to speak with the staff, all of whom have heartbreaking stories of their neighbourhood's destruction. 'I used to live at 247 Caledon St,' begins museum guide Noor Ebrahim, pointing at the map covering the museum's floor.

Noor's grandfather came to Cape Town in 1890 from Surat in India. An energetic man who had four wives and 30 children, he built up a good business making ginger beer. Noor's father was one of the old man's sons to his first wife, a Scot called Fanny Grainger, and Noor grew up in the heart of District Six. 'It was a very cosmopolitan area. Many whites lived there – they owned the shops. There were blacks, Portuguese, Chinese and Hindus all living as one big happy family.'

'We didn't know it was going to happen,' remembers Noor of the 1966 order declaring District Six a white area under the Group Areas Act. 'We saw the headlines in the paper and people were angry and sad but for a while little happened.' Then in 1970 the demolitions started and gradually the residents moved out.

Noor's family hung on until 1976, when they were given two weeks to vacate the house that his grandfather had bought some 70 years previously. By that time they'd seen families, neighbours and friends split up and sent to separate townships determined by their

DON'T MISS

- Floor map of District Six
- Walking tour of area
- Homecoming Centre

PRACTICALITIES

- Map p274
- ☎021-466 7200
- www.districtsix.co.za
- 25A Buitenkant St, East City
- adult/child R30/15, walking tours per person R60
- ⏲9am-4pm Mon-Sat
- 🚌Lower Buitenkant

race. They'd prepared by buying a new home in the coloured township of Athlone.

Noor will never forget the day he left District Six. 'I got in the car with my wife and two children and drove off, but only got as far as the corner before I had to stop. I got out of the car and started to cry as I saw the bulldozers move in immediately. Many people died of broken hearts.'

Homecoming Centre

A block north of the main museum is its annexe, the **Homecoming Centre** (Map p274; 15 Buitenkant St; Lower Buitenkant), occupying part of the Sacks Futeran Building. For many generations the Futeran family traded soft goods and textiles from these premises, and before that part of the building was the Buitenkant Congregational Church. It is now open occasionally for temporary exhibitions and events.

Trafalgar Park

To get an idea of what District Six was like, you could explore (in daytime and preferably in company; the museum runs regular walking tours) the area around Chapel St, north of the raised Nelson Mandela Blvd. Here you'll find old workers cottages and **Trafalgar Park** (Map p274; www.capetown.gov.za/en/parks/Pages/TrafalgarPark.aspx; cnr Victoria Rd & Searle St, Woodstock; Zonnebloem), which contains the remains of the French Redoubt, one of a series of defensive positions built by the Dutch East India Company (Vereenigde Oost-Indische Compagnie; VOC) in 1871 to protect the Cape against a British attack.

The Future of District Six

Since democracy, there have been promises to rebuild the 4200-sq-metre site, but as the largely empty lots prove, it's been very slow going. The **District Six Beneficiary Trust** (www.districtsix.za.org) formed to register land claims and handle the issues and processes of resettlement. However it wasn't until December 2011 that local government committed to having 1500 homes rebuilt by February 2015 and a total of 5000 by 2019, when it's hoped the area will have some 20,000 inhabitants. Both targets are unlikely to be met.

It will be impossible for everyone to return to where they once lived because buildings such as the Cape Peninsula University of Technology now occupy large chunks of the area. Many claimants are also getting very old and some prefer to take financial compensation rather than land restoration from the government who keep failing in their pledges to build homes.

READING UP

Recalling Community in Cape Town (eds Ciraj Rassool and Sundra Posalendis) is an illustrated account of the now-destroyed District Six area and how its memory was kept alive by those who once lived there. Another good book to read is *'Buckingham Palace', District Six* by Richard Rive, an eloquent tale about the inhabitants of five houses in the heart of District Six.

The area gets its name from being the sixth area to become a municipal area; it was designated in 1867. In the 1960s it was renamed Zonnebloem (meaning 'Sunflower' in Afrikaans).

WALKING TOURS

Book with the museum for their sunset walk (R60) at 5.30pm Thursday, or for guided private walking tours. Many township tours also start at the museum, where the history of the apartheid era Pass laws, which regulated where people were allowed to live based on their race, are explained.

SIGHTS

DISTRICT SIX MUSEUM MUSEUM

See p82.

CAPE TOWN SCIENCE CENTRE MUSEUM

Map p276 (☎021-300 3200; www.ctsc.org.za; 370B Main Rd, Observatory; admission R40; 9am-4.30pm Mon-Sat, 10am-4.30pm Sun; P; Observatory) Occupying a rare example of the work of modernist architect Max Policansky, this is a great place to bring kids for attractions such as the giant gyroscope (R5 extra) and tons of Lego. There's also a replica of the Soyuz capsule that returned South African tech billionaire Mark Shuttleworth to earth after his trip to the International Space Station.

HEART OF CAPE TOWN MUSEUM MUSEUM

Map p276 (☎021-404 1967; www.heartofcapetown.co.za; Old Main Bldg, Groote Schuur Hospital, Main Rd, Observatory; overseas visitors R200, South African adult/student R100/50; guided tours 9am, 11am, 1pm & 3pm; P; Observatory) Booking a tour is the only way you can see the theatre in Groote Schuur Hospital where history was made in 1967 when Dr Christiaan Barnard and his team carried out the world's first successful heart transplant operation (sadly, the recipient died a few days later). The displays have a fascinating Dr Kildare quality to them. For R50 extra transfers to and from your hotel can be arranged.

GREATMORE STUDIOS ART STUDIOS

Map p274 (☎021-447 9699; www.greatmoreart.org; 47-49 Greatmore St, Woodstock; 9am-5pm Mon-Fri; Lawley) FREE This pioneer of the Woodstock art scene provides studio space for local artists and visiting overseas artists, with the idea of providing skills transfer and cross-cultural stimulation of ideas and creativity. Visitors are welcome to stroll around and there are occasionally group exhibitions held here.

LOCAL KNOWLEDGE

DISTRICT SIX & WOODSTOCK STREET ART

Vivid works of street art, big and small, decorate the sides of many buildings in District Six and Woodstock. Street artists conducting tours around these areas include Juma Mkwela (p26), a friendly Zimbabwean who also leads tours of Khayelitsha, and **Grant Jurius** (☎079 066 7055; www.facebook.com/thestreetisthegallery), who also offers tours around Mitchell's Plain. Khayelitsha and Mitchell's Plain are both areas where you'll find more eye-catching works.

Substation 13 (Map p274; Canterbury St, District Six; Lower Buitenkant) A blue-hued painting of Nelson Mandela covers one side of this electrical substation building, while on the other is a mural dedicated to District Six. Both images were designed and painted by **Mak1one** (www.mak1one.com) aka Maxwell Southgate. He also decorated the facade of Charly's Bakery, opposite, and his distinctive street art can be spotted at several other locations around town.

I Art Woodstock (Map p274; btwn Gympie & Hercules Sts, Woodstock; Woodstock) The sketchy grid of streets off Albert Rd is a canvas for some amazing street art, much of it created during a collaborative project between **a word of art** (www.a-word-of-art.co.za) and Adidas Originals in 2011. More pieces have been added since, such as *Raised by Wolves* by Nardstar, and the *Freedom Day Mural* by Freddy Sam.

Land & Liberty (Map p274; Keizersgracht, District Six; Hanover St) Prolific street artist **Faith47** (www.faith47.com) created this eight-storey tall mother with a baby strapped to her back pointing up towards Lion's Head.

Harvest (Map p274; Picket Post 59-63 block, cnr Cauvin Rd & Christiaan St, District Six; District Six) Faith47 designed this proud African woman and her crop of reeds, which integrates an electronic lighting system. It's designed to illuminate every time a donation is made to the #ANOTHERLIGHTUP (www.anotherlightup.com) project, which funds lighting for public spaces in the township of Monwabisi Park.

Freedom Struggle Heroes (Map p274; Darling St, District Six; Hanover St) Portraits of Nelson Mandela, Steve Biko, Cissie Gool and Imam Haron are painted on the side of a building as if their faces were carved into the side of Table Mountain. Nearby on the corner of Tennant St you'll find more street art, including a proud-looking Masai woman.

CAPE CRAFT & DESIGN INSTITUTE GALLERY

Map p274 (CCDI; www.ccdi.org.za; 75 Harrington St, East City; Lower Buitenkant) FREE In the works in early 2015 was this new showcase for the CCDI. Up and running is the British Council–sponsored **Maker Library** project with Capetonian designer Heath Nash at the helm. The CCDI will have projects both here and across the road in Harrington House.

BIJOU ART STUDIOS

Map p276 (78 Lower Main Rd, Observatory; 7.30am-4pm Mon-Fri; Observatory) There are studio spaces for artists and craftspeople in this fabulous art deco building, once a cinema, including that of blacksmith **Conrad Hicks** (www.blacksmith.co.za). Some of his work is on display in the shopfront gallery here, which shares space with a branch of the cafe Origin.

Many of the artist studios open up to the public during Art Week at the end of November or early December.

EATING

The three main dining strips to zone in on are Woodstock's Roodebloem Rd, Salt River's Albert Rd and Lower Main Rd in Observatory. Also mark your calendar with a big red cross for Saturday's brunch fest at the Neighbourgoods Market (p89).

★KITCHEN SANDWICHES, SALADS $

Map p274 (www.lovethekitchen.co.za; 111 Sir Lowry Rd, Woodstock; sandwiches & salads R60-70; 8am-3.30pm Mon-Fri; ; District Six) Over all the swanky restaurants in town, it was this little charmer that Michelle Obama chose for lunch, proving the First Lady has excellent taste. Tuck into plates of divine salads, rustic sandwiches made with love, and sweet treats with tea served from china teapots.

A few doors down chef Karen Duddley has opened a more formal second venture, **Dining Room** (Map p274; 021-461 0463; 117 Sir Lowrey Rd; noon-3pm Tue-Fri, 7pm-9pm Thu; District Six), serving a similar menu.

★OCEAN JEWELS SEAFOOD $

Map p274 (083 582 0829; www.oceanjewels.co.za; Woodstock Exchange, 66 Albert Rd, Woodstock; mains R45-50; 9.30am-5pm Mon-Fri, 10am-2pm Sat; Woodstock) Fish straight from Kalk Bay harbour is served at this SASSI-supporting seafood cafe that does a mean tuna burger with wedge fries. Despite being in the industrial-chic Woodstock Exchange, the vibe is as relaxed as the seaside, with whitewashed wooden tables and food served on rustic enamel plates.

HELLO SAILOR BISTRO $

Map p276 (021-447 0707; www.hellosailorbistro.co.za; 86 Lower Main Rd, Observatory; mains R50; 8am-10pm; Observatory) A tattooed mermaid in a round portrait on the wall looks down on the tattooed patrons of this slick bistro serving price-friendly comfort food – burgers, salads, pastas – all done well. The restaurant closes at 10pm, but the bar here can kick on until 2am on the weekend.

THREE FEATHERS DINER BURGERS $

Map p274 (021-448 6606; 68 Bromwell Rd, Woodstock; burgers R70; 11am-3pm Mon & Tue, to 9pm Wed-Fri, to 7pm Sat; Kent) Street art decorates this cavernous space that's a shrine to the owner's beloved American muscle cars, such as the bright orange Pontiac Firebird parked inside next to the pinball machine. Serves giant, juicy burgers (a veg option is available), shakes and craft beers.

CHARLY'S BAKERY BAKERY, CAFE $

Map p274 (www.charlysbakery.co.za; 38 Canterbury St, East City; baked goods R17-35; 8am-5pm Tue-Fri, 8.30am-2pm Sat; Lower Buitenkant) The fabulous female team here, stars of the reality TV series *Charly's Cake Angels,* make – as they say – 'mucking afazing' cupcakes and other baked goods. The heritage building is as colourfully decorated as their cakes.

QUEEN OF TARTS CAFE $

Map p276 (021-448 2420; www.queenoftarts.co.za; 213 Lower Main Rd, Observatory; mains R45-70; 8am-4pm Mon-Fri, to 2pm Sat; Observatory) This charming cafe, decorated like your granny's kitchen, serves sweet and savoury tarts and other delish confections. You'll also find their tarts on stalls at Neighbourgoods and other Cape Town markets.

SUPERETTE CAFE, DELI $

Map p274 (www.superette.co.za; Woodstock Exchange, 66 Albert Rd, Woodstock; mains R50; 9am-4pm Mon-Fri, to 2pm Sat; Woodstock)

From the same guys behind the gallery What If The World and the organisers of the Neighbourgoods Market comes this laid-back, tastefully turned out and oh-so-trendy neighbourhood cafe. Try the all-day breakfast sandwich or baked goods made with natural sugars.

DOWNTOWN RAMEN JAPANESE $

Map p274 (105 Harrington St, East City; noodles R65; ⏲11am-3pm & 5.30-10pm Mon-Sat; 🚌Roeland) Although slightly different items are available at lunch and dinners, the two types of ramen – one with a slice of *char sui* pork, the other a veg version with tofu – are served at both times and should be sampled. Ask for the chilli on the side if you don't like your noodles so spicy. It's upstairs at Lefty's.

LEFTY'S BARBECUE, PIZZA $

Map p274 (105 Harrington St, East City; mains R60-95; ⏲11am-10pm; 🚌Roeland) Appealing to students and lovers of grunge and shabby chic, this artfully crafted dive bar amps up its hipster cred with sticky BBQ pork ribs and Kentucky chicken waffles, alongside brick-oven-baked pizza and beetroot and ginger felafel for nonmeat eaters. There's plenty of craft beers to wash it all down, too.

RAW AND ROXY VEGAN $

Map p274 (302 Albert Rd, Woodstock; mains R70-90; ⏲9am-5pm Mon-Sat; ✎; 🚌Kent) Beatrice Holst has seduced meat-loving Capetonians with delicious raw and vegan repasts and drinks, including super vitamin-charged juices, a raw lasagne that has foodies reaching for superlatives, and a silky smooth and super-rich avocado chocolate ganache cake.

CAFÉ GANESH AFRICAN, INDIAN $

Map p276 (☎021-448 3435; www.cafeganesh.wozaonline.co.za; 38B Trill Rd, Observatory; mains R50-80; ⏲6-11.30pm Mon-Sat; 🚆Observatory) Sample pap (maize porridge) and veg, grilled springbok or lamb curry at this funky hang-out, squeezed into an alley between two buildings. Junkyard decor and matchbox-label wallpaper create that chic-shack look.

TOUCH OF MADNESS BISTRO $

Map p276 (☎021-448 2266; www.touchofmadness.co.za; 12 Nuttall Rd, Observatory; mains R55-70; ⏲noon-late Mon-Sat, 7pm-late Sun; 📶; 🚆Observatory) This long-running bar and restaurant offers an eclectic art-house atmosphere, dressed up in purple with lace trimmings. It serves a range of 'ballistic burgers, potty pitas and radical wraps', which suits the area's boho-student palate and pocket. Check out the spoken-word events on Mondays.

SORBETIERE ICE CREAM $

Map p274 (www.sorbetiere.co.za; Side Street Studio, 48 Albert Rd, Woodstock; ice creams from R22; ⏲8am-4pm Mon-Fri, 10am-2pm Sat; 🚆Woodstock) Cool down with luscious locally made ice creams and sorbets at this tiny cafe inside the street-art decorated Side Street Studios. It also serves coffee and crêpes.

★POT LUCK CLUB INTERNATIONAL $$

Map p274 (☎021-447 0804; www.thepotluckclub.co.za; Silo Top fl, Old Biscuit Mill, 373-375 Albert Rd, Woodstock; dishes R75-100; ⏲12.30-2.30pm & 6-8.30pm Mon-Sat, 11am-12.30pm Sun; 🚌Kent) The more affordable of Luke Dale-Roberts' operations at the Old Biscuit Mill may offer panoramic views of the surrounding area, but it's what's on the plate that tends to take the breath away. The dishes are designed to be shared; we defy you not to order a second plate of the smoked beef with truffle-café-au-lait sauce. Sunday brunch without/with bottomless bubbly is R350/500.

★PESCE AZZURRO ITALIAN $$

Map p274 (☎021-447 2009; www.pesceazzurro.co.za; 113 Roodebloem Rd, Woodstock; mains R85-105; ⏲noon-3pm & 6-10pm Mon-Sat; 🚌Balfour) Tuscan-born chef Andrea Volpe turns out delicious rustic Italian pasta and seafood dishes at this casual joint well patronised by locals. The mussels and crayfish here are excellent. Round off the meal with grandma's tiramisu.

CHANDANI INDIAN, VEGETARIAN $$

Map p274 (☎021-447 7887; www.chandani.co.za; 85 Roodebloem Rd, Woodstock; mains R60-80; ⏲11.30am-3pm & 6.30-10.30pm Mon-Sat; ✎; 🚌Balfour) This long-running and appealing Indian restaurant offers a great selection of dishes for vegetarians including *aloo gobi* (potato and cauliflower curry) and *dal makani* (black lentils in a creamy tomato sauce).

★TEST KITCHEN INTERNATIONAL $$$

Map p274 (☎021-447 2622; www.thetestkitchen.co.za; Shop 104A, Old Biscuit Mill, 375 Albert Rd, Woodstock; 5-course lunch/dinner from

R470/590; ⌚12.30-2.30pm & 7-9pm Tue-Sat; 🚌Kent) Luke Dale-Roberts creates inspirational dishes using top-quality local ingredients. However, the UK-born chef is so famous now that bookings several months in advance are necessary, both for lunch and dinner. Pescatarian and vegetarian menus are available on request.

DRINKING & NIGHTLIFE

★TAPROOM MICROBREWERY

Map p274 (www.devilspeakbrewing.co.za; 95 Durham Ave, Salt River; ⌚8am-4pm Mon, to 11pm Tue-Sat; 🚌Upper Salt River) Devil's Peak Brewing Company make some of South Africa's best craft beers. Their taproom and restaurant provide a panoramic view up to Devil's Peak itself. The food is hearty fare (think burgers and fried chicken), designed to balance the stellar selection of on-tap beers. There are also barrel-aged brews and the new Explorer series of bottled ales.

★TRUTH COFFEE

Map p274 (www.truthcoffee.com; 36 Buitenkant St, East City; ⌚7.30am-6pm Mon-Sat, to 2pm Sun; 📶; 🚌Lower Buitenkant) This self-described 'steampunk roastery and coffee bar', with pressed tin ceilings, naked hanging bulbs and mad-inventor style metalwork, is an awe-inspiring space in which to mingle with city slickers. Apart from coffee, craft beers, baked goods and various sandwiches, burgers and hot dogs are on the menu.

There's also a branch in the Prestwich Memorial (p64).

★AMADODA BRAAI BAR, BRAAI

Map p274 (www.amadoda.co.za; 1-4 Strand St, Woodstock; ⌚noon-9pm Mon-Thu, to 2am Fri-Sun; 🚆Woodstock) Pulling off a township braai (barbecue; menus start at R50) and shebeen atmosphere, this slickly decorated venue, tucked away down a side road beside the railway tracks, attracts a racially mixed crowd. The juke box is stacked with African, jazz and house music tracks; it's worth checking out late on a weekend evening when patrons start to boogie.

★ESPRESSOLAB MICROROASTERS COFFEE

Map p274 (www.espressolabmicroroasters.com; Old Biscuit Mill, 375 Albert Rd, Woodstock; ⌚8am-4pm Mon-Fri, to 2pm Sat; 🚌Kent) Geek out about coffee at this lab staffed with passionate roasters and baristas. The beans, which come from single farms, estates and co-ops from around the world, are packaged with tasting notes such as those for fine wines.

★LADY BONIN'S TEA TEAHOUSE

Map p274 (www.ladybonin.com; Shop AG11b, Woodstock Exchange, 66 Albert Rd, Woodstock; ⌚9am-5pm Mon-Fri, to 3pm Sat; 🚆Woodstock) A charmingly decorated, relaxing place in which to sample organic and sustainable artisan teas, fruity and herbal brews, and vegan baked treats.

ROSETTA ROASTERY CAFE

Map p274 (www.rosettaroastery.com; Shop AG01, Woodstock Exchange, 66 Albert Rd, Woodstock; ⌚8am-4pm Mon-Fri; 🚆Woodstock) Tucked away in the courtyard of the Woodstock Exchange these guys have a singularly appreciative hipster audience on tap to enjoy their single origin and estate coffees from around the world, each roasted differently to bring out the best flavours. No wonder it's been named one of the 25 coffee shops to visit before you die.

FLAT MOUNTAIN CAFE, BAR

Map p274 (www.flatmountainroasters.co.za; 101 Sir Lowry Rd, Woodstock; ⌚6am-3.30pm Mon-Fri, 9am-1pm Sat; 🚌District Six) These artisan coffee guys specialise in blends, including an organic one and a full-flavour decaf. It's handy if you're browsing the galleries in the area and need a caffeine kick. Beers and alcoholic drinks are served in the bar upstairs; the bar's breezy balcony connects up with hipster boutique Smith & Abrahams next door.

SUGARHUT CLUB

Map p274 (www.sugarhutclub.co.za; 44 Constitution St, East City; cover R40; 🚌Lower Buitenkant) Above a working-men's pub on the East City–District Six border, its broad balcony providing panoramic views towards Table Mountain, this glam club-for-hire venue is used for the fab Unofficial Pink Party events organised by the lovely lesbians Janine and Kelly, usually on the last Friday of the month.

RIOT FACTORY MICROBREWERY

Map p274 (The Palms, 145 Sir Lowry Rd, Woodstock; ⌚4-9pm Wed-Fri, 10am-2pm Sat; 🚌District Six) One of Woodstock's many new boutique breweries, Riot makes a quaffable golden ale and and the Valve IPA. It also stocks other local craft beer and the Western Cape artisanal gin Inveroche. Street artist Falco1 created the striking wall mural.

GARAGISTA MICROBREWERY
Map p274 (www.garagista.co.za; 139 Albert Rd, Woodstock; ⏲2-6pm Wed-Fri, 11-3pm Sat; Woodstock) You have to hand it to Garagista – they know how to target and market their craft beers. Teaming up to share space with Lovell Gallery in Woodstock is a smart move, providing a contemporary art edge (and audience) for their ales. Naming one of their brews Tears of the Hipster is inspired.

WOODSTOCK LOUNGE CAFE, BAR
Map p274 (www.woodstocklounge.co.za; 70 Roodebloem Rd, Woodstock; ⏲11.30am-midnight Mon-Sat; Balfour) Wall-sized prints of black-and-white photos of old Woodstock provide some visual relief at this white box cafe-bar. There are pretty good pizzas to go with Jack Black on tap, and TV screens and comfy sofas for watching sport.

TRIBE WOODSTOCK CAFE
Map p274 (www.tribecoffee.co.za; Woodstock Foundry, 160 Albert Rd, Woodstock; ⏲7am-4pm Mon-Fri, 9am-2pm Sat; Woodstock) Woodstock's creative hub developments wouldn't be complete without an on-site artisan coffee roaster and cafe, and the Woodstock Foundary is no exception. Here Tribe does the duties with a pleasant cafe fronting onto a quiet courtyard. They also run **Tribe 112** (Map p268; 112 Buitengracht St, City Bowl; ⏲7am-5pm Mon-Fri, 8am-2pm Sat; Church/Longmarket) in a BMW dealership in the City Bowl.

HAAS CAFE
Map p274 (www.haascollective.com; 19 Buitenkant St, East City; ⏲7am-5pm Mon-Fri, 8am-3pm Sat & Sun; ; Lower Buitenkant) Come more for the arty design boutique – where you can sip artisan coffee, lounge, and work on your laptop – than for the food, which is OK, but not outstanding.

FIELD OFFICE CAFE
Map p274 (www.fieldoffice.co.za; 37 Barrack St, East City; ⏲7am-4pm Mon-Fri; Lower Buitenkant) This cool cafe doubling as a workspace for the laptop-toting classes is also one of the showrooms for furniture and lighting designers **Pedersen & Lennard** (www.pedersenlennard.co.za). Field Office has a similar set up at the **Woodstock Exchange** (Map p274; 66 Albert St, Woodstock; ⏲7.30am-4.30pm Mon-Fri; Woodstock).

ENTERTAINMENT

FUGARD THEATRE THEATRE
Map p274 (☎021-461 4554; www.thefugard.com; Caledon St, East City; Lower Buitenkant) Named in honour of Athol Fugard, South Africa's best-known living playwright, this very impressive arts centre was created from the former Congregational Church Hall. There are two stages, the largest theatre also doubling up as a 'bioscope' – a fancy word for a digital cinema where top international dance and opera performances are screened.

ASSEMBLY LIVE MUSIC
Map p274 (www.theassembly.co.za; 61 Harrington St, East City; cover R30-50; Lower Buitenkant) In an old furniture assembly factory, this live-music and DJ performance space has made its mark with an exciting, eclectic line-up of both local and international artists. It also holds the audiovisual event **Pecha Kucha** (www.pechakucha-capetown.co.za), generally once a month.

STARDUST BAR
Map p274 (☎021-462 7777; www.stardustcapetown.com; 118 Sir Lowry Rd, Woodstock; ⏲6pm-3am Tue-Sat; District Six) This cheesy but hugely popular 'theatrical diner' gets packed with groups who come to enjoy tagines (R110 to R140) and other dishes while listening to the waitstaff – all professional singers – hop up on stage periodically to belt out tunes. There's a spacious bar here so you don't need to eat if you just want to watch the show.

SHACK COMEDY
Map p274 (43 De Villiers St, District Six; ⏲noon-4am; Roeland) This long-running bar hosts the occasional Luna Comedy nights when you can catch local funny guys and girls doing stand-up. Also here is the live-music and DJ venue Mercury Live.

TAGORE LIVE MUSIC
Map p276 (☎021-447 8717; 42 Trill Rd, Observatory; ⏲5pm-midnight; Observatory) Candles, cosy nooks and crannies, and avant-garde music set the scene at this tiny cafe-bar,

a favourite with the Obs alternative set. There's no cover charge for the sets that usually kick off at 9.30pm Wednesday, Friday and Saturday.

MAGNET THEATRE THEATRE

Map p276 (☎021-448 3436; www.magnettheatre.co.za; Unit 1, The Old Match Factory, cnr St Michaels & Lower Main Rds, Observatory; tickets R50; Observatory) This National Lottery-funded project works with youngsters on a variety of performance and theatre projects. Some of their shows have won awards at festivals in South Africa and overseas.

SHOPPING

★OLD BISCUIT MILL SHOPPING CENTRE

Map p274 (www.theoldbiscuitmill.co.za; 373-375 Albert Rd, Woodstock; 9am-5pm Mon-Fri, to 3pm Sat; Kent) This former biscuit factory houses an ace collection of arts, craft, fashion and design shops, as well as places to eat and drink. Favourites include **Clementina Ceramics** (www.clementina.co.za) and **Imiso Ceramics** (www.imisoceramics.co.za) for ceramics; the organic bean-to-shop chocolate factory **Cocofair** (www.cocoafair.com); and **Mü & Me** (www.muandme.net) for super-cute graphic art for cards, wrapping paper, stationery and kids' T-shirts.

★NEIGHBOURGOODS MARKET MARKET

Map p274 (www.neighbourgoodsmarket.co.za; Old Biscuit Mill, 373-375 Albert Rd, Woodstock; 9am-2pm Sat; Kent) The first and still the best of the artisan goods markets that are now common across the Cape. Food and drinks are gathered in the main area where you can pick up groceries and gourmet goodies or just graze, while the separate Designergoods area hosts a must-buy selection of local fashions and accessories. Come early unless you enjoy jostling with crowds.

★SOUTHERN GUILD ARTS & CRAFTS

Map p274 (☎021-461 2856; www.southernguild.co.za; Unit 1, 10-16 Lewin St, Woodstock; 10am-5pm Tue-Fri, to 1pm Sat; District Six) Trevyn

WOODSTOCK'S GALLERIES

Spurring on Woodstock's gentrification has been a crack team of commercial galleries. All put on interesting shows and there's no pressure to buy.

South African Print Gallery (Map p274; www.printgallery.co.za; 109 Sir Lowry Rd, Woodstock; 9.30am-4pm Tue-Fri, 10am-1pm Sat; District Six) Specialising in prints by local artists – both well established and up-and-coming – and likely to have something that is both affordable and small enough to fit comfortably in your suitcase for transport home.

Stevenson (Map p274; www.stevenson.info; 160 Sir Lowry Rd, Woodstock; 9am-5pm Mon-Fri, 10am-1pm Sat; District Six) Exhibitions at this well-respected gallery have included the humorous, subversive work of Anton Kannemeyer, also known as Joe Dog, creator of the darkly satiric comic *Bitterkomix* with Conrad Botes, who is also represented here. You can also browse pieces of the distinctive ceramic art of Hylton Nel.

What If The World (Map p274; www.whatiftheworld.com; 1 Argyle St, Woodstock; 10am-4.30pm Tue-Fri, to 3pm Sat; Kent) In an old synagogue and associated buildings, this gallery can be credited with kicking Capetonian creativity up the backside. Drop by to witness the unruly forces of young South African art. Also on-site is a bakery.

Goodman Gallery Cape (Map p274; ☎021-462 7573; www.goodman-gallery.com; 3rd fl, Fairweather House, 176 Sir Lowry Rd, Woodstock; 9.30am-5.30pm Tue-Fri, 10am-4pm Sat; District Six) A big gun of the Johannesburg art world, the Goodman Gallery was one of the few to encourage artists of all races during apartheid. It represents luminaries like William Kentridge and Willie Bester, as well as up-and-coming artists. The entrance is around the back of the building.

SMAC (Map p274; ☎021-422 5100; www.smacgallery.com; The Palms, 145 Sir Lowry Rd, Woodstock; District Six) This Stellenbosch-based gallery, specialising in works from 1960 to the 1980s, occupies a series of roomy spaces in the Palms, where you'll find a few other smaller art and interior design dealers and galleries.

and Julian McGowan have made a business out of cherry-picking the cream of the South African design community and promoting it to the world in annual collections. This is their new permanent showcase, so the go-to location for spotting emerging talents and buying up incredible, distinctive pieces.

★WOODSTOCK EXCHANGE SHOPPING CENTRE

Map p274 (www.woodstockexchange.co.za; 66 Albert Rd, Woodstock; ⏲9am-5pm Mon-Fri, to 2pm Sat; Woodstock) There's a fair amount of original retail at the Exchange, including the atelier and showroom of **Grandt Mason Originals** (www.g-mo.co.za; Shop 13), which uses luxurious fabrics from ends of rolls and swatch books to make one-off footwear; **Chapel** (www.store.chapelgoods.co.za) leather goods; **Charlie. H**, who crafts kimonos, halter dresses and skirts from printed fabrics; and boutique **Kingdom**, which mixes fashion and accessories with interior design.

★BOOK LOUNGE BOOKS

Map p274 (021-462 2425; www.booklounge.co.za; 71 Roeland St, East City; ⏲9.30am-7.30pm Mon-Fri, 8.30am-6pm Sat, 10am-4pm Sun; Roeland) The hub of Cape Town's literary scene, thanks to its great selection of titles, comfy chairs, simple cafe and busy program of events. There are up to three talks or book launches a week, generally with free drinks and nibbles, and readings for kids on the weekend.

Also look for the handmade Elizabethan bags and brooches here made from recycled pieces of fabric and other found objects.

MNANDI TEXTILES & DESIGN CLOTHING, HANDICRAFTS

Map p276 (021-447 6814; 90 Station Rd, Observatory; ⏲9am-5.30pm Mon-Fri, to 2pm Sat; Observatory) Mnandi sells cloth from all over Africa, including the local *shweshwe* cotton printed with everything from animals to traditional African patterns. You can also have clothes tailor-made and find lots of cute gifts including adorable Zuka cloth dolls of Xhosa women and Desmond Tutu.

WOODSTOCK CO-OP SHOPPING CENTRE

Map p274 (357-363 Albert Rd, Woodstock; ⏲9am-5pm Mon-Sat; Kent) At this co-op you'll find a rough and ready collection of start-ups, try outs and established traders, hawking a range of appealing items including accessories, and old and new interior design. Look out for the skateboards and street wear of **Babith**, up-cycled clothing and objects from **Knobs & Tassles**, and female fashion from **w9apparel**.

ASHANTI HOMEWARES, CRAFT

Map p274 (www.ashantidesign.com; 133-135 Sir Lowry Rd, Woodstock; ⏲9am-5pm Mon-Fri, 10am-3pm Sat; District Six) Baskets, mats, lampshades, pillows, bags and cushions gathered from across Africa are among the many rainbow-coloured products on sale at this great artisan design shop. Often no two pieces are alike. You can also buy fabrics by the metre.

BIBLIOPHILIA BOOKS

Map p274 (www.bibliophilia.co.za; 1 Side Street Studios, 48 Albert Rd, Woodstock; ⏲9am-4pm Mon-Fri, 10am-2pm Sat; Woodstock) Pick up a copy of the beautifully illustrated *Woodstock, Salt River, Observatory Walking Map* at this ace bookshop specialising in art, design and pop-culture titles. You can also find many locally published magazines and books here, as well as a few music CDs.

RECREATE HOMEWARES

Map p274 (www.recreate.za.net; 6 Stowe St, Salt River; ⏲9am-5pm Mon-Fri, to 2pm Sat; Kent) Extraordinary repurposed furniture and lighting by Katie Thompson – think suitcases turned into chairs, crockery as lamp stands, and fridge magnets made from computer keyboard letters.

VAMP HOMEWARES, CRAFT

Map p274 (www.vampfurniture.co.za; 368 Albert Rd, Woodstock; ⏲9.30am-4.30pm Mon-Fri, 8.30am-3pm Sat; Kent) Capetonian interior design adventures can be had at this place, set back from Albert Rd, where you may be able to pick up original framed Tretchikoff prints alongside retro suitcases, globes, and contemporary arts and crafts.

WOODHEAD'S ACCESSORIES

Map p274 (www.woodheads.co.za; 29 Caledon St, East City; ⏲8am-5pm Mon-Fri, 8.30am-1pm Sat; Lower Buitenkant) If you're after a full hide of cow, buffalo, antelope, zebra etc, head over to these savvy guys who've been catering to Cape Town's leather trade since 1867. They also stock locally made flip-flops, hide boots, bags and belts.

WOODSTOCK CYCLEWORKS
SPORTS, CLOTHING

Map p274 (☎021-461 5634; www.woodstockcycleworks.com; 14 Searle St, Woodstock; ⏰9am-6pm Mon-Fri, 9.30am-1pm Sat; 🚌District Six) Swing by this converted warehouse complex, even if you're not in the market for a custom-built bike. It also sells fashionable, locally made biking tops, arty T-shirts and prints, and has Le Jeune cafe (named after a South African brand of bike). In the courtyard, vegetable tanned hides are used for the leather products made by **Stockton Goods** (www.stocktongoods.com).

The side of the building is painted with a bicycle-themed mural by Freddy Sam. This is also the official after-event venue for Thursday Late (p74).

AFRICAN HOME
CRAFT

Map p274 (www.africanhome.co.za; 41 Caledon St, East City; ⏰8.30am-5pm Mon-Fri; 🚌Lower Buitenkant)  There's an appealing range of fair-trade crafts on sale here, including striking white-beaded mirror and picture frames.

BROMWELL BOUTIQUE MALL
FASHION, ARTS

Map p274 (www.thebromwell.co.za; 250 Albert Rd, Woodstock; ⏰8am-5pm Mon-Sat; 🚌Kent) This stylish collection of vendors selling exotic artefacts, fashions, accessories, art and decor is huddled together in the spruced up old Bromwell Hotel, dating back to the 1930s. Following the Woodstock redevelopment blueprint to the T, there's a cafe, bakery and deli on the ground floor.

WOODSTOCK FOUNDRY
SHOPPING CENTRE

Map p274 (www.facebook.com/WoodstockFoundry; 160 Albert Rd, Woodstock; 🚆Woodstock) This is a handsome complex of design studios and shops in a revamped old Woodstock building. The cast-metal foundry **Bronze Age** (www.bronzeageart.com) anchors the place; you'll also find furniture designed by **John Vogel** (www.vogeldesign.co.za); jewellery in brass, silver and gold by **Dear Rae** (www.dearrae.co.za); **Indigi Designs** (www.inidigidesigns.co.za) for interior stuff; and a branch of Mexican restaurant **Fat Cactus**.On Wednesday nights the small **Day Before Thursday** food and goods market is held here.

SALT CIRCLE ARCADE
SHOPPING CENTRE

Map p274 (19 Kent Rd, Salt River; 🚌Kent) Among the retail options to hunt out here are the secondhand bookshop **Blank Books** (www.blankbooks.co.za), the owner of which writes the local blog www.ilovewoodstock; **Miyu** (www.miyuhomeware.com) for quality crafts and interior design; and **Beerguevara** (www.beerguevara.com) for craft beer ingredients and courses. Food trucks gather in the central courtyard.

SPORTS & ACTIVITIES

CITY ROCK
ROCK CLIMBING

Map p276 (☎021-447 1326; www.cityrock.co.za; 21 Anson Rd, Observatory; climbing-wall day pass adult/child R100/75; ⏰9am-9pm Mon-Thu, 9am-6pm Fri, 10am-6pm Sat & Sun; 🚆Observatory) This popular indoor climbing gym offers climbing courses and hires out and sells climbing gear. It also has yoga classes here.

HINTHUNT
GAME

Map p274 (☎021-448 9864; www.hinthunt.co.za; 3rd flr, main courtyard, Old Biscuit Mill, 373-375 Albert Rd, Woodstock; per person from R129; ⏰9am-8.15pm; 🚌Kent) Lots of fun to be had as the clock is ticking and you and your fellow players have just 60 minutes to play Sherlock, solve the puzzles and get yourselves out of a claustrophobic room in the bowels of the Old Biscuit Mill. Minimum two people.

WALK-IN ROBOTICS
PLAY CENTRE

Map p276 (☎021-448 8516; www.ortascape.org.za; 370B Main Rd, Observatory; per hour R55; ⏰9am-4pm; 🚆Observatory) In the same building as the Cape Town Science Centre, this project allows you to create and program your own robot using Lego WeDo Robotics kits. Instructors are on hand to assist, and while you can't take the finished robot away, you can take plenty of photos and video.

Gardens & Surrounds

GARDENS | ORANJEZICHT | TAMBOERSKLOOF | VREDEHOEK | HIGGOVALE

Neighbourhood Top Five

❶ Ride the revolving cableway up **Table Mountain** (p94), then walk across the top to the summit at Maclear's Beacon or abseil off the edge.

❷ View the nation's best visual art at the **South African National Gallery** (p97).

❸ Discover all about South Africa's Jewish immigrants at the **South African Jewish Museum** (p96).

❹ Visit the **Oranjezicht City Farm** (p100) and drop by its farmers market on Saturday.

❺ Climb **Lion's Head** (p97) for a panoramic view of the city and coast, or drive out to the viewpoint on **Signal Hill** (p97).

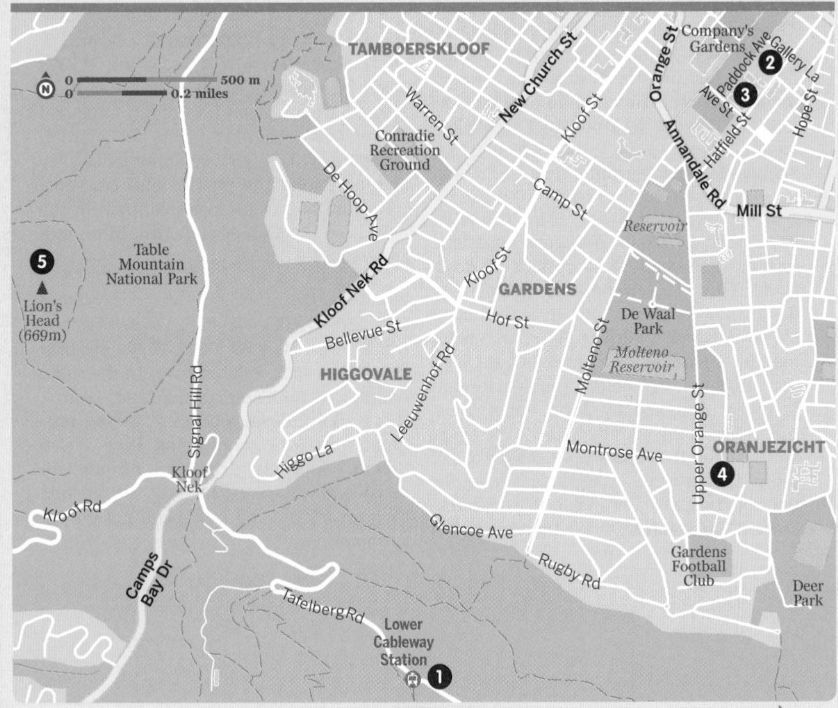

For more detail of this area see Map p277 and p278

Explore Gardens & Surrounds

Taking its name from the Company's Gardens, the City Bowl end of this mountainside region is where you'll find some of Cape Town's premier museums. Further up the slopes are desirable residential areas, home to some of the city's most appealing and individual accommodation options, not least of which is the leafy compound of the Belmond Mount Nelson Hotel.

It goes without saying that the area is dominated by the massive bulk of Table Mountain, as well as the adjacent rocky humps of Lion's Head, Signal Hill and Devil's Peak. You'll hardly be able to keep your eyes off the mountain, especially when the famous tablecloth of cloud is tumbling off its summit – usually in the late afternoon. Climbing it more than repays the effort but, if that's not on the cards, then there's always the cableway.

Kloof St, the Gardens' commercial spine, is perfect for leisurely strolls with its collection of individual boutiques, restaurants and lively bars. West and up Signal Hill you'll find the suburb of Tamboerskloof, while Oranjezicht lies to the east behind De Waal Park. Windblasted Vredehoek is further to the east towards Devil's Peak (it's marked by the trio of residential blocks officially called Disa Park, but more commonly known as the 'Tampon Towers'), while Higgovale, sheltered from the wind, is to the west.

Local Life

- **Dog park** Join locals walking their dogs in leafy De Waal Park (p98); free concerts are occasionally held in the bandstand here on summer Sundays.
- **De-stress** Enjoy a clothed, oil-free massage at contemporary-styled Enmasse (p103).
- **Movies** Catch the latest flick and art-house gems at the Labia (p101), the neighbourhood's cinema.

Getting There & Away

- **Bus** MyCiTi bus routes go up Kloof Nek Rd to Table Mountain and around Orangezicht and Vredehoek.
- **Shared taxi** These shuttle up Kloof St to Kloof Nek Rd, then over to Camps Bay before returning to the City Bowl.
- **Walk** It's easy to walk between the main sights of lower Gardens, but be prepared for quite a workout if you plan on hiking up to the lower cableway.

Lonely Planet's Top Tip

Bertram House (p98) and Rust en Vreugd (p97) are a couple of small museums in the Gardens area that you are likely to have all to yourself. The former is the city's last remaining example of a Georgian-style red-brick house, while the latter has a lovely formal garden and some beautiful watercolours and prints.

Best Places to Eat

- Chef's Table (p99)
- Ferdinando's (p98)
- Blue Cafe (p98)
- Hallellujah (p99)
- Aubergine (p100)

For reviews, see p98.

Best Places to Drink

- Yours Truly (p100)
- Power & the Glory/ Black Ram (p100)
- Blah Blah Bar (p101)
- Perseverance Tavern (p101)
- Chalk & Cork (p101)

For reviews, see p100.

Best Places to Shop

- Coffeebeans Routes (p101)
- KIN (p102)
- Stefania Morland (p102)
- Erf 81 Food Market (p102)
- Bluecollarwhitecollar (p102)

For reviews, see p101.

TOP SIGHT
TABLE MOUNTAIN

NEIL AUSTEN/GETTY IMAGES ©

Around 60 million years old, and a canvas painted with the rich diversity of the Cape's floral kingdom, Table Mountain is truly iconic. You can admire the showstopper of Table Mountain National Park and one of the 'New Seven Wonders of Nature' (www.new7wonders.com) from multiple angles, but you really can't say you've visited Cape Town until you've stood on top of it.

DON'T MISS

- Cableway
- Maclear's Beacon
- Abseil Africa
- Dassies

PRACTICALITIES

- Map p277
- www.tmnp.co.za

Table Mountain Cableway

Riding the **cableway** (☎021-424 0015; www.tablemountain.net; Tafelberg Rd; one way/return adult from R115/225, child R58/110; ⏲8.30am-6pm Feb-Nov, 8am-9.30pm Dec & Jan; 🚌Lower Cable Car) up Table Mountain is a no-brainer: the views from the revolving car and the summit are phenomenal. At the top are souvenir shops, a good cafe and some easy walks to follow.

Departures are every 10 minutes in high season (December to February) and every 15 to 20 minutes at all other times, but the cableway doesn't operate when it's very windy (call in advance or go online to see if it's operating). There's also not much point going up if the top is wrapped in the cloud known as the 'tablecloth'; the best visibility and conditions are likely to be first thing in the morning or in the evening.

From mid-December to mid-January, a limited number of online tickets are available for access to the cable car from 7.30am, before the ticket office opens at 8am. They cost R300 and are valid for two days from purchase.

Climbing the Mountain

In 1503 Portuguese navigator Admiral Antonio de Saldanha bagged the title of 'first European to climb Table Mountain'. He named it Taboa do Cabo (Table of the Cape), although the Khoe-san, the Cape's original inhabitants, knew it as Hoerikwaggo (Mountain of the

Sea). Visitors have been climbing the mountain ever since, and there's a range of ways you can ascend from Gardens.

None of the routes up are easy, but the 3km-long **Platteklip Gorge route**, accessed from Tafelberg Rd, is at least straightforward. It's very steep and you should allow about 2½ hours to reach the upper cableway station at a steady pace. Be warned that the route is exposed to the sun, so climb as early in the morning as possible and bring plenty of water and sunblock.

Another possibility, recommended for very experienced climbers only, is the **India Fenster route**, which starts from directly behind the lower cableway station and heads straight up. The hikers you see from the cableway, perched like mountain goats on apparently sheer cliffs, are taking this route.

Other Hiking Routes

There's no need to climb to the top of the mountain to get brilliant views. A short hike up behind the lower cableway station will bring you to the **Contour Path**, running a fairly level way eastwards around Devil's Peak to the King's Blockhouse and, eventually, Constantia Nek.

The **Pipe Track** runs along the west side of the mountain towards the Twelve Apostles and provides stunning coastal views; the path was originally constructed to carry water along a pipe from Disa Gorge on Table Mountain's Back Table to the Molteno Reservoir in Oranjezicht. This route is best walked in the early morning, before the sun hits this side of the mountain. The **Kasteelspoort Path** off the Pipe Track is an alternative way to the top of the mountain.

At the Top

Concrete paths lead from the upper cableway station to the restaurant, shop and various terraces. These are easy enough to stroll around without a guide, and from them you may even be able to spot a dassie, a large native rodent who – believe it or not – is related to the elephant. Free volunteer-guided walks across Table Mountain's plateau run at 10am and noon daily from beside the upper cableway station.

To reach the mountain's 1088m summit you'll need to go a bit further along the track to **Maclear's Beacon**, a distance of around 5km, which should take one hour for the round trip. Don't attempt this route if there's low cloud or mist on the mountain, as it's very easy to lose your way.

ABSEIL AFRICA

The 112m drop off the top of Table Mountain with **Abseil Africa** (Map p268; ☎021-424 4760; www.abseilafrica.co.za; 297 Long St, City Bowl; abseiling R650) is a guaranteed adrenaline rush – don't even think of tackling it unless you've got a head (and a stomach) for heights. Take your time, because the views are breathtaking. Tag on a guided hike up Platteklip Gorge for R250.

Table Mountain is so distinctive it was used by astronomers to name the Mensa ('table', in Latin) constellation of stars.

EATING & SLEEPING

Near the upper cableway station, the self-serve Table Mountain Cafe offers tasty deli items and meals, compostable plates and containers, and good coffee. It also sells wine and beer, so there's no need to cart your bottle up the slopes to toast the view. Camping isn't allowed on the mountain. Should you wish to spend the night up here, the only option is the self-catering accommodation at the Overseers Mountain Cottage.

TOP SIGHT
SOUTH AFRICAN JEWISH MUSEUM

Jewish life in South Africa and the contributions of local Jews past and present are imaginatively recorded in this museum, located in the beautifully restored Old Synagogue (next to the grand, still functioning Great Synagogue). Photo ID is required for entry to this secure complex, which also includes the pleasant, kosher Café Riteve.

Old Synagogue

Temporary exhibits occupy the museum's first hall, in the Old Synagogue (1863): note the detailed mosaics and stained-glass windows. Downstairs is a partial recreation of a Lithuanian *shtetl* (village); many of South Africa's Jews fled this part of Eastern Europe during the pogroms and persecution of the late 19th and early 20th centuries.

The permanent exhibition *Hidden Treasures of Japanese Art* showcases exquisite *netsuke* (decorative toggles) from the **Isaac Kaplan Collection**. Kaplan, who started out as a blacksmith, never visited Japan, but taught himself Japanese so he could amass and document these small carved pieces of ivory and wood.

DON'T MISS

- Old Synagogue
- Great Synagogue
- Cape Town Holocaust Centre

PRACTICALITIES

- Map p278
- www.sajewishmuseum.co.za
- 88 Hatfield St, Gardens
- adult/child R40/free
- 10am-5pm Sun-Thu, to 2pm Fri
- Annandale

Cape Town Holocaust Centre

Upstairs in the building across the courtyard from the museum, the Cape Town Holocaust Centre offers an emotionally charged, free exhibit that charts the history of anti-Semitism and draws parallels to South Africa's struggle for freedom from apartheid. Downstairs you can watch the fascinating 25-minute documentary *Nelson Mandela: A Righteous Man*.

Great Synagogue

Make time for a short tour of the gorgeously decorated Great Synagogue (1905). Volunteer guides will point out aspects of the building's neo-Egyptian style, including the symbolic stained-glass windows and a pulpit carved by Anton Anreith.

SIGHTS

TABLE MOUNTAIN — MOUNTAIN

See p94.

SOUTH AFRICAN JEWISH MUSEUM — MUSEUM

See p96.

SOUTH AFRICAN NATIONAL GALLERY — GALLERY

Map p278 (021-481 3970; www.iziko.org.za/museums/south-african-national-gallery; Government Ave, Gardens; adult/child R30/15; 10am-5pm; Annandale) The impressive permanent collection of the nation's premier art space harks back to Dutch times and includes some extraordinary pieces. But it's often contemporary works, such as the *Butcher Boys* sculpture by Jane Alexander – looking rather like a trio of Tolkienesque orcs who have stumbled into the gallery – that stand out the most.

Also note the remarkable teak door in the courtyard, carved by Herbert Vladimir Meyerowitz, with scenes representing the global wanderings of the Jews; his carvings also adorn the tops of the door frames throughout the gallery.

SOUTH AFRICAN MUSEUM — MUSEUM

Map p278 (021-481 3805; www.iziko.org.za/museums/south-african-museum; 25 Queen Victoria St, Gardens; adult/child R30/15; 10am-5pm; Michaelis) South Africa's oldest museum may be showing its age, but it does contain a wide and often intriguing series of exhibitions, many on the country's natural history. The best galleries are the newest, showcasing the art and culture of the area's first peoples, the Khoekhoen and San, and including the famous Linton Panel, an amazing example of San rock art. There's an extraordinary delicacy to the paintings, particularly the ones of graceful elands.

Also worth looking out for are the terracotta Lydenburg Heads, the earliest-known examples of African sculpture (AD 500–700) in the African Cultures Gallery; a 2m-wide nest – a veritable avian apartment block – of the sociable weaver bird, in the Wonders of Nature Gallery; and the atmospheric Whale Well, hung with giant whale skeletons and models and resounding with taped recordings of their calls.

SOUTH AFRICAN PLANETARIUM — PLANETARIUM

Map p278 (www.iziko.org.za/museums/planetarium; 25 Queen Victoria St, Gardens; adult/child R40/20; 10am-5pm; Michaelis) The displays and star shows at the Planetarium, attached to the South African Museum, unravel the mysteries of the southern hemisphere's night sky. Daily shows use images caught by the Southern African Large Telescope (in the Karoo region), which has the largest aperture of any telescope in the world. Call ahead or check the website for show times.

LION'S HEAD — VIEWPOINT

(Signal Hill Rd, Tamboerskloof; P; Kloof Nek) It was the Dutch who coined the term Lion's Head (Leeuwen Kop) for the giant, nipple-like outcrop that overlooks Sea Point and Camps Bay. It takes about 45 minutes to cover the popular 2.2km-hike from Kloof Nek to the 669m summit. There are also hiking routes up from the Sea Point side.

A lot of people do the hike as an early-morning constitutional, and it's a local ritual to hike up and watch the sun go down on a full-moon night. The moonlight helps the walk back down, although you should always bring a torch (flashlight) and go with company.

SIGNAL HILL — VIEWPOINT

(Kloof Nek) The early settlement's lookout point is so named because it was from here that flags were hoisted when a ship was spotted, giving the people below time to prepare goods for sale and dust off their tankards. Walk, cycle or drive to the summit, which is part of Table Mountain National Park, by taking the first turn-off to the right off Kloof Nek Rd onto Military Rd.

Signal Hill was also known as Lion's Rump, as it's attached to Lion's Head by a 'spine' of hills.

RUST EN VREUGD — GALLERY, GARDEN

Map p278 (021-464 3280; www.iziko.org.za; 78 Buitenkant St, City Bowl; adult/child R20/10; 10am-5pm Mon-Fri; Roeland) This delightful mansion, dating from 1777–78 and fronted by a period-style garden (re-created in 1986 from the original layout), was once the home of the state prosecutor. It now houses part of the William Fehr Collection of paintings and furniture (the major part is in the Castle of Good Hope; p55); you may see detailed lithographs of Zulus by George Angus and a delicately painted watercolour panorama of Table Mountain (from 1850) by Lady Eyre.

BERTRAM HOUSE MUSEUM

Map p278 (☎021-481 3972; www.iziko.org.za/museums/bertram-house; cnr Orange St & Government Ave, Gardens; adult/child R20/10; ⏲10am-5pm Mon-Fri; 🚌Government Ave) The only surviving Georgian-style red-brick house in Cape Town dates from the 1840s. The interior is decorated appropriately to its era, with Regency-style furnishings and displays of 19th-century English porcelain, as well as a small exhibition upstairs on the San ethnographic archive.

NEW CHURCH MUSEUM GALLERY

Map p278 (www.thenewchurch.co; 102 New Church St, Tamboerskloof; ⏲noon-3pm Tue & Thu, 11am-3pm Sat; 🚌Ludwig's Garden) FREE Open only for a few hours each week, this gallery focuses on contemporary Southern African art. The founding benefactor, Piet Viljoen, has bequeathed his collection of more than 400 pieces to the gallery, and the shows mounted are worth checking out for some striking abstract works.

DE WAAL PARK PARK

Map p277 (Camp St, Gardens; 🚌Lower Reservoir) This leafy park, named in honour of former Cape Town mayor Christiaan de Waal, is much patronised by dog owners. Between December and early April there are sometimes free concerts (usually starting around 3pm on Sunday) in the bandstand, which was made in Glasgow and originally brought to the city for the 1904–05 Cape Town Exhibition at Green Point.

TABLE MOUNTAIN FRAMES

One legacy of Cape Town's 2014 World Design Capital program is the **Table Mountain Frames**. Giant, bright-yellow metal frames are sited at various locations, including Signal Hill; the Waterfront; Eden on the Bay in Bloubergstrand; beside Charly's Bakery in District Six; and Lookout Hill in Khayelitsha. Sponsored by Table Mountain Cableway, they have proved to be popular, with many photos being uploaded to an **online gallery** (www.tablemountain.net/galleries).

EATING

★**FERDINANDO'S** PIZZA $

Map p278 (☎084 771 0485; www.facebook.com/pages/Ferdinandos-pizza/418463764843892; 84 Kloof St, Gardens; pizza R80-110; ⏲6-11pm Wed-Sat; 🚌Welgemeend) Bookings are required for this charming 'secret pizza parla' that shares premises with the Blah Blah Bar. Diego is the pizza maestro and Kikki the bubbly host and creative artist, while their adorable mutt Ferdinando keeps them all in line. Toppings for their fantastic crispy, thin-crust pizzas change with the season.

★**BLUE CAFE** INTERNATIONAL, DELI $

Map p278 (☎021-426 0250; www.thebluecafe.co.za; 13 Brownlow Rd, Tamboerskloof; mains R25-55; ⏲7.30am-10pm; 📶; 🚌Belle Ombre) In business under various owners (and names) as a cafe and mini-deli since 1904, the Blue Cafe's latest incarnation is perhaps one of its best. It's a lovely, casual, all-day dining spot that's particularly good for an early-evening meal at its street tables – some of which afford beguiling views of the surrounding mountains as the sun sets.

YARD BURGERS, SANDWICHES $

Map p278 (www.facebook.com/YARDCT; 6 Roodehek St, Gardens; mains R70-110; ⏲7am-10.30pm Mon-Sat; 🚌Roodehek) The Dog's Bollocks' blockbuster burgers (only 50 served per night, from 5pm) got this hip grunge spot going a few years ago; they've now expanded to all-day dining, with Mucky Mary's for breakfast fry-ups and sandwiches, Bitch's Tits tacos and Deluxe Coffeeworks, who also roast their beans here. Great street art decorates the building.

TAMBOERS WINKEL INTERNATIONAL $

Map p278 (☎021-424 0521; www.tamboerswinkel.com; 3 De Lorentz St, Tamboerskloof; mains R50-70; ⏲8am-8pm Tue, to 10pm Wed-Fri, to 6pm Sat, to 4pm Sun; 🚌Welgemeend) A serious contender for the award for best breakfast or lunch spot around Kloof St, this rustic, country-kitchen-style cafe-shop is a charmer. Chef Karen's chicken pie, wrapped in flaky filo pastry, is indeed legendary. It also has free wine tastings for different vineyards on Wednesdays at 6pm.

MANNA EPICURE BAKERY $

Map p277 (☎021-426 2413; www.mannaepicure.com; 151 Kloof St, Gardens; mains R40-110; ⏲8am-5pm Tue-Sat, to 4pm Sun; 🚌Welgemeend) Come for a deliciously simple breakfast or lunch, or for late-afternoon cocktails and tapas on the verandah of this white-box cafe. The freshly baked breads alone – coconut or pecan and raisin – are worth dragging yourself up the hill for.

LAZARI INTERNATIONAL, GREEK $

Map p277 (☎021-461 9865; www.lazari.co.za; cnr Upper Maynard St & Vredehoek Ave, Vredehoek; mains R60-75; ⏲7.30am-4pm Mon-Fri, 8am-2.30pm Sat & Sun; 📶; 🚌Upper Buitenkant) Few proprietors work as hard as Chris Lazari to be friendly to their customers – who, understandably, are a loyal bunch. It's buzzy, gay-friendly and great for brunch or an indulgent moment over coffee and cake.

LIQUORICE & LIME INTERNATIONAL, DELI $

Map p277 (☎021-423 6921; 162 Kloof St, Gardens; breakfast & sandwiches R40-70; ⏲7am-5pm; 🚌Upper Kloof) Pause at this convivial gourmet deli on your way from climbing up or down Table Mountain or Lion's Head. The French toast with grilled banana is yummy, and there's baked goods and sandwiches.

DEER PARK CAFÉ INTERNATIONAL, VEGETARIAN $

Map p277 (☎021-462 6311; www.deerparkcafe.co.za; 2 Deer Park Dr West, Vredehoek; mains R50-80; ⏲8am-9pm; 📶🌿👪; 🚌Herzlia) Fronting a kids' playground, this relaxed cafe has chunky wooden furniture that gives it the feel of a big nursery. The tasty food is anything but child's play, though. There are some great vegetarian options, as well as a kids' menu.

MELISSA'S INTERNATIONAL, DELI $

Map p278 (www.melissas.co.za; 94 Kloof St, Gardens; mains R50-70; ⏲7.30am-7pm Mon-Fri, 8am-7pm Sat & Sun; 🚌Welgemeend) Pay by weight for the delicious breakfast and lunch buffets, then browse the grocery shelves for picnic fare or gourmet gifts.

★HALLELUJAH INTERNATIONAL $$

Map p278 (☎079 839 2505; www.hallelujahhallelujah.co.za; 11 Kloof Nek Rd, Tamboerskloof; mains R90-130; ⏲6.30-11pm Wed-Sat; 🚌Ludwig's Garden) Emma Hoffmans is the talented young chef of this compact kitchen and its flamingo-decorated dining space (booking only for tables of four to six; counter seats available for walk-ins). Work your way through her short but very sweet menu of small plates, including grilled prawns in steamed buns, duck and cold soba noodles, and a zingy green-papaya tom yam salad.

MARIA'S GREEK $$

Map p278 (☎021-461 3333; 31 Barnet St, Dunkley Sq, Gardens; mains R75-135; ⏲8am-10.30pm Tue-Fri, 9am-10.30pm Sat; 🅿🌿; 🚌Annandale) There are few places more romantic or relaxing for a meal than Maria's on a warm night, when you can tuck into classic Greek meze and dishes such as moussaka on rustic tables beneath the trees in the square. There are tons of vegetarian options on the menu, too.

KYOTO GARDEN SUSHI JAPANESE $$

Map p278 (☎021-422 2001; 11 Lower Kloofnek Rd, Tamboerskloof; mains R80-195; ⏲5.30-11pm Mon-Sat; 🚌Ludwig's Garden) Beechwood furnishings and subtle lighting lend a calm, Zen-like air to this superior Japanese restaurant, owned by an LA expat but with an expert chef turning out sushi and sashimi. The prawn noodle salad is excellent, as is the Asian Mary cocktail.

SOCIETI BISTRO FRENCH, CONTEMPORARY $$

Map p278 (☎021-424 2100; www.societi.co.za; 50 Orange St, Gardens; mains R100-180; ⏲noon-11pm Mon-Sat; 🚌Michaelis) Dine in the courtyard garden for Table Mountain views, or in the atmospheric, brick-walled and wine-rack-covered interior. The unfussy bistro dishes are well prepared and proficiently served.

CAFE PARADISO ITALIAN $$

Map p278 (☎021-423 8653; www.madamezingara.com; 101 Kloof St, Tamboerskloof; mains R80-160; ⏲9am-10pm Mon-Sat, 10am-3pm Sun; 👪; 🚌Welgemeend) Travellers with kids will love this place: it features a kitchen where little ones can make their own pizza, cookies, cupcakes or gingerbread figures (R48 per baking project) while the adults dine in a pleasant garden setting.

★CHEF'S TABLE INTERNATIONAL $$$

Map p278 (☎021-483 1864; www.belmond.com/mountnelsonhotel; Belmond Mount Nelson Hotel, 76 Orange St, Gardens; lunch R500, dinner R595, with wines R995; ⏲noon-3pm Fri, 6.30-9pm Mon-Sat; 🅿🌿; 🚌Government Ave) The

Nellie's swanky Planet restaurant and bar are worth a visit, but for a real treat book one of the four tables with a front-row view onto the drama and culinary magic unfolding inside the kitchen. The food is superb (vegetarians are catered for) and presented by the chefs who will take you on a behind-the-scenes tour.

★AUBERGINE INTERNATIONAL **$$$**

Map p278 (☎021-465 0000; www.aubergine.co.za; 39 Barnet St, Gardens; 2/3-course lunch R240/320, 3/4/5-course dinner R465/565/675; ⏲noon-2pm Wed-Fri, 5-10pm Mon-Sat; ✎; 🚌Annandale) German-born Harald Bresselschmidt is one of Cape Town's most consistent chefs, producing creative, hearty dishes that are served with some of the Cape's best wines. Don't over-order, as portions are large. Vegetarian menus are available and the service and ambience are impeccable.

The restaurant occasionally hosts live music and wine-tasting events at **Auslese** (Map p278; www.auslese.co.za; 115 Hope St), their venue around the corner.

DRINKING & NIGHTLIFE

★YOURS TRULY CAFE, BAR

Map p278 (www.yourstrulycafe.co.za; 73 Kloof St, Gardens; ⏲6am-11pm; 🚌Ludwig's Garden) Fronting the backpackers Once in Cape Town (p203), this place is hopping from early morning to late. Travellers mingle with hipster locals, who come for the excellent coffee, craft beer, gourmet sandwiches, thin-crust pizzas and the occasional DJ event.

The original, smaller branch is on **Long St** (Map p268; www.yourstrulycafe.co.za; 175 Long St, City Bowl; ⏲7am-5pm Mon-Fri, 8am-3pm Sat; 🚌Dorp/Leeuwen).

★POWER & THE GLORY/ BLACK RAM CAFE, BAR

Map p278 (☎021-422 2108; 13B Kloof Nek Rd, Tamboerskloof; ⏲cafe 8am-10pm Mon-Sat, bar 5pm-late Mon-Sat; 🚌Ludwig's Garden) The coffee and food (pretzel hot dogs, crusty pies and other artisan munchies) are good, but it's the smoky, cosy bar that packs the trendsters in, particularly on Thursday to Saturday nights.

TOP SIGHT
ORANJEZICHT CITY FARM & MARKET

Local residents and volunteers created this beautifully laid-out market garden on land where, in 1709, 'Oranje Zigt' – the original farm on the upper slopes of Table Mountain – was established. By the early 20th century, the once large farm had disappeared, swallowed up by urban development, leaving the small Homestead Park and an unused bowling green – which in 2013 began its transformation into the current farm. You are free to wander around or rest on the benches, which provide sweeping views of Table Bay. Guided tours can also be arranged: see the website for details.

The farm's produce and that of other small Western Cape farms is sold at a market every Saturday in Homestead Park: at the time of research the market was being held at **Leeuwenhof** (Map p277; Hof St, Tamboerskloof; 🚌Upper Kloof), the official residence of the Western Cape Premier. A major social event, the market is worth attending whether you need fresh produce or not, as there are plenty of stalls where you can get breakfast or lunch and buy gifts.

DON'T MISS

- Guided tour of the farm
- Saturday market

PRACTICALITIES

- Map p277
- www.ozcf.co.za
- Upper Orange St, Oranjezicht
- ⏲farm 8am-4pm Mon-Sat, market 9am-2pm Sat
- gUpper Orange

★**CHALK & CORK** WINE BAR

Map p278 (☎021-422 5822; www.chalkandcork.co.za; 51 Kloof St, Gardens; ⏲9am-6pm Mon-Wed, to 10pm Thu-Sat; 🚌Lower Kloof) This wine bar and restaurant has a pleasant courtyard fronting Kloof St. The menu runs the gamut from breakfast dishes to tapas and sharing platters, but you're welcome to drop in for just the wines, plenty of which is served by the glass and sourced from some of the region's best estates.

★**BLAH BLAH BAR** BAR

Map p278 (☎082 349 8849; www.facebook.com/BlahBlahBarCPT; 84 Kloof St, Gardens; ⏲5pm-2am; 🚌Welgemeend) Working in conjunction with **Erdmann Contemporary** (www.erdmanncontemporary.co.za; ⏲10am-9pm Wed-Sat), who allow their upstairs gallery to be used for some of the bar's concerts, and with pizza supremos Ferdinando's (p98), Blah Blah is anything but blah. Check their Facebook page for live-music and DJ events that are staged here; some have a cover charge.

PERSEVERANCE TAVERN PUB

Map p278 (www.perseverancetavern.co.za; 83 Buitenkant St, Gardens; ⏲noon-10pm Mon-Sat; 🚌Roeland) This convivial, heritage-listed pub, which is affectionately known as 'Persies' and has been around since 1808, was once Cecil Rhodes' local. There are beers on tap and the pub grub is decent.

ASOKA BAR, RESTAURANT

Map p278 (☎021-422 0909; www.asoka.za.com; 68 Kloof St, Gardens; 🚌Ludwig's Garden) A mellow Zen vibe pervades this groovy Asian restaurant-bar (pronounced 'ashoka') with a tree growing in the middle of it. Live jazz is a regular feature of Tuesday nights (performances from 8pm), while on other nights DJs play suitably chilled sounds.

VAN HUNKS BAR, RESTAURANT

Map p278 (cnr Kloof & Upper Union Sts, Gardens; ⏲12.30pm-1am; 🚌Belle Ombre) Ponder the legend of Van Hunks, who challenged the devil to a smoking match atop the peak that can be seen from this establishment's deck. It's a good spot to watch the comings and goings along Kloof St.

ENTERTAINMENT

LABIA CINEMA

Map p278 (☎021-424 5927; www.thelabia.co.za; 68 Orange St, Gardens; tickets R40; 🚌Michaelis) A Capetonian treasure and lifeline to the independent movie fan, the Labia is named after the old Italian ambassador and local philanthropist Count Labia. The African Screen program is one of the rare opportunities you'll have to see locally made films; check the website for session times.

STRAIGHT NO CHASER JAZZ

Map p278 (☎076-679 2697; www.straightnochaserclub.wordpress.com; 79 Buitenkant St, Gardens; 1/2 sets R60/100; ⏲7pm-2am Wed-Sat; 🚌Roeland) Next to Diva's Pizza, this tiny jazz club aims to recreate the atmosphere of Ronnie Scott's and Village Vanguard. It's run by hard-core jazz cats who take their music seriously – and who also have the connections to get top-class talent on the stage. Bookings are essential for the two sets per night, starting at 8.30pm and 10.30pm.

INTIMATE THEATRE THEATRE

Map p278 (☎021-480 7129; www.facebook.com/TheIntimateTheatre; University of Cape Town Hiddingh Campus, Orange St, Gardens; 🚌Michaelis) This 75-seat venue is the pick of the three stages that can be found at the University of Cape Town's drama department. Read the reviews before going to see any productions, as they vary widely in quality and content.

SHOPPING

★**COFFEEBEANS ROUTES** ARTS & CRAFTS

Map p278 (www.coffeebeansroutes.com; 22 Hope St, Gardens; ⏲9am-5pm Mon-Fri; 🚌Roodehek) As well as running some of the best guided tours you can take in Cape Town, Coffeebeans Routes are championing local creatives with this boutique that stocks an eclectic range of goods. Find great CDs and books by Capetonian musicians and writers, as well as fashion, accessories, art and various crafts.

★KIN — ART, CRAFTS

Map p278 (www.kinshop.co.za; 99B Kloof St, Gardens; 9.30am-5.30pm Mon-Sat; Ludwig's Garden) You're sure to find a unique gift or item for yourself at this creative boutique representing over a hundred South African artists and designers, ranging from ceramics and jewellery to prints and bags. It also has a branch at the **Waterfront** (Map p280; Shop 11B, Alfred Mall, V&A Waterfront; 9am-9pm; V&A Waterfront), which stocks more African-themed designs.

★STEFANIA MORLAND — FASHION

Map p277 (www.stefaniamorland.com; 153A Kloof St, Gardens; 9am-5pm Mon-Fri, to 2pm Sat; Welgemeend) Gorgeous gowns and more casual wear made from silks, linens, lace and other natural fibres seduce fashionistas in this chic showroom and atelier.

★ERF 81 FOOD MARKET — MARKET

Map p278 (www.tyisanabanye.org; cnr Leeuwenvoet & Military Rds, Tamboerskloof; 9am-2pm Sun; Lower Kloof) The latest entrant into Cape Town's booming market scene is this worthy, nonprofit urban agriculture project. Food security activists Tyisa Nabanye (Xhosa for 'growing together') moved from the townships into this former military site, cleaned up a shed and planted a market garden with a spectacular view of Table Mountain. Follow the road uphill to find the market and garden.

★BLUECOLLARWHITECOLLAR — FASHION

Map p278 (www.bluecollarwhitecollar.co.za; Lifestyles on Kloof, 50 Kloof St, Gardens; Lower Kloof) Designer Paul van der Spuy offers a wonderful selection of tailored men's and women's shirts – formal (white collar) and informal (blue collar), as well as T-shirts and shorts. You can also find them at the Old Biscuit Mill (p89) Saturday market.

LIM — HOMEWARES

Map p278 (www.lim.co.za; 86A Kloof St, Gardens; 9am-5pm Mon-Fri, 9.15am-1pm Sat; Welgemeend) Although the shop's name is an acronym for 'Less is More', this interior design shop has been so successful that they've had to add more room by expanding into the neighbouring house. Wander through the rooms admiring the stylish, pared-back selection of homewares, including fashion accessories made from buckskin.

UNKNOWN UNION — FASHION

Map p278 (www.unknownunion.co.za; 24 Kloof St, Gardens; 10am-6pm Mon-Fri, to 4pm Sat; Lower Kloof) The showroom and atelier for this Capetonian streetwear brand is a friendly, colourful and appealing place to shop for fashion statements as well as more casual clothing. They also sell tacos at lunch from a van out front and have a satellite stall in the Watershed (p113) at the Waterfront.

73 ON KLOOF — FASHION

Map p278 (73 Kloof St, Gardens; 10am-6pm Mon-Fri, to 4pm Sat; Ludwig's Garden) On one side of this boutique you'll find clothes such as shirts, shorts and trousers by **Adriaan Kuiters** (www.adriaankuiters.com) for men, as well as accessories such as canvas and leather bags and belts. On the other is something for the gals from **Take Care** (www.takecareclothing.com). Designs for either range share the same clean-line, general monochrome aesthetic.

ASTRA CENTRE — TOYS, GIFTS

Map p277 (www.astrajse.com; 20 Breda St, Gardens; 9am-3.30pm Mon-Thu, to 2.30pm Fri; Gardens) 'Ability rather than disability' is the creed of this admirable organisation that creates meaningful employment for physically and mentally challenged members of Cape Town's Jewish community. They sell beautifully made toys, such as rag dolls and wooden playthings, as well as other colourful woven, needlework and woodwork gifts. Also here is the charming kosher cafe **Coffee Time** (8am-3.30pm Mon-Thu, to 2.30pm Fri).

MR & MRS — FASHION, HOMEWARES

Map p278 (www.mrandmrs.co.za; 98 Kloof St, Gardens; 9am-6pm Mon-Fri, to 4pm Sat; Welgemeend) A tasteful selection of fashion, gifts and homewares from South African and international designers. The choices of products reflect the owners' travels through Indonesia, Argentina and India.

CITY BOWL MARKET — MARKET

Map p278 (www.citybowlmarket.co.za; 14 Hope St, Gardens; 4.30-8.30pm Thu; Roodehek) Based in a lovely old building with a lofty hall and outside courtyard areas, this weekly market sells mainly food and drink, including freshly made salads, roast-pork sandwiches, craft beers, wines and fruit juices. There's also some fashion on sale.

Check the website, as they may soon reopen on Saturday mornings.

GARDENS CENTRE MALL

Map p278 (☎021-465 1842; www.gardensshoppingcentre.co.za; cnr Mill & Buitenkant Sts, Gardens; ⏰9am-7pm Mon-Fri, to 5pm Sat, to 2pm Sun; 🚌Gardens) A handy, well-stocked mall covering all the bases, with good cafes (including an internet cafe), bookshops, Pick 'n' Pay and Woolworths supermarkets, a Flight Centre and a Cape Union Mart for camping and outdoor adventure gear.

LIFESTYLES ON KLOOF MALL

Map p278 (www.lifestyleonkloof.co.za; 50 Kloof St, Gardens; ⏰9am-7pm Mon-Fri, to 5pm Sat, 10am-3pm Sun; 🚌Lower Kloof) Alongside fashion boutiques such as bluecollarwhitecollar and Alexandra Höjer, you'll find the supermarket Woolworths, health-food store and chemist **Wellness Warehouse** (www.wellnesswarehouse.com), and a branch of the boutique vintners **Wine Concepts** (www.wineconcepts.co.za; ⏰9am-7pm Mon-Fri, to 5pm Sat).

MABU VINYL BOOKS, MUSIC

Map p278 (☎021-423 7635; www.mabuvinyl.co.za; 2 Rheede St, Gardens; ⏰9am-8pm Mon-Thu, to 7pm Fri, to 6pm Sat, 11am-3pm Sun; 🚌Lower Kloof) New and secondhand LPs, CDs, DVDs, books and comics are bought, sold and traded at this reputable shop that features in the award-winning documentary *Searching for Sugarman*. Ask here about independently released CDs by local artists.

SPORTS & ACTIVITIES

DOWNHILL ADVENTURES CYCLING

Map p278 (☎021-422 0388; www.downhilladventures.com; cnr Orange & Kloof Sts, Gardens; activities from R750; 🚌Upper Loop/Upper Long) Get the adrenaline pumping with Downhill's cycling trips, including a thrilling ride down from the lower cable station on Table Mountain, as well as more leisurely pedals in the Tokai Forest, or through the Constantia Winelands and the Cape of Good Hope. You can also hire bikes here (R300 per day) and arrange surf or sandboarding lessons.

ENMASSE MASSAGE

Map p278 (☎021-461 5650; www.enmasse.co.za; 123 Hope St, Gardens; 1hr massage R395; ⏰8am-10pm; 🚌Gardens) De-stress with Thai-style and shiatsu massages (performed without oils) in a historic building that was once a hotel. Stay as long as you like afterwards, relaxing in the tea salon and enjoying any of the 13 different blends of mainly local teas (which you can also buy to take home). Enter via Gate 2, Schoonder Rd.

CAPE TOWN TANDEM PARAGLIDING PARAGLIDING

(☎076 892 2283; www.paraglide.co.za; flights R1150) Feel like James Bond as you paraglide off Lion's Head, land near the Glen Country Club, and then sink a cocktail at Camps Bay. Novices can arrange a tandem paraglide, where you're strapped to an experienced flyer who takes care of the technicalities. Make enquiries on your first day in Cape Town as the weather conditions have to be right.

MILL ST BRIDGE SKATE PARK SKATE PARK

Map p278 (Mill St, Gardens; ⏰8am-9pm; 🚌Gardens) FREE Skateboarders of all abilities gather at this purpose-built skate park (beneath the Mill St flyover bridge) to practise their moves, including board flips. Those without wheels can spectate or check out the interesting street art.

Green Point & Waterfront

GREEN POINT | WATERFRONT | MOUILLE POINT | THREE ANCHOR BAY

Neighbourhood Top Five

❶ Journey to **Robben Island** (p109), once an infamous prison and now a historical site, where you can see the cells in which Nelson Mandela and other heroes from the Freedom struggle spent time.

❷ See all kinds of sea life, including sharks, at the **Two Oceans Aquarium** (p115).

❸ Discover the history of the V&A Waterfront on a **walking tour** (p108).

❹ Learn about biodiversity at beautiful **Green Point Urban Park** (p110), then take a tour around **Cape Town Stadium** (p110).

❺ Sail into Table Bay on one of the many **harbour cruises** (p108) from the Waterfront.

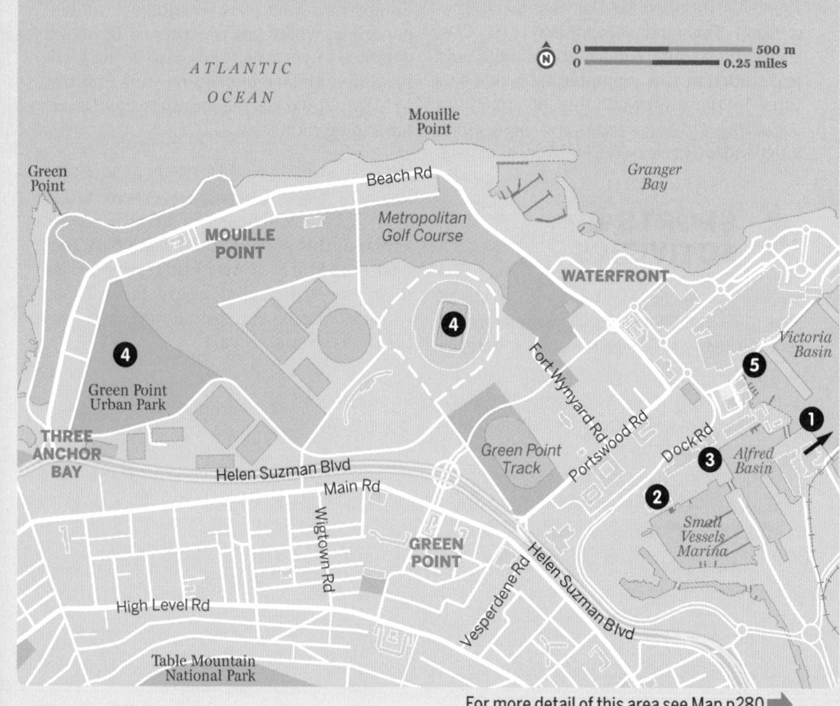

For more detail of this area see Map p280

Explore Green Point & Waterfront

It's easy to see why the V&A Waterfront, commonly called the Waterfront, is not only Cape Town's top tourist attraction – drawing more visitors than the cableway ride to the top of Table Mountain – but also Africa's, seeing more foot traffic than Egypt's pyramids. A textbook example of how to best redevelop a declining dock area, this atmospheric place is always buzzing with plenty to do, not least of which is making a trip out to Robben Island, the infamous jail that is now a thought-provoking museum. Several sleeping options are located around the Waterfront (p205), so it might even end up being the base for your stay.

The outcrop of largely open land west of the Waterfront is Green Point, where you'll find Cape Town Stadium and an excellent municipal park – both legacies of the 2010 FIFA World Cup. Green Point's name has also been applied to the surrounding suburb, which includes rocky Mouille Point – right on the Atlantic Coast and an atmospheric place for a seaside stroll or sunset cocktails and a meal. If shopping and dining at the Waterfront isn't for you, there's also a retail and restaurant cluster along Main Rd, between Braemar and York Rds.

Local Life

➡ **Constitutionals** Catch the sunset and evening breeze on a leisurely stroll or jog around Mouille Point.

➡ **Shopping** Victoria Wharf (p113) is just as popular with locals as it is with tourists. You can also catch a movie at the multiplex.

➡ **Deli** Grab a coffee, a sandwich or picnic supplies at Giovanni's Deli World (p111), a local institution.

Getting There & Away

➡ **Walk and cycle** The pedestrian Walk of Remembrance, created for the 2010 World Cup, provides easy, safe walking or cycling access to and from the city.

➡ **Bus** MyCiTi buses shuttle from the city to stops at the Waterfront and Green Point. Two Oceans Aquarium is also the start/finish point of tours on the City Sightseeing Cape Town (p25) buses.

➡ **Boat** City Sightseeing Cape Town offers a riverboat service along the canals that link the Waterfront to the Cape Town International Convention Centre.

Lonely Planet's Top Tip

The restaurant at Cape Town Hotel School (p111) is one of the city's secret seaside dining spots, with vistas straight onto Granger Bay. In the garden you can also see the base of the original **Mouille Point Lighthouse**.

Best Places to Eat

➡ V&A Market on the Wharf (p110)

➡ Nü (p111)

➡ Café Neo (p111)

➡ Nobu (p111)

➡ El Burro (p111)

For reviews, see p110.

Best Places to Drink

➡ Bascule (p112)

➡ Vista Bar (p112)

➡ Shift (p112)

➡ Shimmy Beach Club (p112)

➡ Tobago's Bar & Terrace (p112)

For reviews, see p112.

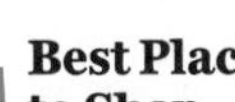

Best Places to Shop

➡ Watershed (p113)

➡ Victoria Wharf (p113)

➡ Rain (p113)

➡ Cape Union Mart Adventure Centre (p114)

➡ Everard Read (p114)

For reviews, see p113.

GEORGE PACHANTOURIS/GETTY IMAGES ©

TOP SIGHT
V&A WATERFRONT

Cape Town's redeveloped Victoria and Alfred (V&A) Docks area is a dazzling beacon of success for the rainbow nation, attracting 24 million visitors a year to its glitzy mix of retail and touristic entertainment. Adding to the carnival atmosphere is the fact that the Waterfront remains a working harbour, with much of its historic fabric preserved.

Evolution of the Waterfront

The Dutch first built the Chavonnes Battery in this area of Table Bay in 1726. In June 1858 a storm wrecked over 30 vessels in the bay, reinforcing the need to create Cape Town's first proper harbour. This began in 1860, with Queen Victoria's second son, Prince Alfred, on hand for the ceremonial duties. The first basin constructed was named after him, the second after his mother (hence the Victoria and Alfred Docks).

By the mid-20th century Cape Town had outgrown these docks. Once Duncan Dock was constructed further west along the Foreshore, the V&A area fell into disuse and creeping decay. Redevelopment began in the late 1980s, when prospects did not look bright for the project – or, for that matter, South Africa in the dying days of apartheid.

Through its ups and downs, the Waterfront is currently very much on the up, with major projects in the pipeline including the transformation of the old grain silo into a major contemporary-art museum and an expansion of the commercial and residential areas eastwards, incorporating part of Duncan Dock and involving a relocation of the Yacht Club.

DON'T MISS

- Two Oceans Aquarium
- Zeitz MOCCA Pavilion
- Chavonnes Battery Museum
- Nobel Square
- Harbour cruises
- Historical walking tour

PRACTICALITIES

- Map p280
- www.waterfront.co.za
- P
- Nobel Square

Two Oceans Aquarium

The excellent **Two Oceans Aquarium** (www.aquarium.co.za; Dock Rd; adult/child R125/60; ⌚9.30am-6pm; 🚸; 🚌Aquarium) is one of the Waterfront's top attractions. It features denizens of the deep from the cold and the warm oceans that border the Cape Peninsula, including ragged-tooth sharks. There are penguins, turtles, an astounding kelp forest, and pools in which kids can touch sea creatures. Qualified divers can get in the water for a closer look (R700, including dive gear). Get your hand stamped on entry and you can return any time the same day.

Zeitz MOCAA Pavilion

Until its Thomas Heatherwick-designed home in a former grain silo opens in 2017, a taster of the Zeitz MOCAA's collection of contemporary African art is displayed in this small **pavilion** (www.waterfront.co.za/activities/land-operators/zeitz-mocca-pavilion; North Wharf; ⌚noon-8pm Wed-Sun; 🚌Nobel Square) FREE next to the Bascule Bridge. Exhibits here change regularly, and several are put on in conjunction with the Chavonnes Battery Museum. Entrepreneur Jochen Zeitz' impressive art collection will provide the finished museum's permanent exhibition within some 80 proposed gallery spaces.

Chavonnes Battery Museum

Along with the Castle of Good Hope, the Dutch built a series of fortifications around Table Bay. The **Chavonnes Battery Museum** (☎021-416 6230; www.chavonnesmuseum.co.za; Clock Tower Precinct; admission R35; ⌚9am-4pm) houses the remains of an early-18th-century cannon battery. Although they had been partly demolished and built over during the construction of the docks in 1860, an excavation of the site in 1999 revealed the remains. You can walk around the entire site and get a good feel for what it was originally like. It's staffed by costumed enthusiasts, who shoot off a real cannon in front of the museum on Sunday at noon.

Nobel Square

Here's your chance to have your photo taken with Desmond Tutu and Nelson Mandela. In Nobel Square stand larger-than-life statues (designed by Claudette Schreuders) of both men, alongside those of South Africa's two other Nobel Prize winners – Nkosi Albert Luthuli and FW de Klerk. Also here is the *Peace and Democracy* sculpture by Noria Mahasa, which symbolises the contribution of women and children to the struggle. It's etched with pertinent quotes by each of the great men.

FIREWORKS

The annual fireworks display on 31 December is one of the Waterfront's biggest events; book well in advance for seats at restaurants with views of the outdoor spectacular. There are two shows, at 7pm and midnight.

The Waterfront's wharves are too small for modern container vessels and tankers, but the Victoria Basin is still used by tugs, fishing boats and harbour vessels of various kinds. In Robinson Dry Dock you'll see ships under repair.

JOGGING & CYCLING

There are marked 2.5km and 5km running routes around the Waterfront that offer great views for your daily jog. Bicycles can also be hired from Up Cycles (p252), near the Clock Tower, and Awol Tours (p252).

Historical Walking Tour

One of the best ways to get an insight into the history of the Waterfront and its development, as well as make sense of this sprawling site, is to sign up for a **historical walking tour** (bookings 021-408 7600; adult R150, min 4 people; 11am & 2pm). Starting at the Chavonnes Battery Museum, the guided two-hour tours take you past buildings and sights such as the **Clock Tower**, from where the harbour master used to control the comings and goings in the docks; **Robinson Dry Dock**, one of the oldest of its kind in the world and still in use today; the **Breakwater Prison**, where you can see carvings made by the prisoners in the slate walls; and the **Time Ball Tower**, previously used to signal the time to ships in the bay.

Bookings can be made at the visitor information centre (p247), where you can also pick up a map for a self-guided walking tour of the Waterfront.

Harbour Cruises

For all the Waterfront's land-lubber attractions, the key way to experience the place is from a boat: nothing quite matches sailing across Table Bay with Table Mountain up ahead, a sight that has been greeting mariners for generations.

There's a wide variety of boat rides available, from luxury yachts to the **Penny Ferry** (R5) row boat, which transports people between Pier Head and the Clock Tower. For listings of cruise-boat operators, see p114.

Maritime Centre

Stocked with model ships and a model of Table Bay harbour made in 1885 by prisoners and warders of Breakwater Prison (another redeveloped part of the Waterfront site), the small **Maritime Centre** (021-405 2880; www.iziko.org.za/museums/maritime-centre; 1st fl, Union-Castle House, Dock Rd; adult/child R20/free; 10am-5pm; Nobel Square) also houses the **John H Marsh Maritime Research Centre** (www.rapidttp.co.za/museum), a resource for those interested in maritime history. The main exhibition at the centre is about the ill-fated voyage of the *Mendi,* which sank in the English Channel in 1917, taking 607 black troops to a watery grave.

Cape Wheel

The **Cape Wheel** (www.capewheel.co.za; Market Sq; adult/child R100/50; 9am-10pm Sun-Thu, to 11pm Fri & Sat; Nobel Square) was supposed to be a temporary attraction but has proved so popular that it's become a permanent fixture. Your ticket gives you four spins (lasting around 15 minutes) on this 40m-tall Ferris wheel. For an extra R20, you can take the 30-minute ride that includes a picnic basket.

Diamond Museum

Really an extended sales pitch for the bling on sale in the attached Shimansky jewellers (p114), the displays at this **museum** (www.capetowndiamondmuseum.org; 1st fl, Clock Tower Shopping Centre; admission R50, free with voucher from website; 9am-9pm; Waterfront Silo) have nonetheless been put together with some style and imagination. There's no obligation to buy, and you can learn a lot about diamonds and how their discovery contributed to the wealth of South Africa. The guided tours are led by one of the sales staff who will point out replicas of famous rocks, such as the Hope and the Taylor-Burton Diamonds.

Springbok Experience

You don't have to be rugby crazy to enjoy the new **Springbok Experience** (021-418 4741; www.facebook.com/SpringbokRugbyMuseum; Portswood House; adult/child R50/30; 10am-6pm; Nobel Square), which celebrates the history of rugby in South Africa and, in particular, the trials and triumphs of the national team, the Springboks. There are several interactive displays (one purports to show whether you'd make the grade as a Springbok player), and the historical aspects – including the international boycotts of the team during apartheid – are covered in detail.

TOP SIGHT
ROBBEN ISLAND

Robben Island's best-known prisoner was Nelson Mandela, which makes it one of the most popular pilgrimage spots in all of Cape Town. Set some 12km out in Table Bay, the flat island, a Unesco World Heritage Site, served as a jail from the early days of VOC (Vereenigde Oost-Indische Compagnie; Dutch East India Company) control right up until 1996.

The Tour

The small island, just 2km by 4km, can only be visited on a tour that starts with a ferry journey (30 to 60 minutes, depending on the vessel) from Nelson Mandela Gateway at the Waterfront. Once on the island you'll be introduced to a guide, typically a former inmate, who will lead a walk through the old prison (with an obligatory peek into Mandela's cell). There's also a bus ride around the island with commentary on the various places of note, such as the lime quarry in which Mandela and many others slaved, the prison house of Pan African Congress (PAC) leader Robert Sobuke, and the church used during the island's stint as a leper colony. All up, the tour lasts two hours.

DON'T MISS

- Nelson Mandela's Cell
- *Cell Stories* exhibit
- Nelson Mandela Gateway
- Jetty 1

PRACTICALITIES

- ☎021-413 4220
- www.robben-island.org.za
- adult/child R280/150
- ⏱ferries depart at 9am, 11am, 1pm & 3pm, weather permitting
- 🚌Nobel Square

Cell Stories

If you're lucky, you'll have about 10 minutes to wander around on your own. The guides may suggest checking out the African penguin colony near the landing jetty or the karamat (Muslim shrine), but a better alternative is to return to the prison's A section to view the *Cell Stories* exhibit. In each of 40 isolation cells is an artefact from and the story of a former political prisoner: chess pieces drawn on scraps of paper, a soccer trophy, a Christmas card from a heartbroken wife. It's all unbelievably moving. This is not part of the regular tour, but there's nothing to stop you slipping away from your guide to view it.

Booking Tickets

While we recommend going to Robben Island, a visit here is not without its drawbacks. One hurdle can be getting a ticket - in peak times these can sell out days in advance, so book well ahead via the website. Another strategy is to book a ticket in conjunction with a township tour - some operators may have access to tickets when regular tours are sold out. (Problems with the island's management has also led to its boats sometimes being out of commission, as was the case at the time of research.)

At the Quayside

Even if you don't make it to the island there are still things to see at the Waterfront. The **Nelson Mandela Gateway** (Map p280; Clock Tower Precinct, V&A Waterfront; ⏱9am-8.30pm; 🚌Nobel Square) FREE has a small museum with displays that focus on the struggle for freedom. Also preserved as a small museum is **Jetty 1** (Map p280; V&A Waterfront; ⏱7am-9pm; 🚌Nobel Square) FREE, the departure point for Robben Island when it was a prison.

SIGHTS

V&A WATERFRONT NEIGHBOURHOOD

The V&A Waterfront includes the following sights: Two Oceans Aquarium (p107), Zeitz MOCAA Pavilion (p107), Chavonnes Battery Museum (p107), Nobel Square (p107), Maritime Centre (p108), Cape Wheel (p108), Diamond Museum (p108) and Springbok Experience (p108).

ROBBEN ISLAND & NELSON MANDELA GATEWAY LANDMARK

See p109.

CAPE TOWN STADIUM STADIUM

Map p280 (021-417 0101; Granger Bay Blvd, Green Point; tours adult/child R45/17; tours 10am, noon & 2pm Tue-Sat; P; Stadium) Shaped like a giant, traditional African hat and wrapped with a Teflon-mesh membrane designed to catch and reflect natural light, this R4.5 billion stadium, built for the 2010 FIFA World Cup, is Cape Town's most striking piece of contemporary architecture. The hour-long tours will take you behind the scenes into the VIP and press boxes as well as the teams' dressing rooms.

The 55,000-capacity stadium is home ground for the soccer team Ajax Cape Town, and has been used for big pop concerts by the likes of Coldplay and U2, as well as a memorial service for Nelson Mandela.

Across from the new stadium, a section of the old Green Point Stadium forms the viewing platform for a running and cycling track.

GREEN POINT URBAN PARK PARK

Map p280 (www.gprra.co.za/green-point-urban-park.html; Bay Rd, Green Point; 7am-7pm; P; Stadium) One of the best things to come out of the redevelopment of Green Point Common for the 2010 World Cup is this park and biodiversity garden. Streams fed by Table Mountain's springs and rivers water the park, which has three imaginatively designed areas – People & Plants, Wetlands, and Discovering Biodiversity – that, along with educational information boards, act as the best kind of outdoor museum. Guided tours (adult/child R35/11) can be arranged through the Cape Town Stadium.

As well as the many types of *fynbos* (literally 'fine bush' – primarily proteas, heaths and ericas) and other indigenous plants, you can see an example of the kind of structure that the Khoe-san used to live in, and spot beautifully made beaded animals, insects and birds among the flower beds. There's plenty of space for picnics with brilliant views of Cape Town Stadium, Signal Hill and Lion's Head, and two kids' play parks (one for toddlers and one for older kids).

GREEN POINT LIGHTHOUSE LIGHTHOUSE, PARK

Map p280 (100 Beach Rd, Mouille Point; adult/child R16/8; 10am-3pm Mon-Fri; P; Three Anchor Bay) Often mistakenly called Mouille Point Lighthouse (the remains of which are in the grounds of the nearby Cape Town Hotel School), this red-and-white candy-striped beacon dates back to 1824 and makes a striking landmark. You can take a self-guided tour inside.

Outside on the grassy common beside the Mouille Point Promenade are a variety of attractions that will appeal to families, including a good playground, **Putt-Putt Golf** (admission R20; 9am-10pm), the **Serendipity Maze** (adult/child R22/11; 10.30am-6pm) and the child-sized locomotive of the **Blue Train** (www.thebluetrainpark.com; admission R15; 9.30am-6pm) amusement park.

THREE ANCHOR BAY BEACH

Map p280 (Beach Rd, Green Point; Three Anchor Bay) This small, rocky beach has easy access from the promenade. It's from here that the bohemian poet Ingrid Jonker, considered the Sylvia Plath of South Africa, committed suicide by drowning in 1965.

CAPE MEDICAL MUSEUM MUSEUM

Map p280 (021-418 5663; Portswood Rd, Green Point; admission by donation; 9am-4pm Tue-Fri; Stadium) The *Disease and History* exhibit at this quirky museum details in length (with some gruesome photographs) the history of major diseases in the Cape, from scurvy to HIV/AIDS. Less horrific are a recreated Victorian doctor's room and pharmacy.

EATING

★V&A MARKET ON THE WHARF FOOD COURT $

Map p280 (www.marketonthewharf.co.za; Pump House, Dock Rd, V&A Waterfront; mains from R50; 10am-5.30pm Jun-Oct, to 7pm Nov-May; P; Nobel Square) There's no need to spend big to eat well (and healthily) at the Waterfront, thanks to this colourful, market-style food court in the old Pump House. Grab a coffee or freshly squeezed juice to go with a wrap or muffin, or opt for a larger meal such as fish and chips.

★NÜ VEGETARIAN $

Map p280 (www.nufood.co.za; Shop 4, Portside, Main Rd, Green Point; mains R50-60; ⏰7am-7pm Mon-Fri, 7.30am-7pm Sat, 7.30am-6pm Sun; 🖉; 🚌Upper Portswood) A great place for a healthy veggie breakfast or lunch, with freshly squeezed juices, smoothies and nutritional salads and multigrain wraps packing out the menu. Order at the counter and enjoy in a bright, unfussy space. There's also a branch in **Sea Point** (Map p284; ☎021-439 7269; Shop 3, Piazza St John, 395 Main Rd, Sea Point; ⏰7.30am-7pm Mon-Sat, to 6pm Sun; 🖉; 🚌Arthur's).

★CAFÉ NEO GREEK, CAFE $

Map p280 (129 Beach Rd, Mouille Point; mains R50-70; ⏰7am-7pm; P📶; 🚌Three Anchor Bay) This favourite seaside cafe has a pleasingly contemporary design and atmosphere that sways from buzzy (at meal times) to more laid-back – great for a late-afternoon drink. Check out the big blackboard menu while sitting at the long communal table inside, or grab a seat on the deck overlooking the red-and-white lighthouse.

GIOVANNI'S DELI WORLD CAFE, DELI $

Map p280 (103 Main Rd, Green Point; mains R30-60; ⏰7.30am-8.30pm; 🚌Stadium) Its menu bursting with flavourful food, Giovanni's can make any sandwich you fancy, which is ideal for a picnic if you're on your way to the beach. The pavement cafe is a popular hang-out.

NEWPORT MARKET & DELI INTERNATIONAL, DELI $

Map p280 (www.newportdeli.co.za; Amalfi, 128 Beach Rd, Mouille Point; mains R50-80; ⏰7am-5pm; P; 🚌Three Anchor Bay) A new location for this long-running deli and cafe sees it expanded over two floors. Grab a smoothie, power-blend or caffeinated beverage and sandwiches and deli goods to enjoy along Mouille Point promenade or in Green Point Park.

TASHAS INTERNATIONAL $$

Map p280 (☎021-421 4350; www.tashascafe.com; Shop 7117, Victoria Wharf, Breakwater Blvd, V&A Waterfront; mains R50-100; ⏰7.30am-9pm Sun-Mon, to 10pm Tue-Sat; P📶🖉; 🚌Waterfront) Muffins that could feed a small family and other delectable baked goods and desserts are the forte of this luxe-design cafe – a hit concept from Johannesburg imported to the Mother City. Also on the menu are plenty of salads, sandwiches and mains; many are served in half-portions for if you're not so hungry.

There's also an outdoor section with some water views across the car park.

★WILLOUGHBY & CO SEAFOOD, JAPANESE $$

Map p280 (☎021-418 6115; www.willoughbyandco.co.za; Shop 6132, Victoria Wharf, Breakwater Blvd, V&A Waterfront; mains R60-160; ⏰noon-10.30pm; P📶; 🚌Waterfront) Commonly acknowledged as one of the better places to eat at the Waterfront – and with long queues to prove it. Huge servings of sushi are the standout from a fish-based menu at this casual eatery inside the mall.

EL BURRO MEXICAN $$

Map p280 (☎021-433 2364; www.elburro.co.za; 81 Main Rd, Green Point; mains R90-175; ⏰noon-10.30pm; P; 🚌Stadium) With a balcony providing views of Cape Town Stadium, this is one stylish donkey: the decor a bit more chic than your average Mexican joint, the menu more inventive. Supplementing the usual tacos and enchiladas are traditional dishes such as chicken mole *poblano*. Booking is advised, as it's popular.

CAPE TOWN HOTEL SCHOOL CONTEMPORARY $$

Map p280 (☎021-440 5736; Beach Rd, Mouille Point; mains R90-150; ⏰11.30am-2.30pm & 6.30-9.30pm Mon-Fri, noon-2.30pm Sun; P; 🚌Mouille Point) The dining room is elegantly decorated in shades of grey and silver and the outdoor patio looks straight onto Granger Bay. Enthusiastic students train here as chefs and servers so things may not all go smoothly, but we found the experience pleasant and the food very tasty and nicely presented on our visit. Their Sunday buffet is R195 per person.

★NOBU JAPANESE $$$

Map p280 (☎021-431 5111; www.noburestaurants.com; One & Only Cape Town, Dock Rd, V&A Waterfront; mains R200-400, set dinners from R190; ⏰6-11pm; P; 🚌Aquarium) This branch of the upmarket global Japanese chain is a smooth-running operation. The chefs turn out expert renditions of Nobu Masahisa's signature ceviches and cod in miso sauce, along with the expected sushi and tempura (best sampled in the good-value set meals). The soaring dining hall offers a New York–metro buzz.

The more intimate bar upstairs is a nice spot to work your way through the extensive sake menu.

HARBOUR HOUSE SEAFOOD **$$$**

Map p280 (021-418 4744; Quay 4, V&A Waterfront; mains R95-260; noon-10pm; P; Nobel Square) The Kalk Bay institution has set up shop at the Waterfront with a good, white-tablecloth restaurant on the ground floor (ask for a table on the deck outside). They've an even better sushi and lounge bar on the upper deck – just the spot for a chilled glass of wine at sunset.

DRINKING & NIGHTLIFE

★BASCULE BAR

Map p280 (021-410 7100; www.capegrace.com; Cape Grace Hotel, West Quay Rd, V&A Waterfront; noon-2am; Nobel Square) Over 450 varieties of whisky are served at the Grace's sophisticated bar, with a few slugs of the 50-year-old Glenfiddich still available (at just R18,000 a tot). Outdoor tables facing the marina are a superb spot for drinks and tasty tapas. Make a booking for one of the whisky tastings (from R240), in which you can sample various drams paired with food.

VISTA BAR COCKTAIL BAR

Map p280 (www.oneandonlyresorts.com; One & Only Cape Town, Dock Rd, V&A Waterfront; noon-1am; Aquarium) The luxury hotel's bar offers plush surrounds and a perfectly framed view of Table Mountain. It's a classy spot for afternoon tea (R195; from 2.30pm to 5.30pm) or a creative cocktail, including classics with a local twist.

SHIFT COFFEE

Map p280 (47 Main Rd, Green Point; 7am-7pm; ; Upper Portswood) Sporting an industrial-chic look with a cosy library corner inside and sheltered, spacious front courtyard outside, this is one of the area's most inviting cafes. Owner Luigi Vigliotti works hard to please customers, and he's come up with a few intriguing signature brews, including the 'Hashtag', which blends espresso with vanilla gelato and Oreo cookies.

★SHIMMY BEACH CLUB CLUB

(021-200 7778; www.shimmybeachclub.com; South Arm Rd, V&A Waterfront; admission before/after 3pm free/R150; 11am-2am Mon-Fri, 9am-2am Sat, 11am-6pm Sun; Waterfront Silo) Drive past the smelly fish processing factories to discover this glitzy mega-club and restaurant, arranged around a small fake beach studded with a glass-sided pool. Perhaps unsurprisingly, it has pool parties with scantily clad dancers shimmying to grooves by top DJs, including the electro-jazz group Goldfish, who have a summer Sunday residency here (bookings advised).

★TOBAGO'S BAR & TERRACE COCKTAIL BAR

Map p280 (021-441 3000; Radisson Blu Hotel Waterfront, Beach Rd, Granger Bay; 11am-midnight; Granger Bay) Walk through the hotel to the spacious deck bar with a prime Table Bay position. It's a great place to enjoy a sunset cocktail; you can take a stroll along the breakwater afterwards.

SOTANO CAFE, BAR

Map p280 (021-433 1757; www.sotano.co.za; 121 Beach Rd, Mouille Point; 7am-11pm; Three Anchor Bay) With a a relaxed vibe and a spacious deck open to Mouille Point promenade, this is an ideal spot for sundowners or a coffee and light bite with an ocean view. There's live music on Friday from 7pm to 9pm and Sunday from 4pm to 7pm.

GRAND CAFÉ & BEACH BAR

Map p280 (072 586 2052; www.grandafrica.com; Granger Bay Rd, Granger Bay; noon-11pm; Somerset Hospital) Sand was dumped here to created the private beach for this oh-so-chic bar and restaurant operating out of a former warehouse. Locals love to gather on weekends here to enjoy the laid-back vibe, rather than the so-so food. DJs kick in later at night.

ALBA LOUNGE COCKTAIL BAR

Map p280 (021-425 3385; www.albalounge.co.za; 1st fl, Hildegards, Pierhead, V&A Waterfront; 11am-2am; Nobel Square) The views across the harbour are grand from this contemporary-design cocktail bar, where the drinks are inventive and there's a roaring fire in winter to add to that inner alcohol glow.

MITCHELL'S SCOTTISH ALE HOUSE & BREWERY PUB

Map p280 (021-418 5074; www.mitchells-ale-house.com; cnr East Pier & Dock Rd, V&A Waterfront; 10am-2am; Nobel Square) Check all airs and graces at the door of South Africa's oldest microbrewery (established in 1983 in Knysna), which serves a variety of freshly brewed ales and good-value meals. The 'Old Wobbly' packs an alcoholic punch.

BELTHAZAR WINE BAR

Map p280 (021-421 3753; www.belthazar.co.za; Shop 153, Victoria Wharf, V&A Waterfront; Breakwater) Claiming to be the world's largest wine bar, Belthazar offers 600 different South African wines, around 250 of which you can get by the (Riedel) glass. The attached restaurant specialises in top-class Karan beef, and it also does plenty of seafood dishes, too.

ENTERTAINMENT

Mainstream movies are screened at the Numetro Multiplex, while art-house titles show at the Ster Kinekor Cinema. Both are located in the Victoria Wharf mall.

MARKET SQUARE AMPHITHEATRE LIVE MUSIC

Map p280 (www.waterfront.co.za/events/overview; off Dock Rd, V&A Waterfront; Nobel Square) The Waterfront's Market Square amphitheatre is the focus for much free entertainment, including buskers and various musical and dance acts. Apart from the giant electronic screen showing videos, the amphitheatre acts as a platform for up-and-coming artists, and there are always live shows from 5pm to 6pm on Saturday and Sundays.

JOU MA SE COMEDY CLUB COMEDY

Map p280 (079-495 3989; www.joumasecomedy.com; Pump House, Dock Rd, V&A Watefront; tickets from R95; 6-10pm, shows 8.30pm; Nobel Square) This long-running comedy club, which hosts the cream of South Africa's comedy talent, has found a permanent home at the back of the old Pump House next to Robinson Dry Dock. The club's name means 'Your Mother's ****', but you don't need to understand Afrikaans slang to get the jokes of host Kurt Schoonraad and the other performers.

GALILEO OPEN AIR CINEMA CINEMA

Map p280 (www.thegalileo.co.za/waterfront.html; Croquet Lawn, off Portswood Rd, V&A Waterfront; tickets R70, blanket/chair hire R10/20; Nov-Apr; Nobel Square) From November to April, this open-air cinema sets up shop to screen classic and crowd-pleasing movies on the croquet lawn next to the Dock House hotel. Sadly, you're not allowed to bring your own blanket or chair, but they're available to rent from the venue. Check online for the current program.

SHOPPING

The bulk of the Waterfront's hundreds of shops and stalls are in Victoria Wharf, although there are a few interesting shops in the smaller Alfred Mall.

★WATERSHED SHOPPING CENTRE

Map p280 (www.waterfront.co.za; Dock Rd, V&A Waterfront; 10am-7pm; Nobel Square) The best place to shop for souvenirs in Cape Town, this exciting revamped retail market gathers together hundreds of top Capetonian and South African brands in fashion, arts, crafts and design – there's something here for every pocket. On the upper level is an exhibition space, and a wellness centre offering holistic products and massages.

Many boutiques and crafts stores you'll find elsewhere in the city have outlets here, but there are also unique stalls such as Township Guitars, which makes and sells the all-electric township 'blik' guitars, made from oil cans, wood and fishing wire (from R3900).

★VICTORIA WHARF SHOPPING CENTRE

Map p280 (www.waterfront.co.za; Breakwater Blvd, V&A Waterfront; 9am-9pm; Breakwater) All the big names of South African retail (including Woolworths, CNA, Pick 'n' Pay, Exclusive Books and Musica), as well as international luxury brands, are represented at this appealing mall – one of Cape Town's best.

★RAIN BEAUTY

Map p280 (www.rainafrica.com; Shop 105, Victoria Wharf, Breakwater Blvd, V&A Waterfront; 9am-9pm; Breakwater) Pamper yourself with the high-quality, hand-made beauty and body products from this Swellendam-based company that's like a chic South

African version of The Body Shop. Their soaps and lotions make lovely gifts.

★CAPE UNION MART ADVENTURE CENTRE OUTDOOR GEAR

Map p280 (www.capeunionmart.co.za; Quay 4, V&A Waterfront; ⌚9am-9pm; Nobel Square) This emporium is packed with backpacks, boots, clothing and practically everything else you might need for outdoor adventures, from a hike up Table Mountain to a Cape-to-Cairo safari. There's also a smaller branch in Victoria Wharf (p113), as well as in the Gardens Centre (p103) and Cavendish Square (p136) malls.

★EVERARD READ ART

Map p280 (☎021-418 4527; www.everard-read-capetown.co.za; 3 Portswood Rd, V&A Waterfront; ⌚9am-6pm Mon-Fri, to 4pm Sat; Nobel Square) Very classy gallery showcasing the best of contemporary South African art, including works by the contemporary realist John Meyer, and Velaphi Mzimba, who works in mixed media.

DONALD GREIG GALLERY & FOUNDRY ART

Map p280 (☎021-418 0003; www.donaldgreig.com; West Quay Rd, V&A Waterfront; ⌚9.30am-5.30pm Mon-Fri, to 1pm Sat; Marina) The striking, life-size bronze animal sculptures of Donald Greig grace many public and private spaces around the Western Cape. At his foundry, set in a 19th-century former customs warehouse, you can watch the casting process and buy pieces small enough to fit easily in your luggage.

SOLVEIG FASHION

Map p280 (www.solveigoriginals.co.za; Albert Mall, Dock Rd, V&A Waterfront; ⌚9am-9pm; Nobel Square) Stocks highly original, colourful and distinctively South African fashions (mainly for women but with a few jackets for men) and accessories.

NAARTJIE CHILDREN, CLOTHING

Map p280 (☎021-421 5819; www.naartjiekids.com; Shop 119, Victoria Wharf, Breakwater Blvd, V&A Waterfront; ⌚9am-9pm; Nobel Square) This attractive range of designer cotton clothing for kids has grown from a stall on Greenmarket Sq to a global brand. There are also branches in **Cavendish Square** (Map p286; ☎021-683 7184; Vineyard St) and Canal Walk (p157), plus a factory shop in Hout Bay (p123).

VAUGHAN JOHNSON'S WINE & CIGAR SHOP WINE

Map p280 (www.vaughanjohnson.co.za; Market Sq, Dock Rd, V&A Waterfront; ⌚9am-6pm Mon-Fri, to 5pm Sat, 10am-5pm Sun; Nobel Square) Sells many South African wines of repute (plus a few more from other countries); unlike most wine sellers here, it's also open on Sundays.

CARROL BOYES HOMEWARES

Map p280 (☎021-418 0595; www.carrolboyes.co.za; Shop 6180, Victoria Wharf, Breakwater Blvd, V&A Waterfront; ⌚9am-9pm; Breakwater) Carrol Boyes' sensuous designs in pewter and steel give a fun feel to cutlery, kitchen products and homewares. You'll also find some rainbow-hued beadworks from Monkeybiz on sale here, as well as Barbara Jackson's ceramics.

SHIMANSKY JEWELLERY

Map p280 (☎021-421 2788; www.shimansky.co.za; 1st fl, Clock Tower Centre, V&A Waterfront; ⌚9am-9pm; Nobel Square) Diamonds are synonymous with South Africa – here you'll find plenty of them, set in a range of jewellery designs. There's also a small museum and a workshop where you can take a peek at how all that bling is made.

SPORTS & ACTIVITIES

WATERFRONT CHARTERS CRUISE

Map p280 (☎021-418 3168; www.waterfrontcharters.co.za; Shop 5, Quay 5, V&A Waterfront; Breakwater) Offers a variety of cruises, including highly recommended 1½-hour sunset cruises (R220), on its handsome wood- and brass-fitted schooner *Esperance*. A 30-minute jet-boat ride is R330.

YACOOB TOURISM CRUISE

Map p280 (☎021-421 0909; www.ytourism.co.za; Shop 8, Quay 5, V&A Waterfront; ; Breakwater) Among the several trips that this company runs are those on the *Jolly Roger Pirate Boat* (adult/child from R120/60) and *Tommy the Tugboat* (R50/25), both perfect for families. Adults may prefer the *Adrenalin* speed-boat jaunts or a cruise on the catamarans *Ameera* and *Tigress*.

KASKAZI KAYAKS KAYAKING, TOUR

Map p280 (☎083 346 1146, 083 230 2726; www.kayak.co.za; Shell petrol station, 179 Beach Rd, Three Anchor Bay; per person R300; ⏰1-5.30pm Tue-Fri, 9am-1pm Sat; 🚌Three Anchor Bay) This outfit runs two-hour guided kayak trips (weather dependent) from Three Anchor Bay to either Granger Bay or Clifton. There are astounding views of the mountains and coastline, as well as possible close encounters with dolphins, seals and penguins. Whale sightings in season are also on the cards. They can also arrange cycle tours and rentals and tandem paraglides.

SPORTS HELICOPTERS SCENIC FLIGHTS

(☎021-419 5907; www.sport-helicopters.co.za/huey-combat-mission; East Pier Rd, V&A Waterfront; flights from R2700; 🚌Waterfront) In this company's fleet is an ex–US Marine Corps Huey chopper from the Vietnam War era, which flies with open doors for that authentic *Apocalypse Now* experience. Standard tours last 30 minutes and take you towards Hout Bay and back; the hour-long tour gets you from the Waterfront to Cape Point.

CAPE TOWN HELICOPTERS SCENIC FLIGHTS

(☎021-418 9462; www.helicopterscapetown.co.za; 220 East Pier, Breakwater Edge, V&A Waterfront; per person from R1300; 🚌Waterfront) Unforgettable views of the Cape Peninsula are guaranteed with these scenic flights. A variety of packages are available from a 30-minute journey out to Robben Island and back to the hour-long journey down to Cape Point (R3500).

TABLE BAY DIVING DIVING

Map p280 (☎021-419 8822; www.tablebaydiving.com; Quay 5, Shop 7, V&A Waterfront; 🚌Breakwater) This reputable operator offers shore dives for R300, boat dives for R350 and full equipment hire for R600 per day. Its open-water PADI course is R4200. You can also arrange shark-cage diving trips to Gansbaai.

TWO OCEANS AQUARIUM DIVING

Map p280 (☎021-418 3823; www.aquarium.co.za; Dock Rd, V&A Waterfront; dives R700; 🚌Aquarium) A guaranteed way to swim with sharks is to dive in the tanks at the Two Oceans Aquarium. No Great Whites, but several ragged-tooth sharks, other predatory fish and a turtle make for a delightful diving experience. The cost includes gear hire, and you need to be a certified diver. They also run PADI diving courses here.

OCEAN SAILING ACADEMY SAILING

Map p280 (☎021-425 7837; www.oceansailing.co.za; Marina Centre, West Quay Rd, V&A Waterfront; 🚌Marina) Contact the only Royal Yachting Association (RYA) school in South Africa to find out about its sailing courses, which are tailored to all skill levels.

METROPOLITAN GOLF CLUB GOLF

Map p280 (☎021-430 6012; www.metropolitangolfclub.co.za; Fritz Sonnenberg Rd, Mouille Point; caddie fees 9/18 holes R100/185, equipment hire 18/9 holes R200/300; 🚌Mouille Point) As part of the revamp of the sports facilities on Green Point Common, this course also got an upgrade, with four species of local grasses planted to give it a more natural look. The wind-sheltered position – between Cape Town Stadium and Green Point Park, with Signal Hill in the background – can't be beat.

Sea Point to Hout Bay

SEA POINT | CLIFTON | CAMPS BAY | HOUT BAY

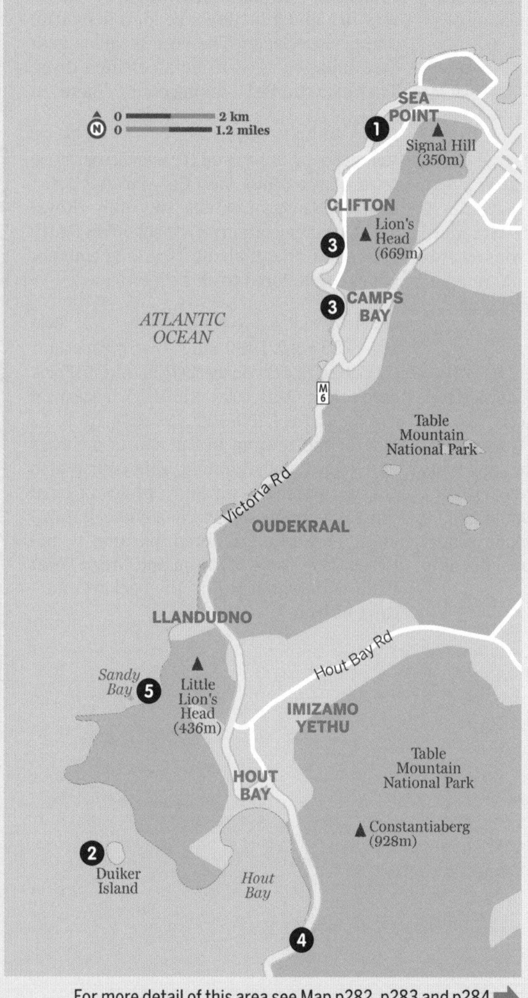

For more detail of this area see Map p282, p283 and p284

Neighbourhood Top Five

❶ Stroll along **Sea Point Promenade** (p118), stopping to admire or ponder the public artworks, then go for a swim at the beautiful art deco **Sea Point Pavilion** (p123).

❷ Snorkel or dive with Cape fur seals off rocky **Duiker Island** (p123).

❸ Lounge on the soft sand at the quartet of beaches at **Clifton** (p118) or ritzy **Camps Bay Beach** (p118).

❹ Gaze down on Hout Bay from thrilling **Chapman's Peak Drive** (p123).

❺ Shed your clothes at secluded **Sandy Bay** (p118) and explore its giant rock formations.

Explore Sea Point to Hout Bay

Long popular with Cape Town's Jewish, gay and Chinese communities, Sea Point sports numerous art deco apartment blocks, lending it an almost Miami Beach elegance. Main Rd and Regent Rd form its commercial spine, lined with many good restaurants, cafes and shops.

Moving south, you'll find prime beach territory: the exclusive and wealthy residential neighbourhoods of Bantry Bay, Clifton and Camps Bay follow hard and fast on each other in a tumble of mansions with to-die-for sea views.

Follow the coastal Victoria Rd over the pass beside Little Lion's Head (436m) to drop down into the fishing community of Hout Bay. Hout means 'wood' in Afrikaans: this is where Jan van Riebeeck found plentiful supplies of timber in the forests that once blanketed the Disa River valley, which helped him to build his original fort in Cape Bowland. The forests are long gone, but Hout Bay's stunning geography – a natural harbour and horseshoe sweep of white sand nestled between the almost vertical Sentinel and the steep slopes of Chapman's Peak – remains eternal.

With its township of Imizamo Yethu (also known as Mandela Park) inland and its coloured district of Hangberg facing the harbour, Hout Bay is like a microcosm of South Africa, and is facing the same post-apartheid integration challenges. Its village atmosphere and handy location midway along the Cape make it a good base for visitors.

If you're not planning on staying in the area, a day or two is fine to see the sights here.

Local Life

- **Markets** Join locals on Friday night grazing at Hout Bay's Bay Harbour Market (p122) and listening to live music.
- **Beaches** Search out lower-profile beaches to escape the crowds, such as Glen Beach (p119) or Llandudno (p118).
- **Constitutionals** Jog or stroll along Sea Point Promenade (p118) in the late afternoon and early evening – and meet legions of locals doing likewise.

Getting There & Away

- **Bus** MyCiTi shuttles run along the coast from Clifton to Hout Bay via Camps Bay.
- **City Sightseeing Cape Town** The hop-on, hop-off tour buses (p25) make stops in Camps Bay and Hout Bay.
- **Shared taxi** These run regularly from the city to Sea Point and Camps Bay.

Lonely Planet's Top Tip

A beautiful spot to watch the sunset over Camps Bay, with the sun's dying rays warming Table Mountain's Twelve Apostles buttresses, is near the top of Camps Bay Drive. There are benches and plenty of grass on which to spread a blanket and toast the view.

Best Places to Eat

- La Boheme (p119)
- La Mouette (p120)
- Duchess of Wisbeach (p120)
- La Perla (p119)
- Kleinsky's Delicatessen (p119)

For reviews, see p119.

Best Places to Drink

- Bungalow (p120)
- La Vie (p120)
- Dunes (p121)
- La Belle (p121)
- Hout Bay Coffee (p121)

For reviews, see p120.

Best Places to Shop

- Bay Harbour Market (p122)
- Hout Bay Craft Market (p122)
- Ethno Bongo (p122)
- T-Bag Designs (p122)

For reviews, see p122.

SIGHTS

★SEA POINT PROMENADE — OUTDOORS

Map p284 (Beach Rd, Sea Point; Promenade) Ambulating along Sea Point's wide, paved and grassy promenade is a pleasure shared by Capetonians from all walks of life – it's a great place to observe the city's multiculturalism. There are kids' playgrounds, a well-maintained outdoor gym, and several public artworks that are worth taking the time to see. The coast here is rocky and swimming is dangerous, although you can get in the water at **Rocklands Beach**. If you're too thin-skinned for the frigid sea, there's Sea Point Pavilion (p123) towards the promenade's southern end.

★CLIFTON BEACHES — BEACH

Map p282 (Victoria Rd, Clifton; Clifton, Clifton 2nd, Clifton 3rd, Clifton 4th) Giant granite boulders break up the four beaches at Clifton, all accessible by steps from Victoria Rd. Almost always sheltered from the wind, they offer top sunbathing spots. Vendors hawk drinks and ice creams along the beach and sun loungers and shades are available, but there are no public toilets. The most northern and longest of the beaches are **Clifton 1st** and **2nd**; **Clifton 3rd** is the gay beach, though plenty of straight folk frequent it, too, while **Clifton 4th** is popular with families. Before hopping in the sea, remember that the water comes straight from the Antarctic, so swimming here is exhilarating (ie freezing).

CAMPS BAY BEACH — BEACH

Map p282 (Victoria Rd, Camps Bay; Camps Bay) With soft white sand and a backdrop of the spectacular Twelve Apostles of Table Mountain, Camps Bay is one of the city's most popular beaches. However, it has drawbacks: it's one of the windiest beaches here; it gets crowded, particularly on weekends; there are no lifeguards on duty; and the surf is strong. So please take care if you do decide to swim. There's a strip of busy bars and restaurants here, ideal for drinks at sunset or general all-day lounging.

SANDY BAY — BEACH

(access from Sunset Ave, Llandudno; Llandudno) This particularly beautiful stretch of sandy beach is roughly a 15-minute walk to the south from the Sunset Rocks parking area at Llandudno. As Cape Town's unofficial nudist beach – though there's no pressure to take your clothes off – it's popular with nature lovers, and with the gay community as a cruising spot. There are incredible rock formations and trails through shrubby *fynbos* (literally 'fine bush'; primarily proteas, heaths and ericas) to explore, too.

ART BY THE SEASIDE

Public art is never going to please everyone, but there was a strident outcry in November 2014, when Michael Ellion's **Perceiving Freedom** – a giant metal-and-plastic pair of Ray-Bans – was unveiled on Sea Point Promenade. Looking out to Robben Island, Ellion's stated intention was to reference Nelson Mandela, who was once photographed wearing a pair of the iconic sunglasses. Dismissed by the local press as 'corporate vandalism' rather than art, by the end of the month the sculpture had been vandalised by the guerrilla graffiti group Tokolos Stencil Collective (www.facebook.com/tokolosstencils).

Perceiving Freedom, which has since been removed, was one of several temporary installations from **Art54** (www.art54.co.za), a World Design Capital–endorsed project that is being piloted along the Atlantic Seaboard, from Mouille Point to Camps Bay, to increase the city's stock of public art. These works tend to be in place for six months to year but a few are permanent: for example, the **Promenade Pets** benches by Rocklands Beach, which has seats held up by pairs of blue seagulls, black sea lions and pink poodles. At Camps Bay you can pose like the king and queen of the beach on Greg Benatar's **Royal View** thrones.

At the Three Anchor Bay end of Sea Point Promenade is Kevin Brand's **White Horses**, which was inspired by the SS *South African Seafarer*'s calamitous visit to Table Bay in 1966. When the ship ran aground some of its cargo, including some plastic white horses, washed up on the shore nearby. Each of the slightly askew horses has a vuvuzela horn in its mouth; speak into one horse and the sound comes out the mouth of another.

LLANDUDNO BEACH BEACH

(Llandudno Rd; Llandudno) The exclusive real estate of Llandudno has a boulder-strewn beach that's a beauty. It's a popular spot with families. There's surfing here on the beach breaks (mostly rights), best at high tide with a small swell and a southeasterly wind. Bring a picnic: there are no shops here.

TWELVE APOSTLES MOUNTAIN

(Kloof Nek/Dal) The name of the Twelve Apostles is said to have been coined by British governor Sir Rufane Donkin in 1820. However, there are well over 12 buttresses on the sea-facing side of Table Mountain, and none is individually named after an apostle. (The Dutch called them De Gevelbergen; Gable Mountains.) They're best viewed around sunset from Camps Bay Drive.

WORLD OF BIRDS BIRD SANCTUARY

(www.worldofbirds.org.za; Valley Rd, Hout Bay; adult/child R85/40; 9am-5pm, monkey jungle 11.30am-1pm & 2-3.30pm; P; Valley) Barbets, weavers and flamingos are among the 3000 birds and small mammals, covering some 400 different species, that are found here. A real effort has been made to make the aviaries, South Africa's largest, as natural-looking as possible, with the use of lots of tropical landscaping. In the **monkey jungle** you can interact with cheeky squirrel monkeys.

OUDEKRAAL PARK, DIVING

(Victoria Rd/M6; adult/child R20/10; 7am-6pm; Oudekraal) There's an attractive picnic spot maintained by Table Mountain National Park on this clump of granite boulders jutting into the Atlantic. The protected coves teeming with marine life and the oldest-known wreck in South Africa (dating from 1670) also make this a prime diving location.

GLEN BEACH BEACH

Map p282 (off Victoria Rd, Camps Bay; Glen Beach) Escape the crowds on this sheltered stretch of sand, split off from Camps Bay's northern end by boulders. Swimming isn't advised, but if the surf's up this is a popular spot with locals for riding the waves. There's stair access from the main road.

GRAAFF'S POOL RUIN

Map p284 (Beach Rd, Sea Point; Graaf's Pool) FREE This natural sea pool was named after the Graaff family, who owned a mansion on the Sea Point beachfront in the mid-19th century and built the walkway and protective wall (now mostly demolished) for it. In the 20th century it became a meeting spot for local gay men. The award-winning short film *Behind the Wall* (viewable on YouTube) reveals the pool's fascinating history.

EATING

★KLEINSKY'S DELICATESSEN DELI $

Map p284 (www.facebook.com/Kleinskys; 95 Regent Rd, Sea Point; mains R20-65; 8.30am-8.30pm; ; Tramway) A homage to classic, Jewish-style delis, this is a great addition to Sea Point's casual dining scene, serving dishes such as toasted bagels with smoked salmon or house-made chopped liver, chicken soup with matzo balls, and *latkes* (potato pancakes). It serves good coffee, too. The walls act as a gallery for local artists.

FISH ON THE ROCKS SEAFOOD $

Map p283 (021-790 0001; www.africasfavourite.com; Harbour Rd, Hout Bay; mains R50; 10.30am-8.15pm; Atlantic Skipper) This place dishes up some of Cape Town's best fish and chips in a breezy bayside location. Watch out for the dive-bombing seagulls if you eat on the rocks, though.

HESHENG CHINESE $

Map p284 (021-434 4214; 70 Main Rd, Sea Point; mains R20-70; 11am-11pm Mon & Wed-Sun, 5-11pm Tue; Sea Point High) Sea Point is stacked with Chinese restaurants, but this inauspicious-looking place is the real deal, run by a friendly Chinese couple and frequented by Chinese expats. All of the dumplings and noodles are made by hand.

★LA BOHEME SPANISH $$

Map p284 (021-434 8797; www.labohemebistro.co.za; 341 Main Rd, Sea Point; 2/3-course dinner R125/160; noon-10.15pm Mon-Fri; ; Firmount) Although you can stoke up on espresso and delicious tapas and light meals during the day, La Boheme is best visited in the evening, when candles twinkle on the tables and you can take advantage of the superb-value two- or three-course menus.

★LA PERLA ITALIAN $$

Map p284 (021-439 9538; www.laperla.co.za; cnr Church & Beach Rds, Sea Point; mains R95-160; 10am-midnight; Sea Point Pool) This eternally stylish restaurant, with its wait-staff in white jackets, has been a fixture of Sea Point's promenade for decades. Enjoy something from the menu of pasta, fish and meat dishes on the terrace shaded by stout palms, or retreat to the intimate bar.

★**MASSIMO'S** ITALIAN $$

(☎021-790 5648; www.pizzaclub.co.za; Oakhurst Farm Park, Main Rd, Hout Bay; mains R55-130; ⏰5-11pm Wed-Fri, noon-11pm Sat & Sun; P 📶 ✎ 👪; 🚌Imizamo Yethu) They do pasta and *spuntini* (tapas-style small plates), but it's the wood-fired thin-crust pizzas that are Massimo's speciality – and very good they are, too. It's all served up with warmth and humour by the Italian Massimo and his Liverpudlian wife Tracy. Plenty of vegetarian options, too.

CHEYNE'S ASIAN, FUSION $$

Map p283 (☎079 067 4919; www.facebook.com/cheyneshoutbay; 1 Pam Arlene Pl, Main Rd, Hout Bay; mains R65-70; ⏰noon-3pm Thu-Sat, 6-10pm Mon-Sat; ✎; 🚌Military) Cheyne Morrisby has gathered quite a following for his inventive Asian and Pacific Rim–inspired small plates, which combine adventurous flavours and textures. Not everything works, but when it does – such as with tiger-prawn tacos or the lush peanut-butter-and-miso butterscotch shake – it can be sublime. The presentation, service and street-art decor are all great.

★**LA MOUETTE** FRENCH $$$

Map p284 (☎021-433 0856; www.lamouette-restaurant.co.za; 78 Regent Rd, Sea Point; mains R125-180, tasting menu R295; ⏰noon-3pm Tue-Sun, 6-10.30pm daily; 🚌Kei Apple) Well-executed classics (such as bouillabaisse and linefish Niçoise) and inventive new dishes (like salt-and-pepper prawns with chorizo popcorn) make this a standout culinary experience. The tasting menu is a great deal. It's delightful to dine in the lush, outdoor courtyard beside the bubbling fountain.

DUCHESS OF WISBEACH FRENCH $$$

Map p284 (☎021-434 1525; Courtyard Bldg, 1 Wisbeach Rd, Sea Point; mains R95-165; ⏰7-10.30pm Mon-Sat; 🚌Sea Point High) Under the stewardship of a celebrated Johannesburg chef, the Duchess raises Sea Point's dining bar by several notches. It serves classic French bistro food with a modern South African spin. All of the ingredients are fresh, with the only thing frozen being the house-made ice creams and sorbets.

KITIMA ASIAN $$$

Map p283 (☎021-790 8004; www.kitima.co.za; Kronendal, 140 Main Rd, Hout Bay; mains R90-190, Sun brunch R250; ⏰5.30-10.30pm Tue-Sat, noon-3pm Sun; P; 🚌Imizamo Yethu) The Kronendal, a Cape Town Dutch farmhouse with parts dating to 1713, has been sensitively restored to house this excellent pan-Asian restaurant specialising in Thai food and sushi. Thai chefs ensure that dishes such as chicken pad Thai are authentically delicious.

ROUNDHOUSE INTERNATIONAL $$$

Map p282 (☎021-438 4347; www.theroundhouserestaurant.com; The Glen; 4-course menu R665; ⏰6-10pm Tue-Sat year-round, noon-4pm Wed-Sat & noon-3pm Sun May-Sep; P ✎; 🚌Kloof Nek) Overlooking Camps Bay, this heritage-listed 18th-century building, set in wooded grounds, is perfect for the elegant restaurant it now houses. The menu can be configured to provide a delicious vegetarian meal. Also consider a relaxed lunch (Tuesday to Sunday) or breakfast (Friday to Sunday) on the lawns at the spring and summer **Rumbullion** restaurant, where you can snack on gourmet pizza and salads (mains R85 to R180).

HARVEY'S INTERNATIONAL $$$

Map p284 (☎021-434 2351; www.winchester.co.za; Winchester Mansions Hotel, 221 Beach Rd, Sea Point; brunch R270; 🚌London) Book for Sunday Jazz brunch (11am to 2pm), where live music and a glass of bubbly will greet you on arrival in the flower-draped central courtyard. The chic sea-facing bar and bistro is also good for lunch, drinks and nibbles.

DRINKING & NIGHTLIFE

★**BUNGALOW** BAR

Map p282 (☎021-438 2018; www.thebungalow.co.za; Glen Country Club, 3 Victoria Rd, Clifton; ⏰noon-2am; 🚌Maiden's Cove) This restaurant lounge bar with a Euro-chic vibe is a great place for beers, cocktails or a boozy meal, after which you can crash on a daybed under a billowing white awning, or dangle your feet in the tiny barside pool. There's a more club-by atmosphere by night. Bookings advised.

★**LA VIE** BAR

Map p284 (☎021-433 1530; www.lavie.co.za; 205 Beach Rd, Sea Point; ⏰9am-11.30pm; 📶; 🚌Promenade) Next to the South African Broadcasting Company studios, this is one of the few places where you can have anything from breakfast to cocktails within sight of Sea Point Promenade. Lounge on the terrace and enjoy the thin-crust pizza (R50 to R100).

★DUNES BAR

Map p283 (www.dunesrestaurant.co.za; 1 Beach Rd, Hout Bay; 9am-11pm; ; Hout Bay) You can hardly get closer to the beach than this – in fact, the front courtyard *is* the beach. Up on the terrace or from inside the restaurant-bar you'll get a great view of Hout Bay, along with some decent pub grub and tapas. There's also a safe play area for kids.

★LA BELLE CAFE, BAKERY

Map p282 (021-437 1278; www.labellecampsbay.co.za; 201 The Promenade, Camps Bay; 7am-11pm; Whale Rock) This belle is one of the loveliest along the Camps Bay dining strip, and a lot more relaxed and less pretentious than some of its neighbours. Coffees, speciality teas, smoothies and a good range of cocktails are on offer – plus some tempting baked goods, cakes and other light meals.

★HOUT BAY COFFEE CAFE

Map p283 (www.facebook.com/HoutbayCoffee; Mainstream Shopping Centre, Main Rd, Hout Bay; 9am-5pm Mon-Fri, to 3pm Sat & Sun; Military) Sip excellent coffee at this rustic cafe, set in an 18th-century add-on to the original 17th-century woodcutters' cottage at Hout Bay. The outdoor area is shaded by a 150-year-old Norfolk Pine, with tables and chairs made from an old fishing boat. They also bake filo-pastry chicken pies, luscious chocolate cakes and wheat-free quiche with free-range eggs.

KOI RESTAURANT & VODKA BAR BAR, RESTAURANT

Map p284 (021-439 7258; www.ambassador-hotel.co.za/food-and-wine; Ambassador Hotel, 34 Victoria Rd, Bantry Bay; noon-10.30pm; ; Bantry Bay) The floor-to-ceiling windows at this minimalist restaurant-bar provide a vertigo-inducing vista over the waves and rocks below. It's perfect for cocktails and nibbles on the way back from Clifton.

DIZZY'S RESTAURANT & PUB PUB

Map p282 (021-438 7328; www.dizzys.co.za; 41 The Drive, Camps Bay; weekend admission around R20; 7.30am-3am; Whale Rock) There's regular nightly entertainment at this convivial British-style pub and restaurant specialising in seafood platters, with karaoke on Tuesday, a pub quiz and DJs on Thursday and a beer-pong battle every Sunday at 8pm. Set back from the seafront, it's a laid-back place for a coffee or beer and to hang out with locals.

MYNT CAFE, BAR

Map p282 (31 Victoria Rd, Camps Bay; 8am-10pm Tue-Sun; Camps Bay) At the northern end of the Camps Bay dining strip, this place offers coffee, cocktails and light meals with a beach view – and it's a tad more relaxed than the self-consciously fashionable cafes (with booming DJ music) nearby.

LEOPARD BAR COCKTAIL BAR

(021-437 9000; www.12apostleshotel.com; Twelve Apostles Hotel & Spa, Victoria Rd, Oudekraal; 11am-2am; Oudekraal) With a dress-circle

LOCAL KNOWLEDGE

LIVE-MUSIC GUIDE

Patrick Craig, musician, gig promoter and creator of Sea Point's Studio 7 (p122), filled us in on the 'jazz cats' and breaking bands of the Capetonian scene.

Best indoor venues? Assembly (p88) and House of Machines (p71) can always be relied on for cool and up-and-coming bands; the former is mainly DJs and electronic music. Weinhaus + Biergarten (p70) also have a great live-music schedule, with al-fresco courtyard gigs in warmer months. For jazz, check out **Kloof St House** (Map p278; 021-423 4413; www.kloofstreethouse.co.za; 30 Kloof St, Gardens; mains R95-175; Lower Kloof) for their Sunday lunch session; the same owners run Asoka (p101), which also has sessions on Tuesday night. If it's Monday, head to Lyra's (p135) in Rondebosch for Dan Shout's weekly jam session.

Best outdoor venues? In summer you can't miss the concerts in Kirstenbosch (p126). Although it's a 45-minute drive out of town, the **Paul Cluver Forest Ampitheatre** (www.cluver.com/amphitheatre) in Elgin is really beautiful – a very different environment in which to catch a gig. Also look for outdoor shows at other wine estates.

Best artists to watch? Electro-jazz combo GoodLuck; local boy Jeremy Loops; Matthew Mole from Jo'burg; Majozi from Durban; the indie pop trio Beatenberg; and symphonic indie-rock band Al Bairre.

view over the Atlantic, the Twelve Apostles Hotel's bar is an ideal spot to escape the hoi polloi of Camps Bay for a classy cocktail or – better yet – deliciously decadent afternoon tea (R175; served from 2pm to 4pm).

TA DA! CAFE

Map p283 (☎021-790 8132; www.theboardroomadventures.co.za; 37 Victoria Rd, Hout Bay; ⏰8am-5pm; 🚌Lower Victoria) There's some shaded outdoor seating and a pleasant interior, including a lounge that occasionally hosts movie nights, at this coffee bar and crêperie. On offer are both sweet and savoury versions of the French pancakes. There's also a branch in Muizenberg, above Gary's Surf School (p150).

ENTERTAINMENT

★STUDIO 7 LIVE MUSIC

Map p284 (www.facebook.com/Studio7Sessions; 8 Calais Rd, Sea Point; 🚌Rhine) Local musician Patrick Craig (p121) has a members-only music club in his living room. Top local and international musicians play acoustic gigs here in very relaxed, intimate surroundings. Usually no more than 40 tickets are sold (online) – check the Facebook page for details, as it's a fantastic venue for true music lovers.

THEATRE ON THE BAY THEATRE

Map p282 (☎021-438 3300; www.theatreonthebay.co.za; 1 Link St, Camps Bay; 🚌Lower Camps Bay) The program here sticks with conventional plays or one-person shows. Should you want to eat before curtain, there's the chic **Sidedish Theatre Bistro**.

SHOPPING

★BAY HARBOUR MARKET MARKET

Map p283 (www.bayharbour.co.za; 31 Harbour Rd, Hout Bay; ⏰5-9pm Fri, 9am-4pm Sat & Sun; 🚌Atlantic Skipper) At the far western end of the harbour is this imaginatively designed indoor market, one of Cape Town's best. There's a good range of things to buy, as well as very tempting food and drink. Live music gives it a relaxed, party-like atmosphere.

★HOUT BAY CRAFT MARKET MARKET

Map p283 (Baviaanskloof Rd, Hout Bay; ⏰10am-5pm Sun; 🚌Military) Browsing the stalls at this little village-green market, a fundraiser for the Lions Club of Hout Bay, is a lovely way to while away an hour or so on a Sunday. You'll find crafts made by locals, including impressive beadwork, colourfully printed cloths and cute guinea fowl made from pine cones.

★ETHNO BONGO JEWELLERY

Map p283 (☎021-790 0802; www.ethnobongo.co.za; 35 Main Rd, Hout Bay; ⏰9.30am-5.30pm Mon-Fri, to 4pm Sat, 10am-4pm Sun; 🚌Military) A court order stopped them using the name Dolce & Banana for their bead jewellery, but otherwise it hasn't put a dent in this long-running shop, set in an original fisherman's cottage, that sells fun fashion items made by local craftspeople. Products include home decor made from materials such as reclaimed wood and driftwood.

★T-BAG DESIGNS ARTS & CRAFTS

Map p283 (☎021-790 0887; www.tbagdesigns.co.za; Klein Kronendal, 144 Main Rd, Hout Bay; ⏰9am-4.30pm Mon-Fri; 🚌Imizamo Yethu) Recycled tea bags are used to produce an attractive range of greetings cards, stationery and other quality hand-made paper products; it's a worthwhile project that employs people from the neighbouring township of Imizamo Yethu. It also has a stall in the Watershed (p113) at the Waterfront.

SHIPWRECK SHOP ANTIQUES

Map p283 (☎021-790 1100; www.marinerswharf.com; Mariner's Wharf, Harbour Rd, Hout Bay; ⏰9am-5.30pm; 🚌Northshore) If you're after anything to do with ships – from scrimshaw (old carved ivory) to charts and models – then this treasure trove, with over 20,000 pieces of memorabilia salvaged from ocean-going vessels, should be on your list.

IZIKO LO LWAZI ARTS & CRAFTS

Map p283 (☎021-790 2273; www.izikoll.co.za; Hout Bay Community Cultural Centre, Baviaanskloof Rd, Hout Bay; ⏰8.30am-4.30pm Mon-Fri; 🚌Military) 🍃 This craftwork collective produces creative recycled-paper products from (among other things) elephant, horse and camel dung! Their beaded cards are delightful.

PEACH FASHION

Map p284 (www.peachsa.com; 2 Marine House, Main Rd, Sea Point; ⏰9am-5pm Mon-Fri, to 1pm Sat; 🚌Arthur's) A well-curated selection of quality imported clothing, scarves, costume jewellery, underwear, bags and other accessories are on display at this colourful boutique, a favourite of local fashionistas.

LOCAL KNOWLEDGE

PROMENADE MONDAYS & SKATEBOARDING IN CAPE TOWN

Every Monday at 6pm, up to 300 skateboarders, cyclists and in-line skaters gather at the parking lot beside Queen's Beach in Sea Point to take part in **Promenade Mondays** (www.facebook.com/pages/PromenadeMondays/128084890690061). This social push/roll/skate-a-thon along Sea Point Promenade is organised by town planner and long-boarder Marco Morgan, a founding member of the National Skate Collective – which has been lobbying the city for years to provide improved facilities for skaters.

The lifting of the ban on cycling along the promenade has paved the way not only for Promenade Mondays, but also for Up Cycles (p252), which has a rental bike station next to Sea Point Pavilion, so visitors can join in the event. Marco recommends hitting skateboard shops along Long St if you want to pick up your own set of wheels, and checking out the scene at the Mill St Bridge Skate Park (p103) in Gardens, where you may even catch South African champion skater (and Cape Town local) **Jean-marc Johannes** (www.facebook.com/jeanmarcskate) practising his moves.

NAARTJIE KIDS — CHILDREN'S CLOTHING

Map p283 (☎021-790 3093; www.naartjiekids.com; 46 Victoria Ave, Hout Bay; ⏰9am-6pm Mon-Fri, to 5pm Sat, 10am-4pm Sun; 🚌Oxford Earl) This designer children's clothing brand has gone global, but it's based in Cape Town. This location is its factory shop.

SPORTS & ACTIVITIES

★CHAPMAN'S PEAK DRIVE — DRIVING, CYCLING

(www.chapmanspeakdrive.co.za; Chapman's Peak Drive; cars/motorcycles R38/25; 🚌Hout Bay) Take your time driving, cycling or walking along 'Chappies', a 5km toll road linking Hout Bay with Noordhoek – it's one of the most spectacular stretches of coastal highway in the world. There are picnic spots and viewpoints, and it's worth taking the road at least one way en route to Cape Point. The toll booth is at the Hout Bay end of the road; you're free to walk up here and along the road. On the approach from Hout Bay look for a bronze **leopard statue**. It has been sitting there since 1963 and is a reminder of the wildlife that once roamed the area's forests (which has also largely vanished).

★ANIMAL OCEAN — SNORKELLING, DIVING

Map p283 (☎079 488 5053; www.animalocean.co.za; Hout Bay Harbour, Hout Bay; snorkelling/diving per person R650/850; 👪; 🚌Fishmarket) Although it's weather dependent (and not for those who suffer seasickness), don't miss the chance to go snorkelling or diving with some of the playful, curious Cape fur seals that live on Duiker Island, and swim in the shark-free waters around it. All necessary gear, including thick neoprene wetsuits, is provided. Trips run only from September to April.

DUIKER ISLAND CRUISES — BOAT TOUR

Map p283 (🚌Fishmarket) From Hout Bay Harbour you can catch a boat to Duiker Island, also known as Seal Island for its colony of Cape fur seals (not to be confused with the official Seal Island in False Bay). Three companies run these cruises daily, usually with guaranteed sailings in the mornings: **Circe Launches** (☎021-790 1040; www.circelaunches.co.za; adult/child R60/30), **Drumbeat Charters** (☎021-791 4441; www.drumbeatcharters.co.za; adult/child R75/30) and **Nauticat Charters** (☎021-790 7278; www.nauticatcharters.co.za; adult/child R75/30).

SEA POINT PAVILION — SWIMMING

Map p284 (Beach Rd, Sea Point; adult/child R20/10; ⏰7am-7pm Oct-Apr, 9am-5pm May-Sep; 🚌Sea Point Pool) This huge outdoor pool complex, with its lovely art deco touches, is a Sea Point institution. It gets very busy on hot summer days – not surprisingly, since the pools are always at least 10°C warmer than the always-frigid ocean.

INTO THE BLUE — DIVING

Map p284 (☎021-434 3358; www.diveschoolcapetown.co.za; 88B Main Rd, Sea Point; open-water PADI courses from R4650, shore/boat dives R275/420, gear hire per day R520; 🚌Sea Point High) Conveniently located near Sea Point's hostels and guesthouses, this operator runs courses and has regular dives on a variety of themes scheduled around the Cape, including shark-cage dives.

Southern Suburbs

MOWBRAY | RONDEBOSCH | CLAREMONT | NEWLANDS | BISHOPSCOURT | WYNBERG | CONSTANTIA

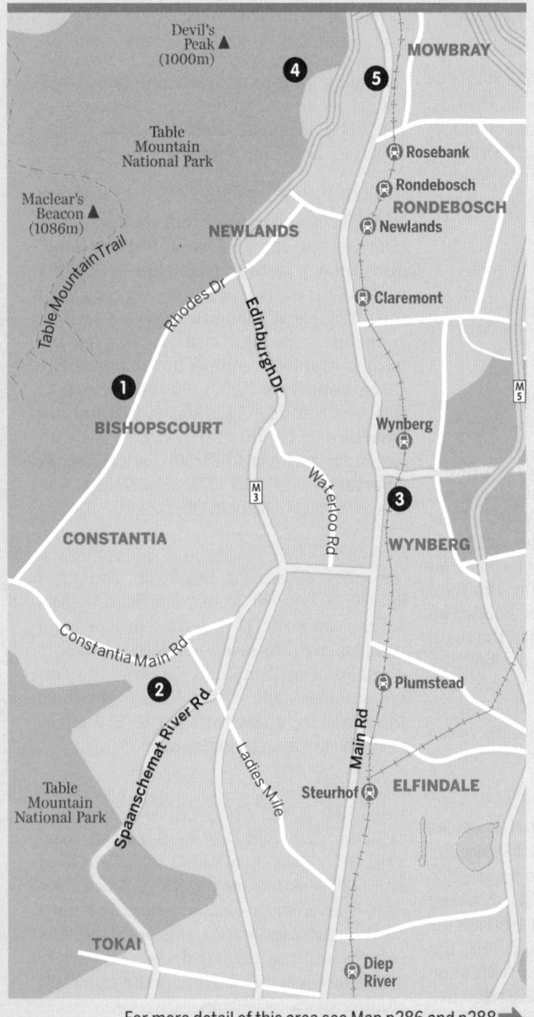

For more detail of this area see Map p286 and p288

Neighbourhood Top Five

❶ Immerse yourself in the diverse splendour of the Cape floral kingdom at **Kirstenbosch Botanical Gardens** (p126), and be sure to attend one of the outdoor summer concerts.

❷ Taste wines along the **Constantia Valley Wine Route** (p127), visiting historic estates such as **Groot Constantia** (p127).

❸ Take a stroll around the lovely urban conservation area of **Wynberg Village** (p129).

❹ Admire the view from the grand **Rhodes Memorial** (p129).

❺ Step into the world of one of South Africa's top 20th-century painters at the **Irma Stern Museum** (p129).

Explore Southern Suburbs

If you want to see how the other half in Cape Town lives – the rich half, that is – visit the Southern Suburbs, the residential areas clinging to the eastern slopes of Table Mountain. Heading south out of the City Bowl and around Devil's Peak you'll first hit Mowbray and Rondebosch; this is the territory of the University of Cape Town (UCT) and the location of one of Cape Town's premier arts spaces, the Baxter Theatre Centre.

Leafy, affluent Newlands and Bishopscourt are where you'll find the area's highlight, Kirstenbosch Botanical Gardens, as well as the city's major cricketing and rugby venues. The area around Claremont station is a fascinating study in contrasts, with black and coloured traders crowding the streets around the ritzy Cavendish Square mall. It's a similar story in Wynberg, another place where the haves rub shoulders with the have-nots. The thatched-roof Cape Georgian homes of Wynberg Village are worth a look.

Immediately to the west is Constantia, home to South Africa's oldest wineries and where the super-wealthy live in huge mansions behind high walls. It's a verdant area that culminates in Tokai, with its shady forest reserve.

Local Life

- **Sports** Join the fans cheering on South African cricket and rugby teams at Sahara Park Newlands (p135) and Newlands Rugby Stadium (p135).
- **Beer** Sample microbrews at Banana Jam (p133), tour South Africa's oldest commercial brewery (p131) or drop by the ever-popular Forrester's Arms (p134).
- **Markets** The Kirstenbosch commons hosts various markets, including a monthly craft market (p136); also head to the Tokai Forest Market (p135) on Saturday for farm-fresh produce and crafts.

Getting There & Away

- **Car** From the city follow the M3, which runs parallel to the east side of Table Mountain and has turn-offs for UCT, the Rhodes Memorial, Newlands and Kirstenbosch. Stay on the M3 for Constantia and Tokai.
- **Bus** The City Sightseeing Cape Town Blue Route bus stops at Kirstenbosch; you can add a free extension bus tour to the Constantia wineries.
- **Shared taxi** Minibus taxis shuttle along Main Rd from Mowbray to Wynberg.
- **Train** Cape Metro Rail has stops at Rondebosch, Newlands, Claremont, Kenilworth, Wynberg, Rosebank and Mowbray.

Lonely Planet's Top Tip

If you're in Cape Town on the second-last Saturdays of March or November and like pottery, head to **Rondebosch Common** for the Potters Market organised by **Ceramics South Africa** (www.ceramics-sa-cape.co.za). Get there around 7am to snag the best pieces and bargains. Every Saturday at 8am there's also a 5km **park run** (www.parkrun.co.za/rondeboschcommon) around the common – anyone can join.

Best Places to Eat

- Greenhouse (p133)
- La Colombe (p133)
- Starlings Cafe (p132)
- Bistro Sixteen82 (p132)
- Four&twenty Cafe & Pantry (p133)

For reviews, see p132.

Best Places to Drink

- Banana Jam (p133)
- Martini Bar (p134)
- Forrester's Arms (p134)
- Localé (p134)

For reviews, see p133.

Best Places to Shop

- Montebello (p135)
- Art in the Forest (p135)
- Balu Legacy Boutique (p135)

For reviews, see p135.

TOP SIGHT
KIRSTENBOSCH BOTANICAL GARDENS

Covering 5 hectares of Table Mountain, these beautiful landscaped gardens – the largest in South Africa – merge almost imperceptibly with the surrounding natural *fynbos* (literally, 'fine bush'; primarily proteas, heaths and ericas) vegetation. They're a wonderful place to relax, take in the scenery and learn about the magnificent Cape floral kingdom. There's always something flowering, but the gardens are at their best between mid-August and mid-October.

History of the Gardens

In 1657 Jan van Riebeeck appointed a forester to the area. A group of French refugees shipwrecked en route to Madagascar were employed in 1660 to plant a wild almond hedge as the boundary of the Dutch outpost (a remnant of it is still here). Van Riebeeck called his private farm Boschheuwel, and it wasn't until the 1700s, when the gardens were managed by JF Kirsten, that they got the name Kirstenbosch. Cecil Rhodes owned the land from 1895 until his death in 1902, when he bequeathed his estate to the nation. It officially became a botanical garden in 1913.

What to See

Apart from the almond hedge, some magnificent oaks, and the Moreton Bay fig and camphor trees planted by Rhodes, the gardens are devoted almost exclusively to indigenous plants. About 9000 of Southern Africa's 22,000 plant species are cultivated here.

Added for the garden's centenary in 2013, the **Tree Canopy Walkway** (informally known as the Boomslang, meaning 'tree snake') is a curvaceous steel and timber bridge that rises through the trees and provides wonderful views.

You'll find a *kopje* (hill) that's been planted with pelargoniums; a sculpture garden; a section of plants used in making medicine; and a fragrance garden with raised beds and plants that can be smelt and felt, developed so that sight-impaired people could enjoy the garden (the plant labels here are also in Braille).

The main entrance at the Newlands end of the gardens is where you'll find plenty of parking, the information centre, an excellent souvenir shop and the atmosphere-controlled **conservatory**, which displays plant communities from a variety of terrains: the most interesting of these is the Namakwa and Richtersveld section, with baobabs and quiver trees.

Make an effort to attend the series of **Summer Sunset Concerts**, usually held on Sundays; some of the biggest names in South African music perform here.

Guided Walks & Hiking Routes

The gardens run free guided walks; you can also hire an electronic device (R40) that plays recorded information about the various plants on the three signposted circular walks.

There are also two popular **hiking routes** up Table Mountain from Kirstenbosch, along either **Skeleton Gorge**, which involves negotiating some sections with chains, or **Nursery Ravine**. These can be covered in three hours by someone of moderate fitness. The trails are well marked and steep in places, but the way to the gardens from the cableway and vice versa is not signposted.

DON'T MISS

- Summer Sunset Concerts
- Tree Canopy Walkway
- Conservatory
- Van Riebeeck's Hedge

PRACTICALITIES

- Map p288
- ☎021-799 8782
- www.sanbi.org/gardens/kirstenbosch
- Rhodes Dr, Newlands
- adult/child R55/15
- 8am-7pm Sep-Mar, to 6pm Apr-Aug, conservatory 9am-5pm year-round

DON BAYLEY/GETTY IMAGES ©

TOP SIGHT
CONSTANTIA VALLEY WINE ROUTE

South Africa's wine industry began here in 1685, when Governor Simon van der Stel chose the area for its wine-growing potential. After his death in 1712, his 7.6-sq-km estate, which he had named Constantia, was split up. The area is now the location for the Constantia Valley Wine Route, comprising 10 vineyards.

DON'T MISS

- Groot Constantia
- Steenberg Vineyards
- Buitenverwachting
- Klein Constantia
- Beau Constantia

PRACTICALITIES

- Map p288
- www.constantiawineroute.com

Groot Constantia

Simon van der Stel's **manor house**, a superb example of Cape Dutch architecture, is maintained as a museum at **Groot Constantia** (pictured above; 021-794 5128; www.grootconstantia.co.za; Groot Constantia Rd; tastings R30, museum adult/child R20/free, cellar tours incl tasting R40; 9am-5.30pm; P). Set in beautiful grounds, the estate can become busy with tour groups but is large enough for you to escape the crowds. In the 18th century, Constantia wines were exported and highly acclaimed around the world; try the sauvignon blanc and the Gouverneurs Reserve bordeaux-style blend.

The large **tasting room** is first on your right as you enter the estate. Further on is the free **orientation centre**, which provides an excellent overview of the estate's history, and the beautifully restored homestead. The interiors have been appropriately furnished; take a look at the tiny slave quarters beneath the main building. The **Cloete Cellar**, with a beautiful moulded pediment, was the estate's original wine cellar. It now houses old carriages and a display of storage vessels. Hour-long tours of the modern cellar depart at 2pm.

Steenberg Vineyards

Enjoy the gorgeous contemporary tasting bar and lounge at **Steenberg Vineyards** (www.steenberg-vineyards.co.za; Steenberg Estate, Steenberg Rd, Tokai; tastings R20 & R40; 10am-6pm; P), in which you can sample its great merlot, sauvignon blanc, semillon and Méthode Cap Classique sparkler. The farm estate is the oldest on the Cape, dating back to 1682, when

KARAMAT

At the entrance to Klein Constantia is the karamat (saint's tomb) of Sheik Abdurahman Matebe Shah, who was buried here in 1661. The tomb is one of several that encircle Cape Town, supposedly providing protection against natural disasters.

There's no shortage of places to dine while out visiting the wineries. Groot Constantia has two restaurants and Steenberg Vineyards has an excellent bistro. Buitenverwachting offers an elegant formal restaurant overlooking its vineyards, as well as a more casual cafe and (in the summer season) picnics. At both Groot Constantia and Eagle's Nest, you can also pre-order picnics to enjoy in the grounds – just bring your own blanket.

WALKING TRAILS

Zandvlei Trust (www.zandvleitrust.org.za/art-constantia%20walking%20trails.html) has online maps of nine easy walking trails in the Constantia Valley. None are more than 45 minutes long, and some run through shady old forests and beside rivers.

it was known as Swaane-weide (Feeding Place of the Swans). Also here is the five-star Steenberg Hotel (p208, in the original manor house), Catharina's Restaurant and an 18-hole golf course.

Buitenverwachting

Buitenverwachting (☎021-794 5190; www.buitenverwachting.co.za; Klein Constantia Rd; tastings R40; ⏲9am-5pm Mon-Fri, 10am-3pm Sat; 🅿) means 'beyond expectation', which is certainly the feeling one gets on visiting this 1-hectare estate. Beg, borrow or steal to snag a bottle of its delicious (but limited-release) Christine bordeaux blend. The creamy chardonnay and richly textured cabernet sauvignon are also standout whites. Order ahead to enjoy a blissful **picnic lunch** (☎083 257 6083; lunch R145; ⏲noon-4pm Mon-Sat Nov-Apr) in front of the 1796 manor house. There's also a casual cafe and a fancier restaurant with a sweeping view of the vineyards.

Klein Constantia

Part of the original Constantia estate, **Klein Constantia** (www.kleinconstantia.com; Klein Constantia Rd; tastings R30; ⏲tastings 10am-5pm Mon-Fri, to 4.30pm Sat, to 4pm Sun; 🅿) is famous for its Vin de Constance, a sweet muscat wine. It was Napoleon's solace on St Helena, and Jane Austen had one of her heroines recommend it for having the power to heal 'a disappointed heart'. Also sample their champagne-style sparkler. Klein Constantia doesn't offer the frills and bonuses of other wineries, but it's worth visiting for its excellent tasting room.

Other Wineries

Constantia Glen (☎021-795 6100; www.constantiaglen.com; Constantia Main Rd; tastings R30; ⏲10am-5pm Mon-Fri, to 4pm Sat & Sun; 🅿) is known for its sauvignon blanc and bordeaux-style blends. There's a view of the vineyards from the terrace in front of the tasting room.

Stuart Botha, the young winemaker at **Eagle's Nest** (☎021-794 4095; www.eaglesnestwines.com; Constantia Main Rd; tasting R40; ⏲10am-4.30pm; 🅿), is one of the stars of an SABC reality TV series *Exploring the Vine*. Try the viognier or shiraz. Book ahead for picnics (R375 for two), which you can enjoy in the shady grounds beside a stream; otherwise there are various food platters and light snacks available.

There are panoramic views from the tasting room and wine and sushi bar at **Beau Constantia** (☎021-794 8632; www.beauconstantia.com; Constantia Nek; wine tastings R55, canapes R90; ⏲tasting room 10am-4.30pm, wine & sushi bar noon-8.30pm Tue-Sun; 🅿), although take care when driving in as the car park is a little tricky to locate. There are five wines to taste.

SIGHTS

KIRSTENBOSCH BOTANICAL GARDENS — GARDENS

See p126.

CONSTANTIA VALLEY WINE ROUTE — WINERIES

See p127.

RHODES MEMORIAL — MONUMENT

Map p286 (www.rhodesmemorial.co.za; off M3, Groote Schuur Estate, Rondebosch; ⏲7am-7pm; P) FREE Partly modelled on the arch at London's Hyde Park Corner, this monumental granite memorial stands on the eastern slopes of Table Mountain, at a spot where the mining magnate and former prime minister used to admire the view. The 49 steps, one for each year of his life, are flanked by pairs of lions; the top provides sweeping vistas to the Cape Flats and the mountain ranges. Rhodes bought all the surrounding land in 1895 for £9000 as part of a plan to preserve a relatively untouched section of the mountain for future generations. His ambition and determination is memorialised by a dynamic statue of a man on a rearing horse (in contrast to the bust of Rhodes himself, which has him looking rather grumpy). Behind the memorial is a pleasant restaurant (p133) and a steep path leading up to the King's Blockhouse, a defensive position built by the British between 1795 and 1803. From here it's possible to follow the contour path above Newlands Forest to Skeleton Gorge and down to Kirstenbosch.

The exit for the memorial is at the Princess Anne Interchange on the M3.

IRMA STERN MUSEUM — MUSEUM

Map p286 (☎021-685 5686; www.irmastern.co.za; Cecil Rd, Rosebank; adult/child R10/5; ⏲10am-5pm Tue-Sat; Rosebank) The pioneering 20th-century artist Irma Stern (1894–1966), whose works are some of the most sought-after among modern South African painters, lived here for almost 40 years, and her studio has been left virtually intact, as if she'd just stepped out into the verdant garden for a breath of fresh air. Her ethnographic art-and-craft collection from around the world is as fascinating as her art, which was influenced by German expressionism and incorporates traditional African elements.

WYNBERG VILLAGE — VILLAGE

Map p288 (around Durban Rd, Wynberg; Wynberg) Declared an urban conservation area in 1981, Wynberg Village is also known as Little Chelsea or Chelsea Village, a nickname it gained in the 1950s in reference to London's Chelsea. Like that British artsy quarter, the village's Cape Georgian buildings (the densest collection in South Africa) house the homes and shops of artists, designers and interior decorators.

Midway between Cape Town and Simon's Town, this charming village of thatched-roof cottages was developed mainly in the 19th century as a garrison for the British army, but there are also older buildings here; it's best explored on a walking tour (p130).

TABLE MOUNTAIN RESERVOIRS

On the area of Table Mountain known as the Back Table are five dams and reservoirs, created in the late 19th and early 20th centuries to provide a secure water supply for the booming population of Cape Town. Work started on the first dam in 1890; the 995-megalitre reservoir, **Woodhead Reservoir** (named after then mayor Sir John Woodhead), was completed in 1897. At the same time the independent municipality of Wynberg began working on a series of dams: **Victoria Reservoir** was completed in 1896, **Alexandra Reservoir** was finished in 1903 and **De Villiers Reservoir** in 1907. In 1904 the city of Cape Town also added the 924-megalitre **Hely-Hutchinson Reservoir**, named after Sir Walter Hely-Hutchinson, the last governor of Cape Colony.

In hikes around the Back Table you can admire the construction skill and detail of these dams and learn something of their history at the **Waterworks Museum** (☎021-686 3408; Back Table, Table Mountain National Park). Call ahead, as this small building at the northern corner of the Hely-Hutchinson Reservoir is often closed. Inside, various bits of machinery used to build the dams are displayed, including the Barclay locomotive made in Scotland in 1898, which was dismantled and reconstructed on top of the mountain. A straightforward way up here is from Constantia Nek, where there's parking, and through the Cecilia Plantation; the route to Hely-Hutchinson dam is around 4km one way.

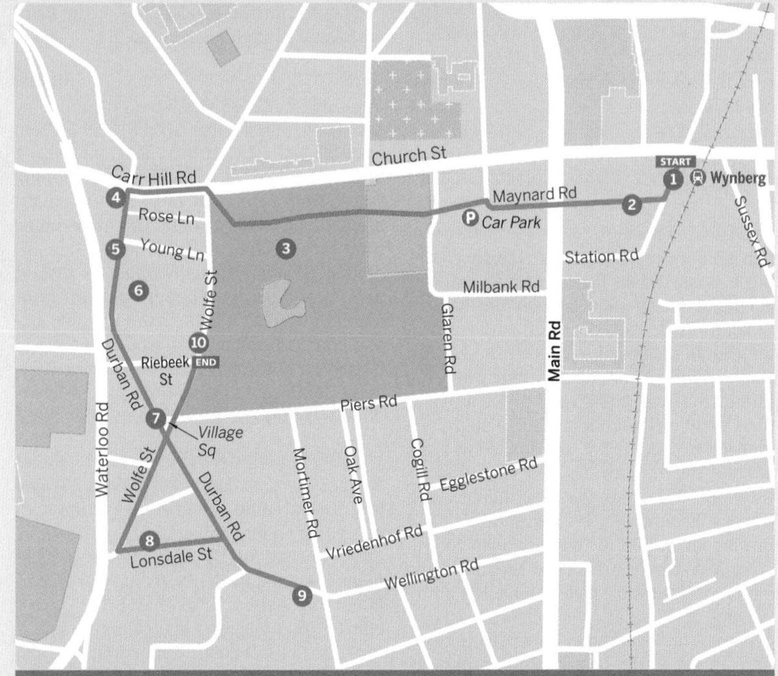

Neighbourhood Walk
Wynberg Village Walk

START WYNBERG STATION
END WOLFE ST
LENGTH 2.5KM; ONE HOUR

This conservation area is packed with Cape Georgian and Victorian buildings, some thatched, and many with lovely flower gardens. The area around 1 **Wynberg Station**, always jammed with taxis and traders, contrasts starkly with the genteel village less than 10 minutes' walk west. Opposite the station is the restored 2 **Town Hall**, designed at the turn of the 19th century by William Black in Flemish revival style.

Cross Main Rd and head down Maynard Rd. Across from the car park (an alternative start/finish point if you're driving) is 3 **Maynardville Park** (p131). Walk through the park, emerging at the junction of Wolfe St and Carr Hill Rd. The neo-Gothic 4 **Dutch Reformed Church**, up the hill at the corner of Durban Rd, dates back to 1831; inside are four granite supporting pillars donated by Cecil Rhodes. Turn left (south) at the church and walk down Durban Rd. Many pretty thatched-roof cottages line this street, including 5 **Winthrop House**, which was once the British army officers' mess, and 6 **Falcon House**, said to be the village's first courthouse.

Where Durban Rd meets Wolfe St is a small square shaded by a pair of oak trees. Around here are interior-design shops; some surround the hidden 7 **Chelsea Courtyard**, a delightful garden. Return to Wolfe St and continue south to Lonsdale St to admire another one located in the 8 **old bakery** (c 1890), with its fish-scale slate turret flanked by griffins.

Turn left (east) into Lonsdale St and continue to Durban Rd. Detour right to peek through the wire fence at the late 18th-century mansion 9 **Tenterden**. The Cape Dutch–revival verandah was added in the 20th century. The Duke of Wellington once slept at the (no longer extant) coach house that was located on the property.

Retrace your steps back along Durban Rd until you reach the village square; 10 **Wolfe St** has shops and places to eat and drink.

MAYNARDVILLE PARK PARK

Map p288 (Wolfe St, Wynberg Village; ⏲8am-6pm; 🚉Wynberg) When the 1870s mansion of Victorian property magnate James Maynard was demolished in the 1950s, the city took over the extensive grounds surrounding it and created this park. The estate's former swimming pool is now a pond, while the archery lawn has been replaced by the Maynardville Open-Air Theatre (p134).

GROOTE SCHUUR HISTORIC BUILDING

Map p286 (☎083 414 7961, 021-686 9100; Klipper Rd, Rondebosch; admission R50; ⏲tours 10am-noon Mon-Fri; 🚉Rondebosch) Advance booking is necessary for the tour around the grandest of Cecil Rhodes' former residences. It was home to a succession of prime ministers, culminating with FW de Klerk. The beautifully restored interior, all teak panels and heavy colonial furniture, and with fine antiques and tapestries, is suitably imposing. The best feature is the colonnaded verandah overlooking the formal gardens, which slope uphill towards an avenue of pine trees and sweeping views of Devil's Peak. Bring your passport to gain entry to this high-security area; the entrance is unmarked but easily spotted on the left as you take the Princess Anne Ave exit off the M3.

TOKAI FOREST FOREST

Map p288 (Tokai Rd, Tokai; adult/child R20/10, car R15; ⏲8am-5pm Apr-Sep, 7am-6pm Oct-Mar; 🅿) This wooded section of Table Mountain National Park, south of Constantia, is a favourite spot for picnics, mountain biking and walks. The most challenging walk is the 6km hike up to **Elephant's Eye Cave**, within the Silvermine section of the park; the zigzag path is fairly steep and offers little shade as you climb higher up Constantiaberg (928m), so bring a hat and water. At the walk's base you'll find the **Tokai Arboretum**, a planting of 1555 different trees representing 274 species, begun in 1885 by Joseph Storr Lister, the conservator of forests for the Cape Colony. Here, too, is the pleasant **Lister's Place Tea Garden** (☎021-715 4512; ⏲9am-5pm Tue-Sun) and the self-catering accommodation Wood Owl Cottage (p208). To reach the forest, take the Tokai exit from the M3 highway and follow the signs.

NEWLANDS BREWERY BREWERY

Map p286 (☎021-658 7440; www.newlandsbrewery.co.za; 3 Main Rd, Newlands; admission R50; ⏲tours 10am, noon & 2pm Mon-Thu, also 6pm Tue & Wed, also 4pm Fri, 10am & 2pm Sat; 🅿; 🚉Newlands) In the early 19th century Jacob Letterstedt built the Mariendahl Brewery in Newlands, a handsome building since granted National Monument status. It's now part of Newlands Brewery and owned by South African Breweries. Fascinating tours of the complex, including the chance to sample the various beers made here (which include Castle and Black Label), will give you an insight into large-scale beer-making.

LOCAL KNOWLEDGE

SWEET SPRING WATERS

In Newlands, just off Kildare Rd, you may be intrigued to see a steady flow of cars pulling into and out of a cul-de-sac. A clue lies in the road's name: Spring Way. At the end of the cul-de-sac flows fresh water that has been piped straight from a spring off Table Mountain. In-the-know Capetonians come to get their drinking water here, as well as at the water spring installed next to the Newlands Brewery. The Khoe-San called the river flowing off of Table Mountain 'Camissa', meaning 'sweet water' – something you can judge for yourself as you fill up your water bottle.

ARDERNE GARDENS GARDENS

Map p286 (www.ardernegardens.org.za; 222 Main Rd, Claremont; ⏲9am-6pm; 🚉Hartfield Rd) FREE Planted by botanist Ralph Arderne in 1845, these shady gardens represent the oldest collection of trees in the southern hemisphere and include bamboo, fir, gum and enormous Moreton Bay fig trees. It's a lovely place to wander around for an afternoon, and is especially colourful on weekends, when many Capetonian wedding parties arrive here to have their photos taken.

MOSTERT'S MILL HISTORIC BUILDING

Map p286 (www.mostertsmill.co.za; Rhodes Ave, Rosebank; 🚉Rosebank) As you're following the M3 from the city, just after the open paddocks on Devil's Peak you'll pass, on the left, a real Dutch windmill dating from around 1796 – the only such working mill south of the Sahara. The thatched cap can rotate to face the wind. Check the website for the few days a year when it's operated.

UNIVERSITY OF CAPE TOWN UNIVERSITY, ARCHITECTURE

Map p286 (UCT; www.uct.ac.za; off Rugby Rd, Rosebank; P; Rosebank) For the non-academic there's no pressing reason to visit the University of Cape Town, but it's nonetheless an impressive place to walk around. UCT presents a fairly cohesive architectural front, with ivy-covered neoclassical facades and a fine set of stone steps leading to the temple-like Jameson Hall. If you approach UCT from Woolsack Dr, you'll pass the **Woolsack**, a cottage designed in 1900 by Sir Herbert Baker for Cecil Rhodes; it's now a student residence. (It's said that Rudyard Kipling wrote the poem 'If' during his residence here between 1900 and 1907.)

EATING

GARDENER'S COTTAGE CAFE $

Map p286 (021-689 3158; Montebello Craft Studios, 31 Newlands Ave, Newlands; mains R45-70; 9.30am-2.30pm Tue-Fri, 8.30am-4.30pm Sat & Sun; Newlands) After exploring the Montebello craft studios, relax at this lovely cafe and tea garden in the grounds. It serves simple, hearty meals in the shade of leafy trees.

O'WAYS TEACAFE VEGETARIAN $

Map p286 (021-617 2850; www.oways.co.za; 20 Dreyer St, Claremont; mains R55-170; 7.30am-5pm Mon-Fri, 9am-2pm Sat; Claremont) Pronounced 'always', this stylish, relaxing place is fully vegetarian, and includes tasty dishes such as dim sum dumplings and portobello mushrooms filled with couscous. It's also one of the best places in Cape Town to come for tea, with 60-odd loose-leaf teas and infusions on offer.

CHART FARM CAFE $

Map p288 (021-762 0067; www.chartfarm.co.za; Klaasens Rd, Wynberg; mains R25-50; 9am-4.30pm; P; Wynberg) Roses, chestnuts, lemons and grapes are among the tasty things grown on this small farm tucked away on the west side of the M3. At the coffee shop, which features a panoramic view across the farm to the mountains, enjoy homemade cakes, breakfasts and lunch treats such as chicken pie. Pick your own roses afterwards for R4 a stem.

KIRSTENBOSCH TEA ROOM INTERNATIONAL $

Map p288 (021-797 4883; www.ktr.co.za; Gate 2, Kirstenbosch Botanical Gardens, Rhodes Dr, Newlands; mains R50-100; 9am-5pm; P; Claremont) Kirstenbosch's best dining option. English tea for two (R210), including cucumber and cream-cheese sandwiches, mini-quiches and homemade scones with strawberry jam and clotted cream, can be ordered to enjoy anywhere you please in the gardens. Picnic lunches are available.

TASHAS BAKERY, INTERNATIONAL $

Map p288 (www.tashascafe.com; Shop 55, Constantia Village, Constantia Main Rd, Constantia; mains R55-80; 7am-6pm; P) Muffins that could feed a small family and other delectable baked goods and desserts are the forte of this luxe-design cafe offering 'easy eating' – a hit Johannesburg concept imported to the Mother City.

BROOKER & WALLER DELI $

Map p286 (087 625 0059; www.brookerwaller.co.za; Shop 1A, Cavendish Pl, Cavendish St, Claremont; salads & sandwiches R30-65; 8am-5pm Mon-Fri, 9am-3pm Sat; Claremont) Nip into this convivial deli with shared tables to pick up epicurean food and drink; the light meals include a selection of salads and pastrami sandwiches.

★**STARLINGS CAFE** INTERNATIONAL $$

Map p286 (021-671 6875; www.starlings.co.za; 94 Belvedere Rd, Claremont; mains R65-100; 7am-4pm Mon-Fri, to 3pm Sat, to 2pm Sun; Claremont) Although it's not at all on the tourist route and a little tricky to spot – hidden as it is behind a big hedge – this cafe is one of the southern suburbs' most charming dining spots. With its relaxed, arty cottage and shady garden environment, it's great for a lazy breakfast or lunch.

★**BISTRO SIXTEEN82** INTERNATIONAL $$

Map p288 (021-713 2211; www.steenberg-vineyards.co.za; Steenberg Vineyard, Tokai; mains R100-185; 9am-8pm; P) Perfectly complementing the slick and contemporary wine-tasting lounge at Steenberg Vineyard is this appealing bistro, serving everything from breakfast with a glass of bubbly to an early supper of tapas with their quaffable merlot. Seating is both indoor and outdoor, with beguiling views of the gardens and mountain.

★**FOUR&TWENTY CAFE & PANTRY** INTERNATIONAL $$

Map p288 (021-761 1000; www.fourandtwentycafe.co.za; 23 Wolfe St, Wynberg Village; mains R65-100; 8am-5pm Tue-Sat; Wynberg) A favourite among the Little Chelsea crowd, this appealing place cooks up delicious food, from fresh salads and sandwiches to inventive dishes such as oxtail stew pie, *imam biyaldi* (caramelised aubergine with an almond crunch) and fish with polenta chips. The courtyard, draped with bougainvillea, is a lovely spot even just for tea and cake.

A TAVOLA ITALIAN **$$**

Map p286 (021-794 3010; www.atavola.co.za; Library Sq, Wilderness Rd, Claremont; mains R90-150; noon-3pm Sun-Fri, 6-10pm Mon-Sat; P; Claremont) This spacious, classy neighbourhood joint, with walls hung with photos of people tucking into food, makes a near-perfect Caesar salad, as well as delicious pasta and other mains. No wonder the people are smiling in those photos.

LA BELLE BAKERY, INTERNATIONAL **$$**

Map p288 (021-795 6336; www.alphen.co.za; Alphen Dr, Constantia; mains R70-160; 7am-7pm; P) In front of the Alphen hotel, this dining spot is appealing both inside and out – for breakfast, lunch or a snack. Treat yourself to a five-star brekkie (R220) or one of the speciality-leaf teas (R25). There's also a branch at Camps Bay (p121).

RHODES MEMORIAL RESTAURANT CAPE MALAY **$$**

Map p286 (021-687 000; www.rhodesmemorial.co.za; Rhodes Memorial, off M3, Groote Schuur Estate, Rondebosch; mains R70-125; 7am-5pm) Behind the memorial is a pleasant restaurant and alfresco tearoom in a 1920 thatched-roof cottage. It's family run and specialises in Cape Malay dishes, such as curries, *bredies* (pot stews of meat or fish and vegetables) and *bobotie* (delicately flavoured ostrich-meat curry with a topping of egg baked to a crust). Bookings are advised on the weekends – especially on Sunday, when there's live jazz from 1pm to 4pm.

JONKERSHUIS CAPE MALAY **$$**

Map p288 (021-794 6255; www.jonkershuisconstantia.co.za; Groot Constantia Rd, Constantia; mains R88-148; 9am-10pm Mon-Sat, to 5pm Sun; P) This casual brasserie-style restaurant in the grounds of Groot Constantia has a pleasant, vine-shaded courtyard and tables looking onto the manor house. Sample Cape Malay dishes (including a tasting plate for R148) or cured meats with a glass or two of the local wines, or satisfy your sweet tooth with the desserts.

GRAZE INTERNATIONAL **$$**

Map p288 (083 655 3332; cnr Kenilworth Rd & 2nd Ave, Harfield Village, Kenilworth; mains R60-125; 7am-9pm Mon-Fri, 8am-9pm Sat & Sun; P; Kenilworth) A handy accompaniment to craft-brew pub Banana Jam across the road is this new venture that zones in on sustainable, nutritional produce with bold flavours, not to mention a living wall of salad leaves. Expect to find free-range chicken and burgers made with beef from cows grazing on biodynamic pastures and the like.

★GREENHOUSE INTERNATIONAL **$$$**

Map p288 (021-794 2137; www.collectionmcgrath.com; The Cellars-Hohenort, 93 Brommerslvei Rd, Constantia; 5-course meal without/with wine R550/870; 7-9.30pm Tue-Sat; P) Chef Peter Tempelhoff's culinary imagination runs riot in this elegant, leafy restaurant, one of the Cape's top dining destinations. The best of local produce, from sustainable kabeljou fish and kroon duck to globe artichokes, may be featured on the five-course menu (which can be vegetarian).

★LA COLOMBE FRENCH **$$$**

Map p288 (021-794 2390; www.lacolombe.co.za; Silvermist, Main Rd, Constantia; lunch mains R135-210, 4/6-course dinner R465/685; 12.30-2.30pm & 7.30-9.30pm; P) There's a new location on the Silvermist estate for this storied restaurant, but little else has changed. Chef Scot Kirton rustles up skilful dishes combining French and Asian techniques and flavours, such as smoked tomato risotto and miso-seared scallops. The elegant setting and personable service couldn't be better.

DRINKING & NIGHTLIFE

★BANANA JAM BEER HALL

Map p288 (www.bananajamcafe.co.za; 157 2nd Ave, Harfield Village, Kenilworth; 11am-11pm Mon-Sat, 5-10pm Sun; ; Kenilworth) Real beer lovers rejoice – this convivial Caribbean restaurant and bar is like manna from heaven, with over 30 beers on tap (including its own brews) and bottled ales from all the top local microbrewers, including Jack Black, Darling Brew and CBC.

★MARTINI BAR COCKTAIL BAR

Map p288 (021-794 2137; www.cellars-hohenort.com; 93 Brommerslvei Rd, Constantia;

⊙11am-11.30pm) Ponder your choice from the 200-strong list of cocktails on the menu (we recommend the Liz McGrath Rose Martini, flavoured with rose petals from the hotel's famous gardens) while admiring the magnificent pink, lemon, burgundy and teal decor of the lounge. Peacocks wander the grounds outside. You can also enjoy afternoon tea here or in the hotel's **Fern Bar**.

★LOCALÉ CAFE, BAR

Map p286 (☎021-685 2155; www.facebook.com/pintxosatlocale; 71 Klipfontein Rd, Little Mowbray; ⊙7am-5pm Mon-Wed, to 10pm Thu & Fri, 8am-midnight Sat & Sun; ; Mowbray) On a shopping strip with a few other decent places to eat is this appealing, shabby-chic cafe-bar decorated with mismatched furniture and even a signed Tretchikoff print. It's a good place for a coffee or a cocktail supplemented by tasty *pintxos* (bite-sized Spanish-style canapes).

★FORRESTER'S ARMS PUB

Map p286 (www.forries.co.za; 52 Newlands Ave, Newlands; ⊙9am-11pm Mon-Thu & Sat, to midnight Fri, to 9pm Sun; ; Newlands) 'Forries' has been around for over a century. This English-style pub offers a convivial atmosphere and a great range of local ales (both large-brewery and craft), good pub meals (including wood-fired pizza), and a very pleasant beer garden with a play area for the kids.

TOAD & JOSEPHINE PUB

Map p286 (☎021-686 1437; www.thetoad.co.za; Boundary Rd, Newlands; ⊙noon-10.30pm; Newlands) Set beside the Liesbeek River, Cape Town's only surviving water mill (built sometime after 1819 by Jacob Lettersted, who went on to become a wealthy brewer and miller) is now part of this pub-restaurant. Watch the giant iron wheel turn as you quaff drinks and nibble on wood-fired pizza on the shaded deck.

BARRISTERS PUB

Map p286 (☎021-674 1792; www.barristersgrill.co.za; cnr Kildare Rd & Main St, Newlands; ⊙11am-11pm Sun-Fri, 9am-midnight Sat; ; Newlands) A locals' favourite watering hole, with a series of cosy rooms hung with an eye-catching assortment of items in ye-olde-country-pub style. It's also an excellent spot for warming pub grub on a chilly night.

CAFFÉ VERDI CAFE, BAR

Map p288 (☎021-762 0849; www.caffe-verdi.co.za; 21 Wolfe St, Wynberg; ⊙9.30am-12.30am Mon-Thu, to 1.30am Fri, to midnight Sat; Wynberg) This handsome cafe-bar, set in a 110-year-old house with a pretty courtyard, is a pleasant place to retire for a drink after exploring Chelsea Village.

TIGER TIGER CLUB

Map p286 (www.tigertiger.co.za; Stadium On Main, 103 Main Road, Claremont; admission R45 Thu, R50 Fri & Sat; ⊙8.30pm-4am Thu-Sat; Claremont) If you're looking for a late-night party and dance spot in the southern suburbs, with a young, up-for-it crowd, then this is the place to head to. Be aware that there's a 'no T-shirt, shorts or sandals' rule on Friday and Saturday night, so dress smart.

☆ ENTERTAINMENT

★BAXTER THEATRE THEATRE

Map p286 (☎021-685 7880; www.baxter.co.za; Main Rd, Rondebosch; tickets from R120; Rosebank) Since the 1970s the Baxter has been the focus of Capetonian theatre. There are three venues – the main theatre, the concert hall and the studio – and between them they cover everything from kids' shows to African dance spectaculars. They have an ongoing relationship with the Royal Shakespeare Company thanks to Capetonian Sir Anthony Sher, who has performed here.

ALMA CAFÉ LIVE MUSIC

Map p286 (☎021-685 7377; www.almacafe.co.za; 20 Alma Rd, Rosebank; cover charge from R100; ⊙8am-4pm Mon-Thu, 6-10pm Wed, 8am-5pm Fri, 8am-1pm Sat & Sun, 6-11pm Sun; Rosebank) This cosy venue, which also serves food and drinks, usually has live music on Wednesday (free) and Sunday (cover charge; bookings necessary). Check the Facebook page for details of upcoming events.

MAYNARDVILLE OPEN-AIR THEATRE THEATRE

Map p288 (☎021-421 7695; www.maynardville.co.za; cnr Church & Wolfe Sts, Wynberg; Wynberg) It wouldn't be summer in Cape Town without a visit to Maynardville's open-air theatre to see some Shakespeare. Bring a blanket, pillow and umbrella, though, as the weather can be dodgy and the seats are none too comfy. At other times of the year, dance, jazz and theatre performances also take place here.

SAHARA PARK NEWLANDS CRICKET
Map p286 (021-657 2043; www.wpca.org.za; 146 Campground Rd, Newlands; tickets R30-250; Newlands) If it weren't for a nearby brewery messing up the view towards the back of Table Mountain, Newlands would be a shoo-in for the title of world's prettiest cricket ground. With room for 25,000, it's used for all international matches. Local team the Nashua Mobile Cape Cobras play here during the season, which runs from September to March.

Under a sponsorship deal its official name is Sahara Park Newlands, but everyone still knows it as Newlands Cricket Ground. Tickets cost around R50 for local matches and up to R200 for internationals. Grab a spot on the grass to soak up the festive atmosphere.

NEWLANDS RUGBY STADIUM RUGBY
Map p286 (021-659 4600; www.wprugby.com; 8 Boundary Rd, Newlands; Newlands) This hallowed ground of South African rugby is home to the **Stormers** (www.thestormers.com). Super-12 games and international matches are played here.

GALILEO OPEN AIR CINEMA CINEMA
Map p288 (www.thegalileo.co.za; Kirstenbosch Botanical Gardens, Rhodes Dr, Newlands; tickets R70, blanket/chair hire R10/20; Wed Nov-Apr; Claremont) Most Wednesday evenings from November to March you can watch a movie outdoors in the gardens (entry is from 6pm; movies start around 7.30pm to 8.15pm, depending on sunset). Check the website for what's showing, but note that screenings will only be cancelled in extreme weather and that you cannot bring your own rugs or chairs.

KENILWORTH RACECOURSE HORSE RACING
Map p288 (021-700 1667; www.itsarush.co.za; Rosemead Ave, Kenilworth; Kenilworth) Racing runs year-round here, but the main event to put down in your diary is the glitzy **J&B Met**, South Africa's equivalent of Ladies Day at Ascot (and often more of a fashion show than a horse race). General admission tickets for it start at R125.

LYRA'S JAZZ
Map p286 (021-685 2871; www.lyras.co.za; Shop 9 & 10, Fountain Centre, cnr Belmont & Main Rds, Rondebosch; 8am-10pm Mon-Sat; Rondebosch) You don't come here so much for the cheap-and-cheerful food (mains R50 to R100) as for the jazz jam session that takes place every Monday night, hosted by local musician Dan Shout.

SHOPPING

★MONTEBELLO ARTS & CRAFTS
Map p286 (www.montebello.co.za; 31 Newlands Ave, Newlands; 9am-5pm Mon-Fri, to 4pm Sat, to 3pm Sun; Newlands) This development project has helped several great craftspeople and designers along the way. In the leafy compound, artists studios are scattered around the central craft shop, where you can buy a great range of gifts, including some made from recycled materials. There's also a plant nursery, the excellent cafe **Gardener's Cottage** and car-washers.

★ART IN THE FOREST CERAMICS
Map p288 (021-794 0291; www.lightfromafrica.com; Cecilia Forest, Constantia Nek, Rhodes Dr, Constantia; 10am-4pm Mon-Sat) Profits from this gallery, hidden away in the Cecilia Forest, go towards supporting the Light From Africa Foundation. But that's not the sole reason for visiting: there's the first-class ceramic art pieces on sale – many created by top Capetonian potters and up-and-coming talents – and the handsome 1950s building, with its panoramic aspect towards Constantia.

★TOKAI FOREST MARKET MARKET
Map p288 (www.tokaiforestmarket.co.za; Chrysalis Academy, Tokai Manor, Tokai Rd, Tokai; parking R5; 9am-2pm Sat;) If you can tear yourself away from the other Saturday markets, this outdoor market with farm-fresh produce and crafts, held in the leafy surrounds of Tokai, is well worth attending. Grab breakfast here and let the little ones run wild in the various activity areas.

★BALU LEGACY BOUTIQUE FASHION
Map p286 (www.balu.co.za; 9 Cavendish Lane, off Cavendish St, Claremont; 9am-5pm Mon-Fri, to 2pm Sat; Claremont) Balu Nivison's designs using original print fabrics are temptingly displayed in this chic boutique in one of the heritage cottages behind Cavendish Square. There's a cafe and juice bar here, too, as well as range of essential oils and body lotions – and a few pieces for men by Balu's son Benjamin.

CAVENDISH SQUARE MALL

Map p286 (021-657 5620; www.cavendish.co.za; Cavendish Square, Dreyer St, Claremont; 9am-7pm Mon-Sat, 10am-5pm Sun; Claremont) The focal point of Claremont's shopping scene, this top-class mall has outlets of many of Cape Town's premier fashion designers, as well as supermarkets, department stores and multiplex cinemas.

KIRSTENBOSCH CRAFT MARKET ARTS & CRAFTS

Map p288 (021-671 5468; cnr Kirstenbosch Dr & Rhodes Ave, Newlands; 9am-5pm last Sun of month; Claremont) Lots to choose from at this large craft market spread across the commons outside Kirstenbosch Botanical Gardens. It's possible to use a credit card to pay for most purchases: payments are made in one of the stone cottages on the site. Proceeds from the market go to the development fund for Kirstenbosch.

HABITS FASHION

Map p286 (021-671 7330; www.habits.co.za; 1 Cavendish Close, Cavendish St, Claremont; 9am-5pm Mon-Fri, to 1.30pm Sat; Claremont) Features women's clothes, made from linen, cotton and silk by Jenny le Roux, that are classical and practical. Bored partners can crash on the sofa, watch TV and sip complimentary drinks.

THE SPACE FASHION

Map p286 (021-674 6643; www.thespace.co.za; L69, Cavendish Square, Dreyer St, Claremont; 9am-7pm Mon-Sat, 10am-5pm Sun; Claremont) Celebrating individual style, this groovy boutique in the bowels of Cavendish Square stocks creative local fashion designs and accessories, as well as fun gift items.

YDE FASHION

Map p286 (021-683 6177; www.yde.co.za; F66, Cavendish Square, Dreyer St, Claremont; 9am-7pm Mon-Sat, 10am-5pm Sun; Claremont) Standing for 'Young Designers Emporium', this place is all a bit of a jumble, but you'll most likely find something reasonably inexpensive to suit among the clothes and accessories, created for both sexes by South African streetwear designers. There are branches at Victoria Wharf (p113) at the Waterfront and at Canal Walk (p157).

CONSTANTIA VILLAGE SHOPPING CENTRE

Map p288 (021-794 5065; www.constantiavillage.co.za; cnr Constantia Main & Spaanschemat River Rds, Constantia; 9am-6pm Mon-Fri, to 5pm Sat, to 2pm Sun) The area's main shopping hub covers all the basics and more with a couple of major supermarkets and many other stores, including music and bookshops and fashion retailers.

ACCESS PARK OUTLET SHOPS

Map p288 (www.accesspark.co.za; 81 Chichester Rd, Kenilworth; 9am-5pm Mon-Fri, to 3pm Sat, 10am-2pm Sun; Kenilworth) Bargain hunters converge on the scores of outlet and factory shops here, which sell everything from Adidas runners to computers and luggage.

SPORTS & ACTIVITIES

SA FOREST ADVENTURES ADVENTURE SPORTS

Map p288 (083 517 3635; www.saforestadventures.co.za; Silvermist Mountain Lodge & Wine Estate, Main Rd, Constantia; per person R480; 9am-4pm Aug-Apr, to 3pm May-Jul) Zigzagging across a ravine on the Silvermist wine estate is one of the longest ziplines in South Africa, made up of seven sections. There's little shade on the rocky hillside but the views are great – once you catch your breath after whizzing down the line, that is. From the estate entrance follow the signs to the Silvermist Eatery for the zipline entrance.

SPORTS SCIENCE INSTITUTE OF SOUTH AFRICA GYM, SWIMMING

Map p286 (021-659 5600; www.ssisa.com; Boundary Rd, Newlands; per day R90; 5.30am-9pm Mon-Fri, 6.30am-7pm Sat, 8am-12.30pm & 4-7pm Sun; ; Newlands) Many of the country's top professional athletes train here. Amenities include a 25m pool, an indoor running track and children's daycare. Day visitors are welcome. It's sandwiched between the Newlands cricket and rugby stadiums.

KENILWORTH RACECOURSE CONSERVATION AREA WALKING

Map p288 (021-700 1843; www.krca.co.za; Kenilworth Race Course, Rosemead Ave, Kenilworth; Kenilworth) In the centre of Kenilworth Racecourse are 5200 sq metres of protected Cape Flats sand *fynbos*, where nature walks and other events are sometimes organised. See the website for details.

Simon's Town & Southern Peninsula

MUIZENBERG | KALK BAY | SIMON'S TOWN | KOMMETJIE | NOORDHOEK

Neighbourhood Top Five

❶ Hike, cycle or just laze on a serene beach at the **Cape of Good Hope** (p139), a nature reserve covering the rugged tip of the peninsula.

❷ Snap photos of the colony of African penguins waddling around **Boulders** (p144).

❸ Go shopping in **Kalk Bay** (p149) and enjoy a bite or a drink overlooking its harbour.

❹ Learn to surf off **Muizenberg Beach** (p141), which is lined with brightly coloured bathing chalets.

❺ Explore caves and walk around the reservoir in Table Mountain National Park's **Silvermine Nature Reserve** (p141).

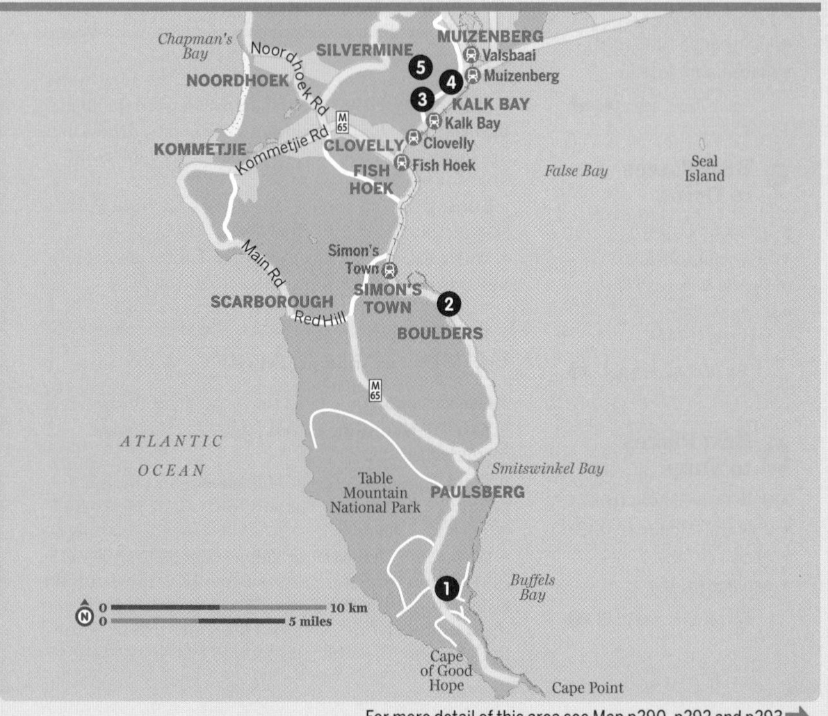

For more detail of this area see Map p290, p292 and p293

Lonely Planet's Top Tip

From late May to early December, False Bay is a favourite haunt of whales and their calves, with October and November the peak viewing season. Southern right, humpback and bryde (*bree*-dah) whales are the most commonly sighted. Good viewing spots include the coastal walk from Muizenberg to St James (p142), the Brass Bell pub (p147) at Kalk Bay, and Jager's Walk (p150) at Fish Hoek. You can also take whale-watching cruises with Simon's Town Boat Company (p150).

Best Places to Eat

- Olympia Café & Deli (p146)
- Flagship (p147)
- Foodbarn (p147)
- Lighthouse Cafe (p147)
- Casa Labia (p146)

For reviews, see p145.

Best Places to Drink

- Brass Bell (p147)
- Slow Life (p147)
- Tiger's Milk (p147)
- Cape Point Vineyards (p148)

For reviews, see p147.

Best Places to Shop

- Blue Bird Garage (p148)
- Kalk Bay Modern (p148)
- Sobeit (p148)
- Artvark (p148)

For reviews, see p148.

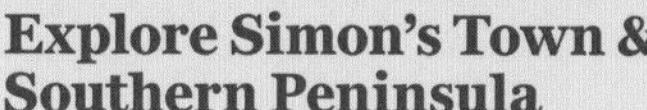

Explore Simon's Town & Southern Peninsula

The Cape's deep south is practically a world unto itself, far-flung from the big-city bustle of the northern end of town. You'll be amply rewarded for taking a few days to explore the area's sights, the principal of which is the magnificent Cape of Good Hope (Cape Point).

Other places to see include the regenerating seaside suburb of Muizenberg, home to the gorgeous Casa Labia; Kalk Bay, packed with antique and craft shops, good cafes and a lively daily fish market; the naval base of Simon's Town, where pleasure boats depart for thrilling cruises to Cape Point; and Boulders, home to the famous colony of African penguins.

On the Atlantic Ocean (western) side of the peninsula, life is even quieter at Noordhoek, famous for its wide, sandy beach, and the surfing mecca of Kommetjie (pronounced *com*-ma-key; also known as just 'Kom'), a quiet and isolated fishing village beside the cast-iron Slangkop Lighthouse. Scarborough is the last coastal community before you round the peninsula to the entry to Cape Point. The beaches on the False Bay (eastern) side of the coast are not quite as spectacular as those on the Atlantic side, but the water is often 5°C or more warmer, and can reach 20°C in summer, making swimming far more pleasant here.

Local Life

- **Markets** Much of Muizenberg decamps to the Blue Bird Garage (p148) on Friday night for eats, drinks and live music; the Thursday-night market at Cape Point Vineyards is also a hit.
- **Surfing** Suit up and join the surfies catching waves at Kommetjie (p144) and Muizenberg (p141).
- **Music** Check for concerts at Casa Labia (p145), Slow Life (p147) and Alive Cafe (p148) in Muizenberg.

Getting There & Away

- **Car** Essential for getting the most out of the region.
- **Taxi** Try **Noordhoek Taxis** (☎021-234 7021; www.noordhoektaxis.co.za).
- **Train** There are stops at Muizenberg and Kalk Bay before the terminus at Simon's Town. Cape Metro Rail offers a R30 day ticket.
- **Water taxi** Take **Mellow Yellow** (Map p292; ☎073-473 7684; www.watertaxi.co.za; single/return R100/150) between Kalk Bay and Simon's Town. (We recommend taking the train to Simon's Town and the water taxi back to Kalk Bay, not the other way around.)

MICHAEL JUNG/GETTY IMAGES ©

TOP SIGHT
CAPE OF GOOD HOPE

Commonly called Cape Point, this 77.5-sq-km section of Table Mountain National Park includes awesome scenery, fantastic walks and often deserted beaches. Some 250 species of birds live here, including cormorants and a family of ostriches that hang out near the Cape of Good Hope, the southwesternmost point of the continent.

Flying Dutchman Funicular

It's not a hard walk uphill, but if you're feeling lazy the **Flying Dutchman Funicular** (Map p293; www.capepoint.co.za; one way/return adult R42/52, child R17/22; ⏲9am-5.30pm) runs up from beside the restaurant to the souvenir kiosk next to the old lighthouse. Dating from 1860, this lighthouse was built too high up (238m above sea level) so was often obscured by mist and fog. (The new lighthouse built at Dias Point in 1919 is 87m above the water.)

Beaches

There are some excellent beaches here, which you may even have to yourself (but take care if you go swimming – there are no lifeguards). The best ones are **Platboom Beach** and **Buffels Bay** (which has a large rockpool for safe swimming). **Maclear Beach**, near the main car park, is good for walks or diving but is too rocky for enjoyable swimming. Further towards Cape Point is the beautiful **Diaz Beach**. Access is on foot from the car park.

Fauna & Flora

It's rare to spot the bonteboks, elands and zebras that live in the reserve; more commonly you'll see dassies and baboons.

DON'T MISS

- Cape of Good Hope
- Cape Point lighthouses
- Cape of Good Hope and Hoerikwaggo Trails
- Buffels Beach
- Platboom Beach

PRACTICALITIES

- Map p293
- www.tmnp.co.za
- adult/child R110/55
- ⏲6am-6pm Oct-Mar, 7am-5pm Apr-Sep
- P

TOURS

Numerous tour companies run day trips to the reserve, which pause at the **Buffelsfontein Visitor Centre** (Map p293; ☎021-780 9204; Cape of Good Hope; ⏰9am-4pm Mon-Thu, to 3pm Fri), allowing you just enough time to walk to Cape Point, grab lunch and get your picture snapped at the Cape of Good Hope on the way back.

Portuguese navigator Bartholomeu Dias coined the name Cabo da Boa Esperança (Cape of Good Hope); a cross carved into the rock near here is believed to indicate the spot where Dias stepped onto the Cape in 1488.

EATING & SLEEPING

Forgot the picnic? Snacks can be bought at the Buffelsfontein Visitor Centre or a shop next to the funicular, where you'll also find the Two Oceans Restaurant, which is set up to deal with tour-bus crowds but has terrific terrace views. Camping is not allowed, but there are three self-catering cottages – Olifantsbos (p210), Eland and Duike – that can be rented, as can the Smitswinkel Tented Camp (p208), just outside Cape Point's main entrance gate.

Heed the signs warning to *not* feed the baboons. After years of interacting with tourists, these monkeys have learned to grab food straight from your hands or climb in the open windows of your car to get it. *Never* challenge them, as they will turn aggressive. The damage inflicted might end up being far more serious than baboon poop on your car seats.

Trees are scarce in the windswept reserve, which is blanketed in *fynbos* (literally 'fine bush', primarily proteas, heaths and ericas). It's particularly beautiful in spring, when wildflowers are in bloom.

Hiking & Cycling

The best way to explore the reserve is on foot or by bike – several tour companies include biking in their itineraries, including Awol (p25), Day Trippers (p26) and Downhill Adventures (p103). A basic map is provided with your ticket at the entrance gate. Serious hikers should pick up the more detailed Slingsby Maps. Bear in mind that the weather can change quickly here.

Cape of Good Hope Trail

Bookings are required for the two-day, one-night Cape of Good Hope Trail (R210, not including the reserve's entry fee), which traces a spectacular 33.8km circular route through the reserve. Highlights along the way include spotting many species of proteas and other *fynbos* and enjoying sweeping vistas on the section between Paulsberg and Judas Peak on the False Bay side of the trail.

Accommodation is at the basic Erica, Protea and Restio huts on the north side of De Gama Peak. The huts' elevated position allows you to see both sunset and sunrise. The dormitory sleeps six in bunk beds; you'll need your own sleeping bag. Cutlery and crockery are provided and there's a hot shower. Contact the Buffelsfontein Visitor Centre in the park.

Other Trails

The reserve is the start (or finish) of the 75km **Hoerikwaggo Trail**. The 15km section of the trail here begins at the Cape Point Lighthouse and runs down the False Bay coast to Smitswinkel Bay; there are some steep sections but from late August to October you may be rewarded with sightings of whales in the bay.

A trail runs from the Cape of Good Hope up to the Cape Point Lighthouse via Diaz Beach. There's also a 3.5km walk from Buffels Bay to the spectacular Paulsberg peak.

The easiest walk is the 1km trail linking the old and new lighthouses. It takes less than 30 minutes walking along a spectacular ridgeway path to look down on the new lighthouse and the sheer ocean cliffs.

SIGHTS

Muizenberg, Kalk Bay & Around

Muizenberg was established by the Dutch in 1743 as a staging post for horse-drawn traffic. Its heyday was the early 20th century, when it was a major seaside resort. Kalk Bay is named after the lime (*'kalk'* in Afrikaans) used for painting buildings in the 17th century, which was produced by burning seashells in kilns. During apartheid it was neglected by government and business as it was mainly a coloured area. Around False Bay, south of Kalk Bay, the communities of Fish Hoek and Clovelly have wide beaches that are safe for swimming.

CASA LABIA CULTURAL CENTRE — ARTS CENTRE

Map p290 (021-788 6068; www.casalabia.co.za; 192 Main Rd, Muizenberg; 10am-4pm Tue-Sun; Muizenberg) FREE This magnificent seaside villa built in 1930 was once the palatial home of Italian ambassador Count Natale Labia and his South African wife. It now hosts a program of concerts, lectures and events, as well as housing works from the Labia family's art collection (including paintings by Irma Stern and Gerald Sekoto) and regularly changing contemporary art exhibitions. The building also houses an excellent cafe (p145) and the top-class arts and crafts shop **CasBah**. The grand building – designed by Capetonian architect Fred Glennie and furnished by a Venetian interior designer with antique fixtures and fittings – doubled as the embassy residency and legation for several decades. After a varied history, the rights to oversee the building were handed back to the Labias' son in 2008. It has since undergone a loving restoration.

MUIZENBERG BEACH — BEACH

Map p290 (Beach Rd, Muizenberg; P; Muizenberg) Popular with families, this surf beach is famous for its row of colourfully painted Victorian bathing chalets. Surfboards can be hired and lessons booked at several shops along Beach Rd; lockers are available in the pavilions on the promenade. The beach shelves gently and the sea is generally safer here than elsewhere along the peninsula. At the eastern end of the promenade is a fun **water slide** (1hr/day

TOP SIGHT
SILVERMINE NATURE RESERVE

Off the main tourist trail, but still a spectacular section of Table Mountain National Park, Silvermine can be accessed from the cross-peninsular road Ou Kaapse Weg, as well as via hiking trails from Boyes Dr. It's named for the fruitless attempts by the Dutch to prospect for silver in this area from 1675 to 1685. The park is popular with locals, who come here for hiking, mountain biking, rock climbing and caving.

The focal point is the **Silvermine Reservoir**, built in 1898. It's a beautiful spot for a picnic or a leisurely 20-minute walk on a wheelchair-accessible boardwalk. Locals often swim in the tannin-stained waters of the reservoir. The **Silvermine River Walk** (45 minutes one-way) from the main car park is also worthwhile.

On the southeastern edge of the reserve is **Peers Cave**: a trail leads here from a marked parking spot on the Ou Kaapse Weg. The cave is named after Victor Peers, who, with his son Bertie, started excavating the site in 1927. They collected evidence of the habitation of the Khoe-San dating as far back as 10,000 years, including a skull – it's thought this was an ancient burial site. Declared a National Monument in 1941, the cave provides a dramatic viewpoint towards Noordhoek and the sea.

DON'T MISS

- Silvermine Reservoir
- Silvermine River Walk
- Peers Cave

PRACTICALITIES

- Map p290
- 021-715 0011
- www.tmnp.co.za
- Ou Kaapse Weg
- adult/child R10/5
- 7am-6pm Oct-Mar, 8am-5pm Apr-Sep

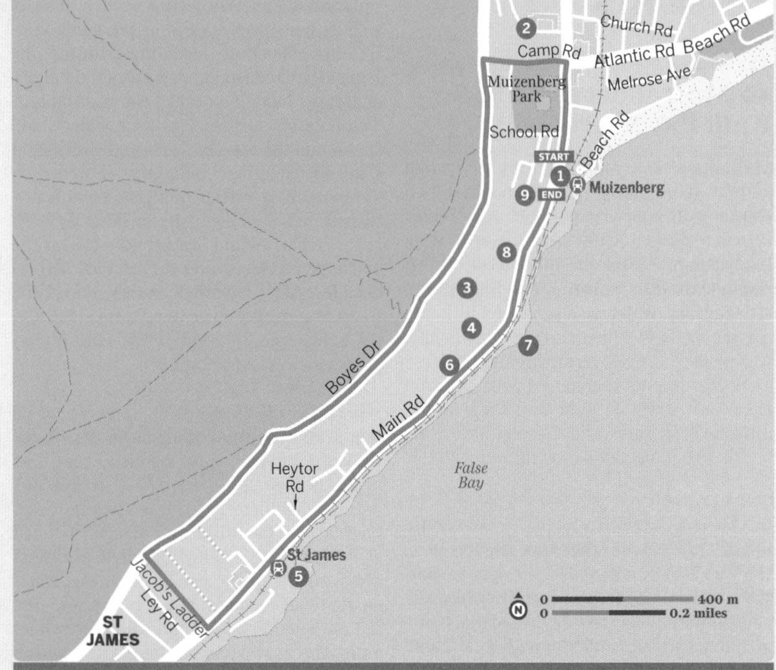

Neighbourhood Walk
Muizenberg–St James Walk

START MUIZENBERG STATION
END MUIZENBERG STATION
LENGTH 3KM; ONE HOUR

This invigorating coastal walk provides spectacular views of False Bay and gives you a sense of the history and once grand nature of this seaside suburb.

From ❶ **Muizenberg Station**, head north past Muizenberg Park to Camp Rd, past the red-and-white-painted ❷ **synagogue**, which dates from the 1920s, when Muizenberg had a large Jewish community. Concrete steps lead up to Boyes Dr, from where there's a commanding view across Muizenberg and its broad, flat beach.

A wrought-iron gate on the left side has steps leading down to the ❸ **grave of Sir Abe Bailey** (1864–1940): 'soldier, former sportsman, philanthropist, mining pioneer'. You should also be able to glimpse Bailey's house, ❹ **Rust-en-Vrede**, with its red tiles and high gables, on Main Rd below. Rust-en-Vrede was commissioned by Cecil Rhodes (p60), but he never lived in it.

Keep walking along Boyes Dr until you reach the Jacob's Ladder steps leading down towards ❺ **St James Station**. Next to the station are a set of brightly painted Victorian-style bathing huts, which this area is best known for, and a tidal rock pool – ideal for a cooling dip. A coastal walking path starts here and heads back towards Muizenberg.

As you approach a grand, Spanish-style mansion with green-glazed roof tiles (called 'Gracelands', after Elvis' pad), you'll see another underpass that lets you nip across to busy Main Rd to visit ❻ **Rhodes Cottage**, where Rhodes passed away in 1902.

Back on the coastal path, on the right side, is ❼ **Bailey's Cottage**, built in 1909 and another of Bailey's residences. Closer to Muizenberg, on Main Rd, is ❽ **Casa Labia** (p141), which belongs to the family of an Italian count who built the property in 1930.

Further along is the whitewashed ❾ **Posthuys**. Built in the 1670s, this one-time lookout post for ships entering False Bay is one of Cape Town's oldest European-style buildings. It's a minute's walk from here back to Muizenberg Station.

pass R40/80; ⏲1.30-5.30pm Mon-Fri, 9.30am-5.30pm Sat & Sun).

KALK BAY HARBOUR HARBOUR

Map p290 (Essex Rd, Kalk Bay; ⏲fish market 9am-5pm; P; 🚆Kalk Bay) This picturesque harbour is best visited in the morning, when the fishing boats pitch up with their daily catch and a lively quayside market ensues. This is an excellent place to buy fresh fish for a braai (barbecue), or to spot whales during the whale-watching season. Nearby, next to Kalk Bay station and the Brass Bell pub, are a couple of tidal swimming pools.

RONDEVLEI NATURE RESERVE WILDLIFE RESERVE

(☎021-706 2404; Fisherman's Walk Rd, Zeekoevlei; adult/child R12/6; ⏲7.30am-5pm daily year-round, 7.30am-7pm Sat & Sun Dec-Feb; P; 🚆Retreat) Hippos hadn't lived in the marshes of this small, picturesque nature reserve for 300 years until they were re-introduced in 1981. There are eight hippos, but they're shy and you're unlikely to spot them unless you stay overnight (R1050 for up to four people, self-catering). For details contact **Imvubu Nature Tours** (☎082 847 4916, 021-706 0842; www.imvubu.co.za), which also runs one-hour guided walks (R400 per person, minimum six people), on which you can spot some 200 species of birds from the waterside trail, viewing towers and hides.

RHODES COTTAGE MUSEUM MUSEUM

Map p290 (☎021-788 1816; 246 Main Rd, Muizenberg; admission by donation; ⏲10am-1pm Wed, Fri & Sat, to 4pm Tue; 🚆Muizenberg) Staffed by dedicated volunteer guides from the Muizenberg Historical Conservation Society, this thatched-roof cottage, designed by Sir Herbert Baker, is now an engaging museum where you can learn all about Cecil Rhodes (p60), who died in the front bedroom in 1902. The cottage has pleasant mountainside gardens, which are a lovely place to rest and spot whales during the season.

SAVE OUR SEAS SHARK CENTRE MUSEUM

Map p290 (☎021-788 6694; www.saveourseas.com; 28 Main Rd, Kalk Bay; 🚆Kalk Bay) Closed for renovations at the time of research, so call ahead to see if this education centre, which encourages awareness, protection, conservation and the sustainable fishing of sharks worldwide, has reopened. You can also find out about the pioneering **Shark Spotters** (www.sharkspotters.org.za) program, which monitors key beaches and raises the alarm if sharks are spotted swimming near them.

LOCAL KNOWLEDGE

AVOIDING TRAFFIC & CROWDS

Main Rd is the coastal thoroughfare linking Muizenberg with Fish Hoek, although a prettier (and often less congested) alternative route between Muizenberg and Kalk Bay is the mountainside Boyes Dr, which provides fantastic views down the peninsula.

If you can spare only a day for the southern peninsula, one strategy for beating the crowds is to head down the Atlantic Coast via Chapman's Peak Dr, then follow Main Rd/M65 to the entrance to Cape Point. Start early and you'll arrive at the tip of the Cape before the bulk of the tourist buses, which tend to stop off at Boulders first (you can hit this on the way back instead).

Simon's Town & Rest of Southern Peninsula

On the False Bay side of the peninsula, Simon's Town is named after Governor Simon van der Stel. The winter anchorage for the Dutch East India Company (Vereenigde Oost-Indische Compagnie; VOC) from 1741, and a naval base for the British since 1814, it remains a naval town.

CAPE OF GOOD HOPE OUTDOORS

See p139.

NOORDHOEK BEACH BEACH

(access from Beach Rd, Noordhoek) This magnificent 5km stretch of beach is favoured by surfers and horse riders. It tends to be windy, and dangerous for swimmers. The Hoek, as it is known to surfers, is an excellent right beach break at the northern end that can hold large waves (only at low tide); it's best with a southeasterly wind. In the middle of the beach, the rusted shell of the steamship *Kakapo* sticks out of the sand like a weird sculpture. It ran aground here in 1900, on its maiden voyage from Britain to Australia.

SIMON'S TOWN MUSEUM MUSEUM

Map p292 (☎021-786 3046; www.simonstown.com/museum/stm_main.htm; Court Rd, Simon's Town; adult/child R10/5; ⏲10am-4pm Mon-Fri, to 1pm Sat; P; Simon's Town) Housed in the old governor's residence (1777), the exhibits in this rambling museum trace Simon's Town's history. Included is a display on Just Nuisance, the Great Dane that was adopted as a navy mascot in WWII – whose grave, above town off Red Hill Rd, makes for a long, pleasant (but uphill) walk from the harbour, with good views.

JUST NUISANCE STATUE STATUE

Map p292 (Jubilee S, Simon's Town; P; Simon's Town) Immortalised in bronze in 1985 by artist Jean Doyle, this famous local mascot lived from 1937 to 1944 and is fondly remembered for befriending naval sailors during WWII. His statue overlooks the marina. There are also craft stalls on the square, which hosts a market every second Saturday from 9.30am to 2.30pm.

HERITAGE MUSEUM MUSEUM

Map p292 (www.simonstown.com/museum/sthm.htm; Almay House, King George Way, Simon's Town; admission R10; 11am-4pm Tue-Thu & Sun; P; Simon's Town) Simon's Town had a 7000-strong community of people of colour before apartheid forcibly removed most of them, mainly to the suburb of Ocean's View, across on the Atlantic side of the peninsula. This small but interesting museum, with a lovely front garden, is dedicated to the evictees and based in Almay House (1858). It's curated by Zainab Davidson, whose family was kicked out in 1975.

IMHOFF FARM FARM

(021-783 4545; www.imhofffarm.co.za; Kommetjie Rd, Kommetjie; P) FREE There's plenty to see and do at this attractive historic farmstead just outside Kommetjie. Among the attractions are craft shops and studios; the good Blue Water Café (p147); a **snake and reptile park** (adult child R35/30; 9am-5pm Mon-Fri); the **Higgeldy Piggeldy Farmyard** (admission R20, cup of feed R5; 9am-5pm), stocked with animals; **camel rides** (082 344 3163; adult/child R50/30; noon-4pm Tue-Sun); and a **shop** (9am-5pm) selling tasty cheeses (made on site) and other provisions.

KOMMETJIE BEACHES BEACH

(access off Kommetjie Rd, Kommetjie; P) A top surfing location, Kommetjie offers an assortment of reefs that hold a very big swell. Outer Kommetjie is a left point out from Slangkop Lighthouse, at the southern end

TOP SIGHT
BOULDERS PENGUIN COLONY

Some 3km southeast of Simon's Town is Boulders, a picturesque area with enormous boulders dividing small, sandy coves that a colony of 2100 delightful African penguins calls home. A boardwalk runs from the Boulders Visitor Centre at the Foxy Beach end of the protected area (another part of Table Mountain National Park) to Boulders Beach, where you can get down on the sand and mingle with the waddling penguins. Don't, however, be tempted to pet them: the penguins have sharp beaks that can cause serious injuries.

The bulk of the colony, which has grown from just two breeding pairs in 1982, seems to prefer hanging out at Foxy Beach, where like nonchalant, stunted supermodels they blithely ignore the armies of camera-touting tourists snapping away from the viewing platform.

The aquatic birds, which are an endangered species, were formerly called jackass penguins on account of their donkey-like braying – you'll have a chance to hear it if you turn up during the main breeding season, which peaks from March to May. Parking is available at either end of the reservation, on Seaforth Rd and on Bellevue Rd, where you'll also find accommodation and places to eat.

DON'T MISS

- Penguins
- Boulders Beach

PRACTICALITIES

- Map p292
- www.tmnp.co.za
- Simon's Town
- adult/child R60/30
- 8am-5pm Apr-Sep, to 6.30pm Feb-Mar & Oct-Nov, 7am-7.30pm Dec & Jan
- P
- Simon's Town

of the village. Inner Kommetjie is a more protected, smaller left, with lots of kelp (only at high tide). They both work best with a southeasterly or southwesterly wind. For breezy beach walks, it doesn't get much better than the aptly named Long Beach, accessed off Benning Dr.

CAPE POINT OSTRICH FARM FARM
Map p293 (021-780 9294; www.capepointostrichfarm.com; Sun Valley; tours adult/child R55/25; 9.30am-5.30pm; P) There's ostriches aplenty at this family-run farm, restaurant and tourist complex just 600m from Cape Point's main gate. Tours of the breeding facilities are conducted at regular intervals. The well-stocked shop is notable if for nothing else than the myriad artistic ways that ostrich eggs, skins and feathers can be turned into decorative objects.

SAS ASSEGAAI MUSEUM
Map p292 (021-786 5243; www.navy.mil.za/museum_submarine; Naval Dockyard, Simon's Town; adult/child R50/25; 10am-3.30pm Dec-Jun, to 2.30pm Jul-Nov; Simon's Town) Call ahead to book a tour out to this Daphne-class, French-built submarine, which served the navy from 1971 to 2003. Groups of up to 12 are guided through the floating vessel and given an explanation of what life onboard was like. The pick-up point for the bus into the Naval Dockyard is Jubilee Sq.

SOUTH AFRICAN NAVAL MUSEUM MUSEUM
Map p292 (021-787 4686; www.simonstown.com/navalmuseum; St George's St, Simon's Town; 9.30am-3.30pm; Simon's Town) FREE Principally for naval enthusiasts, this museum nonetheless has plenty of interesting exhibits, including model ships and submarines, uniforms and a life-sized ship's bridge. The museum occupies the buildings of the original Dockyard Magazine (storehouse), built in the mid-18th century.

EATING

Muizenberg & Kalk Bay

C'EST LA VIE BAKERY, FRENCH $
Map p290 (20 Main Rd, Kalk Bay; mains R50; 7am-3pm Wed-Sun; Kalk Bay) Serving coffee that everyone in Kalk Bay raves about, this compact, French-style artisan bakery and cafe is a good spot for breakfast and light lunches. Also serves freshly squeezed juices.

> LOCAL KNOWLEDGE
>
> **STEAM TRAIN TO SIMON'S TOWN**
>
> Book well ahead for the very popular day trips offered by vintage steam train operator **Atlantic Rail** (021-556 1012; www.atlanticrail.co.za; adult/child R250/150; office 9am-3pm Mon-Fri;), usually on Sundays, from Cape Town to Simon's Town. The wooden-bodied coaches dating from the 1920s and '30s are pulled by a Class 24 steam locomotive built in 1949. One of the coaches is a lounge bar. With prior arrangement, drop-offs and pick-ups in Kalk Bay are also possible.

EMPIRE CAFÉ INTERNATIONAL $
Map p290 (021-788 1250; www.empirecafe.co.za; 11 York Rd, Muizenberg; mains R50-95; 7am-4pm Mon-Tue & Thu-Sat, to 9pm Wed, 8am-4pm Sun; ; Muizenberg) The local surfers' favourite hang-out is a great place for a hearty eggs-on-toast type of breakfast or lunch. Local art exhibitions enliven the walls and a dramatic chandelier dangles from the ceiling. On Wednesday it stays open later and serves gourmet burgers (R70).

KNEAD BAKERY, INTERNATIONAL $
Map p290 (021-788 2909; www.kneadbakery.co.za; Surfer's Corner, Beach Rd, Muizenberg; mains R30-70; 8am-6pm Sun & Mon, to 8pm Tue-Sat; Muizenberg) Breads, brioches, bagels, pastries, pies and pizzas – if it involves dough, it's here. Chandelier and mirrored tiles add glamour to this popular venue.

BOB'S BAGEL CAFE BAKERY $
Map p290 (083 280 0012; 6 Rouxville Rd, Kalk Bay; bagels from R20; 7.45am-1pm Mon-Fri, 8.15am-2pm Sat & Sun; ; Kalk Bay) Sharing premises with a pottery shop, Bob's is the place for your bagel fix. They're freshly baked here and you can have them au naturel, or as sandwiches, along with good coffee and other baked nibbles and organic ice creams. Streetside benches provide a good view of the small children's park opposite.

★CASA LABIA INTERNATIONAL $$
Map p290 (021-788 6068; www.casalabia.co.za; 192 Main Rd, Muizenberg; mains R70-145;

SUNPATHS OF THE CAPE

In his research into the Khoe-San and the even older peoples who lived on the Cape, Dean Liprini, an archaeoastronomer, has developed an astonishing theory. He believes that the Cape is crisscrossed by a grid of sight lines and key points comprising caves, sound chambers, geometrical marker stones, and sun and moon shrines, some in the uncanny shape of giant human faces. Sunrise and sunset are exactly aligned with these points at the summer and winter solstices and the spring and autumn equinoxes, thus indicating that they formed a way for the ancient people to measure the passing of the year and record auspicious dates.

As wacky as it may sound, there may be something in Liprini's theory, as you'll discover if you go for a hike in the hills of the southern peninsula with him or one of his colleagues. Observed from certain angles, unmistakable profiles of faces appear in the rocks, some with 'eye' holes that catch the light. One such rock is a granite boulder on Lion's Head, while another is the Pyramid All-Seeing Eye, just off the M6 between Glencairn and Sunnydale. There's also what Liprini calls the Cave of Ascension, above the ancient burial site of Peers Cave (p141). To find out more about the sunpaths and see when walks are scheduled, check the website www.sunpath.co.za.

⌚10am-4pm Tue-Thu, 9am-4pm Fri-Sun; 🖉; 🚉Muizenberg) Some ingredients at this pleasant cafe in the gorgeously decorated arts and cultural centre (p141) come from the adjoining garden. There are plans to make wine and olive oil from the vines and olive trees that grow on the slopes, too. Enjoy home-baked treats and delicious breakfasts, open sandwiches and plenty of veg options.

★OLYMPIA CAFÉ & DELI BAKERY, INTERNATIONAL $$

Map p290 (☎021-788 6396; www.facebook.com/OlympiaCafeKalkBay; 134 Main Rd, Kalk Bay; mains R60-100; ⌚7am-9pm; 🚉Kalk Bay) Setting a high standard for relaxed rustic cafes by the sea, Olympia bakes its own breads and pastries. It's great for breakfast, and its Mediterranean-influenced lunch dishes are delicious, too – particularly the heaped bowls of mussels.

LIVE BAIT SEAFOOD $$

Map p290 (☎021-788 5755; www.harbourhousegroup.co.za/livebait; Kalk Bay harbour, Kalk Bay; mains R75-200; ⌚noon-4pm & 6-10pm; 🅿; 🚉Kalk Bay) Sit within arm's reach of the crashing waves and the bustle of Kalk Bay harbour at this breezy, Greek island–style fish restaurant; it's one of the best options around for a relaxed seafood meal. The same company runs the fancy Harbour House restaurant upstairs, and the cheap-as-chips Lucky Fish take-away next door.

ANNEX INTERNATIONAL $$

Map p290 (☎021-788 2453; www.theannex.co.za; 124 Main Rd, Kalk Bay; mains R70-110; ⌚8am-9pm; 📶; 🚉Kalk Bay) A great option for all-day-dining, offering a tempting menu running from French toast, croissants, bacon and maple syrup to quiches, salads and more substantial mains.

Simon's Town & Rest of Southern Peninsula

SOPHEA GALLERY & TIBETAN TEAHOUSE VEGETARIAN $

Map p292 (www.sopheagallery.com; 2 Harrington Rd, Seaforth; mains R30-65; ⌚10am-5pm Tue-Sun; 🖉; 🚉Simon's Town) Tasty vegetarian and vegan teahouse food, based on recipes from Tibet, are served in part of this colourful gallery that stocks artefacts and jewellery from the East. From its raised perch there's a nice view out to sea.

CAPE FARMHOUSE RESTAURANT INTERNATIONAL $

Map p293 (☎021-780 1246; www.capefarmhouse.com; cnr M65 & M66, Redhill; mains R50-90; ⌚9am-5pm; 👪🐾) This 250-year-old farmhouse has a scenic setting beside interesting craft stalls and a kids' playground, and serves everything from breakfast to fillet steak, with as much produce as possible coming from its organic garden. In summer it hosts music concerts on Saturdays from 3.30pm; see the website for details.

★LIGHTHOUSE CAFE INTERNATIONAL $$

Map p292 (☎021-786 9000; www.thelighthousecafe.co.za; 90 St Georges St, Simon's Town; mains R75-140; ⌚8.30am-4pm Sun-Tue, to 9.30pm Wed-Sat; 🚉Simon's Town) Relaxed, beachcomber-chic cafe, with a menu big on seafood – there's a delicious and filling Mauritian bouillabaisse and fish and chips made to Jamie Oliver's recipe. It also does burgers, pizza and meze platters.

MEETING PLACE INTERNATIONAL $$

Map p292 (021-786 5678; www.themeetingplaceupstairs.co.za; 98 St George's St, Simon's Town; mains R75-120; 9am-9pm Mon-Sat, to 3pm Sun; Simon's Town) Offering a busy deli-cafe on the ground floor, and an arty restaurant upstairs with a balcony overlooking Simon Town's main drag. Sample gourmet sandwiches or the homemade ice creams.

JUST SUSHI JAPANESE $$

Map p292 (021-786 4340; Simon's Town Waterfront, St George's St, Simon's Town; mains R90-135; noon-10pm; P; Simon's Town) There's plenty of chances to eat fish and chips in Simon's Town, but this is the only place serving sushi and sashimi – and it's pretty good. The location next to the harbour is also a plus.

BLUE WATER CAFÉ INTERNATIONAL $$

(021-783 2007; www.bluewatercafe.co.za; Imhoff Farm, Kommetjie Rd, Ocean View; mains R50-105; 9am-5pm Tue, to 9pm Wed-Sun; P) There's a stunning view of Chapman's Peak from the stoop of this historic property at the heart of Imhoff Farm (p144). It's a lovely place to enjoy breakfast on the way down to Cape Point, or other simple-but-good dishes for lunch, including pasta and pizza.

★FLAGSHIP INTERNATIONAL $$$

Map p293 (021-786 1700; www.chefbrucerobertson.com; 15 Erica Rd, Simon's Town; 5-course lunch with wines R800; set lunch 1-4pm; ; Simon's Town) The untimely death of Bruce Robertson, shortly after he set up this gourmet lunch restaurant and boutique hotel, left big kitchen shoes to fill. Duncan Doherty has proved up to the task: his delicious five-course seafood lunch is served on a communal table next to the open kitchen and is made with locally sourced produce. Booking is essential for the 1pm lunch start. Also bring your swimmers for a mid-meal dip in the pool. If you'd like to stay over, there are four comfortable guest suites (from R1700).

★FOODBARN INTERNATIONAL $$$

(021-789 1390; www.thefoodbarn.co.za; cnr Noordhoek Main Rd & Village Lane, Noordhoek; 4/5-course set menu R450/550; restaurant noon-2.30pm daily, 6.30-9.30pm Tue-Sat, deli 8am-9pm Tue-Sat, to 5pm Sun-Mon, cafe 8am-4.30pm daily, tapas bar 6-9.30pm Tue-Sat; P)  Masterchef Franck Dangereux might have opted for the less stressful life in Noordhoek, but that doesn't mean this operation skimps on quality. Expect rustic, delicious bistro dishes. The separate book-lined deli-bakery-cafe and tapas bar is just as good, and stocks freshly baked goodies, chocolates and other locally sourced food and drinks.

DRINKING & NIGHTLIFE

★SLOW LIFE CAFE

Map p290 (www.facebook.com/slowlifesouthafrica; 152 Main Rd, Muizenberg; cover charge R50-120; 9am-10pm Tue-Sat; ; Muizenberg) Life in Muizenberg can feel pretty laid-back: this concept cafe gets the groove just right with a relaxed, arty atmosphere, long hours, a decent drinks and food menu, and live music or comedy gigs often held on Friday and Saturday nights.

★TIGER'S MILK BAR, RESTAURANT

Map p290 (021-788 1869; www.tigersmilk.co.za; cnr Beach & Sidmouth Rds, Muizenberg; kitchen 9am-10pm, bar to 2am; ; Muizenberg) There's a panoramic view of Muizenberg Beach through the floor-to-ceiling window of this hangar-like bar and restaurant. Although it's open all day for food (good pizza and steaks), the vibe – with its long bar counter, comfy sofas and quirky decor (a BMW bike and a giant golden cow's head hanging on exposed brick walls) – is more nightclub.

★BRASS BELL BAR, RESTAURANT

Map p290 (www.brassbell.co.za; Kalk Bay station, Main Rd, Kalk Bay; 11am-10pm; Kalk Bay) Follow the tunnel beneath the train tracks to reach this institution, lapped by the waves of False Bay. On a sunny day there are few better places to drink and eat (mains R50 to R100) by the sea. You can also take a dip in the adjacent tidal pools before or after.

★CAPE POINT VINEYARDS WINERY

(021-789 0900; www.cpv.co.za; 1 Chapmans Peak Dr, Noordhoek; tastings R45; tastings 10am-6pm, restaurant noon-3pm & 6.30-8.30pm Mon-Wed, Fri & Sat, picnics 11am-6pm, market 4.30-8.30pm Thu;) Known for its fine sauvignon blanc, this small vineyard has a spectacular setting overlooking Noordhoek Beach. Enjoy the wines with a picnic (R395 for two, bookings essential) in the grounds, or at the restaurant. The Thursday-evening community market (selling mainly food) is a weekly highlight for locals and great for kids, who can play on the lawns.

BEACH ROAD BAR BAR
(☎021-789 1783; cnr Beach & Pine Rds, Noordhoek; ⊙11am-11.30pm) If you're down this way (say, after a drive along Chapman's Peak Dr) the bar above the Red Herring restaurant is a pleasant place for a drink or a bite to eat (kitchen closes at 10pm). There's a good view of the beach from the terrace.

ENTERTAINMENT

KALK BAY THEATRE THEATRE
Map p290 (☎079 361 8275; www.kalkbaytheatre.co.za; 52 Main Rd, Kalk Bay; 🚇Kalk Bay) One of the city's several intimate dinner-and-show venues, this theatre is housed in a converted church. You don't need to eat there beforehand to see the productions, which are often reasonably short.

ALIVE CAFE PERFORMING ARTS
Map p290 (☎021-788 9010; www.alivecafe.co.za; 11 Atlantic Rd, Muizenberg; ⊙cafe 8am-5pm; 🚇Muizenberg) Check the website to find out about the wide range of events held at this 'creative experience hub'. Events range from poetry evenings, theatre and documentary screenings to live music, yoga and a market every fourth Saturday of the month. You can drop by its cafe and have a cup of fair-trade coffee any day, too.

MASQUE THEATRE THEATRE
Map p290 (☎021-788 6999; www.masquetheatre.co.za; 37 Main Rd, Muizenberg; 🚇Muizenberg) The program at this small theatre (seating 174) changes on a pretty regular basis, veering from stand-up comedy, live music and ballet to musical revues and more serious plays.

SHOPPING

Muizenberg & Kalk Bay

★**KALK BAY MODERN** ARTS & CRAFTS
Map p290 (☎021-788 6571; www.kalkbaymodern.co.za; 136 Main Rd, Kalk Bay; ⊙9.30am-5pm; 🚇Kalk Bay) This wonderful gallery is stocked with an eclectic, appealing range of arts and crafts, and there are often exhibitions by local artists. Check out the Art-i-San collection of printed cloth, a fair-trade product made by !Kung Bushmen in Namibia.

SOBEIT STUDIO ARTS & CRAFTS
Map p290 (☎021-788 9007; www.sobeitstudio.com; 51 Main Rd, Muizenberg; ⊙8am-5pm Mon-Sat; 🚇Valsbaai) On the top floor of a pink and turquoise art deco building, this modern curiosity shop of crazy creatives includes wax artists, graphic and furniture designers and jewellery makers. Pick up a distinctive souvenir, such as candles in the shape of skulls or busts of Napoleon. You'll also find some of the products for sale at the Kalk Bay Co-op.

BLUE BIRD GARAGE FOOD & GOODS MARKET MARKET
Map p290 (☎082 331 2471; www.bluebirdmarket.co.za; 39 Albertyn Rd, Muizenberg; ⊙4-10pm Fri; 🚇Valsbaai) This hit artisan food-and-goods market is based in a 1940s hangar, once the base for the southern hemisphere's first airmail delivery service, and a garage in the 1950s. It's a fun place to shop, particularly on Friday night, when there's live music.

ARTVARK ARTS & CRAFTS
Map p290 (☎021-788 5584; www.artvark.org; 48 Main Rd, Kalk Bay; ⊙9am-6pm; 🚇Kalk Bay) This contemporary folk-art gallery is a great place to find attractive souvenirs. It stocks a wide range of interesting arts and crafts by local artists, including paintings, pottery and jewellery, as well as goods from India and Central America.

BBELLAMY & BBELLAMY HOMEWARES
Map p290 (www.bbellamyandbbellamy.com; 51 Main Rd, Muizenberg; ⊙9am-5pm Thu-Sat; 🚇Valsbaai) David Bellamy is the designer behind this cornucopia of beautiful imported fabrics and items made from them, such as lampshades, cushion covers, scarves and shirts. Some of the fabrics are block-printed by David's team to create original designs.

BLUE PLANET FINE ART GALLERY
Map p290 (☎021-788 3154; www.blueplanetfineart.com; 25 Main Rd, Muizenberg; ⊙8am-5pm; 🚇Valsbaai) Combining a cafe with an art gallery, Blue Planet has an appealing selection of works, such as painted skateboards, by local artists you're unlikely to find represented elsewhere. Art classes are also offered here.

GINA'S STUDIO ARTS & CRAFTS

Map p290 (www.journeyinstitches.co.za; 38 Palmer Rd, Muizenberg; ⊙10am-4pm Wed-Fri, to 2pm Sat; Muizenberg) Gina Niederhumer is the crafter behind this small boutique packed with appealing items, from crocheted jewellery to patchwork bags and quilts, and origami made from old Afrikaans Braille paper.

KALK BAY BOOKS BOOKS

Map p290 (021-788 2266; www.kalkbaybooks.co.za; 124 Main Rd, Kalk Bay; ⊙9am-6pm Nov-Apr, to 5pm May-Oct; Kalk Bay) This is where the southern peninsula's book lovers gather. Check the Facebook page for details of book launches and readings.

QUAGGA RARE BOOKS & ART BOOKS

Map p290 (021-788 2752; www.quaggabooks.co.za; 84 Main Rd, Kalk Bay; ⊙9.30am-5pm Mon-Sat, 10am-5pm Sun; Kalk Bay) It's hard to pass this appealing bookshop if you're looking for old editions and antiquarian books. It has local and tribal art and artefacts.

POTTERSHOP CERAMICS

Map p290 (021-788 7030; 6 Rouxville Rd, Kalk Bay; ⊙9.30am-4.30pm; Kalk Bay) Pick up works by local ceramicists, including rejects of hand-painted plates and cups by the **Potter's Workshop** (www.pottersworkshop.co.za) – which often have so little wrong with them you'd hardly notice.

CATACOMBS FASHION

Map p290 (021-788 8889; www.facebook.com/pages/Catacombes-Kalkbay/127570887056; 71 Main Rd, Kalk Bay; ⊙9.30am-5pm; Kalk Bay) Get the floaty boho look at this boutique that stocks a beautiful range of dresses, separates and accessories. They're locally made and designed with original prints, some inspired by the Mexican Day of the Dead or flowers. Also carries some art and crafts.

THE STUDIO ARTS, CRAFTS

Map p290 (083 778 2737; www.thestudiokalkbay.co.za; Majestic Village, 122 Main Rd, Kalk Bay; ⊙9am-5pm Oct-Feb, to 4pm Mar-Sep; Kalk Bay) Works by artist Donna McKellar, whose studio used to be here, as well as other artists and creatives. The selection is worth a browse and the stock changes often, with different exhibitions about every two weeks.

BIG BLUE FASHION

Map p290 (021-788 2399; www.bigblue.co.za; 82 Main Rd, Kalk Bay; ⊙9am-5pm; Kalk Bay) This nationwide boutique is good for quirky, affordable T-shirts, fun clubbing gear or beachwear. It also stocks quirky gifts and homewares. Other branches in Cape Town include ones next to the Old Biscuit Mill in **Woodstock** (Map p274; Cavendish Square) and in the Cape Quarter in **De Waterkant** (Map p272; 021-425 1179; www.bigblue.co.za; Somerset Rd; Golden Arrow bus).

KALK BAY CO-OP FASHION

Map p290 (071-124 0667; 100 Main Rd, Kalk Bay; ⊙9am-5pm; Kalk Bay) This section of the Kalk Bay Co-op gathers together fashions and accessories by local designers (mainly for women, with a few pieces for men), while across the road, to either side of the train station entrance, are branches focusing more on colourful arts and crafts, including skull candles and casts from Sobeit. There's also a smaller branch in Simon's Town.

WHATNOT & CHINA TOWN ANTIQUES,

Map p290 (021-788 1823; 70 Main Rd, Kalk Bay; ⊙10am-5pm Mon-Sat, to 3pm Sun; Kalk Bay) This emporium – occupying a maze of rooms – offers all manner of plates, cups, bowls and decorative objects crafted from clay, including rare collectables.

Simon's Town & Rest of Southern Peninsula

RED ROCK TRIBAL ARTS & CRAFTS

Map p293 (021-780 9127; www.redrocktribal.co.za; Cape Farm House, cnr M65 & M66, Redhill; ⊙10am-5pm) Join owner Juliette as she hula-hoops outside her quirky collection of crafts and tribal artefacts, from tin-can planes made in KwaZulu-Natal to old Ethiopian silver and Coptic crosses. Opposite is a giant metal zebra made for an advertisement.

LARIJ WORKS ARTS & CRAFTS

Map p292 (86 St George's St, Simon's Town; ⊙10am-4pm Mon-Fri, to 2pm Sat; Simon's Town) Contemporary, nautical-themed artwork and decor, alongside cotton sleepwear, are sold in this upstairs gallery. The woven rope mats are particularly appealing.

REDHILL POTTERY CERAMICS

Map p293 (021-780 9297; www.redhillpotterycape.co.za; Kilfinan Farm, Scarborough) Specialises in pottery that mimics old enamelware in its glaze and incorporates bright African colours in the designs. It's also possible to decorate your own pot and pick it up later (or have it shipped home).

SPORTS & ACTIVITIES

Muizenberg & Kalk Bay

JAGER'S WALK WALKING

(Fish Hoek; Fish Hoek) Starting at the southern end of Fish Hoek beach, this paved walk provides a pleasant stroll of around 1km to Sunny Cove (which is on the train line). You can walk the remaining 5km from here along an unpaved road to Simon's Town.

GARY'S SURF SCHOOL SURFING

Map p290 (021-788 9839; www.garysurf.co.za; 34 Balmoral Bldg, Beach Rd, Muizenberg; 2hr lessons R380; 8.30am-5pm; Muizenberg) If genial surfing coach Gary Kleynhans can't get you standing on a board within a day, you don't pay for the lesson. His shop, the focus of Muizenberg's surf scene, hires out boards and wetsuits (per hour/day R100/300) and runs sandboarding trips to the sand dunes at Kommetjie (R300).

SURFSTORE AFRICA WATER SPORTS

Map p290 (076 202 3703, 021-788 5055; www.surfstore.co.za; 48-50 Beach Rd, Muizenberg; kitesurfing/SUP/surfing lessons from R690/490/280; Muizenberg) You can take lessons in kitesurfing and stand-up paddleboarding (SUP), as well as regular surfing, with these folks. Also here is a shop stocking a wide range of surf-related gear, and a cafe.

ROXY SURF CLUB SURFING

Map p290 (021-788 8687; www.surfemporium.co.za/roxy-surf-school; Empire Bldg, Surfer's Corner, Beach Rd, Muizenberg; private lessons R330; 8am-6pm; Muizenberg) Roxy started in 2003 as a women-only surf club to encourage more girls and women to get into this male-dominated sport. They still run female-only classes here, but guys can get in on the action, too, as it's now part of the larger Surf Emporium shop.

Simon's Town & Rest of Southern Peninsula

Awol Tours (p252) can arrange cycling tours around the township of Masiphumelele (Xhosa for 'we will succeed').

GOOD HOPE GARDENS NURSERY ECOTOUR

Map p293 (072 234 4804; Sun Valley; R400 per person) This indigenous plants nursery, opposite the Cape of Good Hope nature reserve, runs *fynbos* and coastal foraging courses. Experienced guides will teach you sustainable techniques to harvest edibles, including seaweed and mussels (you need to get a licence for this, available from any post office) from the rock pools around Scarborough.

SIMON'S TOWN BOAT COMPANY BOAT TOUR

Map p292 (083 257 7760; www.boatcompany.co.za; Town Pier, Simon's Town; Simon's Town) Hop aboard the popular *Spirit of Just Nuisance* cruise around the harbour (adult child R50/30), as well as longer boat trips to Cape Point (R550/400) and Seal Island (R400/300). During the whale-watching season there are also cruises that allow you to get up close to these magnificent animals.

APEX SHARK EXPEDITIONS BOAT TOUR

Map p292 (021-786 5717; www.apexpredators.com; Quayside Bldg, Main Rd, Simon's Town; shark-watching tours from R1950; Simon's Town) From February to September this outfit offers shark-watching tours in False Bay (at other times of the year, tours run out of Gansbaai). It also specialises in trips to see pelagic birds (R1800) from November to May – an awesome sight of thousands of sea birds, including up to seven species of albatross.

PISCES DIVERS DIVING

Map p292 (021-786 3799; www.piscesdivers.co.za; Goods Shed, Main Rd, Simon's Town; dives R400, courses from R1050; Simon's Town) Just metres from the water's edge, this recommended PADI dive centre offers a range of courses and scheduled dives.

SEA KAYAK TRIPS KAYAKING

Map p292 (082 501 8930; www.kayakcapetown.co.za; Simon's Town Jetty, Simon's Town; tours from R250; Simon's Town) Paddle out to the African penguin colony at Boulders (R250) with this Simon's Town–based operation.

SLEEPY HOLLOW HORSE RIDING HORSE RIDING

(021-789 2341, 083 261 0104; www.sleepyhollowhorseriding.com; Sleepy Hollow Lane, Noordhoek; per person R460) This reliable operation can arrange horse riding along the wide, sandy beach at Noordhoek, as well as in the mountainous hinterland. Two-hour rides leave at 9am, 1pm and 4.30pm.

Cape Flats & Northern Suburbs

LANGA | GUGULETHU | KHAYELITSHA | PINELANDS | MILNERTON

Neighbourhood Top Five

❶ Learn about the tragedies of South Africa's past and its hopes for the future on a **township tour** (p26), or stay at a township B&B.

❷ Get your fingers sticky eating delicious barbecued meats at **Mzoli's** (p154) in Gugulethu or **Nomzamo** (p154) in Langa.

❸ Watch kitesurfers riding the waves and soaring into the skies off Table View and **Bloubergstrand** (p153), with postcard-perfect views of Table Mountain in the distance.

❹ Sip your way around a dozen wineries on the **Durbanville Wine Route** (p156).

❺ Ride the ferry around the wetlands of **Intaka Island** (p153).

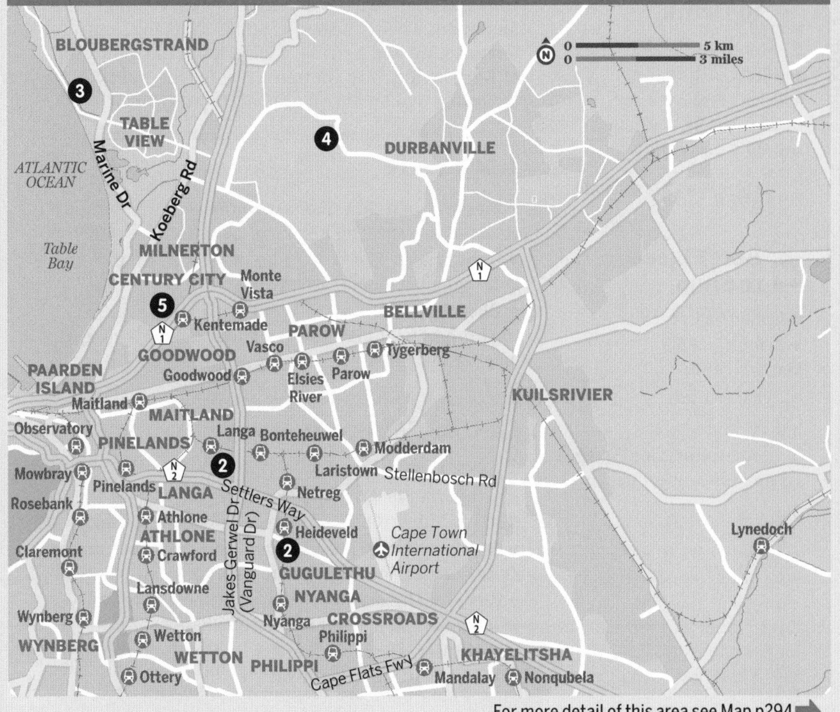

For more detail of this area see Map p294

Lonely Planet's Top Tip

The best township tours (p26) involve walking or cycling around rather than sitting on a bus; there's even a running tour you can do around Gugulethu. Better still is to stay overnight at a township-based B&B or homestay (p210).

Best Places to Eat

- Tables at Nitida (p155)
- Moyo (p155)
- Maestro's on the Beach (p155)
- Clifford & Sandra's (p154)
- Mzoli's (p154)

For reviews, see p154.

Best Places to Drink

- Blue Peter (p156)
- Kefu's (p155)
- Buyel' Embo Village (p155)
- Petit Fours (p156)

For reviews, see p155.

Best Places to Shop

- Canal Walk (p157)
- Milnerton Flea Market (p157)
- Philani Nutrition Centre (p157)

For reviews, see p157.

Explore Cape Flats & Northern Suburbs

Sprawling across the sandy plains east of Table Mountain, the Cape Flats seldom get good press. The down-at-the-heel communities and informal settlements (ie shacks) of the largely black townships may seem unlikely candidates as tourist destinations, but visiting a township might well be one of the most illuminating and life-affirming things you do while in Cape Town.

Langa, founded in 1927, is South Africa's oldest planned township, and has areas of affluence as well as poverty – a pattern repeated in the other main townships of Gugulethu and Khayelitsha (the largest, with an estimated population of over 1.5 million). Complexes such as the spiffy shopping mall Gugulethu Square and Langa's Guga S'Thebe Arts & Cultural Centre are proof that there is much more to life here than crime, poverty and disease. We highlight some of the sights and projects to visit on a township tour or on your own. While most of the places we list will be perfectly safe to visit without guides, be sure to call your destination first and get clear directions or arrange for a local to meet you.

The lush garden suburb of Pinelands lies cheek by jowl with Langa; come here to visit the Oude Molen Eco Village. North of the city centre alongside Table Bay are Milnerton, Table View and Bloubergstrand, all blessed with excellent beaches and spectacular views of Table Mountain. There's also a gigantic shopping centre at Century City, and a string of wineries in the rolling hills of Durbanville. Give yourself a day for the sights in the townships and another for the northern suburbs.

Local Life

- **Markets** Join the hunters of antiques, bargains and curios at the weekend Milnerton Flea Market (p157).
- **Pubs** Enjoy a beer and a slice of pizza in front of Blue Peter (p156), a Bloubergstrand institution.
- **Church** Attend a gospel church service in the townships on Sunday; township tour guides (p26) can help arrange this.

Getting There & Away

- **Car** Take the N2 to Langa, Gugulethu and Khayelitsha; the N1 to Century City; and Marine Dr (R27) to Milnerton, Table View and Bloubergstrand.
- **Township tours** There are set itineraries but tour guides can be flexible in where they go.
- **Bus** MyCiTi buses run through Milnerton to Bloubergstrand and out to Khayelitsha.
- **Train** Metro trains run to Langa, Gugulethu (closest stop Nyanga) and Khayelitsha.

SIGHTS

Cape Flats

GUGA S'THEBE ARTS & CULTURAL CENTRE ARTS CENTRE

Map p294 (021-695 3493; cnr Washington & Church Sts, Langa; 8am-4.30pm Mon-Fri, 8.30am-2pm Sat & Sun; P; Langa) FREE Decorated with polychromatic ceramic murals, this is one of the most impressive buildings in the townships – even more so now it has a new theatre, creatively constructed largely from recycled materials. In one of several studio spaces here you can watch pottery being made and then buy samples from the centre's shop. Performances by local groups are often staged in the outdoor amphitheatre.

LANGA QUARTER CULTURAL BUILDING

Map p294 (iKhaya Le Langa; www.facebook.com/IKhayaLeLanga/timeline; cnr N'Dabeni & Bittenhout Sts, Langa; 8am-5pm; Langa) FREE An old primary school is the base for this impressive social enterprise project, which aims to transform the surrounding area into a precinct for galleries, shops, restaurants, bars and cafes with broad, cross-cultural appeal. There's a cafe, gift shop and Table Mountain yellow frame (p98) here. Opposite, on Bittenhout St, a wall is the canvas for an annual street-art competition.

On nearby Rubusana Ave, several homes are part of the **Langa Township Art Gallery** (Langa TAG) project, with the homeowners displaying and selling the works of local artists.

The organisers of the project can also organise **homestays** in Langa. If enough funds are raised, the official World Design Capital pavilion, a legacy of the 2014 event, will be erected here, too.

LANGA MOSAIC PLINTHS PUBLIC ART

Map p294 (Washington St, Langa; Langa) Near the Guga S'Thebe Arts & Cultural Centre are four colourful, mosaic-decorated plinths. Each side of the plinths has a different theme: one is the only memorial to the *Mendi,* a troop ship that sank in the English Channel in 1917, drowning 607 members of the South African Native Labour Corps.

The huge mural painted on the building opposite the cultural centre was done by Philip Kgosana, the man held aloft in the composition – it commemorates the 1960 defiance campaign against apartheid laws.

LANGA PASS MUSEUM MUSEUM

Map p294 (084 863 3427; cnr Washington St & Lerotholi Ave, Langa; admission by donation; by appointment; P; Langa) Call Thami Siljila to arrange a time to see inside the old Dom Pass Office where locals had to present their identity cards during apartheid. There's a great collection of photographs and documentary evidence showing what life was like in Langa during that time.

GUGULETHU SEVEN & AMY BIEHL MEMORIALS SCULPTURE

(cnr Steve Biko St/NY1 & NY111, Gugulethu; Nyanga) The Gugulethu Seven Memorial commemorates seven young black activists from the townships who were murdered by the police here in 1986. Nearby, next to the Caltex petrol station, the Amy Biehl Memorial marks the spot where the young American anti-apartheid activist died, under tragic circumstances, in 1993.

LOOKOUT HILL VIEWPOINT

(021-367 7087; cnr Mew Way & Spine Rd, Khayelitsha; P; Khayelitsha) FREE Climb the wooden staircase leading to the top of this sand hill for a sweeping view of the Khayelitsha township. For access it's best to go into the cultural and tourism centre at its base, where you'll find the restaurant Malibongwe (p154) and a craft market. Ask there for one of the guards to accompany you, as there have been incidents of muggings.

Northern Suburbs

BLOUBERGSTRAND BEACH, VILLAGE

(Kleinbaai) On the beaches beside this attractive village, the British won their 1806 battle for the Cape. The panoramic view it provides of Table Mountain across Table Bay is fabulous, but it's also popular with kitesurfers and windsurfers; watching them ride the waves on the weekends is an impressive sight. You can also see Robben Island clearly from here.

INTAKA ISLAND BIRD SANCTUARY

Map p294 (021-552 6889; www.intaka.co.za; 2 Park Lane, Intaka Island, Century City; adult/child entrance R12.50/7.50, entrance & ferry ride R35/25; 7.30am-7pm Oct-Apr, to 5.30pm

May-Sep, ferry rides 10am-4pm; P) *Intaka* means 'bird' in Xhosa and you can see some 120 species of these feathered creatures at this 1600-sq-metre wetland reserve that's part of the Century City development. Learn all about the wetlands at the **Eco-Centre**, built and run to the best environmental principles. From here you can take a **ferry ride** through the canals that flow around the island, or follow the 2km walking trail around the reserve.

EATING

Cape Flats

★CLIFFORD & SANDRA'S AFRICAN $

(Khayelisha market, off Ntlazane Rd, Khayelitsha; meals R20; ⏲8am-6.30pm; Khayelitsha) At the market next to Khayelitsha Station, ask around to find this shack cafe serving some of the tastiest – and certainly best-value – traditional chow in Cape Town. Clifford will pour water over your hands before you start using them (no cutlery here) to tuck into beef stew, crispy fried chicken and pap (maize starch).

Juma Mkwela's street-art tour (p26) stops here for lunch, but it's easy to locate if you're alone, too.

★MZOLI'S BRAAI $

(021-638 1355; 150 NY111, Gugulethu; meals R50-100; ⏲9am-6pm; Nyanga) Tourists, TV stars and locals gather at this busy butchery serving some of Cape Town's tastiest grilled meat. First buy your meat and make sure you get them to add their special sauce. Take it to the kitchen to be braaied (barbecued) and then find a table outside. It gets super-hectic here at weekends, so arrive early.

Beers and other drinks are available from vendors nearby. Bring plenty of napkins as cutlery is nonexistent.

NOMZAMO BRAAI $

Map p294 (021-695 4250; 15 Washington St, Langa; meals R50-100; ⏲9am-7pm; Langa) This spotlessly clean butchers is the Langa equivalent of Mzoli's, but with a more relaxed, peaceful vibe since it doesn't sell alcohol. The cuts of meat – beef, lamb, pork, sausages and chicken wings – are top-class. Call ahead if you want to add side dishes such as bread, salads etc, to make a full meal.

EZIKO AFRICAN $

Map p294 (021-694 0434; www.ezikorestaurant.co.za; cnr Washington St & Jungle Walk, Langa; mains R50; ⏲9am-5pm Mon-Sat; P; Langa) Eziko offers simple, good food in a pleasant setting; try the chef's special fried chicken or the breakfast. If you're feeling adventurous go for the 'delectable' tripe. Dishes are served with sides of *samp* (a mixture of maize and beans), pap, bread and vegetables.

MALIBONGWE AFRICAN $

(021-361 6259; www.malibongwerestaurant.co.za; cnr Mew Way & Spine Rd, Khayelitsha; mains R40-60; ⏲8am-6pm Mon-Sat; P; Khayelitsha) Tripe curry and grilled meats are among the traditional dishes served at this pleasantly decorated and spacious restaurant and bar at the base of Lookout Hill. For a more local vibe, head down Spine Rd to the street braai-joints opposite Kefu's bar; Ziba's Chicken is recommended.

LELAPA AFRICAN $$

Map p294 (021-694 2681; www.facebook.com/lelapa; 49 Harlem Ave, Langa; buffet from R180; ; Langa) Sheila has been so successful with her delicious African-style buffets (which include plenty of vegetarian dishes) that she's taken over the neighbour's place, extending her once cosy home restaurant into a space for big tour groups. Book ahead, as there are no set opening hours.

MZANSI AFRICAN $$

Map p294 (021-694 1656; www.mzansi45.co.za; 45 Harlem Ave, Langa; buffet R180; Langa) Next door to Lelapa, a similar buffet deal is offered by this convivial place with a rooftop dining area that has a great view of Table Mountain. They can also arrange a marimba band and African drumming lessons.

Northern Suburbs

MILLSTONE INTERNATIONAL, BAKERY $

Map p294 (021-447 8226; Valkenberg East, Oude Molen Eco Village, Pinelands; meals R50-60; ⏲9am-5pm Tue-Sun; P; Pinelands) This rustic cafe and farm stall specialises

LOCAL KNOWLEDGE

EATING ON SPINE RD, KHAYELITSHA

Walk down Spine Rd from Lookout Hill to Makabeni Rd to get an insight into the Khayelitsha dining scene. There's no sign but you'll know **Groover Park** (Spine Rd, Ilitha Park; meal R50-100; 11am-10pm; P; Khayelitsha) by the many cars parked outside of it on a weekend afternoon – and the patrons tucking into freshly grilled meats. Across the road is a row of outdoor braai (barbecue)stalls (**Ziba's Chicken** is recommended), as well as a pizza stall. Closer to Lookout Hill, **Espinaca** (073 095 0119; www.facebook.com/espinacainnovations/timeline; 42 Spine Rd, Ilitha Park; 7am-6pm Mon-Fri, 8am-6pm Sun; ; Khayelitsha) was set up by young entrepreneur Lufefe Nomjana, who bakes spinach bread and muffins that are a welcome vegetarian respite from Spine Rd's braai brigade.

in organic produce, hand-crafted breads, preserves and jams. Kids will love the tree house in the garden and the pony rides next door.

★TABLES AT NITIDA INTERNATIONAL $$

(021-975 9357; www.tablesatnitida.co.za; Nitida, Tygerberg Valley Rd, Durbanville; mains R55-125; 9am-4pm Mon-Sat, to 3pm Sun; P) Call ahead to pre-book one of the delicious gourmet picnics (R320 for two, R60 for children), which you can enjoy on the outside lawns - or nip into the cafe after a wine tasting at Nitida to sample delightful meals, such as the splendid beetroot *tarte tatin* or lamb kebabs.

★MOYO AFRICAN $$

(021-554 9671; www.moyo.co.za; Shop 50, Eden on the Bay, Blouberg; mains R85-145; 10am-10pm; P; Big Bay) Game meats such as crocodile and warthog are on the menu at this fun African-themed restaurant. Have your face painted and dangle your feet in a cooling paddle-pool beneath a table shaped like a surfboard, with spectacular beach and Table Mountain views outside.

A guitarist strolls around playing each evening from Thursday to Sunday. There's a live band on Sundays from 2pm.

★MAESTRO'S ON THE BEACH INTERNATIONAL $$

Map p294 (021-551 4992; www.maestros.co.za; Bridge Rd, Milnerton; mains R60-130; 10am-11pm Mon-Fri, 9am-11pm Sat & Sun; P; Woodbridge) Next to Milernton Golf Club (you enter through their car park), this all-day dining operation has a grand beachside position with swoon-worthy views of Table Mountain.

DE GRENDEL RESTAURANT INTERNATIONAL $$$

(021-558 6280; www.degrendel.co.za; 112 Plattekloof Rd, Durbanville; 2/3 courses R255/285; noon-2.30pm & 7-9.30pm Tue-Sat, noon-2.30pm Sun; P) If you can drag your eyes away from the panoramic view of Table Mountain for a second, the upmarket bistro food served at this classy wine farm at the southern end of the Durbanville Wine Route (p156; the end closest to the city) is worthy of attention, too. Expect dishes such as confit of duck tart and organic lamb noisette.

DRINKING & NIGHTLIFE

Cape Flats

KEFU'S BAR

(021-361 0566; www.kefus.co.za; 39-41 Mthawelanga St, Ilitha Park, Khayelitsha; 10am-midnight Mon-Thu, to 2am Fri & Sat; Khayelitsha) Ms Kefuoe Sedia has come a long way since she started a six-seater pub in her front lounge in 1990. This spiffy, two-level, 140-seat place, with mellow jazz playing in the background, also serves food. Call ahead from Monday to Thursday to check if it's open.

BUYEL' EMBO VILLAGE BAR

(078 409 5071; www.facebook.com/pages/Buyel-Embo-Village/420612358048631; 8 Alfred Nzo St, Mandela Park, Khayelitsha; Khayelitsha) DJ events and live-music gigs are often held on weekends and holidays at this large complex in traditional African village style,

WORTH A DETOUR

DURBANVILLE WINE ROUTE

About 25km (around a 30-minute drive) north of the City Bowl but still within Cape Town's metropolitan borders is the **Durbanville Wine Route** (www.durbanvillewine.co.za). Vines have been grown here since 1698; the area's signature grape is sauvignon blanc, which benefits from the cooler winds off the coast that the hills receive. Among the dozen wineries on the route are:

De Grendel (021-558 6280; www.degrendel.co.za; 112 Plattekloof Rd, Durbanville; tastings R20-50; 9am-7pm Mon-Sat, 10am-4pm Sun; P) Closest of the Durbanville wineries to Cape Town and with a jaw-dropping view of Table Mountain from its tasting room. There's also a good restaurant (p155) and a large *fynbos* garden.

Durbanville Hills (021-558 1300; www.durbanvillehills.co.za; M13, Durbanville; tastings R45-120; tastings 9am-4.30pm Mon-Wed, to 6pm Thu & Fri, 10am-4pm Sat & Sun, restaurant 8.30am-3pm Tue-Sun year-round, 6-10pm Thu-Sat Nov-Mar, 6-10pm Fri Apr-Oct; P) Set in an ultramodern hilltop building commanding splendid views of Table Bay; the tastings include pairings with chocolates, biltong or tapas-style dishes.

Hillcrest Estate (021-970 5800; www.hillcrestfarm.co.za; M13, Durbanville; tastings R20; tastings 9am-5pm, restaurant 9am-4pm; P) Apart from excellent winemaking, Hillcrest also brews craft beers and grows olives. Its historic **quarry** (www.thequarry.co.za), with a fish-stocked lake, is used for wakeboarding and events such as **Galileo Cinema** (www.thegalileo.co.za) screenings on Tuesday nights.

Meerendal (021-975 1655; www.meerendal.co.za; M48 Visserhok, Durbanville; tastings R10; tastings 9am-6pm Mon-Sat, 10am-5pm Sun; P) Established in 1702 and with some of the oldest pinotage and shiraz vineyards in South Africa, the tastings here are very professional. There's a boutique hotel, the contemporary-styled Crown restaurant and 18km of mountain-biking trails (day pass R30).

Nitida (021-976 1467; www.nitida.co.za; Tygerberg Valley Rd, Durbanville; tastings R20-50; 9.30am-5pm Mon-Fri, to 3pm Sat, 11am-3pm Sun; P) Offering tastings of award-winning wines and the excellent restaurant Tables at Nitida (p155).

with a number of bars, barbecued food spots, and chill areas around a central open courtyard.

DEPARTMENT OF COFFEE — CAFE

(078 086 0093; 158 Ntlazani St, Khayelitsha; 10am-5pm; Khayelitsha) Gourmet coffee comes to Khayelitsha – even though it's served through a kiosk with uninviting barred windows and they keep erratic hours. There are some outdoor tables and chairs nearby for you to sit and sip your coffee and nibble on their muffins.

GALAXY — CLUB

(021-637 9132; www.superclubs.co.za; College Rd, Ryelands Estate; admission R50; 9pm-4am Thu-Sat) This legendary Cape Flats dance venue is where you can get down to R&B, hip hop and live bands with a black and coloured crowd. Women often get in for free. The plush live-music venue **West End** (5pm-4am Fri & Sat) is next door.

Northern Suburbs

★BLUE PETER — BAR

(021-554 1956; www.bluepeter.co.za; Popham St, Bloubergstrand; 9.30am-11pm; Kleinbaai) At this perennial favourite the deal is grab a beer (13 types on draught), order a pizza and plonk yourself on the grass outside to enjoy the classic views of Table Mountain and Robben Island. It's also a hotel.

★PETITS FOURS — CAFE

(021-554 4462; www.petits-fours.co.za; 20 Stadler Rd, Bloubergstrand; 8am-5pm; Kleinbaai) At the southern end of Bloubergstrand is this delightful place in a whitewashed seaside cottage, with a counter loaded with a tempting collection of cakes and baked goods. There's a slight French flavour to the menu (mains run from R60), but toasted sandwiches (jaffles) are also a signature dish here.

DEON NAGEL'S GAT PARTY GAY & LESBIAN

Map p294 (082 821 9185; www.facebook.com/groups/117474602037; Theo Marais Park, Koeberg Rd, Milnerton; cover R30; 9pm-2am1st, 2nd & last Sat of month; Montague Gardens) Camp and Afrikaans cultures collide at these parties where local gays and lesbians gather to twirl around in *langarm* (a local type of ballroom dance) style to country-and-western-style tunes. People go in groups and bring their own food and drink (although there's always a bar), but if you're solo it won't take you long to make friends. The DJs usually play a range of music that anyone can dance to.

Gat means 'hole' in Afrikaans, and the name comes from the original location of the party, at the old Parrow Athletic Club, which was based in a former quarry – literally a hole in the ground.

ENTERTAINMENT

GRANDWEST CASINO CASINO

Map p294 (021-505 7777; www.suninternational.com/grandwest; 1 Vanguard Dr, Goodwood; 24hr; ; Goodwood) Even if gambling isn't your thing, there's plenty to keep you entertained at Grandwest, including a six-screen cinema, many restaurants, a food court, an Olympic-sized ice rink, kids' play areas, a bowling alley, and regular concerts by major international singers and bands. It's 12.5km east of the city centre.

IBUYAMBO LIVE MUSIC, DANCE

Map p294 (021-694 3113, 083 579 0853; www.ibuyambo.co.za; Washington St, Langa; Langa) Dizu Plaatjies and his award-winning group of Xhosa musicians and dancers perform at this cultural centre by arrangement. Drumming sessions can be organised and traditional beadwork explained.

ATHLONE STADIUM SPECTATOR SPORT

(021-637 6607; Cross Blvd, Athlone; Athlone) It's mainly used for soccer matches, although from December to February a contest between the various Cape Town Minstrel groups is also held here.

SHOPPING

Cape Flats

PHILANI NUTRITION CENTRE CRAFT

(021-387 5124; www.philani.org.za; Phaphani St, Site C, Khayelitsha; 8.30am-4.15pm; Nolungile) This long-running, community-based health organisation has six projects in the townships, including a weaving factory in Khayelitsha's Site C that produces rugs and wall hangings, and a printing project.

COMMUNITY CREATIVE DISTRICT ARTS & CRAFTS

(www.artstownship.com; NY147, Gugulethu; 9am-5pm; Nyanga) A collaboration between various local arts and community groups, this street – within walking distance of Mzoli's (p154) – has several homes whose owners have turned their living rooms into art galleries. Like any commercial gallery, they get a commission for each piece sold and may also sell their own crafts.

Northern Suburbs

MILNERTON FLEA MARKET MARKET

Map p294 (021-550 1383; www.milnertonfleamarket.co.za; Marine Dr/R27, Paarden Eiland; 8am-2pm Sat, to 3pm Sun; Zoarvlei) Hunt for vintage pieces and collectables among the junk and cheap goods at this car-boot sale that fills up a car park on the edge of Table Bay. The views of Table Mountain are matched by the interesting characters you'll encounter here.

CANAL WALK SHOPPING CENTRE

Map p294 (021-529 9699; www.canalwalk.co.za; Century Blvd, Century City; 9am-9pm; Canal Walk North) With over 400 shops, 50-odd restaurants, 18 cinema screens and parking for 6500 cars, you'd be a fool to argue with this mall's claim of being the largest in Africa. The food court is so big that acrobatics shows are often held over the diners.

CENTURY CITY NATURAL GOODS MARKET MARKET

Map p294 (www.centurycity.co.za/events/century-city-natural-goods-market-and-art-on-the-island; Central Park Field, Century City; 9am-2pm last Sun of month; ; Canal Walk North) On the last Sunday of the month, this well-established market – with plenty of eating options and kids' entertainment – is held in the park opposite Intaka Island (p153). Go onto the island to see local artists in the Eco-Centre.

SPORTS & ACTIVITIES

OUDE MOLEN ECO VILLAGE VOLUNTEERING, SWIMMING

Map p294 (021-448 6419; www.oudemolenecovillage.co.za; Alexandra Rd, Pinelands; pool adult/youth/child R30/20/10; pool 8am-5pm; Pinelands) Many grassroots-style operations occupy this once-abandoned section of the buildings and grounds of the Valkenberg psychiatric hospital. You can volunteer to work at the village's organic farm through the Willing Workers on Organic Farms (WWOOF) scheme, go horse riding with **Oude Molen Stables** (073 199 7395; per hr R150) or go for a swim in the village's outdoor pool. Also here are the cafe and farm stall Millstone (p154).

RATANGA JUNCTION AMUSEMENT PARK

Map p294 (www.ratanga.co.za; Century Boulevard, Century City; adult/child R172/90; 10am-5pm Sat & Sun Jan-Mar, daily during school holidays; Canal Walk South) The rides and attractions at this African-themed amusement park range from stomach-churning, looping roller coasters to an animal petting zoo. If you don't want to experience any of the rides at all there's a reduced entrance charge of R65.

SKYDIVE CAPE TOWN EXTREME SPORTS

(082 800 6290; www.skydivecapetown.za.net; R1900) Based about 20km north of the city centre in Melkboshstrand, this experienced outfit offers tandem skydives. Needless to say, the views – once you stop screaming – are spectacular. Flights take off from the Delta 200 Airfield at Melkbosstrand; they don't offer Cape Town pickups, but can recommend transport operators if you don't have your own vehicle.

MOWBRAY GOLF CLUB GOLF

Map p294 (021-685 3018; www.mowbraygolfclub.co.za; 1 Raapenberg Rd, Mowbray; 18 holes R350; 7am-6pm; Pinelands) Established in 1910, Mowbray is considered by some to be the best in-town course for its rural setting and abundant birdlife. It certainly has a lovely view of Devil's Peak.

MILNERTON GOLF CLUB GOLF

Map p294 (021-552 1351; www.milnertongolf.co.za; Bridge Rd, Milnerton; 18 holes R315; 7am-6pm; Woodbridge) About 12km north of the city centre on Woodbridge Island, this 18-hole, par-72 course has a magnificent position overlooking Table Bay and great views of Table Mountain. (The wind can be a problem, though.)

BEST KITEBOARDING AFRICA WATER SPORTS

Map p294 (021-556 2765; www.bestkiteboardingafrica.com; Portico Bldg, Athens Rd, Table View; half/full-day lesson R900/1700; 9.30am-5.30pm Mon-Fri, 10am-3pm Sat & Sun; Marine Circle) The long, broad and windswept beach at Table View is ideal for the sport of kitesurfing. This outfit, overlooking the beach, can teach you how to do it, or just rent you some gear if you already know how. They also teach stand-up paddleboarding (SUP).

WINDSWEPT WATER SPORTS

(082 961 3070; www.windswept.co.za; Bloubergstrand; 2hr group/individual lessons R495/990) Philip Baker runs windsurfing and kitesurfing camps out of his base in Bloubergstrand. Two-hour lessons are available for either groups or individuals, or if you already know the ropes you can hire a kite and board for R395. Packages including accommodation are also available.

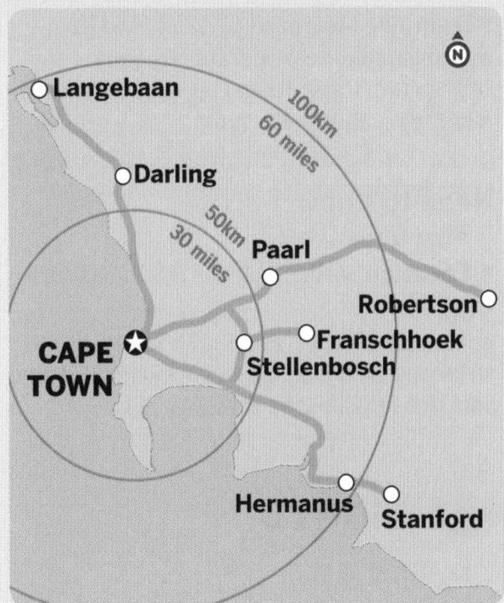

Day Trips & Wineries

Stellenbosch p160

At the heart of hundreds of vineyards, Stellenbosch is an elegant town with colonial architecture and good museums.

Franschhoek p165

Lush vineyards surround Franschhoek's compact town centre, and its main road is dotted with excellent restaurants.

Paarl p169

The largest town in the Winelands, Paarl lies on the banks of the Berg River and has Cape Dutch architecture and vineyards.

Robertson p173

Further afield in the Breede River Valley, Robertson is the largest town on a blissfully uncrowded wine route. Many estates offer free tastings.

Hermanus p174

Clinging to the clifftops, Hermanus has pretty beaches, *fynbos*-covered hills and some of the best land-based whale-watching in the world.

Stanford p178

This picture-perfect village on the banks of the Klein River offers fabulous off-the-beaten-track foodie experiences.

Darling p180

Darling is known for its wine, arty community and inimitable drag show.

Langebaan p181

Come to coastal Langebaan for open-air seafood restaurants, phenomenal sunsets and kite-surfing lessons on the lagoon.

Stellenbosch

Explore

If you only have a day, start at the excellent Village Museum before turning to the reason most people visit this vibrant university town – wine. Choosing vineyards can be a daunting task, so stop at the tourist office to pick up a free copy of *Stellenbosch and its Wine Routes*. You'll need your own wheels (bicycle wheels will do) to explore the vineyards, which are scattered far and wide around the town. Better still, join a tour and enjoy sipping rather than spitting. Tours usually visit up to four vineyards and include lunch – eating at one of the estates is a Stellenbosch must. Those staying overnight will appreciate the town's after-dark vibe, largely revolving around bustling student bars.

The Best...

- **Sight** Villiera
- **Place to Eat** Schoon de Companje (p163)
- **Place to Drink** Brampton Wine Studio (p163)

Top Tip

If you don't want to drive, and a tour group doesn't appeal, try the **Vine Hopper** (021-882 8112; www.vinehopper.co.za; 1-day pass R240), a hop-on, hop-off service that visits 12 vineyards in the Stellenbosch area.

Getting There & Away

- **Bus** The **Baz Bus** (0861 229 287; www.bazbus.com) runs to and from Cape Town (R260, 30 minutes, daily).
- **Train** The **Metrorail** (021-449 6478; www.metrorail.co.za) operates frequent trains from Cape Town (1st/economy class R18.50/12, about one hour).

Need to Know

- **Area Code** 021
- **Location** Stellenbosch is 50km east of Cape Town.
- **Tourist Office** (021-883 3584; www.stellenboschtourism.co.za; 36 Market St; 8am-5pm Mon-Fri, 9am-2pm Sat & Sun;)

A WALKING TOUR OF STELLENBOSCH

If you need to walk off all those wine tastings, you could take a **guided town walk** (per person R100; 11am & 3pm Mon-Fri, 9.30am Sat & Sun) from Stellenbosch Tourism. Bookings are essential for weekend walks. If you prefer to go it alone, pick up the excellent brochure *Historical Stellenbosch on Foot* (R5), which has a walking-tour map and information on many of the town's historic buildings.

SIGHTS

VILLAGE MUSEUM MUSEUM

(www.stelmus.co.za; 18 Ryneveld St; adult/child R35/15; 9am-5pm Mon-Sat, 10am-4pm Sun) A group of exquisitely restored and period-furnished houses dating from 1709 to 1850 make up this museum, which occupies the entire city block bounded by Ryneveld, Plein, Drostdy and Church Sts and is a must-see. Also included are charming gardens and, on the other side of Drostdy St, stately **Grosvenor House**.

TOY & MINIATURE MUSEUM MUSEUM

(Rhenish Parsonage, 42 Market St; adult/child R20/10; 9am-4pm Mon-Fri, 9am-2pm Sat) This delightful museum features a remarkable collection of detailed toys ranging from railway sets to dollhouses. The real highlight, though, is a chat with curator Philip Kleynhans, who is as passionate about local history and architecture as he is about the charming museum exhibits.

BRAAK PARK

(Town Sq) At the north end of the Braak, an open stretch of grass, you'll find the neo-Gothic **St Mary's on the Braak Church**, completed in 1852. To its west is the **VOC Kruithuis** (Powder House; adult/child R5/2; 9am-2pm Mon-Fri Sep-May), built in 1777 to store the town's weapons and gunpowder – it now houses a small military museum. On the northwest corner of the square is **Fick House**, a fine example of Cape Dutch architecture from the late 18th century.

BERGKELDER WINERY

(021-809 8025; www.bergkelder.co.za; tastings R40; 8am-5pm Mon-Fri, 9am-2pm Sat) For wine lovers without wheels, this cellar a short walk from the town centre is

WORTH A DETOUR

HELDERBERG WINERIES

There are around 30 wineries in the Helderberg region, an off-shoot of the Stellenbosch wine route. Sitting on the lower slopes of the Helderberg mountains near Somerset West, this region has some of the country's oldest estates.

Vergelegen (021-847 1334; www.vergelegen.co.za; Lourensford Rd, Somerset West; adult/child R10/5, tastings R30; 9.30am-4pm) Simon van der Stel's son Willem first planted vines here in 1700. The buildings and elegant grounds have ravishing mountain views and a 'stately home' feel to them. You can take a tour of the gardens (R20), a cellar tour (R20) or just enjoy a tasting of four of the estate's wines. Tasting the flagship Vergelegen Red costs an extra R10.There are also two restaurants. The bistro-style Stables (mains R70 to R175) overlooks the Rose Garden. For a more upmarket meal, try Camphors (lunch Wednesday to Sunday, lunch and dinner Friday and Saturday). Picnic hampers (R150 per person, November to April only) are also available – bookings are essential for these and Camphors.

Waterkloof (021-858 1292; www.waterkloofwines.co.za; Sir Lowry's Pass Village Rd, Somerset West; tastings from R30; 10am-5pm, walks 10am & 4.30pm) The stunning contemporary architecture here is a fine contrast to the familiar Cape Dutch buildings at older estates. The estate specialises in biodynamic wines and ecofriendly farming methods – take a two-hour guided tour (R390) around the estate to learn more. Horse riding (R585) is also offered, and if you're feeling particularly flush you could fly in from Cape Town by helicopter (R6500). All activities include a two-course lunch or dinner in the excellent restaurant.

ideal. Hour-long tours are followed by an atmospheric candle-lit tasting in the cellar. The tours run at 10am, 11am, 2pm and 3pm Monday to Friday, and at 10am, 11am and noon Saturday. A wine and salt pairing (R75) is also on offer. Bookings are required for all activities.

UNIVERSITY MUSEUM — MUSEUM

(52 Ryneveld St; admission by donation; 10am-4.30pm Mon, 9am-4.30pm Tue-Sat) This fabulous Flemish Renaissance-style building houses an interesting and varied collection of local art, an array of African anthropological treasures and exhibits on South African culture and history.

★VILLIERA — WINERY

(021-865 2002; www.villiera.com; tastings free; 9am-5pm Mon-Fri, 9am-3pm Sat) Villiera produces several excellent Méthode Cap Classique wines and a highly rated and very well-priced shiraz. Excellent two-hour wildlife drives (R150 per person) with knowledgeable guides take in the various antelope, zebras and bird species on the farm.

WARWICK ESTATE — WINERY

(021-884 4410; www.warwickwine.com; tastings R25, wine safari R50; 10am-5pm;) Warwick's red wines are legendary, particularly its bordeaux blends. The winery offers an informative 'Big Five' wine safari (referring to grape varieties, not large mammals) through the vineyards and picnics to enjoy on the lawns.

SPIER — WINERY

(021-809 1100; www.spier.co.za; tastings from R38; 10am-5pm;) Spier has some excellent shiraz, cabernet and red blends, though a visit to this vast winery is less about wine and more about the other activities available. There are bird of prey displays, Segway tours through the vines, two restaurants, and picnics to enjoy in the grounds. Look out for special events, particularly the Spier Winelands Express, a train trip running from Cape Town in the summer months.

HARTENBERG ESTATE — WINERY

(021-865 2541; www.hartenbergestate.com; Bottelary Rd; tastings R25; 9am-5pm Mon-Fri, 9am-4pm Sat year-round, 10am-4pm Sun Oct-Apr) Thanks to a favourable microclimate, Hartenberg produces superlative red wines, particularly cabernet, merlot and shiraz. Lunch is available (bookings essential) and from October to April picnics (R175) can be arranged to take on a wetland walk through the estate.

Stellenbosch

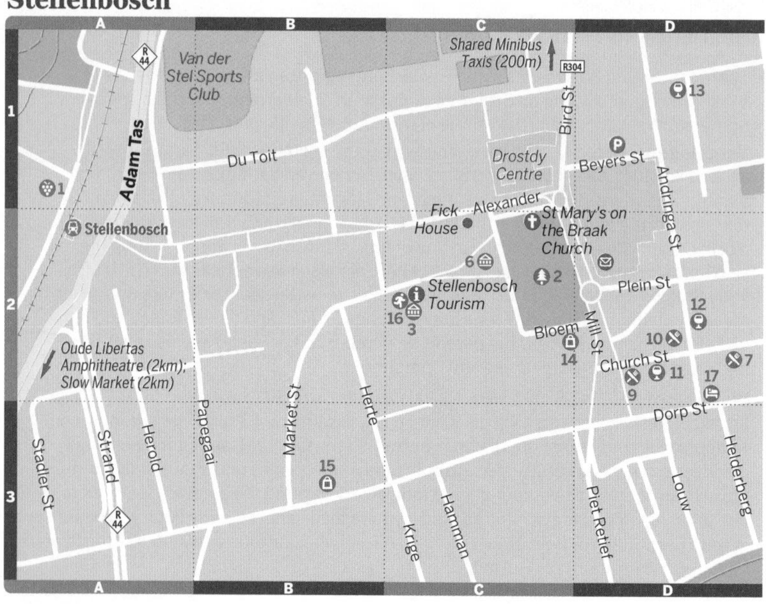

VAN RYN BRANDY CELLAR DISTILLERY

(☎021-881 3875; www.vanryn.co.za; tour & tastings from R50; ⊙9am-5.30pm Mon-Fri, to 3.30pm Sat year-round, 11am-3pm Sun Oct-Apr) This brandy distillery runs superb tours, which include a barrel-making display and end with your choice of tasting. Options include pairing brandy with chocolate or charcuterie and sampling brandy cocktails.

BLAAUWKLIPPEN WINERY

(☎021-880 0133; www.blaauwklippen.com; Rte 44; tastings R35; ⊙10am-5pm, cellar tours 11am & 2pm; 👪) This rustic, 300-year-old estate with several fine Cape Dutch buildings is known for its excellent red wines, particularly its cabernet sauvignon and zinfandel. There's a wine and chocolate pairing option (R80) and lunch is available either at the bistro (call for times; they change according to the season) or, from October to March, with a picnic on the lawn (bookings essential). It's good for kids, especially on weekends when there are horse-and-carriage rides around the estate.

MEERLUST ESTATE WINERY

(☎021-843 3587; www.meerlust.com; Rte 310; tastings R30; ⊙9am-5pm Mon-Fri, 10am-2pm

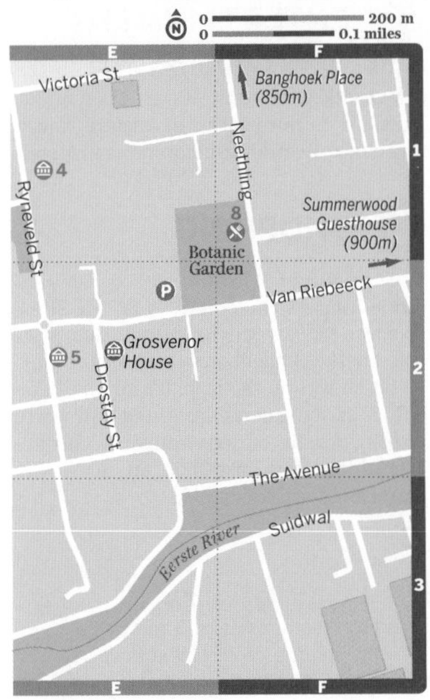

Sat) Hannes Myburgh is the eighth generation of his family to have run this historic wine estate since 1756. They are most famous for Rubicon, a wine that John Platter's guide once called a 'pre-eminent Cape claret'. Its tasting room, decorated with the owner's collection of posters and a fine history of the winery, is worth a look.

TOKARA WINERY

(☎021-808 5900; www.tokara.co.za; Rte 310; tastings free; ⌚9am-5pm Mon-Fri, 10am-3pm Sat & Sun) Tokara is renowned for its excellent wines – particularly chardonnay and sauvignon blanc – and for its upmarket restaurant (lunch Tuesday to Sunday, dinner Tuesday to Saturday), fine-art collection and sleek design. In summer you can enjoy intricate dishes and mountain views outside. In winter, snuggle up by the fire with a taster of the noble late harvest (dessert wine) or pot still brandy (R10). There's a fantastic deli/sculpture gallery for less fancy lunches, and you can taste the olive oil made on the estate.

JONKERSHOEK NATURE RESERVE NATURE RESERVE

(www.capenature.co.za; Jonkershoek Rd; adult/child R40/20; ⌚7.30am-4pm) This small nature reserve is 8km southeast of town and set within a timber plantation. There is a 10km scenic drive, plus hiking trails ranging from 5km to 18km. A hiking map is available at the entrance.

EATING & DRINKING

★SCHOON DE COMPANJE DELI $

(www.decompanje.co.za; 7 Church St; mains R50-100; ⌚breakfast & lunch Tue-Sun, pizzas served until 6pm) A vibrant bakery and deli priding itself on locally sourced ingredients. The menu features salads, sandwiches and meze-style platters, as well as fresh cakes and pastries and local craft beer. There are tables on the pavement, while inside has a market-hall feel, with plenty of seating and some shops to browse.

KATJIEPIERING RESTAURANT CAFE $

(Van Riebeeck St; mains R50-120; ⌚9am-5pm) Tucked away in the corner of the botanic garden and surrounded by exotic plants, this is a lovely spot for coffee, cake or a light lunch. Some traditional meals are served.

HELENA'S SOUTH AFRICAN $$

(☎021-883 3132; www.helenasrestaurant.co.za; Coopmanhuijs Boutique Hotel, 33 Church St; R80-220; ⌚breakfast, lunch & dinner) A little, charming restaurant within a boutique hotel. The menu is small but features some traditional dishes and lots of locally sourced goodies – the wild mushroom risotto is superb. Bookings essential.

96 WINERY ROAD INTERNATIONAL $$

(www.96wineryroad.co.za; Zandberg Farm, Winery Rd; mains R120; ⌚lunch & dinner Mon-Sat, lunch Sun) Off Rte 44 between Stellenbosch and Somerset West, this is a long-established restaurant, known for its dry aged beef.

WIJNHUIS ITALIAN $$

(www.wijnhuis.co.za; cnr Andringa St & Church Sts; mains R100-210; ⌚lunch & dinner) There's an interesting menu and an extensive wine list stretching to more than 500 labels. Around 20 wines are available by the glass and tastings are available (R50).

★BRAMPTON WINE STUDIO WINE BAR

(☎021-883 9097; www.brampton.co.za; 11 Church St; ⌚9am-7.30pm Mon-Fri, from 10am Sat) Play games and scribble on tables while sipping shiraz at this trendy pavement cafe that also serves as Brampton winery's tasting room. Sandwiches and wraps (R50 to R70) are served throughout the day.

MYSTIC BOER BAR

(www.diemysticboer.co.za; 3 Victoria St) This funky bar is a Stellenbosch institution. There's regular live music and decent bar food.

CRAFT WHEAT & HOPS BEER

(Andringa St; ⏲11am-9.30pm Mon-Sat) This place has 15 local micro-brewed beers on tap and another dozen in bottles. There's also a decent wine list and a great selection of spirits. Open sandwiches (R40 to R60) are served and there's a nice tapas menu available after 4pm.

ENTERTAINMENT

OUDE LIBERTAS AMPHITHEATRE ARTS

(www.oudelibertas.co.za; Oude Libertas Rd) Open-air performances of theatre, music and dance are held here November to March.

SHOPPING

OOM SAMIE SE WINKEL SOUVENIRS

(Uncle Sammy's Shop; 84 Dorp St; ⏲8.30am-6pm Mon-Fri, 9am-5pm Sat & Sun) This place was on the Stellenbosch map before Stellenbosch was on the map. It's an unashamedly touristy general dealer but still worth visiting for its curious range of goods – everything from joke-shop tat to African crafts and local foodstuffs.

WINING & DINING

The Cape Winelands boast many of South Africa's top restaurants, and enjoying a spot of fine dining at one of the vineyards is a worthy splurge. Many places have set gourmet menus offering three to six smallish courses. There's often a wine pairing option, where each dish comes with a small glass of wine chosen by the sommelier to complement the food.

Jordan (☎021-881 3612; www.jordanwines.com; Stellenbosch Kloof Rd; bakery mains R60-120, 3-course menu from R345; ⏲breakfast, lunch & dinner Thu-Sat) It's a little off the beaten Stellenbosch path, but it's worth the drive to get to this well-respected restaurant in a winery. The delectable menu is filled with high-end, inventive dishes, and, for those looking for something more casual, the bakery serves salads and cheese platters with freshly baked bread.

Harvest at Laborie (☎021-807 3095; www.harvestatlaborie.co.za; Taillefer St; mains R90-140; ⏲lunch Mon-Sun, dinner Thu-Sat; 👪) Eat on a patio overlooking vines at this elegant wine estate a short walk from Main St. Local produce dominates the menu, including West Coast mussels, Karoo lamb and seasonal game steaks. Bookings recommended for dinner and weekend lunches.

La Petite Ferme (☎021-876 3016; www.lapetiteferme.co.za;Franschhoek Pass Rd; mains R100-180; ⏲lunch; 📶) In a stupendous setting overlooking the valley, this quaint country bistro-style restaurant has a small menu. Sample the boutique wines and smoked, deboned salmon trout, its delicately flavoured signature dish. There are some luxurious rooms if you can't bear to leave.

Haute Cabrière Cellar (☎021-876 3688; www.cabriere.co.za; Franschhoek Pass Rd; mains R140-180; ⏲lunch Tue-Sun, dinner Tue-Sat) As well as the delectable and imaginative à la carte offerings, there is a six-course set menu with accompanying wines (R750). Tastings (from R30) are also available at the cellar and on Saturdays the proprietor performs the *sabrage:* slicing open a bottle of bubbly with a sword.

Rust en Vrede (☎021-881 3757; www.rustenvrede.com; Annandale Rd; 4-course menu R620, 6-course menu with/without wines R1150/750; ⏲dinner Tue-Sat) Chef John Shuttleworth prepares contemporary takes on the classics at this winery restaurant.

Overture Restaurant (☎021-880 2721; www.dineatoverture.co.za; Hidden Valley Wine Estate, off Annandale Rd; 3 courses R375, 6-course menu R540; ⏲lunch Wed-Sun, dinner Thu-Sat) A very modern wine estate and restaurant where TV chef Bertus Basson focuses on local, seasonal produce paired with Hidden Valley wines.

CRAFT MARKET MARKET

(Braak; ⌚9am-5pm Mon-Sat) This open-air market is a great place to haggle for African carvings, paintings and costume jewellery.

SPORTS & ACTIVITIES

Stellenbosch and its immediate surrounds are fairly flat. Cycling the town centre or between wineries is a great way to explore.

★BIKES 'N WINES TOUR

(☎021-823 8790; www.bikesnwines.com; per person R550-790) This carbon-negative company comes highly recommended. Cycling routes range from 9km to 21km and take in three or four Stellenbosch wineries.

ADVENTURE SHOP BICYCLE RENTAL

(☎021-882 8112; www.adventureshop.co.za; cnr Dorp & Mark Sts; per day R150) A good option for bike rental if you're not interested in a tour.

SLEEPING

In addition to the wealth of sleeping options, for all budgets, in the town itself, a number of the wine estates offer accommodation ranging from self-catering chalets to uberluxurious hotels.

★BANGHOEK PLACE BACKPACKERS $

(☎021-887 0048; www.banghoek.co.za; 193 Banghoek Rd; dm/r R150/600;) This stylish suburban hostel is a quieter alternative, away from the town centre. The recreation area has satellite TV and a pool table and there's a nice swimming pool in the garden.

STELLENBOSCH HOTEL HISTORIC HOTEL $$

(☎021-887 3644; www.stellenboschhotel.co.za; 162 Dorp St, cnr Andringa St; s/d incl breakfast from R880/1100;) A comfortable country-style hotel with a variety of rooms, including some with self-catering facilities and others with four-poster beds. A section dating from 1743 houses the Jan Cats Brasserie, a good spot for a drink. The hotel and restaurant were being renovated when we visited.

SUMMERWOOD GUESTHOUSE GUESTHOUSE $$$

(☎021-887 4112; www.summerwood.co.za; 28 Jonkershoek Rd; s/d incl breakfast R1310/2150;) In a suburban neighbourhood bordering a small nature reserve east of the town centre is this elegant guesthouse. The immaculate rooms are bright and spacious, with excellent amenities. Rates drop dramatically between April and September.

Franschhoek

Explore

The most compact of the Winelands towns, Franschhoek is the best option for those without wheels – presuming you don't mind taking a taxi from Stellenbosch to get here. Begin your explorations at the Huguenot Memorial Museum to discover Franschhoek's French roots and how it came to be a prime winemaking town. From here you can amble along Huguenot St, perusing menus and shopping for arts and crafts. Enjoy lunch at one of the country's top restaurants before delving into the myriad wine tasting options – many are within walking distance of the main road. If you have a car – and a designated driver – explore the vineyards west of the town or the Franschhoek Pass to the east.

The Best...

➡ **Sight** Boschendal (p166)

➡ **Place to Eat** Le Quartier Français: Tasting Room (p168)

➡ **Place to Drink** Leopard's Leap (p167)

Top Tip

Franschhoek is considered the gastronomic capital of the Cape and a number of local restaurants offer cooking courses led by award-winning chefs. Enquire at the tourist office for details.

Getting There & Away

➡ **Trains** Take a train from Cape Town to Stellenbosch (1st/economy class R18.50/12, about one hour, frequently). From here you can get a shared taxi (R20) or a **private taxi** (☎082 256 6784).

Need to Know

➡ **Area Code** ☎021

➡ **Location** Franschhoek is 85km east of Cape Town along the N1 and Rte 45.

➡ **Tourist Office** (☎021-876 2861; www.franschhoek.org.za; 62 Huguenot St; ⌚8am-6pm Mon-Fri, 9am-6pm Sat, 9am-4pm Sun)

SIGHTS

HUGUENOT MEMORIAL MUSEUM — MUSEUM

(www.museum.co.za; Lambrecht St; adult/child R10/2; ⌚9am-5pm Mon-Sat, 2-5pm Sun) This museum celebrates South Africa's Huguenots and houses the genealogical records of their descendants. Behind the main complex is a pleasant cafe, in front is the **Huguenot Monument** (⌚9am-5pm) FREE, opened in 1948, and across the road is the annexe, which offers displays on the Anglo-Boer War and natural history.

HUGUENOT FINE CHOCOLATES — FOOD

(☎021-876 4096; www.huguenotchocolates.com; 62 Huguenot St; ⌚8am-5.30pm Mon-Fri, 9am-5.30pm Sat & Sun) An empowerment program gave the two local guys who run this chocolatier a leg up and now people are raving about their confections. There are daily chocolate-making demonstrations including a tasting (R40) at 11am and 3pm – advance bookings recommended.

CERAMICS GALLERY — GALLERY

(☎021-876 4304; www.davidwalters.co.za; 24 Dirkie Uys St; ⌚10am-6pm) Franschhoek boasts many fine galleries, mostly along Huguenot St. At the Ceramics Gallery you can watch David Walters, one of South Africa's most distinguished potters, at work in the beautifully restored home of Franschhoek's first teacher. There are also exhibits of work by other artists.

★BOSCHENDAL — WINERY

(☎021-870 4210; www.boschendal.com; Rte 310, Groot Drakenstein; tastings R35, manor house R20; ⌚9am-5.30pm) This is a quintessential Winelands estate, with lovely architecture, food and wine. There are excellent vineyard (R35) and cellar (R25) tours; booking is essential. For a dose of history with your wine, take the self-guided tour of the manor house. Boschendal has three eating options: the huge buffet lunch (R240) in the main restaurant, light lunches in Le Café or a 'Le Pique Nique' hamper (adult/child R175/75; bookings essential), served under parasols on the lawn from September to May.

★LA MOTTE — WINERY

(☎021-876 8000; www.la-motte.com; Main Rd; tastings R50; ⌚9am-5pm Mon-Sat) There's enough to keep you occupied for a full day

Franschhoek

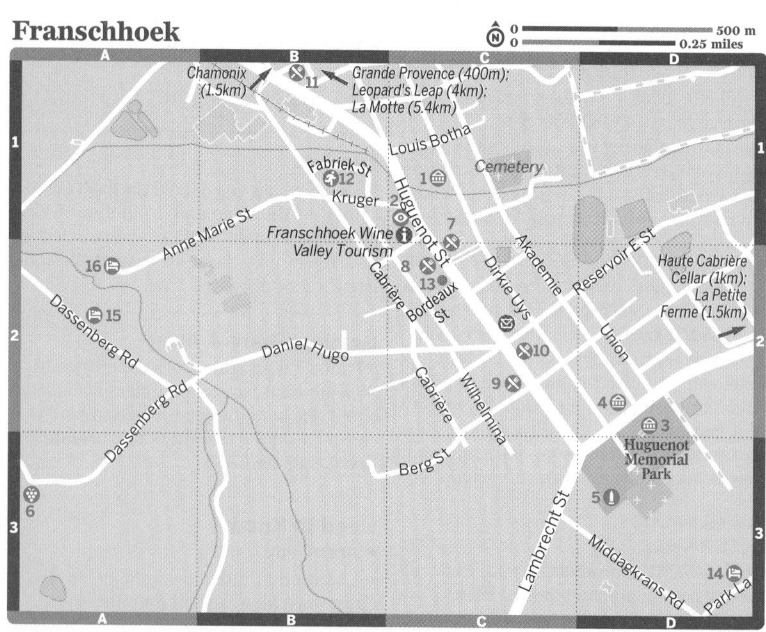

at this vast estate just west of Franschhoek. As well as tastings on offer of the superb shiraz range, wine-pairing lunches and dinners are served at the **Pierneef à la Motte** (mains R100-200; ⏲breakfast Sat & Sun, lunch Tue-Sun, dinner Thu-Sat) restaurant. The restaurant is named for South African artist Jacob Hendrik Pierneef and a collection of his work is on show at the on-site museum.

This is also the starting point for historical walks (R50) through the estate, taking in four national monuments and a milling demonstration and ending with a bread tasting (Wednesday 10am, bookings essential). If you've over-indulged, walk off a few calories on the 5km circular hike that starts at the farm.

FRANSCHHOEK WINE TRAM

If you'd rather ditch the car and properly enjoy the tasting rooms, the **Franschhoek Wine Tram** (☎021-300 0338; www.winetram.co.za; 32 Huguenot Rd; adult/child R200/85) is a fun alternative to the usual Winelands tour. The actual tram line is short and only two wineries have a tram stop. The rest of the hop-on, hop-off service makes use of an open-sided bus to shuttle passengers between the wine farms. There are two routes, each visiting up to seven wineries. Bookings advisable and dress warmly – the bus in particular can get pretty chilly.

LEOPARD'S LEAP — WINERY

(☎021-876 8002; www.leopardsleap.co.za; Rte 45; tastings from R25, restaurant mains R60-120; ⏲9am-5pm Tue-Sat, 11am-5pm Sun; 👪) The bright, modern, barn-like tasting room has comfy couches strewn around – you can either take your tasters to enjoy at leisure or sit at the bar for a slightly more formal affair. The large lawns have a jungle gym for kids, while the rotisserie restaurant (lunch Wednesday to Sunday) offers a very affordable way to eat in the Winelands. Cooking classes are available once a month – booking ahead is essential.

SOLMS-DELTA — WINERY

(☎021-874 3937; www.solms-delta.com; Delta Rd, off Rte 45; tastings R10; ⏲9am-5pm Sun & Mon, to 6pm Tue-Sat) In addition to tastings and sales, various heritage tours are available at this excellent winery. The museum covers Cape history and tells the Solms-Delta story from the perspective of farm workers throughout the years. On the culinary side, there's **Fyndraai Restaurant** (mains R130-155; ⏲lunch), serving original dishes inspired by the Cape's varied cultures and using herbs from the on-site indigenous garden. You can also opt for a picnic, to be enjoyed along an enchanting riverside trail.

GRANDE PROVENCE — WINERY

(www.grandeprovence.co.za; Main Rd; tastings from R40, cellar tours R25; ⏲10am-7pm, cellar tours 11am & 3pm Mon-Fri) A beautifully revamped, 18th-century manor house that is home to a stylish restaurant and a splendid gallery showcasing contemporary South African art. There is a range of tasting options, including grape-juice tasting for the kids (R20). It's within walking distance of the town centre.

Franschhoek

Sights

1 Ceramics Gallery ... C1
2 Huguenot Fine Chocolates ... C1
3 Huguenot Memorial Museum ... D2
4 Huguenot Memorial Museum Annexe ... D2
5 Huguenot Monument ... D3
6 Mont Rochelle ... A3

Eating

7 Franschhoek Market ... C1
8 French Connection ... C2
9 Le Quartier Français: Living Room ... C2
Le Quartier Français: Tasting Room ... (see 9)
10 Reuben's ... C2
11 Ryan's Kitchen ... B1

Sports & Activities

12 Franschhoek Cycles ... B1
13 Franschhoek Wine Tram ... C2

Sleeping

14 La Cabrière Country House ... D3
15 Otter's Bend Lodge ... A2
16 Reeden Lodge ... A2

FOOD MARKETS IN THE WINELANDS

Farmers markets are South Africa's favourite foodie craze, with the Winelands having a particularly good selection. Rather than places to do your shopping, these markets tend to focus more on meals to eat in situ – expect to find anything from freshly baked bread and artisanal cheese to paella, Thai snacks and spicy curries, plus piles of cake, local wine and plenty of craft beer.

Blaauwklippen Market (www.blaauwklippen.com; Rte 44, Blauwklippen Vineyards; ⊙10am-3pm Sun; 👪) A very family-friendly market with carriage and pony rides on offer.

Franschhoek Market (www.franschhoekmarket.wozaonline.co.za; 29 Huguenot Rd; ⊙9am-2pm Sat) Based in the grounds of the church, this market has a real country fete vibe.

Slow Market (www.slowmarket.co.za; Oude Libertas Rd, Oude Libertas; ⊙9am-2pm Sat) Stellenbosch's original farmers market features lots of artisanal produce as well as crafts.

CHAMONIX — WINERY

(☎021-876 8426; www.chamonix.co.za; Uitkyk St; tastings R35; ⊙9.30am-5pm) Cellar tours at 11am and 3pm by appointment (R10). The tasting room is in a converted blacksmith's; there's also a range of schnapps and grappa to sample. The restaurant, **Racine** (mains R100-150; ⊙lunch Tue-Sun, dinner Thu-Sat), has a lovely deck overhanging a stream. It's uphill but you can walk from the town.

HAUTE CABRIÈRE — WINERY

(☎021-876 8500; www.cabriere.co.za; Franschhoek Pass Rd; tastings from R30, cellar tours R60; ⊙9am-5pm Mon-Fri, 10am-4pm Sat, 11am-4pm Sun, cellar tours 11am Mon-Sat) Tasting options include Méthode Cap Classique (MCC; South African sparkling wine) and an excellent range of white and red wines, plus a brandy. During the Saturday session, stand by for the proprietor's party trick of *sabrage:* slicing open a bottle of bubbly with a sword. Ask and you might be able to try your hand.

MONT ROCHELLE — WINERY

(www.montrochelle.co.za; Dassenberg Rd; tastings R20; ⊙tastings 10am-6.30pm) Along with the uberplush hotel of the same name, this winery was bought by Richard Branson in 2014. You can combine your wine tasting with a cheese platter (R115), or enjoy lunch (mains from R95) with a view of the town and the mountains beyond.

EATING

★LE QUARTIER FRANÇAIS: LIVING ROOM — BISTRO $$

(☎021-876 2151; www.lqf.co.za; 16 Huguenot St; tapas R40-95; ⊙breakfast, lunch & dinner) Great for breakfast, light-ish lunches and delectable dinners that won't break the bank. The menu includes Asian-inspired tapas using African ingredients like wildebeest and springbok.

LUST BISTRO & BAKERY — BISTRO $$

(☎021-874 1456; www.lustbistro.com; Rte 45, cnr Simondium Rd; mains R75-130; ⊙breakfast & lunch) At Vrede en Lust winery, this is a refreshingly unfussy place to eat in a region known for haute cuisine. The focus is on sandwiches and pizzas, with all bread baked freshly. Try the sourdough pizza base. On Sunday there's a buffet lunch where you pay by the weight of your plate – bookings essential.

RYAN'S KITCHEN — SOUTH AFRICAN $$

(www.ryanskitchen.co.za; Pl Vendome, Huguenot Rd; mains R75-100, 5-course tasting menu without/with wine R400/590; ⊙lunch & dinner Mon-Sat) Loved by locals, recommended by travellers, this long-running restaurant marries South African ingredients with fine-dining techniques. Watch chefs prepare intricate and surprisingly well-priced dishes. The menu changes every two weeks.

FRENCH CONNECTION — INTERNATIONAL $$

(48 Huguenot St; mains R80-165; ⊙lunch & dinner) No-nonsense bistro-style food using only fresh ingredients is dished up at this deservedly popular place.

★LE QUARTIER FRANÇAIS: TASTING ROOM — FUSION $$$

(☎021-876 2151; www.lqf.co.za; 16 Huguenot St; 5-course meal with wine R750; ⊙dinner Tue-Sat) Consistently rated as one of the world's 50 top restaurants by *Restaurant Magazine* UK. If you're really serious about food, chef Margot Janse will whip up the gourmet, eight-course menu at R1350 with wines.

REUBEN'S FUSION $$$
(☎021-876 3772; www.reubens.co.za; 19 Huguenot St; mains R125-200; ⌚lunch & dinner) The flagship restaurant for this local celebrity chef is a relaxed place offering fusion cuisine with plenty of Asian influence.

SPORTS & ACTIVITIES

PARADISE STABLES HORSE RIDING
(☎021-876 2160; www.paradisestables.co.za; per hr R200; ⌚Mon-Sat) As well as hourly rides through Franschhoek's surrounds, there are four-hour trips taking in two vineyards (R750 including tastings).

FRANSCHHOEK CYCLES CYCLING
(www.franschhoekcycles.co.za; Fabriek St; half/full day R190/290) Rent bikes or have staff arrange a guided cycling tour of surrounding wineries (R385).

SLEEPING

OTTER'S BEND LODGE BACKPACKERS $
(☎021-876 3200; Dassenberg Rd; camping per site R150, dm/d R150/450;) A delightful budget option in a town not known for affordable accommodation. Basic double rooms lead to a shared deck shaded by poplar trees, and there's space for a couple of tents on the lawn. It's a 15-minute walk from town and close to a winery.

★**REEDEN LODGE** CHALET $$
(☎021-876 3174; www.reedenlodge.co.za; Anne Marie St; cottage for 2 ppl from R750;) A good-value, terrific option for families, with well-equipped, self-catering cottages sleeping up to 10 people, situated on a farm about 10 minutes' walk from town. Parents will love the peace and quiet and their kids will love the sheep, tree house and open space.

LA CABRIÈRE COUNTRY HOUSE GUESTHOUSE $$$
(☎021-876 4780; www.lacabriere.co.za; Park Lane; d incl breakfast from R1980;) Under new ownership and after major renovations, this modern boutique guesthouse is better than ever. The sumptuously decorated rooms have underfloor heating and sweeping views to the mountains. Also available is a two-bedroom self-catering cottage in the town centre with a private pool (R2500).

Paarl

Explore

The main drawback to oft-overlooked Paarl is how spread out the town is – the main road stretches for 11km, making your own transport necessary if you want to explore in depth. If you're interested in history, start at the northern end of town, where the two small museums sit a couple of blocks apart. Paarl's restaurants are all in the centre of town, while two wineries flank the southern entrance as you approach from the N1. If you're arriving by train, these are both an easy walk from the station. Paarl's main attractions, though, all lie out of the town itself. There's a cluster of wine estates on the Suid-Agter-Paarl Rd, west of the centre, and another group due south on Simondium Rd.

The Best...

- **Sight** Spice Route (p171)
- **Place to Eat** Bosman's Restaurant (p172)
- **Activity** A balloon ride (p172) over the Winelands.

Top Tip

Some of Paarl's better-known wineries can get incredible busy. Visit midweek, preferably in the morning for a quieter experience.

Getting There & Away

- **Train** Frequent **Metrorail** (☎0800-656 463; www.capemetrorail.co.za) trains are operated from Cape Town (1st/economy class R19/12, 1¼ hours).

Need to Know

- **Area Code** ☎021
- **Location** Paarl is 62km east of Cape Town along the N1.
- **Tourist Office** (☎073 708 2835; www.paarlonline.com; 216 Main St; ⌚8am-5pm Mon-Fri, 10am-1pm Sat & Sun)

SIGHTS

AVONDALE WINERY
(☎021-863 1976; www.avondalewines.co.za; Klein Drakenstein; tastings R50, eco-tours R200; ⌚10am-4pm Mon-Sat) Of the 630-odd wineries across the Western Cape, only 14 make

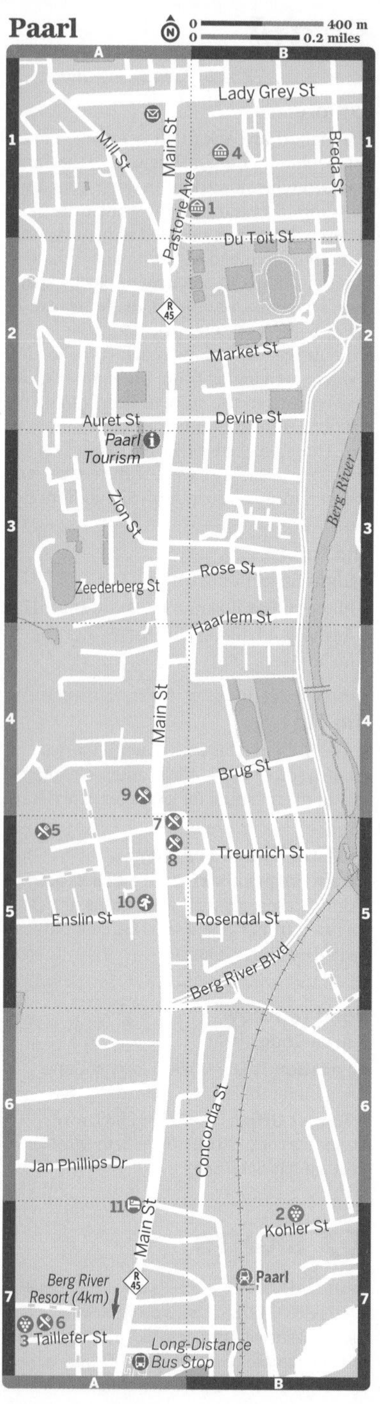

organic wines. Avondale is one of them and it's a great place to visit to find out about their earth-friendly 'biologic' method, and take an eco-tour of the farm on the back of an open van (a 'backie') during which you'll taste their award-winning premium wines.

The handsome Cape Dutch–style 'tasting gallery' is also hung with beautiful landscapes by Scats Esterhuyse. Find out more about Avondale's farming methods at the owner's blog www.biologicwine.co.za.

LABORIE CELLAR WINERY

(www.laboriewines.co.za; Taillefer St; tastings from R25; ⌚9am-5pm Mon-Sat, 11am-5pm Sun) Best known for its award-winning shiraz, Laborie also produces good Méthode Cap Classique and dessert wines. Tasting options include wine and olives (R30) or chocolate (R35).

KWV EMPORIUM WINERY

(www.kwvwineemporium.co.za; Kohler St; tastings R50; ⌚9am-4.30pm Mon-Sat, 11am-4pm Sun, cellar tours 10am, 10.30am & 2.15pm) This winery is a short walk from the train station. Its fortified wines and brandies are award-winning. Cellar tours (R40) are available and there is a range of tasting options, including chocolate and brandy, biltong and wine, and a tea and chocolate pairing for non-drinkers (R45).

PAARL MOUNTAIN NATURE RESERVE NATURE RESERVE

(per vehicle R40, per person R15; ⌚7am-7pm) The three giant granite domes that dominate this reserve glisten like pearls when washed

Paarl

Sights

1 Afrikaans Language Museum B1
2 KWV Emporium B7
3 Laborie Cellar A7
4 Paarl Museum B1

Eating

5 Bosman's Restaurant A5
6 Harvest at Laborie A7
7 Marc's Mediterranean Cuisine & Garden A5
8 Noop A5
9 Terra Mare A4

Sports & Activities

10 Wineland Ballooning A5

Sleeping

11 Oak Tree Lodge A7

BABYLONSTOREN

The 2.5-sq-km wine and fruit farm **Babylonstoren** (☎021-863 3852; www.babylonstoren.com; Simondium Rd, Klapmuts; admission R10; ⏲10am-5pm, restaurant open lunch Wed-Sun, dinner Fri & Sat; P) is on the north slope of the Simonsberg mountain between Klapmuts and Paarl. It's highlight is an 800-sq-metre, formally designed garde: inspired by Cape Town's Company's Gardens, it is an incredible undertaking. It features edible and medicinal plants, lotus ponds and espaliered quince trees, chicken coops and a maze of prickly-pear cacti. Reserve a place on one of the garden tours (10am).

Better yet, check into one of the super-chic guest rooms (from R4900), crafted from the old workers' cottages, so that once the day visitors have left you can enjoy the gardens – not to mention the spa and pool in one of the farm's old reservoir tanks.

There's no need to reserve if you'd like refreshments in the tea garden with its lovely glasshouse. However, bookings are essential for the restaurant Babel (mains R140), which serves delicious meals made with produce from the garden and quaffable wines that the farm has recently resumed making. The new wine cellar (of which tours are available) is a model of contemporary design with interesting exhibits related to the winemaking process. And the tasting room/deli/bakery showcases a selection of wines from estates around Simonsberg, which is said to have some of the best terroir in the Cape.

Babylonstoren has existed for over 300 years, but never used to figure on the Winelands tourism trail. All that began to change in 2007, when Babylonstoren passed to new owners with the vision to transform it into one of the region's must-see destinations.

by rain – hence the name 'Paarl'. The reserve has mountain *fynbos* (literally 'fine bush'; primarily proteas, heaths and ericas), a cultivated wildflower garden that's a delightful picnic spot, and numerous walks with excellent views over the valley. You could also visit the rather phallic **Taal Monument** (www.taalmuseum.co.za; adult/child R20/5; ⏲8am-5pm, 8am-8pm Dec-Mar), a giant needlelike edifice that commemorates the Afrikaans language (*taal* is Afrikaans for 'language').

PAARL MUSEUM — MUSEUM

(303 Main St; admission R5; ⏲9am-4pm Mon-Fri) In the Oude Pastorie (Old Parsonage), built in 1714, this museum has an interesting collection of Cape Dutch antiques and relics of Huguenot and early Afrikaner culture.

AFRIKAANS LANGUAGE MUSEUM — MUSEUM

(www.taalmuseum.co.za; 11 Pastorie Ave; adult/child R20/5; ⏲9.30am-4.30pm Mon-Fri) Paarl is considered the wellspring of the Afrikaans language, a fact covered by this interesting museum. It also shows, thanks to a multimedia exhibition, how three continents contributed to the formation of the language.

★SPICE ROUTE — WINERY

(☎021-863 5200; www.spiceroute.co.za; Suid-Agter-Paarl Rd; tastings from R25; ⏲9am-5pm) Spice Route is known for its complex red wines, particularly the Flagship syrah. Aside from wine there is a lot going on, including glass-blowing demonstrations, wine and chocolate pairings (R75), a chocolatier (tutored tasting R25), grappa distillery (tastings R30) and a superlative microbrewery (tastings R25). As well as the upmarket Spice Route restaurant (mains R95 to R170), there is a pizzeria (mains R50 to R90).

FAIRVIEW — WINERY

(☎021-863 2450; www.fairview.co.za; Suid-Agter-Paarl Rd; wine & cheese tastings R25; ⏲9am-5pm) This hugely popular estate off Rte 101, 6km south of Paarl, is a wonderful winery but not the place to come for a tranquil tasting. It is great value, since tastings include six wines *and* a wide range of cheeses. The well-respected restaurant (mains R70 to R160) is open for breakfast and lunch.

BACKSBERG — WINERY

(☎021-875 5141; www.backsberg.co.za; tastings R15; ⏲8am-5pm Mon-Fri, 9.30am-4.30pm Sat, 10.30am-4.30pm Sun) A hugely popular estate thanks to its reliable label and lavish outdoor lunches – book ahead for the Sunday lamb spit braai (R225). This was South Africa's first carbon-neutral wine farm and its wines include the easy-drinking Tread Lightly range, packaged in lightweight, environmentally friendly bottles.

NEDERBURG WINES WINERY

(☎021-862 3104; www.nederburg.co.za; tastings R25-70; ⏰8am-6pm Mon-Fri, 10am-4pm Sat & Sun) This is one of South Africa's best-known labels, a big but professional and welcoming operation featuring a vast range of wines. Look out for inventive tasting options such as blind food matching, burger pairings and a kids' grape juice and snack pairing experience.

ANURA WINERY

(☎021-875 5360; www.anura.co.za; Off Simondium Rd, Klapmuts; wine & cheese tastings R45; ⏰9.30am-5pm) Foodies could hang out here for a while, tasting cheese made on the premises, grabbing a platter or picnic featuring cured meats from the deli, or swapping grape for grain and sipping a beer from the microbrewery alongside the pretty pond.

GLEN CARLOU WINERY

(☎021-875 5528; www.glencarlou.co.za; Simondium Rd, Klapmuts; tastings R25-35; ⏰9am-5pm Mon-Fri, 10am-4pm Sat & Sun) Sitting south of the N1, the tasting room has a panoramic view of Tortoise Hill. Enjoy a glass of the sumptuous chardonnay or renowned bordeaux blend, Grand Classique, over lunch (three-course meal R340). There's an art gallery too.

DRAKENSTEIN PRISON HISTORIC SITE

On 11 February 1990, when Nelson Mandela walked free from incarceration for the first time in over 27 years, the jail he left was not on Robben Island, but here. Then called the Victor Verster, this was where Mandela spent his last two years of captivity in the warders' cottage, negotiating the end of apartheid. It's still a working prison so there are no tours but there's a superb statue of Mandela, fist raised in *viva* position.

EATING

★TEA UNDER THE TREES TEA ROOM $

(☎082 825 5666; www.teaunderthetrees.co.za; Main Rd, Northern Paarl; mains R40-50; ⏰9am-4pm Mon-Fri Oct-Apr) The only downside to this fabulous tea garden is that it's only open for half the year. Based on an organic fruit farm, it's a wonderful place to sit under century-old oak trees and enjoy an alfresco cuppa, a light lunch or a large slice of home-baked cake. There's no indoor seating.

MARC'S MEDITERRANEAN CUISINE & GARDEN MEDITERRANEAN $$

(129 Main St; mains R65-140; ⏰lunch & dinner Tue-Sat) This laid-back spot is a long-standing Paarl favourite. Patron Marc Friedrich has created a light and bright place with food to match and a Provence-style garden to dine in.

TERRA MARE FUSION $$

(☎021-863 4805; 90A Main St; mains R90-190; ⏰lunch & dinner Mon-Sat) The menu is fairly small but superb, offering intricate takes on the classics. Tables inside can be a little noisy due to the proximity to busy Main St, but there's a delightful garden at the back.

★BOSMAN'S RESTAURANT INTERNATIONAL $$$

(☎021-863 5100; www.granderoche.co.za; Plantasie St; 3-courses R420; ⏰lunch & dinner) This elegant spot within the Grande Roche Hotel is one of the country's top restaurants, serving multi-course dinners and more casual bistro-style lunches (mains from R90). Bookings highly recommended.

NOOP FUSION $$$

(www.noop.co.za; 127 Main St; mains R95-200; ⏰lunch & dinner Mon-Sat) Recommended by locals all over the Winelands, this restaurant and wine bar has a comprehensive menu of upmarket dishes.

SPORTS & ACTIVITIES

WINELAND BALLOONING SCENIC FLIGHTS

(☎021-863 3192; www.kapinfo.com; 64 Main St; per person R3300) You'll need to get up very early in the morning, but a hot-air balloon trip over the Winelands will be unforgettable. Trips run between November and April when the weather conditions are right.

SLEEPING

BERG RIVER RESORT CAMPGROUND $

(☎021-863 1650; www.bergriverresort.co.za; camping per site from R350, d chalets from R715; 🏊👪) An attractive camping ground beside the Berg River, 5km from Paarl on Rte 45 towards Franschhoek. Facilities include canoes, trampolines and a cafe. It gets very crowded during school holidays and is best avoided then.

OAK TREE LODGE GUESTHOUSE $$
(021-863 2631; www.oaktreelodge.co.za; 32 Main St; s/d incl breakfast from R630/840;) Centrally located, this old house has comfortable, well-appointed rooms, some with balconies. The larger garden rooms are quieter, being off the main road.

★**CASCADE COUNTRY MANOR** BOUTIQUE HOTEL $$$
(021-813 6220; www.cascademanor.co.za; Waterfall Rd; s/d incl breakfast R1200/1870;) Tucked away along a dirt road 10km east of the centre, this place will make you feel like you're miles from anywhere here, though it's an easy drive back to town. Rooms are just what you'd expect but it's the grounds that wow, with vast lawns, a large pool, olive groves and a short walk to a pretty waterfall.

Robertson

Explore

Robertson itself holds little for the traveller, save for a particularly good cafe and some delightful guesthouses, but the region around Robertson is filled with uncrowded wineries, many of which offer free tastings. Stop first at the friendly tourism bureau to pick up a map of the Robertson wine route, which also encompasses the neighbouring villages of Ashton, Bonnievale and McGregor. If you end up staying over, or fancy doing something other than sipping, the surrounding mountains offer a range of activities, including hiking, gentle rafting on the river and horse riding – the town is famous for its horse studs.

The Best...

- **Sight** Viljoensdrift
- **Place to Eat** Strictly Coffee (p174)
- **Activity** Horse riding through the vineyards.

Top Tip

It's a two-hour drive from Cape Town to Robertson, so if you're not staying over, be sure to get an early start. Make sure you have cash as the N1 is a toll route.

Getting There & Away

- **Bus** Daily **Translux** (0861 589 282; www.translux.co.za) buses from Cape Town (R200, two hours) stop opposite the police station on Voortrekker St.

Need to Know

- **Area Code** 023
- **Location** Robertson is 160km east of Cape Town along the N1 and Rte 60.
- **Tourist Office** (023-626 4437; www.robertsontourism.co.za; cnr Voortrekker & Reitz Sts; 8am-5pm Mon-Fri, 9am-2pm Sat, 10am-2pm Sun)

SIGHTS

★**VILJOENSDRIFT** WINERY
(023-615 1017; www.viljoensdrift.co.za; tastings free; 9am-5pm Mon-Fri, 10am-4pm Sat;) One of Robertson's most popular places to sip. Put together a picnic from the deli, buy a bottle from the cellar door and take an hour-long boat trip along the Breede River (adult/child R50/20). Boats leave on the hour from noon. Bookings essential.

WORTH A DETOUR

MCGREGOR

Just 20km south of Robertson at the end of a road going nowhere sits the pretty town of McGregor. The main reason to visit, other than a dose of peace and quiet, is to tackle the spectacular **Boesmanskloof Trail** (Greyton McGregor Trail; day permit adult/child R40/20), a 14km hike through the Riviersonderend mountains to Greyton. There's also a shorter hike to a waterfall if you don't feel like a full day of walking.

The town has a superb restaurant, **Karoux** (023-625 1421; www.karoux.co.za; 42 Voortrekker Rd; mains R70-140; dinner Fri-Tue), and a couple of wineries scattered around the outskirts. Try **Tanagra Private Cellar** (023-625 1780; www.tanagra-wines.co.za; tastings free; by appointment) for its range of reds and good grappa.

You need your own wheels to reach McGregor.

EXCELSIOR WINERY
(www.excelsior.co.za; Rte 317; tastings free; ⏲10am-4pm Mon-Fri, to 3pm Sat) Tastings take place on a wooden deck overlooking a reservoir – it's a delightful spot. The real draw is the 'blend your own' experience, where you can mix three wine varieties to your liking and take home a bottle of your creation, complete with your own label (R60).

SPRINGFIELD WINERY
(www.springfieldestate.com; ⏲8am-5pm Mon-Fri, 9am-4pm Sat) Some of the wines here are unfiltered – try the uncrushed Whole Berry for something different. Bring your own picnic to enjoy in the peaceful grounds, overlooking a lake.

VAN LOVEREN WINERY
(www.vanloveren.co.za; tastings R45; ⏲8.30am-5pm Mon-Fri, 9.30am-3pm Sat, 11am-2pm Sun, bistro closed Tue; 👪) Wine-tasting options include pairings with cheese, chocolate and charcuterie as well as a grape-juice tasting for kids (R25). Each tree in the tropical garden tells a story – grab the information pamphlet from reception or join a guided tour (R40). The low-key bistro (mains R55 to R110) serves excellent burgers and pizzas.

GRAHAM BECK WINERY
(www.grahambeckwines.co.za; standard/other tastings free/from R50; ⏲9am-5pm Mon-Fri, 10am-4pm Sat & Sun) Tastings of award-winning syrah and the world-class bubblies (R75) are in a striking modern building with huge plate-glass windows. The winery comes as a breath of fresh air after all those Cape Dutch estates.

EATING

★STRICTLY COFFEE CAFE $
(www.strictlycoffee.co.za; 5 Voortrekker St; mains R40-70; ⏲breakfast & lunch) As well as excellent coffee roasted on-site, you'll find simply wonderful sandwiches with incredibly fresh ingredients. Locals rave about the eggs Benedict for breakfast.

BOURBON STREET INTERNATIONAL $$
(☎023-626 5934; 22 Voortrekker St; mains R60-140; ⏲lunch & dinner Mon Sat, lunch Sun; 📶) A firm favourite with locals and visitors, this New Orleansesque restaurant offers a little of everything. It's also about the only place you'll find nighttime action in Robertson.

SPORTS & ACTIVITIES

NERINA GUEST FARM HORSE RIDING
(☎082 744 2580; www.nerinaguestfarm.com; Goree Rd) This outfit offers horse trails along the river or through the vineyards with an option to swim with the horses afterwards. Rides last from one hour (R150) to half a day (R600).

SLEEPING

ROBERTSON BACKPACKERS BACKPACKERS $
(☎023-626 1280; www.robertsonbackpackers.co.za; 4 Dordrecht Ave; dm/s/d without bathroom R130/250/350, d R450; 📶) A terrific hostel, with spacious dorms and pleasant en suite doubles in the garden. There's a big grassy backyard and a shisha lounge, and wine and activity tours can be arranged. Camping available for R70.

★BALLINDERRY GUESTHOUSE $$
(☎023-626 5365; www.ballinderryguesthouse.com; 8 Le Roux St; s/d incl breakfast from R850/1100; ❄📶🏊) This colourful boutique guesthouse is impeccable, thanks to hosts Luc and Hilde. A champagne breakfast is served, as are superb dinners on request, and Dutch, French and German are spoken. Try to get one of the rooms that opens into the garden.

GUBAS DE HOEK GUESTHOUSE $$
(☎023-626 6218; www.gubas-dehoek.com; 45 Reitz St; s/d from R600/970; 📶🏊) 🍃 Highly recommended by readers is this comfortable home with well-appointed rooms. Owner-chef Gunther Huerttlen will cook you dinner (three courses R270) and there's a shared self-catering kitchen for preparing light meals. The owners are working to produce all of their own electricity.

Hermanus

Explore

On arrival, make a beeline straight for the Old Harbour – still the hub of the town. In whale season (June to December) you're likely to spot whales from here, while year-round it's the site of the town's museums, a permanent craft market and many good restaurants, cafes and hotels. From here, the Cliff Path Walking Trail takes you either southwest to the restaurants, bars and boat trips of the New Harbour or east to Grotto Beach, a 4km walk. In whale season, Hermanus quickly gets overcrowded, but it's easy enough to escape. Try the beaches to the east or the mountains to the north or, if you're keen to follow a lesser-trodden wine-tasting path, seek out the Hemel-en-Aarde Valley.

The Best...

➡ **Activity** Walking the Cliff Path Walking Trail (p177).

➡ **Place to Eat** Burgundy Restaurant (p176)

➡ **Place to Drink** Creation

Top Tip

In whale season keep your eyes – and ears – peeled for the whale crier, who belts out a Morse code signal on his kelp horn whenever he spots a whale.

Getting There & Away

➡ **Taxi** Shuttles to and from Cape Town (R800, 1½ hours) run by **Bernardus Tours** (☎028-316 1093; bniehaus@vodamail.co.za).

Need to Know

➡ **Area Code** ☎028

➡ **Location** Hermanus is 122km east of Cape Town along the N2 and Rte 43.

➡ **Tourist Office** (☎028-313 1602; www.hermanustourism.info; Market Sq; ⏲9am-6pm Mon-Fri, 9am-5pm Sat, 11am-3pm Sun)

SIGHTS

FERNKLOOF NATURE RESERVE — NATURE RESERVE

(☎028-313 0819; www.fernkloof.com; Fir Ave; ⏲9am-5pm) FREE This 15-sq-km reserve is wonderful if you're interested in *fynbos*. There's a 60km network of hiking trails for all fitness levels, and views over the sea are spectacular. A hiking map is available from the tourist information office.

OLD HARBOUR — HISTORIC SITE

This harbour clings to the cliffs in front of the town centre. The **Old Harbour Museum** (adult/child R20/5; ⏲9am-1pm & 2-5pm Mon-Sat, noon-4pm Sun) doesn't really have a lot going for it, but outside there's a display of old fishing boats and the admission fee includes entrance to the more interesting **Whale House Museum** (Market Sq; ⏲9am-4.30pm Mon-Sat, 12pm-4pm Sun) and **Photographic Museum** (Market Sq; ⏲9am-4.30pm Mon-Sat, noon-4pm Sun). There's a permanent craft market in the square as well.

WINE TASTING AROUND HERMANUS

The area is best known for whales, but there are also some superb wineries just outside Hermanus. The **Hemel-en-Aarde** (Heaven on Earth) valley starts 5km west of the town and follows a winding route north for 15km.

Bouchard Finlayson (☎028-312 3515; www.bouchardfinlayson.co.za; tastings R140; ⏲9am-5pm Mon-Fri, 10am-1pm Sat) is a traditional cellar known for its superlative pinot noir, while **La Vierge** (www.lavierge.co.za; tastings R30; ⏲tastings 9am-5pm, lunch Wed-Sun), a little further up the valley, offers tastings and lunch in its ubermodern winery decked out in hot pink and glass. **Newton Johnson** (☎021-200 2148; www.newtonjohnson.com; tastings free; ⏲9am-4pm Mon-Fri, 10am-2pm Sat, restaurant lunch Wed-Sun, dinner Fri & Sat) also has a superb restaurant, while at the far north of the route **Creation** (www.creationwines.com; pairing experiences from R75, restaurant mains R135; ⏲10am-5pm) is known for its food and wine pairing experiences.

If you don't have a nondrinker in your party, the highly recommended **Tuk-Tuk Transporter** (☎084 688 5885; www.hermanustaxi.com) provides transport between three wine farms, including a stop for lunch, and back to your accommodation for R250.

For an alternative way to see the wineries, join a quad-biking tour (R600) with **SA Forest Adventures** (☎083 517 3635; www.saforestadventures.co.za).

Hermanus

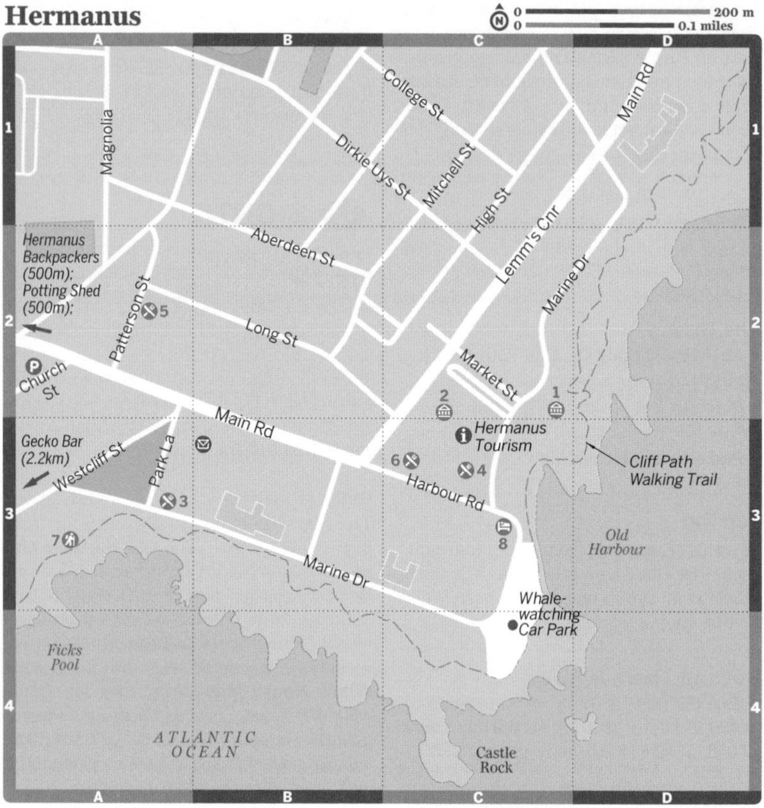

0 200 m
0 0.1 miles

College St
Dirkie Uys St
Mitchell St
High St
Main Rd
Lemm's Cnr
Magnolia
Aberdeen St
Marine Dr
Hermanus Backpackers (500m); Potting Shed (500m);
Patterson St
Long St
Market St
Church St
Main Rd
Hermanus Tourism
Gecko Bar (2.2km)
Westcliff St
Park La
Harbour Rd
Cliff Path Walking Trail
Old Harbour
Marine Dr
Whale-watching Car Park
Ficks Pool
ATLANTIC OCEAN
Castle Rock

EATING & DRINKING

EATERY CAFE $

(Long St Arcade, Long St; mains R50-90; breakfast & lunch Mon-Fri, breakfast & brunch Sat) Tucked away in an arcade, this is a local hang-out lauded for its excellent coffee, fresh salads and sandwiches plus a range of tasty cakes baked on-site.

BISTRO AT JUST PURE CAFE $$

(www.justpurebistro.co.za; cnr Park Lane & Marine Dr; mains R55-95; breakfast & lunch;) Adjoining a natural cosmetics shop, this seafront bistro is all about fresh, local, organic ingredients. Try the 'famous' cheesecake and watch whales from the patio as you eat.

★ **BURGUNDY RESTAURANT** SEAFOOD $$

(028-312 2800; www.burgundyrestaurant.co.za; Marine Dr; mains R70-175; breakfast, lunch & dinner) This long-standing restaurant is going strong, popular with both locals and tourists as much for its superb sea view as for its menu. Seafood is the star, though vegetarians and carnivores are also well served.

Hermanus

Sights

1 Old Harbour Museum....C2
Photographic Museum....(see 2)
2 Whale House Museum....C2

Eating

3 Bistro at Just Pure....A3
4 Burgundy Restaurant....C3
5 Eatery....A2
6 Fisherman's Cottage....C3

Sports & Activities

7 Cliff Path Walking Trail....A3

Sleeping

8 Harbour House Hotel....C3

FISHERMAN'S COTTAGE SEAFOOD $$

(Lemm's Cnr; mains R70-140; ⏱dinner Mon, lunch & dinner Tue-Sat, lunch Sun) The emphasis is on seafood at this 1860s thatched cottage draped with fishing nets, though it also serves steaks and traditional meals.

GECKO BAR BAR

(New Harbour; ⏱11am-2am) The decor is a bit shabby but the ocean views make up for it. There's sushi and pizza on the menu (mains R45 to R75), local beer on tap and live music on weekends.

SPORTS & ACTIVITIES

While Hermanus is renowned for its land-based whale-watching, boat trips are also available. Approaching whales in the water is highly regulated and the boats must stay a minimum of 50m away from the whales.

★CLIFF PATH WALKING TRAIL HIKING

This scenic path meanders for 10km from New Harbour, 2km west of town, along the sea to the mouth of the Klein River; you can join it anywhere along the cliffs. It's simply the finest thing to do in Hermanus, whales or not. Along the way you pass Grotto Beach, the most popular beach; Kwaaiwater, a good whale-watching lookout; as well as Langbaai and Voelklip Beaches. The tourism office has a pamphlet with more details on the trail.

SOUTHERN RIGHT CHARTERS BOAT TOUR

(☎082 353 0550; www.southernrightcharters.co.za; 2hr trip adult/child R650/350) One of four licensed boat operators that run whale-watching trips from New Harbour.

WALKER BAY ADVENTURES WATER SPORTS

(☎082 739 0159; www.walkerbayadventures.co.za; kayaking R350, canoeing R450, boat-based whale-watching R650) Watching whales from a sea kayak is a gobsmacking, if at times rather nerve-racking, experience. Other activities on offer include sandboarding, horse riding and boat trips.

SLEEPING

There is a huge amount of accommodation in Hermanus, but you might still find yourself searching in vain for a bed in the holiday season. Book ahead.

HERMANUS BACKPACKERS BACKPACKERS $

(☎028-312 4293; www.hermanusbackpackers.co.za; 26 Flower St; dm R140, d R410, d without bathroom R380; 📶🏊) A great place with upbeat decor, good facilities and clued-up staff who can help with activities. The simple, help-yourself breakfast is free, and evening braais are R100. It's a pretty chilled spot and the annexe around the corner is even quieter.

WORTH A DETOUR

OCEAN DRIVE

If you have an extra half an hour to spare, taking the ocean road to Hermanus is a spectacular way to arrive and only adds 30 minutes to your trip (plus the time it takes to stop for photos and admire the view). As you reach Strand, veer off the N2 onto Rte 44, a road that hugs the coast once you reach Gordon's Bay. Known as Clarence Dr, this coastal route is a very worthy, toll-free alternative to Cape Town's Chapman's Peak Dr. Allow time to stop at the many lookout points for photos, and between June and December keep an eye on False Bay for frolicking whales. There are a few worthy stops en route, starting with the **Kogelberg Biosphere Reserve** (☎028-271 5138; www.capenature.co.za; adult/child R40/20). The reserve has incredibly complex biodiversity, including more than 1880 plant species. Day walks are available as well as mountain-biking routes, but all activities must be prebooked. Do take the time to stop at the **Stony Point African Penguin Colony** (admission R10; ⏱8am-5pm). It's a much quieter place to watch the diminutive penguins than at the infinitely more famous Boulders Beach, on the other side of False Bay. After driving through Betty's Bay, you'll find the **Harold Porter National Botanical Gardens** (www.sanbi.org; adult/child R24/8; ⏱8am-4.30pm Mon-Fri, 8am-5pm Sat & Sun), worth a quick visit. There are paths exploring the indigenous plant life in the area and, at the entrance, a tearoom and plenty of places to picnic. Pretty **Kleinmond** is a good place for a seafood lunch on the water.

★POTTING SHED GUESTHOUSE $$
(☎028-312 1712; www.thepottingshedaccommodation.co.za; 28 Albertyn St; s/d incl breakfast R715/920;) This friendly guesthouse offers delightful personal touches, including homemade whale-shaped biscuits on arrival. The neat rooms are comfortable and have bright, imaginative decor. There's a spacious loft studio and the owners also operate stylish self-catering apartments (four people R1150) closer to the sea.

HARBOUR HOUSE HOTEL HOTEL $$$
(☎028-312 1799; www.harbourhousehotel.co.za; 22 Harbour Rd; d incl breakfast from R2100;) Some of the bright, modern rooms have kitchenettes and all have a balcony or terrace. It's a delightful seaside hotel and the ocean views from the infinity pool are phenomenal.

Stanford

Explore

As you approach along Rte 43 from Hermanus, look out for Stanford's tranquil wineries, stopping off for tastings, tours or lunch. Once in Stanford, it's best to park and explore the often-deserted streets on foot. Skirt the Village Green and make your way down to the star attraction – the Klein River. Here you'll find boat trips, canoes for hire and plenty of spots for a picnic or birdwatching. Find lunch in one of the eateries whose mantra of 'fresh' and 'local' has Capetonians driving here for lunch every weekend. End your explorations at the brewery just outside the village, or exploring more vineyards to the east of Stanford.

The Best...

- **Sight** Klein River
- **Place to Eat** Marianna's
- **Place to Drink** Birkenhead Brewery

Top Tip

Stanford has become a real foodie destination in recent years. The best place to taste local produce is at the Saturday market (9.30am to noon), held at the Stanford Hotel.

Getting There & Away

- **Car** You really need your own car to reach Stanford. It's 24km east of Hermanus.

Need to Know

- **Area Code** ☎028

LOCAL KNOWLEDGE

ELGIN VALLEY

Once you reach the top of Sir Lowry's Pass in the Hottentots Hollandberge mountains east of Somerset West, you begin to descend into apple country. The region around **Elgin** and **Grabouw** is close enough to visit on a day trip from Cape Town, but is little known to travellers – its wineries (known for sauvignon blanc, chardonnay and pinot noir), hiking trails and other activities remain uncrowded.

Paul Cluver Wines (www.cluver.com; N2, Grabouw; 9am-5pm Mon-Fri, 10am-2pm Sat & Sun) A worthy stop on the Elgin wine route, offering fine wine, a pleasant country-style restaurant and mountain-bike trails.

Green Mountain Trail (www.greenmountaintrail.co.za) A four-day 'slackpacking' hike through the mountains, where your bags are transported as you hike in relative luxury – think white-tableclothed picnics with fine wines and, at the end of the day, a handsome country manor to stay in.

Canopy Tour (www.canopytour.co.za; per person R595) If you are after an exhilarating way to experience the mountains, explore the Hottentots Holland Nature Reserve from above, sliding along a network of cables and resting in the trees as your guide gives punchy ecology lessons.

Peregrine Farmstall (N2; 7.30am-6pm) Locals love to stop for a freshly baked pie and some just-pressed apple juice before heading off on a road trip.

WORTH A DETOUR

GANSBAAI

Gansbaai's star has risen in recent years thanks to shark-cage diving, though most people just visit on a day trip from Cape Town. The unspoilt coastline is perfect for those wishing to explore more out-of-the-way nature spots.

The road from Hermanus leads you past the village of De Kelders – a great spot for secluded whale-watching – straight into Main Rd, which runs parallel to the coastline. Kleinbaai, 7km further east along the coast, is the launch point for **shark-cage diving** tours. There are a number of operators offering similar trips; **Marine Dynamics** (079 930 9694; www.sharkwatchsa.com; adult/child R1500/900) and **White Shark Projects** (028-007 0001; www.whitesharkprojects.co.za; R1500) both have fair-trade accreditation.

Continuing south from Kleinbaai is the **Danger Point Lighthouse** (028-384 0530; adult/child R16/8; 10am-3pm Mon-Fri), dating from 1895, and **Walker Bay Reserve** (adult/child R40/20; 7am-7pm). There's birdwatching here, some good walks and the Klipgat Caves, site of an archaeological discovery of Khoe-San artefacts.

If you're looking for lunch, try **Coffee on the Rocks** (028-384 2017; Cliff St, De Kelders; mains R50-110; 10am-5pm Wed-Sun). All breads here are baked daily on-site and everything is homemade. The ocean-facing deck is a great place for a sandwich, a salad or just a coffee while you watch the sea during whale season.

If you don't have your own wheels, try **Bernardus Tours** (028-316 1093; bniehaus@vodamail.co.za), which has daily shuttles to and from Cape Town (R1000, two hours).

➡ **Location** Stanford is 145km east of Cape Town.

➡ **Tourist Office** (028-341 0340; www.stanfordinfo.co.za; 18 Queen Victoria St; 8.30am-4.30pm Mon-Fri, 9.30am-4pm Sat, 10am-1pm Sun)

SIGHTS

STANFORD HILLS — WINERY

(028-341 0841; www.stanfordhills.co.za; off Rte 43;) Taste the Jacksons pinotage here – a fine example of South Africa's home-grown grape variety. There's also charming self-catering accommodation available (cottage from R700) and a family-friendly restaurant offering a chalkboard menu of rustic fare.

KLEIN RIVER CHEESE FARM — FARM

(028-341 0693; www.kleinrivercheese.co.za; Rte 326; 9am-5pm Mon-Fri, to 1pm Sat;) The cheese from this farm has become wildly popular – the aged Gruyère is particularly good. Taste and buy a selection of cheese or even better, grab one of the picnics (picnics for two R255, children's basket R55; available 11am to 3pm October to March) to enjoy in the grounds. Children will love the petting farm and playground.

BIRKENHEAD BREWERY — BREWERY

(028-341 0013; www.birkenhead.co.za; Rte 326; tours incl tasting R40; 10am-5pm, tours 10am & 3pm Wed-Fri) Try the local beer brewed at Birkenhead, 300m along Rte 326 towards Bredasdorp.

ROBERT STANFORD ESTATE — WINERY

(028-341 0647; www.robertstanfordestate.co.za; Rte 43; tastings free; 8am-4pm Thu-Sun) The white wines here are good, particularly the sauvignon blanc. There's also a small distillery producing grappa and a charming country restaurant open for lunch.

EATING

MARIANNA'S — BISTRO $$

(028-341 0272; 12 du Toit St; mains from R85; lunch Thu-Sun) This award-winning, eclectic place serves a mixture of traditional and contemporary fare, much of it made with produce from the owner's garden. Advance booking is essential. If all the private tables are taken, you might end up sharing a big one with other guests.

HAVERCROFT'S BISTRO $$

(☎028-341 0603; Rte 43; mains from R95; ⏲lunch Thu-Sun) The food from husband-and-wife team Brydon and Innes gets rave reviews. The menu is inventive and refined, utilising plenty of local produce. Sunday lunch is highly recommended. Bookings essential. Havercroft's is based in a farmhouse on Rte 43 as you enter Stanford from Hermanus.

SPORTS & ACTIVITIES

There are three companies offering cruises along the Klein River. **African Queen** (☎082-732 1284; ⏲10am, 2pm & 6pm Sep-May) is the largest boat, while **River Rat** (☎083 310 0952; www.riverratstanford.wordpress.com; ⏲by appointment) and **Platanna** (☎073 318 5078; www.platanna.com) offer a more intimate experience. All companies charge R150 per person for a three-hour trip and allow swimming from the boat. River Rat also offers canoe hire and specialised birdwatching boat trips.

Darling

Explore

For many, the main reason to visit Darling is to watch the poignant and very funny political show performed by satirist Pieter-Dirk Uys. If you want to catch the cabaret, book ahead – shows are generally held on weekend lunchtimes, with some evening shows. There's a small museum in the tourism office, which serves as a good starting point for a day in Darling, and there are a few nice spots for lunch. Once you've explored this dusty *dorp* (village), take time to check out the wineries on its outskirts and to visit the superb !Khwa ttu, south of Darling on Rte 27.

The Best...

- **Sight** Evita se Perron
- **Place to Eat** Hilda's Kitchen
- **Place to Drink** Slow Quarter

Top Tip

In spring (August to September), Darling is the perfect place to witness South Africa's famous flowers burst into bloom, with more than a dozen flower reserves around the town and a wildflower festival in mid-September.

Getting There & Away

- **Car** Rte 27 is the quickest route from Cape Town. For a scenic detour, replace the northern stretch of Rte 27 with the prettier, quieter Rte 307.

Need to Know

- **Area Code** ☎022
- **Location** Darling is 73km north of Cape Town.
- **Tourist Office** (☎022-492 3361; www.darlingtourism.co.za; cnr Pastorie St & Hill Rd; ⏲9am-1pm & 2-4pm Mon-Thu, 9am-3.30pm Fri, 10am-3pm Sat & Sun)

SIGHTS

★**EVITA SE PERRON** THEATRE

(☎022-492 2851; www.evita.co.za; Darling Station; tickets R90; ⏲2pm & 7pm Sat & Sun) This uniquely South African cabaret, featuring Pieter-Dirk Uys as his alter ego Evita Bezuidenhout, touches on everything from South African politics to history to ecology. Nothing is off limits – including the country's racially charged past and the AIDS epidemic. Although the shows include a smattering of Afrikaans, they're largely in English and always hilarious and thought-provoking.

Even if you're not seeing a show, a visit to the complex is well worth it. There's a politically themed sculpture garden and some fascinating apartheid memorabilia on show. The splendidly kitsch **restaurant** (mains R50-75; ⏲lunch Tue-Sun) serves traditional Afrikaner food. Uys also set up the **Darling Trust** (www.thedarlingtrust.org) to assist Swartland communities to empower themselves through participation in education and health programs. The A en C Shop at the complex stocks beading, clothes, wire art and paintings.

!KHWA TTU

Billed as the San Culture & Education Centre, **!Khwa ttu** (www.khwattu.org; Rte 27, Yzerfontein; tours R150; ⏲9am-5pm, tours 10am & 2pm; 📶) is a joint venture by the San people and a Swiss philanthropic foundation (Ubuntu Foundation) and is the only San-owned and operated culture centre in the Western Cape.

Set within the ancestral lands of the San, !Khwa ttu is based on an 8.5-sq-km nature reserve. There's a **restaurant** (mains R50-95; ⏲breakfast & lunch) serving traditional South African cuisine and a wonderful craft shop. **Tours** (2hr tours R250; ⏲10am & 2pm) involve a nature walk in which you learn about San culture, and a wildlife drive – you'll likely see various antelope, zebras and ostriches.

You can stay and self-cater on the reserve in well-equipped **accommodation** (bush camp/cottage per person R250/480, d R1360). !Khwa ttu is off Rte 27 just south of Yzerfontein, 70km from Cape Town.

GROOTE POST WINERY

(☎022-492 2825; www.grootepost.com; tastings free, 2hr wildlife drives per person R130; ⏲9am-5pm Mon-Fri, 10am-4pm Sat & Sun) Of all the Darling wineries, Groote Post has the most to offer the visitor, with wildlife drives, self-guided nature walks, a superb restaurant and, of course, free tastings of its excellent chardonnays and sauvignon blancs. It's 7km along a dirt road, off Rte 307; bookings are essential.

EATING & DRINKING

★MARMALADE CAT CAFE $

(☎022-492 2515; 19 Main Rd; mains R50-95; ⏲breakfast & lunch daily, dinner Fri & Sat) For an afternoon coffee or all-day breakfast, this is the place. It also serves sandwiches, delicious cheeses and homemade sweet treats. Friday night is pizza night – bookings are essential.

HILDA'S KITCHEN BISTRO $$

(☎022-492 2825; www.grootepost.com; Groote Post Winery; mains R110-130; ⏲lunch Wed-Sun) Perhaps Darling's most upmarket place to dine, with a constantly changing menu that is designed to pair with Groote Post's wines.

SLOW QUARTER BAR

(5 Main Rd; ⏲Tue-Sat 10am-6pm) The tap room of the popular local beer, Darling Brew, is a chic place to munch on platters of locally sourced goodies and sip one of its five flagship beers. Light meals R55 to R85.

Langebaan

Explore

When you get to Langebaan, make a beeline for the beach, whether it's for sailing, windsurfing, kitesurfing or just lounging on the white sand. The lagoon can be further explored in the West Coast National Park, which also boasts a pretty beach at Kraalbaai. For most of the year the park's main attractions are ostriches and views of the ocean and lagoon, but in August and September the park gets a temporary facelift when the spring flowers bloom. Entrance fees and visitor numbers increase considerably at this time, but it's still well worth a trip. Langebaan can easily be explored in a day, unless you're keen to take a multiday water-sports course. If you stay over, pick a place close to the beach where everything is within easy walking distance.

The Best...

- **Sight** West Coast National Park (p182)
- **Place to Eat** Die Strandloper (p182)
- **Activity** Learning to kitesurf (p182) on the lagoon.

Top Tip

As well as the eateries mentioned here, there is a small strip of restaurants on Bree St, some on the beachfront with awesome sunset views.

Getting There & Away

- **Bus** Regular **Elwierda** (☎0861 001 094; www.elwierda.co.za) buses run to and from

Cape Town (R100, two to three hours). Bookings a day in advance are essential.

Need to Know

- **Area Code** ☎022
- **Location** Langebaan is 127km north of Cape Town along Rte 27.
- **Tourist Office** (☎022-772 1515; www.capewestcoastpeninsula.co.za; Bree St; ⊙9am-5pm Mon-Fri, 9am-2pm Sat)

SIGHTS

WEST COAST NATIONAL PARK NATIONAL PARK
(www.sanparks.org; adult/child Oct-Jul R64/32, Aug & Sep R128/64; ⊙7am-7pm) This park encompasses the clear, blue waters of the Langebaan Lagoon and is home to an enormous number of birds. The park covers around 310 sq km and protects wetlands of international significance and important seabird breeding colonies. Wading birds flock here by the thousands in summer. The most numerically dominant species is the curlew sandpiper, which migrates north from the sub-Antarctic in huge flocks. The offshore islands are home to colonies of African penguins.

The park is famous for its wildflower display, which is usually between August and September – it can get fairly crowded during this time. Aside from the white-sand beaches and turquoise waters of the ocean and lagoon, the park's greatest allure is that it is under-visited. If you visit midweek (and outside school holidays) you might find that you're sharing the roads only with zebras, ostriches and the occasional leopard tortoise ambling across your path.

★WEST COAST FOSSIL PARK ARCHAEOLOGICAL SITE
(☎022-766 1606; www.fossilpark.org.za; adult/child R20/15; ⊙8am-4pm Mon-Fri, 10am-1pm Sat & Sun) The first bear discovered south of the Sahara, lion-size sabre-toothed cats, three-toed horses and short-necked giraffes are all on display at this excellent fossil park on Rte 45 about 16km outside Langebaan. Fascinating tours depart hourly from 10am to 3pm (until 1pm on weekends) and take you to the excavation sites – among the richest fossil sites in the world. There are also mountain-biking and walking trails, and a coffee shop.

EATING

★DIE STRANDLOPER SEAFOOD $$$
(☎022-772 2490; www.strandloper.com; buffet R260; ⊙lunch Sat & Sun, dinner Fri & Sat Feb-Nov, lunch & dinner daily Dec-Jan) The West Coast life exemplified – a *10*-course fish and seafood braai (barbecue) right on the beach. There's also freshly made bread, bottomless *moerkoffie* (freshly ground coffee) and a local crooner who wanders the tables strumming his guitar. You can BYO (corkage free) or get drinks from the rustic bar, whose view is sensational. Bookings highly recommended.

CLUB MYKONOS SEAFOOD, MEDITERRANEAN $$$
(☎0800 226 770; www.clubmykonos.co.za; 👪) This Greek-themed, pseudo-Mediterranean resort might not appeal as a place to stay over, but it is a fun spot to spend an evening. There are eight restaurants to choose from as well as numerous bars and a casino, all open to nonguests.

SPORTS & ACTIVITIES

CAPE SPORTS CENTRE WATER SPORTS
(☎022-772 1114; www.capesport.co.za; 98 Main Rd) Langebaan is a water-sports mecca, particularly for windsurfing and kitesurfing. This cheery office offers kitesurfing courses (three-day course R2650) and windsurfing lessons (two hours R700), and rents out surfboards, SUPs and kayaks (R295/345/385 per day).

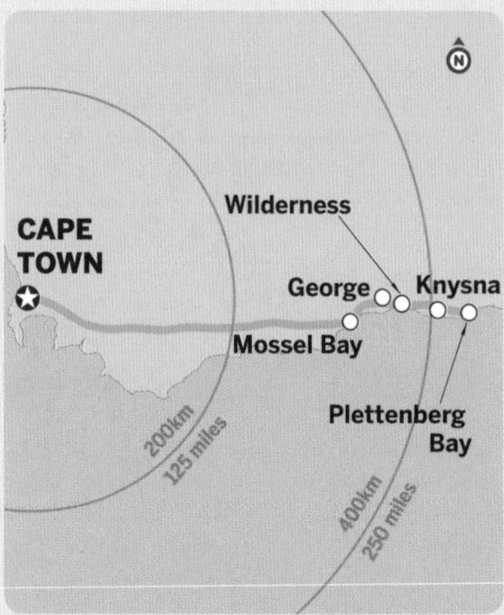

The Garden Route

High on the must-see list of most visitors to Cape Town is the Garden Route, named for the year-round greenery of its forests and lagoons along the coast. It stretches some 200km from Mossel Bay to just beyond Plettenberg Bay.

Mossel Bay p184

Beyond the gas-to-oil refinery you'll find beaches, gnarly surfing spots and a host of activities including shark-cage diving and coastal hikes.

George p187

The largest town along the Garden Route boasts attractive old buildings, world-class golf courses and superb mountain drives.

Wilderness p189

Living up to its name, Wilderness is blessed with gorgeous beaches, bird-rich estuaries and sheltered lagoons backed by densely forested hills.

Knysna p190

Embracing an exquisitely beautiful lagoon and surrounded by ancient forests, Knysna is a place for hiking, sailing, mountain biking or sampling the home-grown oysters and local beer.

Plettenberg Bay p194

The verdant mountains, white sand and crystal-blue waters make 'Plett' one of the country's top tourist spots, loved by locals and foreign visitors alike.

Garden Route

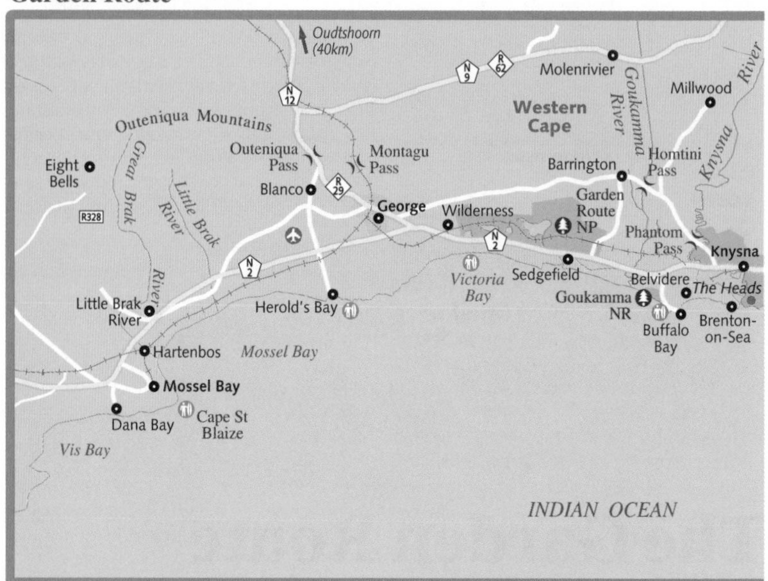

Mossel Bay

Explore

Start your explorations at the excellent Dias Museum Complex to gain insight into Mossel Bay's role in South African history. From here it's a short hop to the harbour to take a dolphin-watching boat trip or enjoy a seafood braai (barbecue) at the water's edge. Head to Santos Beach to swim or relax, or peruse the restaurants and bars of Marsh St, slowly ambling to the Point. Here you'll find a laid-back vibe and restaurants overlooking the ocean, as well as the Cape St Blaize caves and lighthouse. Spend a second day shark-cage diving, surfing, skydiving or hiking along the coast.

The Best...

- **Sight** Dias Museum Complex
- **Place to Eat** Kaai 4
- **Place to Drink** Blue Shed Coffee Roastery

Top Tip

Send a postcard home from South Africa's oldest 'postbox' – a tree inside the Dias Museum Complex where sailors left messages from as early as the 16th century. All letters get a special postmark.

Getting There & Away

- **Bus** Regular **Translux** (www.translux.co.za), **Greyhound** (www.greyhound.co.za) and **Intercape** (www.intercape.co.za) services are operated from Cape Town (R380, six hours, twice daily).

Need to Know

- **Area Code** ☎ 044
- **Location** Mossel Bay is 390km east of Cape Town along the N2.
- **Tourist Office** (☎044-691 2202; www.visitmosselbay.co.za; Market St; ⏰8am-6pm Mon-Fri, 9am-4pm Sat & Sun)

SIGHTS

★DIAS MUSEUM COMPLEX MUSEUM
(www.diasmuseum.co.za; Market St; adult/child R20/5; ⏰9am-4.45pm Mon-Fri, 9am-3.45pm Sat & Sun; P) This excellent museum includes the spring from which Bartholomeu Dias watered the postal tree, the 1786 Dutch East India Company (Vereenigde Oost-Indische Compagnie; VOC) granary, a shell museum (with some interesting aquarium

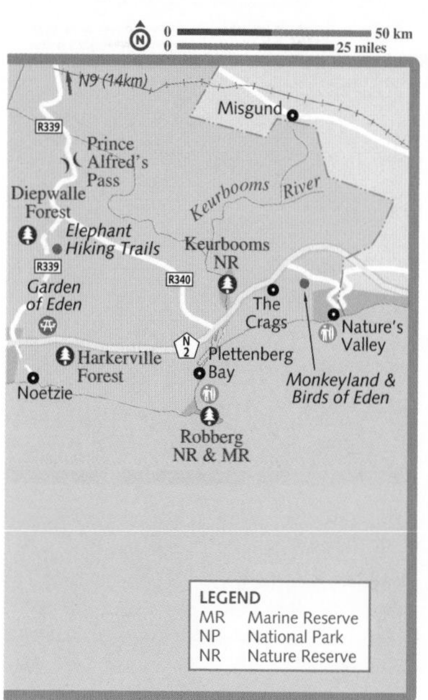

tanks) and a local history museum. The highlight of the complex is the replica of the caravel that Dias used on his 1488 voyage of discovery (adult/child R20/5). Its small size brings home the extraordinary skill and courage of the early explorers.

The replica was built in Portugal and sailed to Mossel Bay in 1988 to commemorate the 500th anniversary of Dias' trip.

BOTLIERSKOP PRIVATE GAME RESERVE WILDLIFE RESERVE
(☎044-696 6055; www.botlierskop.co.za; Little Brak River) This reserve contains a vast range of wildlife, including lions, elephants, rhinos, buffaloes and giraffes. Day visitors are welcome for a variety of activities including three-hour wildlife drives (adult/child R420/210), horse riding (per hour R270) and elephant rides (R820). The reserve is about 20km northeast of Mossel Bay along the N2 (take the Little Brak River turn-off and follow the signs towards Sorgfontein). Bookings essential.

CAPE ST BLAIZE LIGHTHOUSE LIGHTHOUSE
(adult/child R16/8; ⏲10am-3pm) There are wonderful views from the lighthouse. Sadly, the St Blaize Cave, dating back to the Stone Age era, is rather neglected and frequented by vandals.

EATING & DRINKING

★KAAI 4 BRAAI $$
(www.kaai4.co.za; Mossel Bay Harbour; mains R30-95; ⏲lunch & dinner) With one of Mossel Bay's best locations, this low-key restaurant has picnic tables overlooking the ocean. Most dishes – including stews, burgers, boerewors (farmer's sausage) and some seafood – are cooked on massive fire pits and there's local beer on tap.

CAFÉ HAVANA INTERNATIONAL $$
(www.cafehavana.co.za; 38 Marsh St; mains R50-110; ⏲breakfast, lunch & dinner; Wi-Fi) A long-running Cuban-themed restaurant that's as popular as ever. Stews, steaks and seafood all make it on to the menu and there's a good cocktail list. It stays open late and is the best place for some after-hours action.

BIG BLU INTERNATIONAL $$
(Point Rd; mains R50-95) This ramshackle place right on the rocks at the Point is great for a sundowner and serves burgers, seafood and steaks.

VILLA POINT SOUTH AFRICAN $$$
(☎044-691 1923; 11 Marsh St; mains R105-180; ⏲lunch & dinner Mon-Sat) A well-respected restaurant based in an old house. The menu is small and includes plenty of South African meat, including rack of lamb, kudu osso bucco and the very popular springbok shank.

★BLUE SHED COFFEE ROASTERY CAFE
(33 Bland St; ⏲6.30am-8pm; Wi-Fi) Enjoy great coffee and homemade cakes at this funky cafe with eclectic decor and ocean views from the deck. It's an awesome spot to spend a couple of hours chilling or playing vinyl on the old-school jukebox.

SPORTS & ACTIVITIES

OYSTERCATCHER TRAIL HIKING
(www.oystercatchertrail.co.za; full board/self catering from R3200/5400) Hikers tackle this fabulous coastal trail in three or four days. It follows the coastline from Mossel Bay to Dana Bay via Cape St Blaize, where you're likely to see the endangered black oystercatcher.

BILLEON SURFING
(www.billeon.com; 2hr lessons R350) Mossel Bay is well known for its surf, and this company

Mossel Bay

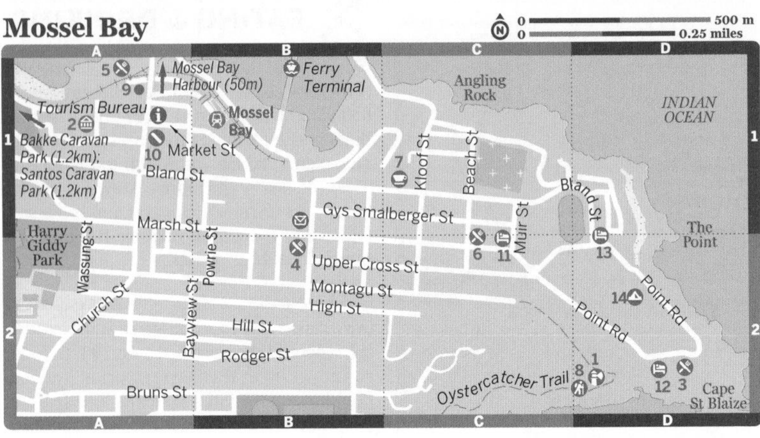

Mossel Bay

Sights
1 Cape St Blaize Lighthouse D2
2 Dias Museum Complex A1

Eating
3 Big Blu D2
4 Café Havana B2
5 Kaai 4 .... A1
6 Villa Point C2

Drinking
7 Blue Shed Coffee Roastery C1

Sports & Activities
8 Oystercatcher Trail D2
9 Romonza A1
10 White Shark Africa A1

Sleeping
11 Mossel Bay Backpackers C2
12 Point Hotel D2
13 Point Village Hotel D2
14 Punt Caravan Park D2

offers lessons for beginners, as well as three-hour sandboarding experiences (R380).

POINT OF HUMAN ORIGINS CULTURAL TOUR
(044-691 0051; www.humanorigin.co.za; tours R395) Led by an archaeology professor, this fascinating four-hour tour includes a hike to the Pinnacle Point Caves, where discoveries have shed light on human life from 162,000 years ago.

ROMONZA BOAT TOUR
(044-690 3101; 1hr boat trips R140) Regular boat trips head out to Seal Island to see the seals, birds and dolphins that frequent these waters. In late winter and spring this outfit also runs whale-watching trips (R640, 2½ hours).

WHITE SHARK AFRICA DIVING
(044-691 3796; www.whitesharkafrica.com; 7 Church St; dives R1350) Full-day cage-diving trips to view great white sharks, including lunch, drinks and snacks.

SKYDIVE MOSSEL BAY ADVENTURE SPORTS
(082 824 8599; www.skydivemosselbay.com; Mossel Bay Airfield; from R2000) Tandem skydives start from 3000m. When the weather and tides cooperate you land on Diaz Beach.

SLEEPING

There are three municipal caravan parks in town. **Bakke** (044-690 3501, 044-691 2915; camping per site from R210, chalets from R520) and **Santos** (044-690 3501, 044-691 2915; camping per site from R210) are next to each other on pretty Santos Beach; Bakke is the one with chalets. **Punt** (044-690 3501, 044-691 2915; camping per site R210) is on the Point and very close to the surf. Prices rise steeply in December and January.

MOSSEL BAY BACKPACKERS BACKPACKERS $
(044-691 3182; www.mosselbayhostel.co.za; 1 Marsh St; dm R140-160, d without/with bathroom R380/450;) This well-run and long-

established backpackers has swallowed the adjoining guesthouse, meaning there are some excellent en suite rooms on offer alongside dorms and basic doubles. There's even a honeymoon suite, complete with spa bath. Staff can arrange all sorts of activities.

★POINT VILLAGE HOTEL HOTEL **$$**
(☎044-690 3156; www.pointvillagehotel.co.za; 5 Point Rd; s/d R500/840) The quirky, fake lighthouse on this exceptionally well-priced hotel's exterior is a sign of what's inside: a range of fun, funky, bright rooms and friendly service. Rooms have a kitchenette and some have balconies. There are also two- and three-bedroom apartments with good sea views (R1800).

POINT HOTEL HOTEL **$$$**
(☎044-691 3512; www.pointhotel.co.za; Point Rd; s/d R1285/1710;) This modern hotel boasts a spectacular location, right above the rocks at the Point. There's a decent restaurant (mains R60 to R120) and the spacious rooms have balconies with ocean views – request a south-facing room for the best vistas.

George

Explore

For many people, George is little more than a transport hub, but there are gems to be found in the Garden Route's largest town. Start at the museum for a little historical perspective, then pick up a brochure from the tourist office detailing a self-guided historical walk. Stroll down York St to the diminutive St Mark's Cathedral and the 'Slave Tree'. Spend the afternoon playing golf or exploring the surrounding Outeniqua mountains on foot, by car or on the quirky Outeniqua Power Van.

The Best...

- **Place to Eat** Old Townhouse (p188)
- **Place to Drink** Robertson Brewery (p188)
- **Activity** Outeniqua Power Van (p189)

Top Tip

Take a drive south of George to the picturesque beaches at Herold's Bay and at Victoria Bay, both surfing hot spots. The latter has a tidal pool for kids.

Getting There & Away

Bus Frequent **Translux** (www.translux.co.za), **Greyhound** (www.greyhound.co.za) and **Intercape** (www.intercape.co.za) buses run from Cape Town (R380, seven hours).

Aeroplane Both **Airlink** (☎0861 606 606; www.flyairlink.com) and **SA Express** (☎0861 729 227; www.flyexpress.aero) fly from Cape Town to George Airport (50 minutes), 7km west of town.

GARDEN ROUTE RETREATS

Parts of the Garden Route can get pretty crowded, especially during South African school holidays. Escape to a hidden lodge to avoid the throngs.

Eight Bells Mountain Inn (☎044-631 0000; www.eightbells.co.za; s/d from R750/1200;) This country inn is 35km north of Mossel Bay on Rte 328 to Oudtshoorn (50km). It's in a lovely mountain setting at the foot of the Robinson Pass and its large grounds have something for everyone from children to squash players. You'll find a variety of rooms; the *rondavels* (round huts) are fun. There's a tea garden and restaurant, and opportunities to hike and ride horses. Prices rise sharply during school holidays.

Hog Hollow (☎044-534 8879; www.hog-hollow.com; Askop Rd, The Crags; s/d incl breakfast R2170/3100;) Hog Hollow, 18km east of Plett along the N2, provides delightful accommodation in African-art-decorated units overlooking the forest. Each unit comes with a private wooden deck and hammock. You can walk to Monkeyland (p195) from here; staff will collect you if you don't fancy the walk back.

Phantom Forest Eco-Reserve (☎044-386 0046; www.phantomforest.com; Phantom Pass Rd; s/d from R2935/4275;) This small private ecoreserve, 6km west of Knysna, comprises 14 elegantly decorated tree houses built with sustainable materials. Various activities, including nature walks, are available. If nothing else, visit for the lavish six-course African dinner (R400) served in the Forest Boma daily; booking is essential.

Need to Know

- **Area Code** ☎044
- **Location** George is 430km east of Cape Town, along the N2.
- **Tourist Office** (☎044-801 9295; www.georgetourism.org.za; 124 York St; ⏰7.45am-4.30pm Mon-Fri, 9am-1pm Sat)

SIGHTS

GEORGE MUSEUM MUSEUM

(Courtenay St; admission by donation; ⏰9am-4.30pm Mon-Fri, 9am-12.30pm Sat) George was the hub of the indigenous timber industry and, thus, this museum contains a wealth of related artefacts.

OUTENIQUA TRANSPORT MUSEUM MUSEUM

(cnr York & Courtenay Sts; adult/child R20/10; ⏰8am-4.30pm Mon-Fri, 8am-2pm Sat) The starting point and terminus for journeys on the Outeniqua Power Van, this museum is worth a visit if you're interested in trains. A dozen locomotives and 15 carriages, as well as many detailed models, have found a retirement home here, including a carriage used by the British royal family in the 1940s.

EATING & DRINKING

OLD TOWNHOUSE STEAKHOUSE $$

(☎044-874 3663; Market St; mains R50-130; ⏰lunch & dinner Mon-Fri, dinner Sat) In the one-time town administration building dating back to 1848, this longstanding restaurant is known for its excellent steaks and ever-changing game-meat options.

ROBERTSON BREWERY BREWERY

(www.robertsonbrewery.com; 1 Memoriam St; tastings R35, light meals R60; ⏰10am-7pm Mon-Sat) There's not a lot to keep you occupied in George, so this family-run microbrewery is a welcome addition. Sip a taster tray of the six staple beers brewed on-site and munch on simple platters while admiring the quirky mural detailing the brewing process.

SPORTS & ACTIVITIES

George is the golfing capital of the Western Cape, and perhaps the entire country. There are a dozen courses – including short courses – scattered around the town's outskirts as well as three golf schools if you're not quite up to par. The most elite and famous is the **Links at Fancourt** (☎044-804 0000;

SURFING ALONG THE GARDEN ROUTE

With the water warming up as you round Cape Agulhas, where the Indian Ocean takes over, you can be happy surfing in just board shorts or a short suit during summer. You'll need a full suit in winter, though. There are good waves along the coast; Mossel Bay and Victoria Bay are considered the best places.

In **Mossel Bay**, the main surf spot is Outer Pool (left of the tidal pool) – a great reef and point break. There's also a soft wave called Inner Pool to the right of the tidal pool. Elsewhere there's a good right in a big swell called Ding Dangs that's best at a lowish tide, especially in a southwesterly or easterly wind. It might be a bit of a hassle paddling out, but the right is better than the left.

You might find something at Grootbrak and Kleinbrak, but better is **Herold's Bay**. When it's on, there's a left-hand wedge along the beach, and it's unusual in that it works in a northwesterly wind.

Best of all though is **Victoria Bay**, which has the most consistent breaks along this coast. It's perfect when the swell is about 1m to 2m and you get a great right-hander.

A little further along is **Buffalo Bay** (Buffel's Bay) where there's another right-hand point. Buffalo Bay is at one end of Brenton Beach; at the northern end, you'll find some good peaks, but watch out for sharks.

On to **Plettenberg Bay**: avoid Robberg Peninsula as that's home to a seal colony. But the swimming area at Robberg Beach (where lifeguards are stationed) can have good waves if the swell isn't too big. Central Beach has one of the best known waves, the Wedge, which is perfect for goofy-footers. Lookout Beach can have some sandbanks and the Point can be good, but there's a lot of erosion here and the beach is slowly disappearing. Watch out for rip currents, especially when there are no lifeguards on duty.

www.fancourt.co.za) designed by Gary Player. **Little Eden** (044-881 0018; www.edenforest.co.za) is a secluded nine-hole course while **Oubaai** (044-851 1263; www.oubaaigolfestate.co.za) is an opulent spot offering ocean vistas from the greens.

OUTENIQUA POWER VAN TOUR
(082 490 5627; adult/child R130/110; Mon-Sat) A trip on this motorised trolley van is one of the best things to do in George. It takes you from the Outeniqua Transport Museum on a 2½-hour trip into the Outeniqua mountains. You can even take a bike and cycle back down the Montagu Pass.

WORTH A DETOUR

MONTAGU & OUTENIQUA PASSES

The Montagu Pass is a quiet dirt road that winds away from George through the mountains; it was opened in 1847 and is now a national monument. Take some sustenance, because there are great picnic sites along the way, then head back on the Outeniqua Pass, where views are even better, but, because it's a main road, it's more difficult to stop when you want to.

Wilderness

Explore

After a brief stop at the tourist office, head straight for that which gives Wilderness its soul and its name: the outdoors. Start with a gentle hike in the Garden Route National Park or a canoeing stint on one of the lagoons. Wilderness is a quieter, more laid-back alternative to Knysna and Plettenberg Bay, but its ultracompact town centre has a surprising number of decent eateries. From here it is a short stroll under the N2 to the beach – but be warned: a strong rip tide means swimming is not advised. After a spot of sun-worshipping, drive out to Timberlake Organic Village to eat at Zucchini; the village is also a great place to shop for crafts and organically grown fresh produce.

The Best...

- **Sight** Garden Route National Park
- **Place to Eat** Girls Restaurant (p190)
- **Activity** Canoeing on the lagoon

Getting There & Away

- **Bus** Both **Greyhound** (www.greyhound.co.za) and **Translux** (www.translux.co.za) operate services from Cape Town (R300, seven hours, two daily).

Need to Know

- **Area Code** 044
- **Location** Wilderness is 445km east of Cape Town and sits right on the N2.
- **Tourist Office** (044-877 0045; George Rd; 7.45am-4.30pm Mon-Fri, 9am-1pm Sat)

 SIGHTS

GARDEN ROUTE NATIONAL PARK (WILDERNESS SECTION) NATIONAL PARK
(044-877 1197; www.sanparks.org; adult/child R106/53; 7am-6pm) Formerly the Wilderness National Park, this section has now been incorporated into the vast and scattered Garden Route National Park along with the Knysna Forests and Tsitsikamma. The park covers a unique system of lakes, rivers, wetlands and estuaries that are vital for the survival of many species. There are several nature trails in the national park for all levels of fitness, taking in the lakes, the beach and the indigenous forest.

The Kingfisher Trail is a day walk that traverses the region and includes a boardwalk across the intertidal zone of the Touws River. The lakes offer anglers, canoeists, windsurfers and sailors an ideal venue. Canoes (R250 per day) can be hired from Eden Adventures, which also offers abseiling (R375) and canyoning (R495).

There are two similar camping grounds in the park with basic but comfortable accommodation, including in *rondavels* (round huts with conical roofs): **Ebb & Flow North** (campsites from R150, d rondavel without/with bathroom R280/325), which is the smaller, and **Ebb & Flow South** (campsites from R150, forest cabins R540, 4-person log cottage R1015).

EATING & DRINKING

BEEJUICE CAFE $

(Sands Rd; light meals R45-85; ⊙breakfast & lunch year-round, dinner Nov-Apr) Although no trains ply the tracks any more, this cafe filling the old station building is still a nice spot for salads and sandwiches. In the evenings, traditional South African fare is served.

★**GIRLS RESTAURANT** INTERNATIONAL $$

(1 George Rd; mains R100-285; ⊙dinner Tue-Sun) It doesn't look much from afar – a restaurant tucked down the side of a petrol station – but Girls gets rave reviews. Try the fresh prawns in a range of divine sauces or the venison fillet.

ZUCCHINI EUROPEAN $$

(www.zucchini.co.za; Timberlake Organic Village; mains R60-130; ⊙breakfast & lunch daily, dinner Fri & Sat;) Stylish decor combines with home-grown organic produce, free-range meats and lots of vegetarian options at this delightful place.

SERENDIPITY SOUTH AFRICAN $$$

(044-877 0433; Freesia Ave; 5-course menu R415; ⊙dinner Mon-Sat) Readers and locals recommend this elegant restaurant with a deck overlooking the lagoon. The South African-inspired menu changes monthly but always features original takes on old classics. It's the town's fine-dining option. Bookings essential.

LOCAL KNOWLEDGE

SEDGEFIELD FARMERS MARKET

Wild Oats Community Farmers Market (www.wildoatsmarket.co.za; ⊙7.30am-noon Sat) A Garden Route institution, this farmers market has been operating for over a decade. Get there early to get your pick of the pies, biltong, cheese, cakes, bread, beer, fudge – all from small, local producers. The market is just off the N2, 1.5km east of Sedgefield's town centre.

SLEEPING

FAIRY KNOWE BACKPACKERS BACKPACKERS $

(044-877 1285; www.wildernessbackpackers.com; Dumbleton Rd; camping R80, dm/d without bathroom R130/400, d R500;) Set in leafy grounds overlooking the Touws River, this long-running hostel is based in an 1874 farmhouse. The bar and cafe are in another building some distance away, so boozers won't keep you awake. Staff can arrange all manner of activities. If you're driving, head into Wilderness town and follow the main road for 2km to the Fairy Knowe turn-off.

★**INTERLAKEN** GUESTHOUSE $$

(044-877 1374; www.interlaken.co.za; 713 North St; s/d incl breakfast R695/1100;) It gets rave reviews from readers, and we can't argue: this is a well-run and friendly guesthouse offering magnificent lagoon views. Delicious dinners are available on request.

★**VIEWS BOUTIQUE HOTEL** BOUTIQUE HOTEL $$$

(044-877 8000; www.viewshotel.co.za; South St; s/d incl breakfast R3200/4200;) With bright, modern, glass-fronted rooms looking on to the glorious beach, this hotel makes the most of its awesome location. It's worth paying the premium for an ocean-facing room if you can, though the mountain-view rooms are also delightful. The hotel has a rooftop pool, spa and steps leading straight to the sand.

Knysna

Explore

Timber played a vital role in Knysna's history so there is no better place to start exploring than in the forests surrounding the town. Hikes range from short strolls to multiday treks. Main St has a plethora of shops and cafes, as well as the quaint Old Gaol Museum. Read up on local history, then head to the bustling, touristy Knysna Waterfront for a seafood lunch and a boat trip on the lagoon. Enjoy craggy ocean views from the eastern head and dine in one of the chic new eateries on Thesen's Island. If you're sticking around, take a township tour and indulge in one of the many outdoor activities this region is known for.

The Best...

- **Sight** Knysna Forests (p193)
- **Place to Eat** Ile de Pain (p192)
- **Place to Drink** Mitchell's Brewery

Top Tip

If you want to stay overnight in either the Rastafarian community or in the township, contact Knysna Tourism and ask for the brochure, *Living Local.*

Getting There & Away

- **Bus** Regular **Translux** (www.translux.co.za), **Greyhound** (www.greyhound.co.za) and **Intercape** (www.intercape.co.za) buses operate from Cape Town (R450, eight hours, twice daily).
- **Shared taxi** Catch a shared taxi from the corner of Main and Gray Sts. Routes include Plettenberg Bay (R20, 30 minutes, daily) and Cape Town (R150, 7½ hours, daily).

Need to Know

- **Area Code** ☎044
- **Location** Knysna is 490km east of Cape Town.
- **Tourist Office** (☎044-382 5510; www.visitknysna.co.za; 40 Main St; ⏲8am-5pm Mon-Fri, 8.30am-1pm Sat year-round, plus 9am-1pm Sun Dec, Jan & Jul)

SIGHTS

KNYSNA LAGOON — PARK

The Knysna Lagoon opens between two sandstone cliffs known as the Heads – once proclaimed by the British Royal Navy to be the most dangerous harbour entrance in the world. There are good views from the eastern head, and from the Featherbed Nature Reserve on the western head.

The best way to appreciate the lagoon is by boat. The **Featherbed Company** (☎044-382 1693; www.featherbed.co.za; Remembrance Dr, off Waterfront Dr; boat trips adult/child from R100/55) operates various vessels and also runs a trip that allows you to explore the nature reserve on foot (adult/child R380/130).

> **KNYSNA'S RASTAFARIAN COMMUNITY**
>
> Knysna is home to South Africa's largest Rastafarian community, **Judah Square**. You can take an impassioned walking tour of the community, which is within the township, with **Brother Zeb** (☎076 649 1034; tours from R70), an unforgettable local character.

MITCHELL'S BREWERY — BREWERY

(☎044-382 4685; www.mitchellsbrewing.com; 10 New St; tastings R75, tours & tastings R150; ⏲10am-6pm Mon-Sat, tours 11am, 12.30pm & 2.30pm) South Africa's oldest microbrewery has moved to bright, new premises on the edge of the lagoon. You can join a tour, or just taste its range of English-style beers in the beer garden. Pub meals (R45 to R70) are also served. Bookings essential for tours.

OLD GAOL MUSEUM — MUSEUM

(☎044-302 6320; cnr Main & Queen Sts; ⏲9.30am-4.30pm Mon-Fri, to 12.30pm Sat) FREE Since this region has plenty of wet weather, a rainy-day option is welcome. The main museum is a pleasant complex in a mid-19th-century building that was once the gaol. There's a gallery showcasing local art, a display on the Knysna elephants and a community art project.

MILLWOOD HOUSE — MUSEUM

(Queen St; ⏲9.30am-4.30pm Mon-Fri, to 12.30pm Sat) FREE Around the corner from the Old Gaol Museum, Millwood House is a mini complex of museums detailing Knysna's history. It's a quaint set of buildings dating back to the town's booming timber era. This is the main focus of the museum, though it also houses information on Knysna's involvement in the Anglo-Boer War and details on the town's founder George Rex.

GOUKAMMA NATURE RESERVE — NATURE RESERVE

(www.capenature.co.za; adult/child R40/20; ⏲8am-6pm) This reserve is accessible from the Buffalo Bay road, and protects 14km of rocky coastline, sandstone cliffs, dunes covered with coastal *fynbos* and forest, and Groenvlei, a large freshwater lake.

BELVIDERE — VILLAGE

Belvidere, 10km from Knysna, is so immaculate it's positively creepy. But it's worth a

Knysna

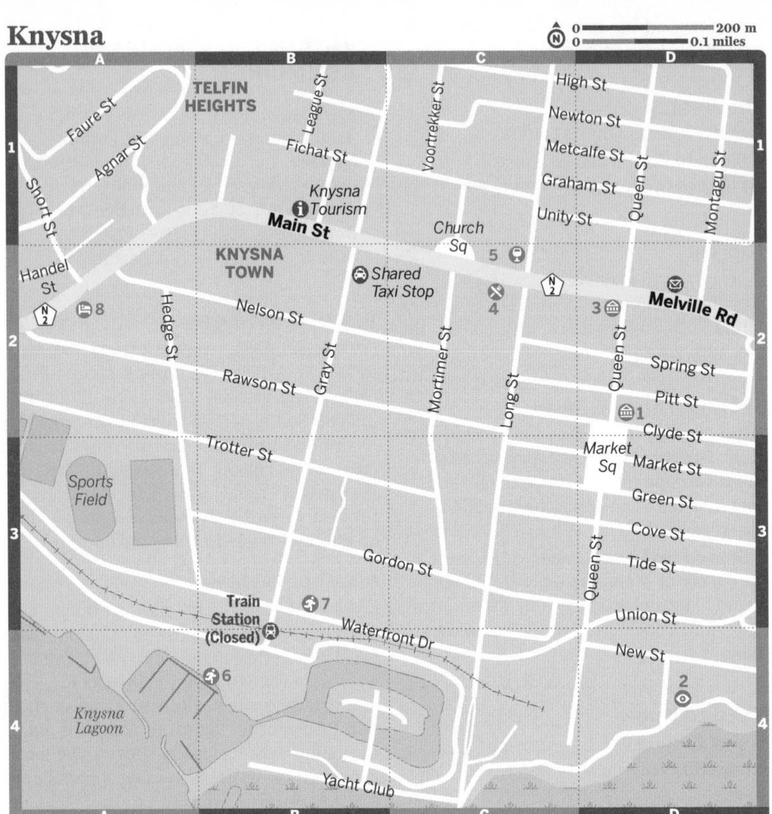

quick look for the beautiful Norman-style Belvidere **church** that was built in the 1850s by homesick English expats. Further on is the **Featherbed Nature Reserve** and, on the seaward side, Brenton-on-Sea.

NOETZIE BEACH

Reached by a turn-off along the N2 10km east of Knysna, Noetzie is a quirky little place with holiday homes in mock-castle style. There's a lovely surf beach (spacious but dangerous) and a sheltered lagoon running through a forested gorge. The trail between the car park and beach is steep.

EATING & DRINKING

★ILE DE PAIN CAFE, BAKERY $

(www.iledepain.co.za; Thesen's Island; mains R50-90; breakfast & lunch Tue-Sun;) A wildly popular bakery and cafe that's as much a hit with locals as it is with tourists. There's an excellent breakfast menu, lots of fresh salads, some inventive lunch specials and quite a bit for vegetarians.

EAST HEAD CAFÉ CAFE $$

(044-384 0933; www.eastheadcafe.co.za; 25 George Rex Dr, Eastern Head; mains R75-145; breakfast & lunch;) There's an outdoor deck overlooking the lagoon and ocean, lots of fish and seafood, plus a few vegetarian dishes. It's a very popular spot so expect to wait for a table in high season.

OLIVE TREE BISTRO $$

(044-382 5867; 21 Main St; mains R90-170; dinner Mon-Sat) One of Knysna's more upmarket restaurants is a romantic spot with a blackboard menu that changes regularly. Bookings advisable.

SIROCCO INTERNATIONAL $$

(044-382 4874; www.sirocco.co.za; Main Rd, Thesen's Island; mains R50-130; lunch & dinner)

Knysna

Sights

1 Millwood House ... D2
2 Mitchell's Brewery ... D4
3 Old Gaol Museum ... D2

Eating

4 Olive Tree ... C2

Drinking

5 Zanzibar Lounge ... C2

Sports & Activities

6 Featherbed Company ... B4
7 Knysna Cycle Works ... B3

Sleeping

8 Island Vibe ... A2

Inside, it's a stylish place to dine on steak and seafood; outside, it's a laid-back bar with wood-fired pizzas and the full range of Mitchell's beers.

ZANZIBAR LOUNGE CLUB

(Main St; ⌚Tue-Sat) Knysna's top spot for late-night dancing offers a relaxed vibe and a balcony area for lounging.

SPORTS & ACTIVITIES

The tourism office has an up-to-date list of the numerous operators offering tours to Knysna's hilltop townships. There are plenty of other activities on offer in the area, including abseiling, canyoning, horse riding, kayaking and quad biking.

EMZINI TOURS CULTURAL TOUR

(☎044-382 1087; www.emzinitours.co.za; adult/child R350/100) Led by township resident Ella, the three-hour trip visits some of Emzini's community projects. Tours can be tailored to suit your interests but generally end at Ella's home for tea, drumming and a group giggle as you try to wrap your tongue around the clicks of the Xhosa language.

MAD ABOUT ART CULTURAL TOUR

(☎044-375 0242; www.madaboutart.org; suggested donation R180) A nonprofit organisation that offers 90-minute walking tours to visit various art and education projects.

KNYSNA CYCLE WORKS CYCLING

(☎044-382 5152; www.knysnacycles.co.za; 20 Waterfront Dr; per day R200; ⌚8.30am-5pm Mon-Fri, 9am-1pm Sat) Long-running agency that rents out mountain bikes and supplies maps of the region's trails.

TRIP OUT WATER SPORTS

(☎083 306 3587; www.tripout.co.za; 2hr surfing class R350) Offers surfing classes for beginners, snorkelling around the Heads (R300) and boat cruises, as well as a full-on kloofing (canyoning) day trip (R850).

SLEEPING

Low-season competition between the several backpackers and many guesthouses in town keeps prices down, but in high season expect steep rate hikes (except at the backpackers), and book ahead.

HIKING THE KNYSNA FORESTS

Now part of the Garden Route National Park, the Knysna Forests are the perfect place for hikers of all levels. At the easy end of the scale is the **Garden of Eden** (adult/child R36/18), where there are lovely forest picnic spots and a wheelchair-friendly path. The **Millwood Gold Mine Walk** is also a gentle hike, while the **Elephant Trails** (adult/child R60/30) at Diepwalle offer varying degrees of difficulty.

For those looking for something more challenging, the **Harkerville Coast Trail** (per person R210) is a two-day hike that leads on to the popular Outeniqua Trail. The **Outeniqua Trail** (☎044-302 5606; adult/child R72/38) is 108km long and takes a week to walk, although you can also do two- or three-day sections. The trail costs R66 per night to stay in a basic hut; bring your own bedding. For permits, maps and further information, contact **SANParks** (☎044-302 5600; www.sanparks.org).

There are also plenty of mountain-biking trails – contact Knysna Cycle Works for rentals and maps.

Around Knysna

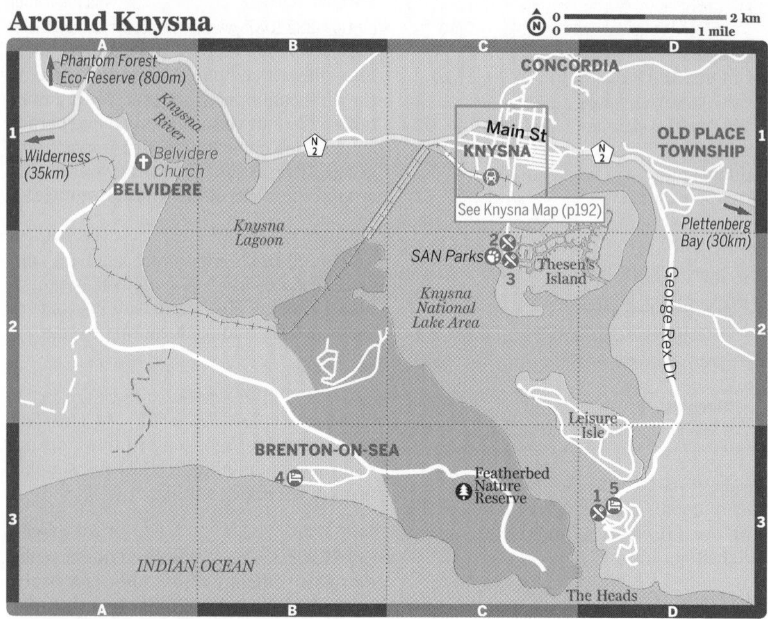

ISLAND VIBE BACKPACKERS $
(☎044-382 1728; www.islandvibe.co.za; 67 Main St; dm R150, d without/with bathroom R480/550;) A funky backpackers with excellent communal areas, cheery staff and nicely decorated rooms. There's a lively bar and a small pool on the deck.

★**BRENTON COTTAGES** CHALET $$
(☎044-381 0082; www.brentononsea.net; 242 CR Swart Drive, Brenton-on-Sea; 2-person cabin R680, 6-person chalet R1380;) On the seaward side of the lagoon, the hills drop to Brenton-on-Sea, overlooking a magnificent 8km beach. The cottages have a full kitchen while cabins have a kitchenette; many have ocean views. There are plenty of braai (barbecue) areas dotted around the manicured lawns.

UNDER MILK WOOD CHALET $$$
(☎044-384 0745; www.milkwood.co.za; George Rex Dr; cabin from R1200) Perched on the shores of Knysna Lagoon are these highly impressive self-catering log cabins, each with its own deck and braai area. There's no pool but there is a small beach.

Plettenberg Bay

Explore

Plett, as the town is known, is compact and most amenities are concentrated around a single thoroughfare, Main Rd. It's a pleasant place to begin, lined with restaurants and some decent cafes, good for breakfast or brunch. Of course, the main reason people visit Plett is for its beaches.

Start at Lookout Beach, close to the town, where the Keurbooms River Lagoon meets the Indian Ocean. Further stretches of sand await east of town – the main beach at Keurboomstrand is a stunner. Inland you can hike or horse ride through the forests, or get up-close with a range of African animals. Return to town for dinner either on Main Rd or at one of the restaurants overlooking the water. Spend a second day exploring the cliffs and dunes of the Robberg Nature Reserve, and end with a dolphin-watching trip departing from Central Beach.

The Best...

- **Sight** Monkeyland
- **Place to Eat** Ristorante Enrico
- **Activity** Hiking in Robberg Nature Reserve

Top Tip

If you're getting wine-withdrawal symptoms, ask at the tourism bureau for the brochure detailing the region's burgeoning wine route – at last count there were nine wineries, most offering Méthode Cap Classique (MCC; South African of sparkling wine).

Getting There & Away

- **Bus** Two daily **Intercape** (www.intercape.co.za) buses operate from Cape Town (R450, nine hours).

Need to Know

- **Area Code** ☎044
- **Location** Plett is 520km east of Cape Town.
- **Tourist Office** (☎044-533 4065; www.plett-tourism.co.za; Melville's Corner Shopping Centre, Main St; ⏲9am-5pm Mon-Fri, 9am-1pm Sat)

SIGHTS

ROBBERG NATURE & MARINE RESERVE — PARK

(☎044-483 0190; www.capenature.org.za; adult/child R40/20; ⏲8am-6pm May-Sep, 7am-8pm Oct-Apr) This reserve, 9km southeast of Plettenberg Bay, protects a 4km-long peninsula with a rugged coastline of cliffs and rocks. There are three circular walks of increasing difficulty, but it's very rocky and not for the unfit or anyone with knee problems! Basic accommodation is available at the spectacularly located **Fountain Shack** (4 people R875), which is reachable only by a two-hour hike. To get to the reserve head along Robberg Rd, off Piesang Valley Rd, until you see the signs.

You can also take a boat trip to view the peninsula – and its colony of Cape fur seals – from the water. You can even get in the water to swim with seals. Contact **Offshore Adventures** (www.offshoreadventures.co.za; boat trip R250, swimming with seals R500) to book.

MONKEYLAND — WILDLIFE RESERVE

(www.monkeyland.co.za; 1hr tours adult/child R175/88; ⏲8am-5pm) This very popular attraction helps rehabilitate wild monkeys that have been in zoos or private homes. The walking safari through a dense forest and across a 128m-long rope bridge is superb. A combo ticket with Birds of Eden costs R280/140 per adult/child.

BIRDS OF EDEN — BIRD SANCTUARY

(www.birdsofeden.co.za; adult/child R175/88; ⏲8am-5pm) This is one of the world's largest free-flight aviaries with a 200-sq-metre dome over the forest. A combo ticket with Monkeyland costs R280/140 per adult/child.

EATING & DRINKING

RISTORANTE ENRICO — SEAFOOD $$

(☎044-535 9818; www.enricorestaurant.co.za; Main Beach, Keurboomstrand; mains R90-140; ⏲lunch & dinner daily, closed Mon in winter) Highly recommended by readers and right on the beach, this is *the* place for seafood in Plett. Enrico has his own boat that, weather permitting, heads out each morning. If you book ahead you can join the fishing trip and have your catch cooked at the restaurant.

TABLE — ITALIAN $$

(www.thetable.co.za; 9 Main St; mains R70-130; ⏲lunch & dinner Mon-Sat, lunch Sun) A funky, minimalist venue with pizzas featuring an array of inventive toppings.

LE FOURNIL DE PLETT — CAFE $$

(cnr Church & Main Sts; mains R70-85; ⏲breakfast & lunch; 📶) Enjoy a good cup of coffee and a freshly baked pastry in the courtyard or on the balcony overlooking Plett's main road. There's also a small lunch menu, largely focusing on salads and sandwiches.

Plettenberg Bay

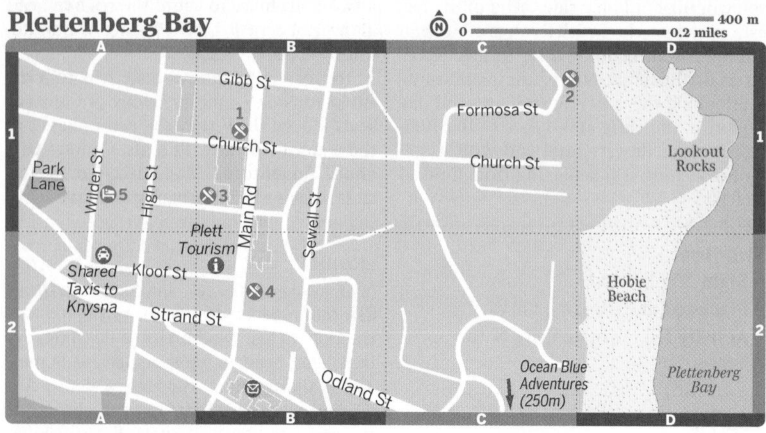

Plettenberg Bay

Eating

1 Le Fournil de Plett B1
2 Lookout C1
3 Nguni B1
4 Table B2

Sleeping

5 Nothando Backpackers Hostel A1

LOOKOUT SEAFOOD $$

(☎044-533 1379; www.lookout.co.za; Lookout Rocks; mains R70-130; ⏰breakfast, lunch & dinner) With a deck overlooking the beach, this is a great place for a simple meal and perhaps views of dolphins surfing the waves.

 STEAKHOUSE $$$

(☎044-533 6710; www.nguni-restaurant.co.za; 6 Crescent St; mains R115-240; ⏰lunch Mon-Fri, dinner Mon-Sat) Tucked away in a quiet courtyard, this is one of Plett's most upscale eateries. The speciality is Chalmar beef, though you'll also find lots of South African favourites including ostrich, Karoo lamb and traditional dishes such as *bobotie* (curry with a topping of egg baked to a crust). Reservations recommended.

SHOPPING

OLD NICK VILLAGE ARTS & CRAFTS

(www.oldnickvillage.co.za) For a bit of retail therapy, head for this complex 3km east of town, with resident artists, a weaving museum, antiques and a restaurant.

SPORTS & ACTIVITIES

OCEAN BLUE ADVENTURES BOAT TOUR

(☎044-533 5083; www.oceanadventures.co.za; Milkwood Centre, Hopewood St; dolphin-/whale-watching R440/700) Trips on 30-person boats to view dolphins and whales in season.

OCEAN SAFARIS BOAT TOUR

(☎044-533 4963; www.oceansafaris.co.za; Milkwood Centre, Hopewood St; dolphin-/whale-watching R440/700) Boat trips to view dolphins and whales in season. The trips are permitted on 30-person boats.

SKY DIVE PLETTENBERG BAY ADVENTURE SPORTS

(☎082 905 7440; www.skydiveplett.com; Plettenberg Airport; tandem jumps R1850) This recommended operator offers dives with outstanding views on the way down.

LEARN TO SURF PLETT SURFING

(☎082 436 6410; www.learntosurfplett.co.za; 2hr group lesson incl equipment R350) A long-running surfing outfit that also offers stand-up paddle-boarding lessons (R150 per hour).

SLEEPING

★NOTHANDO BACKPACKERS HOSTEL BACKPACKERS $

(☎044-533 0220; www.nothando.com; 5 Wilder St; dm R160, d without/with bathroom R420/500; 📶) This excellent, five-star budget option is owner-run and it shows. There's a great bar area with satellite TV, yet you can still find peace and quiet in the large grounds. Rooms are worthy of a budget guesthouse.

ABALONE BEACH HOUSE BACKPACKERS **$**

(☎044-535 9602; www.abalonebeachhouse.co.za; 50 Milkwood Glen, Keurboomstrand; d without/with bathroom R500/600; 📶) This upmarket and extremely friendly backpackers is two minutes' walk from a magnificent beach; surf and body boards are provided free. To reach the house follow the Keurboomstrand signs from the N2 (about 6km east of Plett), then turn into Milkwood Glen.

MILKWOOD MANOR HOTEL **$$$**

(☎044-533 0420; www.milkwoodmanor.co.za; Salmack Rd, Lookout Beach; d from R1520; 📶) A remarkable location, right on the beach and overlooking the lagoon. Rooms have had a revamp and their bright new look has a beachy feel. There's a restaurant on-site and kayaks are free for guests.

Road Trip – Route 62

If you reached the Garden Route along the N2 and you're travelling with your own car, highly recommended for the return trip is Route 62. Billed as the world's longest wine route, the road begins in the Little Karoo and winds its way along mountain passes before ending in the Langeberg region.

If you're heading back to Cape Town from the Garden Route, first take the N12 from George as it climbs the Outeniqua Pass, ending up in Oudtshoorn. The 'ostrich capital of the world' has a range of **ostrich show farms**, the interesting **CP Nel Museum** (www.cpnelmuseum.co.za; 3 Baron van Rheede St; adult/child R20/5; ⏲8am-5pm Mon-Fri, 9am-1pm Sat) and the commercialised but impressive **Cango Caves** (☎044-272 7410; www.cango-caves.co.za; adult/child R80/45; ⏲9am-4pm). If you're not claustrophobic, take the **Adventure Tour** (adult/child R100/60) for a better look at the caves.

Route 62 takes you through Calitzdorp, renowned for its port-style wines. There are four **wineries** within walking distance of the main road. If you're looking for lunch, try **Porto Deli** (cnr Calitz & Voortrekker Sts; mains R70-130; ⏲lunch & dinner Mon-Sat, lunch Sun), an authentic Portuguese restaurant on the main drag.

Passing through unremarkable Ladismith you reach Barrydale, an often-overlooked gem offering stylish accommodation, craft shops and quirky restaurants with a Bohemian feel. There are wineries in the area, and nearby is the inimitable **Ronnie's Sex Shop** (Rte 62; mains R50-90; ⏲8.30am-9pm); the fairly dingy, bra-adorned bar here draws a constant stream of bikers and curious passersby.

Finally you arrive in gorgeous Montagu, tucked away in the Cogmanskloof Mountains. Its wide streets are bordered by 24 restored national monuments, including some fine art deco architecture. There's a wide range of activities, including **hot springs** (www.avalonsprings.co.za; entrance R50; ⏲8am-10pm), a number of **walks** and superlative **rock climbing** (☎023-614 3193; www.montaguclimbing.com; 45 Mount St; 2hr climbing trip R550), as well as excellent accommodation and some good restaurants.

Sleeping

From five-star pamper palaces and designer-chic guesthouses to creatively imagined backpackers, Cape Town's stock of sleeping options caters to all wallets. Choose your base carefully depending on your priorities – not everywhere is close to a beach or major sights.

Booking Accommodation

If there's somewhere you particularly want to stay, make reservations well in advance, especially if visiting during school holidays (from mid-December to the end of January and at Easter). The best budget stays especially fill up quickly.

SA-Venues.com (www.sa-venues.com) Directory of accommodation in Cape Town and the Western Cape.

Cape Town Tourism (www.capetown.travel) Accommodation bookings through member hotels.

Portfolio Collection (www.portfoliocollection.com) Curated listings of top hotels, guesthouses and boutique rental properties.

Lonely Planet (lonelyplanet.com/south-africa/cape-town/hotels) Hotel and hostel bookings.

Facilities

As always, you get what you pay for, but you may be pleasantly surprised at how good the quality of what you get can be. Among the few things to watch out for are:

Internet access Wi-fi is common and often complimentary, but service may be slow, unsecure and have download limits; if you need a reliable connection make detailed enquiries beforehand and check additional costs carefully.

Swimming pools Often more accurately described as plunge pools, particularly when found in guesthouses, though some top hotels have tiny pools, too.

Secure parking Not everywhere has it; some places that do, particularly in the City Bowl area, will slap on an extra daily charge of anything up to R100.

Self-Catering & Serviced Apartments

For longer-term stays, a self-catering or serviced apartment or villa can be a good deal. Reliable agencies include the following:

African Elite Properties (Map p272; ☎021-421 1090; www.africaneliteproperties.com) Agency handling rental of luxury apartments atop the Cape Quarter, starting from R2530 for one-bed units.

Cape Breaks (Map p268; ☎083 383 4888; www.capebreaks.co.za) Offers a range of studios and apartments in St Martini Gardens, beside the Company's Gardens.

Cape Stay (www.capestay.co.za) Accommodation across the Cape.

De Waterkant Cottages (Map p272; ☎021-421 2300; www.dewaterkantcottages.com) Classy villas and apartments in De Waterkant, sleeping from two to eight people.

FZP Property Investment (☎021-426 1634; www.fzp.co.za) Self-catering rental apartments in the City Bowl and beyond.

In Awe Stays (☎083 658 6975; www.inawestays.co.za) Stylish studios and cottages in Gardens and Fresnaye, from R850 a double.

Village & Life (Map p272; ☎021-437 9700; www.villageandlife.com) Focused mainly on properties in De Waterkant and Camps Bay.

Lonely Planet's Top Choices

Tintswalo Atlantic (p207) Spot whales from your balcony at this luxe lodge on the edge of Hout Bay.

Mannabay (p204) Contemporary-art-decorated boutique hotel on the slopes of Table Mountain.

Backpack (p203) Slickly run operation with colourful rooms to suit all budgets.

La Grenadine (p204) Old stables creatively reimagined, with charming rooms around an oasis of fruit trees.

Best by Budget

$

Scalabrini Guest House (p201) City-centre guesthouse; your stay will help the disadvantaged.

La Rose B&B (p201) Enjoy fresh crêpes at this charming Bo-Kaap guesthouse.

African Soul Surfer (p209) Stylish backpackers steps from Muizenberg beach.

$$

Villa Zest (p205) Retro groovy pad in a Bauhaus-style villa in Green Point.

Hippo Boutique Hotel (p204) Extra-spacious rooms, each with a small kitchen.

Cape Heritage (p201) Elegant boutique property in the town centre.

$$$

Ellerman House (p207) Play billionaire at this Bantry Bay beauty.

Belmond Mount Nelson Hotel (p205) Going strong since 1899; still a major player.

Cape Grace (p206) One of the nicest places to stay at the Waterfront.

Best for Backpackers

Ashanti Gardens (p203) Party on at this fun hostel with Table Mountain views.

Atlantic Point Backpackers (p205) Walking distance to the Waterfront.

Once in Cape Town (p203) Cool crash pad, with the most happening cafe-bar in Gardens.

Best Boutique Stays

Marly (p207) Live it up at this exclusive Camps Bay property.

Kensington Place (p205) Watch the city lights twinkle far beneath this luxury hotel.

Dutch Manor (p201) Historic house stocked with antiques on the edge of the Bo-Kaap.

Best B&Bs

Chartfield Guest House (p209) The classiest place to stay in Kalk Bay.

St Paul's B&B Guesthouse (p201) Great budget alternative to city-centre hostels.

Bella Ev (p209) Beautifully decorated, family-run property in Muizenberg.

Best for Greenery

Vineyard Hotel & Spa (p208) Surrounded by lush gardens with views onto Table Mountain.

Camps Bay Retreat (p207) Set in a secluded nature reserve; also near the beach.

Thulani River Lodge (p206) Peace and tranquillity at a thatched mansion in Hout Bay.

NEED TO KNOW

Unless noted, prices quoted are for rooms with private bathrooms during high season (mid-December to mid-January), including breakfast and all taxes.

Price Ranges

$ less than R800 per room or dorm bed

$$ R800 to R2500 per room

$$$ more than R2500 per room

Discounts

Online booking discounts are often available, particularly for longer stays, with rates dropping by anything up to 50% from May to October (during the slow winter season).

Nonsmoking Rooms

Available at most places.

Transport

If a hotel is within easy walking distance of a MyCiTi bus stop or a train station, details are listed in the reviews.

Where to Stay

Neighbourhood	For	Against
City Bowl, Foreshore, Bo-Kaap & De Waterkant	Ideal for exploring city on foot, with plenty of transport to other regions. Bo-Kaap and De Waterkant have characterful guesthouses and hotels.	No beaches. City Bowl is dead on Sundays, when most businesses close. Mosques in the Bo-Kaap and the nightlife of De Waterkant can disturb peace and tranquillity.
East City, District Six, Woodstock & Observatory	The hip urban vibes of these edgy, slowly gentrifying areas.	Safety can still be an issue; short on both greenery and beaches.
Gardens & Surrounds	Tons of lovely boutique guesthouses; easy access to Table Mountain.	The hikes up and down the hills will keep you fit; pack earplugs for the howling wind factor.
Green Point & Waterfront	Direct access to the V&A Waterfront; breezy promenade walks and Green Point Park.	Coping with the crowds at the Waterfront.
Sea Point to Hout Bay	Good seaside bases. Camps Bay is one of the city's ritziest suburbs. Hout Bay is handy for both Atlantic Coast beaches and Constantia vineyards.	Sea Point has its grungy areas. Popularity of Camps Bay pushes up prices and the crowd factor. From Hout Bay it's a longish drive to main city-centre sights.
Southern Suburbs	Leafy and upmarket areas; near Kirstenbosch Botanical Gardens and vineyards of Constantia.	No beaches; city-centre sights also a drive away.
Simon's Town & Southern Peninsula	Good for families and surfers wanting nice beaches; vibey village atmosphere. Simon's Town is historic and has easy access to quiet beaches and the rugged landscapes of Cape Point.	Nearly an hour's drive from the City Bowl. Lack of big-city atmosphere and attractions.
Cape Flats & Northern Suburbs	Close to airport and on way to Stellenbosch. Firsthand experience of black African culture.	Cape Flats suffers wind and dust storms. The surrounding poverty. Distance from city centre.

City Bowl, Foreshore, Bo-Kaap & De Waterkant

LA ROSE B&B B&B $

Map p268 (021-422 5883; www.larosecapetown.com; 32 Rose St, Bo-Kaap; s/d from R600/800; Old Fire Station) A welcoming South African–French couple run this charming B&B, which has been so successful it's expanded into nearby properties. It's beautifully decorated and has a rooftop garden with the best views of the area. Yoann's speciality is making authentic crêpes for the guests.

ROSE LODGE B&B $

Map p268 (021-424 3813; www.rosestreet28.com; 28 Rose St, Bo-Kaap; s/d R600/650; Old Fire Station) Inside a grey-painted corner house is this cute B&B. The Canadian owner likes to play the grand piano and has two adorable dogs. There are just three cosy rooms (with private bathrooms), all decorated in contemporary style. They manage several more similar properties in the Bo-Kaap.

ST PAUL'S B&B GUESTHOUSE B&B $

Map p268 (021-423 4420; www.stpaulschurch.co.za/theguesthouse.htm; 182 Bree St, City Bowl; s/d R550/900, with shared bathroom R450/750; Upper Long/Upper Loop) This spotless B&B in a handy location is a quiet alternative to noise-plagued Long St backpackers. Simply furnished and spacious rooms have high ceilings, and there's a vine-shaded courtyard where you can relax or eat breakfast.

SCALABRINI GUEST HOUSE HOSTEL $

Map p268 (021-465 6433; www.scalabrini.org.za; 47 Commercial St, City Bowl; dm/s/d R240/420/600; Roeland) The monastic order Scalabrini Fathers have provided welfare to Cape Town's poor and refugees since 1994. Housed in a former textile factory, they run social programs, and a pleasant guesthouse with 11 immaculately clean en suite rooms – plus a great kitchen for self-catering where you can watch satellite TV.

LONG STREET BACKPACKERS HOSTEL $

Map p268 (021-423 0615; www.longstreetbackpackers.co.za; 209 Long St, City Bowl; dm/s/d R140/260/370; Dorp/Leeuwen) Little has changed at this backpackers since it opened in 1993 (making it the longest-running of the many on Long St). In a block of 14 small flats, with four to eight beds and a bathroom in each, accommodation is arranged around a leafy, courtyard decorated with funky mosaics, in which the resident cat pads around.

★**DUTCH MANOR** HISTORIC HOTEL $$

Map p268 (021-422 4767; www.dutchmanor.co.za; 158 Buitengracht St, Bo-Kaap; s/d R1400/1900, parking per day R60; Dorp/Leeuwen) Four-poster beds, giant armoires and creaking floorboards lend terrific atmosphere to this six-room property crafted from a 1812 building. Although it overlooks busy Buitengracht, the noise is largely kept at bay thanks to modern renovations. Dinners can be prepared on request by the staff, who can also arrange Bo-Kaap walking tours for R70 (nonguests R100) with a local guide.

CAPE HERITAGE HOTEL BOUTIQUE HOTEL $$

Map p268 (021-424 4646; www.capeheritage.co.za; Heritage Sq, 90 Bree St, City Bowl; d/ste from R2250/3490, parking per day R75; Church/Longmarket) Each room at this elegant boutique hotel, part of the Heritage Sq redevelopment of 18th-century buildings, has its own character. Some have four-poster beds and all have modern conveniences such as satellite TV and clothes presses. There's a roof terrace and a Jacuzzi pool.

GRAND DADDY HOTEL BOUTIQUE HOTEL $$

Map p268 (021-424 7247; www.granddaddy.co.za; 38 Long St, City Bowl; r or trailer from R1910, parking per day R40; Mid-Long/Church) The star attraction is the rooftop 'trailer park' of penthouse suites, made from vintage, artistically renovated Airstream trailers. The regular rooms are also stylish and incorporate playful references to South African culture. Its Daddy Cool bar has been blinged out with gold paint and trinkets.

DADDY LONG LEGS HOTEL BOUTIQUE HOTEL $$

Map p268 (021-422 3074; www.daddylonglegs.co.za; 134 Long St, City Bowl; r/apt from R1175/1275; Dorp/Leeuwen) A stay at this boutique hotel-cum-art installation is anything but boring. Thirteen artists were given free rein to design the boudoirs of their dreams; the results range from a bohemian garret to a hospital ward! Our favourites include the karaoke room (with a mike in the shower) and a room decorated with cartoons of South African pop group Freshlyground. Breakfast is extra. Super-stylish **apartments** (Map p268; 263 Long St, City Bowl; 1/2bedroom apt from R1275/1775; Upper Long/Upper Loop) are also offered – ideal if you crave hotel-suite luxury but want to self-cater.

ROUGE ON ROSE BOUTIQUE HOTEL $$
Map p268 (021-426 0298; www.rougeonrose.co.za; 25 Rose St, Bo-Kaap; s/d R1000/1500; ; Old Fire Station) This great Bo-Kaap option offers nine rustic-chic suites with kitchenettes, lounges and lots of workspace. The fun wall paintings are by a resident artist and all rooms have luxurious, open bath spaces with stand-alone tubs.

PURPLE HOUSE B&B, APARTMENT $$
Map p272 (021-418 2508; www.purplehouse.co.za; 23 Jarvis St, De Waterkant; s/d/apt from R950/1050/1500; ; Alfred) Apart from their stylish and cosy B&B, set in the eponymous purple-painted house, the personable Dutch owners Hank and Guido also offer a self-catering cottage on the same street and a two-bed apartment on Loader St.

DE WATERKANT HOUSE B&B $$
Map p272 (021-409 2500; www.dewaterkant.com; cnr Napier & Waterkant Sts, De Waterkant; s/d from R1000/1250; ; Old Fire Station) A pleasant B&B in a renovated Cape Georgian house, with tiny plunge pool for hot summers and a lounge fireplace for chilly winters. Management also runs another appealing guesthouse, **The Charles** (Map p272; 021-409 2500; www.thecharles.co.za; 137 Waterkant St, De Waterkant; s/d from R1000/1250; ; Alfred), and rent a wide range of serviced apartments in the area.

VICTORIA JUNCTION HOTEL, APARTMENT $$
Map p272 (021-418 1234; www.proteahotels.co.za; cnr Somerset St & Ebenezer Rd, De Waterkant; s/d from R2079/2392, parking per day R45; P; Gallow's Hill) Vintage suitcases hang on the lobby walls like artwork at this Protea hotel offering something edgier than usual, with industrial-loft-style rooms and self-catering apartments with exposed brick walls. There's a reasonably sized lap pool.

VILLAGE LODGE B&B, APARTMENT $$
Map p272 (021-421 1106; www.thevillagelodge.com; 49 Napier St, De Waterkant; s/d from R850/1400; ; Alfred) Rooms are smart but not spacious. The rooftop plunge pool and bar is a prime spot for guests to check out the view. Breakfast is extra.

DE WATERKANT LODGE B&B $$
Map p272 (021-419 2476; www.dewaterkantplace.com; 35 Dixon St, De Waterkant; s/d/apt R600/900/1000; ; Old Fire Station) This appealing guesthouse with friendly management offers good-value, fan-cooled rooms decorated with antiques, plus a self-catering unit sleeping up to six.

CAPE TOWN HOLLOW HOTEL $$
Map p278 (021-423 1260; www.seasonsinafrica.com; 88 Queen Victoria St, City Bowl; r from R1200, parking per day R55; P; Upper Long/Upper Loop) Overlooking the Company's Gardens and Table Mountain, this hotel's online rates and special deals make it a great-value midrange option. A recent renovation has given public area and rooms a pleasant, contemporary look. The pool is minuscule, but there's a restaurant with leafy aspect.

TOWNHOUSE HOTEL $$
Map p268 (021-465 7050; www.townhouse.co.za; 60 Corporation St, City Bowl; s/d from R1595/1945, parking per day R45; P; Groote Kerk) Sharing the good service and high standards of its big sister the Vineyard Hotel & Spa (p208), this is a justly popular inner-city choice. Rooms have been given a contemporary makeover, with wooden floors and chic black-and-white decor.

LONG STREET BOUTIQUE HOTEL BOUTIQUE HOTEL $$
Map p268 (021-426 4309; www.longstreethotel.com; 230 Long St, City Bowl; r from R1250; ; Upper Long/Upper Loop) Offers 12 stylish rooms, with decent bathrooms and soundproofing, we're assured, to deal with its location on one of Long St's noisiest corners.

TAJ CAPE TOWN LUXURY HOTEL $$$
Map p268 (021-819 2000; www.tajhotels.com; Wale St, City Bowl; r/ste R7000/10,000; P; Groote Kerk) India's luxury hotel group has breathed new life into the Board of Executors building at the corner of Wale and Adderley. There's plenty of heritage here but a new tower also houses chic contemporary rooms, many offering spectacular views of Table Mountain. Service and facilities, including excellent restaurant **Bombay Brasserie** (p69), are top-grade.

East City, District Six, Woodstock & Obervatory

★**WISH U WERE HERE** BACKPACKERS $
Map p274 (021-447 0522; www.wishuwerehere capetown.com; 445 Albert Rd, Salt River; dm/s/d with shared bathroom R200/450/600, d with private bathroom R700; ; Kent) The designers

clearly had a lot of fun with this place just a short stroll from the Old Biscuit Mill. One dorm is Barbie-doll pink; a romantic double has a bed made from a suspended fishing boat; another is styled after an intensive care unit! The wraparound balcony overlooks the Salt River roundabout (noisy in daytime).

OBSERVATORY BACKPACKERS BACKPACKERS $

Map p276 (021-447 0861; www.observatoryback packers.com; 235 Lower Main Rd, Observatory; dm/s/d with shared bathroom from R160/360/460, r with private bathroom R530; ; Observatory) There's a funky African theme to this very appealing backpackers, just a short walk from the heart of the Obs action further down Lower Main Rd. The spacious, shady backyard and lounges are a plus. No breakfast but Dolce Bakery is right next door.

GREEN ELEPHANT BACKPACKERS $

Map p276 (021-448 6359; www.greenelephant.co.za; 57 Milton Rd, Observatory; dm/s/d with shared bathroom R140/400/500, s/d with private bathroom R450/540, camping per tent R90; P@; Observatory) This long-running backpackers, split between three houses, is a popular alternative to city-centre hostels. Camping is possible and they can arrange climbs up Table Mountain with a qualified guide (R300 per person). Rates don't include breakfast.

33 SOUTH BOUTIQUE BACKPACKERS BACKPACKERS $

Map p276 (021-447 2423; www.33southback packers.com; 48 Trill Rd, Observatory; dm/s/d with shared bathroom from R150/400/460, d with private bathroom R580; @; Observatory) Not exactly boutique but certainly imaginative, this cosy backpackers in a Victorian cottage has sought inspiration from different Cape Town suburbs as themes for its rooms. There's a delightful shared kitchen and a pretty courtyard. Staff conduct free tours of Observatory. Rates don't include breakfast.

DISTRICT SIX GUEST HOUSE B&B $

Map p274 (021-447 0902; www.districtsixguest house.co.za; 2 Chester Rd, District Six; s/d/t R600/750/850; P; Zonnebloem) In three cottages once attached to historic Zonnebloem Farm House, this spacious guesthouse, surrounded by a broad stoop and with views over the harbour, provides a taste of simple Cape Malay hospitality. It's far from luxurious, but it's all spotless and efficiently run. The four-bed room is ideal for a family.

DOUBLETREE BY HILTON HOTEL CAPE TOWN – UPPER EASTSIDE HOTEL $$

Map p274 (021-404 0570; www.doubletree.hil ton.com; 31 Brickfield Rd, Woodstock; r/ste R1195/2195, parking per day R40; P@; Upper Salt River) This snazzily designed property is tucked away in the revamped buildings of the old Bonwitt clothing factory. Rooms are large and pleasant, offering either mountain or city views. Loft suites (ask for 507, the largest) have kitchenettes. There's an indoor pool and a gym. Rates exclude breakfast.

Gardens & Surrounds

BACKPACK BACKPACKERS $

Map p278 (021-423 4530; www.backpackers.co.za; 74 New Church St, Tamboerskloof; dm/s/d with shared bathroom from R270/720/1060, s/d/apt with private bathroom from R780/1320/1600; P@; Upper Long/Upper Loop) This Fair Trade in Tourism–accredited operation offers affordable style, a buzzy vibe and fantastic staff. Its dorms may not be Cape Town's cheapest but they're among its nicest, while the private rooms and self-catering apartments are charmingly decorated. There's a lovely mosaic-decorated pool and relaxing gardens with Table Mountain views to chill out in. Rates exclude breakfast.

ONCE IN CAPE TOWN BACKPACKERS $

Map p278 (021-424 6169; www.onceincapetown .co.za; 73 Kloof St, Gardens; dm/s/d R235/850/910; P@; Ludwig's Garden) Great vibe and location for this new place, where every room has its own bathroom and breakfast is included (it's served in the hip cafe that fronts the building). There's a courtyard to chill in and a big kitchen for self-catering.

ASHANTI GARDENS BACKPACKERS $

Map p278 (021-423 8721; www.ashanti.co.za; 11 Hof St, Gardens; dm/s/d with shared bathroom from R190/450/650, d with private bathroom R990; P@; Government Ave) One of Cape Town's slickest backpackers, with much of the action focused on the lively bar and deck that overlook Table Mountain. The beautiful old house, decorated with contemporary art, holds the dorms; there's also a lawn where you can camp (R110 per person). Excellent, self-catering en suite rooms are in two separate heritage-listed houses around the corner. There's also another branch in Green Point (p205).

BLENCATHRA BACKPACKERS $

Map p277 (☎073 389 0702, 021-424 9571; www.blencathra.co.za; cnr De Hoop & Cambridge Aves, Tamboerskloof; dm/d with shared bathroom from R150/500; P@; Cotswold) You're well on the way up Lion's Head at this delightful family home, which offers a range of rooms, mostly frequented by long-stay guests. It's ideal for those looking to escape the city and the more commercialised backpacker options. Rates are negotiable for longer stays.

★**LA GRENADINE** GUESTHOUSE $$

Map p278 (☎021-424 1358; www.lagrenadine.co.za; 15 Park Rd, Gardens; r/2-bed cottage from R1300/2500; @; Ludwig's Garden) Expat couple Maxime and Mélodie ladle on the Gallic charm at this imaginatively renovated former stables, where the ancient stone walls are a feature of the rooms. The garden planted with fruit trees is a magical oasis, the lounge is stacked with books and vinyl LPs, and breakfast is served on actress Mélodie's prize collection of china.

HIPPO BOUTIQUE HOTEL BOUTIQUE HOTEL $$

Map p278 (☎021-423 2500; www.hippotique.co.za; 5-9 Park Rd, Gardens; d/ste R1550/2200; P@; Lower Kloof) A brilliantly located and appealing boutique property that offers spacious, stylish rooms, each with a small kitchen for self-catering. Larger, arty suites, with mezzanine-level bedrooms and themes such as Red Bull and Mini Cooper, are worth the extra spend.

FOUR ROSMEAD GUESTHOUSE $$

Map p277 (☎021-480 3810; www.fourrosmead.com; 4 Rosmead Ave, Oranjezicht; d/ste from R2500/3150; P@; Rayden) A heritage-listed building dating from 1903 has been remodelled into this luxury guesthouse. Special touches include a saltwater swimming pool and a fragrant Mediterranean herb garden. The pool-house suite with lofty ceiling is great if you want extra privacy.

CAPE MILNER HOTEL $$

Map p278 (☎021-426 1101; www.capemilner.com; 2A Milner Rd, Tamboerskloof; s/d from R1785/2380, parking per day R60; P@; Upper Long/Upper Loop) Silks and velvets in metallic colours add a sophisticated touch to the contemporary-style rooms here, which are good value for this area. Friendly service and sweeping views of Table Mountain from the luxurious suites and swimming pool area are other pluses.

ABBEY MANOR B&B $$

Map p277 (☎021-462 2935; www.abbey.co.za; 3 Montrose Ave, Oranjezicht; s/d from R2000/2600; P@; Montrose) Occupying a grand Arts and Crafts–style home, built in 1905 for a shipping magnate, the interiors of this luxury guesthouse marry fine linen and antique furnishings with whimsical art-nouveau flourishes. A decent-sized pool and courteous staff enhance the experience.

AN AFRICAN VILLA B&B $$

Map p278 (☎021-423 2162; www.capetowncity.co.za; 19 Carstens St, Tamboerskloof; s/d from R1500/1900; @; Belle Ombre) There's a sophisticated, colourful 'African modern' design theme at this appealing guesthouse, sheltering behind the facade of three 19th-century terrace houses. Relax in the evening in one of two comfy lounges while sipping the complimentary sherry or port.

TREVOYAN B&B $$

Map p278 (☎021-424 4407; www.trevoyan.co.za; 12 Gilmour Hill Rd, Tamboerskloof; r from R1650; P@; Belle Ombre) This heritage building, with high-ceiling rooms, parquet floors and a faint art deco style, has been transformed into a relaxed guesthouse that is smart but not too posh. A big plus is its lovely courtyard garden, partly shaded by a giant oak, with a pool big enough to swim in.

DUNKLEY HOUSE GUESTHOUSE $$

Map p278 (☎021-462 7650; www.dunkleyhouse.com; 3B Gordon St, Gardens; s/d from R800/1025, s/d apt from R1250/1650; @; Annandale) A stylish place, with neutral-toned rooms featuring a mix of retro and modern furnishings, CD players, fresh fruit and flowers and a bamboo grove. There's a plunge pool in the courtyard, while the honeymoon suite has a private pool and separate Jacuzzi.

PLATTEKLIP WASH HOUSE HOUSE $$

Map p277 (☎012-428 9111, 021-712 7471; www.tmnp.co.za; Deer Park, Vredehoek; d R850, extra person R425; P; Herzlia) The old wash houses on the edge of Table Mountain National Park have been converted into some very stylish accommodation. The decoration in the living room includes pieces by top Capetonian craftspeople, while outside is a sunken campfire circle and hammocks.

★**MANNABAY** BOUTIQUE HOTEL $$$

Map p277 (☎021-461 1094; www.mannabay.com; 8 Bridle Rd, Oranjezicht; r/ste from R5000/6000;

P❄@ᯤ≋; ⓑUpper Orange) Nothing seems too much bother for the staff at this knockout property decorated with stunning pieces by local artists. The seven guest rooms are decorated in different themes: Versailles, world explorer, Japan etc. Its high hillside location on the edge of the national park provides amazing views. Rates include high tea, which is served in the library lounge.

BELMOND MOUNT NELSON HOTEL HOTEL **$$$**

Map p278 (☎021-483 1000; www.mountnelson.co.za; 76 Orange St, Gardens; r/ste from R5000/7465; P❄@ᯤ≋; ⓑGovernment Ave) The sugar-pink-painted 'Nellie' is a colonial charmer with its chintz decor and doormen in pith helmets. Rooms sport elegant silver and moss-green decorations. It's great for families since it pushes the boat out for the little ones, with kid-sized robes and bedtime cookies and milk – not to mention the large pool and 3 hectares of gardens, including tennis courts.

KENSINGTON PLACE BOUTIQUE HOTEL **$$$**

Map p277 (☎021-424 4744; www.kensingtonplace.co.za; 38 Kensington Cres, Higgovale; r from R3553; P❄@ᯤ≋; ⓑUpper Kloof) High up the mountain, this exclusive, chic property offers eight spacious and tastefully decorated rooms, all with balconies and beautifully tiled bathrooms. Fresh fruit and flowers in the rooms are a nice touch.

CAPE CADOGAN BOUTIQUE HOTEL **$$$**

Map p278 (☎021-480 8080; www.capecadogan.com; 5 Upper Union St, Gardens; s/d from R2190/2920; P❄@ᯤ≋; ⓑBelle Ombre) This *Gone with the Wind*-style heritage-listed villa presents a very classy boutique operation, with some rooms opening onto the secluded courtyard. They also run the **More Quarters** (www.morequarters.co.za) self-catering apartments around the corner on Nicols St.

15 ON ORANGE HOTEL **$$$**

Map p278 (☎021-469 8000; www.africanpridehotels.com/15onorange; cnr Grey's Pass & Orange St, Gardens; r/ste from R3650/3350, parking per day R65; P❄@ᯤ≋; ⓑMichaelis) The lipstick-red marble walkway to the lobby gives an indication of the luxe nature of this hotel, which is built around a soaring atrium onto which some rooms face (perfect for exhibitionists). It's all very plush and design-savvy. Rates exclude breakfast.

Green Point & Waterfront

ATLANTIC POINT BACKPACKERS BACKPACKERS **$**

Map p280 (☎021-433 1663; www.atlanticpoint.co.za; 2 Cavalcade Rd, Green Point; dm from R225, d with shared/private bathroom from R820/940; P@ᯤ; ⓑUpper Portswood) Playfully designed, well run and steps away from Green Point's main drag. Features include a big balcony and bar, a loft lounge, a tiny pool to cool off in and bicycle rental (R70 per day).

B.I.G. BACKPACKERS BACKPACKERS **$**

Map p280 (☎021-434 0688; www.bigbackpackers.co.za; 18 Thornhill Rd, Green Point; dm/s/d/tr R300/705/965/1400; P❄@ᯤ≋; ⓑSkye Way) Tucked away on the slopes of Green Point, this new backpackers has a fun, laid-back atmosphere with decently decorated rooms, chill areas and a big kitchen (with an honesty bar). They also bake their own bread for breakfast and have a guitar and bicycles handy should you require either.

ASHANTI GREEN POINT BACKPACKERS **$**

Map p280 (☎021-433 1619; www.ashanti.co.za; 23 Antrim Rd, Three Anchor Bay; dm/s/d with shared bathroom R180/450/650, d with private bathroom R900; P@ᯤ≋; ⓑSt Bedes) More chill than the branch in Gardens (p203), this Ashanti has a breezy hillside position with sea views and is nicely decorated with old Cape Town photos. Pancakes are served for breakfast.

VILLA ZEST BOUTIQUE HOTEL **$$**

Map p280 (☎021-433 1246; www.villazest.co.za; 2 Braemar Rd, Green Point; s/d from R1490/1590; P❄@≋; ⓑUpper Portswood) This Bauhaus-style villa has been converted into a quirkily decorated boutique hotel. The lobby is lined with an impressive collection of '60s and '70s electronic goods, including radios, Polaroid cameras and eight-track cassette players. The seven guest rooms have bold, retro-design furniture and papered walls accented with furry pillows and shag rugs.

HEAD SOUTH LODGE BOUTIQUE HOTEL **$$**

Map p280 (☎021-434 8777; www.headsouth.co.za; 215 Main Rd, Three Anchor Bay; d from R995; P❄@≋; ⓑEllerslie) A homage to the 1950s, with retro furnishings and collection of Tretchikoff prints in the bar. Its big rooms, decorated in cool white and grey, are hung with equally striking modern art by Philip Briel.

LA SPLENDIDA HOTEL **$$**

Map p280 (021-439 5119; www.lasplendida.co.za; 121 Beach Rd, Mouille Point; s/d from R1460/2010, parking per day R25; P ❄ @ ; Lighthouse) You'll pay slightly extra for rooms with sea views at this hotel, but the ones looking towards Signal Hill are just as nice. There's a retro pop-art feel to the decor. Breakfast is served in the buzzy cafe-bar on the ground floor, Sotano (p112).

CAPE STANDARD BOUTIQUE HOTEL **$$**

Map p280 (021-430 3060; www.capestandard.co.za; 3 Romney Rd, Green Point; s/d R1390/1780; P @ ; Ravenscraig) A chic property offering whitewashed beach-house rooms downstairs or contemporary rooms upstairs. The mosaic-tiled bathrooms have showers big enough to dance in.

CAPE GRACE LUXURY HOTEL **$$$**

Map p280 (021-410 7100; www.capegrace.com; West Quay Rd, V&A Waterfront; r/ste from R6700/13,200; P ❄ @ ; Nobel Square) One of the Waterfront's most appealing hotels, with an arty combination of antiques and crafts decoration – including hand-painted bed covers and curtains – providing a unique sense of place and Cape Town's history.

ONE & ONLY CAPE TOWN HOTEL **$$$**

Map p280 (021-431 5888; www.oneandonlycapetown.com; Dock Rd, V&A Waterfront; r/ste from R6495/12,595; P ❄ @ ; Aquarium) Little expense has been spared creating this luxury resort. Choose between enormous, plush rooms in the main building (with views of Table Mountain) or the even more exclusive island, beside the pool and spa. The bar turns out inventive cocktails and is a nice place to plonk yourself before a meal at celeb-chef restaurants Nobu or Reuben's.

DOCK HOUSE BOUTIQUE HOTEL **$$$**

Map p280 (021-421 9334; www.dockhouse.co.za; Portswood Close, Portswood Ridge, V&A Waterfront; d/ste R6830/8260; P ❄ @ ; Nobel Square) Butlers in white kurta-style pyjamas greet you at this super-elegant, six-bedroom property crafted out of the former harbour master's house. The luxurious bedrooms are decorated in dove-grey and olive and have spacious bathrooms. It's at the heart of the Waterfront but feels almost a world away. The same company runs the appealing (and slightly cheaper) **Queen Victoria Hotel** (Map p280; 021-427 5900; www.queenvictoriahotel.co.za; Portswood Close, Portswood Ridge, V&A Waterfront; d/ste R5820/8260; P ❄ @ ; Nobel Square) nearby.

Sea Point to Hout Bay

★**GLEN BOUTIQUE HOTEL** BOUTIQUE HOTEL **$$**

Map p284 (021-439 0086; www.glenhotel.co.za; 3 The Glen, Sea Point; d/ste from R1950/4900; P ❄ @ ; The Glen) This gorgeous 'straight-friendly' boutique hotel occupies an elegant old house and a newer block behind. Spacious rooms are decorated in natural tones. In the middle is a fabulous pool and spa, and outdoor dining for the restaurant.

THULANI RIVER LODGE B&B **$$**

(021-790 7662; www.thulani.eu; 14 Riverside Tce, Hout Bay; s/d from R1150/1300; P @ ; Imizamo Yethu) *Thulani* is Zulu for 'peace and tranquillity' – the perfect description for this treasure, an African-thatched mansion tucked away in a lush valley through which the Disa River flows towards Hout Bay. Lie in the four-poster bed in the honeymoon suite and you'll be treated to a sweeping panorama of the back of Table Mountain.

WINCHESTER MANSIONS HOTEL HOTEL **$$**

Map p284 (021-434 2351; www.winchester.co.za; 221 Beach Rd, Sea Point; s/d from R2007/2397, ste s/d from R2521/2911; P ❄ @ ; London) Offering a seaside location (you'll pay extra for rooms with views), old-fashioned style and even some corridors lined with putting greens for golf practice. The pool is a decent size and there's a lovely courtyard with a central fountain – a romantic place to dine.

CASCADES ON THE PROMENADE HOTEL **$$**

Map p284 (021-434 5979; www.cascadescollection.com; 11 Arthurs Rd, Sea Point; s/d R1750/1950; ❄ @ ; Boat Bay) Not technically on the promenade, but close enough that the rooms with balconies at this trendily monochrome designer hotel have sea views. All rooms have USB ports and Apple computers. The cafe on the verandah at the front is a lovely spot for breakfast, brunch or lunch.

HUIJS HAERLEM B&B **$$**

Map p284 (021-434 6434; www.huijshaerlem.co.za; 25 Main Dr, Sea Point; s/d from R900/1850; P @ ; Rhine) Walk up one of Sea Point's steeper slopes to this excellent, gay-friendly (but not exclusively gay) guesthouse. It comprises two houses joined by delightful gardens with a decent-sized pool.

CHAPMAN'S PEAK HOTEL HOTEL $$
Map p283 (021-790 1036; www.chapmanspeakhotel.co.za; Chapman's Peak Dr, Hout Bay; original s/d from R1300/1600, newer s/d from R1470/2200; P; Hout Bay) Take your pick between the chic, contemporary-designed rooms with balconies and to-die-for views across the bay (in a new addition), or the much cheaper and smaller rooms in the original building, which also houses a very popular bar and restaurant.

AMBLEWOOD GUESTHOUSE B&B $$
Map p283 (021-790 1570; www.amblewood.co.za; 43 Skaife St, Hout Bay; r from R1180; P @; Military) June and Trevor are the genial hosts of this convivial upmarket B&B, which has a range of rooms decorated with period furniture. You can cool off in the small pool on the deck with a view over the beautiful sweep of Hout Bay.

★**TINTSWALO ATLANTIC** LUXURY HOTEL $$$
(021-201 0025; www.tintswalo.com; Chapman's Peak Dr, Hout Bay; s/d/ste from R5070/7800/25,000; P; Hout Bay) Destroyed in a disastrous fire in March 2015, this heralded hotel should be back to its best before 2016 is rung in. The only luxury lodge within Table Mountain National Park, Tintswalo hugs the edge of a beautiful rocky bay, a favourite resting ground for whales. Expect sublime views and rooms rich with natural materials. Rack rates include dinner and breakfast. The complex will again be built on raised platforms to keep environmental impact to a minimum.

POD BOUTIQUE HOTEL $$$
Map p282 (021-438 8550; www.pod.co.za; 3 Argyle Rd, Camps Bay; r/ste from R3950/12,120; P; Camps Bay) Offering clean, contemporary design, POD is perfectly angled to catch the Camps Bay action from its bar and spacious pool and deck area. The cheapest rooms have mountain rather than sea views; luxury rooms have their own private plunge pools.

ELLERMAN HOUSE LUXURY HOTEL $$$
Map p284 (021-430 3200; www.ellerman.co.za; 180 Kloof Rd, Bantry Bay; d/ste/villa from R8300/17,270/53,460; P; Bantry Bay) Imagine you've been invited to stay with an immensely rich, art-collecting Capetonian friend. This elegant mansion overlooking the Atlantic, and its more contemporary-styled pair of private villas, houses an incredible contemporary art gallery. Beautiful gardens and oodles of luxe services and conveniences are all on hand.

TWELVE APOSTLES HOTEL & SPA LUXURY HOTEL $$$
(021-437 9000; www.12apostleshotel.com; Victoria Rd, Camps Bay; r/ste from R5511/12,100; P; Oudekraal) Silky wallpaper, piles of pillows and lovely artworks enhance the atmosphere of this seaside option that sits in splendid isolation above the rocks at Oudekraal. Other pluses include a 16-seat cinema and walking trails behind the hotel that lead to secluded picnic spots.

CAMPS BAY RETREAT LUXURY HOTEL $$$
Map p282 (021-437 8300; www.campsbayretreat.com; 7 Chilworth Rd, The Glen; d/ste from R5050/7850; P; Glen Beach) Based in the grand Earl's Dyke Manor (dating from 1929), this splendid option is set in a secluded nature reserve. Choose between rooms in either the main house or the contemporary Deck House, reached by a rope bridge over a ravine. There are also four pools, including some fed by a stream from Table Mountain.

HOUT BAY MANOR HOTEL $$$
Map p283 (021-790 0116; www.houtbaymanor.co.za; Baviaanskloof Rd, Hout Bay; s/d from R2570/3905; P; Military) Your eyes will pop at the fab Afro-chic makeover that the 1871 Hout Bay Manor has been treated to. Tribal artefacts are mixed with brightly coloured contemporary furnishings and handicrafts in rooms that all contain the expected electronic conveniences.

MARLY HOTEL $$$
Map p282 (021-437 1287; www.themarly.co.za; 201 The Promenade, Camps Bay; mountain/sea view ste R5600/10,100; P; Whale Rock) So exclusive it's tricky to find the entrance, exquisite Marly sits high above the Camps Bay throng, but is close enough for you to hear the crash of waves (not to mention the Victoria Rd traffic). If a good night's sleep is needed, we recommend the quieter mountain-view rooms.

Southern Suburbs

OFF THE WALL BACKPACKERS $
Map p286 (076 322 4053, 021-671 6958; www.offthewallbackpackers.com; 117 Roscommon St, Claremont; dm/s/d with shared bathrooms R175/

450/570; ; Claremont) In the thick of Claremont's shopping strip, this is a handy and appealing hostel should you wish to be based close to this area's sights. It's colourfully painted inside and out and has a great communal kitchen. Breakfast not included.

WOOD OWL COTTAGE HOUSE **$$**

Map p288 (021-712 2337; www.tmnp.co.za; Tokai Forest, Tokai Rd, Tokai; 1-3 people R1095, extra adult/child R360/180; P) This elegantly decorated former forester's cottage with three bedrooms, sleeping up to six, is surrounded by trees. The open-plan kitchen and living room has a fireplace and there's a separate TV room. It's ideal for a family.

VINEYARD HOTEL & SPA LUXURY HOTEL **$$$**

Map p286 (021-657 4500; www.vineyard.co.za; Colinton Rd, Newlands; s/d from R2150/2600, ste s/d from R4500/5040; P@; Claremont) Built around the 1799 home of Lady Anne Barnard, this delightful hotel has a contemporary look and is decorated in soothing natural tones. It's surrounded by lush gardens with views onto Table Mountain. Friendly staff, the fabulous **Angsana Spa**, a great gym and pool, and top gourmet restaurant **Myoga** complete the picture.

ALPHEN BOUTIQUE HOTEL **$$$**

Map p288 (021-795 6300; www.alphen.co.za; Alphen Dr, Constantia; ste from R4000; P@; Wittebome) A glitzy makeover has transformed this historic estate into a bling-tastic property with 19 suites variously dubbed 'cool', 'amazing' and 'stunning'. This translates into a fearless mix of antiques and bold, contemporary styling. The property's convivial **La Belle** cafe and bakery and chic **Rose Bar**, overlooking the manicured gardens and pool, are both worth a trip on their own. To get here by car, take the Constantia exit from M3 and follow the signs to Alphen.

STEENBERG HOTEL LUXURY HOTEL **$$$**

Map p288 (021-713 2222; www.steenberghotel.com; Steenberg Estate, Steenberg Rd, Tokai; r/ste from R2650/11,450; P@) You get fresh flowers in plush rooms decorated in soft tones at this luxury hotel that's part of the wine estate (p127). Guests receive complimentary wine tastings and there's a daily shuttle back and forth from the Waterfront.

SLEEPING IN TABLE MOUNTAIN NATIONAL PARK

Private camping is banned here, but Table Mountain National Park has places to stay.

Hoerikwaggo Tented Camps

Partly constructed from materials gathered from the park (so as to blend with nature), these properties are dotted along the five-day, 75km Hoerikwaggo Trail connecting Cape Point with Tafelberg Rd. The 'tents' are canvas, army-camp types, protected by wooden structures and housing comfortable beds. The bathroom facilities at all are excellent, as are the fully equipped communal kitchen and braai (barbecue) areas. You can drive to within relatively easy hiking reach of each. The rates are R500 (R615 for Smitswinkel) per twin-bedded units; bring your own bedding and towels.Bookings can be made online (www.tmnp.co.za) or by phone (021-712 7471; 8am-4pm Mon-Fri).

Orange Kloof (Map p288; off Hout Bay Rd, Cecelia Forest) Perhaps the best, tucked away in a beautiful area near Constantia Nek and providing direct access to the last strand of Afromontane forest in the park.

Silvermine (Silvermine Nature Reserve, off Ou Kaapse Weg) In a breezy location near the reservoir in the Silvermine section of the park.

Slangkop (off Lighthouse Rd, Kommetjie) Near the lighthouse at Kommetjie, beneath a forest of rare, indigenous milkwood trees and decorated with the bones of a whale that washed up on the beach in 2006.

Smitswinkel (Map p293; Cape Point) The only camp to offer en suite bathrooms in its tents, this location is steps from the entrance to the Cape of Good Hope section of the park. Note that it does get windy here.

Cottages

The best of these are Platteklip Wash House (p204), Wood Owl Cottage (p208) and Olifantsbos Guest House (p210). They are all in lovely spots and and you can drive right up to their doors. Linens are provided.

Simon's Town & Southern Peninsula

AFRICAN SOUL SURFER BACKPACKERS $

Map p290 (021-788 1771; www.africansoulsurfer.co.za; 13-19 York Rd, Muizenberg; dm/s/tw/d with shared bathroom R150/300/400/450; ; Muizenberg) In a heritage-listed building with splendid sea views, this backpackers is for those who don't want to be more than 30 seconds from the sand. Nicely designed rooms, a huge kitchen, comfy lounge and ping-pong table. Rates exclude breakfast.

SIMON'S TOWN BOUTIQUE BACKPACKERS BACKPACKERS $

Map p292 (021-786 1964; www.capepax.co.za; 66 St George's St, Simon's Town; dm/s/d with shared bathroom R190/450/550, d with private bathroom R625; ; Simon's Town) Best-value place to stay in Simon's Town, with spacious, ship-shape rooms, several overlooking the harbour. Friendly staff can help you arrange activities in the area, and there's bike hire for R200 per day. Rates exclude breakfast.

SAMHITAKASHA COB HOUSE B&B $

Map p290 (021-788 6613; www.cobhouse.co.za; 13 Watson Rd, Muizenberg; s/d R450/750; P ; Muizenberg) It took two years for English- and French-speaking tour guide Simric Yarrow to build his unique organic home out of mud, wood and straw; one room above the garage is for guests. Hot water is provided via a solar-powered heater and rates include an organic breakfast.

STOKED BACKPACKERS BACKPACKERS $

Map p290 (021-709 0841; www.stokedbackpackers.com; 175 Main Rd, Muizenberg; dm/s/d with shared bathroom R155/400/550, d with private bathroom R715; @; Muizenberg) Some dorms are far nicer than others, so check out the options. Otherwise, you can't fault the location – next to the train station and with beach views. Breakfast is excluded from the rates but there's a pleasant cafe.

GLEN LODGE HOTEL $

(021-782 0314; www.theglenlodgeandpub.co.za; 12-14 Glen Rd, Glencairn; dm/s/d R200/400/750; P; Glencairn) Simple, appealingly furnished rooms, four with sea views. Rates for the dorm (just four bunks) exclude breakfast. Convenient for Glencairn beach and the station, and not far from Simon's Town. A convivial pub and cafe are on the premises.

ECO WAVE LODGE BACKPACKERS $

(073-927 5644; www.ecowave.co.za; 11 Gladioli Way, Kommetjie; dm/s/d with shared bathroom R150/400/450, d with private bathroom R550; P) Less than 100m from the beach – perfect for surfers – this is a spacious, slightly scruffy house with a giant dining room (replete with chandelier) and big sun deck. Surf lessons and gear can be arranged. Turn onto Somerset Way off Kommetjie Rd (M65); this leads into Gladioli Way.

★**BELLA EV** GUESTHOUSE $$

Map p290 (021-788 1293; www.bellaevguesthouse.co.za; 8 Camp Rd, Muizenberg; s/d from R700/1000; P @; Muizenberg) This charming guesthouse, with a delightful courtyard garden, could be the setting for an Agatha Christie mystery, one in which the home's owner has a penchant for all things Turkish, hence the Ottoman slippers for guests' use.

CHARTFIELD GUEST HOUSE B&B $$

Map p290 (021-788 3793; www.chartfield.co.za; 30 Gatesville Rd, Kalk Bay; r from R900; P @; Kalk Bay) This rambling, wooden-floored 1920s guesthouse is decorated with choice pieces of contemporary local arts and crafts. There's a variety of rooms, each with crisp linen, and bathrooms with a rain-style shower. There's also a lovely terrace and garden overlooking the harbour, where you can eat breakfast. Wi-fi access is R35 per day.

MONKEY VALLEY BEACH NATURE RESORT RESORT $$

(021-789 1391; www.monkeyvalleyresort.com; Mountain Rd, Noordhoek; s/d from R1210/1660, cottages from R2550; P) Choose between sea-facing rooms or spacious self-catering cottages (all with thatched, open-rafter roofs) at this imaginatively designed, rustic resort shaded by a milkwood forest; the wide beach is moments away. A great place to stay if you have kids. Follow signs from Noordhoek end of Chapman's Peak Rd (M6).

BOULDERS BEACH LODGE B&B $$

Map p292 (021-786 1758; www.bouldersbeach.co.za; 4 Boulders Pl, Simon's Town; s/d/apt from R650/1100/2400; P @; Simon's Town) Penguins waddle right up to the doors of this smart guesthouse, with rooms decorated in wicker and wood and a range of self-catering units, where rates also include breakfast. Its excellent restaurant has an outdoor deck. Penguins are not the quietest creatures so you may want to bring earplugs.

TOWNSHIP HOMESTAYS

It's possible to do homestays in the townships. These can be arranged in Langa by Siviwe Mbidna (p26) and Langa Quarter (p153), and in Khayelitsha by Kopanong (p210) and **Khayelitsha Travel** (021-361 4505; www.khayelitshatravel.com; Lookout Hill complex, cnr Mew Way & Spine Rd, Ilitha Park).

DE NOORDHOEK HOTEL HOTEL $$
(021-789 2760; www.denoordhoek.co.za; cnr Chapman's Peak Dr & Village Ln, Noordhoek; s/d from R1250/1750;) This hotel was so well constructed it seems it has always been part of Noordhoek Village. The rooms, some specially adapted for use by guests with disabilities, are spacious and comfortable and surround a pretty inner courtyard planted with *fynbos* (literally 'fine bush') and lemon trees. Follow signs to Noordhoek Farm Village from Chapman's Peak Rd (M6).

OLIFANTSBOS GUEST HOUSE HOUSE $$$
Map p293 (021-780 9204; www.tmnp.co.za; Cape of Good Hope; 1-6 people R3285, extra adult/child R360/180;) Escape to this pretty whitewashed cottage, with an isolated position just steps from the beach. Together with its annexe, it sleeps a maximum of 12 people.

Cape Flats & Northern Suburbs

★LIZIWE GUEST HOUSE B&B $
(021-633 7406; www.sa-venues.com/visit/lizivesguesthouse; 121 NY 111, Gugulethu; r from R500; ; Nyanga) Liziwe has made her mansion into a palace, with four delightful rooms all with TVs and African-themed decor. She was featured on a BBC cooking show, so you can be sure her food is delicious; breakfast is R70 extra, dinner R80. Plus her place is walking distance to Mzoli's (p154).

EKHAYA EKASI B&B $
(083 681 0604, 076 658 3426; www.capetownshiptour.com; 6 Gaba St, Makhaza, Khayelitsha; s/d with shared bathroom R275/550; Kuyasa) There are just two cosy rooms decorated in pop-art-bright colours at this ace art and education centre crafted from shipping containers. There's a cafe and gift shop here, as well as a small vegetable garden on the roof. Various entrepreneurship and education projects run out here, including **heArt of a Woman** (www.heartofawomanproject.com/heart-south-africa), which teaches women the art of smartphone photography; the best images are turned into postcards.

COLETTE'S B&B $
Map p294 (083 458 5344, 021-531 4830; www.colettesbb.co.za; 16 The Bend, Pinelands; s/d from R420/600; ; Pinelands) The lovely Colette runs this women-friendly B&B in her spacious, pretty Pinelands home with pet ducks in the garden. All rooms, including a couple in the loft, have private bathrooms.

KOPANONG B&B $
(082 476 1278, 021-361 2084; www.kopanong-township.co.za; 329 Velani Cres, Section C, Khayelitsha; s/d R390/780; ; Khayelitsha) Thope Lekau, called 'Mama Africa' for obvious reasons, runs this excellent B&B with her daughter, Mpho. Her brick home offers two stylishly decorated guest rooms, each with their own bathroom. Dinner (R120) is delicious. If it's already booked, Thope can assist with finding homestays in the area.

★HOTEL VERDE HOTEL $$
(021-380 5500; www.hotelverde.com; 15 Michigan St, Airport Industria; s/d R1485/1625; ; Airport) It's easy to see why the self-proclaimed 'greenest hotel in Africa' has won awards. Rooms are comfy, and local arts and crafts abound throughout. Solar panels and wind generators cut down on power-grid use; there's a beautiful garden made from the preserved wetlands behind the hotel and an eco-friendy pool. There's also a complimentary shuttle to the airport, although it's almost so close you could walk.

MAJORO'S B&B B&B $$
(082 537 6882; majoros@webmail.co.za; 69 Helena Cres, Khayelitsha; s/d with shared bathroom R450/900; ; Khayelitsha) Friendly Maria Maile runs this B&B in her small brick bungalow in an upmarket part of Khayelitsha. She can put up four people in her two homely rooms. Dinner is available for R120 and there's safe parking should you drive.

MALEBO'S B&B $$
(0834751125, 021-3612391; malebo12@webmail.co.za; 18 Mississippi Way, Khayelitsha; s/d R450/900; Khayelitsha) Lydia Masoleng has been opening up her spacious home to guests since 1998. Three of her comfy rooms have bathrooms. Dinner (R120) is available and includes self-brewed *umqombothi* (beer).

Understand Cape Town

Cape Town Today

The legacy of the city's stint as World Design Capital 2014 (WDC2014); the threat of electricity blackouts (known as 'load shedding') due to a struggling national grid; political tussles between the Democratic Alliance (DA), who run the city and the Western Cape, and national governing party the African National Congress (ANC); and is Cape Town the most racist city in South Africa? These are among the ongoing conversation topics across the Mother City.

Best on Film

Black Butterflies Biopic about Afrikaans poet Ingrid Jonkers (a powerful performance by Carice van Houten) set in Cape Town in the 1950s and '60s.

Sea Point Days (www.seapointdays.co.za) Documentary by François Verster focusing on the suburb and its promenade as a multicultural crossroads.

Love the One You Love A phone-sex operator, a dog handler and an IT technician are the main characters in Jenna Bass' debut feature, set in Cape Town.

Best in Print

A City Imagined (ed Stephen Watson) Fine selection of original essays by local writers, revealing different aspects of the Mother City.

Reports from before Daybreak (Brent Meersman) Cape Town is the principal setting for this impressive novel about the turbulent decade before democracy and its damaging effect on people of all races. Also read the follow-up *Five Lives at Noon*.

The Last Train to Zona Verde (Paul Theroux) The great travel writer shines a light on Cape Town at the start of an overland trip to Angola in 2011.

WDC2014 Legacy

The impact and lessons learned from the 460 official WDC2014 projects – some new, others ongoing – were under the microscope at the start of 2015. From the city's point of view, it's the event's legacy that's crucial, in particular a change of mindset from identifying problems to solving them. Such a collaborative approach was captured by switching the city government's slogan from 'This City Works for You' to 'Making Progress Possible. Together.'

What will you notice as a visitor, apart from the Yellow Frames angled at Table Mountain? A list of ongoing initiatives can be found at www.capetown.gov.za/WDC2014 and makes for enlightening reading. Projects of note include 543 public-housing units created in Ocean View, built partly from stone found in the location – the construction of which trained a score of locals in stonemasonry; the Art54 project, to be used as a model for temporary public art around the city; and a series of co-creation workshops, such as the one on developing the tourism and community potential of Khayelitsha's Lookout Hill.

The Politics of Name-Calling

The renaming of Table Bay Boulevard to FW de Klerk Boulevard in early 2015 proved controversial. Both the ANC and the Congress of SA Trade Unions came out against the name change, citing the former president's role under apartheid. It was a similar story with the revamped Company Garden's Restaurant. It had reopened in November 2014 as Haarlem & Hope (after the Dutch ship, the *Nieuwe Haarlem,* shipwrecked in Table Bay in 1647), but when this was branded a 'callous celebration of colonial power' by activist Zackie Achmat on social media, the restaurant decided to revert back to the original name.

Speaking at the ANC's 103rd birthday celebrations in Cape Town in January 2015, President Jacob Zuma blamed apartheid for the recent failures of the national power grid run by Eskom. At an earlier township rally he delved further back into history, saying 'All the trouble [in South Africa] began in 1652 when Jan van Riebeeck landed in the Cape.' That comment provoked a storm of protest from white South Africans, including Mandela's former personal assistant, Zelda la Grange. It's all proof that the deep wounds of South Africa's troubled history still run raw, and particularly so in Cape Town, where the divide between the largely white rich and the majority black and coloured poor is starkly evident.

Murder City?

It's a common view internationally that Cape Town suffers (along with the rest of South Africa) from high crime rates. Newsworthy cases, such as the kidnapping and murder of Shrien Dewani in Gugulethu in 2010, feed into this perception. However, the truth is more complex. Suburbs such as Camps Bay and Claremont are among the safest places to live – not just in South Africa, but the world – with no murders occurring in 2014. In comparison, Khayelitsha clocked up 146 murders, while Nyanga had 305, making it the nation's most deadly location.

Drill down further into the stats and you'll find that the killings generally don't involve unfortunate tourists, but are between family members or drug gangs. Bringing it home vividly was the murder of Vicky Ntozini in November 2012. A pioneer of township B&Bs in Khayelitsha when she opened her shack home to paying guests in 2000, as well as a mother of six, Vicky was killed by her husband.

Township Trials & Triumphs

Turning a spotlight on the daily trials faced by township residents are organisations such as Ndifuna Ukwazi (www.nu.org.za) who report on safety, policing and justice issues, and the community journalism project Ground Up (www.groundup.org.za). Both would recognise, though, that the bad news is only part of the overall picture.

In our opinion it has never been a better time to see how the vast majority of Capetonians live. Alongside grim shack neighbourhoods you'll discover places such as Gugulethu Square, a glittering mall that would not be out of place in Camps Bay; many clean streets lined with impressive houses; and spiffy public complexes such as Khayelitsha District Hospital and Langa's Guga S'Thebe Arts & Cultural Centre. Langa is also the focus for two ambitious social support programs, the Langa Quarter and Langa Cultural Precinct.

if Cape Town were 100 people

48 would be coloured
31 would be black
19 would be white
2 would be Indian/Asian

if South Africa were 100 people

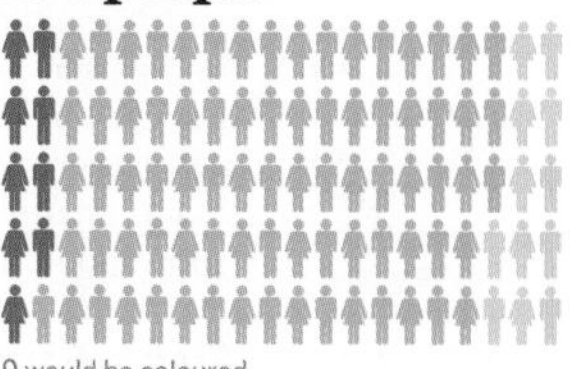

9 would be coloured
79 would be black
9 would be white
3 would be Indian/Asian

population per sq km

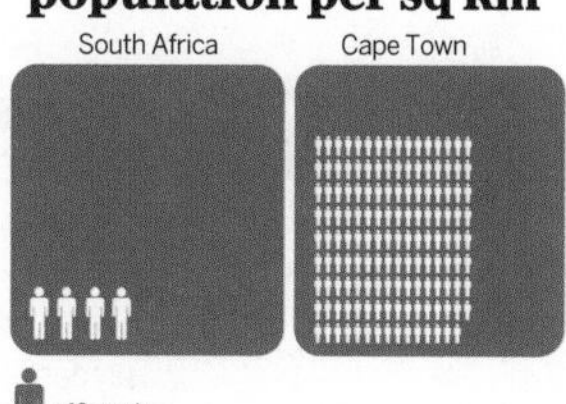

History

Humans lived on the Cape for millennia before the first Europeans visited in the 15th century. Dutch rule lasted nearly 200 years before the British took over in 1814, prompting many Afrikaners (Boers) to trek inland – only to come back with a vengeance during the apartheid years. In 1990 Nelson Mandela became a free man, hailing the start of a democratic South Africa.

South Africa lays strong claim to being the cradle of mankind. At Langebaan Lagoon (north of Cape Town), the discovery of 117,000-year-old fossilised footprints prompted one researcher to speculate that 'Eve' (the very first human or common ancestor of us all) lived here.

The Khoekhoen & San People

Academics don't know whether the earliest-recorded inhabitants of South Africa – the San people – are direct descendants or if they returned to the area after aeons of travel, between 40,000 and 25,000 years ago. For centuries, perhaps even millennia, the San and the Khoekhoen, another early Southern African people, intermarried and coexisted. The distinction is by no means clear, hence the combined term Khoe-San.

Culturally and physically, the Khoe-San developed differently from the Negroid peoples of Africa, but it's possible that they came into contact with pastoralist Bantu-speaking tribes as – in addition to hunting and gathering food – they too became pastoralists, raising cattle and sheep. There's evidence that the Khoe-San lived on the Cape of Good Hope about 2000 years ago.

First European Visitors

The first Europeans to record a sighting of the Cape were the Portuguese, who passed by on their search for a sea route to India and spices. The land here offered the Portuguese little more than fresh water, since their attempts to trade with the Khoe-San often ended in violence. But by the end of the 16th century, English and Dutch traders were beginning to challenge the Portuguese, and the Cape became a regular stopover for ships. In 1647 the Dutch vessel the *Nieuwe Haarlem* was wrecked in Table Bay; its crew built a fort and stayed for a year before they were rescued. This crystallised the value of a permanent settlement in the minds of the directors of the Dutch East India Company

TIMELINE

c 40,000 BC

Middens – ancient garbage heaps packed with shells, bones and pieces of stone tools and pottery – indicate that the antecedents of the Khoekhoen and San tribes were living on the Cape.

AD 1488

Bartholomeu Dias, the first European to sail around the Cape, dubs it Cabo da Boa Esperança (Cape of Good Hope). Others prefer Cabo das Tormentas (Cape of Storms).

1510

The Khoe-San fight back when Portuguese soldiers try to kidnap two of their number; Captain de Almeida and 50 of his troops are killed.

(Vereenigde Oost-Indische Compagnie; VOC). They had no intention of colonising the country, but simply wanted to establish a secure base where ships could shelter and stock up on fresh food supplies.

The San were nomadic hunters and gatherers, and the Khoekhoen (also known as Khoikhoi, possibly meaning 'Men of Men') were semi-nomadic hunters and pastoralists. European settlers later called the Khoekhoen 'Hottentots' and the San 'Bushmen'.

The Dutch Arrive

The task of establishing the VOC station fell to Jan van Riebeeck (1619–77), Commander of the Cape from 1652 to 1662. The Dutch were not greeted with open arms by the Khoe-San and intermittent hostilities broke out. But the locals – who are thought to have numbered between 4000 and 8000 people – hardly stood a chance against the Europeans' guns and diseases.

With the Khoe-San uncooperative, the Cape settlement was soon suffering a chronic labour shortage. From 1657 Van Riebeeck started releasing VOC employees, allowing them to farm land independently, thus beginning the colonisation of Southern Africa and giving birth to the Boers. The following year he began to import slaves from West Africa, Madagascar, India, Ceylon, Malaya and Indonesia. By the time the slave trade ended in 1807, some 60,000 slaves had been brought to the Cape, laying the foundation for its unique mix of cultures and races.

Bartholomeu Dias rounded the Cape in 1488, but didn't linger, as his sights were fixed on the trade riches of the east coast of Africa and the Indies.

The Settlement Grows

The process of colonisation kicked off a series of wars between the Dutch and the Khoe-San further inland, who were no match for the well-armed Europeans. The Dutch also allowed some 200 Huguenots (French Calvinists fleeing religious persecution) to settle on the Cape in 1688. There was a shortage of women in the colony, so female slaves and Khoe-San women were exploited for both labour and sex. In time, the slaves intermixed with the Khoe-San, too. The children of these unions were the ancestors of some of today's coloured population.

WHO ARE THE BOERS?

South Africa's Afrikaner population has its roots in the Dutch and early European settlers of the Cape. The more independent of these settlers soon began drifting away from the strict regime of the VOC and into the countryside. These were the first of the Trekboers (literally 'trekking farmers'), later known as Boers.

Fiercely independent and with livelihoods based on rearing cattle, the Boers were not so different from the Khoe-San that they came into conflict with as they colonised the interior. Many Boers were illiterate and most had no source of information other than the Bible. Isolated from other Europeans, they developed their own separate culture and eventually their own language, Afrikaans, derived from the argot of their slaves.

1652

Jan van Riebeeck, instructed by the Dutch East India Company (Vereenigde Oost-Indische Compagnie; VOC) to establish a supply station en route to India, arrives on 6 April.

1660

Van Riebeeck plants a wild almond hedge to protect his European settlement from the Khoe-San – a section of it remains in the Kirstenbosch Botanical Gardens.

1679

Simon van der Stel, the son of a VOC official and a freed Indian slave, arrives in the Cape as its commander. Two years later he is promoted to governor.

1699

After retiring to develop his estate of Constantia, the birthplace of the Cape's wine industry, Van der Stel is succeeded by his son Willem Adriaan.

Under the VOC's almost complete control, Kaapstad (the Dutch name for Cape Town) provided a comfortable European lifestyle for a growing number of artisans and entrepreneurs servicing ships and crews. By the middle of the 18th century there were around 3000 people living in the riotous port, known as the 'Tavern of the Seas' by every sailor travelling between Europe and the East.

The British Take Over

As the 18th century progressed, the global power of the Dutch was waning and under challenge by the British. Between 1795 and 1806 the Cape was passed like a parcel between the two colonial powers, with the French also briefly drawn into the power play. Even before the colony was formally ceded to the British Crown on 13 August 1814, the British had abolished the slave trade. The remaining Khoe-San were given the explicit protection of the law in 1828. These moves contributed to Afrikaners' dissatisfaction and their mass migration inland from the Cape Colony, which came to be known as the Great Trek.

Despite outlawing slavery, the British introduced new laws that laid the basis for an exploitative labour system little different from it. Thousands of dispossessed blacks sought work in the colony, but it was made a crime to be in the colony without a pass – and without work. It was also a crime to leave a job.

During the first half of the 19th century, before the Suez Canal opened, British officers serving in India would holiday at the Cape.

Cape Economy Booms

Under a policy of free trade Cape Town's economy flourished. In 1854 a representative parliament was formed in Cape Town, but much to the dismay of Dutch and English farmers to the north and east, the British government and Cape liberals insisted on a multiracial constituency (albeit with financial requirements that excluded the vast majority of blacks and coloureds).

The opening of the Suez Canal in 1869 dramatically decreased the amount of shipping that sailed via the Cape, but the discovery of diamonds and gold in the centre of South Africa in the 1870s and '80s helped Cape Town maintain its position as the country's premier port. Immigrants flooded into the city and the population trebled, from 33,000 in 1875 to over 100,000 people at the turn of the century.

Boer War

After the Great Trek, the Boers established several independent republics, the largest being the Orange Free State (today's Free State province) and the Transvaal (today's Northern Province, Gauteng and Mpumalanga). When the world's richest gold reef was found in the

1795

The British take control of the Cape after winning the Battle of Muizenberg. Eight years later the Treaty of Amiens puts the Dutch back in power.

1806

As part of the Napoleonic Wars, the British return. With their decisive victory at the Battle of Blouberg, they secure the Cape for the Crown.

1808

The new government proclaims free trade and abolishes the local slave trade. Still, slaves in the Malmesbury and Tygerberg area revolt and march on Cape Town.

1814

The Cape Colony is formally ceded to Britain, making it the empire's second possession in Africa after Sierra Leone. English replaces Afrikaans as the official language.

Transvaal (a village called Johannesburg sprang up beside it), the British were miffed that the Boers should control such wealth – which precipitated war in 1899. The Boers were outnumbered, but their tenacity and local knowledge meant the war dragged on until 1902, when the British triumphed. Cape Town was not directly involved in any of the fighting, but did play a key role in landing and supplying the half-million imperial and colonial troops who fought for Britain.

Within months of opening in 1899, the Mount Nelson Hotel became the headquarters for the British Army, led by Lords Roberts and Kitchener, during the Boer War. Winston Churchill recuperated at the hotel and filed newspaper dispatches from here after escaping a Boer prison camp.

Act of Union

After the war, the British made some efforts towards reconciliation, and instituted moves towards the union of the separate South African provinces. In 1910 the Act of Union was signed, bringing the republics of Cape Colony, Natal, Transvaal and Orange Free State together as the Union of South Africa. Under the provisions of the act, the Union was still a British territory, with home-rule for Afrikaners. In the Cape, blacks and coloureds retained a limited franchise (although only whites could become members of the national parliament, and eligible blacks and coloureds constituted only around 7%), but did not have the vote in other provinces.

The first government of the new Union was headed by General Louis Botha, with General Jan Smuts as his deputy: statues of both these figures are found in the City Bowl. Their South African National Party (later known as the South African Party or SAP) followed a generally pro-British, white-unity line.

Apartheid Rules

In 1948 the National Party (NP), which championed Afrikaner interests, came to power on a platform of apartheid (literally, 'the state of being apart'). Non-whites were denied the vote, mixed marriages were prohibited, interracial sex was made illegal and every person was classified by race. The Group Areas Act defined where people of each 'race' could live and the Separate Amenities Act created separate public facilities: separate beaches, separate buses, separate toilets, separate schools and separate park benches. Blacks were compelled to carry passes at all times and were prohibited from living in or even visiting towns without specific permission.

Fictional Homelands

A system of homelands was set up in 1951, whereby the proportion of land available for black ownership in South Africa increased very slightly to 13%. Blacks then made up about 75% of the population. The homelands idea was that each black group had a traditional area where it belonged – and must now stay. The area around Cape Town was

1834

Following emancipation, Cape Town's free slaves establish their own neighbourhood, the Bo-Kaap. In the same year the Cape Town Legislative Council is also founded.

1835

Afrikaner dissatisfaction with British rule prompts the start of the Great Trek; some 10,000 families go in search of their own state, opening up the country's interior.

1849

Governor Sir Harry Smith, anxious that the Cape not become a penal colony, bars 282 British prisoners from leaving the ship *Neptune*, forcing it to continue to Tasmania.

1867

The discovery of the world's largest diamond deposit in Kimberley and gold in the Transvaal boosts Cape Town's economy as the port becomes the gateway for mineral wealth.

declared a 'coloured preference area', which meant no black person could be employed unless it could be proved that there was no coloured person suitable for the job. The plan ignored the huge numbers of blacks who had never lived in their 'homeland'. Millions of people who had lived in other areas for generations were forcibly removed into bleak, unproductive areas with no infrastructure.

The homelands were regarded as self-governing states, and it was planned that they would become independent countries. Four of the 10 homelands were nominally independent by the time apartheid was demolished (though not recognised as independent countries by the UN), and their leaders held power with the help of the South African military.

Meanwhile, white South Africa depended on cheap black labour to keep the economy booming, so many black 'guest workers' were ad-

NELSON MANDELA

Nelson Rolihlahla Mandela, one of the world's greatest leaders, was born on 18 July 1918 in the village of Mveso on the Mbashe River. After attending the University of Fort Hare, this son of the third wife of a Xhosa chief headed to Johannesburg, where he overcame prejudice and poverty to qualify as a lawyer. Together with Oliver Tambo, he opened South Africa's first black law firm.

In 1944, Mandela formed the Youth League of the African National Congress (ANC) with Tambo and Walter Sisulu. During the 1950s, Mandela was at the forefront of the ANC's civil disobedience campaigns, for which in 1952 he was arrested, tried and acquitted. After the ANC was banned in the wake of the Sharpeville massacre, Mandela led the establishment of its underground military wing, Umkhonto we Sizwe. In 1964 Mandela was brought to stand trial for sabotage and fomenting revolution in the widely publicised Rivonia Trial. After brilliantly arguing his own defence, he was sentenced to life imprisonment and spent the next 18 years in the infamous Robben Island prison before being moved onto the mainland.

Throughout his incarceration, Mandela repeatedly refused to compromise his political beliefs in exchange for freedom, saying that only free men can negotiate. In February 1990, Mandela was released and in 1991 he was elected president of the ANC. In 1993 Mandela shared the Nobel Peace Prize with FW de Klerk and, in the first free elections the following year, was elected president of South Africa. In 1997 Mandela – or Madiba, his traditional Xhosa name – stepped down as ANC president, although he continued to be revered as an elder statesman. On 5 December 2013, Nelson Mandela died, aged 95 years, from an ongoing respiratory infection.

Madiba's legacy, which reverberates far beyond his country's borders, is what he achieved with unswerving determination, a generosity of spirit and lack of vengeance. His gift to South Africans was the major role he played in bringing peace and reconciliation to a country torn by racial discrimination.

1890	1899	1902	March 1902
Two decades after first arriving in Cape Town, self-made mining magnate Cecil Rhodes, founder of De Beers, becomes the colony's prime minister at the age of 37.	Lord Kitchener dubs the British campaign to gain control of the Boer republics as 'a teatime war', but the Anglo-Boer War is fiercely fought for three years.	Bubonic plague arrives on a ship from Argentina, giving the government an excuse to introduce racial segregation – 6000 blacks are forcibly sent to live on the Cape Flats.	Rhodes dies at Muizenberg; his vast estate is bequeathed to the city, providing the grounds for both the University of Cape Town and Kirstenbosch Botanical Gardens.

mitted back to the country. But unless a black person had a job and a pass, they were liable to be jailed and sent back to their homeland. This caused massive disruption to black communities and families. Unsurprisingly, people without jobs gravitated to cities such as Cape Town to be near their spouses and parents. But no new black housing was built; as a result, illegal squatter camps mushroomed on the sandy plains to the east of Cape Town. In response, government bulldozers flattened the shanties, and their occupants were forced into the homelands. Within weeks, inevitably, the shanties would rise again.

Mandela Jailed

In 1960 the African National Congress (ANC) and the Pan African Congress (PAC) organised marches against the hated Pass laws, which required blacks and coloureds to carry passbooks authorising them to be in a particular area. At Langa and Nyanga on the Cape Flats, police killed five protesters. The Sharpeville massacres in Gauteng were concurrent and resulted in the banning of the ANC and PAC. In response to the crisis, a warrant for the arrest of Nelson Mandela and other ANC leaders was issued. In mid-1963 Mandela was captured; at trial he was sentenced to life imprisonment on Robben Island.

The government tried for decades to eradicate squatter towns, such as Crossroads, which were focal points for resistance to the apartheid regime. Violent removals and killings failed and the government, forced to accept the inevitable, began to upgrade conditions. Since then, vast townships have sprung up across the Cape Flats. No one knows exactly how many people call them home, but it's thought to be in excess of 1.5 million.

The Dutch Reformed Church justified apartheid on religious grounds, claiming the separateness of the races was divinely ordained: that the *volk* (literally, the 'people'), meaning Afrikaners, had a holy mission to preserve the purity of the white race in its promised land.

The Coloured Experience

Apartheid's divide-and-rule tactics – favouring coloureds above blacks – stoked the animosity that still lingers between those Cape communities today. Even so, coloureds did suffer under apartheid, such as the residents of the poor inner-city area of District Six, which in 1966 was classified as a white area. Its 50,000 people, some of whose families had been there for five generations, were gradually evicted and removed to bleak and soulless Cape Flats suburbs like Athlone, Mitchell's Plain and Atlantis. Friends, neighbours and relatives were separated. Bulldozers moved in and the multiracial heart was ripped out of the city, while in the townships, depressed and dispirited youths increasingly joined gangs and turned to crime.

The coloured Muslim community of the Bo-Kaap, on the northeastern edge of Signal Hill, was more fortunate. Home to Cape Town's first mosque (the Auwal Mosque on Dorp St dates back to 1798), the district

1910

The British colonies and the old Boer republics are joined in the Union of South Africa. Cape Town is made the seat of the legislature.

1914

Lingering bitterness over the Boer War and Afrikaners' distaste at competing with blacks and coloureds for low-paying jobs leads to formation of the National Party.

1923

The Black Urban Areas Act restricts the entry of blacks into the city centre. Three years later the prison-like settlement of Langa becomes the first planned township for blacks.

1939

The peninsula's rugged tip is protected within the Cape of Good Hope Nature Reserve. It's 60 years before a single Cape Peninsula national park is created.

was once known as the Malay Quarter, because it was where many of the imported slaves from the start of the Cape Colony lived with their masters. In 1952 the entire Bo-Kaap region was declared to be a coloured area under the terms of the Group Areas Act. There were forced removals, but the residents of the community, which was more homogeneous than that of District Six, banded together in order to successfully fight for and retain ownership of their homes. Many were declared National Monuments in the 1960s, which saved them from the bulldozers.

The Sunday Times Heritage Project (www.sthp.saha.org.za) is an online collaboration between the newspaper and the South African History Archive. It includes a map detailing the stories of many prominent activists and events in South Africa's 20th-century history.

Path to Democracy

In 1982 Nelson Mandela and other ANC leaders were moved from Robben Island to Pollsmoor Prison in Cape Town. (In 1986 senior politicians began secretly talking with them.) Concurrently, the state's military crackdowns in the townships became even more pointed. In early 1990 President FW de Klerk began to repeal discriminatory laws, and the ANC, PAC and Communist Party were legalised. On 11 February the world watched in awe as a living legend emerged from Victor Verster Prison near Paarl. Later that day Nelson Mandela delivered his first public speech since being incarcerated 27 years earlier to a massive crowd overspilling from Cape Town's Grand Parade.

From this time onwards virtually all the old apartheid regulations were repealed; in late 1991, the Convention for a Democratic South Africa (Codesa) began negotiating the formation of a multiracial transitional government, and a new constitution extending political rights to all groups. Two years later a compromise was reached and an election date set. In the frustration of waiting, political violence exploded across the country during this time, some of it sparked by the police and the army.

Despite this, the 1994 election was amazingly peaceful, with the ANC winning 62.7% of the vote. In Western Cape, the majority coloured population voted in the NP as the provincial government, seemingly happier to live with the devil they knew than with the ANC.

For more about the Truth & Reconciliation Commission read the award-winning account *Country of My Skull*, by journalist and poet Antjie Krog.

Truth & Reconciliation Commission

One of the first acts of the new ANC government was to set up the Truth & Reconciliation Commission (TRC) to expose the crimes of the apartheid era. This institution carried out Archbishop Desmond Tutu's dictum: 'Without forgiveness there is no future, but without confession there can be no forgiveness.' Many stories of horrific brutality and injustice were heard during the commission's five-year life, offering some catharsis to individuals and communities shattered by their past.

The TRC operated by allowing victims to tell their stories and perpetrators to confess their guilt, with amnesty offered to those who

1940

Cape Town's pier, built in 1925, is demolished as an ambitious reclamation project extends the city centre 2km from the Strand into Table Bay, creating the Foreshore district.

1948

The National Party wins government. The right of coloureds to vote in the Cape is removed (blacks had been denied the vote since 1910) as apartheid is rolled out.

1964

Following the Rivonia Trial, Nelson Mandela, Walter Sisulu and others escape the death penalty, but are sentenced to life imprisonment on Robben Island in Table Bay.

1976

Students in Langa, Nyanga and Gugulethu march against the imposition of Afrikaans as the teaching medium in schools; 128 people are killed and 400 injured.

came forward. Those who chose not to appear before the commission face criminal prosecution if their guilt can be proven. Although some soldiers, police and 'ordinary' citizens have confessed their crimes, it seems unlikely that those who gave the orders and dictated the policies will ever come forward (former president PW Botha was one famous no-show), and gathering evidence against them has proven difficult.

South Africa's constitution is one of the most enlightened in the world. Apart from forbidding discrimination on practically any grounds, among other things it guarantees freedom of speech and religion, and access to adequate housing and health care and basic adult education.

Rise, Fall & Rise Again of Pagad

The governmental vacuum that existed between Mandela's release from jail and the election of a democratic government left Cape Town in a shaky social position. The early 1990s saw drugs and crime become such a problem that communities began to take matters into their own hands. People against Gangsterism and Drugs (Pagad) was formed in 1995 as an offshoot of the Islamic organisation Qibla. The group saw itself as defending the coloured community from the crooked cops and drug lords who allowed gangs to control the coloured townships.

At first the police tolerated Pagad, but their vigilante tactics turned sour in 1996 with the horrific (and televised) death of gangster Rashaad Staggie. A lynch mob burned then repeatedly shot the dying gangster. Other gang leaders were killed, but Capetonians really began to worry when bombs, some believed to have been planted by the more radical of Pagad's members, began to go off around the city. The worst attack was in 1998, when an explosion in the Planet Hollywood restaurant at the Waterfront killed one woman and injured 27 other people. In September 2000 a magistrate presiding in a case involving Pagad members was murdered in a drive-by shooting.

DESMOND TUTU

Few figures in South Africa's anti-apartheid struggle are as recognisable as Desmond Mpilo Tutu, the retired Anglican Archbishop of Cape Town. Tutu, born in 1931 in Klerksdorp, Transvaal (now in North West Province), rose from humble beginnings to become an internationally recognised activist. During the apartheid era, Tutu was a vigorous proponent of economic boycotts and international sanctions against South Africa. Following the fall of the apartheid government, Tutu headed South Africa's Truth & Reconciliation Commission, an experience that he chronicles in his book *No Future Without Forgiveness*.

Today, Tutu continues to be a tireless moral advocate. He has been a particularly outspoken critic of the ANC government, taking it to task for failing to adequately tackle poverty, corruption and the AIDS crisis. Tutu has been awarded the Nobel Peace Prize, the Gandhi Peace Prize and numerous other distinctions. He is generally credited with coining the phrase 'rainbow nation' as a description for post-apartheid South Africa.

1982

Mandela and other senior ANC leaders are moved from Robben Island to Pollsmoor Prison in Tokai, facilitating the beginning of discreet contact between them and the National Party.

1986

An estimated 70,000 people are driven from their homes and hundreds killed as the government tries to eradicate the squatter towns of Nyanga and Crossroads in the Cape Flats.

1989

President PW Botha suffers a stroke and is replaced by FW de Klerk, who continues the secret negotiations that lead to the ANC, PAC and Communist Party becoming legalised.

1990

Mandela walks a free man from Victor Verster Prison in Paarl, and delivers his first public speech in 27 years from the balcony of the old Cape Town City Hall.

Pagad leader Abdus Salaam Ebrahim was imprisoned in 2002 for seven years for public violence, but no one has ever been charged, let alone convicted, for the Cape Town bombings. For a time, Pagad was designated a terrorist organisation by the government. However, in 2009 it began a comeback campaign, rebranding itself the 'new Pagad', yet still operating like the organisation of old by marching on the homes of suspected drug dealers and demanding they cease their activities. In 2013, murder charges were dropped against Ebrahim, who had been arrested following the slaying of three Tanzanians (alleged to be drug dealers) in Cape Town.

Shifting Alliances

In 1999, two years after Mandela had stepped down as ANC president and was succeeded by his deputy, Thabo Mbeki, South Africa held its second free elections. Nationally, the ANC increased its vote, coming within one seat of the two-thirds majority that would allow it to alter the constitution, but in the Western Cape a pact between the old NP (restyled as the New National Party, or NNP) and the Democratic Party (DP) created the Democratic Alliance (DA), bringing them victory not only in the provincial elections but also in the metropolitan elections.

In 2002 the political landscape shifted radically when the NNP completed a merger with the ANC, which gave the ANC control of Cape Town and brought the city its first black female mayor, Nomaindia Mfeketo. In national and provincial elections two years later the ANC were equally triumphant, and Ebrahim Rasool – a practising Muslim whose family had been moved out of District Six when he was 10 – was appointed premier of the Western Cape.

Conscious of their core vote in the Cape Flats, the ANC-led city council vowed to improve the lot of township folk by upgrading the infrastructure in the informal settlements and boosting investment in low-cost housing, such as the N2 Gateway Project. Urban renewal projects were also announced for Mitchell's Plain, one of the deprived coloured areas of the city blighted, like so many Cape Flats suburbs, by the murderous drug trade. Particularly deadly has been the rise in addiction to methamphetamine, known locally as 'tik'.

More Mandela

Long Walk to Freedom (Nelson Mandela)

Mandela: The Authorized Biography (Anthony Sampson)

The Long Walk of Nelson Mandela (www.pbs.org/wgbh/pages/frontline/shows/mandela)

Nelson Mandela Foundation (www.nelsonmandela.org)

Xenophobia & Soccer

The Democratic Alliance (DA) has held power in Cape Town since 2006 and in Western Cape since 2009. For the poorest Capetonians, however, the political circus counted for little against lives blighted by dire economic, social and health problems. In May 2008 frustrations in the townships, fuelled by spikes in food and fuel prices, boiled over in a

1994

Following democratic elections, Mandela succeeds FW de Klerk as president, saying 'This is the time to heal the old wounds and build a new South Africa.'

1998

After three years of emotionally painful testimonies the Truth & Reconciliation Commission in Cape Town delivers its verdict, condemning both sides in the liberation struggle.

2002

Cape Town elects its first black female mayor, Nomaindia Mfeketo, as the New National Party (NNP) ditches the Democratic Party (DP) to join forces with the ANC.

2004

Ebrahim Murat, 87, and Dan Mdzabela, 82, are handed keys to new homes in District Six, the first returnees among thousands who hope to rebuild lives in the demolished suburb.

ZILLE & DE LILLE

Helen Zille (pronounced Ziller, hence her nickname 'Godzille') and Patricia de Lille are the dynamic duo dominating Capetonian politics. Zille was Cape Town's mayor for three years from 2006, and was awarded the international accolade of World Mayor. In the May 2009 elections she became premier of the Western Cape. She also led the official national opposition party, the Democratic Alliance (DA), between 2007 and 2015.

Johannesburg-born Zille began her career as a journalist in 1974, during which time she exposed the circumstances of the freedom fighter Steve Biko's death while in police custody. As mayor and the state's premier, she has impressed (and sometimes infuriated) locals with her no-nonsense, practical style of government, fearlessly wading into issues as thorny as drugs and gangsterism, teenage pregnancies and prevention of HIV/AIDS transmission. De Lille has been no less fiery and controversial in her political career, which has taken her from being a union rep in her hometown of Beaufort West to one-time leader of the Independent Democrats (ID) and a campaigner to shed light on a shady arms deal that still dogs the upper echelons of the ANC. The ID merged with the DA in 2010, and in 2011 De Lille was chosen as the mayoral candidate, a post she was elected to that year.

series of horrific xenophobic attacks on the most vulnerable members of society – immigrants and refugees from wars and political violence. As some 30,000 people fled in panic, the vast majority of Capetonians rallied to provide assistance.

Despite controversies over the location and spiralling costs of the new Cape Town Stadium, the city's various factions united to support the hosting of the FIFA World Cup in 2010. The event was judged a huge success but, facing global recession and social problems, many locals wonder if the money could not have been better spent.

2014 Elections

Prior to the 2014 national and provincial elections, disenchantment with corruption, crime and slow progress on providing critical services to poor communities fed a growing desire for change; one beneficiary was firebrand politico Julius Malema's Economic Freedom Fighters (EFF) party. Nationally the ANC won comfortably with 62.1% of the vote (down from 65.9% in 2009), with the the DA lagging way behind on 22.2%. However, in the Western Cape, the DA held onto power with 59.4% of the vote, and the ANC at 32.9%. The ANC are attacking hard in the run-up to the next local government elections in 2016, but Patricia de Lille, mayor since 2011, and her DA compatriot Helen Zille, the Western Cape premier, both look pretty secure given their party's track record in governing both the province and the city.

History Reads

Dinosaurs, Diamonds & Democracy: A Short, Short History of South Africa (Francis Wilson)

Beyond the Miracle: Inside the New South Africa (Allister Sparks)

Diamonds, Gold & War (Martin Meredith)

Cape Lives of the Eighteenth Century (Karel Schoeman)

2008

African immigrants are targeted in the xenophobic violence that engulfs Cape townships. Over 40 people are killed and 30,000 driven from their homes in nearly two weeks of attacks.

2010

World Cup Soccer fever grips Cape Town. Over 60,000 spectators in the new Cape Town Stadium, and hundreds of thousands more on the streets, watch the games.

2013

The Mother City joins the nation in mourning the death of Nelson Mandela, projecting a giant laser image of Madiba's face on Table Mountain.

2014

As World Design Capital, the city plans and implements projects that will 'Live Design, Transform Life', such as expanding the MyCiTi bus routes.

People & Culture

Cape Town's racial mix is different from the rest of South Africa. Of its population of 3.1 million, more than half are coloured; blacks account for about a third of the total, while whites and others comprise the balance. However, this is just the starting point for the rich mix of cultures that coexists here.

Racial Groups

Although there are many people who find the old apartheid racial terms 'white', 'black', 'coloured' and 'Indian' distasteful and want to break away from the stereotypes they imply, it's a fact that in South Africa the words are used by everyone, quite often without any rancour or ill feeling.

Many South Africans proudly identify themselves as black, white or coloured – for example, you'll meet black South Africans who happily refer to themselves as black rather than South African or African (which is the African National Congress' preferred collective expression for all people of African, Indian and mixed-race origin).

Coloureds

Coloureds, sometimes known as Cape coloureds or Cape Malays, are South Africans of long standing. Although many of their ancestors were brought to the early Cape Colony as slaves, others were political prisoners and exiles from the Dutch East Indies. Slaves also came from India and other parts of Africa, but their lingua franca was Malay (at the time an important trading language), hence the term Cape Malays.

Many coloureds practise Islam, and Cape Muslim culture has survived intact over the centuries, resisting some of the worst abuses of apartheid. The slaves who moved out with the Dutch to the hinterland, many losing their religion and cultural roots in the process, had a much worse time of it. And yet practically all of the coloured population of the Western Cape and Northern Cape provinces today are bound by Afrikaans, the unique language that began to develop from the interaction between the slaves and the Dutch over three centuries ago.

Cape Town Minstrel Carnival

The most public secular expression of coloured culture today is the riotous Cape Town Minstrel Carnival. This parade, also known in Afrikaans as the Kaapse Klopse, is a noisy, joyous and disorganised affair, with practically every colour of satin, sequin and glitter used in the costumes of the marching troupes, which can number over a thousand members.

Although the festival dates back to the early colonial times when slaves enjoyed a day of freedom on the day after New Year, the look of today's carnival was inspired by visiting American minstrels in the late 19th century – hence the face make-up, colourful costumes and ribald song-and-dance routines. The vast majority of participants come from the coloured community.

Despite the carnival being a permanent fixture on Cape Town's calendar, it has had a controversial history with problems over funding, clashes between rival carnival organisations and allegations of gangster involvement. It has also always been something of a demonstration of coloured people power: whites who came to watch the parade in apartheid times would risk having their faces blacked-up with boot polish. Today it still feels like the communities of the Cape Flats coming to take over the city.

Blacks

Although most blacks in Cape Town are Xhosa, hailing from Eastern Cape province, they are not the only group in the city. Cape Town's economy has attracted people from all over Southern Africa, including many immigrants from the rest of the continent – a lot of the car-parking marshals, traders at the city's various craft markets and waiters in restaurants are from Zimbabwe, Nigeria, Mozambique and the like.

Xhosa culture is diverse, with many clan systems and subgroups. Within the black community there are also economic divisions and subgroups based on culture, such as the Rastafarian community in the Marcus Garvey district of the township of Philippi.

Whites

There are distinct cultural differences in the white community here, depending on whether people are descendants of the Boers or the British and other later European immigrants to South Africa. The Boers' history of geographical isolation and often deliberate cultural seclusion has created a unique people who are often called 'the white tribe of Africa'.

Afrikaans, the only Germanic language to have evolved outside Europe, is central to the Afrikaner identity, but it has also served to reinforce their isolation from the outside world. You'll find Afrikaans to be a much stronger presence in the northern suburbs of Cape Town and in the country towns of the Cape, especially around Stellenbosch, which has a prominent Afrikaans university.

The ethnic composition of Afrikaners is difficult to quantify but it has been estimated at 40% Dutch, 40% German, 7.5% French, 7.5% British and 5% other. Some historians have argued that the '5% other' figure includes a significant proportion of blacks and coloureds.

DEALING WITH RACISM

Cultural apartheid still exists in South Africa. To an extent, discrimination based on wealth is replacing that based on race; most visitors will automatically gain high status. There are, however, still plenty of people who think that a particular skin colour means a particular mindset. A few believe it means inferiority.

The constant awareness of race, even if it doesn't lead to problems, is an annoying feature of travel in South Africa, whatever your skin colour. Racial discrimination is illegal, but it's unlikely that the overworked and under-resourced police force will be interested in most complaints. Tourism authorities are likely to be more sensitive. If you encounter racism in any of the places mentioned by us, please let us know.

African

If you are of African descent, you may well encounter racism from some white and coloured people. Do not assume a special bond with black South Africans either. The various indigenous peoples of South Africa form distinct and sometimes antagonistic cultural groups.

Indian

Although Indians were discriminated against by whites during apartheid, blacks saw them as collaborating with the whites. If you are of Indian descent this could mean some low-level antagonism from both blacks and whites.

Asian

East Asians were a problem for apartheid – Japanese were granted 'honorary white' status, but Chinese were considered coloured. Grossly inaccurate stereotyping and cultural ignorance will probably be the main annoyances you will face.

Most other white Capetonians are of British extraction. Cape Town, as the seat of British power for so long, is somewhat less Afrikaner in outlook than other parts of the country. White liberal Capetonians were regarded with suspicion by more-conservative whites during the apartheid years.

Religion

Islam

Islam first came to the Cape with the slaves brought by the Dutch from the Indian subcontinent and Indonesia. Although the religion could not be practised openly in the colony until 1804, the presence of influential and charismatic political and religious figures among the slaves helped a cohesive Cape Muslim community to develop. One such political dissident was Imam Abdullah Ibn Qadi Abdus Salaam, commonly known as Tuan Guru, from Tidore (now in Indonesia), who was exiled to Robben Island in 1780 and released 13 years later in Cape Town. Four years later he helped establish the city's first mosque, the Auwal Mosque, in the Bo-Kaap, thus making this area the heart of the Islamic community in Cape Town – as it still is today.

During his 13 years on Robben Island, Tuan Guru is said to have transcribed three copies of the Quran from memory. He's buried in Bo-Kaap's Tana Baru Cemetery.

Tuan Guru's grave is one of the 20 or so karamats (tombs of Muslim saints) encircling Cape Town and visited by the faithful on mini pilgrimages. Other karamats are found on Robben Island (that of Sayed Abdurahman Matura); on Signal Hill, which has two (for Sheikh Mohammed Hassen Ghaibie Shah and Tuan Kaape-ti-low); at the gate to the Klein Constantia wine estate (for Sheik Abdurahman Matebe Shah); and at Oudekraal, where there are another two (that of Sheikh Noorul Mubeen and possibly his wife or one of his followers). For a full list see www.capemazaarsociety.com.

THE RITES OF INITIATION

Male initiation ceremonies, which can take place from around age 16 to the early 20s, are a consistent part of traditional black African life (and coloured Muslim life, where teenage boys are also circumcised, albeit with much less ritual). Initiations typically take place around the end of the year and in June to coincide with school and public holidays.

In the Eastern Cape, young Xhosa men once would go into a remote area in the mountains to attend the Ukwaluka, the initiation school where they would be circumcised, live in tents and learn what it is to be a man in tribal society. Some still do return to the Eastern Cape for the ceremony, but others cannot afford to or choose not to do so, so similar initiation sites are created in makeshift tents erected amid the wastelands around the townships.

Initiations used to take several months, but these days they're likely to last a month or less. Initiates shave off all their hair, shed their clothes and wear just a blanket, and daub their faces in white clay before being circumcised. They receive a stick that symbolises the traditional hunting stick; they use it instead of their hands for shaking hands during the initiation period. For about a week immediately after the circumcision, while the wound heals, initiates eat very little and drink nothing. No women are allowed to go near the initiation ground.

Initiations are expensive – around R6000 to R8000, mainly for the cost of the animals (typically sheep or goats) that have to be slaughtered for the various feasts that are part of the ceremony. At the end of the initiation all the items used, including the initiate's old clothes, are burned together with the hut in which he stayed, and the boy emerges as a man. You can spot recent initiates in the townships and Cape Town's city centre by the smart clothes they are wearing, often a sports jacket and a cap.

Cape Town has managed to avoid becoming embroiled in violent Islamic fundamentalism, an outcome that had seemed unlikely in the early 1990s. You'll encounter many friendly faces while wandering around the Bo-Kaap, where you can drop by the local museum to find out more about the community. A sizeable Muslim community also lived in Simon's Town before the Group Areas Act evictions of the late 1960s; its history can be traced at Simon's Town's Heritage Museum.

Christianity

The Afrikaners are a religious people and the group's brand of Christian fundamentalism, based on 17th-century Calvinism, is still a powerful influence. Urbanised middle-class Afrikaners tend to be considerably more moderate. Whites of British descent tend to be Anglican and this faith, along with other forms of Christianity, are also popular among sections of the black and coloured communities.

Spirit Worship

Few blacks in Cape Town maintain a fully traditional lifestyle on a daily basis, but elements of traditional culture do persist, lending a distinctively African air to the townships. At important junctions in life, such as birth, coming of age and marriage, various old rites and customs are followed as well.

Herbal medicine shops are regularly used, and *sangomas* (traditional medicine practitioners, usually women) are consulted for all kinds of illnesses. Certain *sangomas* can also help people get in touch with their ancestors, who play a crucial role in the lives of many black Capetonians. Ancestors are believed to watch over their kin and act as intermediaries between this world and that of the spirits. People turn to their ancestors if they have problems or requests – an animal may be slaughtered in their honour and roasted on an open fire, as it's believed the ancestors eat the smoke.

Judaism

South Africa's oldest Jewish community is in Cape Town. Even though the rules of the Dutch East India Company (Vereenigde Oost-Indische Compagnie; VOC) allowed only for Protestant settlers at the Cape, there are records of Jews converting to Christianity in Cape Town as early as 1669. Jewish immigration picked up speed after the British took charge, with settlers coming mainly from England and Germany. The first congregation was established in 1841, while the first synagogue (now part of the South African Jewish Museum) opened in 1863.

Jewish immigration boomed between 1880 and 1930, when an estimated 15,000 families arrived in South Africa, mainly from Lithuania, Latvia, Poland and Belarus. During this period Jews began to make a large contribution to the city's civic and cultural life. Max Michaelis donated his art collection to the city and Hyman Lieberman became the first Jewish mayor of Cape Town in 1905, the same year the Great Synagogue was consecrated.

Cape Town's Jewish population has dropped from 25,000 (second in number only to the community in Johannesburg) in 1969 to around 15,000 today. Sea Point is the most visibly Jewish area of the city.

Architecture

From the 17th-century Castle of Good Hope to the 21st-century towers rising on the Foreshore, Cape Town's range of architecture is one of its most attractive features. Much that might have been destroyed in other places has been preserved and can be viewed on walking or cycling tours of the city and surroundings.

Dutch Colonial

When the Dutch colonists arrived in 1652, they brought their European ideas of architecture with them, but had to adapt to local conditions and available materials. There was plenty of stone on hand from Table Mountain to build the Castle of Good Hope between 1666 and 1679. The first Capetonian houses were utilitarian structures, such as the thatched and whitewashed Posthuys in Muizenberg, dating from 1673. This simple rustic style of building is one that you'll still find today along the Western Cape coast.

Governor Simon van der Stel's quintessential manor house, Groot Constantia, went up in 1692, setting a precedent for other glorious estates to follow further inland in the Winelands. On Strand St, the fancy facade of the late-18th-century Koopmans-de Wet House is attributed to Louis Thibault, who, as lieutenant of engineers for the Dutch East India Company (Vereenigde Oost-Indische Compagnie; VOC), was responsible for the design of most of Cape Town's public buildings in this period. Thibault also had a hand in the handsome Rust en Vreugd: completed in 1778, the house is notable for its delicately carved rococo fanlight above the main door, as well as its double balconies and portico.

Of course, not everyone lived in such a grand manner. In the city centre, the best place to get an idea of how Cape Town looked to ordinary folk during the 18th century is to take a stroll through the Bo-Kaap. You'll notice flat roofs instead of gables and a lack of shutters on the windows, all the result of VOC building regulations.

Best Dutch Colonial

- *Castle of Good Hope (1679)*
- *Groot Constantia (1692)*
- *Vergelegen (1700)*
- *De Tuynhuis (1700)*
- *Rust en Vreugd (1778)*

British Colonial

When the British took over from the Dutch in the early 19th century, they had their own ways of doing things, and this extended to the architectural look of the city. British governor Lord Charles Somerset made the biggest impact during his 1814–26 tenure. It was he who ordered the restyling of De Tuynhuis – first built as a guesthouse and later a summer residence for the Dutch governors of the Cape – to bring it into line with Regency tastes for verandahs and front gardens, and renamed it Government House.

As the British Empire reached its zenith in the late 19th century, Cape Town boomed and a slew of monumental buildings were erected. Walk down Adderley St and through the Company's Gardens and you'll pass many, including the Standard Bank building, with its pediment, dome and soaring columns; the Houses of Parliament; and the Byzantine-influenced Old Synagogue, dating from 1863. The neighbouring and neo-Egyptian-styled Great Synagogue, with its twin tow-

Best British Colonial

- *Bertram House (1840)*
- *Standard Bank (1880)*
- *Houses of Parliament (1885)*
- *Cape Town Town Hall (1905)*
- *Centre for the Book (1913)*

ers, is from 1905. Long St is where you can see Victorian Cape Town at its most appealing, with the wrought-iron balconies and varying facades of shops and buildings.

Another building boom in the 1920s and '30s led to the construction of many fine art deco buildings in the city centre. Prime examples include the blocks around Greenmarket Sq and the handsome 1939 Mutual Heights building – the continent's first skyscraper – decorated with friezes and frescoes, all with South African themes.

Township Architecture

From the early 1920s out on the empty, sandy Cape Flats, homes were being built for the coloured and black labourers. Langa was established in 1927 and is South Africa's oldest planned township; today it's home to 250,000 people – the same number who live in the city centre, but squashed into a suburb some 48 times smaller.

Although shacks (properly called 'informal settlements') are the constructions most widely associated with the townships, this is far from the only architecture in these areas; the buildings you'll find can be broken into five main categories.

Shacks

It's estimated that there are around one million people living in self-built shacks. Cobbled together from a variety of materials, such as old packing crates, and decorated with (among other things) magazine pages and old food-tin labels, the design and structure of a shack depends on the financial situation of the owner and how long they have lived there.

Hostels

Built originally for migrant labourers before WWII, these two-level brick dormitories were broken up into basic units, each accommodating 16 men, who shared one shower, one toilet and one small kitchen. Tiny bedrooms housed up to three men each. After the Pass laws (which stated that those without a job outside the homelands were not allowed to leave) were abolished, most men brought their families to

SIR HERBERT BAKER

Like his patron Cecil Rhodes, Herbert Baker (1862–1946) was an ambitious young Englishman who seized the chance to make his mark in South Africa. Baker arrived in Cape Town in 1892 and a year later, through family connections, had gained himself an audience with Rhodes and been commissioned to remodel Groote Schuur, the prime minister's mansion on the slopes of Table Mountain. This kicked off a style known as Cape Dutch Revival.

Many more commissions followed, and Cape Town is littered with buildings of Baker's design, including several cottages in Muizenberg (where Baker lived for a while), St George's Cathedral and the First National Bank on Adderley St. In 1900, Rhodes sent Baker to Italy, Greece and Egypt to study their classical architecture to inspire him to design the sort of grand buildings Rhodes wished to see constructed in South Africa. Two years later, though, Rhodes was dead – and Baker was designing his memorial.

Among Baker's grandest work is the imposing Union Buildings in Pretoria (1909). In 1912 he left South Africa to join Edwin Lutyens in designing the secretariat buildings in New Delhi. Back in the UK, he worked on South Africa House in London's Trafalgar Sq, and was knighted in 1926. He's buried in Westminster Abbey.

live with them. Each unit became home to up to 16 families, with each room sleeping up to three families. Although some families still live in such conditions, other hostels have been modernised to provide less cramped and much more habitable apartments.

Architecture Books

Hidden Cape Town (Paul Duncan & Alan Proust)

Cape Town: Architecture & Design (Pascale Lauber)

Cape Dutch Houses & Other Old Favourites (Phillida Brooke Simons)

Shack Chic (photographed by Craig Fraser)

Terrace Houses

In the older townships of Langa and Gugulethu you'll come across one-storey terrace housing built between the 1920s and '40s. Like the hostels, conditions in these 30-sq-metre 'railway carriage' houses were very basic and crowded. Since the end of apartheid these houses have been owned by the former tenants, who are now responsible for their maintenance. Residents have sometimes expanded them (when possible) into the front and back yards.

Social Housing

Since 1994, the South African government has striven to build proper houses in the townships, first through the Reconstruction and Development Programme (RDP) and currently through the Breaking New Ground (BNG) scheme, both of which provide a very basic, free house to former shack residents. Averaging around 28 sq metres in size, these 'matchbox' houses are little more than four concrete-block walls topped with a roof of corrugated iron. There's no insulation, ceilings or hot water provided.

So called 'gap' housing is also being built in the townships for low-income families who earn between R3500 and R10,000 a month. Residents are expected to contribute towards buying these subsidised homes, which are typically of a better quality than BNG housing.

Township Villas

There are areas of Gugulethu, Langa and Khayelitsha that are very middle-class, and where you'll find spacious, bungalow-style houses and villas of a high standard.

Apartheid Era

The election of the National Party to government in 1948 was bad news for Cape Town's architecture in more ways than one. Apartheid laws labelled Cape Town a mainly coloured city – this meant that the national government was unwilling to support big construction projects (hampering the development of the Foreshore for decades), while the local authorities went about applying the Group Areas Act, demolishing areas such as District Six and rezoning Green Point (including De Waterkant) as a whites-only area.

At the Foreshore end of Bree St, the 42-floor, 142m-high Portside Tower (2014) is Cape Town's tallest building. Designed by DHK and Louis Karol Architects, the building is South Africa's first Green Star–rated skyscraper.

Examples of rationalist architecture from this era include the hideous Artscape arts centre and the adjoining Civic Centre on the Foreshore, which demonstrate the obsession with concrete that was typical of international modernism. Such poor design wasn't necessarily a function of apartheid planning, as the Baxter Theatre proves. Designed by Jack Barnett, its flat roof is famously dimpled with orange fibreglass downlights that glow fabulously at night. Also notable is the striking Taal Monument in Paarl, with a 57m-concrete tower designed by Jan van Wijk.

The lack of planning or official architectural concern for the townships has long been criticised, although it is worth mentioning the tremendous ingenuity and resilience that residents have shown in creating liveable homes from scrap. A visit to the townships today reveals colourfully painted shacks and murals, homes and churches made from shipping crates, and more recent imaginative structures, such as the Guga S'Thebe Arts & Cultural Centre in Langa.

Contemporary Architecture

The death knell of apartheid coincided with the redevelopment of the Victoria & Alfred Waterfront in the early 1990s. More recent architectural additions to the Waterfront include the Nelson Mandela Gateway and Clock Tower Precinct, built in 2001 as the new departure point for Robben Island, and the ritzy millionaire's playground of the V&A Marina, with some 600 apartments and 200 boat moorings.

The recent Cape Town property boom has created an environment for some interesting new residential buildings and conversions of old office blocks into apartments, such as the Mutual Heights building, the three old buildings that are part of Mandela Rhodes Place, and the adjacent Taj Cape Town hotel, all of which sensitively combine the original structures with new towers.

Opening in 2003, the Cape Town International Convention Centre (CTICC), with its ship-like prow and sleek glass-and-steel hotel, drew favourable nods and has helped push the City Bowl down towards the waterfront, from which it had been cut off for decades. An extension to the CTICC is currently rising across Heerengracht. In late 2014, the city announced plans to extend the commercially successful Waterfront area along the Foreshore, with a new cruise liner terminal, housing, commercial buildings and landscaped public space.

At the end of 2014 the new theatre at the Guga S'thebe Arts & Cultural Centre in Langa was opened. An innovative collaboration between the city's Department of Arts and Culture and architectural students from faculties in Cape Town, Germany and the USA, it was constructed using recycled materials, including shipping crates, straw, and wood from fruit crates. All eyes will be on the Waterfront in 2017, when the new art museum Zeitz MOCAA, designed by Thomas Heatherwick to use the old grain silos there, is set to open.

Best Modern & Contemporary

Baxter Theatre (1977)

Guga S'Thebe Arts & Cultural Centre (2000)

Green Point Stadium (2010)

Fugard Theatre (2010)

Arts

Cape Town's mash-up of cultures and the sharply contrasting lives of its citizens make it a fertile location for the arts. Music is a pulsing constant in the Mother City, with jazz a particular forte. There's a surprisingly good range of performing arts, and a host of imaginative authors shed light on more obscure corners of the urban experience.

Visual Arts

Public Artworks

Africa by Brett Murray

The Knot by Edoardo Villa

Nobel Square by Claudette Schreuders

Olduvai by Gavin Younge

At the South African National Gallery, you may find paintings by Gerard Sekoto, a black artist whose works capture the vibrancy of District Six, and Peter Clarke, a distinctive printer, poet and painter hailing from Simon's Town. Irma Stern's German-expressionism-inspired works can be found in the Irma Stern Museum and at Casa Labia in Muizenberg.

Notable among contemporary local artists is Conrad Botes, who first made his mark with his weird cult comic *Bitterkomix,* founded with Anton Kannemeyer. Botes' colourful graphic images, both beautiful and horrific, have been shown in exhibitions in New York, the UK and Italy, as well as at the Havana Biennale in 2006.

Also look out for works by the painter Ndikhumbule Ngqinambi; Willie Bester (www.williebester.co.za), whose mixed-media creations of township life are very powerful; and the more conventional John Kramer (www.johnkramer.net), who captures the ordinary, serene quality of the South African landscape.

THE PEOPLE'S PAINTER

Across Cape Town you'll see the striking multiracial faces that inspired the portraits of Vladimir Tretchikoff (1913–2006). The most famous of these is the iconic *Chinese Girl* – a mesmerising image of a blue-faced, red-lipped Asian beauty as instantly recognisable as the *Mona Lisa*.

The twists of fate that transported Tretchikoff – born in Petropavlovsk in present-day Kazakhstan– to Cape Town via Harbin, Shanghai, Singapore and Indonesia just after WWII is the stuff of high adventure. Against all odds, and with little assistance from Cape Town's established art circles, Tretchikoff made a fortune marketing his art as prints around the world; the 252 exhibitions organised by the skilled businessman and self-promoter were attended by over two million people.

However it wasn't until 2011 that a major retrospective of his work, which included many of the originals oils, was held at the South African National Gallery in Cape Town. The accompanying book *Tretchikoff: The People's Painter* is a fine introduction to the artist's work.

Natasha Mercorio, Tretchikoff's granddaughter, has also launched the Tretchikoff Trust (www.vladimirtretchikoff.com) with the aim of helping creative youths realise their dreams. A percentage of sales of new prints from Tretchikoff's collection help fund the project.

Music

Jazz

Cape Town has produced some major jazz talents, including the singer-songwriter Jonathan Butler and the saxophonists Robbie Jansen and Winston 'Mankunku' Ngozi. So important has the city been to the development of jazz that there is a subgenre of the music called Cape Jazz, which is improvisational in character and features instruments that can be used in street parades, such as the drums and trumpets favoured in the Cape Town Minstrel Carnival.

The elder statesman of the scene is pianist Abdullah Ibrahim (www.abdullahibrahim.co.za). Born Adolph Johannes Brand in District Six in 1934, he began performing at 15 under the name Dollar Brand, and formed the Jazz Epistles with the legendary Hugh Masekela. In 1962, after moving to Zurich, he was spotted by Duke Ellington, who arranged recording sessions for him at Reprise Records and sponsored his appearance at the Newport Jazz Festival in 1965. Brand converted to Islam in 1968 and took the name Abdullah Ibrahim. In 1974 he recorded the seminal album *Manenberg* with saxophonist Basil Coetzee. He occasionally plays in Cape Town and, in 2006, spearheaded the formation of the 18-strong Cape Town Jazz Orchestra.

Goema-style jazz takes its rhythmic cues from the goema drum and has been popularised by musicians such as Mac McKenzie and Hilton Schilder. Other respected local artists to watch out for include guitarists Jimmy Dludlu and Reza Khota (www.rezakhota.com), pianist Paul Hamner and singer Judith Sephuma.

Dance, Rock & Pop

Few Afro-fusion groups have been as big recently as the multiracial seven-piece band Freshlyground (www.freshlyground.com), who draw huge crowds whenever performing in their hometown. Their song 'Waka Waka', with Colombian artist Shakira, was the official 2010 FIFA World Cup anthem; on their 2013 album *Take Me to the Dance* they collaborated with Steve Berlin of Los Lobos.

Bridging the divide between jazz and electronic dance music are Goldfish (www.goldfishlive.com), aka the duo David Poole and Dominic Peters, who combine samplers, a groove box, keyboards, vocoder, upright bass, flute and saxophone in their live performances. Dominic's brother Ben Peters is a member of Goodluck (www.goodlucklive.com), who are also gaining a strong following for their similar sound.

Techno, trance, hip hop, jungle and rap are wildly popular. Afrikaans rapper Jack Parow (www.jackparow.com) is the Capetonian answer to the national rap sensation Die Antwoord (www.dieantwoord.com) – both acts embody the subculture of 'zef', a 'white trash'-style fashion with lots of exaggerated bling, tattoos and the like. Also tune in to kwaito, a mix of *mbaqanga* (a Zulu style of music), jive, hip hop, house and ragga. The music of local singing superstar Brenda Fassie (1964–2004) has a strong kwaito flavour – listen to her hits such as 'Weekend Special' and 'Too Late for Mamma'. Dubbed 'Madonna of the Townships' by *Time* magazine, Fassie, who was born in Langa, struggled with drug problems throughout her brief life.

Among the many indie rock bands and singers to catch at gigs around town are Ashtray Electric (www.ashtrayelectric.co.za); Arno Carstens (www.arnocarstensmusic.wordpress.com), the one-time lead singer of the legendary Springbok Nude Girls; the incredible one-man-band Jeremy Loops (www.jeremyloops.com); and 13-member ska/reggae/hip-hop/dance/you-name-it band The Rudimentals (www.facebook.com/rudimentals).

For a preview of the Capetonian art scene check out the website Artthrob (www.artthrob.co.za), which showcases the best in South African contemporary art (and has plenty of up-to-the-minute news), and the magazine *ArtSouthAfrica* (www.artsouthafrica.com).

Literature

Cape Town has nurtured several authors of international repute, including Nobel Prize-winner JM Coetzee (the first part of his Man Booker Prize-winning novel *Disgrace* is set in Cape Town); André Brink, professor of English at the University of Cape Town; and the Man Booker-Prize-nominated Damon Galgut.

Out of the coloured experience in District Six came two notable writers, Alex La Guma (1925–85) and Richard Rive (1931–89). La Guma's books include *And a Threefold Cord,* which examines the poverty, misery and loneliness of slum life, and *A Walk in the Night,* a collection of short stories set in District Six. Rive's *'Buckingham Palace', District Six* is a thought-provoking and sensitive set of stories.

Sindiwe Magona grew up in Gugulethu in the 1940s and '50s. The feisty writer's early life experiences inform her autobiographical works *To My Children's Children* (1990) and *Forced to Grow* (1992). *Beauty's Gift* (2008) deals unflinchingly with AIDS in the black community and, in particular, its impact on five women who consider themselves to be in faithful relationships.

The Cape's incredible true crime stories have provided easy inspiration for a slew of thriller writers, including Mike Nicol, Deon Meyer, Margie Orford, Sarah Lotz and Andrew Brown – whose novel *Refuge,* shortlisted for the Commonwealth Writers Prize in 2009, provides an unflinching look at the city's dark underbelly.

Capetonian Lauren Beukes (www.laurenbeukes.com) has had international hits with her fantasy/sci-fi/social-realism mash-ups *Moxyland* and *Zoo City* (which won the 2011 Arthur C Clarke Prize), and the fantasy/crime novels *The Shining Girls* (2013) and *Broken Monsters* (2014).

Cinema

Cape Town is a major centre for South African movie-making and, increasingly, for international productions. The city acts as a magnet for many talented people in the industry and you'll frequently see production crews shooting on location around town. On the city's outskirts are the Cape Town Film Studios (www.capetownfilmstudios.co.za), where several major Hollywood productions have been shot, including *Safe House,* the Cape Town–set thriller with Denzel Washington and Ryan Reynolds.

CONTROVERSIAL ARTISTS

'It is an incitement of violence,' said artist Michael Elion, expressing a fear for his life after his sculpture of a giant pair of Ray-Bans, entitled *Perceiving Freedom*, was vandalised on Sea Point Promenade in November 2014. In creating a controversial piece of art, Elion has joined a long list of fellow Capetonian artists who have upset the establishment and/or the public.

Censorship of the arts was standard under apartheid. In recent years, such government-sanctioned censorship has again reared its ugly head. Capetonian cartoonist Zapiro (www.zapiro.com) has twice been sued by President Jacob Zuma for defamation (both cases were eventually dropped). Zuma and the ANC also took umbrage against *The Spear,* by Brett Murray (www.brettmurray.co.za), when it was displayed at the Goodman Gallery in Johannesburg in 2012; this provocative painting of Zuma was later defaced by two members of the public. Murray's sculpture *Africa,* standing in St George's Mall, was also a controversial winner of a Cape Town public sculpture competition in 1998.

Oliver Hermanus followed up his 2009 debut feature *Shirley Adams,* a bleak Ken Loach-style drama set in Mitchell's Plains on the Cape Flats, with *Skoonheid* (Beauty); it was the first ever Afrikaans movie to play at the Cannes Film Festival (in 2011) and won the Queer Palm award. Among other recent local movies to feature Cape Town are *Long Street,* directed by Revel Fox and starring his daughter and wife, and the charming *Visa/Vie* directed by Elan Ganmaker.

On DVD, keep an eye out for the American documentary *Long Night's Journey into Day,* nominated for Best Documentary at the 2001 Oscars. This very moving Sundance Film Festival winner follows four cases from the Truth & Reconciliation Commission hearings, including that of Amy Biehl, the white American murdered in the Cape Flats in 1993. *U-Carmen e Khayelitsha,* winner of the Golden Bear at the 2005 Berlin International Film Festival, is based on Bizet's opera *Carmen* and was shot entirely on location in Khayelitsha.

The Labia's African Screen is the only Cape Town cinema that regularly screens South African movies. At the multiplexes you might also catch the odd South African–made feature. Otherwise, your best chance of watching home-grown product is at the city's several film festivals.

Theatre & Performing Arts

Cape Town's lively and diverse performing arts scene mounts large-scale musicals, one-man shows, edgy dramas reflecting modern South Africa and intimate poetry reading soirees. The city has produced some notable actors, including the Sea Point–born Sir Anthony Sher, who returns occasionally to the city to perform.

Among local theatre companies that have gone international are Handspring Puppet Company (www.handspringpuppet.co.za), whose amazingly lifelike creations formed the heart of the hit UK National Theatre production *War Horse,* and director Brett Bailey's Third World Bunfight (www.thirdworldbunfight.co.za), which specialises in using black actors to tell uniquely African stories – their thought-provoking show *Exhibit B* sparked controversy across Europe in 2014.

Songwriter and director David Kramer (www.davidkramer.co.za) and musician Taliep Petersen (1950–2006) teamed up to work on two musicals, *District Six* and *Poison,* before hitting the big time with their jazz homage *Kat and the Kings,* which swept up awards in London in 1999 and received standing ovations on Broadway. Their collaboration *Goema* celebrates the tradition of Afrikaans folk songs while tracing the contribution made by the slaves and their descendants to the development of Cape Town.

In early 2015 Kramer premiered his new musical *Orpheus in Africa,* about American impresario Orpheus McAdoo and his African American Virginia Jubilee Singers, who visited South Africa in the 1890s.

The Natural Environment

Cape Town is defined by its magnificent natural environment, part of the World Heritage–status Cape Floristic Region (CFR) – the richest and smallest of the world's six floral kingdoms and home to some 8200 plant species, more than three times as many per square kilometre as in the whole of South America.

The Land

Table Mountain's flat-top shape as we know it today probably first came about 60 million years ago, although the mountain as a whole started forming about 250 million years ago, making it the elder statesman of world mountains. (For comparison, the Alps are only 32 million years old and the Himalayas 40 million years old.)

The types of rock that make up the mountain and the Cape Peninsula are broken into three major geological types. The oldest, dating back 540 million years, is Malmesbury shale – this forms the base of most of the City Bowl and can be seen along the Sea Point shoreline, on Signal Hill and on the lower slopes of Devil's Peak. It's fairly soft and weathers easily. The second-oldest is the tough Cape granite, which forms the foundation for Table Mountain and can also be seen on Lion's Head and the boulders at Clifton and Boulders Beaches. The third type of rock is called Table Mountain Sandstone, a combination of sandstone and quartzite.

It's thought that originally the summit of Table Mountain was a couple of kilometres higher than it is today. Over time this rock was weathered to create the distinctive hollows and oddly shaped rocks found on the mountain's summit and at Cape Point.

Reading Up

- *Wild About Cape Town (Duncan Butchart)*
- *The Rocks and Mountains of Cape Town (John Compton)*
- *How the Cape Got Its Shape (fold-out map and chart by Map Studio)*

Flora

Fynbos (*fine*-bos; from the Dutch, meaning 'fine bush') thrives in the Cape's nitrogen-poor soil – it's thought that the plants' fine, leathery leaves improve their odds of survival by discouraging predators. There are three main types of *fynbos* that you'll come across: proteas (including the king protea, South Africa's national emblem), ericas (heaths and mosses) and restios (reeds). Examples of *fynbos* flowers that have been exported to other parts of the world include gladiolus, freesias and daisies.

On Signal Hill and the lower slopes of Devil's Peak you'll find *renosterbos* (literally, 'rhinoceros bush'), composed predominantly of a grey ericoid shrub and peppered with grasses and geophytes (plants that grow from underground bulbs). In the cool, well-watered ravines on the eastern slopes of Table Mountain you'll also find small pockets of Afro-montane forest, such as at Orange Kloof, where only 12 entry permits are issued daily.

Table Mountain and the peninsula alone contain 2285 plant species – more than in all of Britain – and it's also home to over 100 invertebrates and two vertebrates not found anywhere else on earth.

While the biodiversity of the Cape Peninsula is incredible, it is also threatened. More than 1400 *fynbos* plants are endangered or vulnerable to extinction; some have minute natural ranges. Most *fynbos* plants need fire to germinate and flower, but unseasonal and accidental fires can cause great harm. The fires can also burn far longer and more fiercely because of the presence of invasive alien plants, such as the various pines and wattles that also pose a threat because of the vast amounts of water they suck up.

In the wake of the devastating forest fires that swept across the Cape in 2000, Table Mountain National Park and the public works project Working for Water undertook an alien-plant-clearing program to rehabilitate fire-damaged areas and to educate vulnerable communities, such as the townships, about fires. Around 85% of the park's management area has so far been cleared of alien plants.

The first farms were granted at Cape Point in the 1780s, but the area really didn't become fully accessible until 1915, when the coastal road from Simon's Town was completed.

Fauna

The animal most closely associated with Table Mountain is the dassie, also known as the rock hyrax. Despite the resemblance to a plump hamster, these small furry animals are – incredibly – distantly related to the elephant. You'll most likely see dassies sunning themselves on rocks around the upper cableway station.

Among the feral population of introduced fallow deer that roam the lower slopes of Table Mountain (around the Rhodes Memorial) is an animal once regarded as extinct: the quagga. This partially striped zebra was formerly thought to be a distinct species, but DNA obtained from a stuffed quagga in Cape Town's South African Museum showed it to be a subspecies of the widespread Burchell's zebra. A breeding program started in 1987 has proved successful in 'resurrecting' the quagga. Mammals found at the Cape of Good Hope include eight antelope species, Cape mountain zebras and a troupe of chacma baboons.

The Cape's most famous birds are the African penguins (formerly called jackass penguins for their donkey-like squawk). You'll find some 3000 of the friendly penguins at Boulders Beach.

Marine Life

The seas surrounding the Cape Peninsula host many types of marine life. Southern right and humpback whales, dolphins, Cape fur seals and loggerhead and leatherback turtles are among the species you might be able to spot. One you would hope to not see – unless you're in the safety of a diving cage or on board a boat – is the great white shark.

In order to protect and conserve threatened marine species (such as abalone and west coast rock lobster) that had until recent times flourished in the waters around the Cape, Table Mountain National

SCORING CAPE TOWN'S ENVIRONMENT

In 2014, Cape Town scored highly on Siemens' African Green Cities Index (www.siemens.co.za/sustainable-development), and was praised for its comprehensive Energy and Climate Change Action Plan and policies to contain urban sprawl and protect green space. Areas for improvement include having the highest carbon-dioxide emissions per capita from electricity consumption in the index (which covers 15 major African cities), and the second highest generation of waste. That said, the report notes city initiatives to tackle waste generation, including schemes to separate recyclables before collection and an Integrated Waste Exchange program to facilitate the exchange of potentially useful materials.

Park created a Marine Protected Area (MPA) in 2004. Covering around 1000 sq km of waters from Moullie Point to Muizenberg, the MPA includes six 'no-take' zones, where no fishing or extractive activities are allowed.

Creating Table Mountain National Park

Cape Point itself isn't exactly where the warm waters of the Indian Ocean meet the cold seas of the Atlantic. The actual meeting point fluctuates along the southwestern coast between Cape Point and Cape Agulhas.

The campaign to designate the Cape Point area a nature reserve first got underway in the 1920s, when there was a chance that the land could have been turned over to developers. At the same time, future prime minister General Jan Smuts – a keen hiker – started a public appeal to secure formal protection for Table Mountain; today there's a track on the mountain named after him. The Cape of Good Hope Nature Reserve was eventually secured in 1939.

This was the first formal conservation on the Cape, although mining magnate and South African politician Cecil Rhodes had used a small part of his vast fortune to buy up much of the eastern slopes of Table Mountain; he gifted this land, which includes Kirstenbosch and the Cecilia Estate stretching to Constantia Nek, to the public in his will.

In the 1950s the Van Zyl Commission baulked at creating a single controlling authority for the park, but in 1958 all land on Table Mountain above the 152m-contour line was declared a National Monument. The city of Cape Town proclaimed the Table Mountain Nature Reserve in 1963 and the Silvermine Nature Reserve in 1965.

By the 1970s, 14 different bodies were in control of the publicly owned natural areas of the Cape. It wasn't until 1998 that a single Cape Peninsula National Park became a reality. In 2004 the park was renamed Table Mountain National Park.

Wine

Although Jan van Riebeeck, the founder of the Cape Colony, planted vines and made wine himself, it was not until the arrival of Governor Simon van der Stel in 1679 that winemaking in South Africa began in earnest. Van der Stel created the estate Constantia (later subdivided into the several estates in the area today), and passed on his winemaking skills to the burghers who settled around Stellenbosch.

The French Influence

Between 1688 and 1690, some 200 Huguenots arrived in the country. They were granted land, particularly in the region around Franschhoek (which translates as 'French Corner'). Although only a few had any winemaking experience, they gave the infant industry fresh impetus.

For a long time, Cape wines (except those produced at Constantia) were not in great demand, and most grapes ended up in brandy. The industry received a boost in the early 19th century, as war between Britain and France – and preferential trade tariffs between the UK and South Africa – led to more South African wine being imported to the UK.

'Today, praise be the Lord, wine was pressed for the first time from Cape grapes.'

Jan van Riebeeck, 2 February 1659

Apartheid-era sanctions and the power of the Kooperatieve Wijnbouwers Vereeniging (KWV; the cooperative formed in 1918 to control minimum prices, production areas and quota limits) didn't exactly encourage innovation, and instead hampered the industry. Since 1992 the KWV, now a private company, has lost much of its former influence.

Many new and progressive winemakers are leading South Africa's re-emergence onto the world market. New production regions are being established in the cooler coastal areas east of Cape Town, around Mossel Bay, Walker Bay and Elgin, and to the north around Durbanville and Darling. The older vines of the Swartland, northwest of Paarl (and in particular the Paardeberg area), are also producing some very high-quality wines.

The Human Cost

The black and coloured workforce in the wine industry currently numbers over 160,000, most of whom are toiling in vineyards owned by around 4500 whites. Workers often receive the minimum monthly wage of R105 a day. When this was increased from R69 a day in 2013, following a crippling strike among fruit pickers, some farms responded by cutting back on hiring pickers, with female workers in particular taking the brunt of the cuts.

Ripe with Abuse, a 2011 report by Human Rights Watch (HRW; www.hrw.org), damned the industry, citing low wages, appalling housing conditions, lack of access to toilets or drinking water while working, no protection against pesticides and barriers to union representation.

There is labour legislation on the books, but it's not always complied with, and unfortunately many workers are unaware of their rights. Wines of South Africa (www.wosa.co.za) runs various programs to improve the industry's human rights and sustainability record. The industry has also increased cooperation with the Wine Industry and Ethical Trade Association (WIETA; www.wieta.org.za), which lobbies for a better deal for those working in the wine industry.

Wine Varieties

Reds

Regular pinotage, a cross between pinot noir and cinsaut, which produces a very bold wine, is the Cape's signature grape. Together with other robust red varieties such as shiraz (syrah) and cabernet sauvignon, it's being challenged by lighter blends of cabernet sauvignon, merlot, shiraz and cabernet franc, which are closer in style to bordeaux.

Grape (Jeanne Viall, Wilmot James and Jakes Gerwel; 2012) is a well-rounded, thought-provoking account of the development of South Africa's wine industry.

Whites

The most common variety of white wine is chenin blanc. In the last decade or so, more fashionable varieties such as chardonnay and sauvignon blanc have been planted on a wide scale. Other widely planted whites include colombard, semillon and sweet muscats. Table whites, especially chardonnay, once tended to be heavily oaked and high in alcohol, but lighter, more fruity whites are now in the ascendancy. For good sauvignon blancs, look to wineries in the cooler regions of Constantia, Elgin and Hermanus.

Sparkling

Méthode Cap Classique (MCC) is the name that South Africa's wine industry has come up with for its champenoise-style wines: many are as good as, or even better than, the real thing.

Fortified

The Worcester, Calitzdorp and Karoo regions are the country's leading producer of fortified wines, including port, brandy and South Africa's own *hanepoot*. This dessert wine is made from the Mediterranean

TOP TIPPLES

Cathy Marston (www.cathymarston.co.za), Cape Town–based wine educator and writer, recommends the following wines:

Reds

MR de Compostella (www.raats.co.za) This elegant, restrained wine created by Mzokhona Mvemve and Bruwer Raats wouldn't be out of place in any line-up of top bordeaux blends, and knocks most of the competition into a cocked hat. Alas – short of begging at the cellar door, it's so popular you're unlikely to be able to get it.

Hartenberg's cabernet sauvignon–shiraz (www.hartenbergestate.com) For under R100 you can't get a better-value red wine. It's a great blend that goes well with everything for everyday drinking.

Fairview's Beacon shiraz There's quite a lot of pepper in the flavour of this wine, but it's very modern and forthright with a spicy, black-fruit finish.

Whites

Tokara's Director's Reserve White An elegant blend of sauvignon and semillon.

DeMorgenzon's White 12 (www.demorgenzon.co.za) Seriously lovely chenin-based blend.

AA Badehorst Secateurs chenin blanc (www.aabedenhorst.com) A great everyday, crowd-pleasing white.

Graham Beck Blanc de Blancs One of the classiest, freshest bubblies you'll find in the Cape. Among MCC sparklers, those of **Silverthorn Wines** (www.silverthornwines.co.za) in Robertson are also worth seeking out.

WORKER'S WINE

It's worth noting that South Africa has more fair-trade-accredited wines than any other country. Various wineries are leading the way in setting improved labour and fair-trade standards. Both Solms-Delta and Van Loveren (www.vanloveren.co.za) in Robertson have made their employees shareholders in joint-venture wine farms, while part of the Nelson Wine Estate (www.nelsonscreek.co.za) has been donated to the workers to produce wines under the label New Beginnings.

Other worker or black-owned and -empowerment brands:

Thandi (www.thandiwines.com) Meaning 'love' or 'cherish' in Xhosa (isiXhosa), and located in the Elgin area, this was the first winery in the world to be fair-trade–certified. It's half owned by the 250 farm worker families and produces good single varietals and blends.

M'hudi (www.mhudi.com) Owned by the Rangaka family, their range includes a cabernet sauvignon, chenin blanc, pinotage and sauvignon blanc.

Lathithá (www.lathithawines.co.za) Made by winemakers at Blaauwklippen on behalf of Sheila Hlanjwa, it's part of a project to popularise wine drinking in township communities.

Fairvalley Wines (www.fairvalley.co.za) The fair-trade–accredited wines from this venture, located next door to Fairview, are owned by 42 families.

grape variety known as muscat of Alexandria to produce a sweet, high-alcohol tipple for the domestic market.

Wine Trends

South African winemakers blend grape varieties for many of their top wines. Red blends, mostly based on cabernet sauvignon, have been around for decades, but recent years have seen something of an explosion in white blends in two distinct, but equally exciting, main styles. First, those mixing sauvignon blanc and semillon, à la white bordeaux. Vergelegen has been the leader here, with its well-oaked and rather grand semillon-based wine. But now there are many fine versions – like Oak Valley's OV blend, Tokara White and Steenberg's Magna Carta.

The other strand in the white blend story is more indigenous. These wines are often from warmer inland districts, like the Swartland. Most follow the lead of the 'inventor' of this style, Eben Sadie, with his wine Palladius, and use plenty of chenin blanc, along with varieties like chardonnay, roussanne and viognier.

Rosé wines – lightly fruity, crisp and dry – are gaining popularity. Look out for 'pinotage' on the label – not everyone admires this local variety in red wines, but all agree it's great for pink ones.

Winemakers are also moving to the coast or climbing mountains in search of cooler areas to make different styles of wine; these wines are more delicate and often have lower alcohol levels and greater freshness. Elgin, a high inland plateau, is gaining increasing recognition for its fine chardonnay, sauvignon blanc and pinot noir. Sauvignon blanc is a favourite for wineries in maritime areas, too – such as Lomond and Black Oystercatcher, both not far from Cape Agulhas; or Fryer's Cove up the West Coast, whose vineyards are just inland from the chilly Atlantic. There's also a trend for using muscat to make light, sparkling moscato-style wines, such as those produced by De Krans in the Karoo and Imbuko in Wellington.

Pinotage also features in the growing band of 'chocolate coffee' styles of red wine, a trend kicked off by Diemersfontein in Wellington. While these wines, with their distinctive coffee and chocolate aromas and flavours, are generally sniffed at by the critics, they have been a hit with the public.

Glossary of Wine Terms

Aroma The smell of a wine; 'bouquet' is usually used for the less fruity, more developed scents of older wine.

Balance The all-important harmony of the components in a wine: alcohol, fruitiness, acidity and tannin (and oak, when used).

Blend A mix of two or more varieties in one wine, eg colombard-chardonnay. You'll see 'Cape Blend' appearing on some reds' labels; it implies at least 20% pinotage.

Shops in the UK that support Wine Industry & Ethical Trade Association (WIETA) include Asda, Tesco, Marks & Spencer and Waitrose, while in South Africa, Woolworths is on board; check WIETA's website (www.wieta.org.za) for details.

Corked Not literally cork fragments in the wine, but when the cork has tainted the wine, making it (in the extreme) mouldy-tasting and flat.

Estate wine This term is permitted only for wine grown, made and bottled on a single property.

Finish The impression a wine leaves in the mouth: the longer the flavour persists (and the sadder you are when it goes), the better.

Garage wine Wine made in minuscule quantities, sometimes by passionate amateurs – and occasionally actually in a garage.

Oaked or **wooded** Most serious red wines, and a lot of smart whites, are matured for a year or two in expensive wooden barrels; it affects the texture of the wine and the flavour. A cheap way of getting oak flavour is to use wood chips or staves in a metal tank.

Organic It's the grapes, rather than the winemaking, that can be organic (naturally grown without pesticides, chemical fertilisers etc).

Tannin Mostly in red wine and derived from grape skins and pips, or oak barrels; the mouth-puckering dryness on gums and cheeks, which softens as the wine matures.

Vintage The year the grapes were harvested; also used to describe a port-style wine made in a particularly good year (the best are often called 'vintage reserve').

Survival Guide

Directory A–Z

Customs Regulations

There are the usual duty-free restrictions on entering South Africa: you're only allowed to bring in 1L of spirits, 2L of wine and 400 cigarettes. Motor vehicles must be covered by a carnet (customs permit). For more info, contact the **Department of Customs & Excise** (☎0800 007 277, 011-602 2093; www.sars.gov.za).

Electricity

The electricity system is 230V AC at 50 cycles per second. Appliances rated at 240V AC will work.

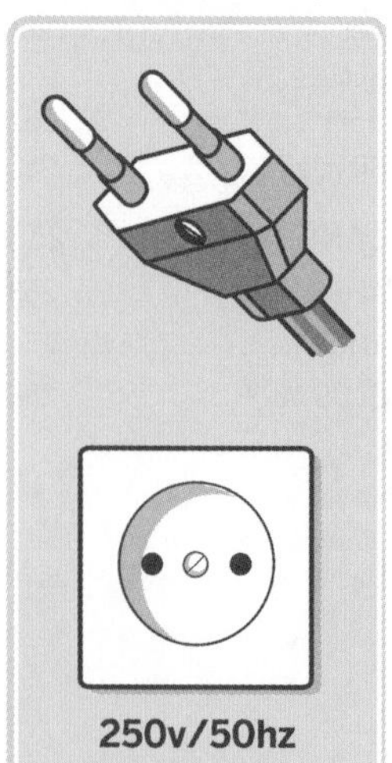

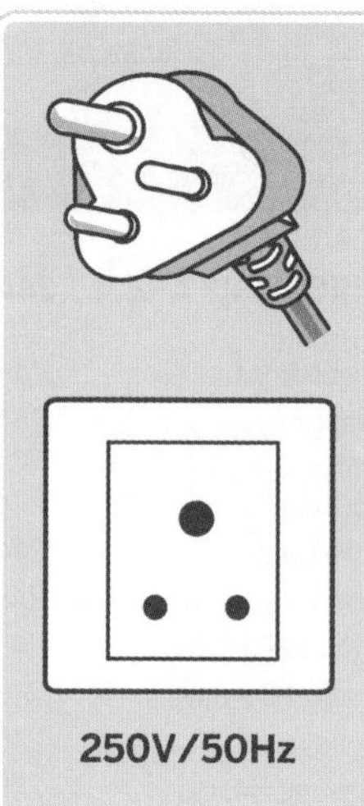

Embassies & Consulates

Most foreign embassies are based in Johannesburg (Jo'burg) or Pretoria, but a few countries also maintain a consulate in Cape Town. Most are open from 9am to 4pm Monday to Friday.

Angolan Consulate (☎021-425 8700; www.angolanembassy.org/consular.html; 15th fl, Metropolitan Bldg, 7 Coen Steytler Ave, Foreshore; 🚌Convention Centre)

Dutch Consulate (☎021-421 5660; http://southafrica.nlembassy.org; 100 Strand St, City Bowl; 🚌Strand)

French Consulate (☎021-423 1575; www.consulfrance-lecap.org; 78 Queen Victoria St, Gardens; 🚌Upper Long/Upper Loop)

German Consulate (☎021-405 3052; www.southafrica.diplo.de; 19th fl, Triangle House, 22 Riebeeck St, Foreshore; 🚌Lower Long/Lower Loop)

Italian Consulate (☎021-487 3900; www.conscapetown.esteri.it/Consolato_Capetown; 2 Grey's Pass, Queen Victoria St, City Bowl; 🚌Upper Long/Upper Loop)

UK Consulate (☎021-405 2400; www.gov.uk/government/world/organisations/british-consulate-general-cape-town; 15th fl, Norton Rose House, 8 Riebeeck St, Foreshore; 🚌Adderley)

US Consulate (☎021-702 7300; http://southafrica.usembassy.gov; 2 Reddam Ave, Westlake)

Emergency

In any emergency call ☎107 (landlines only), or ☎021-480 7700 if using a mobile. Other useful phone numbers:

Table Mountain National Park (☎0861 106 417)

Sea Rescue (☎021-449 3500)

Health

Tap water is drinkable here, and with the exception of HIV/AIDS, there's little need to worry about health issues in Cape Town. But hundreds do die daily from HIV/AIDS, so make sure you protect yourself while having sex. For more information on health in South Africa, read Lonely Planet's *Healthy Travel Africa* and *South Africa, Lesotho & Swaziland*.

Internet Access

Wi-fi access is available at many hotels and hostels, as well as several cafes and restaurants throughout the city. We list those where it is available, often for free (just ask for the password).

Paid wi-fi rates are pretty uniform at R30 per hour; general providers include **Red Button** (www.redbutton.co.za) and **Skyrove** (www.skyrove.com).

Medical Services

Medical services here are of a high standard; make sure you have health insurance and be prepared to pay for services immediately. In an emergency call ☎107 (landlines only), or ☎021-480 7700 if using a mobile phone, for directions to the nearest hospital.

Many doctors make house calls; look under 'Medical' in the phone book or ask at your hotel.

Netcare Christiaan Barnard Memorial Hospital (☎021-480 6111; www.netcare.co.za/139/netcare-christiaan-barnard-memorial-hospital; 181 Longmarket St, City Bowl; 🚌Church/Longmarket) The best private hospital. Reception is on the 8th floor.

Netcare Travel Clinic (☎021-419 3172; www.travelclinic.co.za; 11th fl, Picbal Arcade, 58 Strand St, City Bowl; ⏰8am-4pm Mon-Fri; 🚌Adderley) For vaccinations and travel health advice.

Groote Schuur Hospital (Map p276; ☎021-404 9111; www.westerncape.gov.za/your_gov/163; Main Rd, Observatory; 🚆Observatory) In an emergency, you can go directly to the casualty (emergency) department.

Money

The unit of currency is the rand (R), which is divided into 100 cents (¢). The coins are 5¢, 10¢, 20¢ and 50¢, and R1, R2 and R5. The notes are R10, R20, R50, R100 and R200. Rand is sometimes referred to as 'bucks'.

ATMs

If your card belongs to the worldwide Cirrus network you should have no problem using ATMs in Cape Town. However, it pays to follow some basic procedures to ensure safety:

➡ Avoid ATMs at night and in secluded places. Machines in shopping malls are usually the safest.

➡ Most ATMs in banks have security guards. If there's no guard around when you're withdrawing cash, watch your back, or get someone else to watch it for you.

➡ Watch the people using the ATM ahead of you carefully. If they look suspicious, go to another machine.

➡ Use ATMs during banking hours and, if possible, take a friend. If your card is jammed in a machine then one person should stay at the ATM while the other seeks assistance from the bank.

➡ When you put your card into the ATM press 'cancel' immediately. If the card is returned then you know there is no blockage in the machine and it should be safe to proceed.

➡ Politely refuse any offers of help to complete your transaction. If someone does offer, end your transaction immediately and find another machine.

➡ Carry your bank's emergency phone number, and if you do lose your card report it immediately.

Changing Money

Most banks change cash and travellers cheques in major currencies, with various commissions. You'll also find exchange bureaux at the major shopping malls, including Victoria Mall at the Waterfront.

Tipping

A tip of 10% is standard for most services.

Opening Hours

Exceptions to the following general hours are listed in reviews.

Banks 9am to 3.30pm Monday to Friday, 9am to 11am Saturday.

Post offices 8.30am to 4.30pm Monday to Friday, 8am to noon Saturday.

Shops 8.30am to 5pm Monday to Friday, 8.30am to 1pm Saturday. Major shopping centres, such as the Waterfront and Canal Walk, are open 9am to 9pm daily.

Cafes 7.30am to 5pm Monday to Saturday. Cafes in the City Bowl are open 8am to 3pm on Saturday and closed on Sunday.

Restaurants 11.30am to 3pm and 6pm to 10pm Monday to Saturday.

Post

There are post office branches across Cape Town; see www.sapo.co.za to find the nearest. The post is reliable but can be slow. If you're mailing anything of value, consider using private mail services, such as **Postnet** (www.postnet.co.za), which uses DHL for international deliveries.

Public Holidays

On public holidays government departments, banks, offices, post offices and some museums are closed. Public holidays in South Africa include the following:

New Year's Day 1 January

Human Rights Day 21 March

Easter (Good Friday/Easter Monday) March/April

Family Day 13 April

Constitution Day (Freedom Day) 27 April

Worker's Day 1 May

Youth Day 16 June

Women's Day 9 August

Heritage Day 24 September

Day of Reconciliation 16 December

Christmas Day 25 December

Boxing Day (Day of Goodwill) 26 December

PRACTICALITIES

Newspapers & Magazines

Cape Times (www.iol.co.za/capetimes) Local morning newspaper, Monday to Friday.

Cape Argus (www.iol.co.za/capeargus) Local afternoon newspaper, Monday to Saturday.

Mail & Guardian (www.mg.co.za) National weekly, published Friday; includes excellent investigative and opinion pieces and arts-review supplement.

Cape Etc (www.capetownetc.com) Quarterly listings and features magazine.

Big Issue (www.bigissue.org.za) Monthly magazine that helps provide an income for the homeless; sold at many of Cape Town's busiest traffic intersections.

TV & Radio

South African Broadcasting Corporation (SABC; www.sabc.co.za) National radio and TV channels.

Cape Talk (www.capetalk.co.za) 567 MW; talkback radio.

Fine Music Radio (www.fmr.co.za) 101.3FM; jazz and classical.

KFM (www.kfm.co.za) 94.5FM; pop music.

Good Hope FM (www.goodhopefm.co.za) Between 94 FM and 97FM; pop music.

Heart (www.1049.fm) 104.9FM; pop music, soul, R&B.

Taxi Radio (www.thetaxi.co.za) Woodstock-based internet radio.

Safe Travel

Cape Town is one of the most relaxed cities in Africa, which can instill a false sense of security. People who have travelled overland from Cairo without a single mishap or theft have been known to be cleaned out in Cape Town – generally when doing something like leaving their gear on a beach while they go swimming.

Paranoia is not required, but common sense is. There is tremendous poverty on the peninsula and the 'informal redistribution of wealth' is reasonably common. The townships and suburbs on the Cape Flats have an appalling crime rate and unless you have a trustworthy guide or are on a tour they are not places for a casual stroll.

Always listen to local advice about where to go and not to go. Remember that there is safety in numbers.

Swimming at any of the Cape beaches is potentially hazardous, especially for those inexperienced in the surf. Check for warning signs about rips and rocks, and only swim in patrolled areas. Parents should certainly keep an eye on their kids, bearing in mind the hypothermia-inducing water temperatures!

Taxes & Refunds

Value-added tax (VAT) is 14%. Foreign visitors can reclaim some of their VAT expenses on departure, but this applies only to goods that you are taking out of the country. Also, the goods must have been bought at a shop participating in the VAT foreign tourist sales scheme.

To make a claim, you need your tax invoice. This is usually the receipt, but make sure that it includes the following:

- the words 'tax invoice';
- the seller's name, address and VAT registration number;
- a description of the goods purchased;
- the cost of the goods and the amount of VAT charged;
- a tax invoice number;
- the date of the transaction.

For purchases over R5000, your name and address and the quantity of goods must also appear on the invoice. All invoices must be originals, not photocopies. The total value of the goods claimed for must exceed R250.

At the point of your departure, you will have to show the goods to a customs inspector. At airports make sure you have the goods checked by the inspector before you check in your luggage. After you have gone through immigration, you make the claim. Your refund will be issued either with a rand cheque (which you can cash straight away at the currency-exchange office) or on a Visa electron cash card, which can be used globally.

You can also make your claim at Johannesburg international airport and several border crossing posts – for full details see www.taxrefunds.co.za.

Telephone

South Africa's country code is ☎27 and Cape Town's area code is ☎021, as it also is for Stellenbosch, Paarl and Franschhoek; this must be included even when dialling locally. Sometimes you'll come across phone numbers beginning with ☎0800 for free calls or ☎0860 for calls shared 50/50 between the caller and receiver. Note that it's cheaper to make a call between 7pm and 7am.

Forget about public telephones, which rarely work (if you can even find them).

Mobile Phones

South Africa's mobile-phone networks are all on the GSM digital system. The main three operators are **Vodacom** (www.vodacom.co.za), **MTN** (www.mtn.co.za) and **Cell C** (www.cellc.co.za). Both Vodacom and MTN have desks at Cape Town International Airport, where you can sort out a local prepaid or pay-as-you-go SIM card to use in your phone during your visit. Otherwise you'll find branches of each company across the city, as well as many places where you can buy vouchers to recharge the credit on your phone account. Call charges average about R2.50 per minute.

Time

South African Standard Time is two hours ahead of Greenwich Mean Time (GMT; at noon in London, it's 2pm in Cape Town), seven hours ahead of USA Eastern Standard Time (at noon in New York, it's 7pm in Cape Town) and eight hours behind Australian Eastern Standard Time (at noon in Sydney, it's 4am in Cape Town). There is no daylight-saving time.

Tourist Information

Staff at the head office of **Cape Town Tourism** (Map p280; ☎021-487 6800; www.capetown.travel; Pinnacle Bldg, cnr Burg & Castle Sts, City Bowl; Mid-Long) can book accommodation, tours and car hire, and provide information on national parks and reserves. There are several other branches around town as well.

Blaauwberg Coast Visitor Information Centre (☎021-521 1080; 1 Marine Dr, Table View; 9am-5.30pm Mon-Fri, to 1pm Sat & Sun; Marine Circle)

Muizenberg Visitor Information Centre (Map p290; ☎021-787 9140; The Pavilion, Beach Rd; 8am-5pm Mon-Fri, 9am-1pm Sat & Sun; Muizenberg)

Simon's Town Visitor Information Centre (Map p292; ☎021-786 8440; 111 St George's St; 8am-5pm Mon-Fri, 9am-1pm Sat & Sun; Simon's Town)

V&A Waterfront Visitor Information Centre (Map p280; ☎021-408 7600; Dock Rd; 9am-6pm; Nobel Sq)

Travellers with Disabilities

While sight- or hearing-impaired travellers should have few problems in Cape Town, wheelchair users will generally find travel easier with an able-bodied companion. Very few accommodation places have ramps and wheelchair-friendly bathrooms. It's possible to hire vehicles converted for hand control from many of the major car-hire agencies.

The path around the reservoir in Silvermine is designed to be wheelchair-accessible. **Linx Africa** (www.linx.co.za/trails/lists/disalist.html) has province-by-province listings of trails suitable for people with disabilities.

There are also several South African tour companies specialising in travel packages for travellers with disabilities, including a couple of Cape Town–based operations:

Endeavour Safaris (☎021-556 6114; www.endeavour-safaris.com)

Epic Enabled (☎021-785 7440; www.epic-enabled.com)

Flamingo Adventure Tours & Disabled Ventures (☎082 450 2031, 021-557 4496; www.flamingotours.co.za)

For more tour operators catering for travellers with disabilities, enquire with **Access-Able Travel Source** (www.access-able.com).

For further general information contact **National Council for Persons with Physical Disabilities in South Africa** (☎011-726 8040; www.ncppdsa.org.za).

Visas

Visitors on holiday from most Commonwealth countries (including Australia and the UK), most Western European countries, Japan and the USA don't require visas. Instead, you'll be issued with a free entry permit on arrival, which is valid for a stay of up to 90 days. But if the date of your flight out is sooner than this, the immigration officer may use that as the date of your permit expiry, unless you request otherwise.

From June 2015, new immigration regulations require that all children aged under 18 show an unabridged birth certificate, with additional paperwork needed in some cases. Your airline will likely alert you to these new immigration regulations when you buy your flight. For further information and updates, check www.southafrica.info, www.home-affairs.gov.za, or with your government's travel advisory or your airline.

If you aren't entitled to an entry permit, you'll need to get a visa (also free) before you arrive. These aren't issued at the borders, and must be obtained from a South African embassy or consulate in your own country. Allow several weeks for processing.

For any entry – whether you require a visa or not – you need to have at least two completely blank pages in your passport, excluding the last two pages.

Apply for a visa extension or a re-entry visa at the **Department of Home Affairs** (☎021-468 4500; www.home-affairs.gov.za; 56 Barrack St, City Bowl; ⏲7.30am-4.30pm Mon-Fri, 8.30am-12.30pm Sat; 🚇Lower Buitenkant).

Volunteering

Useful starting points for information are the Cape Town–based **Greater Good SA** (www.myggsa.co.za), with details on many local charities and development projects, and **Uthando South Africa** (www.uthandosa.org/projects), a tour company that supports a vast range of charitable projects. Also recommended is **How 2 Help** (www.h2h.info).

Women Travellers

In most cases, women will be met with warmth and hospitality in Cape Town. However, paternalism and sexism run strong, especially away from the city centre, and these attitudes – much more than physical assault – are likely to be the main problem.

South Africa's sexual assault statistics are appalling. Yet while there have been incidents of female travellers being raped, these cases are relatively rare. It's difficult to quantify the risk of assault – and there is a risk – but it's worth remembering that plenty of women do travel alone safely in South Africa.

Use common sense and caution, especially at night. Don't go out alone in the evenings on foot: always take a taxi. Avoid isolated areas, roadways and beaches during both day and evening hours; avoid hiking alone; and don't hitchhike. Carry a mobile phone if you're driving alone. Talk with local women about what and where is OK, and what isn't.

Transport

ARRIVING IN CAPE TOWN

Most likely you'll arrive at Cape Town International Airport. If coming from within South Africa, it's possible that your arrival point will be Cape Town's combined rail and bus station. The city is also on the international cruise circuit, with liners docking either at the Waterfront or in the docks. Flights, cars and tours can all be booked online at www.lonelyplanet.com/travelservices.

Air

There are many direct international flights into Cape Town. Generally it's cheaper to book and pay for domestic flights within South Africa on the internet (rather than via a local travel agent).

Cape Town International Airport (CPT; ☎021-937 1200; www.airports.co.za) The airport, 22km east of the city centre, has a tourist information office located in the arrivals hall.

Getting into Town

BUS

MyCiTi buses Run every 30 minutes between 4.45am and 10.15pm to the city centre and the Waterfront. A single-trip fare is R75; if you use a 'myconnect' card (which costs a non-refundable R35; see p251), the fare varies between R45.30 and R68.70 – depending on whether you travel in peak or off-peak hours, and use a standard fare or the MyCiTi Mover fares package.

Backpacker Bus (☎082 809 9185; www.backpackerbus.co.za) Book in advance for airport transfers (from R180 per person) and pick-ups from hostels and hotels.

TAXI

Expect to pay around R250 for a nonshared taxi.

CAR

Major car-hire companies have desks at the airport. Driving along the N2 into the city centre from the airport usually takes 15 to 20 minutes, although during rush hours (7am to 9am and 4.30pm to 6.30pm) this can extend up to an hour.

Train

Long-distance trains arrive at Cape Town Train Station on Heerengracht in the City Bowl. There are services Wednesday, Friday and Sunday to and from Johannesburg (Jo'burg) via Kimberley on the **Shosholoza Meyl** (☎086 000 8888; www.shosholozameyl.co.za): these sleeper trains offer comfortable accommodation and dining cars. Other services include the luxurious **Blue Train** (☎021-449 2672; www.bluetrain.co.za) and **Rovos Rail** (☎021-421 4020; www.rovos.com).

Bus

Interstate buses arrive at the bus terminus at Cape Town Train Station, where you'll find the booking offices for the following bus companies, all open from 6am to 6.30pm daily.

Greyhound (Map p268; ☎021-418 4326; www.greyhound.co.za)

Intercape Mainliner (Map p268; ☎0861 287 287; www.intercape.co.za)

Translux (Map p268; ☎0861 589 282, 021-449 6209; www.translux.co.za)

Baz Bus (☎0861 229 287, 021-422 5202; www.bazbus.com) Offers hop-on, hop-off fares and door-to-door service between Cape Town and Jo'burg/Pretoria via Northern Drakensberg, Durban and the Garden Route.

Boat

Many cruise ships pause at Cape Town. Useful contacts:

Cruise Compete (www.cruisecompete.com) Site with an up-to-date list of all cruises visiting Cape Town.

MSC Starlight Cruises (☎0860 114 411; www.msccruises.co.za) South African–based operator.

Royal Mail Ship St Helena (☎+44 020 7575 6480; www.rms-st-helena.com) Sails from the UK via St Helena – the most isolated inhabited island on earth – to Cape Town.

GETTING AROUND CAPE TOWN

Car & Motorcycle

Driving

Cape Town has an excellent road system. The morning and early-evening rush hours are 7am to 9pm and 4.30pm to 6.30pm. Road signs alternate between Afrikaans and English. You'll soon learn, for example, that Linkerbaan isn't the name of a town – it means 'left lane'.

Petrol costs around R12.50 per litre, depending on the octane level you choose. Most petrol stations accept credit cards. An attendant will always fill up your tank for you, clean your windows and ask if the oil or water needs checking – tip them 5% to 10% for the service.

Drive with caution, as Capetonian drivers are inveterate rule breakers. Breath-testing for alcohol exists, but given the lack of police resources and the high blood-alcohol level permitted (0.08%), drunk drivers remain a danger. It's highly unlikely that the police will bother you for petty breaches of the law, such as breaking the speed limit (although you may well end up with a fine if caught on a speed camera).

Buying a Car

Cape Town is a very pleasant place to spend the week or two that it will inevitably take to buy a car or motorbike. Many used-car dealers are clustered along Victoria Rd between Salt River and Observatory and Voortrekker Rd/R102. Online classified ad sites to check include **Junk Mail** (www.junkmail.co.za/cape-town) and **Auto Trader** (www.autotrader.co.za).

A good car costs about R30,000; you'd be lucky to find a decent vehicle for much less than R20,000. You might be thinking of getting a Land Rover, new or old, for a trans-Africa trip; Land Rover expert **Graham Duncan Smith** (☎021-797 3048) charges a consultation fee of R180 for initial inspections and R300 per hour for subsequent mechanical work.

Before buying always ask for a current roadworthy certificate. If needed, these certificates – required when you pay tax for a licence disc, and register the change-of-ownership form – can be obtained from **Dekra** (www.dekraauto.co.za) testing stations in several locations across Cape Town; they charge R340 for a test.

Whoever you're buying a car from, make sure the car's details correspond accurately with those on the ownership (registration) papers; that there is a *current* licence disc on the windscreen and that there's police clearance on the vehicle. The police clearance department can be contacted on ☎021-945 3891.

Register your newly purchased car at the City Treasurer's Department, **Motor Vehicle Registration Division** (☎0860 212 414; Civic Centre, Hertzog Blvd, Foreshore; ⏰8am-3.30pm Mon-Fri; 🚌Civic Centre); bring along the roadworthy certificate, a current licence disc, an accurate ownership certificate, a completed change-of-ownership form (signed by the seller) and a clear photocopy of your ID (passport), along with the original.

Obtaining insurance for third-party damages and damage to or loss of your vehicle is a very good idea.

Hire

CAR

Rates range from R230 per day for a Kia Picanto to around R3000 for a Porsche convertible. It's unlikely you'll need to pay higher rates for unlimited kilometres. For meandering around, 400km a day should be more than enough, and if you plan to stop for a day here and there, 200km a day might be sufficient.

When you're getting quotes make sure that they include value-added tax (VAT), as that 14% slug makes a big difference.

One problem with nearly all car-hire deals is the 'excess', or the amount you are liable for before the insurance takes over. Even with a small car you can be liable for up to at least R6000 (although there's usually the choice of lowering or cancelling the excess for a higher insurance premium). A few companies offer 100% damage and theft insurance at a more expensive rate. You may also be charged extra if you nominate more than one driver. If a non-nominated driver has an accident, then you won't be covered by insurance. Always make sure you read the contract carefully before you sign.

Car-hire companies include the following:

Around About Cars (☎021-422 4022; www.aroundaboutcars.com; 20 Bloem St; ⏰7.30am-7pm Mon-Fri, to 4pm Sat, 8am-1pm Sun; 🚌Upper Long/Upper Loop) Friendly local operation offering one of the best independent deals in town, with rates starting at R230 per day.

Avis (☎021-424 1177; www.avis.co.za; 123 Strand St, City Bowl; ⏰7.30am-6pm

Mon-Fri, 8am-noon Sat & Sun; 🚌Strand)

Hertz (☎021-410 6800; www.hertz.co.za; 40 Loop St, City Bowl; ⏰7am-6pm Mon-Fri, 8am-4pm Sat & Sun; 🚌Strand)

Status Luxury Vehicles (☎021-510 0108; www.slv.co.za) Contact them if you wish to cruise around town in a Bentley or a sporty Porsche Boxter S Cab convertible (R5500 per day).

MOTORCYCLES & SCOOTERS

The following places hire out two-wheeled motors:

Cape Sidecar Adventures (☎021-434 9855; www.sidecars.co.za; 2 Glengariff Rd, Three Anchor Bay; 🚌Ellerslie) Hire a chauffeur to drive you around in one of this company's vintage CJ750s sidecars, manufactured for the Chinese army to pre-WWII BMW specifications. An eight-hour trip costs R3140; two hours is R1570.

Harley Davidson Cape Town (☎021-401 4260; www.harley-davidson-capetown.com; 9 Somerset Rd, De Waterkant; ⏰8.30am-5.30pm Mon-Fri, 8am-2pm Sat; 🚌Alfred)

Scoot Dr (☎021-418-5995; www.scootdr.com; 61 Waterkant St, Foreshore; ⏰8am-5pm Mon-Fri, to 1pm Sat; 🚌Strand) Rents out Vespa and Yamaha scooters.

Parking

Monday to Saturday during business hours there will often be a one-hour limit on parking within the city centre in a particular spot – check with a parking marshal (identified by their luminous yellow vests), who will ask you to pay for the first half-hour up front (around R5).

If there's no official parking marshal you'll almost always find someone on the street to tip a small amount (say, R5) in exchange for looking after your car. Charges for off-street parking vary, but you can usually find it for R10 per hour.

Taxi

Consider taking a nonshared taxi at night or if you're in a group. Rates are about R10 per kilometre. **Uber** (www.uber.com) is very popular and works well.

Excite Taxis (☎021-448 4444; www.excitetaxis.co.za)

Marine Taxi (☎0861 434 0434, 021-447 0329; www.marinetaxis.co.za)

Rikkis (☎0861 745 547; www.rikkis.co.za)

SA Cab (☎0861 172 222; www.sacab.co.za)

Telecab (☎082 222 0282, 021-788 2717) For transfers from Simon's Town to Boulders and Cape Point.

Shared Taxi

In Cape Town (and South Africa in general) a shared taxi means a minibus. These private services, which cover most of the city with an informal network of routes, are a cheap and fast way of getting around. On the downside they're usually crowded and some drivers can be reckless.

The main rank, on the upper deck of Cape Town Train Station, is accessible from a walkway in the Golden Acre Centre or from stairways on Strand St. It's well organised and finding the right rank is easy. Anywhere else, you just hail shared taxis from the side of the road and ask the driver where they're going.

Bus

Golden Arrow

Golden Arrow (☎0800 656 463; www.gabs.co.za) buses run from the **Golden Acre Bus Terminal** (Map p268; Grand Pde), with most services stopping early in the evening. You might find them handy for journeys into the Cape Flats, Northern Suburbs and even as far south as Simon's Town. Fares start from R5.

MyCiTi buses

The **MyCiTi** (☎0800 656 463; www.myciti.org.za) network of commuter buses runs daily between 5am and 10pm, with the most frequent services being between 8am and 5pm. Routes cover the city centre up to Gardens and out to the Waterfront; along the Atlantic seaboard to Camps Bay and Hout Bay; up to Tamboerskloof along Kloof Nek Rd, with a shuttle service to the cableway; Woodstock and Salt River; Khayelitsha; and the airport.

Fares have to be paid with a stored-value 'myconnect' card (a non-refundable R35), which can be purchased from MyCiTi station kiosks and participating retailers. It's also possible to buy single-trip tickets (R30 or R75 to or from the airport). A bank fee of 2.5% of the loaded value (with a minimum of R1.50) will be charged, eg if you load the card with R200 you will have R195 in credit. The card, issued by ABSA (a national bank), can also be used to pay for low-value transactions at shops and businesses displaying the MasterCard sign.

Fares charged depend on the time of day (peak-hour fares are charged from 6.30am to 8.30am and 4pm to 6pm, Monday through Friday) and whether you have pre-loaded the card with the MyCiTi Mover package (amount of between R50 and R1000), which can cut the standard fares by 30%.

For journeys of under 5km (eg from Civic Centre to Gardens or the Waterfront), standard fares are R8.90 at peak times (as above) and R6.80 at all other times; city centre to Table View is peak/off-peak R12.50/9.40; city centre to airport R68.70/65.60; city centre to Hout Bay R12.50/9.40.

Train

Cape Metro Rail (☎0800 656 463; www.capemetrorail.co.za) trains are a handy way to get around, although there are few (or no) trains after 6pm on weekdays and after noon on Saturday.

The difference between MetroPlus (first class) and Metro (economy class) carriages in price and comfort is negligible. The most important line for visitors is the Simon's Town line, which runs through Observatory and around the back of Table Mountain, through upper-income suburbs such as Newlands, and on to Muizenberg and the False Bay coast. These trains run at least every hour from 6am to 9pm and during peak times (6am to 9am and 3pm to 6pm) as often as every 15 minutes.

Metro trains also run out to Strand on the eastern side of False Bay, and into the Winelands to Stellenbosch and Paarl. They are the cheapest and easiest means of transport to these areas; security is best at peak times.

Some MetroPlus/Metro fares are: Observatory R9.50/7, Muizenberg R12.50/8.50, Simon's Town R15.50/9.50, Paarl R18.50/12 and Stellenbosch R18.50/12. A tourist ticket R30 allows unlimited one-day travel between Cape Town and Simon's Town and all stations in between.

Bicycle

If you're prepared for the many hills and long distances between sights, the Cape Peninsula is a terrific place to explore by bicycle. Dedicated cycle lanes are a legacy of the World Cup: there's a good one north out of the city towards Table View, and another runs alongside the Walk of Remembrance from Cape Town Train Station to Green Point. Bear in mind it's nearly 70km from the centre to Cape Point. Unfortunately, bicycles are banned from suburban trains.

Hire

There are numerous places in Cape Town that offer bicycle hire:

Awol Tours (Map p280; ☎021-418 3803; www.awoltours.co.za; Information Centre, Dock Rd, V&A Waterfront; 🚌Nobel Square) Bikes can be rented from R200/300 per half/full day.

Bike & Saddle (☎021-813 6433; www.bikeandsaddle.com)

Cape Town Cycle Hire (☎084 400 1604, 021-434 1270; www.capetowncyclehire.co.za; per day from R250) Delivers and collects bikes free of charge to the City Bowl, and down the Atlantic seaboard to Llandudno.

Downhill Adventures (☎021-422 0388; www.downhilladventures.com; cnr Orange & Kloof Sts, Gardens; ⏰8am-6pm Mon-Fri, to 1pm Sat)

Up Cycles (☎076 135 2223; www.upcycles.co.za; 1hr/half-day/full-day R50/150/200; ⏰8.30am-6.30pm May-Oct, 8am-9pm Nov-Apr) Pick up or drop off bikes at any of three stations: Sea Point Pavilion, Clock Tower Square (at the Waterfront) and Mandela Rhodes Place Hotel (in the City Bowl).

Language

South Africa has 11 official languages: English, Afrikaans, Ndebele, North Sotho, South Sotho, Swati, Tsonga, Tswana, Venda, Xhosa and Zulu. In the Cape Town area only three languages are prominent: Afrikaans, English and Xhosa.

AFRIKAANS

Afrikaans developed from the dialect spoken by the Dutch settlers in South Africa from the 17th century. Until the late 19th century it was considered a Dutch dialect (known as 'Cape Dutch'), and in 1925 it became one of the official languages of South Africa. Today, it's the first language of around six million people. Most Afrikaans speakers also speak English, but this is not always the case in small towns and among older people.

If you read our coloured pronunciation guides as if they were English, you'll be understood. The stressed syllables are in italics. Note that aw is pronounced as in 'law', eu as the 'u' in 'nurse', ew as the 'ee' in 'see' with rounded lips, oh as the 'o' in 'cold', uh as the 'a' in 'ago', kh as the 'ch' in the the Scottish *loch*, r is trilled, and zh is pronounced as the 's' in 'pleasure'.

Basics

Hello.	*Hallo.*	ha·*loh*
Goodbye.	*Totsiens.*	tot·*seens*
Yes./No.	*Ja./Nee.*	yaa/ney
Please.	*Asseblief.*	a·si·*bleef*
Thank you.	*Dankie.*	*dang*·kee
Sorry.	*Jammer.*	*ya*·min

How are you?
Hoe gaan dit? — hu khaan dit

Fine, and you?
Goed dankie, en jy? — khut *dang*·kee en yay

What's your name?
Wat's jou naam? — vats yoh naam

My name is ...
My naam is ... — may naam is ...

Do you speak English?
Praat jy Engels? — praat yay *eng*·ils

I don't understand.
Ek verstaan nie. — ek vir·*staan* nee

WANT MORE?

For in-depth language information and handy phrases, check out Lonely Planet's *Africa Phrasebook*. You'll find it at **shop.lonelyplanet.com**, or you can buy Lonely Planet's iPhone phrasebooks at the Apple App Store.

Accommodation

Where's a ...?	*Waar's 'n ...?*	vaars i ...
campsite	*kampeerplek*	kam·*peyr*·plek
guesthouse	*gastehuis*	*khas*·ti·hays
hotel	*hotel*	hu·*tel*

Do you have a single/double room?
Het jy 'n enkel/ dubbel kamer? — het yay i *eng*·kil/ *di*·bil *kaa*·mir

How much is it per night/person?
Hoeveel kos dit per nag/ persoon? — *hu*·fil kos dit pir nakh/ pir·*soon*

Eating & Drinking

Can you recommend a ...?	*Kan jy 'n ... aanbeveel?*	kan yay i ... *aan*·bi·feyl
bar	*kroeg*	krukh
dish	*gereg*	khi·*rekh*
place to eat	*eetplek*	*eyt*·plek

NUMBERS – AFRIKAANS

1	*een*	eyn
2	*twee*	twey
3	*drie*	dree
4	*vier*	feer
5	*vyf*	fayf
6	*ses*	ses
7	*sewe*	*see*·vi
8	*agt*	akht
9	*nege*	*ney*·khi
10	*tien*	teen

I'd like ..., please.	*Ek wil asseblief ... hê.*	ek vil a·si·*bleef* ... he
a table for two	*'n tafel vir twee*	i *taa*·fil fir twey
that dish	*daardie gereg*	*daar*·dee khi·*rekh*
the bill	*die rekening*	dee *rey*·ki·ning
the menu	*die spyskaart*	dee *spays*·kaart

Emergencies

Help!	*Help!*	help
Call a doctor!	*Kry 'n dokter!*	kray i *dok*·tir
Call the police!	*Kry die polisie!*	kray dee pu·*lee*·see

I'm lost.
Ek is verdwaal. ek is fir·*dwaal*

Where are the toilets?
Waar is die toilette? vaar is dee toy·*le*·ti

I need a doctor.
Ek het 'n dokter nodig. ek het i *dok*·tir *noo*·dikh

Shopping & Services

I'm looking for ...
Ek soek na ... ek suk naa ...

How much is it?
Hoeveel kos dit? *hu*·fil kos dit

What's your lowest price?
Wat is jou laagste prys? vat is yoh *laakh*·sti prays

I want to buy a phonecard.
Ek wil asseblief 'n foonkaart koop. ek vil a·si·*bleef* i *foon*·kaart koop

I'd like to change money.
Ek wil asseblief geld ruil. ek vil a·si·*bleef* khelt rayl

I want to use the internet.
Ek wil asseblief die Internet gebruik. ek vil a·si·*bleef* dee *in*·tir·net khi·*brayk*

Transport & Directions

A ... ticket, please.	*Een ... kaartjie, asseblief.*	eyn ... *kaar*·kee a·si·*bleef*
one-way	*eenrigting*	*eyn*·rikh·ting
return	*retoer*	ri·*tur*

How much is it to ...?
Hoeveel kos dit na ...? *hu*·fil kos dit naa ...

Please take me to (this address).
Neem my asseblief na (hierdie adres). neym may a·si·*bleef* naa (*heer*·dee a·*dres*)

Where's the (nearest) ...?
Waar's die (naaste) ...? vaars dee (*naas*·ti) ...

Can you show me (on the map)?
Kan jy my (op die kaart) wys? kan yay may (op dee kaart) vays

What's the address?
Wat is die adres? vat is dee a·*dres*

XHOSA

Xhosa belongs to Bantu language family, along with Zulu, Swati and Ndebele. It is the most widely distributed indigenous language in South Africa, and is also spoken in the Cape Town area. About six and a half million people speak Xhosa.

In our pronunciation guides, the symbols b', ch', k', p', t' and ts' represent sounds that are 'spat out' (only in case of b' the air is sucked in), a bit like combining them with the sound in the middle of 'uh-oh'. Note also that hl is pronounced as in the Welsh *llewellyn* and dl is like hl but with the vocal cords vibrating. Xhosa has a series of 'click' sounds as well; they are not distinguished in this chapter.

Basics

Hello.	*Molo.*	*maw*·law
Goodbye.	*Usale ngoxolo.*	u·*saa*·le ngaw·*kaw*·law
Yes./No.	*Ewe./Hayi.*	e·*we*/haa·*yee*
Please.	*Cela.*	*ke*·laa
Thank you.	*Enkosi.*	e·*nk'aw*·see
Sorry.	*Uxolo.*	u·*aw*·law
How are you?	*Kunjani?*	k'u·*njaa*·nee

Fine, and you?
Ndiyaphila, unjani wena? ndee·yaa·*pee*·laa u·*njaa*·nee *we*·naa

What's your name?
Ngubani igama lakho? ngu·*b'aa*·nee ee·*gaa*·maa laa·*kaw*

My name is ...
Igama lam ngu ... ee·*gaa*·maa laam ngu ...

Do you speak English?
Uyasithetha isingesi? u·yaa·see·*te*·taa ee·see·*nge*·see

I don't understand.
Andiqondi. aa·ndee·*kaw*·ndee

Accommodation

Where's a ...?	*Iphi i ...?*	ee·*pee* ee ...
campsite	*ibala loku-khempisha*	ee·*b'aa*·laa law·k'u·*ke*·mp'ee·shaa
guesthouse	*indlu yama-ndwendwe*	ee·*ndlu* yaa·maa·*ndwe*·ndwe
hotel	*ihotele*	ee·*haw*·t'e·le

Do you have a single/double room?
Unalo igumbi kanye/kabini? u·*naa*·law ee·*gu*·mb'ee k'aa·*nye*/k'aa·*b'ee*·nee

How much is it per night/person?
Yimalini ubusuku/umntu? yee·*maa*·lee·nee u·*b'u*·su·k'u/*um*·nt'u

Eating & Drinking

Can you recommend a ...?	*Ugakwazi ukukhuthaza ...?*	u·ngaa·*k'waa*·zee u·k'u·*ku*·taa·zaa ...
bar	*ibhari*	ee·*baa*·ree
dish	*isitya*	ee·see·*ty'aa*
place to eat	*indawo yokutya*	ee·*ndaa*·waw yaw·k'u·*ty'aa*

I'd like ..., please.	*Ndiyafuna ...*	ndee·yaa·*fu*·naa ...
a table for two	*itafile yababini*	ee·*t'aa*·fee·le yaa·b'aa·*b'ee*·nee
that dish	*esasitya*	e·*saa*·see·ty'aa
the bill	*inkcukacha ngama-xabiso*	ee·*nku*·k'aa·haa ngaa·maa·*kaa*·b'ee·saw
the menu	*isazisi*	e·saa·*zee*·see

Emergencies

Help!	*Uncedo!*	u·*ne*·daw
I'm lost.	*Ndilahlekile.*	ndee·laa·*hle*·k'ee·le
Call a doctor!	*Biza ugqirha!*	*b'ee*·zaa u·*gee*·khaa

Call the police!
Biza amapolisa! b'ee·zaa aa·maa·*paw*·lee·saa

Where are the toilets?
Ziphi itoylethi? zee·*pee* ee·*taw*·yee·le·tee

I need a doctor.
Ndifuna ugqirha. ndee·*fu*·naa u·*giee*·khaa

Shopping & Services

I'm looking for ...
Ndifuna ... ndee·*fu*·naa ...

How much is it?
Yimalini? yee·*maa*·li·nee

What's your lowest price?
Lithini ixabiso elingezantsi? lee·*tee*·nee ee·*kaa*·b'ee·saw e·lee·nge·*zaa*·nts'ee

I want to buy a phonecard.
Ndifuna uku thenga ikhadi lokufowuna. ndee·*fu*·naa u·*k'u* te·ngaa ee·*kaa*·dee law·k'u·*faw*·wu·naa

I'd like to change money.
Ndingathanda tshintsha imali. ndee·ngaa·*taa*·ndaa *ch'ee*·nch'aa ee·*maa*·lee

I want to use the internet.
Ndifuna uku sebenzisa i intanethi. ndee·*fu*·naa u·*k'u* se·b'e·*nzee*·saa ee ee·*nt'aa*·ne·tee

Transport & Directions

A ... ticket, please.	*Linye ... itikiti nceda.*	lee·*nye* ... ee·*t'ee*·k'ee·t'ee *ne*·daa
one-way	*ndlelanye*	*ndle*·laa·nye
return	*buyela*	b'u·*ye*·laa

How much is it to ...?
Kuxabisa njani u ...? ku·*kaa*·b'ee·saa *njaa*·nee u ...

Please take me to (this address).
Ndicela undise (kule dilesi). ndee·*ke*·laa u·*ndee*·se (k'u·*le dee*·le·see)

Where's the (nearest) ...?
Iphi e(kufutshane) ...? ee·*pee* e·(k'u·*fu*·ch'aa·ne) ...

Can you show me (on the map)?
Ungandibonisa (kwimaphu)? u·ngaa·ndee·*b'aw*·nee·saa (k'wee·*maa*·pu)

What's the address?
Ithini idilesi? ee·*tee*·nee ee·*dee*·le·see

NUMBERS – XHOSA

English numbers are commonly used.

1	*wani*	*waa*·nee
2	*thu*	tu
3	*thri*	tree
4	*fo*	faw
5	*fayifu*	*faa*·yee·fu
6	*siksi*	*seek'*·see
7	*seveni*	se·*ve*·nee
8	*eyithi*	e·*yee*·tee
9	*nayini*	*naa*·yee·nee
10	*teni*	*t'e*·nee

GLOSSARY

ANC – African National Congress

apartheid – literally 'the state of being apart'; the old South African political system in which people were segregated according to race

bobotie – traditional Cape Malay dish of delicate curried mince with a topping of savoury egg custard, usually served on turmeric-flavoured rice

braai – barbecue featuring lots of grilled meat and beer; a South African institution, particularly in poorer areas, where having a communal braai is cheaper than using electricity

bredie – traditional Cape Malay pot stew of vegetables and meat or fish

cafe – in some cases, a pleasant place for a coffee, in others, a small shop selling odds and ends, plus unappetising fried food; also kaffie

coloureds – South Africans of mixed race

DA – Democratic Alliance

farm stall – small roadside shop or shelter that sells farm produce

fynbos – literally 'fine bush'; the vegetation of the area around Cape Town, composed of proteas, heaths and reeds

karamat – tomb of a Muslim saint

kloof – ravine

line fish – catch of the day

mealie – an ear of maize; also see mealie meal and mealie pap

mealie meal – finely ground maize

mealie pap – mealie porridge; the staple diet of rural blacks, often served with stew

Mother City – another name for Cape Town; probably so called because it was South Africa's first colony

NP – old apartheid-era and now defunct National Party

PAC – Pan-African Congress

Pagad – People against Gangsterism and Drugs

rondavel – round hut with a conical roof; frequently seen in holiday resorts

SABC – South African Broadcasting Corporation

sangoma – traditional African healer

shared taxi – relatively cheap form of shared transport, usually a minibus; also known as a black taxi, minibus taxi or long-distance taxi

shebeen – drinking establishment in a township; once illegal, now merely unlicensed

strand – beach

township – black residential district, often on the outskirts of an otherwise middle-class (or mainly white) suburb

venison – if you see this on a menu it's bound to be some form of antelope, usually springbok

VOC – Vereenigde Oost-Indische Compagnie (Dutch East India Company)

Voortrekkers – original Afrikaner settlers of the Orange Free State and Transvaal who migrated from the Cape Colony in the 1830s

Behind the Scenes

SEND US YOUR FEEDBACK

We love to hear from travellers – your comments keep us on our toes and help make our books better. Our well-travelled team reads every word on what you loved or loathed about this book. Although we cannot reply individually to your submissions, we always guarantee that your feedback goes straight to the appropriate authors, in time for the next edition. Each person who sends us information is thanked in the next edition – and the most useful submissions are rewarded with a selection of digital PDF chapters.

Visit **lonelyplanet.com/contact** to submit your updates and suggestions or to ask for help. Our award-winning website also features inspirational travel stories, news and discussions.

Note: We may edit, reproduce and incorporate your comments in Lonely Planet products such as guidebooks, websites and digital products, so let us know if you don't want your comments reproduced or your name acknowledged. For a copy of our privacy policy visit lonelyplanet.com/privacy.

OUR READERS

Many thanks to the travellers who used the last edition and wrote to us with helpful hints, useful advice and interesting anecdotes:
Andreas Ziegler, Christina Jaki, Irene Hollebrandse, Jose Verhelst, Kanji Nakatsu, Marie Frei, Melanie Robertson, Ross Shardlow, Roxy David

AUTHOR THANKS

Simon Richmond

Many thanks to all the people who made my time in Cape Town such a pleasure and continuing education, including: fellow author Lucy and Shawn, Brent Meersman, Iain Harris, Lee Harris, Toni Shina, Nicole Biondi, Alison Foat, Sally Grierson, Patrick Craig, Cathy Marston, Tony Elvin, Rashiq Fataar, Zayd Minty, Daniel Sullivan, Sheryl Ozinsky, Bulelwa Makalima-Ngewana, Juma Mkwela, Gamidah Jacobs, Cindy Taylor, Iain Manley, Marco Morgan and Caroline Jordan.

Lucy Corne

Thanks to Cathy Marston for her encyclopaedic knowledge of every winery in the Western Cape, to Simon for his help and suggestions, as always; to Hakon, Scott, Debbie and James for the tips and to everyone at the various tourist information offices, particularly those in Hermanus, Knysna, Mossel Bay and Robertson. Thanks most of all to Shawn, for coping wonderfully as a single father while I was on the road.

ACKNOWLEDGMENTS

Cover photograph: Muizenberg Beach, Grant Medium Format/Alamy

THIS BOOK

This 8th edition of Lonely Planet's *Cape Town & the Garden Route* guidebook was researched and written by Simon Richmond and Lucy Corne, who also wrote the previous edition. This guidebook was produced by the following:

Destination Editor Matt Phillips

Product Editors Kate James, Amanda Williamson

Senior Cartographer Diana Von Holdt

Book Designer Mazzy Prinsep

Assisting Editors Imogen Bannister, Ali Lemer, Gabrielle Stefanos, Saralinda Turner

Cover Researcher Naomi Parker

Thanks to Karyn Noble, Martine Power, Tony Wheeler, Juan Winata

Index

See also separate subindexes for:

EATING P261
DRINKING & NIGHTLIFE P263
ENTERTAINMENT P263
SHOPPING P263
SPORTS & ACTIVITIES P264
SLEEPING P265

Sights 000
Map Pages **000**
Photo Pages **000**

INDEX K-S

Sights 000
Map Pages **000**
Photo Pages **000**

EATING

Sights 000
Map Pages **000**
Photo Pages **000**

DRINKING & NIGHTLIFE

ENTERTAINMENT

SHOPPING

SPORTS & ACTIVITIES

SLEEPING

Cape Town Maps

Sights
- Beach
- Bird Sanctuary
- Buddhist
- Castle/Palace
- Christian
- Confucian
- Hindu
- Islamic
- Jain
- Jewish
- Monument
- Museum/Gallery/Historic Building
- Ruin
- Shinto
- Sikh
- Taoist
- Winery/Vineyard
- Zoo/Wildlife Sanctuary
- Other Sight

Activities, Courses & Tours
- Bodysurfing
- Diving
- Canoeing/Kayaking
- Course/Tour
- Sento Hot Baths/Onsen
- Skiing
- Snorkelling
- Surfing
- Swimming/Pool
- Walking
- Windsurfing
- Other Activity

Sleeping
- Sleeping
- Camping

Eating
- Eating

Drinking & Nightlife
- Drinking & Nightlife
- Cafe

Entertainment
- Entertainment

Shopping
- Shopping

Information
- Bank
- Embassy/Consulate
- Hospital/Medical
- Internet
- Police
- Post Office
- Telephone
- Toilet
- Tourist Information
- Other Information

Geographic
- Beach
- Hut/Shelter
- Lighthouse
- Lookout
- Mountain/Volcano
- Oasis
- Park
- Pass
- Picnic Area
- Waterfall

Population
- Capital (National)
- Capital (State/Province)
- City/Large Town
- Town/Village

Transport
- Airport
- Border crossing
- Bus
- Cable car/Funicular
- Cycling
- Ferry
- Metro station
- Monorail
- Parking
- Petrol station
- Subway station
- Taxi
- Train station/Railway
- Tram
- Underground station
- Other Transport

Note: Not all symbols displayed above appear on the maps in this book

Routes
- Tollway
- Freeway
- Primary
- Secondary
- Tertiary
- Lane
- Unsealed road
- Road under construction
- Plaza/Mall
- Steps
- Tunnel
- Pedestrian overpass
- Walking Tour
- Walking Tour detour
- Path/Walking Trail

Boundaries
- International
- State/Province
- Disputed
- Regional/Suburb
- Marine Park
- Cliff
- Wall

Hydrography
- River, Creek
- Intermittent River
- Canal
- Water
- Dry/Salt/Intermittent Lake
- Reef

Areas
- Airport/Runway
- Beach/Desert
- Cemetery (Christian)
- Cemetery (Other)
- Glacier
- Mudflat
- Park/Forest
- Sight (Building)
- Sportsground
- Swamp/Mangrove

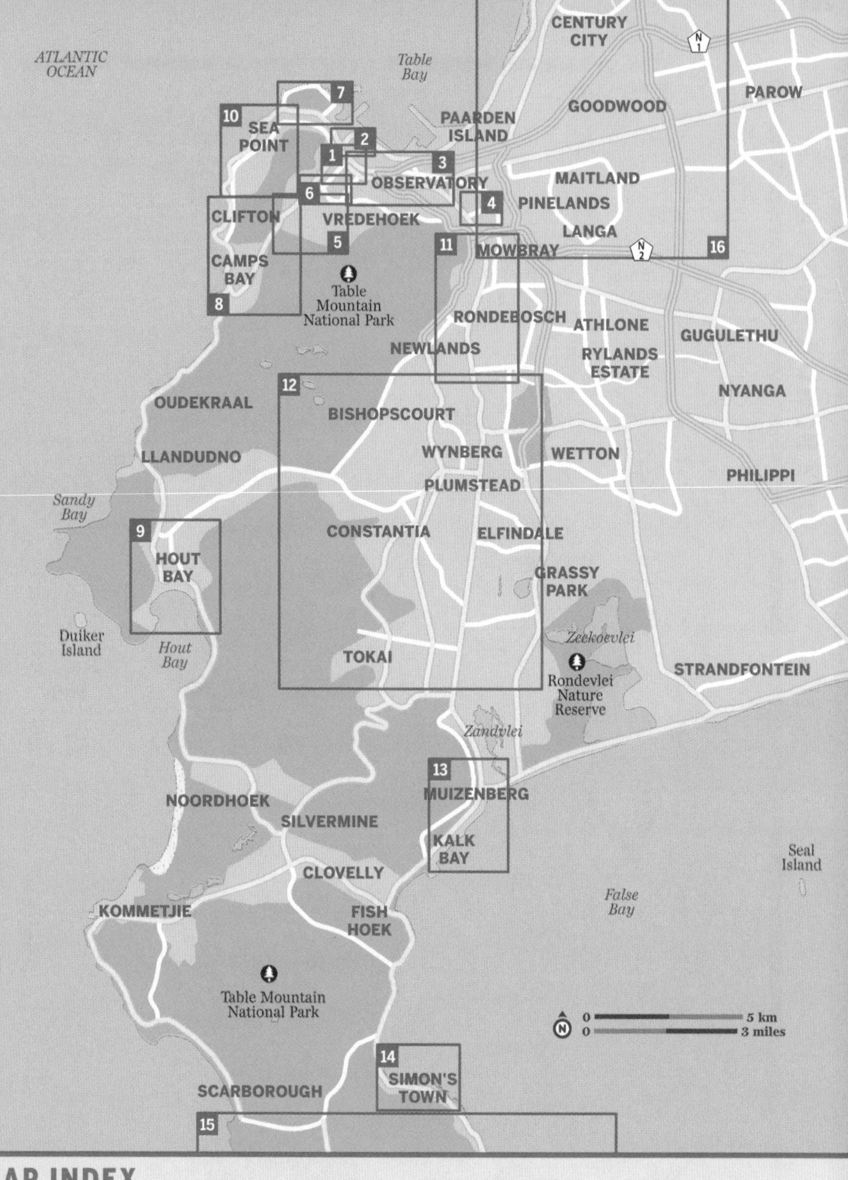
ATLANTIC OCEAN
Table Bay
CENTURY CITY
PAROW
GOODWOOD
PAARDEN ISLAND
SEA POINT
OBSERVATORY
MAITLAND
PINELANDS
LANGA
CLIFTON
VREDEHOEK
MOWBRAY
CAMPS BAY
Table Mountain National Park
RONDEBOSCH
ATHLONE
GUGULETHU
NEWLANDS
RYLANDS ESTATE
NYANGA
OUDEKRAAL
BISHOPSCOURT
WYNBERG
WETTON
LLANDUDNO
PLUMSTEAD
PHILIPPI
Sandy Bay
CONSTANTIA
ELFINDALE
HOUT BAY
GRASSY PARK
Zeekoevlei
Duiker Island
Hout Bay
TOKAI
Rondevlei Nature Reserve
STRANDFONTEIN
Zandvlei
MUIZENBERG
NOORDHOEK
SILVERMINE
KALK BAY
Seal Island
CLOVELLY
False Bay
KOMMETJIE
FISH HOEK
Table Mountain National Park
0 5 km
0 3 miles
SIMON'S TOWN
SCARBOROUGH

MAP INDEX

Key on p270

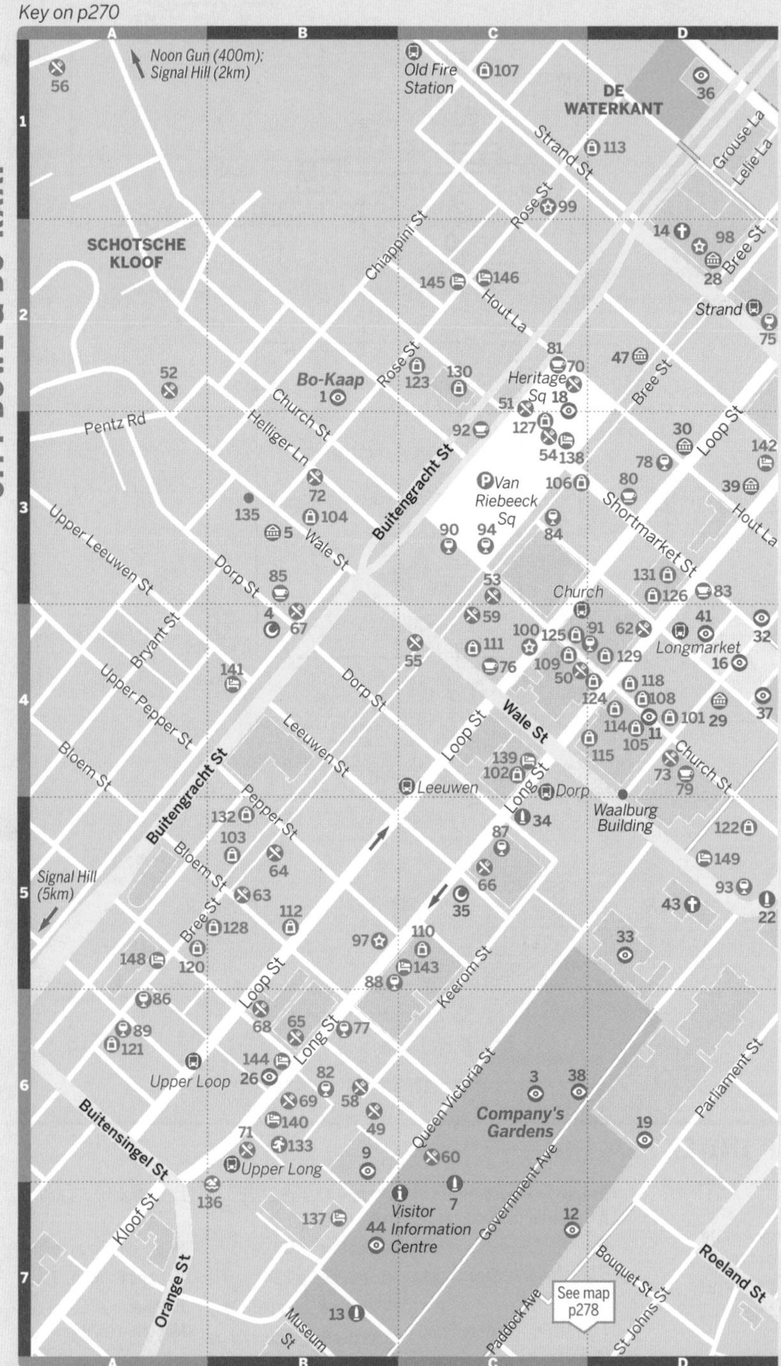

Noon Gun (400m); Signal Hill (2km)
Old Fire Station
DE WATERKANT
SCHOTSCHE KLOOF
Bo-Kaap
Heritage Sq
Van Riebeeck Sq
Church
Longmarket
Leeuwen
Dorp
Waalburg Building
Signal Hill (5km)
Upper Loop
Upper Long
Company's Gardens
Visitor Information Centre
Strand
See map p278
Strand St
Rose St
Chiappini St
Hout La
Grouse La
Lelie La
Bree St
Church St
Helliger Ln
Pentz Rd
Buitengracht St
Loop St
Shortmarket St
Upper Leeuwen St
Dorp St
Wale St
Bryant St
Upper Pepper St
Bloem St
Leeuwen St
Pepper St
Long St
Keerom St
Queen Victoria St
Government Ave
Parliament St
Buitensingel St
Kloof St
Orange St
Museum St
Paddock Ave
Bouquet St
St Johns St
Roeland St

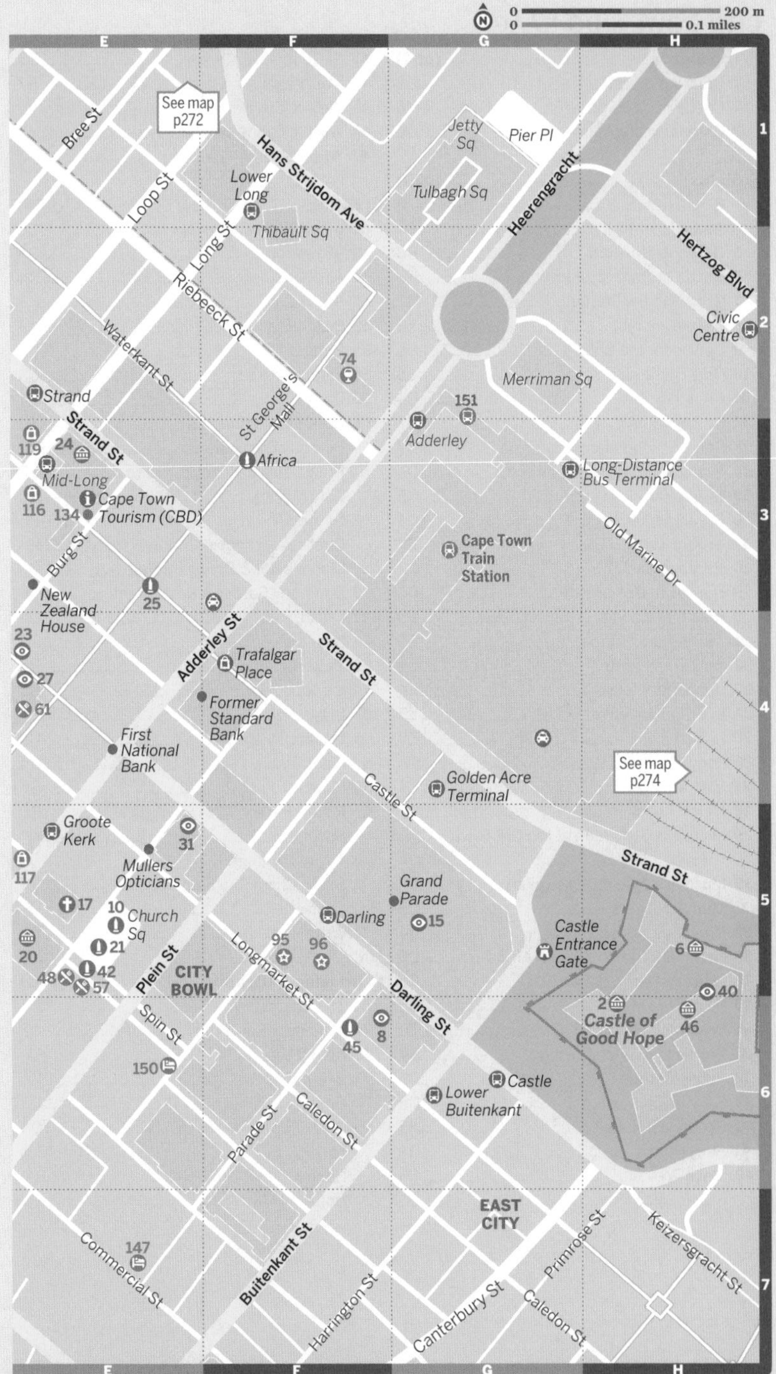

0
200 m
0
0.1 miles
E
F
G
H
1
2
3
4
5
6
7
See map p272
Bree St
Loop St
Lower Long
Hans Strijdom Ave
Thibault Sq
Jetty Sq
Pier Pl
Tulbagh Sq
Heerengracht
Hertzog Blvd
Long St
Riebeeck St
Waterkant St
Civic Centre
74
Merriman Sq
St George's Mall
Strand
Strand St
151
Adderley
119
24
Africa
Long-Distance Bus Terminal
Mid-Long
116
134
Cape Town Tourism (CBD)
Old Marine Dr
Cape Town Train Station
Burg St
New Zealand House
25
Adderley St
23
Trafalgar Place
Strand St
27
61
Former Standard Bank
First National Bank
See map p274
Golden Acre Terminal
Castle St
Groote Kerk
31
Mullers Opticians
117
Strand St
Grand Parade
17
10
Church Sq
Darling
15
21
Castle Entrance Gate
20
95
96
6
48
42
57
Plein St
CITY BOWL
Longmarket St
Darling St
2
40
Castle of Good Hope
46
Spin St
45
8
150
Castle
Lower Buitenkant
Caledon St
Parade St
EAST CITY
Primrose St
Keizersgracht St
Commercial St
147
Buitenkant St
Harrington St
Canterbury St
Caledon St

CITY BOWL & BO-KAAP *Map on p268*

Top Sights (p54)

1 Bo-Kaap B2
2 Castle of Good Hope H6
3 Company's Gardens C6

Sights (p59)

6 Spin St (see 48)
4 Auwal Mosque B4
5 Bo-Kaap Museum B3
6 Castle Military Museum H5
7 Cecil Rhodes Statue C7
8 Central Library F6
9 Centre for the Book B6
10 Church Square E5
11 Church St D4
12 De Tuynhuis C7
13 Delville Wood Memorial B7
14 Evangelical Lutheran Church D2
15 Grand Parade & Around G5
16 Greenmarket Square D4
17 Groote Kerk E5
18 Heritage Square C2
19 Houses of Parliament D6
20 Iziko Slave Lodge E5
21 Jan Hendrik Statue E5
22 Jan Smuts Statue D5
23 Kimberley House E4
24 Koopmans-de Wet House E3
25 Krotoa Place E3
26 Long Street B6
27 Market House E4
28 Martin Melck House D2
29 Michaelis Collection at the Old Town House D4
30 Museum of Gems & Jewellery D3
31 Mutual Heights E5
32 Namaqua House D4
33 National Library of South Africa D5
34 Open House C5
35 Palm Tree Mosque C5
36 Prestwich Memorial D1
37 Protea Insurance Building D4
38 Public Garden C6
39 SA Mission Museum D3
40 Secunde's House H5
41 Shell House D4
42 Slave Tree E5
Slavery Memorial (see 21)
43 St George's Cathedral D5
44 VOC Vegetable Garden B7
45 We Are Still Here F6
46 William Fehr Collection H6
47 Youngblood Africa D2

Eating (p66)

48 6 Spin St Restaurant E5
49 95 Keerom B6
50 Addis in Cape C4
51 Africa Café C2
52 Biesmiellah A2
53 Birds Café C3
54 Bistro Bizerca C3
55 Bocca C4
56 Bo-Kaap Kombuis A1
Bombay Brasserie (see 149)
57 Bread, Milk & Honey E5
Café Mozart (see 114)
58 Carne SA B6
Chef's Warehouse & Canteen (see 138)
59 Clarke's Bar & Dining Room C4
60 Company Garden's Restaurant C6
61 Crush E4
62 Dear Me D4
63 Jason Bakery B5
64 Latitude 33 B5
65 Lola's B6
66 Masala Dosa C5
67 Plant B4
68 Plant B6
69 Royale Eatery B6
Sababa (see 121)
70 Savoy Cabbage C2
71 South China Dim Sum Bar B6
72 Spasie B3
73 Woza! D4

Drinking & Nightlife (p70)

74 31 F2
75 Alexander Bar & Café D2
76 Bean There C4
77 Beerhouse B6
78 Coco D3
79 Deluxe Coffeeworks D4
Fork (see 126)
Honest Chocolate Cafe (see 111)
80 House of Machines D3

Entertainment **(p74)**

Shopping **(p75)**

Sports & Activities **(p79)**

Sleeping **(p201)**

Transport **(p249)**

Sights (p64)
1 Prestwich Memorial Garden......B4

Eating (p66)
2 Anatoli......B2
3 Beefcakes......A2
4 Borage Bistro......D3
5 Gold......B1
6 Hemelhuijs......B4
7 Izakaya Matsuri......B2
8 La Petite Tarte......A3
9 Loading Bay......A4

Drinking & Nightlife (p70)
10 Amsterdam Action Bar & Backstage......B2
11 Bar Code......B2
12 Beaulah......B2
13 Cafe Manhattan......A3
14 Crew Bar......B2
15 Fireman's Arms......C3
16 Hard Pressed Cafe......D3
17 Origin......A3
18 Truth......B4

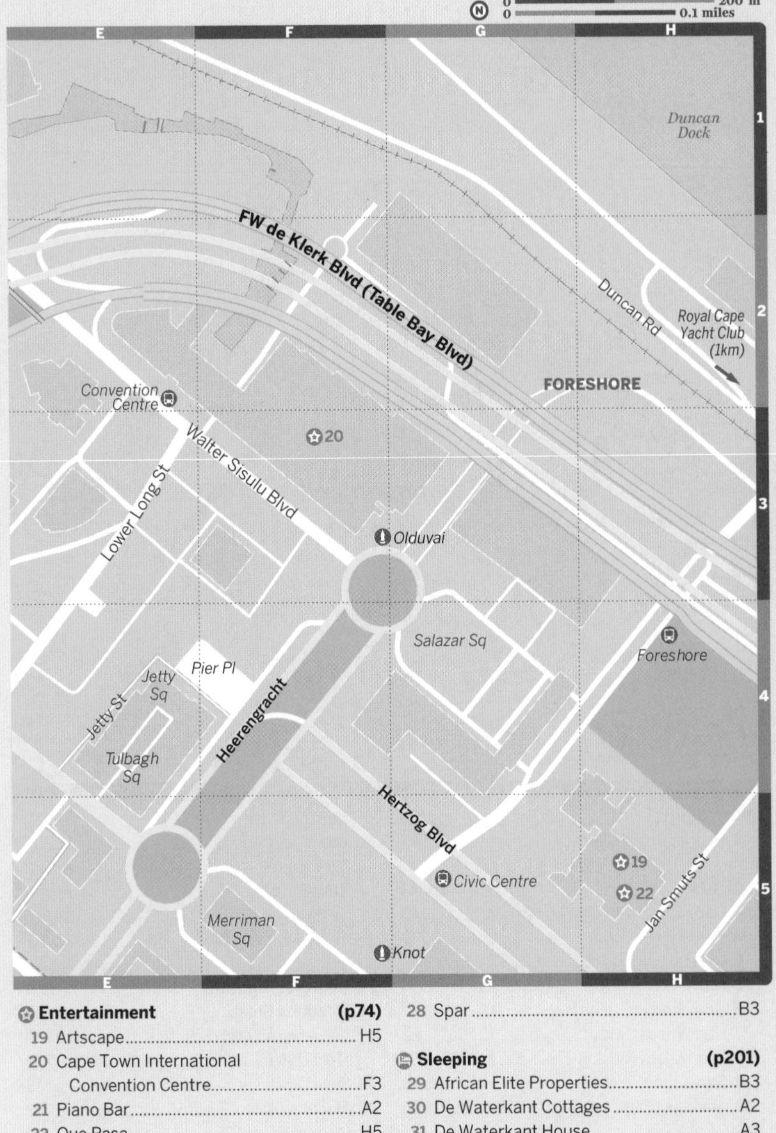

Entertainment (p74)
19 Artscape H5
20 Cape Town International Convention Centre F3
21 Piano Bar A2
22 Que Pasa H5

Shopping (p78)
23 Africa Nova A3
24 Baraka A3
25 Big Blue A1
26 Cape Quarter B3
27 Klûk & CGDT C5
28 Spar B3

Sleeping (p201)
29 African Elite Properties B3
30 De Waterkant Cottages A2
31 De Waterkant House A3
32 De Waterkant Lodge A3
33 Purple House A2
34 The Charles A3
35 Victoria Junction A1
36 Village & Life A3
37 Village Lodge A2

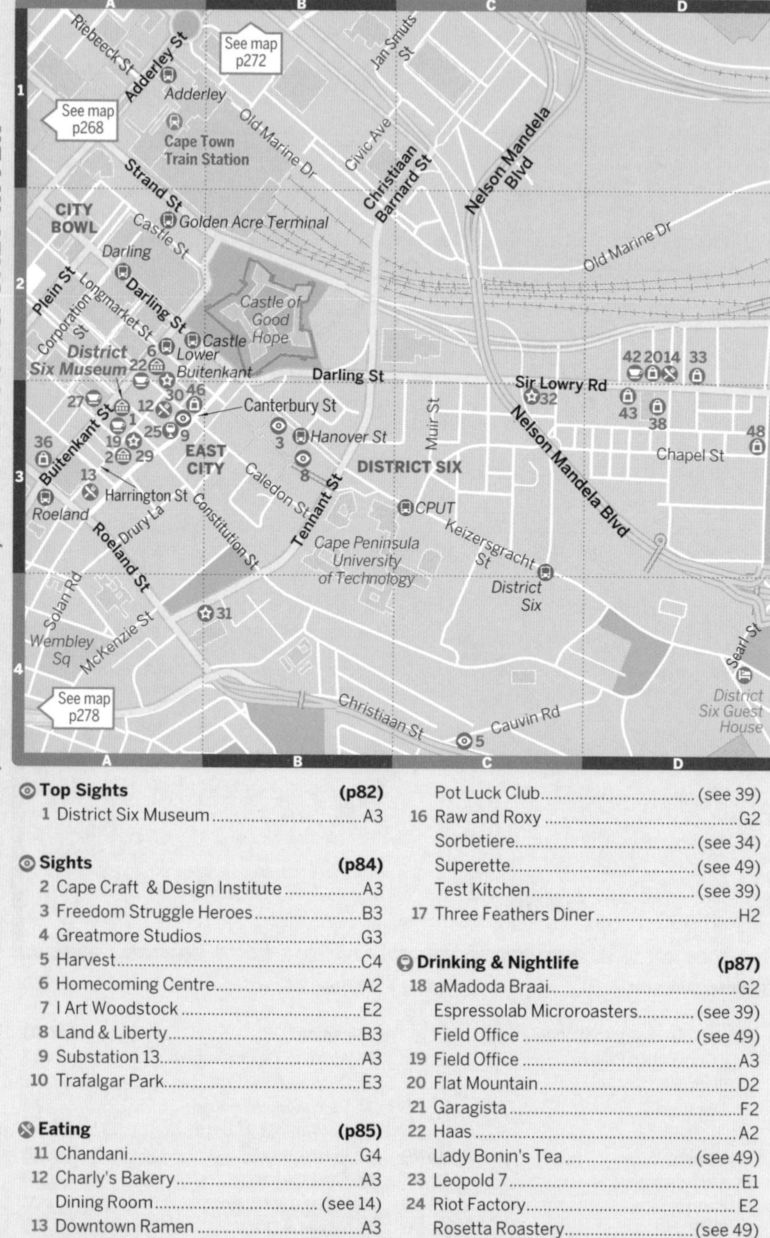

Top Sights (p82)

1 District Six Museum A3

Sights (p84)

2 Cape Craft & Design Institute A3
3 Freedom Struggle Heroes B3
4 Greatmore Studios G3
5 Harvest C4
6 Homecoming Centre A2
7 I Art Woodstock E2
8 Land & Liberty B3
9 Substation 13 .... A3
10 Trafalgar Park E3

Eating (p85)

11 Chandani G4
12 Charly's Bakery A3
Dining Room .... (see 14)
13 Downtown Ramen A3
14 Kitchen D2
Lefty's .... (see 13)
Ocean Jewels .... (see 49)
15 Pesce Azzurro G4
Pot Luck Club .... (see 39)
16 Raw and Roxy G2
Sorbetiere .... (see 34)
Superette .... (see 49)
Test Kitchen .... (see 39)
17 Three Feathers Diner H2

Drinking & Nightlife (p87)

18 aMadoda Braai G2
Espressolab Microroasters .... (see 39)
Field Office .... (see 49)
19 Field Office A3
20 Flat Mountain D2
21 Garagista F2
22 Haas A2
Lady Bonin's Tea .... (see 49)
23 Leopold 7 .... E1
24 Riot Factory E2
Rosetta Roastery .... (see 49)
25 Sugarhut A3
26 Taproom H4
Tribe Woodstock .... (see 50)
27 Truth A3

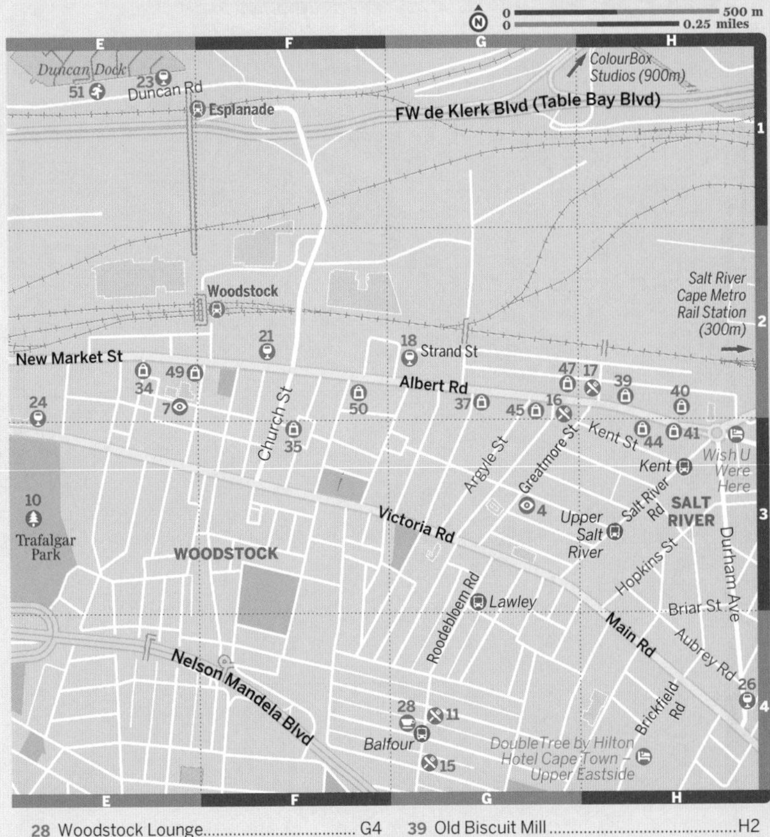

Duncan Dock
51
23
Duncan Rd
Esplanade
FW de Klerk Blvd (Table Bay Blvd)
ColourBox Studios (900m)
Woodstock
Salt River Cape Metro Rail Station (300m)
21
18
Strand St
New Market St
49
34
Albert Rd
47
17
39
40
24
7
50
37
45
16
Church St
35
Kent St
44
41
Wish U Were Here
Kent
Argyle St
Greatmore St
10
Trafalgar Park
4
Upper Salt River
Salt River Rd
SALT RIVER
Victoria Rd
WOODSTOCK
Hopkins St
Durham Ave
Roodebloem Rd
Lawley
Briar St
Main Rd
Aubrey Rd
26
Nelson Mandela Blvd
Brickfield Rd
28
11
Balfour
15
DoubleTree by Hilton Hotel Cape Town – Upper Eastside

OBSERVATORY

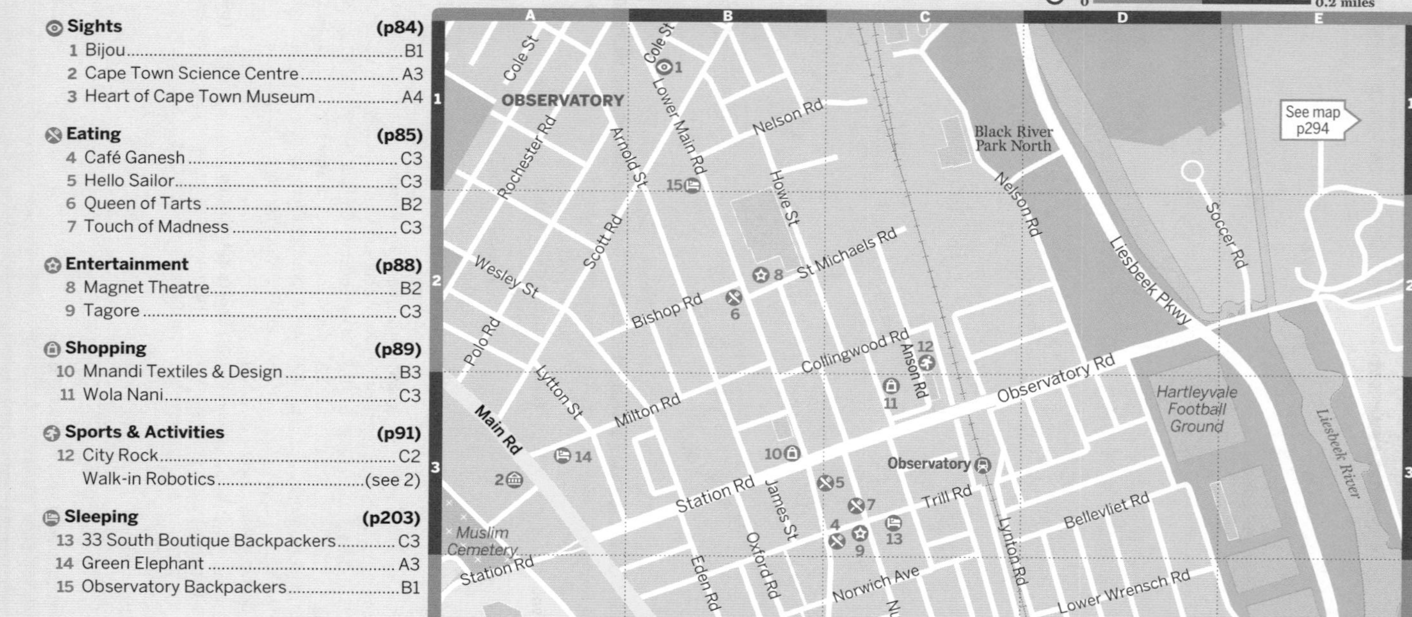

Sights (p84)

1 Bijou B1
2 Cape Town Science Centre A3
3 Heart of Cape Town Museum A4

Eating (p85)

4 Café Ganesh C3
5 Hello Sailor C3
6 Queen of Tarts B2
7 Touch of Madness C3

Entertainment (p88)

8 Magnet Theatre B2
9 Tagore C3

Shopping (p89)

10 Mnandi Textiles & Design B3
11 Wola Nani C3

Sports & Activities (p91)

12 City Rock C2
Walk-in Robotics .... (see 2)

Sleeping (p203)

13 33 South Boutique Backpackers C3
14 Green Elephant A3
15 Observatory Backpackers B1

HIGGOVALE, ORANJEZICHT & UPPER TAMBOERSKLOOF

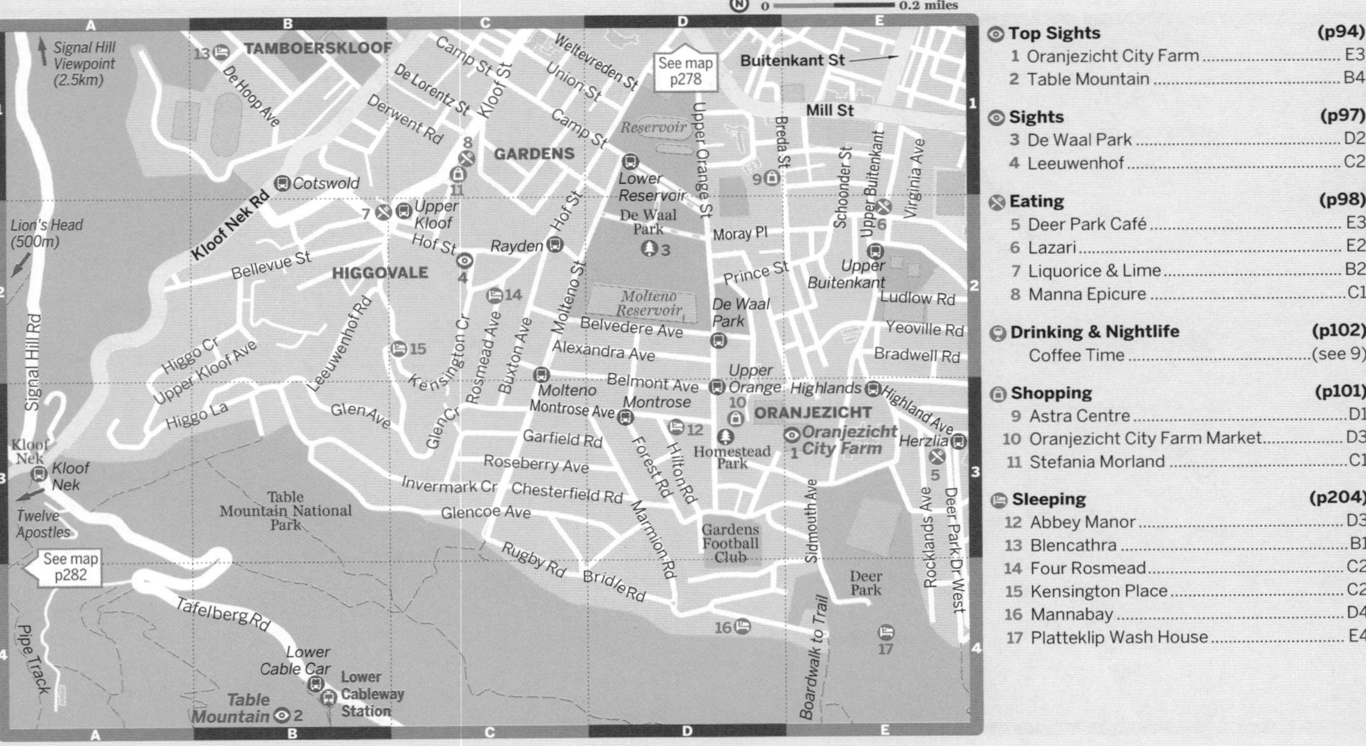

Top Sights (p94)
1 Oranjezicht City Farm E3
2 Table Mountain B4

Sights (p97)
3 De Waal Park D2
4 Leeuwenhof C2

Eating (p98)
5 Deer Park Café E3
6 Lazari E2
7 Liquorice & Lime B2
8 Manna Epicure C1

Drinking & Nightlife (p102)
Coffee Time .... (see 9)

Shopping (p101)
9 Astra Centre D1
10 Oranjezicht City Farm Market D3
11 Stefania Morland C1

Sleeping (p204)
12 Abbey Manor D3
13 Blencathra B1
14 Four Rosmead C2
15 Kensington Place C2
16 Mannabay D4
17 Platteklip Wash House E4

GARDENS & TAMBOERSKLOOF

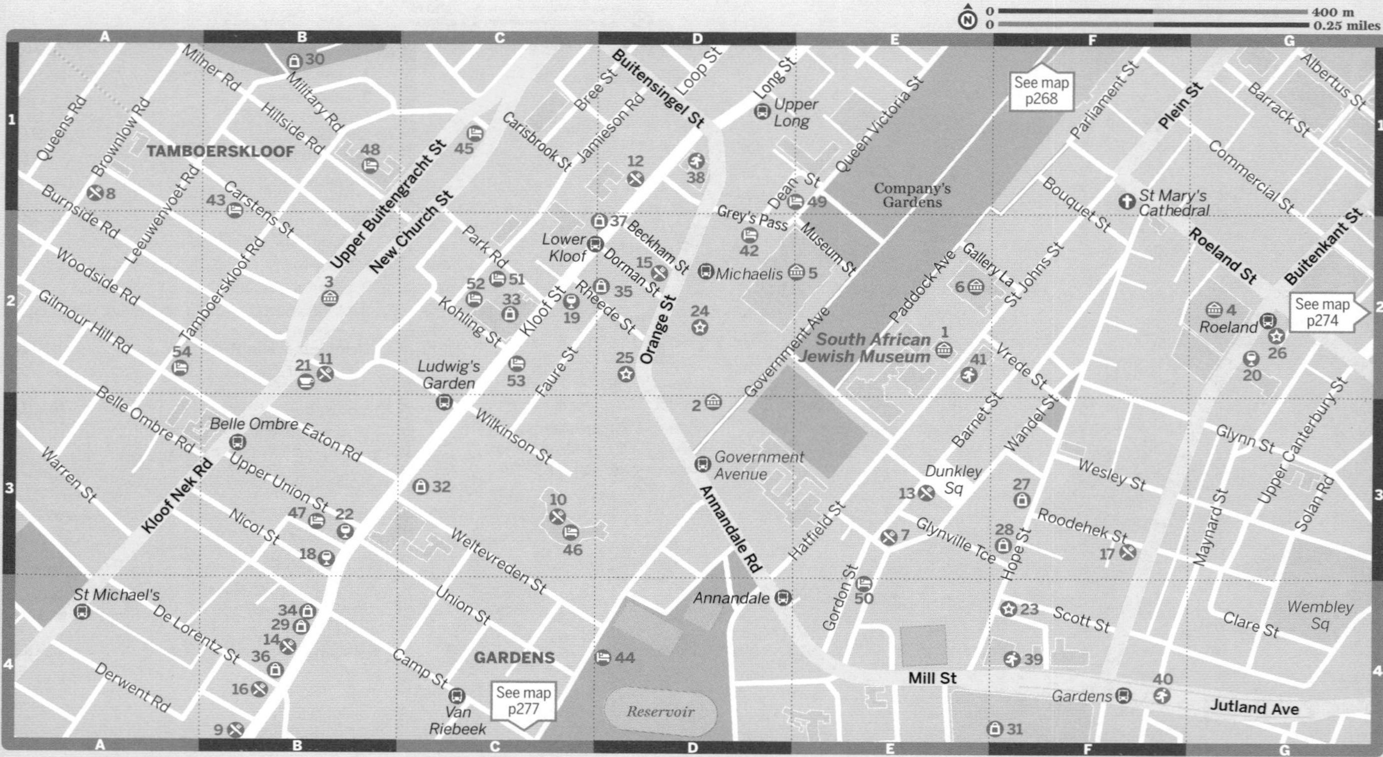

GARDENS & TAMBOERSKLOOF

Top Sights **(p96)**
1 South African Jewish Museum E2

Sights **(p97)**
2 Bertram House D3
3 New Church Museum B2
4 Rust en Vreugd G2
5 South African Museum E2
6 South African National Gallery E2
South African Planetarium ...... (see 5)

Eating **(p98)**
7 Aubergine E3
8 Blue Cafe A1
9 Cafe Paradiso B4
Café Riteve ...... (see 1)
10 Chef's Table C3
Ferdinando's ...... (see 29)
11 Hallellujah B2
12 Kloof St House D1
Kyoto Garden Sushi ...... (see 11)
13 Maria's E3
14 Melissa's B4
15 Societi Bistro D2
16 Tamboers Winkel B4
17 Yard F3

Drinking & Nightlife **(p100)**
18 Asoka B3
Blah Blah Bar ...... (see 34)
19 Chalk & Cork C2
Deluxe Coffeeworks ...... (see 17)
20 Perseverance Tavern G2
21 Power & the Glory/Black Ram B2
22 Van Hunks B3
Yours Truly ...... (see 53)

Entertainment **(p101)**
23 Auslese F4
24 Intimate Theatre D2
25 Labia D2
26 Straight No Chaser G2

Shopping **(p101)**
73 On Kloof ...... (see 53)
Bluecollarwhitecollar ...... (see 33)
27 City Bowl Market F3
28 Coffeebeans Routes F3
29 Erdmann Contemporary & Photographers Gallery B4
30 Erf 81 Food Market B1
31 Gardens Centre F4
32 KIN C3
33 Lifestyles on Kloof C2
34 LIM B4
35 Mabu Vinyl D2
36 Mr & Mrs B4
37 Unknown Union D2
Wine Concepts ...... (see 33)

Sports & Activities **(p103)**
Coffeebeans Routes ...... (see 28)
38 Downhill Adventures D1
39 Enmasse F4
40 Mill St Bridge Skate Park F4
41 Mountain Club of South Africa E2

Sleeping **(p203)**
42 15 on Orange D2
43 An African Villa B1
44 Ashanti Gardens D4
45 Backpack C1
46 Belmond Mount Nelson Hotel C3
47 Cape Cadogan B3
48 Cape Milner B1
49 Cape Town Hollow E1
50 Dunkley House E4
51 Hippo Boutique Hotel C2
52 La Grenadine C2
53 Once in Cape Town C2
54 Trevoyan A2

GREEN POINT & WATERFRONT

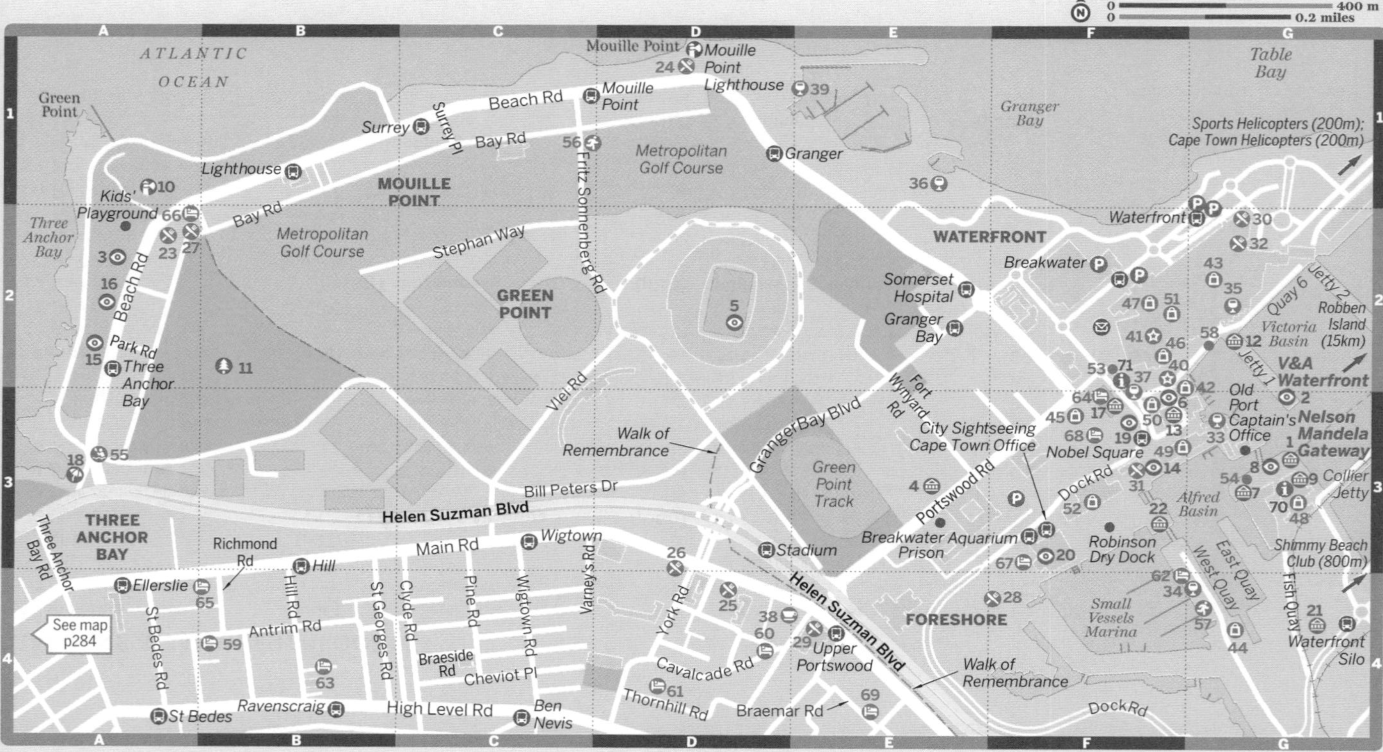

GREEN POINT & WATERFRONT

Top Sights (p106)
1 Nelson Mandela Gateway G3
2 V&A Waterfront G3

Sights (p110)
3 Blue Train A2
4 Cape Medical Museum E3
5 Cape Town Stadium D2
6 Cape Wheel F3
7 Chavonnes Battery Museum G3
8 Clock Tower G3
9 Diamond Museum G3
10 Green Point Lighthouse A1
11 Green Point Urban Park B2
12 Jetty 1 ..... G2
13 Maritime Centre F3
14 Nobel Square F3
15 Putt-Putt Golf A2
16 Serendipity Maze A2
17 The Springbok Experience F3
18 Three Anchor Bay A3
19 Time Ball Tower F3
20 Two Oceans Aquarium F3
21 Zeitz MOCAA Museum G4
22 Zeitz MOCAA Pavilion F3

Eating (p110)
23 Café Neo A2
24 Cape Town Hotel School D1
25 El Burro D4
26 Giovanni's Deli World D3
Harbour House ..... (see 42)
27 Newport Market & Deli A2
28 Nobu F4
29 Nü E4
30 Tasha's G2
31 V&A Market on the Wharf F3
32 Willoughby & Co G2

Drinking & Nightlife (p112)
33 Alba Lounge G3
34 Bascule G4
35 Belthazar G2
36 Grand Café & Beach E1
37 Mitchell's Scottish Ale House & Brewery F3
38 Shift D4
Sotano ..... (see 66)
39 Tobago's Bar & Terrace E1
Vista Bar ..... (see 28)

Entertainment (p113)
Galileo Open Air Cinema ..... (see 64)
Jou Ma Se Comedy Club ..... (see 31)
40 Market Square Amphitheatre F2
41 Nu Metro F2

Shopping (p113)
42 Cape Union Mart Adventure Centre F2
43 Carrol Boyes G2
44 Donald Greig Gallery & Foundry ... G4
45 Everard Read F3
KIN ..... (see 49)
46 Naartjie F2
47 Rain F2
48 Shimansky G3
49 Solveig F3
50 Vaughan Johnson's Wine & Cigar Shop F3
51 Victoria Wharf F2
52 Watershed F3

Sports & Activities (p114)
53 Awol Tours F2
54 Historical Walking Tour G3
55 Kaskazi Kayaks A3
56 Metropolitan Golf Club C1
57 Ocean Sailing Academy G4
Table Bay Diving ..... (see 58)
Two Oceans Aquarium ..... (see 20)
58 Waterfront Charters G2
Yacoob Tourism ..... (see 58)

Sleeping (p205)
59 Ashanti Green Point B4
60 Atlantic Point Backpackers D4
61 B.I.G. Backpackers D4
62 Cape Grace F4
63 Cape Standard B4
64 Dock House F3
65 Head South Lodge B4
66 La Splendida A2
67 One & Only Cape Town F3
68 Queen Victoria Hotel F3
69 Villa Zest E4

Information (p247)
70 Cape Town Tourism G3
71 Information Centre F2
V&A Waterfront Visitor Information Centre ..... (see 37)

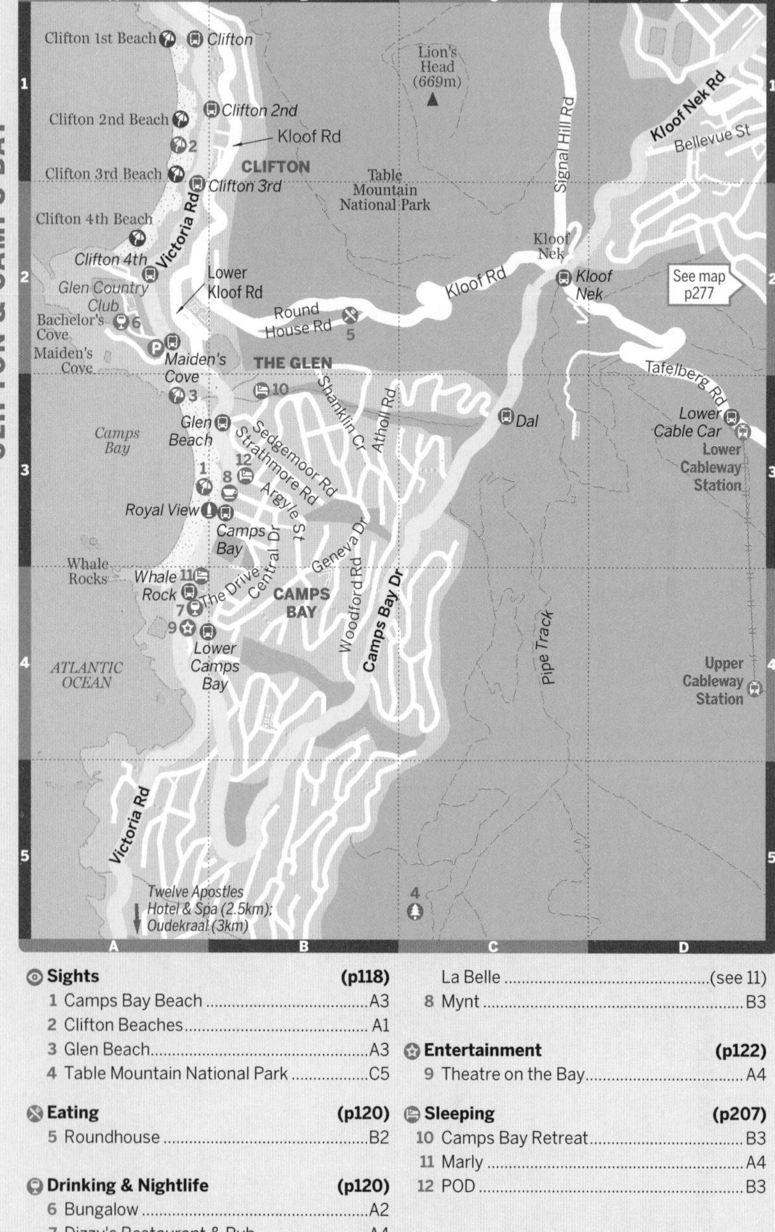

Sights (p118)

1 Camps Bay Beach A3
2 Clifton Beaches A1
3 Glen Beach A3
4 Table Mountain National Park C5

Eating (p120)

5 Roundhouse B2

Drinking & Nightlife (p120)

6 Bungalow A2
7 Dizzy's Restaurant & Pub A4
La Belle .... (see 11)
8 Mynt B3

Entertainment (p122)

9 Theatre on the Bay A4

Sleeping (p207)

10 Camps Bay Retreat B3
11 Marly A4
12 POD B3

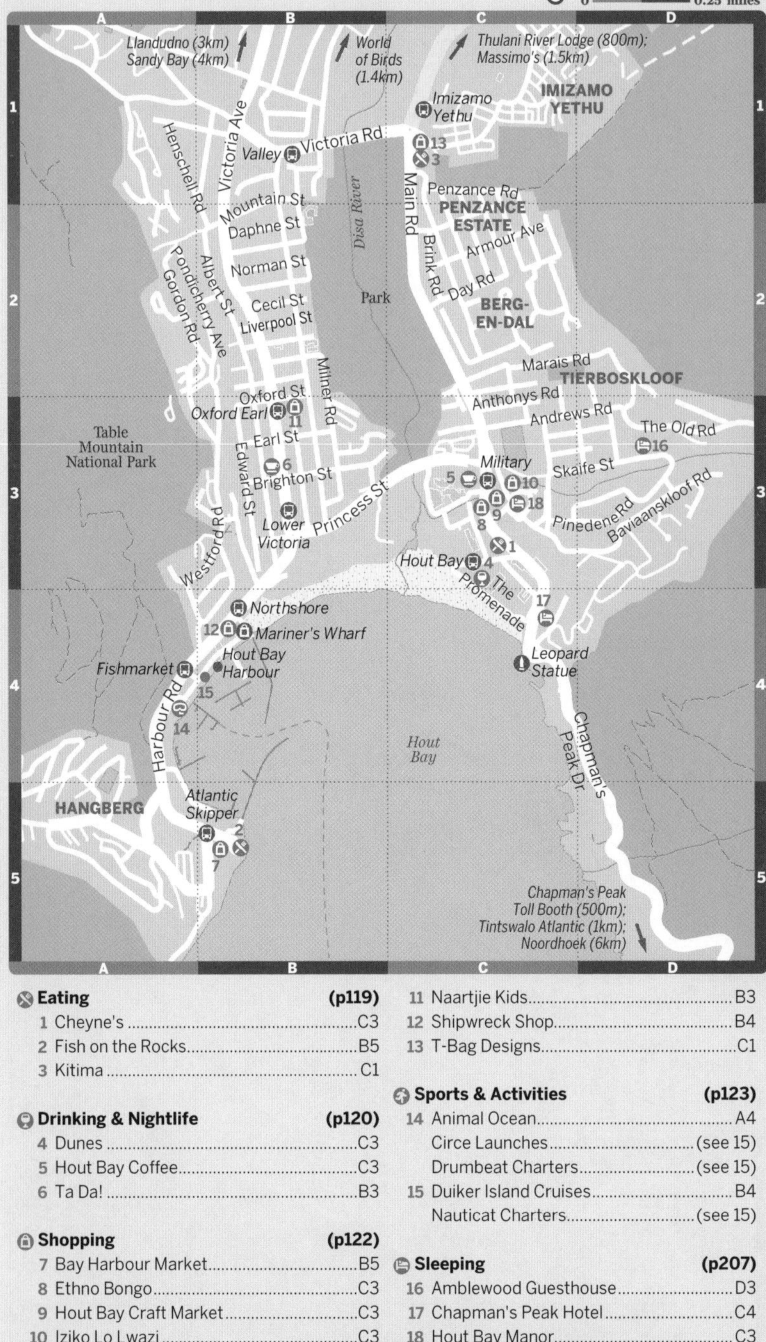

Eating (p119)

1 Cheyne's C3
2 Fish on the Rocks B5
3 Kitima C1

Drinking & Nightlife (p120)

4 Dunes C3
5 Hout Bay Coffee C3
6 Ta Da! B3

Shopping (p122)

7 Bay Harbour Market B5
8 Ethno Bongo C3
9 Hout Bay Craft Market C3
10 Iziko Lo Lwazi C3
11 Naartjie Kids B3
12 Shipwreck Shop B4
13 T-Bag Designs C1

Sports & Activities (p123)

14 Animal Ocean A4
Circe Launches .... (see 15)
Drumbeat Charters .... (see 15)
15 Duiker Island Cruises B4
Nauticat Charters .... (see 15)

Sleeping (p207)

16 Amblewood Guesthouse D3
17 Chapman's Peak Hotel C4
18 Hout Bay Manor C3

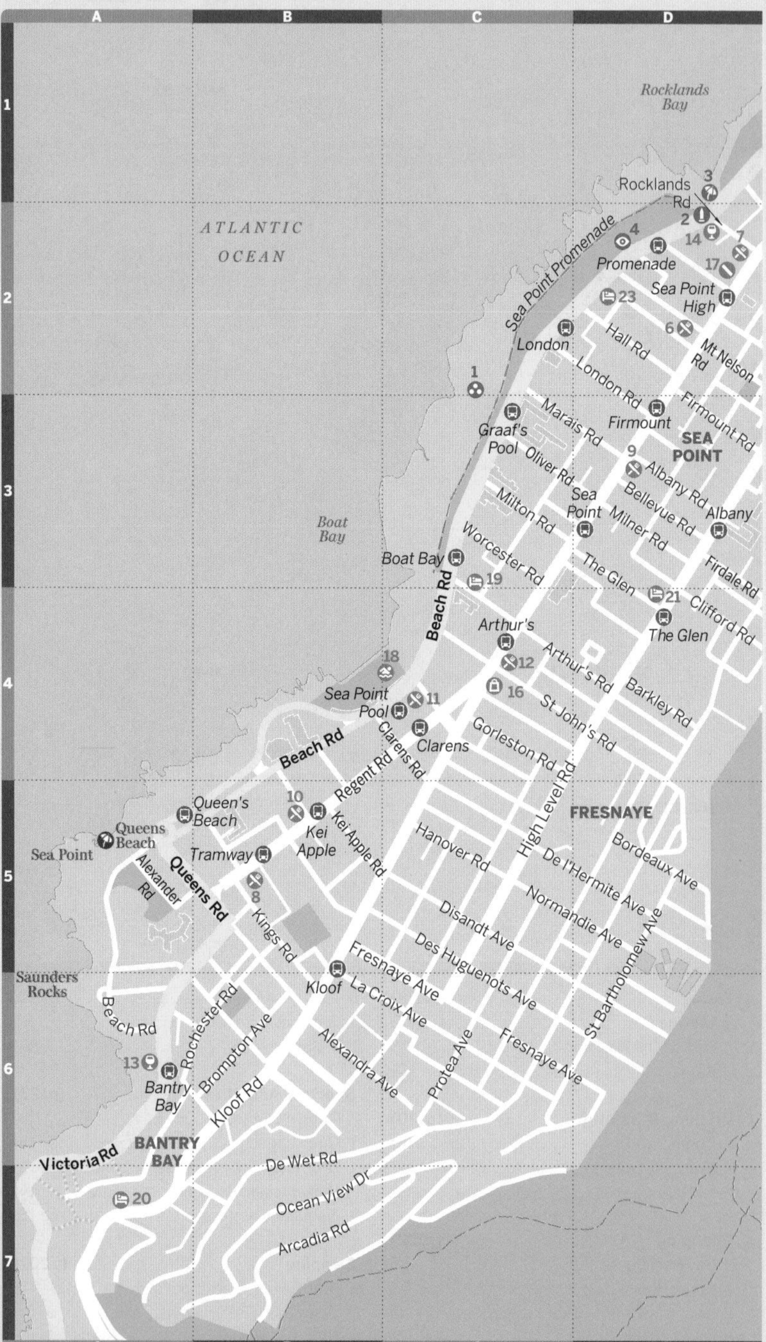

ATLANTIC OCEAN
Rocklands Bay
Boat Bay
Rocklands Rd
Sea Point Promenade
Promenade
Sea Point High
London
Hall Rd
Mt Nelson Rd
London Rd
Firmount
Firmount Rd
Graaf's Pool
Marais Rd
SEA POINT
Oliver Rd
Albany Rd
Sea Point
Milton Rd
Bellevue Rd
Albany
Milner Rd
Worcester Rd
Boat Bay
The Glen
Firdale Rd
Beach Rd
Clifford Rd
Arthur's
The Glen
Arthur's Rd
Sea Point Pool
Barkley Rd
St John's Rd
Clarens Rd
Clarens
Gorleston Rd
Beach Rd
Regent Rd
High Level Rd
FRESNAYE
Queen's Beach
Queens Beach
Kei Apple
Kei Apple Rd
Sea Point
Tramway
Hanover Rd
De l'Hermite Ave
Bordeaux Ave
Alexander Rd
Queens Rd
Normandie Ave
Kings Rd
Disandt Ave
Des Huguenots Ave
Fresnaye Ave
Saunders Rocks
Kloof
La Croix Ave
St Bartholomew Ave
Beach Rd
Rochester Rd
Brompton Ave
Alexandra Ave
Protea Ave
Fresnaye Ave
Bantry Bay
Kloof Rd
BANTRY BAY
Victoria Rd
De Wet Rd
Ocean View Dr
Arcadia Rd

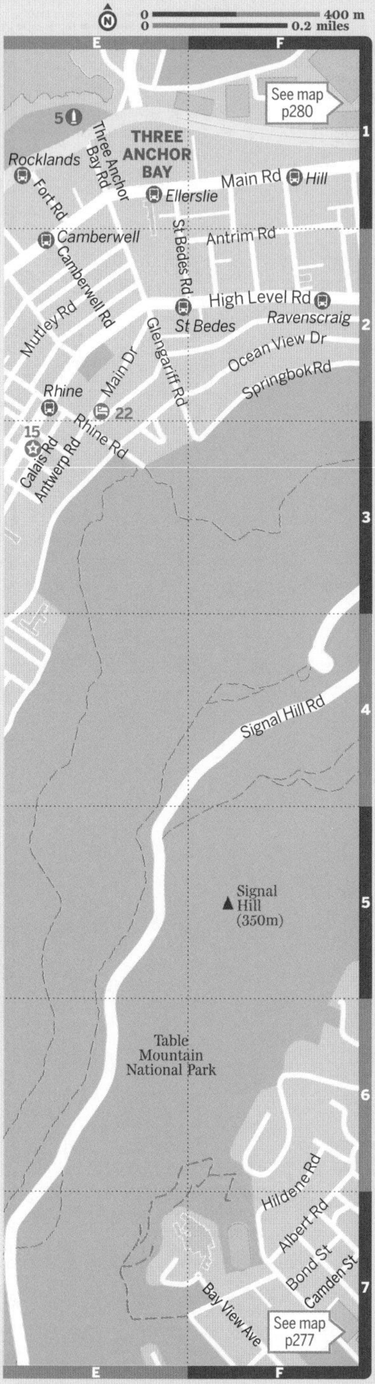

Sights (p118)

1 Graaff's Pool ... C2
2 Promenade Pets ... D2
3 Rocklands Beach ... D1
4 Sea Point Promenade ... D2
5 White Horses ... E1

Eating (p119)

6 Duchess of Wisbeach ... D2
Harvey's ... (see 23)
7 Hesheng ... D2
8 Kleinsky's Delicatessen ... B5
9 La Boheme ... D3
10 La Mouette ... B5
11 La Perla ... C4
12 Nü ... C4

Drinking & Nightlife (p120)

13 Koi Restaurant & Vodka Bar ... A6
14 La Vie ... D2

Entertainment (p122)

15 Studio 7 ... E3

Shopping (p122)

16 Peach ... C4

Sports & Activities (p123)

17 Into the Blue ... D2
18 Sea Point Pavilion ... C4

Sleeping (p206)

19 Cascades on the Promenade ... C3
20 Ellerman House ... A7
21 Glen Boutique Hotel ... D4
22 Huijs Haerlem ... E2
23 Winchester Mansions Hotel ... D2

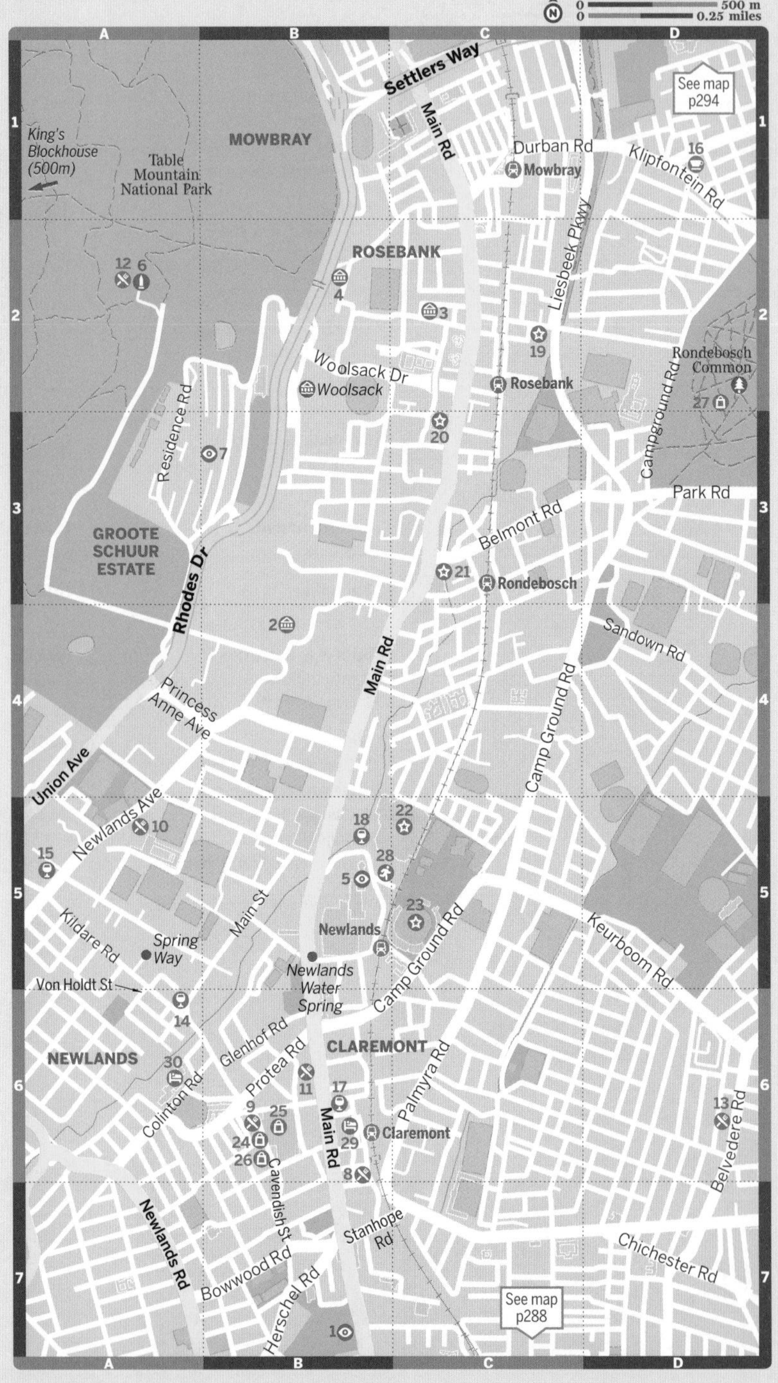
0 500 m
0 0.25 miles
See map p294
King's Blockhouse (500m)
Table Mountain National Park
MOWBRAY
Settlers Way
Main Rd
Durban Rd
Mowbray
Klipfontein Rd
Liesbeek Pkwy
ROSEBANK
Woolsack Dr
Woolsack
Rosebank
Rondebosch Common
Campground Rd
Residence Rd
Park Rd
Belmont Rd
GROOTE SCHUUR ESTATE
Rhodes Dr
Rondebosch
Sandown Rd
Main Rd
Princess Anne Ave
Camp Ground Rd
Union Ave
Newlands Ave
Main St
Newlands
Kildare Rd
Spring Way
Von Holdt St
Newlands Water Spring
Camp Ground Rd
Keurboom Rd
Glenhof Rd
Protea Rd
CLAREMONT
Palmyra Rd
NEWLANDS
Colinton Rd
Main Rd
Claremont
Belvedere Rd
Cavendish St
Stanhope Rd
Newlands Rd
Bowwood Rd
Herschel Rd
Chichester Rd
See map p288

SOUTHERN SUBURBS

Sights (p129)
1 Arderne Gardens B7
2 Groote Schuur B4
3 Irma Stern Museum C2
4 Mostert's Mill B2
5 Newlands Brewery B5
6 Rhodes Memorial A2
7 University of Cape Town B3

Eating (p132)
8 A Tavola B6
9 Brooker & Waller B6
10 Gardener's Cottage A5
11 O'ways Teacafe B6
12 Rhodes Memorial Restaurant A2
13 Starlings Cafe D6

Drinking & Nightlife (p133)
14 Barristers A6
15 Forrester's Arms A5
16 Localé D1
17 Tiger Tiger B6
18 Toad & Josephine B5

Entertainment (p134)
19 Alma Café C2
20 Baxter Theatre C3
21 Lyra's C3
22 Newlands Rugby Stadium C5
23 Sahara Park Newlands C5

Shopping (p135)
24 Balu Legacy Boutique B6
25 Cavendish Square B6
26 Habits B6
Montebello (see 10)
Naartjie (see 25)
27 Rondebosch Potters Market D2
The Space (see 25)
YDE (see 25)

Sports & Activities (p136)
28 Sports Science Institute of South Africa B5

Sleeping (p207)
29 Off the Wall B6
30 Vineyard Hotel & Spa A6

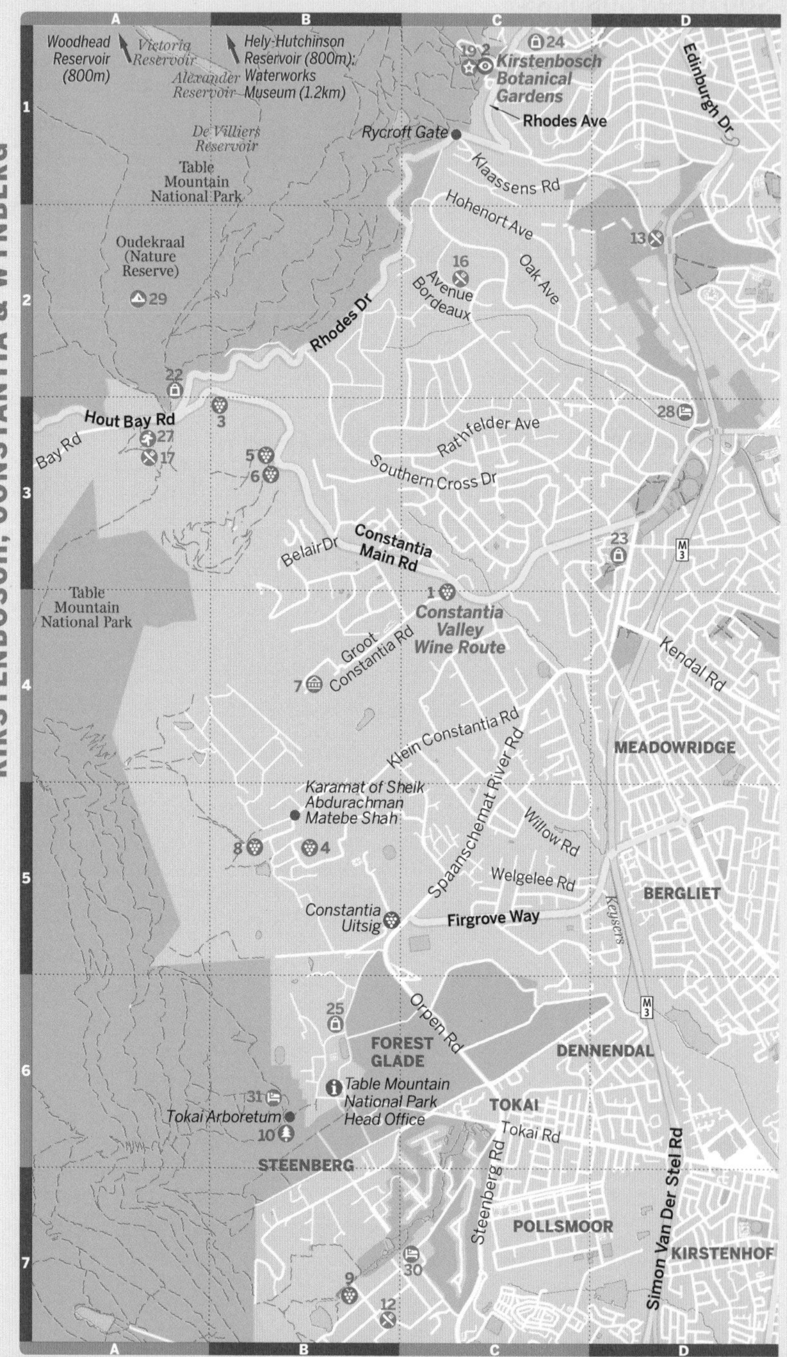

A
B
C
D
1
2
3
4
5
6
7
Woodhead Reservoir (800m)
Victoria Reservoir
Alexander Reservoir
Hely-Hutchinson Reservoir (800m); Waterworks Museum (1.2km)
De Villiers Reservoir
Table Mountain National Park
Oudekraal (Nature Reserve)
29
19
2
24
Kirstenbosch Botanical Gardens
Rhodes Ave
Rycroft Gate
Edinburgh Dr
Klaassens Rd
Hohenort Ave
13
16
Avenue Bordeaux
Oak Ave
Rhodes Dr
22
Hout Bay Rd
Bay Rd
3
27
17
5
6
28
Rathfelder Ave
Southern Cross Dr
Constantia Main Rd
Belair Dr
23
M3
1
Constantia Valley Wine Route
Table Mountain National Park
Groot Constantia Rd
7
Kendal Rd
Klein Constantia Rd
Spaanschemat River Rd
MEADOWRIDGE
Karamat of Sheik Abdurachman Matebe Shah
8
4
Willow Rd
Welgelee Rd
BERGLIET
Keysers
Constantia Uitsig
Firgrove Way
25
Orpen Rd
FOREST GLADE
DENNENDAL
31
Table Mountain National Park Head Office
TOKAI
Tokai Arboretum
10
Tokai Rd
STEENBERG
Steenberg Rd
Simon Van Der Stel Rd
POLLSMOOR
KIRSTENHOF
30
9
12

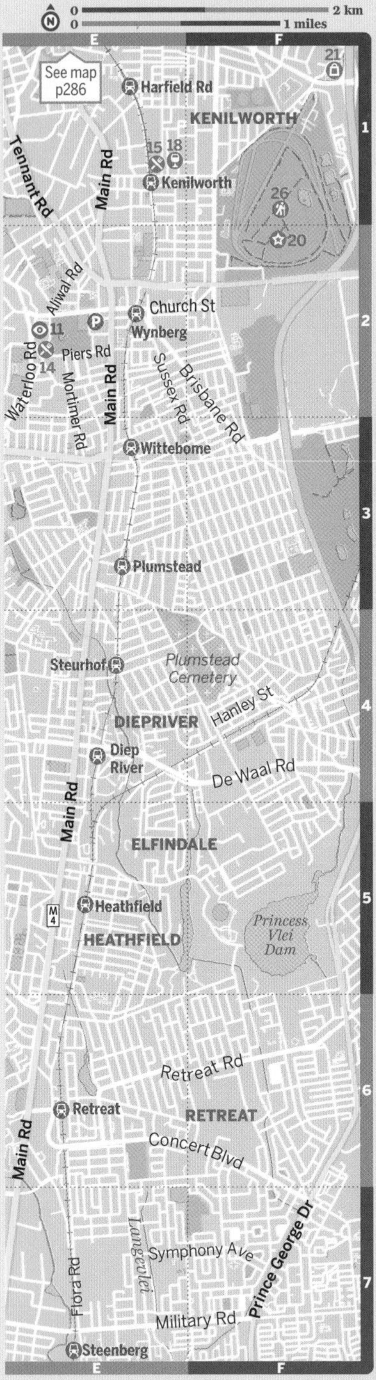

Top Sights (p126)

- 1 Constantia Valley Wine Route C4
- 2 Kirstenbosch Botanical Gardens C1

Sights (p129)

- 3 Beau Constantia B3
- 4 Buitenverwachting B5
- 5 Constantia Glen B3
- 6 Eagle's Nest B3
- 7 Groot Constantia B4
- 8 Klein Constantia B5
- Maynardville Park ..... (see 11)
- 9 Steenberg Vineyards B7
- 10 Tokai Forest B6
- 11 Wynberg Village E2

Eating (p132)

- 12 Bistro Sixteen82 ..... B7
- 13 Chart Farm D2
- 14 Four&twenty Cafe & Pantry E2
- 15 Graze E1
- 16 Greenhouse C2
- Jonkershuis ..... (see 7)
- Kirstenbosch Tea Room ..... (see 2)
- La Belle ..... (see 28)
- 17 La Colombe A3
- Picnic Lunch ..... (see 4)
- Tashas ..... (see 23)

Drinking & Nightlife (p133)

- 18 Banana Jam E1
- Caffé Verdi ..... (see 14)
- Lister's Place Tea Garden ..... (see 10)
- Martini Bar ..... (see 16)

Entertainment (p134)

- 19 Galileo Open Air Cinema C1
- 20 Kenilworth Racecourse F2
- Maynardville Open-Air Theatre ..... (see 11)

Shopping (p135)

- 21 Access Park F1
- 22 Art in the Forest A2
- 23 Constantia Village D3
- 24 Kirstenbosch Craft Market C1
- 25 Tokai Forest Market B6

Sports & Activities (p136)

- 26 Kenilworth Racecourse Conservation Area F1
- 27 SA Forest Adventures A3

Sleeping (p208)

- 28 Alphen D3
- 29 Orange Kloof Camp Site A2
- 30 Steenberg Hotel C7
- 31 Wood Owl Cottage B6

MUIZENBERG & KALK BAY

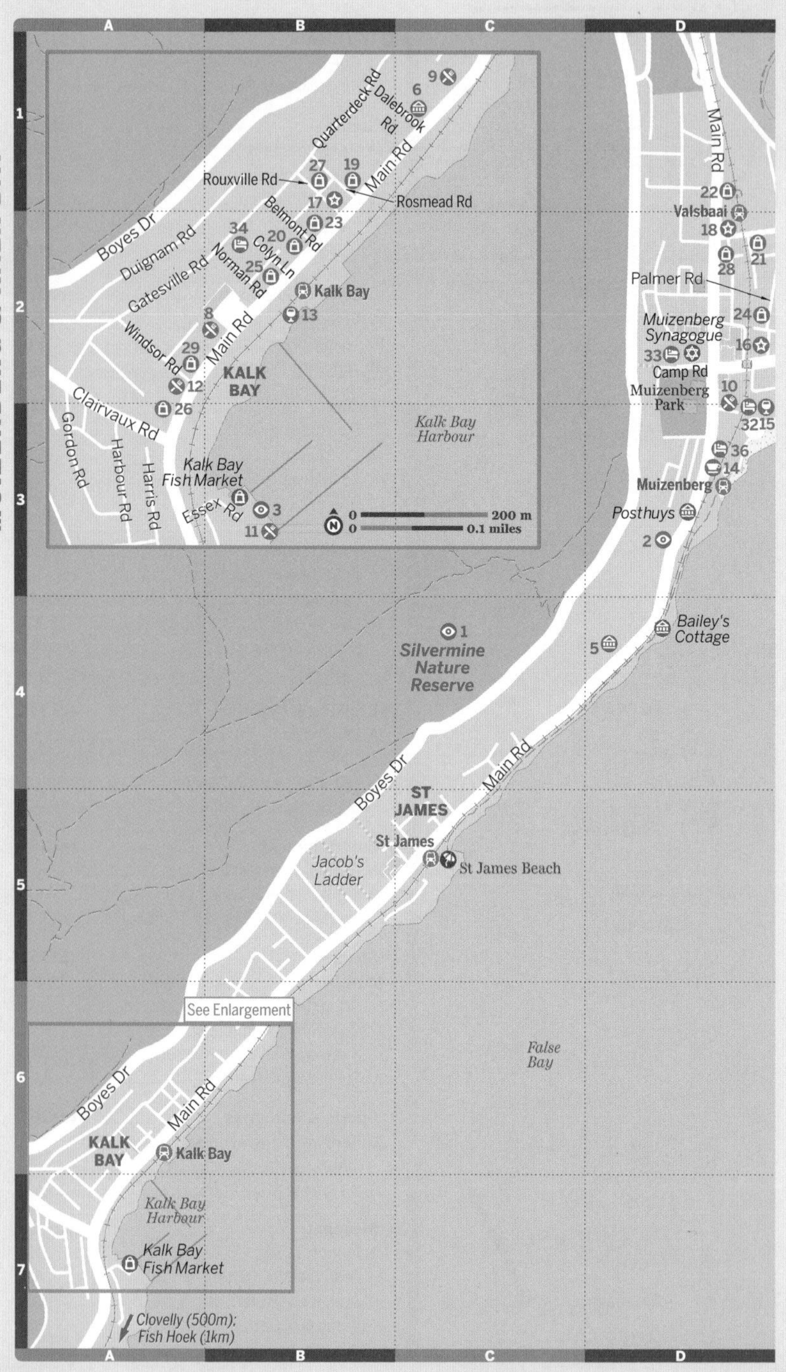

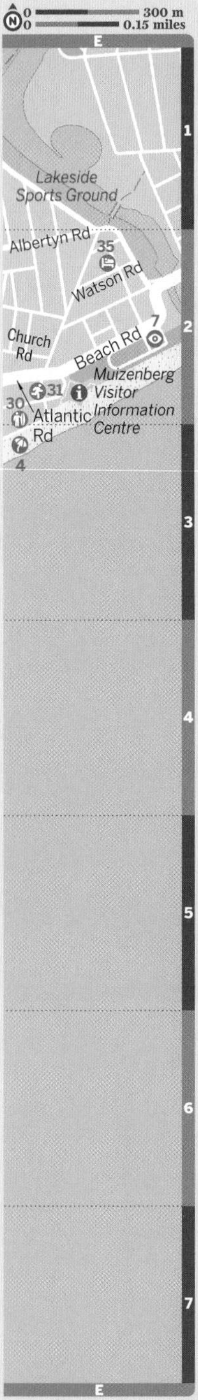

0 300 m
0 0.15 miles
E
Lakeside Sports Ground
Albertyn Rd
35
Watson Rd
Church Rd
Beach Rd
7
Muizenberg Visitor Information Centre
31
30
Atlantic Rd
4
E

SIMON'S TOWN

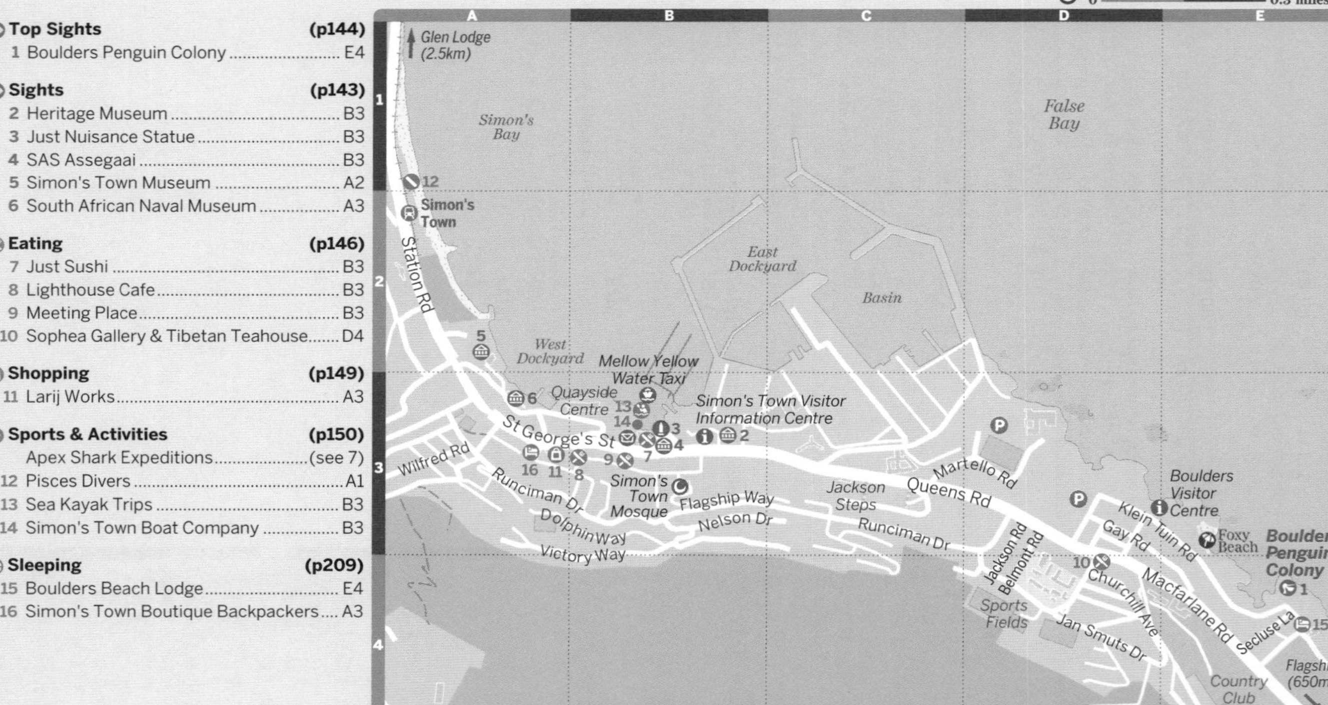

0 600 m
0 0.3 miles
Glen Lodge (2.5km)
Simon's Bay
False Bay
Simon's Town
Station Rd
East Dockyard
Basin
West Dockyard
Mellow Yellow Water Taxi
Quayside Centre
Simon's Town Visitor Information Centre
St George's St
Wilfred Rd
Runciman Dr
Simon's Town Mosque
Flagship Way
Nelson Dr
Dolphin Way
Victory Way
Jackson Steps
Queens Rd
Martello Rd
Runciman Dr
Jackson Rd
Belmont Rd
Sports Fields
Boulders Visitor Centre
Klein Tuin Rd
Gay Rd
Foxy Beach
Boulders Penguin Colony
Churchill Ave
Macfarlane Rd
Jan Smuts Dr
Secluse La
Country Club
Flagship (650m)

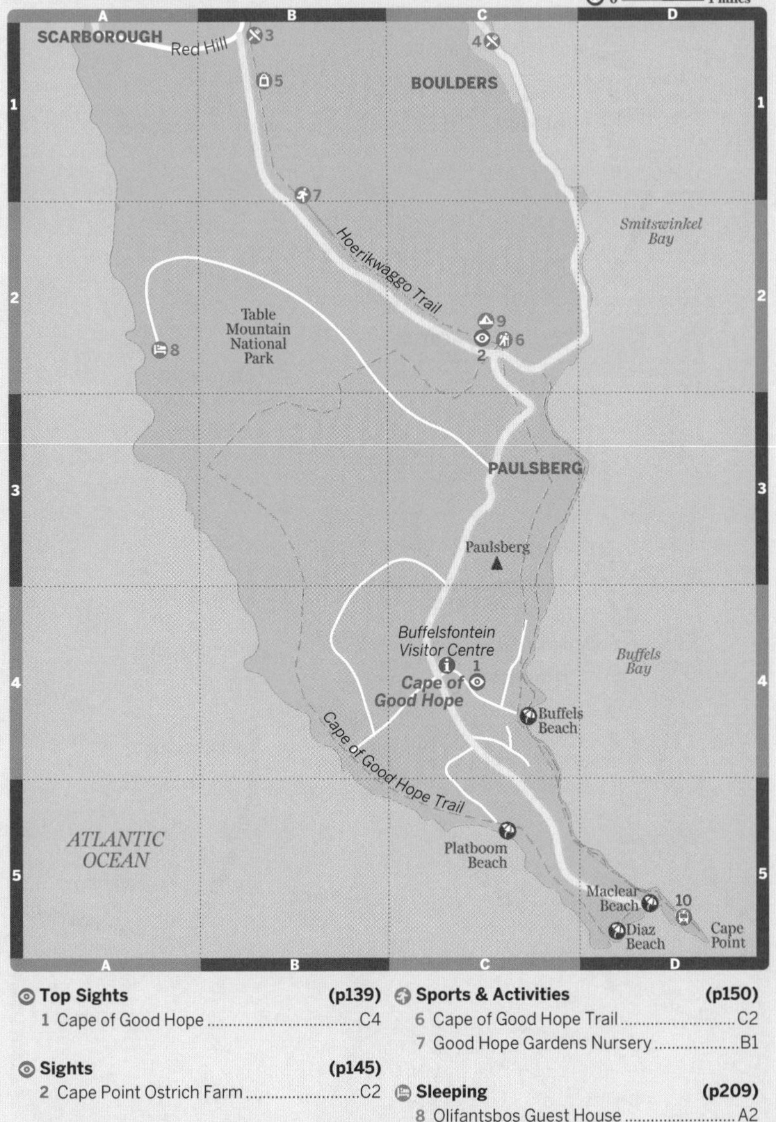

Top Sights (p139)
1 Cape of Good Hope C4

Sights (p145)
2 Cape Point Ostrich Farm C2

Eating (p146)
3 Cape Farmhouse Restaurant B1
4 Flagship C1

Shopping (p149)
Red Rock Tribal .... (see 3)
5 Redhill Pottery B1

Sports & Activities (p150)
6 Cape of Good Hope Trail C2
7 Good Hope Gardens Nursery B1

Sleeping (p209)
8 Olifantsbos Guest House A2
9 Smitswinkel Camp Site C2

Transport (p139)
10 Flying Dutchman Funicular D5

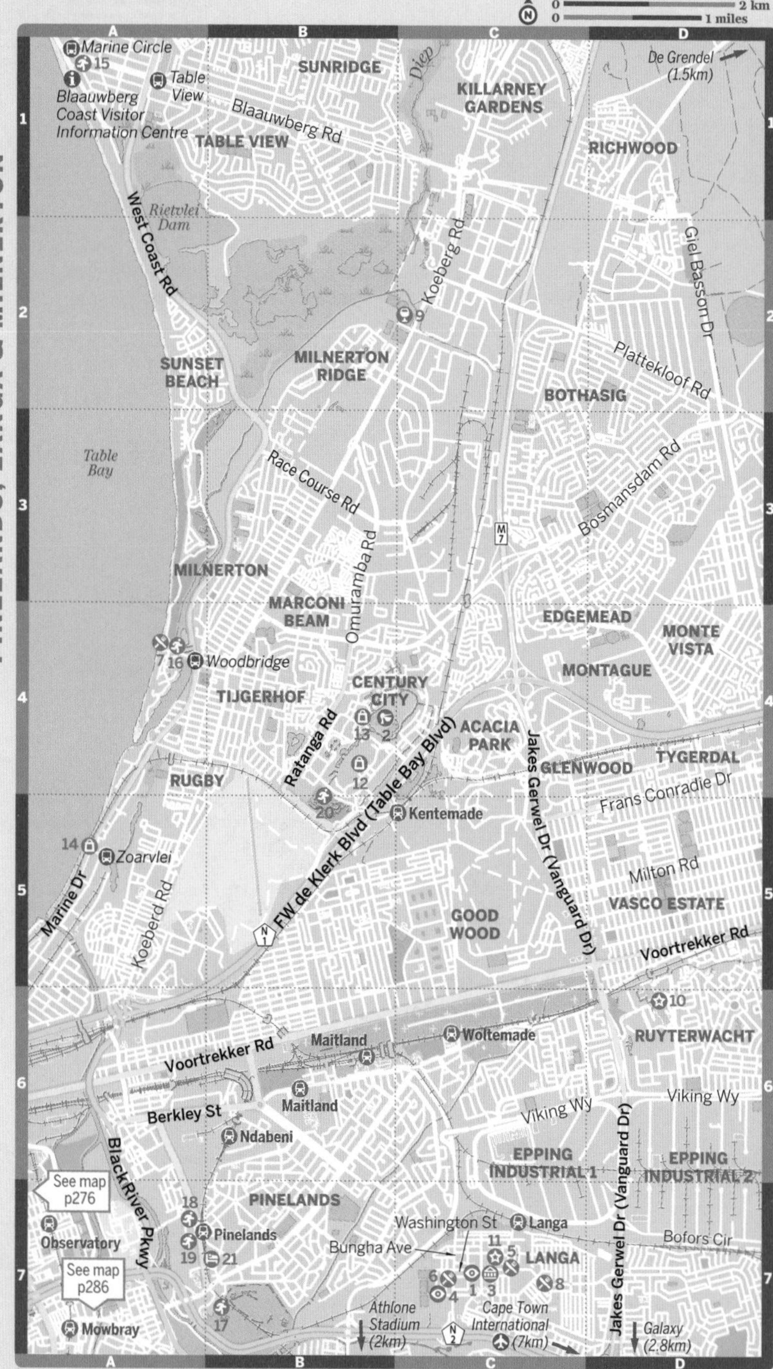

Marine Circle
Blaauwberg Coast Visitor Information Centre
Table View
SUNRIDGE
Diep
KILLARNEY GARDENS
De Grendel (1.5km)
RICHWOOD
Blaauwberg Rd
TABLE VIEW
West Coast Rd
Rietvlei Dam
Koeberg Rd
Giel Basson Dr
SUNSET BEACH
MILNERTON RIDGE
Plattekloof Rd
BOTHASIG
Table Bay
Race Course Rd
Bosmansdam Rd
Omuramba Rd
MILNERTON
MARCONI BEAM
EDGEMEAD
MONTE VISTA
MONTAGUE
Woodbridge
TIJGERHOF
CENTURY CITY
ACACIA PARK
Ratanga Rd
FW de Klerk Blvd (Table Bay Blvd)
Jakes Gerwel Dr (Vanguard Dr)
GLENWOOD
TYGERDAL
RUGBY
Frans Conradie Dr
Kentemade
Zoarvlei
Milton Rd
Marine Dr
Koeberd Rd
GOOD WOOD
VASCO ESTATE
Voortrekker Rd
RUYTERWACHT
Woltemade
Maitland
Berkley St
Viking Wy
Ndabeni
Black River Pkwy
EPPING INDUSTRIAL 1
EPPING INDUSTRIAL 2
See map p276
PINELANDS
Observatory
Pinelands
Washington St
Langa
Bungha Ave
LANGA
Bofors Cir
See map p286
Athlone Stadium (2km)
Cape Town International (7km)
Galaxy (2.8km)
Mowbray